# BIBLICAL ARCHAEOLOGY

# BIBLICAL ARCHAEOLOGY

## THE WORLD.
## THE MEDITERRANEAN.
## THE BIBLE

Henry O. Thompson

PARAGON HOUSE PUBLISHERS

New York

Published in the United States by

**Paragon House Publishers**
90 Fifth Avenue
New York, N.Y. 10011

**Library of Congress Cataloging-in-Publication Data**

Thompson, Henry O.
  Biblical archaeology.

  Includes bibliographical references and index.
  1.Archaeology.  2.Bible — Antiquities.  I.Title.
CC165.T49  1987      930.1      86–25434
ISBN 0–913729–58–2
ISBN 0–913729–76–0 (pbk.)

DEDICATED TO

*Joyce Elaine Beebe Thompson*

JOY

&

INSPIRATION

# Table of Contents

## SECTION VI.   Archaeology and Religion

# Acknowledgments

The Talmud says that the day of redemption comes a little closer when a scholar acknowledges *all* his sources. I am not able to share in this cause. In over twenty-five years of reading, digging, studying, and writing, one accumulates a sense of obligation without always knowing to whom it is owed. Much of the following comes from experience, museum study, conversations along the way, staring at vague lines in the archaeological record, and then reading, studying, and writing some more. I hereby acknowledge my debt to all who have gone on before me — to those who have dug, and those who came afterwards and have helped us to know what was found. Special tribute is paid to my first mentors — Lawrence E. Toombs and Robert J. Bull — and to regular friend and friendly critic, Roger S. Boraas. But that is only the beginning as the list quickly expands to my first Director, G. Ernest Wright of blessed memory, Ted Campbell, Jim Ross, Siegfried Horn, Larry Geraty, Adnan Hadidi, Fawzi Zayadine, Moawiyah Ibrahim, Muhammad Murshed Khadijah, Bill Dever, Sy Gitin, Jim Sauer and many, many more. My appreciation for Jim Sauer multiplies with the years. That includes the ongoing friendship of Sue, Tommy, and Katy. It extends to his fine leadership of the American Schools of Oriental Research, for sharing developments in the field, for his review of this manuscript, and the offer of constructive comments. Any errors of fact or interpretation, of course, are my own. Colleagues of the written word are in the footnotes and bibliographies. Here too, the number is beyond counting! Particular thanks go to Clifford C. Slocum for his fine photographic work that went beyond the call of duty. A note of very special appreciation for sketches and encouragement goes to my wife, Joyce, to whom this volume is respectfully dedicated.

HENRY O. THOMPSON

# Introduction

Archaeology in general and biblical archaeology in particular have many facets. We know a great deal about the Bible, for example — as literature, as history, as theology, as a book of faith. When I look at the Bible, I see all of these. But I see much more. Or, to put it another way, I am aware that what I see is illuminated by light coming through those other facets which I associate with biblical archaeology. This is a book about the latter, but it is biblical archaeology set in a context of the Mediterranean world and the world in general. References to Denmark, China, and the Yucatan may seem odd in a book about the Bible, but archaeology does not exist in an air tight vacuum apart from culture, and biblical archaeology exists within the framework of archaeology in general. We cannot deny that context but we can enjoy it.

At first glance, methods of excavation and related concerns do not appear to have much to do with the Bible. It is all so mechanical that it seems distant indeed from the book that some call the Word of God. But then, so does shelf after shelf of multi-volumed studies of systematic theology. So I have come to think of the methods of biblical archaeology as an ongoing, improving process that continues to illuminate human history generally and the Bible in particular.

How did we get to where we are? We have a scientific art (or an artistic science) such as medicine and we know it did not just appear. It grew and developed. The growth and development of archaeology is as interesting as the growth and development of a person. It is indeed a fascinating story in its own right. And part of the fascination is that it is still growing and developing. As we move into the twenty-first century, I can hear some sophomoric excavator looking back and castigating us for our poor methods, just as his sophomoric colleagues of today castigate the methods of earlier generations of excavators. Each age thinks it has the most scientific techniques. A hundred years ago, someone wanted to close the patent office because everything that could be invented had been! But there is always more to learn. Tomorrow's techniques will be new, yet old, with roots in today as ours are rooted in yesterday.

There are techniques and there are techniques. The modern scientific laboratory has produced electronic equipment and new insights that add a new facet to biblical archaeology. The application of physical and biological science to excavation and to the things we find has opened a new chapter in our work. Some of this information is so technical that many field or "dirt" archaeologists do not know it. Neither does the more traditional biblical student or scholar, unless s/he has a background in these other sciences. An introduction to this field can give both new and experienced archaeologists a sense of the revolution we have created here.

These things — history, methods, and science — tell us something about archaeology itself. But "Rik" Wheeler was fond of reminding us that we are not digging up things. The past really comes alive when we realize we are uncovering the lives of real people. Their daily life is spread out before us as we find out how they baked their bread and carried their water and learned how to read and write. This facet of archaeology sheds light, allows it to spread across the spectrum and show us the many-colored coat of the ancient world — so different and yet so like our own.

All these facets bear on the Bible itself. Our vision is broadened, deepened, enlightened by the discoveries of the explorer, the excavator, the translator, the pottery expert, the coin expert, the art expert, the bone specialist, the linguist, the medical historian, and all who have a part in the art or science or human study we call biblical archaeology.

But in the end, the Bible is a book of religion. While thinking involves abstraction and theology is a formal type of thinking, archaeology is concerned with material things — specific objects which have survived the ravages of time. How do we move from rocks to abstractions? The distinction is, of course, overdrawn, for we find words inscribed and engraved and inked on these objects and we are already dealing with abstractions. But there is more than that. The human mind does not dig up something and forget it. The mind leaps ahead to question the identity of what the hand now holds. Images of those real, live people leap into view. Here a priest lifts up a sacrifice to the gods and there an architect plans out a temple to the glory of the nation's deities. Over the years, a picture comes into focus and we see the faith of ancient peoples, including those who walk through the pages of the Bible. Our understanding deepens and we ourselves continue our own growth and development.

# Abbreviations

| | |
|---|---|
| AA | American Antiquity |
| AASOR | Annual of the ASOR |
| ADAJ | Annual of the Department of Antiquities of Jordan |
| AIA | Archaeological Institute of America |
| AINAN | American Institute of Nautical Archaeology Newsletter |
| AJA | American Journal of Archaeology |
| ANEP | Pritchard, James B., ed. *The Ancient Near East in Pictures Relating to the Old Testament.* 2nd ed. Princeton: Princeton University, 1969. |
| ANET | Pritchard, James B., ed. *Ancient Near Eastern Texts Relating to the Old Testament.* 3rd ed. Princeton: Princeton University, 1969. |
| AOP | Albright, William F. *The Archaeology of Palestine.* Baltimore: Penguin, 1961. |
| AOTS | Thomas, D. Winton, ed. *Archaeology and Old Testament Study.* Oxford: Clarendon Press, 1967. |
| ASOR | American Schools of Oriental Research |
| ASORN | ASOR Newsletter |
| AUSS | Andrews University Seminary Studies |
| BA | Biblical Archaeologist |
| BANE | Wright, G. Ernest, ed. *The Bible and the Ancient Near East.* Garden City: Doubleday, 1961. |
| BAR | Biblical Archaeology Review |
| BASOR | Bulletin of the ASOR |

BGA        Bacon, Edward, ed. *The Great Archaeologists*. London: Secker and
           Warburg, 1976.
BHI        Bright, John. *A History of Israel*. 3rd ed. Philadelphia: Westminster, 1981.

CAH        Cambridge Ancient History
CBQ        Catholic Biblical Quarterly
CCEA       Cottrell, Leonard, ed. *The Concise Encyclopedia of Archaeology*. New York:
           Hawthorne, 1960.
CHP        Ceram, C.W. *Hands on the Past*. New York: Knopf, 1966.
CPHA       Ceram, C.W. *A Picture History of Archaeology*. London: Thames and
           Hudson, 1958.
CS         Cross, Frank M., ed. *Symposia*. Cambridge: ASOR, 1979.

DFP        Detroit Free Press
DHYA       Daniel, Glyn. *A Hundred Years of Archaeology*. London: Duckworth, 1950.

EAEHL      *Encyclopedia of Archaeological Excavations in the Holy Land*
EI         *Eretz Israel*

FGNDBA     Freedman, David Noel, and Greenfield, Jonas, eds. *New Directions in
           Biblical Archaeology*. Garden City: Doubleday, 1969.

HTR        Harvard Theological Review
HUCBAS     Hebrew Union College Biblical and Archaeological School
HWP        Hawkes, Jacquetta. *The World of the Past*. Vol. I. New York: Knopf, 1963.

IAMS       Institute for Archaeo-Metallurgical Studies
IDB        *The Interpreter's Dictionary of the Bible*. Vols. 1–4. Nashville: Abingdon,
           1962.
IDBSV      *IDB Supplementary Volume*, 1976.
IECW       Yonah, Michael Avi, and Shatzman, Israel, eds. *Illustrated Encyclopedia of
           the Classical World*. New York: Harper & Row, 1975.
IEJ        *Israel Exploration Journal*
IES        Israel Exploration Society
IJNAUE     *International Journal for Nautical Archaeology and Undersea Exploration*
ILN        *Illustrated London News*

JAOS       *Journal of the American Oriental Society*
JNES       *Journal of Near Eastern Studies*

KAHL       Kenyon, Kathleen M. *Archaeology of the Holy Land*. 4th ed. New York:
           Norton, 1979.

MASCAJ    *Museum Applied Science Center for Archaeology Journal*
MASCAN    *MASCA Newsletter*

NEATC     Sanders, James A., ed. *Near Eastern Archaeology in the Twentieth Century*;
          Garden City: Doubleday, 1970.
NERT      Beyerlin, Walter, ed. *Near Eastern Religious Texts Relating to the Old
          Testament*. Philadelphia: Westminster, 1978.
NG        *National Geographic Magazine*

PAE       Pettinato, Giovanni. *The Archives of Ebla*. Garden City: Doubleday, 1981.
PDBW      Parrot, Andre. *Discovering Buried Worlds*. London: SCM, 1955.
PEF       Palestine Exploration Fund
PEQ       *Palestine Exploration Quarterly*
PRS       Pritchard, James B. *Recovering Sarepta: A Phoenician City*. Princeton:
          Princeton University, 1978.

SA        *Scientific American*
SAAMT     Schiffer, Michael B., ed. *Advances in Archaeological Method and Theory*.
          Vols. 1– ; New York: Academic Press, 1978– .
SBAF      Schoville, Keith N. *Biblical Archaeology in Focus*. Grand Rapids:
          Baker, 1978.
SN        *Science News*

TA        *Tel Aviv*
TDOTT     Thomas, D. Winton. *Documents of Old Testament Times*. New York:
          Harper & Row, 1958.

WAFE      Wheeler, R.E. Mortimer. *Archaeology from the Earth*; Baltimore:
          Penguin, 1954.
WBA       Wright, G. Ernest. *Biblical Archaeology*, rev. Philadelphia:
          Westminster, 1962.
WDUP      Woolley, Leonard. *Digging Up the Past*. Baltimore: Penguin, 1950.

# Illustrations

# Archaeological Ages[*]

**STONE AGE**

Old Stone Age — Paleolithic
    Lower [deeper in the ground] Paleolithic                         Before 70,000 B.C.
    Middle Paleolithic                                      c. 70,000 – c.  35,000 B.C.
    Upper [higher in the ground] Paleolithic                    c. 35,000 – c.  12,000 B.C.
Middle Stone Age — Mesolithic                  c. 12,000 – c. 10,000 B.C.
New Stone Age — Neolithic                      c. 10,000 – c.  4,500 B.C.

**CHALCOLITHIC AGE — COPPER-STONE AGE**     c.  4,500 – c.  3,200 B.C.

**EARLY BRONZE AGE — EB**                   c.  3,200 – c.  2,000 B.C.

    EB I      c. 3200 – 2900
    EB II     c. 2900 – 2600
    EB III    c. 2600 – 2300
    EB IV    c. 2300 – 2000

**MIDDLE BRONZE AGE — MB**              c.  2,000 – c.  1,550 B.C.

    MB I     c. 2000 – 1900
    MB II    c. 1900 – 1550

**LATE BRONZE AGE — LB**                 c.  1,550 – c.  1,200 B.C.

    LB I      c. 1550 – 1400
    LB II    c. 1400 – 1200

**IRON AGE**                                            c.  1,200 – c.      300 B.C.

    Iron I    c. 1200 –  900
    Iron II   c.  900 –  600
    Iron III  c.  600 –  300

**NEO-BABYLONIAN PERIOD**                               c. 625 – 540 B.C.

**PERSIAN PERIOD**                                      c. 550 – 532 B.C.

**HELLENISTIC PERIOD**                                  c. 533 –  63 B.C.

**ROMAN PERIOD**                                        63 B.C. – 324 A.D.

**BYZANTINE PERIOD**                                    325 – 640 A.D.

**ISLAMIC PERIOD**                                      630 – 1918 A.D.

**CRUSADER PERIOD**                                     1099 – 1291 A.D.

**MODERN PERIOD**                                       1918 – present

*There is considerable debate about transition times from one age to another. The beginning of Chalcolithic varies from 4500–3500. Some think EB IV = MB I. Kathleen Kenyon postulated an EB-MB Age as a transition between EB and MB. The earlier ages are approximations, usually related to cultural change as found in the archaeological record, but sometimes related to historic events, e.g., Ahmose expelled the Hyksos from Egypt c. 1550. The later dates are based on particular people coming to power. There was often some overlap when a new king, such as Cyrus the Great, came to power but took several years to conquer surrounding territories. The change from Roman to Byzantine represents Constantine's move from Rome to Byzantium, renamed Constantinople. Ottoman rule ended in 1917. Others start the modern period with Napoleon's invasion of Egypt in 1799 and the beginning of stronger European influence. There are numerous subdivisions found in some reports, e.g., MB II, Iron I and Iron II may be subdivided into A, B, and C. There are many early/late subdivisions which may be even further subdivided, e.g., Early Roman (63 B.C.–135 A.D.) may be divided into ER I-IV.

The Mediterranean World and The Near or Middle East (Drawn by Joyce E. Thompson)

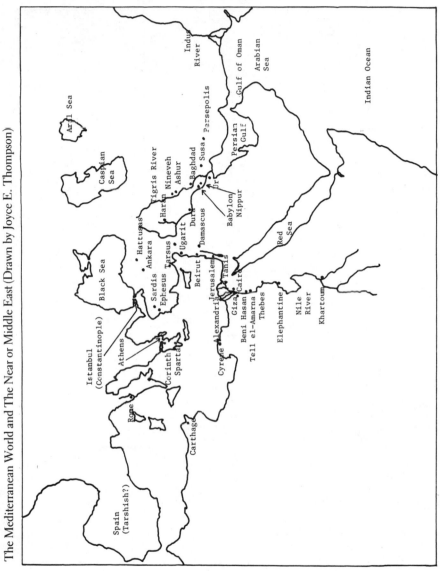

# ARCHAEOLOGY ITSELF

Throughout my years of teaching archaeology, lecturing, seminars, workshops, special appearances and also in general conversation, I have been frequently asked several questions. These questions have come up both in academic circles and outside the university. One of the first questions is, "How do you know where to dig?" A close second is, "How do you dig?" Close behind or even ahead is, "What do you find?" Sooner or later, the curious will ask, "Why do you dig?" These questions form the outline of this introductory section on archaeology itself.

# CHAPTER 1

# Basic Questions

## A. "WHERE DO YOU DIG?"

### An Accident

Frequently knowledge of a site is gained by sheer accident. For example, road work may uncover an ancient tomb. Persian tombs (539–330 B.C.) were uncovered this way in Nablus in the Holy Land, forty miles north of Jerusalem. Digging for new telephone and sewage lines in Jordan's capital, Amman — ancient Rabbah (II Samuel 11:1) — uncovered several Roman tombs. The responsible supervisor contacts the appropriate authorities who rush (we hope) to see what, if anything, can be salvaged.

Accidental discoveries are often made during the digging of building foundations. A hoard of bronze tools and weapons were discovered in Balata, now within the municipality of Nablus. This stimulated the excavation of Tell Balata, ancient Shechem (Genesis 33:18) by the German Archaeological Institute in the years 1913–1934. A *tell* (Arabic) or *tel* (Hebrew) is an artificial hill or mound formed from the ruins of a city. The excavation of Khirbet ("ruin") al-Hajjar ("stone"), near Amman, was prompted by the discovery of Ammonite statues by workers digging foundations for a house. Foundation excavation for a new hotel on the Mount of Olives, east of Jerusalem, uncovered some pre-Israelite tombs.

Accidental finds from airport construction are worldwide. Included are Maya ruins on Cozumel (an island near the coast of Yucatan), prehistoric camps in England, Roman mansions in Italy, ancient tombs in Beirut, and a Late Bronze (1500–1200 B.C.) temple near Amman.

3

**Figure 1–1.** An ancient tell: Beth-shan. Tell el-Husn, the "Mound of the Fortress," biblical Beth-shan has the classical conical shape of a near eastern tell, built up from the accumulation of debris against remains of the city walls.

The everyday life and work of people is perhaps a more classic source of accidental discovery of archaeological materials leading to excavation. In 1928, a farmer was plowing near Ras Shamra on the coast of Syria. The tip of his plow broke through the ceiling of a buried Mycenean tomb. Ras Shamra excavations have uncovered ancient Ugarit and a previously unknown civilization. In an excavated temple library were copies of religious texts which describe the Canaanite religion. A woman digging (1887) for nitrous clay for fertilizer at Tell el-Amarna 200 miles south of Cairo in Egypt, found a group of clay tablets. The Amarna letters tell us about political conditions in Palestine during the reign of Pharaoh Ikhnaton (c. 1370–1335 B.C.). He is sometimes called the "heretic king" because he worshipped the sun disc, the Aton. He built a new capital at Akhetaton, now called Tell el-Amarna.

The accidental discovery of the fabulous Dead Sea Scrolls of Qumran is well known. A Ta'amira Bedouin boy, Muhammed Adh-Dhib, was looking for a lost goat. He tossed a rock into a cave and heard something break. He was scared and

**Figure 1–2.** Qumran Cave 4. The hole in the outer end of the cliff, left of the people, in the center of the picture, is the fourth of 11 caves in which scroll material was found. Hundreds of caves were explored by an international team.

**Figure 1–3.** Qumran Cave 4 Interior. There are two levels within the cave. Remains of jars and inscriptions were found on the floor buried in the dust of centuries.

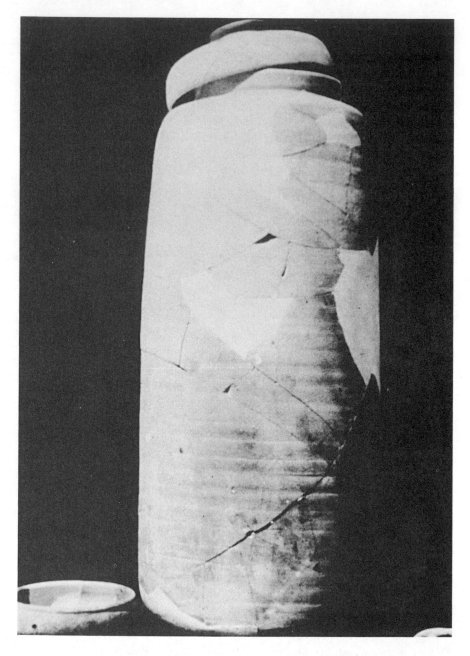

**Figure 1–4.** Qumran jar, typical of those in which scrolls were stored.

**Figure 1–5.** Qumran scroll. Several scrolls were quite complete but hundreds of fragments were found, some with only a few letters.

ran away. But he came back with a friend to take a look, and started one of the greatest manuscript discoveries of modern times.

A fisherman's net may bring up a pottery jar or some other evidence of a shipwreck. Underwater archaeology is a new discipline which we will look at in a later section.

## The Higher View

Aerial photography accidentally acquired importance for archaeology. Reconnaisance photographs made during World War I revealed Roman fortifications in Britain and Etruscan tombs in Italy. An aerial photograph led Zakariah Goneim in 1951 to the discovery of a lost pyramid at Sakkara, Egypt.

A photograph taken from the air shows light and shadow in a way that a person on the ground might not normally see. Buried remains may cause a slight ridge, invisible on the spot, but which casts a slight shadow discernable from the air. The aerial view may also show differences in the color of vegetation. Since the soil over an ancient wall is not as deep as next to the wall, the vegetation over the wall is not as luxuriant and dries out or dies more quickly than the rest. Aerial archaeology has a history all its own and we will return to this later.

Here we note that aerial observation is not limited to the airplane. Sir Leonard
Woolley tells of a discovery of tombs in Egypt as he and a companion sat on a hillside late in the afternoon. The sun cast shadow at just the right angle to make visible
the slightly heaped up gravel of each burial. One might note also the prehistoric
discoveries of L.S.B. Leakey in Olduvai Gorge in Tanzania, Africa. Late afternoon shadows showed some buried remains previously unnoticed. Olduvai Gorge
is significant too, for the erosion which formed it in the first place. The remains
discovered by Leakey were partially exposed by erosion in the sides of the canyon.
Similar erosion aided Sir Flinders Petrie in his excavations of Tell Jemmeh (Gerar?
— Genesis 20:1) in Southern Palestine.

**Figure 1–6.**    Bab edh-Dhra' cemetery with plan of some of the excavation and in-set map
showing its location west of Karak. Courtesy of G. Ernest Wright.

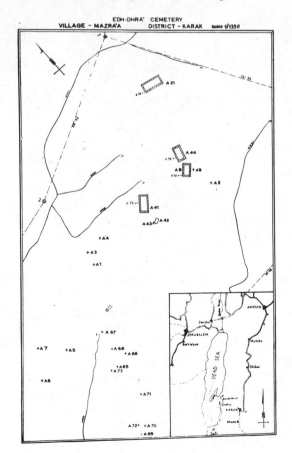

**Figure 1–7.**   Charnel house A 51 entrance. The two well-cut orthostat slabs forming the doorway show up better in the next picture. Here note the rectangular mud brick wall that apparently sealed the door. Above the bone pile were large quantities of cloth, mostly burned but some still strong enough to resist tearing in spite of the fact that it was still less than 10 cm below the ground surface. The view is from the inside of the house. Courtesy of G. Ernest Wright.

## For Sale

Ancient objects may "find" their way into an antiquity shop or the market place. The search for some "dragon bones" in China led to the discovery of Anyang, royal capital of the Shang dynasty (1765–1123 B.C.). The dragon bones, sold to drug stores (apothecary shops) to be ground into powder for "nerves," were "oracle" bones. When the king inquired of the oracle, a priest cracked a bone or shell with heat, and figured out an answer by the direction of the crack. The answer might then be written on the bone, sometimes with a note on the outcome. The bones were discovered by farmers plowing, c. 1860, but it was 1928 before the source was tracked down in northeast China and scientific explorations could begin. In the meantime, the peasants had begun digging and clandestine treasure of all sorts had reached the market.

**Figure 1–8.**  Charnel House A 51 entrance after clearing. Note the two stone steps that lead down to a packed clay floor. To the right at the end of the meter stick is a broken copper dagger. In addition to hundreds of pots, there were over a thousand beads and several stone plaques. Courtesy of G. Ernest Wright.

**Figure 1–9.**  The interior of Shaft Tomb A 72 NW Chamber showing some of the piled up bowls and jugs. Courtesy of G. Ernest Wright.

The appearance of a great deal of Early Bronze (c. 3000–2000 B.C.) pottery in the shops of Jerusalem led to the partial excavation of Bab edh-Dhra. Its location had been known for some time. Bab edh-Dhra is on the east side of the Dead Sea at the point where the "tongue" (the Lisan) extends out into the Sea. The site includes a huge cemetery. Excavation uncovered the usual tombs, but also a fascinating series of *charnel houses* in which ancient peoples cremated their dead. One house had over 600 bowls, jars and other pottery vessels. Over 347 came from the entry-way alone. Underground tombs contained between ten and fifteen bowls and jugs. Some of the bowls were neatly stacked and the lower ones were not even dusty. Paul Lapp, the first excavator, estimated the whole cemetery must have contained 3,000,000 pots.

## Seek and Ye Shall Find (Maybe)

Tracking down the source of something helps us see that the "where" of digging may be accidental. Some excavation sites, however, are carefully chosen in advance. A site like Jerusalem (II Samuel 5:6–9) has always been known. The location of Jericho (Joshua 6) has been known, although some caution is necessary

**Figure 1–10.** Shechem guarded the pass between Mt. Ebal (right) and Mt. Gerizim (left) and the road between them through the pass to Samaria, as well as the road to Tirzah which goes off to the right. The Shechem Plain from which the picture was taken, is good farmland that grew the food to support the city. The low, 7 acre mound lies just beyond the modern olive oil factory, seen here in the misty dawn.

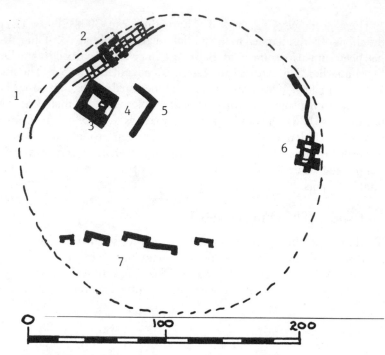

**Figure 1–11.** Sketch Plan of Shechem: 1. Cyclopean (boulders) wall; 2. Northwest Gate; 3. Migdol Temple; 4. Palace; 5. Temenos Wall (separated palace from the rest of the city); 6. East Gate; 7. Village of Balata. (Drawn by Joyce E. Thompson)

here. "New Testament" Jericho (Luke 10:29) is several miles away from "Old Testament" Jericho, Tell es-Sultan. The modern town of Jericho spreads out from the base of the latter so one could say there are three different sites for Jericho.

Shechem was once identified with Nablus, which is built over the ruins of the Roman city of Neapolis ("new city"). Nablus is within the east – west pass that lies between Mount Ebal and Mount Gerazim. Hermann Thiersch discovered the remains of a large wall sticking out of the side of a low mound, Tell Balata. The tell is two miles east of the center of Nablus at the mouth of the pass. The mound is partly under the village of Balata and it overlooks the fertile valley called the Plain of Shechem. Thiersch reasoned that this strategic location better suited our knowledge of this important city from Genesis 34, Joshua 24, I Kings 12, etc. It is also named in several Egyptian inscriptions and probably in the Ebla tablets of Syria.

The Bible, of course, is tremendously helpful in locating a place referred to in its pages. But the location is not always pinpointed to the exact spot. Hence the confusion over Jericho, Shechem, and other places.

**Figure 1–12.**    Ramses III (1198–1167 B.C.). This statue was found at Beth-shan and suggests his control of the city.

## A Name

Some sites, such as Beisan, Biblical Beth-shan (Joshua 17:11), twenty miles north of Shechem, are chosen for excavation because of their size, location, or suggested identity. The latter is the reason for excavating Tell Beit Mersim, which William F. Albright, the excavator, identified as biblical Debir (Joshua 10:38), and also el-Jib, identified as Gibeon (Joshua 9). Beth-shan was dug (1921–1934) by the University Museum of the University of Pennsylvania. Egyptian inscriptions found during the excavation refer to the city and assure the tell's identity. Earlier Egyptian records helped identify its location. The Egyptian "Letter of Hori" (c. 1200 B.C.) demands that a potential scribe "explain Beth-shan" in relation to other cities (apparently geography was part of scribal knowledge). It was assumed that Beth-shan was near these other cities. The tell today is in the *wadi* (canyon) below the village of Beisan which is on the southern rim of the wadi. This Arabic name is similar to the Biblical name (Beth-shan-Bei-san) and so it gives a clue to the location of the Biblical city and a clue as to where to dig.

This is also true for Gibeon, excavated by James B. Pritchard of the University Museum. Earlier scholars questioned whether Arabic "Jib" could be related to "Gib-eon." Like Schechem, the biblical description is vague enough so Gibeon's location could be that of a neighboring tell. Pritchard settled the argument by excavating el-Jib and discovering some jar handles with the name of "Gibeon" inscribed on them. Similarly, Yohanan Aharoni's excavation of Arad uncovered a *potsherd* with the city name scratched on the surface. The Israeli excavation of Tell el-Areini was successful in the opposite way. The site was checked for its possible identification as biblical Gath — which it is not.

## Research

Sometimes a site may be carefully researched in extra-biblical sources. This was true for the temple remains on Tell er-Ras, the northern peak of Mount Gerazim, overlooking Shechem. Robert J. Bull of Drew University carefully checked historical records, studied the coins of Neapolis, and studied the contours of the hill. On the basis of this study, the expedition discovered a temple of Hadrian, which in turn was built over what may be the temple of the Samaritans (John 4:20).

The newer forms of research will be explored in Section III.

## Folklore

Traditions are related to historical records — possibly one should call them historical memories. Ever since Heinrich Schliemann followed the Iliad of Homer to discover ancient Troy in 1870, tradition has been taken more seriously. The identification of Hissarlik in Turkey with Troy is not accepted by everyone (very

**Figure 1–13.**    Tell er-Ras, "Mound of the Head" is the first and most prominent of Mt. Gerizim's three peaks. Here Robert J. Bull and associates of the Shechem Expedition found remains of a Hadrianic temple (Roman Emperor Hadrian, c. 135 A.D.). Under this temple was an altar, perhaps that of the Samaritan temple, c. 300 B.C.

little is in the scientific world). The evidence is ambiguous enough to be a reminder that traditions vary and must be used cautiously. The tomb of Jonah at Tell Quyuniq in modern Iraq suggests the tell's identity with Nineveh, although not everyone believes that Jonah was an historical figure. The present day Samaritans of Nablus follow their historical memory and hold their Passover on the main peak of Mount Gerizim. The evidence noted earlier suggests that the smaller but more prominent Tell er-Ras was the site of their temple from about 300–100 B.C. Their historical memory may have moved the site of their temple to another peak, possibly when the temple of Hadrian was built c. 135 A.D. Such movement has already been noted for Jericho.

## Goals

Excavation in search of a special goal should not be overlooked. The work of Schliemann and Leakey was noted. Howard Carter searched the Valley of the Kings across the Nile River from Luxor, Egypt. He looked for and finally found (1922) the remains of King Tut (Pharaoh Tut-ankh-Amun, c. 1353–44 B.C.) in all his regal splendor.

## Re-excavate

Deliberately seeking a place to dig involves re-excavation as well. The Germans excavated Shechem between 1913 and 1934. Unfortunately the final report was never published. It was destroyed during World War II when Allied fire bombs burned the house of Ernst Sellin, the director of the German excavations. Another reason for re-excavation, far more important than fire-bombs and unpublished results, is the continuing refinement of archaeological methods. Thus very important sites should perhaps be re-excavated as a matter of policy every twenty-five years or so. This means that excavators should deliberately leave a major portion of the mound for the future, as suggested by Kathleen Kenyon. Some of the most recent re-excavations of biblical sites besides Shechem include Jerusalem, Jericho (1952–1958), Taanach (1962–1968), Gezer (1964–1972, 1984), Ai (1964–69), Megiddo (1960–1971), and Tell el-Hesi (1970–1984.)

## Pots

The lowly potsherd should not be overlooked in answering the question, "Where?" While pottery is readily broken, the pieces — potsherds or simply *sherds* — seemingly last forever. Over the centuries, ancient pottery changed in style, use, decoration, etc. A detailed knowledge of these changes (the science of typology) helps date different types of vessels giving us a pottery chronology. Potsherds are churned up from previous destructions of a site by building, quarrying, and the farmer's plow, just as Indian arrowheads turn up in America. A survey or preliminary study of the types of sherds on the surface of an ancient site gives a rough indication of the place's history. This survey may attract an excavator who is interested in the particular historical period(s) represented. The survey may relate to other reasons for selecting a specific site. It may substantiate or negate an earlier reason. An excavator looking for an Iron Age (1200–300 B.C.) site might be encouraged to dig a site if there is Iron Age pottery on the surface. However, a site may have been occupied in a given period even if no pottery from that period is found on the surface. That type may not have been churned up to the surface. The survey method is good, but it is not infallible. Pottery is so important that we shall come back to it again and again.

## Surveys

In one sense, the early travellers discussed in the next section were conducting surveys. They looked around and reported on the sites they visited. In 1838, Edward Robinson made this a more systematic effort. He relied heavily on Arabic names for places. The development of pottery chronology gave Nelson Glueck a tool for dating sites in his surveys (1931–1964) in Transjordan and in the Negev desert in today's Israel. Since this time, pottery chronology has been refined and his work revised but he remains the pioneer.

These surveys have become increasingly sophisticated and precise. Surveyors now use landrovers rather than camels. Photography, including aerial photography, aids in both discovery and recording. New electronic search equipment will be discussed in Section III. In recent years, more attention has been given to settlement patterns and agricultural remains such as terrace walls, cisterns, olive and grape working installations. Thousands of sites are now known throughout the Near East and more are being discovered each year.

## B. "HOW DO YOU DIG?"

"What do you do when you dig?" The circular answer is that when you dig, you dig. But *how* do you dig? The point must quickly be made that you do not "just dig." This is true for any kind of archaeology and biblical archaeology is no exception. The "how" depends upon what is there when you start. The typical Near Eastern site is a mound of earth and debris called a tell. Sometimes a tell is a truncated cone: a cone with no peak so that it is flat on top. It frequently turns out that in its original state, it was a natural hill, but subsequent human habitation has increased the height of the hill. The increase varies from a few feet to seventy or eighty feet or more. The site of Shechem is more of a shoulder (Shechem means "shoulder") of Mount Ebal sticking out into the pass. The original soil just above bedrock is like that found on the slopes of Ebal.

A simplified diagram of the build-up of a tell might remind one of a many-layered chocolate cake. Dark layers, or *strata*, of human occupation debris are interspersed with layers of fill or even darker layers of ash from the fires of destruction. But we are getting ahead of our story. The chocolate cake analogy leads to another, however. If excavators were giants, they could simply cut a wedge out of the cake and see what is there. Instead, ideally, we start at the top and slowly inch our way down, only to find that the layers or strata are not as neat as the cake analogy implies. Ancient cities had hills and valleys, chuck-holes in the streets, eroded ditches and terraces.

## Here's What You Do

Before digging actually starts, the tell or area is mapped by a surveyor. A map is drawn with grid lines related to the lines of latitude and meridian on an ordinary geographical map. The grid lines help to locate on the survey map the exact spot of the digging. The lines may be used to form the limits of the square holes that are dug.

The basic unit of digging is often called a *square*, about fifteen feet on a side. The number and direction of these squares is determined largely by the "lay on the land" and the purpose of digging. The digging takes place in different areas or *fields* on the mound. One field might be concerned with the history of city walls. Hence a series of squares may be marked off on the slope of the mound, forming, in effect, a trench from top to bottom. Another field might be in the approximate center of the mound. Here it is hoped the complete *stratigraphy*, the complete number of *strata* or layers in the history of the city, might be found. Instead of a trench, squares may be arranged to form a large rectangle. We should pause here and note that in between each of the squares is a segment or wall of dirt about three feet thick, called a *balk* or *baulk*.

**Figure 1–14.** Getting ready to dig. A major excavation requires major amounts of supplies, ranging from food for the staff to tents, digging tools, notebooks, string. The buckets are used for soaking pottery overnight. This makes it easier to wash and easier to find ostraca—sherds with writing on them.

**Figure 1–15.**    Stratigraphy inside the Shechem temple. The man is standing on the original floor of the temple, c. 1650 B.C. The plaster floor even with his hand [to the right, his left] is from the rebuilding of the temple, c. 1450 B.C. A thin white line level with his shoulder marks the last phase of the temple, probably destroyed by Abimelech, Judges 9. The rough stone on top is from the foundation of an Iron Age granary.

The balk serves as a walkway between squares. More importantly, we dig straight down. The straight digging and balks serve as a check on the digging. Some strata differ so little in color or consistency that it is virtually impossible to see the difference as the digging deepens. However, the distinction may appear like the cake layers in the side of the balk where you can see or "read" them. As the hole gets deeper, it is necessary to leave steps in the dirt along one or more sides. This makes the square smaller. Eventually the hole may get so deep and the digging room so cramped that it becomes necessary or desirable to remove the balks. They may be simply knocked down and cleared out, or, to serve as a check on one's stratigraphy, they may be carefully dug layer by layer.

**Figure 1–16.** This conglomeration of walls, ancient and modern, is a reminder that excavation is not simply digging a hole in the ground!

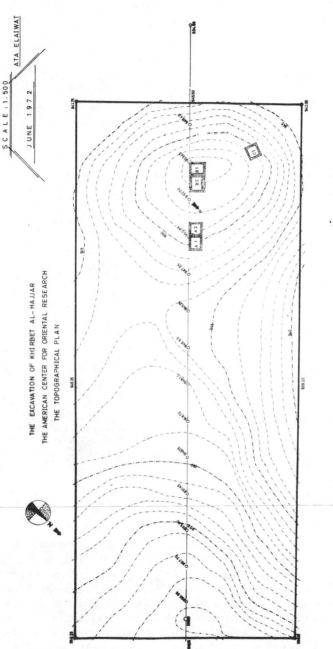

**Figure 1–17.** A survey of Khirbet al-Hajjar and the neighboring hill. The dotted lines are contour lines showing elevation in meters above sea level. The closer the lines, the steeper the slope. Note how the squares are planned along the line of the surveyor's line. Area A was planned to intersect an outer defense wall, not seen but suspected from the surface. The wall was found in Square 1. Area C was planned perpendicular to a wall that appeared above the surface. Area B was the highest point of the hill where one might expect to find the completest stratigraphy for the entire occupation of the hill since ancient peoples tended to live on the high point of the hill for visibility of an approaching enemy. Surveyed and drawn by Ata Elaiwat. Courtesy of Department of Antiquities of Jordan.

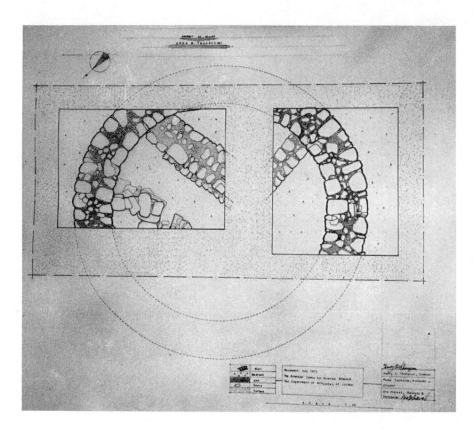

**Figure 1–18.** Plan of Area B. Excavation uncovered a completely unexpected tower, typical of a series around Amman. Some are round and some are square or rectangular. The 18 previously known were plotted and each found to be within sight of 2–3 others. A smoke signal in day time and a fire signal at night would warn of an approaching enemy. A Viet Nam veteran noted the similarity to conflict in that country where guard posts were chosen so their fire power covered the valleys in between to catch infiltrators in a cross fire. The top plan shown here shows several internal walls which would strengthen upper floors as well as provide separate rooms. A door is shown in the lower left wall. Drawn by Ata Elaiwat. Courtesy of Department of Antiquities of Jordan.

**Figure 1–19.** The stratigraphy against the tower wall. The wall of dirt on the left is the outer balk of the square. Locus 31 is the foundation trench. To build their tower, the builders dug through earlier occupation debris represented by loci or strata 21, 22, 25, 26, 28. Most of the wall was on bed rock but in a few spots, Locus (Stratum) 32 ran partly under the wall. Loc. 19 was the first stratum after the wall was built. Drawn by Safe Haddad. Courtesy of Department of Antiquities of Jordan.

# KH AL_HAJJAR

P. 1
SUBSIDIARY BULK
SCALE 1:25
19_20 JULY
S. HADDAD

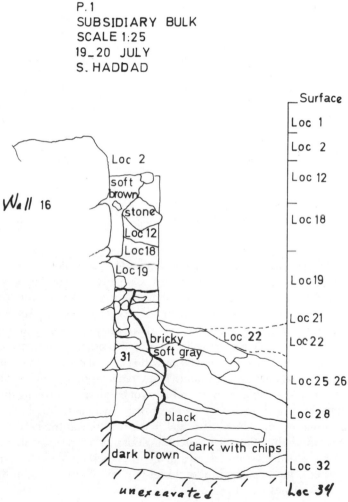

**Figure 1–20.**    Top plan at Tell Siran. The wide space between contour lines shows that the top is nearly flat. This time the squares were planned north-south, in an open area among trees. Only 1 and 2 were dug in this season. Surveyed and drawn by Ata Elaiwat. Courtesy of Department of Antiquities of Jordan.

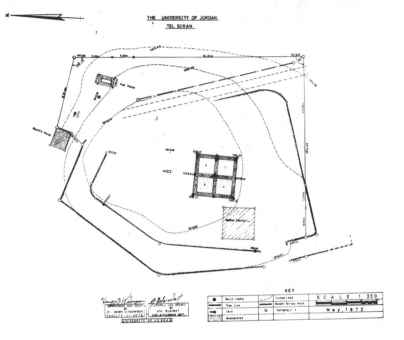

To retrace the procedure just a moment, it should be noted that in starting to dig, the entire fifteen foot square is not dug at once. One uses a pickaxe to mark off part of the area and loosen the top few inches of dirt. A second person with a hoe can scrape the loose dirt into a basket which can be carried away by a basket boy or girl (aged eight to ninety). They carry the baskets of dirt away to be dumped, hopefully where it will not have to be moved again. During this process, pickman, hoeman and basket carriers as well as the supervisor will keep a sharp eye out for pieces of pottery or man-made objects of any kind. These range from the minutest of beads to huge chunks of building stone or the remains of buildings. If nothing unusual is uncovered in the area cleared, the supervisor may have the rest of the area excavated to a similar depth. Then again, he or she may repeat the process and go deeper in the same half-or quarter-square. If in doubt, or simply to be cautious, one might dig a *probe trench* — a small area in a corner, perhaps three feet square, is dug to a greater depth to give a hint of things to come, but it is dug in the same fashion — a few inches at a time.

A new stratum or layer can be detected by changes in the color or consistency of the soil. This new layer can sometimes be traced across the square, with finer tools such as a hand pickaxe, and a mason's trowel. The potsherds from this layer are carefully kept separate from others and when these sherds are dated they in turn date the layer in the earth.

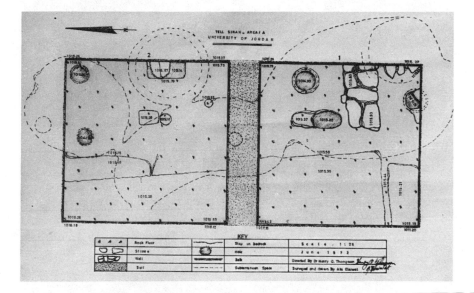

**Figure 1–21.** Plan of Squares 1 and 2. The dotted lines are the outlines of underground rooms. These may have been enlarged from cisterns. The one under the number 2 was still plastered in the lower part. The gray area between Squares 1 and 2 is the unexcavated balk. Drawn by Ata Elaiwat. Courtesy of Department of Antiquities of Jordan.

**Figure 1–22.** Square 1 at Tell Siran. The center balk is on the left. The hole in the middle goes down into an underground room. The wall under the meter stick is probably the foundation of a house. Courtesy of Department of Antiquities of Jordan.

**Figure 1–23.** A "section" or balk at Tell Hesban, Area B, showing a series of plastered layers—strata—perhaps representing a Roman street or paved area, re-paved several times. The "Plains of Moab" are in the background.

**Figure 1–24.**   Strata in excavation. The upper left corner shows the side or section of the square. When the wall was found, a sub-sidiary section or balk was made perpendicular to it. As the digging deepened, several lower sections were made against it.

## And the Walls Came Tumbling Down

In the course of digging, a wall of some nature may appear. The previous square digging may then have to take a slant, for the probe trench or excavation against a wall must always be perpendicular to it. The reasons are twofold. A straight balk is easier to analyze and this straight balk (perpendicular to the wall as well as vertically straight) helps to reveal the history of the wall. A layer or stratum that butts up against the wall would be contemporary with it or a rebuilding of it. But in any event, it was put there after the wall was built. There may be several of these layers and the lowest, or earliest, may be a floor for the building, or a ground surface outside the building or against a defensive or terrace wall.

One of the most interesting aspects of wall excavation is the *foundation trench*. At the bottom of the wall there may be a stratum that is broken — that is, it does not touch the wall. However, the layer above it does. The original builders dug a trench in the ground through the surface which we see as the broken layer. They laid the first courses of the wall under the surface of their day just as modern wall builders do. After building, they back-filled the trench and laid the floor over the filled trench and up to the wall.

This explains in part the build-up of an ancient city mound. Lacking bulldozers, the ancients did not simply "clear the decks," as in urban renewal. If an enemy or the decay of time had sufficiently destroyed the walls of an ancient city, newcomers or returnees would simply smooth out the rubble and build anew. If walls showed

**Figure 1–25.** The pottery shed. The pottery dug in the excavations is kept separate by location in baskets or buckets and washed in the shade of the canvas cover. The wet potsherds are spread out to dry in the hot sun. A preliminary sorting picks out handles, bases, rims, decoration and other elements that can be dated. Specialists then date these and given the excavators the date of the level, layer, or other feature that was excavated.

here and there, they might utilize them in some of their modern construction. Sometimes fill from other parts of the mound or nearby sources would be used to cover the ruins. This was the case when the ancient builders wanted to increase the height of the natural mound for new building. They did this in building the temple at Shechem, c. 1650 B.C. The ground level was raised by about fifteen feet. This made the temple more prominent. Then again, fill may be brought in to eliminate a defensive system. After the conquest of Shechem c. 100 B. C., the defensive system was simply covered up with a massive fill. This building on top of old buildings, or the use of fill, plus the natural accumulation of human debris, accounts for the increase in height of a natural hill to form a tell. This is aided by stumps of the surrounding city wall. The charred or ruined remains of destruction or decay hold back debris washed down from higher levels. This "wall action" helps develop the conic shape of an ancient tell.

## Finer Things

With thin strata, or finer remains such as fragile bones or tiny beads, the excavation may move progressively from the use of a pickaxe to a hand axe, to a trowel, to dental tools, to a brush, and finally to puffs of air with a syringe. Brooms can be used to

**Figure 1–26.**    Ancient peoples and some people today re-use stones from ancient construction. In this wall in Ankara, the long stones with ridges are architraves or the tops of doors. The ones with holes are door sockets. Note the variety of shapes and color, and the bricks built on top of the stone part of the wall.

clean or dust off some surfaces and larger things like rocks or walls. Camel's hair brushes may be too strong for the decayed bones of an infant burial or a bit of ivory carving.

The care used is of course appropriate to the material at hand. A rule of thumb might be, "When in doubt, be careful." The excavator destroys the evidence as digging procedes. The old aphorism holds: better safe than sorry.

## History

The history of the where and the how, and the record of the way in which modern archaeology developed, is the concern of Section II. The people who developed it all are as interesting as the development itself. They are very much a part of the story.

## C.  "WHAT DO YOU FIND?"

The above details on how to dig have given some idea of what we find. We find architecture — city walls and gates, homes, temples, palaces. We find the layers, or strata, which give us the history of the site. The nature of a stratum tells about the

**Figure 1–27.**    Pottery mold for bronze tools and weapons.

history of that city level. It may be ash from a destruction or the hard packed earth of a dirt floor. Objects or *artifacts* found in the stratum give some indication of the culture and the wealth of the town. These artifacts illuminate at least two major aspects of the site's history.

## The City

One of these aspects is what we learn about the life of the place. The German excavations of Shechem discovered two pottery molds for making copper and bronze tools and weapons, such as adzes and spear heads. It was the discovery of such bronze tools in 1908 which had given impetus to the excavation of Shechem. In the Drew University–McCormick Theological Seminary excavations (1956–1964) of Shechem, the broken end of a smaller but similar mold was found in a Middle Bronze Age context, dating from c. 1750 B.C. Two adzes, one in remarkably good condition, were found in a similar context. These adzes fit neatly into the remaining portion of the mold. These finds, plus several objects called blast furnace nozzles, plus quantities of copper slag and miscellaneous other bronze and copper objects, would seem to indicate a small but flourishing bronze industry in Shechem at that time.

The remains of a large, two-story house excavated on top of the tell had an industrial fire-pit, possibly for slaking lime. This was a patrician-sized house. It was surrounded by the wall stumps of small rough huts which suggested poor workers, or possibly slaves, who may have been involved in the industrial work.

## Dating

A second major aspect of the search for artifacts is the help they give in dating the stratum in which they are found. Some of these items are rather explicit, such as *scarabs* inscribed with the name of a particular Egyptian pharaoh. The date of the pharaoh, known from Egyptian sources, thus gives a clue to the date of the layer. Some caution is necessary. Scarabs were sometimes handed down from one generation to another as heirlooms, precious stones, or magic amulets. The stratum would probably not be any earlier than the pharaoh, but could be much later, dating to the last owner of the scarab rather than the first.

Other things help correct this initial impression by providing independent sources of dating. The lowly potsherd noted earlier is a major source for dating. Pottery was invented c. 7000–5000 B.C. It broke easily. Under ordinary circumstances, people did not keep broken potsherds as heirlooms. The broken bits were trampled under foot or thrown into the street or into the village trash heap. There they lay like precious stones waiting for the eager grasp of the modern archaeologist. Pottery, like clothing, changes style from generation to generation and from people to people. We study the decoration, style, form of handles, shape of rims and bases, and the quality of manufacture. Broken pottery in the bottom layers is normally older than that in the strata on top or nearer the top. A date for a specific layer, from a scarab or inscription or obtained by some other means, gives a date to a particular type of pottery. Several dated layers give us dates for several types of pottery. The dates of other styles from other strata can then be interspersed. This method of sequence dating for pottery *(typology)* was developed by Sir Flinders Petrie and refined by William F. Albright. Refinement continues with each generation of archaeologists. Now pottery typology is itself a reliable tool for the dating of the layers in a site's history.

Scarabs and pottery are but two means of dating. Another obvious way is by using coins. One of the oldest coins discovered in the Holy Land was found at Shechem. It is a late sixth century B.C. Greek coin from the island of Thasos. In 1960, a small horde of coins was discovered at Shechem. The dates indicated that they were hidden in the second century B.C., since the latest was made in 193 B.C. In the overall context of the Bible, however, coins are a relatively recent innovation. Coinage was developed in the seventh century B.C. in Lydia, part of today's Turkey.

The very latest methods of dating are discussed later but other aids in determining archaeological chronology can be considered here. Art history shows how the study of painting, decoration, sculpture and architecture can help in dating a find or city level. There is a type of construction, for example, called *terra pisee*, or beaten earth. The Hyksos, c. 1700 B.C., often built ramparts with a glacis of beaten earth. They brought horse-drawn chariots with them and built huge encampments for their horses and chariots. There is one at Hazor, north of the Sea of Galilee, that covers about 160 acres. Around these camps, or simply around the outside of the city wall, they built a long sloping embankment. This was plastered to prevent erosion. An enemy charging up the embankment would be fully exposed to the defenders spears and arrows.

Inscriptions are important for dating purposes. The vocabulary, the grammar, the date of use of a language in a given area — all of these help with chronology. Aramaic became a common language *(lingua franca)* c. 550 B.C. Thus "Aramaisms" suggest a later date than Assyrian words or inscriptions. The use of Akkadian as the "lingua franca" of the Late Bronze Age (1500–1200 B.C.) is an earlier example of dating by language. Over the centuries, the way in which letters or signs were formed also changed. A study of these changes helps date inscriptions. This was an important means of dating the Dead Sea Scrolls.

Like pottery, inscriptions help date other archaeological finds. Their contents provide historical records which are frequently helpful. A destruction layer which is loosely dated c. 1450 B.C., perhaps by pottery or art, might be more accurately dated to 1479 by an inscription in Egypt which tells about the conquest of the city by Pharaoh Tuthmosis III.

## Daily Life

Ancient pottery was a part of daily life. So were houses, city walls, and a great deal more. Excavators find the remains of food — olive pits, grain, animal bones. These are fragile and decay easily so only parts may remain like the hard outer shell of pollen grains or the impression of a stalk of wheat left in a mud brick. Grinders and sickles and storage bins are found. The luxuries of life also appear — cosmetics or cosmetic holders or implements, jewelry or the molds in which it was made, ivory in the form of decorated pieces for furniture.

Organic material such as furniture or clothing does not usually last but in very dry regions, fragments may remain. Cloth of finely woven linen and wool were found at Kintillet Ajrud south of Kadesh Barnea. At Jericho, Kenyon found some tomb furniture preserved underground. Some of the Dead Sea Scrolls were

**Figure 1–28.** A modern diamond toothed saw is used for cutting pottery. Photo courtesy Lawrence T. Geraty, Director, Hesban Expedition.

**Figure 1–29.**    Cut pottery can be drawn by tracing, which is much faster than older methods involving careful measurements with calipers and transfer to paper of connectable points. Photo courtesy L. T. Geraty.

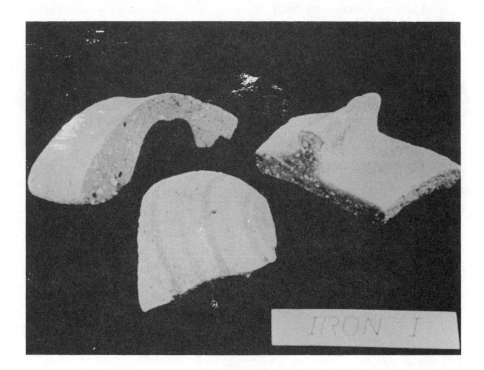

wrapped in linen. Scrolls may be of *papyrus* which survives rarely, or of *parchment* (animal skins), which has a better chance. One of the Dead Sea Scrolls is made of copper.

"What has been found" and its illumination of the Bible is the running theme of Sections V and VI. Who found what is also of interest. We note also Sir Mortimer Wheeler's oft-quoted aphorism that we are not digging up things, but people. They too are of interest. For archaeology in general, David P. Williams claims "Man's self-understanding is the ultimate guest." In a sense, we are digging up ourselves. [1]

## D. "WHY DO YOU DIG?"

This last question and its answers have been hinted at already. What is the significance of all this digging? One could echo Sir Edmund Hilary who was asked why
he climbed Mount Everest. In some surprise that the question should even come
up, he answered, "Why, because it's there." That is certainly one reason for digging. In another famous aphorism, Wheeler noted that pragmatically, archaeology
is useless. But he thought it had other qualities. It is a robust, adventurous science,
one which has the manifold task of revealing in three dimensions the works of
man's unconquerable mind, a science which can stimulate the human mind to
fresh conquests as few other disciplines can.[2]

For Wheeler, the traditional view of archaeology as the "Handmaid of History"
belongs to the era of the dodo.[3] Without succumbing to the reductionism
("nothing but. . .") of "handmaid" we can still be interested in history as one, or
even the primary, reason for digging. In the early years of archaeology, the major
motivation for archaeological excavation seems to have been the search for
"treasure." Of course, no modern excavator dislikes finding material of museum or
display interest. Still less will he throw it away. In fact, it is against the antiquities
law in most countries to do much of anything with such artifacts except turn them
over to the antiquities department of the host country. Since the late 1880s, however, archaeological interest has turned more and more directly to the detailed history represented by the strata and artifacts.

Now if history is a major or direct motive for digging, it is appropriate to press the
issue and ask why we have this interest in history. It has been said that we are our
past and that we cannot divorce ourselves from our past. We need to understand
that past if we want to understand ourselves. Thus we need to know how earlier
people lived. What did they do for a living? What was their religion? What was their
standard of living? What did they eat? What did they wear? What were their ideals?
Did they have any literature? What kind of government did they have? Did they
have any connections with other ancient peoples? What relationship, if any, do
they have with the present day?

All these questions and more are implied by our interest in history. Palestine or
Canaan is frequently called the crossroads of Africa and Asia, or the bridge between
Egypt and Mesopotamia, the whole forming a *fertile crescent* (James Breasted's
term) of river valleys that saw the birth of Western civilization. Biblical archaeology has an additional interest not normally found in American Indian, African,
South Sea Island, Chinese, and other archaeologies. It is related to the Jewish,
Christian and Islamic heritage. People who have read or heard about the Bible are
frequently interested in trying to acquire a deeper understanding of it. In a famous
lecture, "Babel und Bibel," Friedrich Delitzsch (1850–1922) asked a rhetorical
question on why people should be interested in all the churning and digging of

ancient Babylon. He answered his own question, "The Bible!" Modern scholarship claims that the Bible and history come together in a unique way. Whether we consider the Hebrew Tenak (the Christian Old Testament) or the Christian combination of the Old and New Testaments, the Bible has a great deal of history in it. Archaeology contributes to an understanding of that history. Biblical archaeology contributes to an understanding of the Bible.

Shechem illustrates this understanding. The city plays an important part in several areas of biblical history. Genesis 12 and 33 tell us about Abraham and Jacob, c. 1800–1700 B.C. Joshua 24 describes the covenant of Joshua with the people of Israel at Shechem c. 1225 B.C. Judges 9 describes the rule of Abimelech c. 1150 B.C. Jeroboam I had his capital there c. 922 B.C. (I Kings 12). The site's last destruction was by the Maccabean King John Hyrcanus c. 107 B.C., perhaps because it was a stronghold of the Samaritans. The latter still hold their annual Passover on nearby Mount Gerazim. Samaritans still live in Nablus which has incorporated Balata into its city limits. The Samaritan temple on Tell er-Ras, the first of the three peaks of Mount Gerizim, was noted earlier. The Samaritans built it c. 330 B.C. and it was destroyed c. 128 B.C. by Hyrcanus. Later the Romans built a temple on this peak and later still, the Christians built one or more churches on Gerizim.

A clearer picture of the history of ancient Palestine will clarify and aid our understanding of the Bible. Sometimes archaeology seems to confirm the biblical picture of historical events. In contrast to other sites, the Bible gives no description of Joshua's conquest of Shechem, and yet he controlled it (Joshua 8:30, 23, 24). Somehow he took it over peacefully or at least it came into the Israelite confederacy without a battle. Excavations of Shechem have not found any evidence of major or total destruction in this period (c. 1250–1230 B.C.). Archaeology, of course, does not solve all the problems. For example, how did Joshua acquire control of Shechem in the first place?

This last statement serves as a reminder that archaeology is not ordinarily a "now-it-is-done-for-all-time" operation. There is still a great part of the mound of Shechem which has not been excavated. Just as the Americans followed the Germans after an interlude of twenty-two years, so yet another Shechem dig may be under way some day, unless the current suburban expansion from Nablus completely covers the rest of the mound.

"Why do you dig?" is a theological question. It concerns the meaning of what we are doing. The theological significance of archaeology is the theme of Section VI.

Whole volumes have been and will continue to be written on the subject matter covered here. These four questions give a thumbnail sketch of archaeology itself. How do we know where to dig? We know from accidental finds, biblical descriptions, perhaps historical identification of the site. How do we dig? Carefully — often with painstaking care — sometimes switching from a pickaxe to a small hand pick to a mason's trowel, and finally to a brush, perhaps a camel's hair brush. What do we find? We discover the stratified history of a site, plus pottery and other arti-facts such as figurines, tools and weapons; sling stones; masonry and building remains; animal and vegetable remains; and human bones. What is the signifi-cance of all this? Why do we dig? A more accurate picture of the history of a site, a country, and a people leads to a clearer understanding of that people's history. In the case of biblical cities, this knowledge leads to a clearer understanding of the Bible.[4]

# NOTES

1. Williams, "As a Discipline Comes of Age." *Archaeology* 29 (no. 4; Oct. 1976), pp. 229–231.
2. Wheeler, *Alms for Oblivion: An Antiquary's Scrapbook* (London: Weidenfeld and Nicholson, 1966), p. 97.
3. Wheeler, *Alms for Oblivion*, p. 95.
4. Much of the content of this chapter came out of the writer's own field work. The attached bibliog-raphy may be helpful for those who wish to continue their study. Abbreviations are listed in the front matter.

# ADDITIONAL READING

Aharoni, Yohanan. 1973. "Remarks on the 'Israeli' Method of Excavation." EI 11:48–53 (Hebrew), 23 (English summary).

Aharoni, Yohanan. *Arad Inscriptions*. Jerusalem: IES, 1981.

Albright, William F. 1932–38. "The Excavation of Tell Beit Mirsim I, IA, II." AASOR 12, 13, 17.

Albright, William F. *The Archaeology of Palestine*. Baltimore: Penguin, 1961 (original 1949).

Albright, William F. 1969. "The Impact of Archaeology on Biblical Research — 1966." pp. 1–14 in FGNDBA.

AINAN 1, no. 1, Spr. 74.

Amiran, Ruth. *Ancient Pottery of the Holy Land*. Jerusalem: Masada, 1963.

Bade, William F. *A Manual of Excavation in the Near East*. Berkeley: University of California, 1934.

Banning, Edward F. 1982. "The Research Design of the Wadi Ziqlab Survey, 1981." ASORN 8:4–8.

Barker, Philip A. *Techniques of Archaeological Excavation*. New York: Universe, 1983.

Bass, George F. *Archaeology Beneath the Sea*. New York: Walker, 1976.

Bevan, Bruce W. *Aerial Photography for the Archaeologist*. Philadelphia: University Museum, 1975.

Blakely, Jeffrey A. and Toombs, Lawrence E. *The Tell El-Hesi Field Manual: The Joint Archaeological Expedition to Tell El-Hesi*, Vol. I. Cambridge: ASOR, 1980.

Breiner, Sheldon. *Applications Manual for Portable Magnetometers*. Palo Alto, CA: Geometrics, 1973.

Breiner, Sheldon. 1965. "The Rubidium Magnetometer in Archaeological Exploration." *Science* 150 (no. 3690): 185–193.

Brothwell, Don and Higgs, Eric S. eds., *Science in Archaeology*. New York: Praeger, 1970.

Bull, Robert J. 1968. "The Excavation of Tell er-Ras on Mt. Gerizim," BA 31: 58–72.

Burrows, Millar. *What Mean These Stones?*. New York: Meridian, 1957 (original 1941).

Ceram, C. W. *A Picture History of Archaeology*. London: Thames and Hudson, 1958.

Courbin, P. "How to Locate a Site." *Larousse Encyclopedia of Archaeology*, pp. 57–71; ed. Gilbert Charles-Picard; NY: Putnam, 1972.

Courbin, P. "The Excavation," *Larousse Encyclopedia* pp. 73–93.

Daniel, Glyn. *The Origins and Growth of Archaeology*. Baltimore: Penguin, 1967.

Daniel, Glyn, ed. *Towards a History of Archaeology*. New York: Thames and Hudson, 1980.

Daniels, Steve and David, Nicholas. *The Archaeology Workbook*. Philadelphia: University Museum, 1982.

Deuel, Leo. *Flights Into Yesterday*. New York: St. Martin's, 1969.

Dever, William G. 1980. "Archaeological Method in Israel: A Continuing Revolution." BA 43 (no. 1): 41–48.

Dever, William G. "Archaeology." *IDBSV*.

Dever, William G. 1973. "The Gezer Fortifications and the 'High Place': An Illustration of Stratigraphic Methods and Problems." PEQ 105: 61–70.

Dever, William G. 1973. "Two Approaches to Archaeological Method — The Architectural and the Stratigraphic." EI 11: 1–8.

Dever, William G. 1986. "Late Bronze Age and Solomonic Defenses at Gezer: New Evidence." BASOR 262: 9–34.

Dever, William G. and Lance, H. Darrel, eds. *A Manual of Field Excavation: Handbook for Field Archaeology*. New York: Hebrew Union College, 1978.

Dumas, Frederic. *Deep-Water Archaeology*. London: Routledge and Kegan Paul, 1962.

Fagan, Brian M. *Corridors in Time*. Boston: Little, Brown, 1974.

Franken, H.J. and Franken-Battershill, C.A. *A Primer of Old Testament Archaeology*. Leiden: Brill, 1963.

Glueck, Nelson, 1934–51. Explorations in Eastern Palestine. AASOR 14, 13, 18–19, 25–28.

Hawkes, C.F.C., 1954. "Archaeological Theory and Method: Some Suggestions from the Old World." *The American Anthropologist* 56: 155–168.

Heizer, Robert F., ed. *Man's Discovery of His Past*. Englewood Cliffs, NJ: Prentice-Hall, 1962.

Herzog, Ze'ev, et al., 1984. "The Israelite Fortress at Arad." BASOR 254. (Spr. 1984) 1–34.

Hester, Thomas R., et al. *Field Methods in Archaeology*. 6th ed.; Palo Alto, CA: Mayfield, 1975.

Joukowksy, Martha. *A Complete Manual of Field Archaeology*. Englewood Cliffs, NJ: Prentice-Hall, 1980.

Kelso, James L. "Jericho". IDB 2:835–839.

Kenyon, Kathleen M. *Beginning in Archaeology*. 4th ed.; New York: Norton, 1972.

Lance, H. Darrel. *Excavation Manual for Area Supervisors*. New York: HUCBAS, 1967.

Lapp, Paul W. 1968. "Bab edh-Dhra Tomb A 76 and Early Bronze I in Palestine." BASOR 189: 12–41.

Lapp, Paul W. *Palestinian Ceramic Chronology 200 B.C.– 70 A.D.* New Haven: ASOR, 1961.

Lapp, Paul W. *Biblical Archaeology and History*. Cleveland: World, 1969.

Lapp, Paul W. *The Tale of the Tell*. Pittsburgh: Pickwick, 1975.

MacDonald, Burton. 1981. "The Wadi el Hasa Survey, 1981," ASORN 3: 8–15.

Mazar, Benjamin, ed. *Thirty Years of Archaeology in Eretz-Israel 1948–1978*. Jerusalem: IES, 1981.

Piggott, Stuart. *Approach to Archaeology*. New York: McGraw-Hill, 1959.

Pyddoke, Edward, ed. *The Scientist and Archaeology*. New York: Roy, 1963.

Pyddoke, Edward. *Stratification for the Archaeologist*. London: Phoenix House, 1961.

Renfrew, Colin. 1980. "The Great Tradition versus the Great Divide: Archaeology as Anthropology." AJA 84 (no. 3): 287–298.

Schaub, R. Thomas and Rast, Walter E. 1984. "Preliminary Report of the 1981 Expedition to the Dead Sea Plain, Jordan." BASOR 254: 35–60.

Schiffer, Michael B., ed. *Advances in Archaeological Method and Theory*. New York: Academic Press, 1978.

Schoville, Keith N. *Biblical Archaeology in Focus*. Grand Rapids: Baker, 1978.

Seger, Joe D. 1981. "A Capsule History of Archaeological Methods." BAR 7 (no. 1): 49–51.

Seger, Joe D. 1967. "Why We Dig — At Gezer!" *The Hartford Quarterly* 7 (no. 4, Summer): 9–39.

Shennan, Stephen. "Investigation in the Field," pp. 29–39 (in *The Cambridge Encyclopedia of Archaeology*, ed. Andrew Sherratt; New York: Cambridge University and Crown Publishers, 1980).

Thompson, Henry O. 1977. "Thoughts on Archaeological Method." BAR 3 (no. 3): 25–27. (Sep 77), 25–27.

Thompson, Henry O. "What's in a Name," in *Put Your Future in Ruins*, ed. Thompson; Bristol, IN: Wyndham Hall, 1985.

Toombs, Lawrence E. 1982. "The Development of Palestinian Archaeology as a Discipline" BA 42 (no. 3): 89–91.

Toombs, Lawrence E. *Excavation Manual*. Wooster, OH: Wooster College, 1966.

Toombs, Lawrence E. "Principles of Field Technique" pp. 185–190 in *Shechem* by G. Ernest Wright; New York: McGraw–Hill, 1965.

Van Beek, Gus W., "*Archaeology*." IDB 1:195–207.

Wheeler, R. E. Mortimer. *Archaeology from the Earth*. Baltimore: Penguin, 1954.

Williams, David P. 1976. "As a Discipline Comes of Age: Reflections on Archaeology and the Scientific Method." *Archaeology* 29, (no. 4): 229–231.

Wilson, David, ed. *Aerial Reconnaissance for Archaeology*. London: The Council for British Archaeology, 1975.

Wilson, David. *The New Archaeology*. New York: New American Library, 1974.

Wiseman, James. 1980. "Archaeology in the Future: An Evolving Discipline." AJA 84 (no. 3): 279–285.

Wright, G. Ernest, 1969. "Archaeological Method in Palestine — An American Intepretation. EI 9: 125–129.

Wright, G. Ernest. *Biblical Archaeology*. Philadelphia: Westminster, 1962.

Wright, G. Ernest. "Biblical Archaeology Today." FGNDBA 149–165.

Wright, G. Ernest, 1969. "Is Glueck's Aim to Prove that the Bible is True?" BA 22 (no. 4): 101–108.

Wright, G. Ernest. "The Phenomenon of American Archaeology in the Near East." NEATC 3–40.

Woolley, Leonard. *Digging Up the Past*. Baltimore: Penguin, 1950.

Young, Gordon D., ed. *Ugarit in Retrospect: 50 years of Ugarit and Ugaritic*. Winona Lake, IN: Eisenbrauns, 1981.

# THE HISTORY OF ARCHAEOLOGY

Archaeology began as a treasure hunt. In a sense it still is. Several of the famous Dead Sea Scrolls were sold for $250,000. Yigael Yadin bought them for Israel. More recently, he paid $105,000 for the Temple Scroll. Antiquities bring high prices, not only in the Near East but all over the world. In time, archaeology became a science. However, scientific archaeology is much like other sciences, with origins in more popular interests than the advancement of knowledge. Astronomy and space exploration are rooted in astrology, a way of reading the future or the will of the gods. Chemistry started in alchemy, which searched for ways to turn ordinary metals into gold. Modern chemistry is a continuing search for "treasure" and the "finding" of the treasure is apparent in the value of chemical company shares on the stock markets of the world.

In chapter 2, we review some of the "unscientific" beginnings, while chapter 3 covers the major developments of archaeology in the nineteenth century. Chapter 4 is on the development of "modern" archaeology and some of the many excavations since World War II.

# How it all Began

## A. THE FORERUNNERS

### Thou Shalt Not Steal

It could be said that archaeology began as a treasure hunt, with the tomb robbers who went after the gold and jewelry buried with kings and nobility. Tomb robber excavations included the pyramids of Giza, near modern Cairo, Egypt. The first European did not enter the second great pyramid (Chephren's) until 1818, but the robbers had already been there. Rare and exciting, indeed, is the discovery of an unlooted tomb such as that of "King Tut" (Tut-ankh-Amon) in 1922 in the Valley of the Kings near Luxor. The prolonged and detailed excavation by Howard Carter commanded newspaper headlines for months. Unfortunately, tomb robbers merely smash in, grab the loot and fade away without publicity — and without accurate records of what was found, where it was in the tomb, etc.

King Tut belonged to the Eighteenth Dynasty (family group) of Egyptian pharaohs. This dynasty ruled from c. 1550–1310 B.C. In contrast to the public splendor of the pyramids built about 2600 B.C., the tombs of the pharaohs began to be hidden, because of tomb robbers, as early as 1515 B.C. The hidden tombs were soon found, however. A papyrus inscription has been recovered from the time of Ramses IX, c. 1125 B.C. The papyrus is a record of a court trial of eight tomb robbers. In 1881, Maspero and Brugsch of the Egyptian Department of Antiquities traced tomb robberies to a family that had made it an art for six centuries! Many of the antiquities on sale in today's market are stolen from plundered tombs, whether

43

**Figure 2–1.** Chephren's Pyramid. The second of the three big pyramids on the Giza plateau across the Nile from Cairo. The smooth limestone still covering the peak may have covered all three pyramids in ancient times but over the years it has been removed for other building projects.

in the Near East or elsewhere. Someone has waggishly suggested that since it is apparently impossible to stop all the tomb robberies, we should teach local people to write reports on their "excavations" so the results will not be lost to science. Maspero solved his problem by hiring one of the family members as chief of antiquities for the region!

The tomb robber tradition continues today in the *pot hunters*, both amateur and commercial thieves. The latter include diggers and dealers who traffic in stolen goods. In the United States, fifty per cent of the ancient sites have already been plundered and the rest of the world is catching up with "civilization."[1]

**Figure 2–2.**    The Sphinx at Giza stares unblinking into the desert sun while modern tourists turn to dark glasses or squint doggedly against the intense glare.

## For the Gods

Other examples of early "archaeology" had different motives. A pharaoh's son, later Tuthmosis IV (1421–13 B.C.), stopped to rest while out hunting. He fell asleep in the shadow of a huge head sticking out of the sand. What we now call the Sphinx spoke to him in a dream. He claimed to be the god Harmakis. The Sphinx told the young man he was the divine choice to be pharaoh and then complained about "the sands of the desert. . .encroaching upon me." A later copy of the story was carved on a slab of rock — a *stela* (Greek for "pillar of stone"). This was set up between the paws of the *Sphinx*, which has a man's head and a lion's body. The end of the text is lost but it would seem Tuthmosis cleared the sand away from the part natural rock and part brick body, 840 feet long and 66 feet high at the head. This is the first recorded excavation according to Jacquetta Hawkes. The Sphinx was cleared again by the Twenty-Sixth Dynasty (c. 600 B.C.), the Romans, the French, and the Egyptians.

A similar category of "clearance" fits the efforts of King Nabonidus (556–539 B.C.) of the Chaldeans or Neo-Babylonians. He has been nicknamed "the royal archaeologist." Before he was defeated by Cyrus the Persian, Nabonidus excavated a number of ancient temples, especially of the moon god Sin (pronounced "seen"). He wanted these temples and the worship of the gods properly restored. At one point, he found the temple foundation stone laid by Naram-Sin (c. 2350 B.C.) thirty feet below the surface of Nabonidus' day. His predecessor, Nebuchadnezzar (605–562) collected antiquities from his diggings. These were kept in a special room in his palace — the first museum! Nabonidus' daughter continued the royal museum tradition.

What may have been the first example of archaeological interpretation involves the Greek historian Thucydides. A number of graves were cleared as part of the purification of the temple on the island of Delos in 426 B.C. Half of these were identified as "Carian" because the type of weapons found in the graves and the method of burial resembled that of the Carians of Thucydides' own time.[2]

## Kings and Things

Since archaeology literally means the study of, or the science of, the ancient, we might include here the archaizing tendencies of the ancient world. This tendency continues to appear in the present. It was very prominent in ancient Egypt where art forms followed those of the Old Kingdom from about 2500 B.C. There were rare exceptions like the naturalism of Pharaoh Ikhnaton's period c. 1350 B.C., which lasted through the reign of King Tut. The cumbersome *hieroglyphics* continued in use for centuries after a more usuable script had developed. This was also true for the *cuneiform* (wedge-shaped) writing in Mesopotamia although later writing included some simplification.

A good example of this concern with the old is the Assyrian King Ashurbanipal (669–633 B.C.). He was apparently following an even earlier tradition when he had old inscriptions collected. Where necessary, new copies were made for his library in Nineveh. Later, Alexander the Great (336–323 B.C.) took scholars along on his military campaigns. These men reported their observations to Alexander's teacher, Aristotle, who used the new information for writing natural history.

Napoleon Bonaparte, perhaps deliberately following Alexander's example, took a Commission of the Sciences and Arts along with his expedition to Egypt in 1798. These 167 men included antiquarians and architects who documented the visible remains of ancient Egypt while the army fought the Muslim rulers of the Nile. These French studies are considered to be the beginning of the academic study of Egyptology. Among the results was the publication (by James Ridgeway) in 1802 of *Travels in Upper and Lower Egypt* by Dominique Vivant Denon (1745–1825) in London. This brought many antiquities to European attention. This was even more true for the Commission's *Description of Egypt* (1809–26). This massive study created a sensation. The treasures Napoleon's scholars collected for France ended up in the British Museum when the "Island Kingdom" brought his whole Near Eastern effort to an end. The treasures included the famous Rosetta Stone, discussed later.

Such looting on a national scale followed ancient precedent. The French themselves had recently acquired a substantial amount of Italian art as "war reparations." The Romans helped themselves to the art of Greece, both visible and invisible. When Caesar's legions rebuilt Corinth, they discovered antiquities that stirred Roman society and helped create a market for a new wave of tomb robberies. The latter sought vases and bronzes for collectors. The Emperor Hadrian (117–138 A.D.) both collected and copied antiquities. We could go back even further to the French discovery of the stela of Hammurabi's law code (c. 1700 B.C.) in ancient Susa (in today's Iran). The Elamites had set it up there after "lifting" this copy when they raided their Babylonian neighbors (in today's Iraq). A later king of Elam, Shutruk-Nahunte (c. 1160 B.C.) raided Mesopotamian cities also, and deposited the booty in a temple at Susa. Conflict between today's Iran and Iraq has a long history.[3]

## B. TRAVELERS

Pilgrims and travelers sometimes recorded their experiences, with various degrees of accuracy. These records now help us locate the sites of ancient cities and give us information on the conditions of ruins in a given period. Since some of these ruins no longer exist, their descriptions are all we have. In their own day, they contributed to an interest in antiquities which eventually led to modern archaeology. We can note here that Palestine and adjacent areas have been the goal of Jewish pilgrims from the time of the first dispersions (*diaspora*) in the seventh century B.C. In time, Christian pilgrims added to the throng and eventually Muslims took to the road on their way to Jerusalem and Mecca. Later still, the Crusaders created enormous interest in the Near East. The European Renaissance quickened a fascination with the Classical Era of Greece and with all things ancient.

## To Begin

The ancient Greeks set a few records with their travels, which some of them recorded. Herodotus of Halicarnassus (c. 484–30 B.C.) went as far as the First Cataract in Egypt, c. 450. Diodorus Siculus of Sicily lived in Egypt c. 59 B.C. Strabo, a Greek speaking native of Pontus, lived in Alexandria and also traveled to the First Cataract, c. 25 B.C. Other early writers were the Latins, Pliny the Elder (23–79 A.D.) and Claudius Ptolemaeus who wrote a geography c. 150 A.D.

The Jewish historian Josephus (37–100 A.D.) refers to many Palestinian places. His work is an important, though not always accurate, source of information for the archaeology of this area. This is also the case for the writings of the Christian historian Eusebius (c. 260–340 A.D.), especially his Onomasticon. A writer known simply as the Bordeaux Pilgrim traveled through Palestine in 333 A.D. His record includes such places as Shechem and the Constantinian church at Bethlehem.

The earliest Muslim records still in existence to do not begin until the ninth century A.D. but continue in a steady stream thereafter. Ya'akubi (Ibn Wadhih) wrote both geography and history. He wrote in 874 about the Dome of the Rock in Jerusalem, the site of Solomon's Temple of biblical fame. Another important description of Jerusalem is by Mukaddasi, perhaps a native of the city, who wrote in 985. Ibn Hauqal, in 978, made a new edition of Istakhri's writing (951 A.D.), the first systematic Arab geography. Babylon is one of the many places he describes. One of the greatest Muslim works is the *Geographical Dictionary* by Yakut (1225). This is a detailed description of Muslim countries and towns from India to Spain. Abu el-Fida (1273–1331), Prince of Hama in Syria, wrote a geography in 1321. It has personal observations of the Palestine-Syria area. Amman was in ruins and Hesban was the capital of the Belga region. Arabic writers were not well known in the West so they had little effect on Europe until translations began to appear in the second half of the nineteenth century. The development of modern archaeology occurred primarily in Europe.

In 1172, Benjamin ben Jonah, a rabbi of Tudela, Navarre (Spain) visited Palmyra in Syria and Babylon and Mosul in Iraq. He correctly identifed the ruins across the Tigris River from Mosul as those of ancient Nineveh, one time capital of Assyria which fell in 612 B.C. to the Babylonians and their nomad allies. The rabbi's writings, however, were not published until 1575, so his influence was felt later. Ciriaco de' Pizzicolli (1391–1455), a merchant from Ancona in Italy, made

several journeys to Greece and the East (1435–6, 1443–7). He methodically collected antiquities and information, and made drawings and descriptions of monuments. His care in recording suggests to some that he is "the father of archaeology,"
a title given to a number of people.

In 1543, Persepolis, capital of the Persian Empire (555–321 B.C.), was brought
to European attention by Geosofat Barbaros, Venice's ambassador to Persia. A
German doctor, Leonhard Rauchwolff (or Rauwolf) visited Palestine in 1575. He
made systematic observations in natural history, especially botany. He also
described a visit to Babylon and Nineveh. A contemporary, John Eldred, an
English merchant, traveled to Baghdad in 1583. A Flemish traveler, Johann Zual-
lart, related architecture and archaeology in his drawings in 1586.

In 1579, Johannes Helfrich published an account of his tour (1565) of the pyramids and the Sphinx. An Italian nobleman, Pietro della Valle (died 1658), seeking
solace from a rejected love, journeyed into the Near East. In 1616, he identified
Babylon and Ur (Tell al-Muqayyar). He sent the first samples of cuneiform writing
to Europe from Persepolis and Babylon. Three volumes of his travels were printed
in 1650–58. The Jesuit mathematician, Athanasium Kircher (1601–80) published
*Lingua Aegyptiaca* in 1643. He believed he had succeeded in translating the Egyptian hieroglyphics which Valle had found in Cairo in 1615. Kircher also published
*The Tower of Babel* (1674), based on Valle's travels.[4]

## More Serious

The newly founded (1660) Royal Society of London asked for an accurate description of Persepolis in 1666. In that same year a traveling jeweler, Jean Chardin
(1643–1713) went to Baghdad and later to India. Along the way, he made the accurate observations of Persepolis. He also published the first complete inscription
from the site. Another doctor, Jacob Spon, critically described (1674) what he saw
while traveling in Greece and Asia Minor. He may have coined the term,
"archaeology" for modern use although in the sense of ancient history the term was
used by Plato, Thucydides and Josephus.

In 1685, Engelbert Kampfer visited Persepolis. He brought back many drawings
and the first lengthy cuneiform text to reach Europe. In 1697, an English Chap-
lain, Henry Maundrell, added new archaeological data in the account of his travels
(published 1703) from Aleppo to Jerusalem to Jericho. His diary was so accurate it
served as a guide book for the area for over 150 years and has now been reprinted.

A monumental handbook, *Palestine Illustrated by Ancient Monuments*, was
published in 1709 by a Dutchman. Adrian Reland collected all the available information of the time and critically analyzed it. An English bishop, Richard Pococke
(1704–65) traveled (1737–43) in the Near East. He reached the Valley of the Kings
in Upper Egypt and often left the beaten track of the usual traveler. His book, A

**Figure 2–3.** Jerash was rediscovered by Seetzen. Here is a view of the unusual elliptical forum, seen from the top steps of the theater (which has been restored for plays, concerts, festivals). The lighter color along the bottom of the columns shows the depth of centuries of rubble and sand. Similarly, the lighter colored architraves are those restored or put back in place on top of the columns. The Ionic columns and the forum itself are from the earlier building boom in Jerash. The city continued through Hellenistic, Roman, Byzantine, and Islamic periods, until felled by an earthquake. Photo courtesy Jordan Information Bureau, Washington, D.C.

**Figure 2–4.** The Roman Theater in Amman, Jordan. When Seetzen re-discovered ancient Rabbath Ammon, capital of the Ammonites in the Iron Age, Amman was just a dusty village. As this picture shows, it is now a bustling capital city of the modern Hashemite Kingdom. The theater was built into the hillside when Amman was ancient Philadelphia, one of the Decapolis (Ten Cities). The hill itself is but one of seven, paralleling the seven hills of Rome. The theater has been restored to its original seating capacity of 6,000 people (it's one of the biggest in the near east) and is used for concerts. A number of the columns of the Roman Forum have been set up again and part of the Forum restored as a garden. The Philadelphia Hotel stands at one end.

*Description of the East* (1743) had more plans, drawings, and inscriptions than any previous volume.

A Danish mathematician, Carsten Niebuhr (1733–1815) was the only survivor of an expedition in 1762. His book, *Travels through Arabia and other Countries in the East* (1774–78) was of interest to Napoleon. Niebuhr's accurate copying of cuneiform signs from Persepolis aided in the later decipherment of the language. He also made sketches and drawings of Nineveh. Ulrich Jasper Seetzen explored Transjordan for the first time in a scientific way in the years 1805–07. He rediscovered Amman and Jerash. One of the most fascinating travelers was Johann Ludwig Burckhardt (1784–1817). He became a Muslim and traveled as Sheik Ibrahim to the holy cities of Mecca and Medina. Burckhardt is perhaps most famous for his rediscovery of the Nabataean city of Petra in southern Jordan, in the area of biblical Edom.[5.]

**Figure 2–5.** Petra—The Monastery (Ed-Deir). This gigantic building carved into a mountain top cliff is believed to have been a Nabataean temple, but at some time was used as a Christian church, as indicated by crosses carved into its walls. Probably dates from the 3rd century B.C. Photo courtesy Jordan Information Bureau, Washington, D.C.

**Figure 2–6.** Edward Robinson, American Biblical Scholar. Photo courtesy *Biblical Archaeologist*. Drawing by Linda Huff.

## Climax

These travelers reached their epitome in the American, Edward Robinson (1794–1863). For the last twenty years of his life, he was a professor at Union Theological Seminary in New York City. Earlier, he had taught at Andover (Massachusetts) Theological Seminary where he studied under Moses Stuart. Robinson had already become so well versed in Greek that he had prepared a new edition of eleven books of the Iliad. Under Stuart, he extended his expertise to Hebrew. Over the next twenty years, over four of which were spent in Germany and in continental travel, he became the United States', if not the world's, acknowledged expert in biblical languages. He published many translations of German works as well as his own material. He started a magazine, *Biblical Repository*, where he published his own and Stuart's articles as well as others. In 1851, it merged with *Bibliotheca Sacra*, which he had started in 1843. It was his linguistic fame which brought the offer to teach at Union. However, his interests had turned to geography also. He accepted the chair at Union only with the stipulation that he first be allowed to spend several years traveling in the Near East.

His traveling companion there was the Rev. Eli Smith, a protestant missionary in Beirut, who knew Arabic fluently. Robinson often credited Smith with the success of the 1838 journey of 105 days from Cairo to Beirut via Sinai, Aqaba, Arabia

Petrea, Jerusalem, Nazareth, Safed, Tyre and Sidon. The result was three volumes, *Biblical Researches in Palestine, Mount Sinai and Arabia Petraea*; NY: Ayer, 1977 (original 1841). The significance of this work can hardly be overestimated. It replaced myth and tales with scientific observation. Biblical geography was at last put on a scientific foundation. He kept a journal like Maundrell and Burckhardt, but he included with it minute, detailed, careful, on-the-spot observations. The long term influence of the study is from the recognition by Smith and Robinson that Arabic place names often preserve the ancient Semitic place names. For example, 'Anata = biblical Anathoth, Rammun = ancient Rimon, Mukhmas = the old Michmash, etc.

In 1852, the two went from Beirut through Galilee and Samaria and by a new route to Jerusalem, exploring sections of the country they had missed. This time, they went to Damascus, Baalbek and the northern coast. This seventy-seven day trip was described in *Later Biblical Researches in Palestine and in Adjacent Regions*; Ayer, 1977 (original 1856). In addition to *Researches*, Robinson wrote a *Physical Geography* (1861) of Palestine before blindness and death ended his career.

It has been said that Robinson's work surpassed all previous contributions to Palestinian geography. In turn, it has only been surpassed in recent decades by the explorations of Nelson Glueck (1900–71) on both sides of the Jordan River, and in the Valley of the Ghor south of the Dead Sea. Intermediate to these were the German explorations (1887) of Gottlieb Schumacher in northern Transjordan, and the team of Conder and Kitchner. The Palestine Exploration Fund sent out a British expedition in 1872–78. Claude Reignier Conder (1848–1910) and Horatio H. Kitchner (Lord Kitchner who became famous at Khartoum in 1885) made a detailed "inch to a mile" *Survey of Western Palestine* (west of the Jordan River). Conder later surveyed 510 square miles of Eastern Palestine (Transjordan) in 1881. The final work in mapping the Sinai peninsula was done by T.E. Lawrence ("Lawrence of Arabia").[6]

## C. UNDERGROUND BEGINNINGS

### How It Started

Interest expanded early from surface remains to the underground. The robbers, and Tuthmosis and Nabonides were, in a sense, excavators. The excavations of Caesar's legions at Corinth have been noted. An architect, Filippo Brunelleschi, was digging in Rome in 1400 A.D. In 1709, the Austrian Prince d'Elbeuf (General Emanual Moritz) needed more water for his estate near Naples, according to one of several versions of this incident. Workmen dug a well. Instead of water, they discovered ancient Herculaneum buried under tons of lava by Mount Vesuvius in

**Figure 2–7.**    Pompeii. Mt. Vesuvius framed by the city gate.

**Figure 2–8.**    Dr. John Holladay examines the remains of a shop at Pompeii.

79 A.D. Elbeuf smashed things up a bit but seems to have done little more than remove three classical female statues. He had the statues "restored" by an artist in Rome. By 1738, his estate had been bought by Charles of Bourbon, King of the Two Sicilies (Charles III of Naples).

Various candidates have been nominated as the founder of modern archaeology. One of them is Charles' Keeper of the Royal Library, the Marchese Don Marcello Venuti, an antiquarian expert. He reopened Elbeuf's well shaft, supervised the workmen to avoid unnecessary damage, and translated inscriptions which proved the site to be Herculaneum.[7]

**Figure 2–9.**   The "treasury" at Petra. Carved out of the "living rock" of red sandstone, this ancient tomb is the first sight of Petra after coming through the mile long siq (narrow canyon leading into Petra). The idea of a treasury may come from the tradition that the rock urn on top is hollow and contains gold.

## System

Nearby Pompeii was opened in 1748 by Charles' Chief of Engineers, Col. Rocco Gioacchine de Alcubierre (Roch Joachim Alcunierre) who had already been digging at Herculaneum. It is said he knew as much about antiquities as the moon knows about lobsters, and the work suffered accordingly. His successor, Maj. Charles Weber, a Swiss architect, was an improvement. He made measurements and plans of the architecture and the city. Weber has been put in a class with Heinrich Schliemann as a pioneer, but the modern scientific excavation of Pompeii had to wait for Giuseppe Fiorelli in 1861.

Fiorelli kept a journal in which he not only recorded the objects that were found but their position, the earth around them, and possible conclusions. This is probably the first archaeologist's field book. He even started a school of Pompeii where foreigners and Italians alike could learn archaeological technique. Prof. Amadeo Maiuri directed the work from 1911 to 1963. Recent work has been carried on by the University of Maryland. Excavation has continued at Herculaneum under the direction of Giuseppe Maggi and the sponsorship of Italy's Ministry of Public Works with assistance from the National Geographic Society in the United States.

The discoveries at Herculaneum and Pompeii led to a significant contribution to archaeology in the work of Johann Joachim Winckelmann (1717–68). His *History of the Art of Antiquity* was published in 1764. He tried to relate the objects and artifacts of the two cities to their cultural and historical, i.e., their archaeological, context. For this he too has been called the "father of archaeology," especially in Germany. One can recognize some truth to the title because such systematic interpretation is so necessary for subsequent understanding of archaeological data.

Though little noted at the time, another attempt at systematic interpretation took place to satisfy the curiosity of Thomas Jefferson. In 1784 he opened an American Indian burial mound. Two of his observations were that the age of the skeletons varied and that they included some children. Secondly, the context of the skeletons indicated different times of burial. These two observations eliminated the notion that the mounds were burials of warriors fallen in battle. He also noted the different kinds of stones and their sources, thus relating geology to archaeology.

The latter relationship and this kind of systematic study were of considerable importance to the developing science of archaeology. In 1650, the Irishman James Ussher (1581–1656), Archbishop of Armaugh, published his *Annals of the Ancient and New Testaments*. He decided the world was created in 4004 B.C. This was refined by Bishop John Lightfoot of Cambridge to nine a.m. on 23 October! Glyn Daniel noted this kind of dating as the background for Rev. John William Burgon's (1813–88) poem on "Petra" whose discovery by Burckhardt was noted earlier:

Match me such marvel save in Eastern clime!
A rose-red city "half as old as time."

However, as early as 1669 a Dane, Nicholas Steno (1638–1686) had suggested that sedimentary rocks were similar in structure to the bed of the sea. He was a medical doctor in the court of Ferdinand II, Duke of Tuscany. *Steno's Law* is the principle of superposition or stratification. James Hutton (1726–97) considered rock *strata* (layers) as coming from natural processes still going on in seas, rivers and lakes as noted in his *Theory of the Earth* (1785).

In 1816, William Smith (1769–1839) published his *Strata Identified by Organized Fossils* in which he stated that strata could be identified in chronological order by the remains of extinct animals and that the earth was a good bit older than Bishop Ussher had thought. Smith's work marks the beginning of modern geology. He was shortly followed by Charles Lyell (1797–1875) with his *Principles of Geology*, published 1830–33. Archaeology borrowed the concept of *stratigraphy* — the idea that the earth consists of layers or strata one above the other — from geology. This concept has had a major role in the development of scientific archaeology.

Another important phase in this early development is the age and origin of man. When flints and stone tools were found with the remains of prehistoric animals, some realized man had also been around before 4000 B.C. The studies of stratified remains near Abbeville, France, led a French customs official, Jacques Boucher de Crevecoeur de Perthes (1788–1868) to this idea. Most geologists still believed in Noah's worldwide Flood, so he had a cold reception from them, but he published five volumes, *Of the Creation: Essays on its Origins and the Progress of its Existence* (1838–41), on the finds. His work climaxed in a book on the age of *predeluvian* (before the biblical flood) man, *Of Predeluvian Man and his Works* (1860).

The previous year Charles Darwin (1809–82) had published his *Origin of Species by Means of Natural Selection*. This was followed in 1871 with his *Descent of Man* but it was Darwin's earlier book that is sometimes nominated as the origin of archaeology. Archaeology is concerned with people and their cultural remains, remains which have a chronological development similar to evolution in natural species. To that extent, perhaps Darwin's work can be said to play such a role in archaeology, though we have seen a number of earlier "origins."

Darwin's concept was reinforced by the 1857 discovery of the long bones and skullcap of a primitive man in the Neanderthal ravine of the Dussel River in Rhenish Prussia. But the idea of evolution goes back to the Greeks, such as Thales, Empedocles, Anaximander, and Aristotle, and to the medieval philosophers such as al-Masudi, the Baghdad scientist who proposed a development from mineral to plant to animal to man. Lyell had discussed the transmutation of species and followed this with his book, *The Geological Evidences of the Antiquity of Man*. Others had considered the matter, including Herbert Spencer who had a fully developed concept of evolution before 1859.

Darwin's presentation (1858) of his findings to the Linnaean Society had been a paper co-authored with Alfred Russel Wallace (1823–1913). Wallace "stumbled" on the idea and worked it out in a very short time. But Darwin spent the years 1831–36 on the naval survey ship "Beagle" collecting massive amounts of data from the Galapagos Islands and elsewhere. In the end it was this scientifically collected data which carried the argument, rather than philosophical speculation.[8]

## The Development of Museums

Nebuchadnezzar's collection was noted earlier as was that of Nabonidus' daughter, Bel-shalti-nannar. A princess of northern Greece in the fifth century B.C. had a collection of prehistoric stone axes buried with her. The collections of Roman emperors might be added to the museum story. Henry, the English Bishop of Winchester, sent home a collection of classical statues from Rome c. 1150 A.D. Pope Sixtus IV collected (1471) sculpture in the Palazzo del Campidoglio. Several families of the nobility and church cardinals followed his example. In 1506, Pope Julius II created the Vatican's Belvedere Museum. Kircher (noted earlier for his travels) began the first systematic collection of antiquities at the "Collegium Romanum" in Rome, c. 1635. The English Lord Arundel began a similar collection in 1640.

The Society of Dilettanti was started in London in 1733 to encourage collecting and excavating. The Capitoline Museum was started the following year in Rome, preceding by almost a hundred years (1829) the establishment of the Archaeological Institute in Rome — Instituto di Corrispondenza Archeologica. The years 1753–59 marked the beginning of the British Museum. The Louvre was started in Paris in 1793 with a new twist — the public was admitted free. Museums began with older private collections, but the nationalistic spirit was moving and with it came the demand for greater and bigger displays.

This demand might be seen as the origin of a new wave of treasure hunts which brought the Elgin Marbles from the Parthenon to the British Museum during the years 1803–12. Lord Elgin (Thomas Bruce) saved the Marbles from being burned for lime, to his everlasting credit, though he has since been condemned for theft. The scientific collections of Napoleon's Commission and the Institute of Egypt which he created in 1799, passed to the British when Gen. Menou surrendered in 1801.

A British consul named Salt added to the plunder with the help of an Italian, Giovanni Battista Belzoni (1778–1823). A six-foot seven-inch former circus strongman, Belzoni plundered tombs and temples for profit, but, strangely, did not profit from his 1818 "breaking and entering" of Chephren's pyramid, noted earlier. It was empty and simply "open to the public." A year earlier he had penetrated the sands to enter the buried temple of Abu Simbel. In the process of his collecting activity, he discovered the tomb of Pharaoh Seti I (c. 1308–1290 B.C.) in the Valley of the Kings. His own account, *Narratives of the Operations and Recent Discoveries within the Pyramids, Temples, Tombs and Excavation in Egypt and Nubia* (London: Murray, 1820) shows him clumsily smashing mummies by the dozens. He described his own purpose as "to rob the Egyptians of their papyrii." His ruthless vandalism, however, has been called the most scientific archaeological exploration up to that time. He brought back many sketches, imprints, and measurements, some of which he used in a museum display he set up in London. One might add that his methods were less violent than those of Col. Richard William Howard Vyse, who has been called more scientific than Belzoni. Vyse used gun-powder to try to get into a pyramid in 1837. Fifty years later, Marriette was still blasting his way into buried ruins.

The English were already involved in Mesopotamia as well. The East India Company had discovered the linguistic ability of a cadet named Claudius James Rich (1787–1821). His short life ended during a cholera epidemic, but not before he produced several books on Babylon. His wife extracted several more posthumously from his notes, while his manuscripts and cuneiform tablets went to the British Museum. His first visit (1811) to Babylon included a ten-day, ten-man dig which yielded inscriptions and seals.

The French had already been involved in Mesopotamia through their vicar-general in Baghdad. Abbé J. de Beauchamp made the first modern excavations in Mesopotamia in 1781–85. Working at Babylon, he uncovered a now famous sculpture called the "Lion of Babylon." Beauchamp was the first to describe the even more famous Ishtar Gate. His writings (1790) may have inspired the East India Company's interest expressed through Rich.

It has been suggested, however, that modern excavation in Mesopotamia really began in 1842 when the French appointed a physician as their consul in Mosul. Paul Emile Botta (1802–70) poked around in Tell Quyunjik (Nineveh) but was discouraged by lack of immediate success. He turned to Khorsabad and spent a year and a half (1843–44) digging out the capital of the Assyrian King Sargon II (722–705 B.C.) mentioned in Isaiah 20:1. Many of the sculptures he excavated quickly deteriorated in air and sun. A large shipment sank in the Tigris River when the rafts capsized in rapids. But the next shipment arrived at the Louvre. Fortunately the French government had supplied him with a draftsman, Eugene Napoleon Flandin (1809–76) whose drawings saved at least a view of the lost. In Botta's day he could claim to be systematically excavating, though in retrospect it seems like sheer looting. This continued (1852–55) under Botta's successor, Victor Place (1822–75) who had the unfortunate distinction of also losing a shipment of Khorsabad sculptures in the Tigris. Bandits attacked the rafts and 308 cases went to the bottom in 1855.

England and the British Museum shared the loot of ancient Assyria through the efforts of a worthy successor of Rich, one Sir Austen Henry Layard (1817–94), a descendent of Hugeunot refugees (1685) from France. Layard's job was "to obtain the largest possible number of well-preserved objects of art at the least possible outlay of time and money." He traveled through the country in Arab dress but was robbed and left destitute by bandits. However, he was digging into Nimrud (Calah in Genesis 10:11) by 1845. Almost immediately he found the palaces of the Assyrian Kings Assurnasirpal II (883–59 B.C.), Shalmaneser III (859–24), and Esarhaddon (681–69). Turning to Nineveh (Quyunjik), Layard succeeded where Botta had failed. He not only lay bare the palace of Sennarcherib (704–681; II Kings 18:13) but the library of Ashurbanipal as well. Layard did not really know what he had in the thousands of tablets and their shipment to London probably caused more damage than the ravages of time.

Of special interest is Layard's discovery of the Black *Obelisk* of Shalmaneser III. Its four sides are carved in a series of panels, one of which shows "Jehu, the son of Omri," on his knees before Shalmaneser. Jehu was king of Israel, though not the biological son of Omri, whose dynasty Jehu liquidated (II Kings 9:10). Layard added Asshur to his "conquests" and solved the problem of river transport, so his treasures flowed in increasing numbers to England until he quit in 1850. His large volumes on *Nineveh and its Remains* (1848–49) were followed by other descriptions of travel and excavation. He was elected to Parliament and returned to Istanbul as England's ambassador to the Ottoman Empire.

His is a "rags to riches" story. While he made money on his books, his real wealth came as chairman of the Imperial Ottoman Bank, with branches throughout the Near East. Thus Layard goes down in history as a man who made quite a "success" out of archaeology. It is a material success not matched until modern times, when Wendell Phillips (1921–75) sought excavation permits in Oman, received a sideline concession for oil exploration, and became a millionaire. While exploring and digging, Layard took note of military, political and commercial activity which served him well in later years. He sent reports at the time to British officials. His "spying" activities have haunted archaeologists ever since. The current charge against Americans is that we are with the CIA!

Layard's work was continued in 1852–53 and again in 1878–82 by his former assistant, Hormuzd Rassam (1826–1910), a Chaldean Christian and a British citizen. He discovered Ashurbanipal's palace and library at Nineveh. The hall was decorated with sculptures of a lion hunt in bas-relief. These scenes now decorate the British Museum as do Rassam's later finds such as the famous bronze gates of Shalmaneser II at Balawat, and the inscription of Nabonidus recording his "archaeological" excavation of Naram-Sin's temple at Sippar. Rassam dug into many mounds all over the country. He has been called a looter, though in his day he was but one among many.[9]

## Hunters vs. Hunters

The difference between these nineteenth century treasure hunters and their tomb robbing predecessors lay in their interest in museum pieces. They were after the obelisks, stelae, statues, inscriptions, carvings, whole pottery vessels, coffins, and so forth, and less interested in merely collecting gold and jewelry for melting and resale. The same could be said of the early Renaissance private collectors, the early barrow diggers in England, and the pothunters who continue to pilfer American Indian sites. But tomb robbing also continues in the grand style with a view to the antiquities market, among the Etruscan tombs of Italy, the ancient cemeteries of the Near East, the temples of the Aztecs and Incas, shipwrecks under water, and probably every place that antiquities are found. UNESCO has recommended protection for archaeological sites and the Council of Europe has drawn over twenty nations into a regional plan of protection.

One can rightly deplore the continuation of the tomb robber tradition. This includes the market place that provides a receivership for the stolen goods. Museums as well as private purchasers keep the process of supply and demand operating, although some museums are now publicly refusing to buy artifacts out of context. UNESCO has urged international controls for the illicit traffic in antiquities — some simply stolen from other museums! The first such theft recorded was of some of Layard's Assyrian antiquities, stolen from the British Museum in 1877 and never recovered. The United States Congress agreed to the 1972 UNESCO Convention on Cultural Property in Dec. 1982 on condition that European countries would too. The Congress did not want others to get ahead of U.S. antiquities dealers.

Mixed and ambiguous emotions surface for the likes of Layard and company. They destroyed more than they gained. Yet, as with alchemy and other early sciences, without this spur of fame and pelf the modern science might never have been born. So it might be appropriate here to establish an "apologia," a "defense" of the early museum piece treasure hunters.

Glyn Daniel has duly noted that every generation says it is scientific and says that every previous generation was prescientific. He goes on to claim honestly that we today are working accurately. Perhaps the judgment of Robert Silverberg is to be preferred when he notes that "the man who digs today is all too thoroughly aware of the archaeological crimes committed by his well meaning predecessors, and all too uncomfortably fearful that future excavators may heap imprecations on his head for destroying irreplaceable evidence." Gary Pratico has noted that revision is inevitable. The refinements of archaeology today make that of the 1930s look like prehistory. "Those who are unwilling to concede that time will do the same to the archaeology of 1982 delude themselves."

The transportation of yesterday was incredibly slow compared to the car and jet of today, but we will seem just as slow to the rocket age of tomorrow. As late as 1960 one of the most prominent archaeologists in the world suggested that neither electromagnetic apparatus nor dousing rods are of appreciable use in most archaeological efforts. The use of electromagnetic equipment is in full swing and our tomorrow has already arrived, but some archaeologists do not know it. [10]

## The Ages of Man

Out of the efforts of Herculaneum and Pompeii came the systematic efforts of Winckelmann in the history of art. Out of museum collecting came an effort for systematic display. Christian Jurgensen Thomsen (1788–1856) organized the royal collection of antiquities in Copenhagen into a National Museum which opened to the public in 1819. Viewers found the objects presented according to material — stone, bronze, iron — and the philosophical speculations (1813) of a Danish historian, L.S. Vedel Simonsen. The latter suggested three successive periods of man's past — a Stone Age, a Bronze Age, and an Iron Age. He followed two other Danes, P.F. Suhm (1776) and Skuli Thorlacius (1802) who had similar proposals. Thomsen's Guide Book (1836) was translated into English (1848) and gradually spread his ideas.

Hesiod in his *Works and Days* (eighth century B.C.) presents what may be the first chronological system for humanity. He proposed a series of Ages — Gold, Silver, Bronze, Heroic and Iron — for civilization. Lucretius, *Concerning the Nature of Things* (second century B.C.) thought man first used his teeth and nails, then stones, wood and fire, later copper, and finally iron. Plato, Ovid, and other Greeks could be added. The sequence — Gold, Silver, Bronze and Iron Ages — appears in the Iranian Avesta, in Buddhist doctrine, and in the Bible (Daniel 2:31). The Chinese had arrived at a Stone, Jade, Bronze, and Iron Age sequence by the first century B.C. The philosophical idea is one of the decline of human society from a Golden Age to an inferior age — the philosopher's present age of iron. Still, R.A.S. Macalister has called this three-age system the cornerstone of modern archaeology. In 1865, John Lubbock (1834–1913) divided the Stone Age into the Old and the New Stone Ages, and by 1900, the Mesolithic Stone Age had been inserted between them. These remain the archaeological ages still used for classification, modified by local terms such as the Minoan in Crete.

Thomsen's assistant was probably the first professional archaeologist in the world. Jens Jacob Asmussen Worsaae (1821–85) excavated in his native Jutland with a platoon of soldiers provided by the king (a lesson for peacetime armies). He published the results in the *Primeval Antiquities of Denmark* (1842), which was translated in English in 1849. The book is a landmark in archaeology.

Worsaae explained the need for the three-age system as an organizing principle. He gave the first exposition of the principles of excavation. These include the need for a complete description of the site before excavation, as well as a description of the artifacts. He urged excavators to save both human and animal bones for science, a principle which still has not been fully accepted by some archaeologists today. Worsaae was also aware of the need to interest the general public in archaeology — to preserve sites, encourage finances, and to enrich human culture. For all of this, he too has been called a "father of archaeology." We might add that he was the first archaeologist to record different stratigraphical levels, though John Frere (1740–1807) wrote about this in 1797. In a letter to the Society of Antiquaries in London, Frere described a Paleolithic site at Hoxne, England. Worked flints, "weapons of war, fabricated and used by a people who had not the use of metal, were found under twelve feet of stratified soil. There were four strata which consisted of vegetable earth (one and a half feet), argill (seven and a half feet), sand with shells (one foot), gravelly soil with the flints and the bones of extinct animals (two feet)."[11]

## D.  IT IS WRITTEN

### On the Nile

We have wandered far from the dust of field archaeology in the Near East. Before we go back to the dirt, we must note some extremely important developments in linguistics. In August 1799, Captain Pierre Francois Xavier Bouchard of Napoleon's Army of the Nile was supervising repairs on the fort of St. Julien, according to one of several versions of the story. This was near Alexandria, at the Rosetta (Arabic "Rashid") branch of the Nile, one of several places where the Nile flows through the Delta and into the Mediterranean.

While digging foundation trenches the troops discovered the Rosetta Stone. It is a slab of black basalt about eleven inches thick and roughly forty-five inches high by twenty-eight inches wide. One side is inscribed with two languages and three scripts: fourteen lines of Egyptian hieroglyphics (top) remain with thirty-two lines (middle) of Egyptian demotic (a strongly cursive — handwritten rather than printed — form of hieroglyphics) and fifty-four lines of Greek at the bottom. The Greek could be read fairly readily (it was translated in 1802 by Rev. Stephen Weston) and was probably the original language of the priestly decree from an ancient capital city, Memphis, c. 196 B.C. The priests were paying tribute to Ptolemy V Epiphanes (203–181 B.C.), a Greek king of Egypt of the Ptolemaic Dynasty (one of the heirs of Alexander the Great's empire). Scholars assumed that the other two inscriptions said the same thing and this led to the decipherment of Egyptian hieroglyphics.[12]

**Figure 2–10.** The Rosetta Stone. Photo courtesy The British Museum.

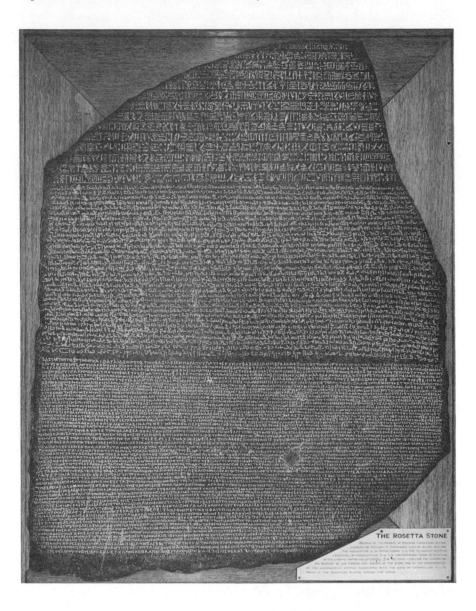

## From Palette to Papyrus

The earliest example of Egyptian writing, c. 3000 B.C., is the Palette of Narmer (perhaps the first pharaoh to unify Egypt into a single nation). It is a combination of picture writing and symbols for sounds and ideas. Shortly after this, the true hieroglyphic system was established — pictographs were dropped and *determinatives* (symbols to show the true sound or meaning of a word) were added. The system lasted for more than 3000 years.

The traditional view of language development is from picture writing to symbols. However, some have questioned this and wonder if hieroglyphics was an artificial development if not by Narmer, at least under his First Dynasty. A cursive form called hieratic, more convenient for writing on papyrus, may have been in use as early as hieroglyphics (Greek for "sacred carving"). Hieratic became increasingly cursive and by the seventh century B.C. was obscure and limited to priestly use (the Greek "heratikos" means priestly).

About this time an even more cursive but simplified form, the *demotic* (Greek for "people") developed from the hieratic. Demotic increased in significance until royal decrees came to be put into hieroglyphics, demotic and Greek, with demotic in the place of importance in the center, as on the Rosetta Stone.

The Egyptian language eventually became written as *Coptic,* Egyptian rendered into Greek, with five additional signs borrowed from the older scripts. All three of the older scripts went out of use with the end of Egyptian paganism in the fifth century A.D. Coptic became the language of Christianity and except for church use, was largely superseded by Arabic when the Muslims conquered Egypt.

## Success

Several efforts at translation, such as Kircher's (whose interest was noted earlier), failed in the sixteenth, seventeenth, and eighteenth centuries. The Rosetta Stone became the key. Contributions to its decipherment were made by the Swedish diplomat, Jan David Akerbald, the French scholar, Silvestre de Sacy, and an English physicist, Dr. Thomas Young (1773–1829) of Cambridge. The latter worked with a bilingual text — an obelisk (hieroglyphics) and its pedestal (Greek) found on the Nile island of Philae in 1815. Akerblad deciphered several words in demotic, and Young identified proper names in hieroglyphics. It was the French Egyptologist, Jean Francois Champollion (1790–1832), however, who succeeded.

Champollion was born at Figeac, France. A linguistic genius, he knew Greek and Latin by age eleven and published his first book when he was twelve. He attended the Academy of Grenoble, and in Paris the School of Oriental Languages and the College de France. At nineteen, he returned to Grenoble as a professor of history. Champollion worked with the contributions just mentioned, his own knowledge of Coptic, and the Rosetta Stone. The French had made copies of the latter before turning it over to the English. He decided that the hieroglyphic script was a system of sounds. It was a forerunner of the alphabet which did not itself become an alphabet.

In 1821, Champollion published "On the Writing of Hieratic" and in 1822 he wrote a "Letter to M. Dacier. . ." with the key for the decipherment of hieroglyphics. Later (1829) he published "On the Writing of Demotic," though demotic was not fully translated until Karl Heinrich Brugsch wrote his *Hieroglyphic-demotic Wordbook* (1868). Champollion went on with his *Precis to the System of the Ancient Egyptians. . .* He was appointed Director of the Egyptian section of the Louvre in 1827. In the following two years, with the Italian professor Niccolo Ipplit Rosellini, he led a joint expedition to Egypt. In 1831, Champollion was appointed to the first university chair in Egyptology — created for him — in Europe at the College de France. His *Grammar* (1836) and *Dictionary* (1841) were published posthumously by his brother.[13]

## Paper Treasure

We began this history of archaeology with the treasure hunt story of the Dead Sea Scrolls. A journalist has reported that one of the scrolls (11QPss – Cave Eleven at Qumran, a scroll of psalms) was opened with a penknife and guts. Dr. James A. Sanders also used a camel's hair brush and a museum room turned into a giant humidifier. The present writer found a Siamese letter opener helpful!

When the famous copper scroll (also called the treasure scroll because its contents report a mythical treasure) was opened, a modern "penknife" — a high powered diamond saw — cut the scroll into strips. We have no idea how the Bedouin opened the papyrus and parchment scrolls when they first found them. But this carries us back to an early interest in scrolls, papyrus rolls, and inscriptions. One report cites the use of a razor rather than a penknife. The razor was used to cut off the outer carbonized part of the roll, which was thrown away.

A Franciscan father, Antonio Piaggio (1701–1794?), gave his attention to the problem. Some 1800 manuscripts were found, charred and gummed, in 1752–54 in Herculaneum. Some of these have still not been unrolled, but Piaggio developed a system for unrolling the less charred ones. He glued threads to the unlettered back and with the threads tied to a straight bar, gently pulled, while using a small knife and some kind of spirit liquid to encourage unrolling with the greatest possible preservation. Would that such care had "caught on." Untold numbers of manuscripts have been tossed to the winds, used to light campfires, and in an earlier day wrapped around and stuffed inside mummies (from which some have been recovered.)

Mummies of course are associated with Egypt. Egypt originated the writing material called papyrus from which English gets the word paper, which was

**Figure 2–11.**   A pond with papyrus reeds in front of the Cairo Museum.

invented in China and reached Europe c. 800 A.D. Papyrus was made from the
reed *cyperus papyrus* which at one time grew profusely in the Delta. These reeds
are the bulrushes among which the Egyptian princess found the baby Moses in a
basket. For 3000 years papyrus was a symbol for Lower Egypt (the Delta). The pithy
core of the reed is laid in horizontal strips, while another layer is laid vertically.
Glued together and smoothed down, sheets could be pasted end to end forming a
strip about nine inches high and as long as necessary. The longest known example
is 133 feet. Writing was on the horizontal strip side.

  Papyrus was invented before 3000 B.C., since that is the approximate date of the
oldest known papyrus fragment. Some Greek and Latin fragments were given to the
Basel library in Switzerland by Johann Jakob Grynaeus in the late 1500s. In 1778,
some Egyptians found fifty rolls of papyrus, probably in the Fayum. An antiquities
dealer took one out of curiosity. The rest it is said, the peasants burned because they
liked the smell. The one roll eventually came to Cardinal Stefan Borgia who gave
it to the Museum of Vellatri. This "Charta Borgiana Papyrus," in Greek, was the
first papyrus published in Europe (1788).

Napoleon's scholar, D.V. Denon, tells of taking a roll from the hands of a mummy. While the French did not yet appreciate papyrii, the hunt and plunder were under way. This increased appreciably after Champollion deciphered hieroglyphics. Most Egyptian papyrii contain religious matter, with medicine second in frequency. Most of the religious texts are funeral texts. The most famous of these is the *Book of the Dead*. It is a collection of sayings, formulae, and prayers to get the deceased safely past judgment in the afterlife. The collection varies from scroll to scroll with no standard text of canon.

In 1877, Mariette appealed to tourists and interested people to buy papyrii and save the inscriptions for posterity. Some did. In 1891, Heinrich Brugsch alone brought 3000 rolls to Europe. Other papyrii were picked up singly or in groups for museums and private collections. In the same year as Mariette's appeal, the Fayum was discovered as the source of a new flood of papyrii on the antiquities market. As with so many things, the earliest scientific investigations began with Sir Flinders Petrie, about whom more later. Earlier he had salvaged 150 documents at Tanis in 1883. One of his first discoveries in the Fayum was a large roll containing the second book of the Iliad. The Egyptian Exploration Society sponsored work at Oxyrhynchus from 1895–1907. Here in huge city dumps, tens of thousands of papyrii were found. Many were government records, kept until no longer needed and then discarded by the basketful, sometimes basket and all. Later, digging in the Fayum, the Expedition found a crocodile cemetery. One of the mummies was broken open and found stuffed with papyrii!

Most finds after Oxyrhynchus (125 miles south of Cairo) were pale in comparison, until new discoveries came to light in the 1940s. In 1945 at Nag Hammadi, a thousand pages making up forty-eight Gnostic documents were discovered. They are the third and fourth century A.D. documents of a Judeo-Christian sect. While details of the original find are obscure, these materials shed light on this obscure sectarian movement, and on the Bible as well. The Bible was also illuminated by the Dead Sea Scrolls, also representing a sect, perhaps the Essenes. [14]

## Between the Rivers

Mesopotamia ("between the rivers"), the land of the Tigris and Euphrates, produced the oldest system of writing known today. Cuneiform (Latin "cuneus" = "wedge") goes back to obscure origins in about 3500 B.C. The term was first applied by Thomas Hyde (1709) writing for Old Persian, although he thought the wedges were decoration. The first cuneiform signs arrived in Europe in 1621 with Pietro della Valle. A longer inscription came from Persepolis in 1685 with Englebert Kampfer (1651–1716), a German doctor who traveled through Persia, sketchbook in hand. Others followed with Cornelis de Bruin (1652–1727), Carsten Neibuhr (noted earlier), the German orientalist Olav Gerhard Tyschsen, the Danish scholar Friedrich Munter, and Chardin's first complete inscription for Persepolis (1711).

Niebuhr recognized three different systems in the writing at Persepolis, sorted out forty-two different characters, and noted that the script ran from right to left. Tyschsen identified the sign for dividing words in 1798. Munter theorized in 1802 that Persepolis belonged to the Persian (Achaemenid) kings in the period 500–330 B.C. George Friedrich Grotefend (1775–1853), an obscure German high school classics teacher, bet a friend that he could decipher the cuneiform of Persepolis. The friend collected the literature to date, and Grotefend did it, using recent developments in Sanskrit and Pahlevi (a linguistic descendent of Old Persian). At least, he assigned correct sound values to a dozen cuneiform signs, including the names Darius, Xerxes, and Hystaspes. He achieved enough fame so that Rich sent him new inscriptions. The final achievement, however, belongs to another researcher.[15]

## Wedges

The Sumerians were the first people to use cuneiform. We do not know where they came from. They were neither Indo-European (ancestors of the Greeks, Hittites and Aryans of India) nor Semites (Akkadians, Babylonians, Assyrians, Canaanites, Hebrews, Arameans, and Arabs). Their earliest writing has been discovered in Uruk level IV (Arabic Warka and biblical Erech, Genesis 10:10), northwest of Ur. It is picture writing with some 900 symbols. By the time of Uruk III, c. 3200, this writing was in straight lines on clay tablets. The scribes turned the tablets so that the finished symbols were lying on their backs. These turned symbols developed into the wedge-shaped signs for sounds, probably through the use of a stylus, such as a piece of reed, which is wedge-shaped in cross-section. By the Babylonian period c. 1750 B.C., there were 600–700 of these signs. Semites took over the cuneiform script c. 2500. From these Akkadians it passed on to Babylonians, Indo-European Kassites (successors of the Babylonians in Southern Mesopotamia, 1500–1200 B.C.) and the Assyrians. In the hands of the Assyrian royal scribes it reached its epitome of physical perfection and even beauty.

In the second millennium, 2000–1000 B.C., Akkadian (which includes Babylonian and Assyrian cuneiform) became the "lingua franca" (common language) of the ancient Near East. It appeared in Asia Minor, Palestine and Egypt as well as its homeland. The Elamites (also neither Semitic nor Indo-European) in Persia had their own script, derived from picture writing. About 2500 B.C., they adopted cuneiform but simplified it to 113 symbols of which 80 are syllabic. In the sixth century, the Persians adapted their Indo-European language to cuneiform and further simplified it to forty-one signs, which was as close to an alphabet as Mesopotamian cuneiform ever came. The latter development may have been influenced by the Aramaic alphabet which was already common. We'll come back later to alphabetic Ugaritic. An interesting recent estimate noted that only ten per cent of the half million known cuneiform inscriptions have been published.

**Figure 2–12.** Sir Charles Creswicke Rawlinson. Photo courtesy Biblical Archaeologist. Permission of British Museum.

## At Last

It was the Persian form of cuneiform that Grotefend translated, and which was deciphered or re-deciphered later. The French orientalist Eugene Burnouf made some progress, translating several names. His Norwegian pupil Christian Lassen went further, showing that the signs represented syllables rather than letters of an alphabet.

A British army officer, Sir Charles Creswicke Rawlinson (1810–95), was in India as a cadet for the East India Company in 1827. Sir John Malcom, Governor of Bombay, inspired the young cadet with a fascination for things oriental. By 1835, Rawlinson was in Persia (Iran) helping reorganize the Shah's troops. While there, he had time to look at the Behistun ("Place of God") inscription in the Zagros Mountain range 11 miles east of Kermanshah, 200 miles northeast of Baghdad, on the ancient road from Ecbatana to Babylon.

Darius the Great (521–485 B.C.) had a relief of himself in victory over his enemies carved on a "blackboard" 100 by 150 feet wide on the face of a 2000 foot high cliff. In three panels with eleven foot high columns of writing, the story is told in three cuneiform languages: Persian, Elamite and Babylonian. Rawlinson, an accomplished athlete, scaled the 340 feet from the base of the cliff and copied the first and third panels from the 60 foot long panorama.

In 1845, after a stint as a political agent in Afghanistan, Arabia, and finally Iraq (Baghdad), Rawlinson returned for more copying which included part of the Elamite inscription. With the help of a Kurdish boy, he made paper *squeezes* — putting wet paper on the inscription and brushing it into the carving to get an impression of the letters. He followed the work of his predecessors and used the inscriptions collected by Niebuhr, Le Brun, and C.J. Rich. He added new ones from Persepolis and the nearby tombs of Nagsh-i-Rustam, combining them with his knowledge of Sanskrit (an Indo-European language), Pahlevi, and Zend (a cognate of Old Persian). He published a translation of 200 lines of the Darius inscription, *The Persian Cuneiform Inscriptions of Behistun* (1846). "Rosetta Stone" fashion, he translated the Babylonian as well in 1851.

Rawlinson did for cuneiform what Champollion had done for hieroglyphics. The Elamite inscription was fully transcribed and translated by George Glenn Cameron (1905–1979) in 1948 and 1957. Cameron made his readings with the help of the Anglo-American Oil Company's riggers. Bedouin boys led them around the back of the mountain to a ledge up above the inscriptions. There are 515 lines of Old Persian, 141 long lines of Babylonian and 650 lines of Elamite. The inscription says that a usurper named Gaumata (possibly the brother of King Cambyses, 530–522) had taken over the throne of Persia. Darius Hystaspes, third cousin to Cambyses, with the help of the imperial army, ousted Gaumata and took over the Empire. The relief shows him with his foot on Gaumata and nine rebel chieftains tied up in front of him.

Some skepticism greeted the translation of Babylonian cuneiform. In 1857, the Royal Asiastic Society became the instrument for four independent translations of portions of the eight-sided clay prism of Tiglath-Pileser III (744–27). The four translators — Rawlinson, W.H. Fox Talbot, Jules Oppert and Edward Hincks — were in substantial agreement. This confirmed the fact that cuneiform had indeed been translated.

There are four footnotes to this discussion, three (Ugaritic, Hittite and Eblaite) of which will be taken up in due time. Here it is appropriate to note again the chance find of 300 Akkadian tablets at Tell el-Amarna, half way between Cairo and Thebes. The peasant woman who found them in 1887 sold the 300 for less than a dollar. The group was split up and marketed, some going for hundreds of dollars. More were found later and eventually 350 were translated and collated; the definitive study (1907–15) was made by J.A. Knudtzon. The tablets are primarily letters between various rulers of the ancient Near East and Pharaoh Ikhnaton (1370–53 B.C.) and his father, Amenophis III (1406–1370). The rulers include Egyptian puppet princes and governors in Palestine. Since the initial discovery, several more Amarna tablets have been found, bringing the total to over 378. These Amarna tablets remain the only cuneiform tablets found in Egypt.[16]

Once again, the early explorers and travelers, the early diggers, and the written or inscribed material are not always considered part of the archaeological record. Some restrict this record to excavation, even excluding all but modern excavation at times. But simple observation shows a continuity from one to another as the history of archaeology flows on through time.

# NOTES

1. Yigael Yadin, "The Temple Scroll," BAR 10, no. 5 (Sep/Oct 84), pp. 32–49. CPHA, pp. 138–39. Roland W. Robbins and Evan Jones, Hidden America (NY: Knopf, 1959). Mark P. Michel, "Preserving America's Prehistoric Heritage," Archaeology 34, no. 2 (Mar/Ap 81), pp. 61–63. Ian M. Thompson, "Looters and Losers in the San Juan Country," Early Man 4, no. 2 (Sum. 82), pp. 28–34.

2. HWP, pp. 7–9. Lionel Casson, "The World's First Museum and the World's First Archaeologists," BAR 5, no. 1 (Jan/Feb 79), p. 32. CPHA, p. 91. The Museum of Belshazzar's Sister (Philadelphia: University Museum, 1937). Thomas H. Charlton, "Archaeology, Ethnohistory, and Ethnology: Interpretive Interfaces," in SAAMT, Vol. 4, pp. 129–76. Dora Jane Hamblin, "A Unique Approach to Unraveling the Secrets of the Great Pyramids," Smithsonian 17, no. 1 (Ap 86), pp. 78–93.

3. J. Christopher Herold, Bonaparte in Egypt (NY: Harper & Row, 1962). C.M. Watson, "Bonaparte's Expedition to Palestine in 1799," PEQ 43 (1917), pp. 17–35. PDBW, p. 37. Leslie

Greener, *The Discovery of Egypt* (London: Cassell, 1966), p. 38. SBAF, p. 192. Casson, "The World's First Museum." HWP, pp. 448–449. CPHA, pp. 90–95. Brian M. Fagin, *The Rape of the Nile* (NY: Scribner's, 1975), and *Return to Babylon: Travelers, Archaeologists and Monuments in Mesopotamia* (Boston: Little, Brown, 1979).

4. Sir Alan Gardiner, *Egypt of the Pharaohs* (Oxford: Oxford University, 1961), pp. 3–7, CCEA, pp. 215–16. Guy le Strange, *Palestine Under the Moslems* (Beirut: Khayats, 1965). AOP, p. 23. Albert R. al-Haik, *Key Lists of Archaeological Excavations in Iraq, 1842–1965* (Coconut Grove, Florida: Field Research Projects, 1968), pp. ix–xiv. Samuel N. Kramer, *The Sumerians* (Chicago: University of Chicago, 1963), p. 7. CHP, p. 143. PDBW, p. 38. SBAF, pp. 81–2. CPHA, pp. 186–190. *Evliya Tshelebi's Travels in Palestine (1648–1650)*, tr. from Turkish by St. H. Stephen (Jerusalem: Ariel, 1980).

5. Henry Maundrell, *A Journey from Aleppo to Jerusalem in 1697* (Beirut: Khayats, 1963). Carsten Niebuhr's two volume work has also been reprinted in Beirut by the Librairie du Liban. M.C.W. Hunter, "The Royal Society and the Origins of British Archaeology: I," *Antiquity* XLV, no. 178 (June 71), pp. 113–123. AOP, p. 24. HWP, p. 446. Kramer, *The Sumerians*, p. 7. SBAF, p. 82. CHP, pp. 116–119. CPHA, pp. 194–204, 126–127. John Lewis Burckhardt, *Travels in Arabia* (London: Cass, 1968) (original 1829). Iain Browning, *Petra*, (2nd ed.; Salem, NH: Merrimack, 1982). Philip C. Hammond, "Petra, the Timeless," *Archaeology* 39, no. 1 (Jan/Feb 86), pp. 18–25. For the nineteenth century as a whole, including Burckhardt, see Yehoshua Ben-Arieh, *The Rediscovery of the Holy Land in the Nineteenth Century* (Jerusalem and Detroit: Magnes and Wayne State, 1979).

6. Henry B. Smith and Roswell D. Hitchcock, *The Life, Writings and Character of Edward Robinson* (New York: Ayers, 1977) (original 1863). G. Ernest Wright, "The Phenomenon of American Archaeology in the Near East," NEATC, pp. 3–40. Philip J. King, "The American Archaeological Heritage in the Near East," BASOR 217 (Feb 75), pp. 55–65, and, "Edward Robinson: Biblical Scholar," BA 46, no. 4 (Dec 83), pp. 230–232. AOP, pp. 25–34. CHP, p. 307. SBAF, pp. 85–86. A complete list of Glueck's publications through 1969 is in NEATC, pp. 382–394. His explorations are described in AASOR and BASOR. Major books include *The River Jordan* (Philadelphia: Westminster, 1946). *Rivers in the Desert* (rev.; NY: McGraw-Hill, 1968). *The Other Side of the Jordan* (rev.; Cambridge: ASOR, 1970). Conder and Kitchner, *The Survey of Western Palestine* (Jerusalem: Kedem, 1970) (original 1881). Conder, *The Survey of Eastern Palestine* (London: PEF, 1889). George R.H. Wright, "T.E. Lawrence and Middle Eastern Archaeology," MDOG 117 (1985), pp. 5–20.

7. Joseph J. Deiss, *Herculaneum* (NY: Crowell, 1966), pp. 22–3 gives d'Elbeuf's name in the French, Maurice de Lorraine. He was part of the Austrian occupation army which was in turn driven out by Charles III. Deiss says it was the monastery which needed water. The discovery was then brought to d'Elbeuf's attention. CPHA, pp. 25–27.

8. Marcel Brion and Edwin Smith, *Pompeii and Herculaneum* (New York: Crown, 1960), pp. 55–59. DHYA, p. 165, pp. 16–17, pp. 37–38. Charles Seltman, "A Mine of Statues," pp. 81–91 (in *Archaeology*, ed. Samuel B. Rapport and Helen Wright; NY: NYU, 1963). CHP, pp. 61–65. CPHA, pp. 23–25. Dr. Giuseppina Cerulli Irelli has been director of excavations in recent years. For the University of Maryland work, cf. Wilhelmina F. Jashemski, *The Gardens of Pompeii, Herculaneum and the Villas Destroyed by Vesuvius* (New Rochelle, NY: Caratzas, 1981), and her earlier reports in the AJA. Joseph Judge, "A Buried Roman Town Gives Up Its Dead," NG 162, no. 6 (Dec 82), pp. 686–693. SBAF, pp. 82–83. William H. Stiebling, Jr., "Who First Excavated Stratigraphically?," BAR 7, no. 1 (Jan/Feb 81), pp. 52–53. Robbins and Jones, *Hidden America*, pp. 3, 71–72. WAFE, pp. 58–59. This was not the first excavation in America. The Plymouth settlers excavated an Algonquin grave in 1622. Shortly after Jefferson's work in 1797, an excavation

located a French settlement on the St. Croix River. The discovery helped settle a boundary dispute between the United States and England. Kathleen Deagan, "Avenues of Inquiry in Historical Archaeology," in vol. 5 (1982), SAAMT, pp. 151–177. She is citing A. Young, *Chronicles of the Pilgrim Fathers* (Boston: 1841), and Robert Schuyler, "Images of America: The Contributions of Historical Archaeology to National Identity," *Southwestern Lore* 42, No 4 (1976), pp. 27–39. Siegfried H. Horn, "From Bishop Ussher to Edwin R. Thiele," *Andrews University Seminary Studies* 18, no. 1 (Spr 80), pp. 37–49. Adnan Hadidi, "The Pottery from Tell Siran," *Faculty of Arts Journal* (University of Jordan) 4, Nos. 1–2 (1973), pp. 23–38. Robert F. Heizer, ed., *Man's Discovery of His Past* (Englewood Cliffs, NJ: Prentice-Hall, 1962), pp. 5–10. CCEA, pp. 117, 490, 294. Kurt Bittel, "The German Perspective and the German Archaeological Institute," AJA 84, No. 3 (July 80), pp. 271–277.

9. Bittel, "The German Perspective." Massimo Pallotino, *The Meaning of Archaeology* (London: Thames and Hudson, 1968), p. 42. DHYA, pp. 16–24, 165–166. CHP, pp. 41, 47–50, 125–143, 223, 239–248. Stanley Mayes, *The Great Belzoni* (NY: Walker, 1961). Donald P. Ryan, "Giovanni Battista Belzoni," BA 219 no. 3 (Sep 86), pp. 133–138. CCEA, pp. 113–114, 270. PDBW, pp. 38, 40, 43. CPHA, pp. 102, 209–210, 221–223, 235–243. Arnold C. Brockman, *The Luck of Nineveh: Archaeology's Great Adventure* (New York: McGraw-Hill, 1978). BGA, pp. 420–421. John Quinn, "An Unchic Sheik who Digs," *Daily News* (5 Feb 69), p. 42. "American Lawrence of Arabia Dies," BAR II, No. 1 (Mar 76), p. 16.

10. CHP, pp. 13–37. Robert McC. Adams, "Illicit International Traffic in Antiquities," *American Antiquity* 36, no. 1 (Jan 71), pp. ii–iii. Dora Jane Hamblin, *Pots and Robbers* (NY: Simon and Schuster, 1970). Grace Glueck, "Someone is Stealing the Great Pots of America," *New York Times* (17 June 79), p. 20E. Arthur Miller, "Archaeological Looting: A New Approach to the Problem", *Expedition* 24, no. 3 (Spr 82), pp. 35–45. "Clamp-down on Plunder," SN 93 (20 Ap 68), p. 381. Rex L. Wilson and Gloria Loyola, eds., *Rescue Archaeology* (Washington, D.C.: Preservation Press, 1982). Clemency Coggins, "New Legislation to Control the International Traffic in Antiquities," *Archaeology* 29, No. 1 (Jan 76), pp. 14–15. Homer A. Thompson, "UNESCO and the Exchange of Cultural Property," *Archaeology* 29, No. 3 (July 76), p. 206. Michel, "Prehistoric Heritage." "On the Trail of Hot Pots," *New York Times* ( 2 Jan 83), p. 14E. Stephen Salisbury, "A hope for an end to the pillaging of the past," *The Philadelphia Inquirer* (30 Dec 82), p. Cl. Ellen Herscher, "Stolen Treasures–Missing Links," *Archaeology* 36, No. 5 (Sep/Oct 83), pp. 58–62. Over fifty countries have now ratified the UNESCO treaty. She describes 700 pieces of art stolen from Peru which the United States returned to Peru in 1982. Wendy Ashmore, "Historic Shipwreck Legislation," *Newsletter AIA* 4, No. 1 (Sep 85), pp. 1, 4, notes new legislation protecting shipwrecks from treasure hunters. Glyn E. Daniel, *Man Discovers His Past* (New York: Crowell, 1968). Robert Silverberg, *Great Adventures in Archaeology* (New York: Dial, 1964). Gary Pratico, "A Reappraisal of Nelson Glueck's Excavations at Tell el-Kheleifeh," ASORN No. 6 (Mar 82), pp. 6–10, and, "Nelson Glueck's 1938–1940 Excavations at Tell el-Kheleifeh: A Reappraisal," BASOR 259 (Aug 85), pp. 1–32.

11. M.L. West, ed., *Hesiod's Works and Days* (London: Oxford University, 1978). HWP, p. 7. DHYA, p. 14. Heizer, *Man's Discovery*, pp. 70–71, 153. R.J. Forbes, *Studies in Ancient Technology* (Vol. 8 Leiden: Brill, 1964). George C. MacCurdy, *Human Origins* (New York: Appleton-Century, 1933), pp. 1–9. Kwang-chih Chang, *The Archaeology of Ancient China* (New Haven: Yale, 1963), pp. 1–2.

12. David Diringer, *The Alphabet* (New York: Philosophical Library, 1948), and, *Writing* (New York: Praeger, 1962). Ignace J. Gelb, *A Study of Writing* (Chicago: Universy of Chicago, 1963). Maurice Pope, "Origins of Near Eastern Writing," *Antiquity* XL, No. 157 (1966), pp. 17–23. Ronald J. Williams, "Writing and Writing Materials," IDB 4 pp. 909–921. Millar Burrows, *What Mean These Stones?* (New York: Meridian, 1957) (original 1941), pp. 30–59. SBAF, pp. 127–152.

13. Barbara Watterson, *Introducing Egyptian Hieroglyphics* (Edinburgh: Scottish Academic Press, 1981). CHP, pp. 162–170. CPHA, pp. 104–110. CCEA, p. 129.
14. Naphtali Lewis, "Papyrus and Ancient Writing," *Archaeology* 36, no. 4 (July/Aug 83), pp. 31–37. James A. Sanders, "The Scroll of Psalms (11QPss) from Cave 11: A Preliminary Report," BASOR 165 (Feb 68), pp. 11–15. Leo Deuel, *Testaments of Time* (New York: Knopf, 1969). Jack Finegan, *Light from the Ancient Past* (2nd ed.; Princeton: Princeton University, 1959), pp. 385–414. CPHA, pp. 44–45, 178–180. James M. Robinson, ed., *The Nag Hammadi Library* (San Francisco: Harper & Row, 1977).
15. Kramer, *The Sumerians*, pp. 3–32. CPHA, pp. 204–205, 207. CCEA, pp. 206–207.
16. Philip G. Coutre, "Sir Henry Creswick Rawlinson: Pioneer Cuneiformist," BA 47, no. 3 (Spr. 84), pp. 143–145. George G. Cameron, "Darius Carved History on Ageless Rock," NG 98, no. 6 (Dec. 50), pp. 825–844, and, "The Monument of King Darius at Bisitun," *Archaeology* 13 (1960), pp. 162–171. Matthew W. Stolper, "George G. Cameron 1905–1979," BA 43, no. 3 (Sum. 80), pp. 183–189. Elizabeth N. Von Voigtlander, *The Bisitum Inscription of Darius the Great, Babylonian Version* (Lund: Humphries, 1978). WBA, p. 21. CHP, pp. 215–222, 182–184. CPHA, pp. 226–234. CCEA, pp. 113, 405–407. SBAF, pp. 258–261. Charles F. Pfeiffer, *Tell el Amarna and the Bible* (Grand Rapids: Baker, 1963). Thomas O. Lambdin, "Tell el-Amarna," IDB 4, pp. 529–533. S.A.B. Mercer, *The Tell el-Amarna Tablets* (Toronto: Macmillan, 1939). ANET, pp. 483–490.

# CHAPTER 3

# Business Picks Up

## A. THE NINETEENTH CENTURY ROLLS ON

### Egypt

About the time Layard was transferring pieces of ancient Assyria to the British Museum, Karl Richard Lepsius (1810–84) was conducting an expedition (1842–46) in Egypt for King Frederick Wilhelm IV of Prussia. Systematically surveying, he pushed knowledge of Egyptian affairs back before 3000 B.C. He upped the number of known pyramids and *mastabas* (a forerunner of the pyramid but with a flat top). A side trip to Sinai collected some workers' graffiti near the copper mines of Serabit el-Khadem. Expedition results were published (1849–59) in twelve large volumes.

The second university chair for Egyptology in Europe (Berlin, 1848) was created for him. In 1866, he found a limestone stela at Canopus, chief trading port of the Greeks before the founding of Alexandria. This Table of Canopus was another trilingual inscription in hieroglyphics, demotic and Greek. The priests expressed (239 B.C.) their gratitude to Ptolemy III Euergetes for reforming the calendar. The intention was to keep the festivals at the right time. The reform failed.

Lepsius was followed by another Frenchman, Auguste Ferdinand Francois Mariette (1821–81). He was born at Boulogne-sur-Mer in France. As a young man he worked for a while with his father in the Marine Department, then as a drawing master in Stratford-on-Avon, and later taught art at the College of Art in Boulogne. He was also a journalist and essayist. His cousin, Nestor Lhote, a pupil of Champollion, died in 1842. Mariette served as executor of the estate. He was fascinated by the Egyptian material in his cousin's effects and later wrote, "The Egyptian duck is a dangerous animal. With a peck of his beak, he injects you with his poison and you find yourself an Egyptologist for life." He taught himself hieroglyphics and Coptic and published a *Catalogue of the Egyptian Objects in the Boulogne Museum.*

During vacations from his new post as Director of the College of Art, Mariette studied in the Louvre. His friend Vicomte Charles de Rougé offered him a minor job there in 1849, and in the following year Mariette was sent to Egypt to buy Coptic, Syriac, Arabic and Ethiopic manuscripts. He turned to digging instead.

He had seen several small sphinxes in wealthy gardens of Alexandria and Cairo. At Saqqara, he saw a similar sphinx sticking out of the sand and thought of Strabo's famous statement, "One finds also (at Memphis) a temple of Serapis in a spot so sandy that the wind causes the sand to accumulate in heaps, under which we could see many sphinxes." Between 1851 and 1855, he uncovered (sometimes by blasting with gunpowder!) an avenue of 140 sphinxes leading to the Serapeum, the temple and cemetery of the mummified Apis bulls at Saqqara.

The ancient Egyptians worshipped their gods in the forms of a variety of animals and birds. These earthly representatives were frequently mummified and the remains of crocodiles, hawks, cats, etc. have been found. Mariette returned to the Louvre as assistant curator but then was appointed Conservateur of Egyptian Monuments in 1855. In thirty years, he dug thirty sites including Abydos, Dendera, Tanis, Edfu, Meydun, Thebes and the temple between the paws of the sphinx. Although he had sent materials from Saqqara back to the Louvre, he became convinced that Egyptian antiquities should stay in Egypt. Finding strong support in Napoleon III and Ferdinand de Lessups (who built the Suez Canal), Mariette encouraged the Khedive, Said Pasha, to start (1858) the Egyptian Antiquities Service with himself as Director. This was the first department of antiquities in the Near East.

One of Mariette's major concerns was protection of the monuments. The first legislation for this protection became law with his encouragement. This is to his credit, though his enemies said it was for his personal advantage. Neither Egyptians nor Europeans practiced field archaeology while Mariette was in power. He did all the digging himself!

An exception was Henry Alexander Rhind (1833–63), a Scottish lawyer in Egypt for his health. In 1855–7, he cleared some tombs near Thebes. In sharp contrast to Mariette, Rhind's methods included careful plotting of the exact locations of all finds. He could distinguish secondary uses this way — some burials were made later than the first ones. Rhind wanted to leave originals intact and sent casts, drawings, and photographs to the museums. Unfortunately these words fell on deaf ears and his methods had little continuing influence.

In retrospect, Mariette's own methods were not all that bad for his day. Petrie condemned Mariette for using dynamite, for not having a uniform plan, for starting work and leaving it unfinished, etc. While his slap dash methods may not sound like "protection," he did stop much of the pillaging. He also "conserved" by starting a museum. The Khedive refused to start one at first. Then came the discovery (1859) of the tomb of Queen Aahotep near the entrance to the Valley of the Kings at Thebes (Luxor). The local *mudir* (chieftain) of Qena stole the contents. He took the jewelry and started for Cairo to give it to the Khedive as a gift. Mariette gave chase in a fast steamboat, overtook the mudir, and violently took back the jewelry. Mariette then took the jewelry and the tale to the Khedive. In amusement, the gift was accepted and the plea for a museum was granted. The offices of a defunct steamship company were turned into a museum which was opened at Boulaq in 1863 by Ismail Pasha as the first national museum in the Near East. In 1889, it was moved to an unused palace at Giza and in 1902 to its present location in the Qasr-el-Nil. Here near the Nile Hilton Hotel, one can see the great treasure of King Tut and mummies stacked like firewood.

Mariette organized the Egyptian antiquities for the Paris Exposition in 1867. This was probably the first time Egyptian art had been properly displayed in Europe. The Empress Eugenie admired the jewelry, and remarked that she would be pleased to have the entire collection as a gift! Khedive Ismail had to admit that a man in Boulaq was more powerful than himself. But Mariette refused to hand over the collection and lost French favor for several years. This incident has been called "the birth of a conscience" about the expropriation of antiquities. Mariette's concern is also revealed in a letter published in 1877 in which he appealed to tourists to stop scribbling and carving their names on temples, obelisks, etc., a childish practice started by the ancient Greeks. He noted a young American traveler who took a brush and a pot of tar all over Egypt, leaving his name smeared hither and yon. Mariette also noted that tourists buy lots of antiquities — there were excellent "factories" at Luxor! This writer can testify that the manufacturing of antiques continues even today.

While visiting in Paris, Mariette met a young student whom he encouraged to pursue Egyptology. Gaston Camille Charles Maspero (1846–1916) was an Italian born in Paris. At the time he met Mariette, Maspero was in his second year at the Normal School. He later became de Rouge's assistant at the School of Higher Studies where he taught Egyptian languages and archaeology. By 1874, Maspero held Champollion's Chair at the College de France. In 1880, he was in Egypt leading a team of excavators which opened the small pyramid of Unas at Saqqara. The following year, he found 4000 lines of hieroglyphics in the pyramids. This disproved Mariette's thesis that the pyramids had no inscriptions. The "Pyramid Texts" are a collection of spells. There were 228 in the Unas pyramid out of over 700 known. More came to light in the pyramids of Pepi II and Teti (also excavated by Maspero), Pepi I, Merenre, and Ibi.

Maspero followed Mariette as Director of Antiquities. In this office (1881–86), he continued Mariette's efforts to protect the ancient remains from tomb robbers and souvenir hunters. In his first year, his assistant Emil Brugsch tracked down the Abd-el-Rasul family which had been robbing tombs around Thebes for six centuries. With the help of Mohammed Ahmed Abdel-Rasul, Brugsch found a cache of forty mummies and hundreds of other treasures. Loyal priests had first rescued them from the robbers of the original tombs and then stored them for safe-keeping in a secret hiding place. Mohammed was given a reward of $1500 and made *reis* (director) of excavations at Thebes.

Maspero continued to excavate at Saqqara and elsewhere. He also removed the sand from the Great Sphinx. He retired in 1886 to write several books including a three volume *History of the Ancient Peoples of the Classic East* (1894–1900). Lord Cromer invited him back in 1889 and he again served as Director until he retired in 1912. During this period, he wrote a guide to the museum collections and directed a complete recording of buildings and inscriptions at Philae and other Nubian temples before they were inundated by the first Aswan dam. These materials were published in 1911 as *Les Temples immerges de la Nubie*.

Maspero also continued Mariette's methods of digging. However, he was much freer in letting others excavate and in sharing the artifacts discovered, while retaining Egypt's right to the first choice of objects. The British, French, Germans, Swiss and Americans were soon at work in Egypt. Maspero's work and studies were extensively published in over 200 books and articles.[1]

## Palestine

One of Maspero's acquaintances was Felician de Saulcy, who explored and excavated around Egypt, Palestine, and Syria in the period 1850–63. Among other activities, he cleared the so-called Tombs of the Kings on the north edge of Jerusalem. He thought they belonged to the Kings of Judah but the tombs were those of the royal family of Adiabene, which ruled 650 years later. However, he is said to be the first modern excavator in Palestine — though it is also said he cleared the tombs as one might clean a sewer!

Another Frenchman, Ernest Renan, arrived in the Levant (the area of today's Lebanon) in 1860 with the expeditionary force sent by Napoleon III. After digging around such places as Byblos, Amrit, Tyre, and Sidon, he produced *Mission de la Phenecie* (1864) on Phoenician archaeology, the first extended study. By today's standards, his digging was ruthless pillaging but it was admirable for his own time because he transformed casual collecting into a systematic search.

The following year the Palestine Exploration Fund was started. While not a religious society, the Fund's aim was "the accurate and systematic investigation of the archaeology, the topography, the geology and physical geography, the manners and customs of the Holy Land, for biblical illustration." A young British ordinance officer, Captain (later, Major-General Sir) Charles Warren, was sent to Jerusalem two years later (1867). Without reliable criteria for dating he too missed the mark by centuries, but his accurate plans and drawings laid the foundations for all subsequent work in that much excavated city. His method of tunneling into hillsides to find old walls, in order to get the plan of the ancient city, curls the hair of modern archaeologists. One also wonders how he got out alive.

His *Underground Jerusalem* (1876) also includes a report on his excavations of ancient Jericho. He was looking for statues and when he found none, he quit. But he thought that if special techniques could be developed to excavate the mud-brick walls, it would be worthwhile to clear the entire mound. He estimated that this might be done for $1200. The PEF also sponsored *The Survey of Western Palestine* (1881) by Conder and Kitchner, and Conder's *Survey of Eastern Palestine* (1889).[2]

We might note in passing several more attempts to excavate in Jerusalem by Guthe (1881), Maudsley (1884) and F.J. Bliss and A.C. Dickie (1894–97). Two important inscriptions were also discovered in this period. Children playing in a tunnel by the Pool of Siloam (Arabic "Silwan") in Jerusalem discovered the Siloam Inscription in 1880. It describes the digging of a tunnel through Mount Ophel, under the city, from the Gihon Spring to the pool of Siloam, during the reign of King Hezekiah c. 700 B.C. The Mesha Stone was discovered in Dhiban (biblical Dibon) in Transjordan in 1868 by a German missionary, F.A. Klein. The French orientalist, Charles Clermont-Ganneau (1846–1923), had a Palestinian assistant make a *paper squeeze* of it. Before he could arrange transportation, local people built a fire, heated the stone, and threw cold water on it, which broke it into many pieces. Some say they thought there was gold inside while others think people simply resented foreign intrusion into their affairs. Clermont-Ganneau rescued some pieces and others rescued a few more. About a third of the inscription was lost but it was partly restored from the impression made in the paper squeeze. The pieces ended up in the Louvre in 1870.

In addition to Edward Robinson, American efforts in this area included the 1848 explorations of Lt. W.F. Lynch (U.S. Navy), who floated down the Jordan River in two metal boats. He spent three weeks exploring the Dead Sea and determined its actual depth. A short-lived American Palestine Exploration Society was started in New York in 1870 but with only meager results. It failed in several efforts to map Transjordan. Its purpose was "the illustration and defense of the Bible." A British Society of Biblical Archaeology lasted from 1870 to World War I. The first president noted the Society's work as archaeology rather than theology, but said the archaeology would help understand theology. Two years later a banknote engraver turned cuneiformist, George Smith (1840–76), publicized his translation of cuneiform tablets pieced together from eighty fragments in the dusty archives of the British Museum. It was part of the Babylonian flood tradition. The story was incomplete. Commissioned by the "Daily Telegraph," he went off to Nineveh and discovered the missing part of the story in five days! The year 1870 saw not only the establishment of two societies but also marked a new era in archaeology.[3]

## Troy

Heinrich Schliemann (1822–1890) was born in Mecklenburg, Germany, the son of a poor German pastor. He was given an illustrated history book for his seventh birthday. In it was an imaginary but very dramatic picture of the destruction of Troy. While working in a grocery store, he heard a drunken miller (another version says sailor) recite the Iliad in classical Greek. Schliemann applied himself Horatio Alger style, learned a number of languages, and became a rich merchant. He made a fortune in the gold rush in California while looking for his brother, Louis, and became an American citizen in 1850 when California became a state. He divorced his Russian wife, apparently when she declined to share his interests in antiquities. He chose a seventeen year old Greek girl, Sophia, as a bride when he was 46. One of her qualifications was an interest in antiquities. Together they went treasure hunting. But this time the treasure sought was literary.

Schliemann considered the Iliad accurate history and set out to prove it. He chose the site of Hissarlik as ancient Troy by following descriptions in the Iliad. Digging started in 1870. The initial work covered three years but he returned several times until his death twenty years later. His wild enthusiasm was restrained and modified with considerable deliberation and diligent record-keeping by an architect, Wilhelm Dorpfeld (1853–1940), who came to Troy in 1882 after five years with the German excavations of Ernest Curtius (1814–96) at Olympia in Greece. The German Archaeological Institute (1874) had strengthened that country's contribution to archaeology.

The Schliemann-Dorpfeld work has been hailed as a great scientific advance, and so it was. However, Schliemann's outstanding contribution may owe itself to his publishing methods as much as anything. He is noted as the first archaeologist to publish his results in modern form — as a report rather than a popular travel-ogue. He himself gives the credit for this to Layard. Schliemann was considerably aided by having apparently proved that the story of ancient Troy was not pure fiction even if the whole Iliad might not be true. The combination of his life and his discoveries caught the public eye. Rarely has an archaeologist received such public acclaim. At any rate, in the course of excavating careful note was made of the layers or strata. Schliemann is credited with this as a scientific advance, though Worsaae dug by layers thirty years earlier. Troy's stratigraphy was interpreted as representing nine different periods of the city's history. When Schliemann found massive walls and a palace in City II (second from the bottom), he decided he had Priam's fortress. This seemed confirmed when at the end of 1873, he reported that he had found "Priam's treasure," a collection of gold vessels and jewelry. He refused to turn half of it over to the Ottoman Empire and was fined 10,000 francs. He refused to pay the fine, but gave the government a gift of 50,000 francs. In 1881, Schliemann took the treasure to the Volker Museum in Berlin from which it was removed to several locations for safe keeping during World War II. One portion was destroyed in the bombing while another was found by American forces and is now in West Berlin. The Russians found the gold treasure in a bunker under the Berlin zoo and it has not been seen since.

Dorpfeld continued the excavations of Troy in 1893–94 with financing from Sophia Schliemann and the Kaiser after Schliemann's death. Later, he assisted William T. Semple, the University of Cincinnati and Carl William Blegen (1887–1971) in a re-excavation from 1932–38. Their work subdivided the major city levels (forty-six strata), corrected minor details, and identified city VIIa as Priam's Troy. However, it was Schliemann's belief in the Iliad and his excavations that laid the foundations for the later refinements. He also began the study of pottery types (typology) in relation to other objects from the same stratum.

Schliemann's work is a landmark in the history of archaeology in the Near East. This was enhanced by his discovery of the civilization of Mycenae. His work there (1874–76) on the Peloponessus, southeast of Athens, north of Sparta, led him to believe he had found the graves of Agamemnon and friends. At Orchomenos, he excavated (1880) a beehive tomb which Schliemann identified as Pausanias' Treasury of Minyas. He and Dorpfeld dug at Tiryns in 1884. Here they excavated cyclopean walls like those described by Pausanias and a palace with a megaron or hall resembling that of Odeysseus as described by Homer. Shortly before his death, Schliemann surveyed Crete with plans to excavate the Palace of Minos.[4]

## The Proper Dimensions

As early as 1851, Captain Meadows Taylor was digging scientifically in India. His reports show careful records of the stratigraphy and the exact location of artifacts. Taylor is also nominated for an archaeological "first." His efforts unfortunately did not catch on any more than his predecessors.

We do not know whether he influenced another British officer, General Augustus Henry Lane-Fox (1827–1900). Lane-Fox was born in Yorkshire, England. From 1845–80, he was in the Grenadier Guards where he studied the use and improvement of the rifle. An amateur anthropologist, he was influenced by Darwinism and applied evolution to human artifacts as well as in biology. This led to collections of weapons, boats, looms, dresses and musical instruments. The first of these collections eventually became a special annex in the Oxford University Museum.

His early work already merited entry into the Royal Society. It also prepared him for things to come. He felt that all things are important, but that the common piece is more significant than the unique or unusual piece because common things reveal development and hence evolution. He realized, however, that such evolution was not automatic and there were times of deterioration as well as advance. His collections also led him to a sociological approach (a view of the culture or society as a whole) and away from a concentration on the artistic aspect of the past, as in early museum and *dilettanti* collecting. The sociological approach has been applied in recent years to biblical studies.

In his earlier years, he excavated *barrows* (burial mounds) and hillforts at Kensington, Sussex, etc. In 1880, he inherited an estate in Dorset, England. The terms of the will led to a change of name and he became known as Pitt-Rivers. For the next twenty years, until his death, he explored and excavated his own estate. His desideratum was total excavation, in contrast to Kathleen Kenyon's later observation that the excavator should leave something for future diggers who will have improved methods. Our interest is in what he called three dimensional recording: in vertical and both horizontal directions. This includes stratigraphy. With military precision, his aim was to be able to put every single artifact back into its original position (at least on paper) in the mound or grave. The emphasis is not only on the recording, but on each single artifact. This method contrasts sharply with the hack and slash methods of previous excavations with an interest in museum pieces — whole or restorable. The recording had to be done as soon as possible. Today we say it should be done on the spot before the artifact is even moved, or immediately thereafter. All of this requires constant supervision and a large staff, for which Pitt-Rivers had both time and money. He also emphasized and practiced the adequate publication of his finds. Pitt-Rivers' methods have been followed and refined by Mortimer Wheeler, although they remained largely unknown and did not catch on at the time. Perhaps this was because his reports were privately published and did not achieve wide circulation.[5]

## Seventy Years

A figure with Pitt-Rivers' own variety of military precision, but almost as romantic a character as Schliemann, is Sir William Matthew Flinders Petrie (1853–1942), born in Charlton, England. He never went to school because of chronic asthma. Yet he was professor of Egyptology of University College, London, for forty-one years (1892–1933) and was knighted in 1923. His autobiography, *Seventy Years in Archaeology* (NY: Holt, 1931) has a fairly literal title. A highly controversial figure in retrospect, he has been called a quiet little man who spent his first two years in Egypt living in a tomb.

**Figure 3–1.**    Sir Flinders Petrie. Photo courtesy Biblical Archaeologist.

**Figure 3–2.** The Great Pyramid of Cheops at Giza which Petrie measured.

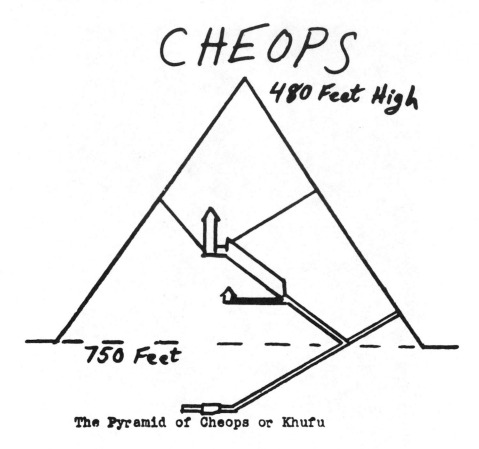

When he arrived in Egypt, Petrie was appalled at the quality of field work — destruction was so rapid, it was like a house on fire. This was the closing year of Conservateur Mariette's work, work which Petrie said was sickening in its destructiveness. His own methodical plodding produced ninety volumes of writing. These included his measurements of the Great Pyramid and excavations at Naucratis, Daphnae, Fayum, Kahun, Gurob, Amarna, Abydos, and Nagada in Egypt, and Tell el-Hesi in Palestine. These volumes are not only excavation reports but syntheses of what was found.

Several volumes were published by the Egypt Exploration Fund with which he worked for several years. The EEF (now the EES — Egyptian Exploration Society) was founded in 1882 by Amelia Ann Stanford Edwards (1831–92), a British novelist, and others. She was the first secretary, and Petrie was the first field director. The Fund's purpose was "to organize expeditions in Egypt with a view to the elucidation of the History and Arts of Ancient Egypt and the Illustration of the Old Testament narrative, so far as it has to do with Egypt and the Egyptians." Petrie noted that Miss Edwards opposed him at first but later supported his work. Her will established his chair of Egyptology in University College, London. His teaching collection of Egyptian antiquities there remains unrivalled. In 1893, he established the ERA — Egyptian Research Account — to train students. In 1905, after disagreement with the EEF governing committee, he developed the ERA into the British School of Egyptian Archaeology which supported excavations, publications, and students. His old Department began working with the EES in 1952 and the BSAE was disbanded in 1953. A six week campaign sponsored by the PEF took him to Palestine in 1890. In 1926, Eqyptian antiquity laws became so rigid that he moved to Palestine ("Egypt over the Border") permanently.

Petrie is hailed as a genius who was the first to put archaeology on a truly scientific basis (Egypt 1880; Palestine 1890), especially with his systematic recording of all finds and prompt publication (see Pitt-Rivers). He is also the first archaeologist to regularly confirm the substance of artifacts — metal was examined by a metallurgist, plant remains by a botanist, etc. Other estimates of Petrie's scientific precision acknowledge that he did not use dynamite or a battering ram. Yet he describes workmen being left for several days without supervision, except for a telescope and secret approaches to the site to catch them loafing! He considered constant supervision too much trouble. His own descriptions lead some to say his excavations are examples of "charnel houses of murdered evidence" — words *he* used to describe the museums of his day.

Petrie has also been credited with digging on a horizontal level — mechanically (with complete scientific objectivity!) removing ten to twenty inches of debris without regard to the true stratigraphy. An artifact or wall at seven feet thus risks being dated to the same period as another artifact at seven feet, though in fact they may be thousands of years apart if one of them is near the slope of the mound and in a quite different stratum of the occupation debris. He describes this along with his statement (when he was eight years old) that "the earth ought to be pared away inch by inch to see all that is in it and how it lies." Reisner, Fisher and Albright (see later) have been credited with (or accused of) following Petrie. It is also a method associated with French archaeology, although Petrie visited the work of Dunand at Byblos in 1929 and was horrified by the way the earth was moved away from its context and dumped into the sea without sifting (rumor had it that a local sheikh anchored his boat at the bottom of the dump and collected numerous artifacts for the antiquities market). Petrie's methods and their perpetuation led Wheeler to describe Palestine as a place "where more sins have been committed in the name of archaeology than on any commensurate portion of the earth's surface." One can admit the truth of this, while also noting that the four men in question, especially Reisner, were far more aware of stratigraphy than this horizontal leveling indicates.

Controversy over Petrie raged in his lifetime and continues. However, as with travelers and treasure hunters, Petrie's contribution remains monumental. He laid the groundwork for pottery typology with his recognition of changing styles, shapes, decoration, the rise and decline of techniques, including manufacturing. He saw the changes in terms of a mound's stratigraphy and related the pottery (and associated artifacts) to varying periods of history.

In a sense we pick up Winckelmann's trail and the initial steps of Schliemann here. In 1870, Alexander Conze, excavator of Samothrace and the first person to use photographs in his reports, discerned a distinct style of decoration on Greek pottery. This "geometric" style showed the possibility of pottery typology for dating purposes.

Petrie pushed on and used even undecorated pottery in his development of *Sequence Dating* (S.D.) with a numbering system of 1–100. S.D. is simply the observation that lower strata are earlier than higher strata, combined with the correlation of pottery types at one site with similar and intervening types elsewhere. A number was assigned to the different types in sequence of appearance from bottom to top giving an absolute chronology (sequence in time) to the types. Eventually comparison with Egyptian artifacts of known date (e.g., by inscriptions) allowed approximate calendar dates for the Sequence Dates. Thus S.D. 40 is c. 3300 B.C.; S.D. 65 is c. 2900 B.C.

This development alone assures Petrie a preeminent place in the annals of archaeology, regardless of deficiences in his methods. In his later years he refused to accept the contributions of others to pottery typology and misdated strata by up to 1000 years. We might add to his credit the Merneptah stela he discovered at Thebes in 1896 and the proto-Sinaitic inscriptions near Mount Sinai in 1904. With his strong judgments on others, and later, others' strong judgment on him, he exemplifies the tendency noted earlier to criticize earlier researchers as "unscientific" while seeing oneself as using truly "scientific" methods. He was still directing field work in his 80s and still living simply and "roughing it" as he had as a young man in his Egyptian tomb. He died in Jerusalem. His body is buried there and his head was taken to London for scientific studies — a scientist to the end![6]

## Carefully With Love

Petrie's pottery chronology was further confirmed by an American, Frederick Jones Bliss, who continued (1891–93) Petrie's dig at Tell el-Hesi. This was the site in southern Palestine where excavation in 1890 helped establish Petrie's S.D. Petrie and Bliss thought the site was biblical Lachish (Josh 10:32). Albright identified it as Eglon (Josh 10:3). This is also questioned. An American expedition re-excavated the thirty-seven acre site with its seven acre acropolis from 1970–84.

Another American of this period was George Andrew Reisner (1867–1942). Born in Indianapolis, he was trained at Harvard and in Berlin under Kurt Sethe, the German Egyptologist. Reisner was Harvard's first and last professor of Egyptology. Like Petrie he began his archaeological career in Egypt (1897). Two years later he organized the University of California's Egyptian Expedition. In 1905 this became the Joint Egyptian Expedition of Harvard University and the Boston Museum of Fine Arts. Reisner directed the Expedition until his death. He dug at Quft, Deir el-Ballas, Naga ed Deir, Giza (the third pyramid — of Mycerinus — and the necropolis around the pyramids); in the Sudan (Meroe, Kerma, Semneh); and briefly in Palestine. At Kerma he found a "death pit" similar to the one found by Woolley at Ur in the 1920s. Reisner's excavations, 1912–14, uncovered a chieftain's grave filled with human sacrifices. The dig in Palestine was in Samaria (1908–10). This was the biblical city built as his capital by Omri (876–869 B.C.) and his son Ahab (869–60), perhaps better known because of Ahab's wife, the notorious Jezebel.

Reisner's excavation at Samaria was one of the few truly scientific excavations in Palestine prior to World War I. Unfortunately the reports were not published until 1922, so its scientific value had no immediate effect. In addition to walls and buildings of Omri and Ahab, the expedition found a temple of Augustus built by Herod the Great. Among the finds were seventy ostraca (ostracon = "shell" or "tile"), broken pieces of pottery with writing on them. Potsherds were the scratch paper of the ancient world. The word "ostracize" comes from Greece where sherds were used in voting on whether an offender should be exiled.

Like Pitt-Rivers and Petrie, Reisner saw the need to record everything, no matter how trivial. His work can be illustrated with the example of the tomb of Queen Hetepheres near the Great Pyramid, excavated in 1924–25:

"In a walled-up recess behind the rock-cut chamber [with] the empty stone coffin of the mother of [Pharaoh Chephren] the pyramid builder [was] a mass of decayed and powdered wood and bits of gold plate. Scattered over the floor were tiny figures cut in gold, hieroglyphs which had been inlaid in the wood and had fallen out as that crumbled to dust. Had these just been gathered up they would have been a pretty illustration of the elaborate fashion in which the royal furniture of Egyptian kings 5000 years ago was adorned, and that would have been all. . . As it was the excavators cleared the chamber laboriously, square inch by square inch, recording the exact position of every tiny fragment; they spent [321 days working there, took 1701 pages of notes and 1057] photographs. From three bits of wooden frame and one panel, shrunk to a sixth of their original size, but preserving traces of the joints, tenons and mortices, they were able to re-construct a unique object, the carrying-chair of the queen.. The gold hieroglyphs, assembled according to the position in which they lay on the floor, formed groups which could be arranged so as to give sense, proper texts which decorated the upright panels of the chair. . . From the other remains of gold and wood the same painful methods recovered an elaborate armchair, a jewel-box and a bed; but after all had been removed from the tomb, the work of reconstruction took Dr. Reisner's men two whole years."

Like Petrie, Reisner trained Egyptians as foremen, photographers, and technical assistants who could excavate stratigraphically.[7]

## B. "NEW" PEOPLES

### Ancient Sumer

Of the ancient peoples whose existence came to light in this period of archaeology, the Sumerians are the oldest and most fascinating. As noted earlier, they developed the first system of writing. By 1852 Rawlinson concluded that one of the systems of cuneiform belonged to a new, unknown people. The common Akkadian title, "King of Sumer and Akkad" furnished the clue. In 1869 Jules Oppert, a French cuneiformist, suggested the "new" people must be Sumerians. Like the Greeks later on, the Sumerians left a cultural heritage far outweighing their political power, influencing the Mesopotamian world until Roman times.

The French made notable contributions in recovering ancient Sumer. Their vice-consul at Basra (a seaport at the mouth of the Tigris-Euphrates River near the Arabian gulf) was Gaston Ernest Choguin de Sarzec (1836–1901). He learned of some stone statues found (1874) at Telloh, the Sumerian city of Lagash (others now say the site of al-Hiba is ancient Lagash). Proceeding illegally, but later with a permit, de Sarzec directed eleven campaigns here between 1877 and 1900. Both the Louvre and the Imperial Ottoman Museum (founded 1887) in Istanbul were the richer for his "considerable haul of antiquities," as another Frenchman described it.

The "haul" included portrait statues of the governors of Lagash, with six of Gudea alone. Gudea, c. 2150 B.C., had built extensively and left numerous remains of temples and statuary. Many statues and figurines were votive offerings — left in a temple or holy place as an act of worship. A large number of inscriptions also came to light.

More digging followed in 1903–09 under a French soldier, Captain Gaston Cros. Illegal burrowing in 1923 led to the resumption of digging by the French in 1929 under the Abbé Henri de Genouillac (who also dug at Kish, 1912–14) and from 1931–33 under André Parrot, for a total of twenty seasons.

Figure 3–3.    The American Expedition to Nippur. Photo courtesy the University Museum, University of Pennsylvania.

**Figure 3–4.** A Cuneiform Tablet from Nippur. Courtesy of the University Museum, University of Pennsylvania.

Americans "got into the act" with their first archaeological efforts in Mesopotamia, the ill-fated expedition to Nippur (modern Nuffar), 100 miles south of Baghdad. Four campaigns were conducted in the period 1889–1900 by the University of Pennsylvania. Squabbles among the troika directorship, friction with local people (the 1889 camp was burned by irate Afaq tribes), and hack and slash methods, all combined to lead to a dismal near-failure. Several seasons had no architect, no photographer and no linguist.

The "near" replaces total failure because they did find 30,000 tablets. Since the studies of the Sumerologist Samuel Noah Kramer began in 1937, these inscriptions have been steadily contributing to knowledge of ancient Sumer as tablet after tablet has been translated. Secondly, the Assyriologist Hermann Volrath (Vollart) Hilprecht (1858–1925) gained control of the expedition at the end (1899–1900). Hilprecht had been born in Hohenerxleben, Germany and studied at the University of Leipzig. In 1886 he went to Philadelphia to the Department of Assyriology in the University of Pennsylvania. He became Curator of the Babylonian Section of the University Museum. He was at the first season's dig but was not allowed to continue until the fourth campaign. In the latter his "orderly and well-stocked mind" (as G. Ernest Wright has described him) insisted on architects and systematic digging rather than the tunneling and hacking treasure hunt of previous years.

Between 1893–1905 Hilprecht organized the finds from Nippur in the Imperial Museum in Istanbul. His work is summarized in his *Explorations in Bible Lands*; Philadelphia: Holman, 1903.

Excavations at Nippur were resumed in 1948 by the Universities of Chicago and Pennsylvania, and later the American Schools of Oriental Research. In addition to temples and other public buildings, more than 1,000 new tablets have appeared.[8]

## The Minoans

Schliemann earned his money. Sir Arthur John Evans (1851–1941) was born to it, in Hertfordshire, England, where his family were wealthy manufacturers. After study at Harrow, Oxford and Gottingen, he traveled in Finland and the Balkans studying folk history. In 1875 his interests turned to archaeology (especially numismatics) in the Balkans but he was also concerned with the freedom movement there. Dispatches to the "Manchester Guardian" disturbed the Austrians who expelled him. While he returned later, his focus had shifted. After visiting Schliemann's work at Mycenae in 1883, he became curator of the Ashmolean Museum in Oxford (1884–1908) and turned to the Mediterranean area.

Inscriptions from Crete came to Evans' attention. He visited there in 1894 and published his first study in 1896. In 1898 he bought the hill of Kaphala, Knossos, near Heraklion (Candia) where ruins had been known to exist for some time (Schliemann had looked, but died before he could do anything). In nine weeks of

**Figure 3–5.** The Lion Gate at Boghazkoy, Hittite capital of Hattusas.

**Figure 3–6.** The Procession of the Hittite Gods in a shrine at Yazlakiya near Boghazkoy.

**Figure 3–7.**   Dr. Wolfgang Roth of Garrett-Evangelical Seminary (Illinois) inspects a mudbrick wall excavated at Tirzah. This baked brick is easy to see but unbaked brick tends to blend with the soil. Sometimes it is greasy like cheese and may have a greenish tinge.

digging at Knossos, he cleared a palace, and a new civilization was brought to light. The Greek myth about King Minos and the Minotaur centered in Crete. The great palace had a labyrinth of rooms and passageways. In memory of the minotaur's labyrinth, palace and culture became known as that of Minos and the Minoans.

Evans not only uncovered a palace that housed a thousand people. He set out to restore it. Restoration included the numerous frescoes in bits and tatters on the walls, and some of the artifacts as well. In recent decades, there have been many questions about this restoration because much of it was based on scanty evidence. He used reinforced concrete, but that did not stop an opponent from labeling Evans' theories "shaky." Reconstruction, however, has become a common element of Near Eastern archaeology, sometimes for preservation and sometimes for purposes of tourism.

Evans went to Crete for inscriptions, and he found them. Most of these inscriptions were not published until after his death, which helped slow decipherment. Cretan seals from c. 2800 B.C. (Early Minoan I) have picture symbols, but true picture writing appears c. 2000 (Middle Minoan I). This picture writing gave way c. 1700 (Middle Minoan III) to what Evans called Linear A. Up to half of the signs can be derived from the last stages of picture writing. This "A" has been called Semitic, but the designation is not widely accepted. A second script, Linear B, has eighty-nine characters of which forty-eight can be traced to Linear A. Hundreds of Linear B inscriptions have been found at Mycenean sites on the mainland. This Linear B was deciphered as a Greek language by an architect, Michael George Francis Ventris (1922–56), with the aid of the new discoveries from Pylos on the mainland, in 1952. Because Linear A has been found on the mainland, its future may also lie there.

Scholars continue to debate the relationship between the Minoan culture on Crete, which came to a violent downfall (earthquake? or invasion?) c. 1400 B.C., and the Mycenean culture discovered by Schliemann. Who controlled whom? Or was it merely the influence of trade? Perhaps future excavations will tell. The Mycenean civilization may represent the Achaeans of Homer's Iliad. They in turn were pushed out by the Dorians c. 1200 B.C., and we hear of them again in the invasions of the Sea Peoples and the biblical Philistines. [10]

## What's New With the Hittites?

Developments and discoveries had also been taking place in central Asia Minor and vicinity. As early as 1736 Jean Otter had discovered an unusual relief at Ibriz in southern Cappadocia. In 1833–37, Charles Texier was wandering around Turkey. He looked over Boghazkoy in 1834 without suspecting that he was standing on the capital of an ancient civilization that once rivaled Egypt. Some years later (1861) an art historian, Georges Perrot, was collecting inscriptions and studying monuments in the Anatolian plateau. He recognized a different art in the reliefs we now call Hittite.

William Wright, a Protestant missionary at Damascus, made some squeezes of strange "hieroglyphics" on stone (first noted by Burckhardt in 1812) in Hamath in 1872. These were published by Richard Burton. Wright "rescued" the inscribed stones and had them sent to Constantinople, with plaster casts to the British Museum. To Burton the script was simply unknown. To Wright they represented the biblical Hittites, and he wrote a book, *The Empire of the Hittites*. In 1876 and again in 1880, a Welshman, Archibald Henry Sayce (1845–1933) of Oxford, put these and other observations together and lectured on the empire of the biblical Hittites to the Society of Biblical Archaeology (to which George Smith read the Flood Story in 1872). Later (1888) he published *The Hittites: The Story of a Forgotten Empire*. While the name appears in Egyptian and Assyrian records as well as in the Bible (e.g., Genesis 15 and 23), the existence of the Hittites was only a guess. With help from the excavations of Carchemish and Zinjirli in northern Syria, some ninety-six monuments and many seals were published in 1900 to illustrate Hittite hieroglyphics.

All of this, and the 1893–94 discovery of tablets at Boghazkoy, encouraged the 1906–12 excavation of the 419 acre site Hattusas of the Land of Hatti. The work was carried out by Hugo Winckler (1863–1914) and the Deutsche Orient Gesellschaft (DOG) — The German Oriental Society (organized 1898; it also sponsored work in Egypt, Palestine and Mesopotamia). The excavations were renewed in 1931 by Kurt Bittel and continued after World War II. Winckler had been appointed to the Chair of Oriental Languages at Berlin University (1904). He had already contributed to the translation of the Amarna tablets. That was his interest — so he sat in the shade during the excavations and let the workers bring him the inscriptions! There was no stratigraphic digging, but luckily the diggers dug into the royal archives and brought him 10,000 cuneiform tablets. Some of these were in Akkadian, while others were in the strange language of two of the Amarna letters, which were addressed to the king of Arzawa. This "Arzawan" language was Hittite cuneiform, which was translated by the Czech scholar Bedrich (Friedrich) Hrozny (1879–1952) in 1915 and presented in his *The Language of the Hittites*. Hrozny was born at Lysa, lived in Bohemia, and studied at Prague, Vienna, Berlin and London. He was on an expedition in northern Palestine in 1904, and in 1905 became a professor at Prague University. While he served as a common soldier in World War I, his commanding officer recognized the importance of Hrozny's linguistic studies and gave him time off to work on the decipherment.

The language is Indo-European, as already suggested by the Norwegian C.A. Knudtzon in 1902. It had been adapted to cuneiform sometime before 1500 B.C. It continued in use until sometime after 1200. The date of the archive was uniquely established by a copy of the Hittite-Egyptian peace treaty, already known from the records of Pharaoh Ramses II (1290–24 B.C.).

Hittite "hieroglyphics" (linguists prefer to restrict the latter term to Egypt) continued to accumulate along with expanded knowledge of the empires — an Old Kingdom, c. 1740–1460 B.C. and a New Kingdom c. 1460–1190. This was helped by improved knowledge of the cuneiform but the hieroglyphs stubbornly resisted translation. Finally (1945), Helmuth T. Bossert (1889–1962) explored the Hittite remains at Karatepe in south-central Turkey. Bossert was Professor of Near Eastern Languages and Culture at the University of Berlin and Director of the University of Istanbul's Institute for the Exploration of Near Eastern Languages and Culture. He was born in London and educated at the Universities of Heidelberg, Strasbourg, Frieburg and Munich. He began excavating at Karatepe in 1947 and discovered a fortress with north and south gates. The entry ways had duplicate inscriptions with Hittite hieroglyphics on one side of the gate and Phoenician on the other. While the contents of the two are not exactly alike they are close enough to be a "Rosetta Stone" type of key. This form of hieroglyphics lasted from c. 1500–600 B.C. Its origins are obscure but its earliest form is pictorial, and there are some similarities to Cretan picture writing. Of the 220 characters, 60 are sound symbols while the rest are idea symbols. While there remain scholarly disputes, by and large it can be read thanks to Bossert and Karatepe.[11]

## Old and New Babylon

Rich and Layard among others had dabbled in Babil, the site of the great city of Nebuchadnezzar (605–562 B.C.) and Hammurabi (c. 1728–1686), fifty-five miles south of Baghdad. They found little of "importance." Perhaps part of the lack of immediate reward was lack of stone for the original building in the southern mud flats of Mesopotamia. Since there was plenty of river mud, mud-brick had been the building material in the area from an early age. Early diggers went through mud-brick remains like green cheese.

Robert Koldewey (1855–1925) studied architecture, archaeology and ancient history at Berlin, Munich and Vienna. He worked at the Acropolis of Assos (1862–63) and on the island of Lesbos. The Berlin Museum had him make brief soundings (1887) at Surghul and Tell al-Hiba near Telloh. He worked in Neandria, Zinjirli, Sicily and in southern Italy, besides teaching at Gorlitz. In 1897 the DOG had Koldewey make a survey of Iraq to select a site for excavation. He suggested Babylon. By this time Koldewey and archaeology were ready for both Brick and Babil. He worked from 1899–1917, until the eighteenth season was ended by the British advance in World War I. By that time he had uncovered only a small portion of the city's 2500 acres, but he had spent half a million dollars and found huge walls, the palaces and the hanging gardens of Nebuchadnezzar. The Ishtar gate,

named after the processional way to the goddess' temple, is among his more spectacular finds, with its lions and dragons in glazed (enameled) brick relief. It took
two years to dig it out of its eighty feet of debris. The ziggurat of Babylon has been
compared to the Tower of Babel in the Bible. Among many inscriptions was a copy
of Hammurabi's Laws.

Koldewey also excavated the ziggurat at Borsippa (Birs Nimrud) and made
soundings at Sharuppak (Fara) and Abu Hateb. His excavation reports were dull
and failed to reach the general public, but he enjoyed the financial support of the
kaiser. Koldewey was the first to use hand pushed railroad cars for earth moving.
His care for stratigraphy inaugurated scientific excavation in Mesopotamia.

Assur (Qalah Sherqat) also had been dabbled in by the treasure hunters (Rich,
Layard, Rassam, Place, Rawlinson) but the German Oriental Society took serious
action under Walter E. Andrae (Koldewey's assistant in 1899) from 1902–14.
Andrae's careful vertical stratigraphic digging of successive temples of Ishtar
brought to light the temple plan and contents covering a period of 3000 years.[12]

## C.   THE HOLY LAND

In 1880 Pere Lagrange established the French Dominican School of Archaeology,
the "Ecole Biblique et Archeologique Francaise" in Jerusalem. The following
year, Louis Hugues Vincent (1871–1960) took up his lifetime residence at the
school. Vincent is perhaps most noted for his multiple volume study on Jerusalem
and his own excavations of what he thought was the Antionia, Pontius Pilate's
headquarters in Jerusalem.

Americans responded strongly with the founding of the American School of Ori-
ental Research (ASOR) in 1900 sponsored by the Archaeological Institute of Amer-
ica (founded 1879) and others. Charles Torrey was ASOR's first director. The
Harvard Expedition to Samaria in 1908 under Reisner was mentioned earlier.
Clarence Stanley Fisher was the architect. Harvard's first director at Samaria was
David Gordon Lyon, founder and director (1891–1922) of the Harvard Semitic
Museum. The British continued especially with the work of Robert Alexander
Stewart Macalister (1870–1950) who excavated Gezer (1902–09) with himself as
the sole staff, trying to do all the surveying, supervising, etc. — not exactly in the
spirit of Pitt-Rivers! Macalister's obituary noted that his work at Gezer "might
almost be said to mark the beginning of scientific archaeology" in Palestine. His
three massive volumes (1912) added a mass of objects to archaeological data. They
continue to be a mine of comparative material though it is difficult to detect where
he found each item. In 1909 he moved to the chair of Celtic Archaeology at
Dublin. The PEF's work continued under Duncan Mackenzie. Many corrections
were made when Hebrew Union College re-excavated the site (1964–73, 1984).

**Figure 3–8.**   R.A.S. Macalister. Photo courtesy Biblical Archaeologist. Published by permission Royal Irish Academy.

The DOG, as noted earlier, was started in 1897 for work throughout the Fertile Crescent. The Germans worked at Taanach (1901–04) under Ernst Sellin, Megiddo (1903–05) under Gottlieb Schumacher, and Jericho (1907–09) under Sellin and Carl Watzinger. The first two, like Gezer, were under-staffed. Taanach has since (1962–68) been re-excavated by an American team under Paul W. Lapp. Megiddo (Tell el-Mutesellim) underwent major work by the Rockefeller expedition in the 1920s and 30s — more on that later. Jericho (already penetrated by Warren, 1867, who gave up when no statutes appeared) was hailed as the scientific excavation of the day, with plans, pottery, and stratigraphy. Finds stretched from 5000 B.C. to 500 A.D. but Sellin refused to use Petrie's pottery typology and eventually the chronology had to be re-written. Sellin began the excavation of Shechem in 1913, a work which was to last for ten seasons over twenty years. In contrast to his work at Jericho, this was marked by inadequate reports, little concern for stratigraphy or pottery, and quarrels between Sellin and G. Welter, the expedition archaeologist — shades of the American expedition to Nippur. One is reminded of Wheeler's observation that at times, archaeology is neither art nor science but a vendetta. The last season at Shechem, directed by Hans Steckeweh, was an improvement for its study of the mound's stratification.

The Jewish Palestine Exploration Society (now the Israel Exploration Society) was started in 1913 by Abraham J. Brawer and others. The traditional geographical exploration came first, with excavation coming to the fore after World War I.[13]

## D.   PHARAOHS AND NOBLES

Reisner's primary field of activity was Egypt. The Germans continued working there. A major figure is Ludwig Borchardt (1863–1938). Sponsored by DOG, he excavated Fifth Dynasty (c. 2500 B.C.) pyramids and temples at Abu Sir, south of Giza (1898–1908). In an overlapping campaign, he and the Society also worked at Amarna (1904–14) following up Petrie's work there in 1891. The outstanding discovery was the royal sculptor's studio and a magnificent bust of Nefertiti, Ikhnaton's lovely queen. Carved in soft limestone, it was filled out with plaster and painted. The flesh color and the headdress with its blue, black, green, white and yellow retain their brilliance.

The EES was noted earlier. The Society sponsored Petrie's work at Abydos (1899) with finds on the early dynasties. The Society continued there with Thomas Eric Peet (1882–1934) and Henri Edouard Naville (1844–1926), discovering among other things a cemetery of mummified ibis birds and thousands of other animals as well, which had been sacrificed to the god Osiris. Naville, a Swiss Egyptologist, had already worked for the EES at several places including Tell el-Maskhuta on the Suez Canal and Deir el Bahri ("the River Monastery") across the Nile at

Thebes (1894–1908). At Bahri he cleared parts of a temple of Hatshepsut (1511–1490 B.C.), one of the first women in history to rule a nation. Nearby he discovered a sun temple from c. 2000 B.C. EES did extensive work in Amarna in postwar years and in Nubian rescue excavations before the completion of the Aswan High Dam in the 1950s and 1960s.

The EES work at Deir el Bahri was continued by the New York Museum of Art (1911–31). The Museum had already worked (1907–10) in the necropolis (city of the dead) at Thebes. Much of that period is synonymous with the career of Herbert Eustis Winlock (1884–1950) who joined the Museum's field work in Egypt in 1906. He dug at Lisht, the Khargeh Oasis, and Thebes, where he became the director in 1928. In 1932 he was made director of the museum itself. One of his most fascinating discoveries at Thebes was in an already cleared tomb of the Eleventh Dynasty (c. 2000 B.C.). A workman noticed a crack in the floor. Winlock stuck a flashlight down and found a group of little people looking at him! They were small wooden models of people herding cattle, rowing a boat, harvesting, working in the butcher shop and the bakery. They were probably intended to serve the nobleman Meket-Re in the afterlife.

James Henry Breasted (1865–1935) was born in Rockford, Illinois. Educated in Illinois, Yale, and Berlin, he was the first professor of Egyptology in America (University of Chicago). He is more noted for translation and synthesis than excavation. His *Ancient Records* (1906–07) ran to five volumes. Covering all the known texts (personally re-examined by Breasted), the work remains a standard reference.

His *Ancient Times* (1916) is perhaps better known. It educated several generations of high school students and adults on the value of studying ancient history. Even better known is the Oriental Institute of the University of Chicago, the first department of Egyptology in America. Breasted founded it in 1919 with the aid of John D. Rockefeller, Jr., with Breasted as Director until his death. The impact of the Institute has been felt throughout the Fertile Crescent — Egypt, Nubia, Yemen, Palestine (Megiddo), Iran (Persepolis), Iraq (Khorsabad, the Diyala Valley, the Hamrin Basin) and Turkey. Work continues today on this broad front. Lawrence Stager has extended the effort across north Africa to Carthage. Breasted coined the term "Fertile Crescent" to designate the arc of fertile land over the Arabian-Syrian Desert and south of the mountains of Armenia, stretching from the Arabian Gulf through Iraq, Syria and Palestine, to the Nile.[14]

# NOTES

1. CHP, pp. 113–5, 149–153. CCEA, pp. 299–301.
2. Frontispiece, *Palestine Exploration Quarterly*. The PEF succeeded where two predecessors failed. These were each named the Palestine Exploration Society. The first (1804) later merged (1839)

with the Royal Geographical Society, while the second (1840) later merged with the Syro-Egyptian Society which in turn became the Biblical Archaeology Society (see Smith, Sayce). Noted in Conder and Kitchner, Vol. I:1. KAHL, p. 1. George R.H. Wright, "T.E. Lawrence and Middle Eastern Archaeology," MDOG 117 (1985), pp. 5–20.

3. Nahman Avigad, "Tombs of Jerusalem," EAEHL, pp. 627–641. Cf. also pp. 565, 605–7, 643–5. Marcel Brion, *The World of Archaeology*, I–II (New York: Macmillan, 1961–2), Vol. II, p. 261. PDBW, p. 43. Siegfried H. Horn, "Why the Moabite Stone Was Blown to Pieces," BAR 12, no. 3 (May/June 86), pp. 50–61, and, "The Discovery of the Moabite Stone," pp. 497–505 in *The Word of the Lord Shall Go Forth* ed. Carol L. Meyers and Murphy O'Connor (Winona Lake, IN: Eisenbrauns, 1983). Emanuel Levine, "The United States Navy Explores the Holy Land," BAR II, no. 4, (Dec. 76), pp. 9–18. Barry Hoberman, "George Smith (1840–1876): Pioneer Assyriologist," BA 46, no. 1 (Wint. 83), pp. 41–2.

4. Several studies now suggest that Schliemann doctored his reports. "Priam's treasure" may have been put together from different finds over a period of three years, and may have included stray items he bought from peasants who found them in tombs. David A. Traill, "Schliemann's 'Discovery' of 'Priam's Treasure'," AJA 86, no. 2 (Ap. 82), p. 288. Machteld J. Mellink notes that the vendetta against Schliemann threatens to obscure his archaeological contributions: "Archaeology in Asia Minor," AJA 86, no. 4 (Oct. 82), pp. 557–76. Carl W. Blegen, *Troy and the Trojans* (London: Thames & Hudson, 1963). Lynn and Gray Poole, *One Passion, Two Loves* (New York: Crowell, 1966). "Treasures of Troy," *MD Journal* (Oct. 65), pp. 290–298. BGA, pp. 419, 421. SBAF, p. 87. CHP, pp. 57–60. CPHA, pp. 49–66. CCEA, p. 413. Kurt Bittel notes that the German Institute grew out of the Archaeological Institute in Rome established in 1829. It had German, French, Italian, and British sections. "The German Perspective and the German Archaeological Institute," AJA 84, no. 3 (July 80), pp. 271–7.

5. M.W. Thompson, *General Pitt-Rivers* (Bradford-on-Avon: Moonraker, 1977). WAFE, pp. 22, 13, 18, 25–29, 209–11, 218–19. BGA, p. 422. CCEA, p. 374.

6. Barbara Adams, "The Petrie Museum of Egyptian Archaeology, University College London," BA 47, no. 4 (Dec. 84), pp. 240–244. Valerie M. Fargo, "Sir Flinders Petrie," ibid., pp. 220–223. Joseph A. Callaway, "Sir Flinders Petrie: Father of Palestinian Archaeology," BAR VI, no. 6 (Nov./Dec. 80), pp. 44–55. T.G.H. James, ed., *Excavating in Egypt: The Egyptian Exploration Society, 1882–1982* (Chicago: University of Chicago, 1982). WAFE, p. 30. C.A. Franken-Battershill and H.J. Franken, *A Primer in Old Testament Archaeology* (Leiden: Brill, 1963). G. Ernest Wright, "Archaeological Method in Palestine — An American Interpretation," EI 9 (1969), pp. 120–133. Adolf Furtwangler and Georg Loeschke are credited with having the first publication which considered the chronological significance of decorated pottery, in their *Mykenische Thongefasse* (Berlin, 1879), and *Mykenische Vasen* (Berlin, 1886). Paul W. Lapp, *Palestinian Ceramic Chronology* (New Haven: ASOR, 1961), p. 1. Adnan Hadidi, "The Pottery from Tell Siran," *Faculty of Arts Journal* IV, nos. 1–2 (1973), p. 23. DHYA, pp. 141, 167, 175. BGA, pp. 419–421. CHP, pp. 177–181. CPHA, pp. 340–42, 122–4. SBAF, pp. 87–9. CCEA, pp. 367–9. WAFE, p. 30.

7. WDUP, pp. 95–96. David O'Conner, "Ancient Egypt and Black Africa — Early Contacts," *Expedition* 14, no. 1 (Fall 71), pp. 2–9. NEATC, pp. 4–40. Christopher S. Johnson, "Ruined Seat of Faithless Kings," *Harvard Magazine* 81, no. 5 (May–June 79), p. 57. D. Glenn Rose, "Eglon (City). 2. Tell el-Hesi?," IDBSV, pp. 252–3. Gus W. Van Beek, "Samaria," IDB 4, pp. 182–3. EAEHL, pp. 1035–7.

8. Samuel N. Kramer, *The Sumerians* (Chicago: University of Chicago, 1963), p. 22. Tom B. Jones, ed., *The Sumerian Problem* (New York: Wiley, 1969). SBAF, pp. 175–181. PDBW, pp. 43–6, 54. Albert R. al-Haik, *Key Lists of Archaeological Excavations in Iraq, 1842–1965* (Coconut Grove, FL: Field Research, 1968), pp. 95–6. CHP, pp. 254–7. CPHA, pp. 247–8. James Knudstad,

"A Report on the 1964–1965 Excavations at Nippur," *Sumer* 22, nos. 1–2 (1966), pp. 111–114, and, "Excavations at Nippur (1966–1967)," *Sumer* 24, nos. 1–2 (1968), pp. 95–106. David I. Owens, *Neo-Sumerian Archival Texts Primarily from Nippur in the University Museum, The Oriental Institute, and the Iraq Museum* (Winona Lake, IN: Eisenbrauns, 1982).

9. Sylvia L. Horowitz, *The Find of a Lifetime: Sir Arthur Evans and the Discovery of Knossos* (New York: Viking, 1981). Evans, *The Palace of Minos*, I–V (New York: Biblo and Tannen, 1964) (original 1921–5). J.D.S. Pendlebury, *The Archaeology of Crete* (New York: Norton, 1965) (original 1939). Leonard Cottrell, *The Bull of Minos* (New York: Grosset & Dunlap, 1962) (original 1953). BGA, p. 419. CHP, pp. 95–101. CPHA, pp. 67–80.

10. CHP, pp. 102–10. CPHA, pp. 80–82.

11. O.R. Gurney, *The Hittites* (Baltimore: Penguin, 1954). Helmuth Bossert, *Karatepe* (Istanbul: Istanbul University, 1946). HWP, pp. 61–4. SBAF, pp. 219–29. CHP, pp. 249–53, 277–94.

12. Robert Koldewey, *The Excavations at Babylon* (New York: Macmillan, 1914). Seton Lloyd, *The Archaeology of Mesopotamia* (London: Thames & Hudson, 1978). James D. Newsome, Jr., *By the Waters of Babylon* (Atlanta: Knox, 1979). Andre Parrot, *Babylon and the Old Testament* (New York: Philosophical Library, 1958). J.W.F. Saggs, *The Greatness that Was Babylon* (London: Sidgwick and Jackson, 1962). James Wellard, *Babylon* (New York: Schocken, 1974). PDWB, p. 46. SBAF, pp. 188–92, 207–8. CHP, pp. 230–235. CPHA, pp. 249–55.

13. William F. Albright, "In Memory of Louis Hugues Vincent," BASOR 164 (Dec. 61), pp. 2–4. Phoebe S. Sheftel, "The American Institute of Archaeology, 1879–1979," AJA 83, no. 1 (Jan. 79), pp. 3–17. Homer A. Thompson, "In Pursuit of the Past: The American Role 1879–1979," AJA 84, no. 3 (July 80), pp. 263–270. Philip J. King, *American Archaeology in the Near East: A History of the American Schools of Oriental Research* (Philadelphia: ASOR, 1983), and, "ASOR at 85," BA 47, no. 4 (Dec. 84), pp. 197–205. Page A. Thomas, "The Success and Failures of Robert Alexander Stewart Macalister," BA 47, no. 1 (Mar. 84), pp. 33–35. R.W. Hamilton, "Gezer," IDB 2, pp. 388–9. EAEHL, pp. 432–4, 1139, 831–2, 551–3. Gus W. Van Beek, "Archaeology," IDB 1, pp. 195–207, and, "Megiddo," IDB 3, pp. 335–42. Yigael Yadin, "Megiddo," IDBSV, pp. 583–5. Albert E. Glock, "Taanach," IDBSV, pp. 855–6. James L. Kelso, "Jericho," IDB 2, pp. 835–9. William L. Reed, "Shechem," IDB 4, pp. 313–5.

14. Charles Breasted, *Pioneer to the Past* (Chicago: University of Chicago, 1977) (original 1943). John A. Brinkman, ed., *The Oriental Institute* (Chicago: University of Chicago, 1980). John A. Wilson, "James Henry Breasted — The Idea of an Oriental Institute," NEATC, pp. 41–56. James H. Breasted, *Development of Religion and Thought in Ancient Egypt* (New York: Scribner's, 1912).

# CHAPTER 4

# The Twentieth Century

## A.  BETWEEN THE WARS

The pace in quantity if not quality of excavation was gathering speed. The post-World War I era saw an explosion of activity. The mind reels at the sheer amount of digging, a process which repeated itself after World War II. In one year there were sixty-eight expeditions in Turkey alone. At this point, a review becomes sketchier and the selection of highlights almost sure to irritate someone whose favorite has been slighted.

### Egypt

In Egypt, Reisner's work continued right up to his death in 1942, although in his later years he was almost blind. Breasted continued his surveys and the copying of inscriptions, work which the Oriental Institute carried on after his death in 1935. Chicago House, the Institute headquarters at Luxor, continued the epigraphic survey there. In 1936 the Metropolitan Museum moved to the Sudan after twenty-four seasons of work at Thebes. In the same year the Egyptian Exploration Society (EES) finished at Amarna.

The outstanding event in Egypt was, of course, the discovery of King Tut-ankh-Amun's tomb. Howard Carter (1873–1939) was seventeen when he went to work with the EES. He arrived in Egypt in 1891 to do copy work for the Archaeological Survey. He excavated under Petrie and Naville, spent several years (1899ff) as an Inspector of Antiquities for the government, and worked in the Valley of the Kings

**Figure 4–1.** The Third Gold Coffin of Pharaoh Tut-Ankh-Amun is still kept in his Tomb in the Valley of the Kings at Thebes. The other two are in the Cairo Museum.

for Theodore Davis (1837–1915). They discovered the tombs of Tuthmosis IV and Queen Hatshepsut. Davis was an American copper magnate who sponsored excavation in the Valley from 1903–12, by which time he could say that it was exhausted of finds. It was probably a kind providence that passed him on to his reward before Carter made his fabulous discovery under a second patron, the Fifth Earl of Carnarvon, George Edward Stanhope Molyneux Herbert (1866–1923). Carnarvon himself died five months after the tomb was discovered in 1922, helping to give rise to a superstition that all those involved in opening the tomb were doomed.

When Carnarvon was looking for an excavator, Maspero recommended Carter, to Maspero's everlasting credit. Tut's tomb is the first pharaoh's tomb ever discovered intact, though a broken but resealed doorway suggests an attempted robbery in antiquity. The extensive finds of wooden statues, thrones, chariots, three gold coffins, etc., are perhaps not as important in the discussion here as the extreme care which Carter used in clearing the tomb. He spent ten years at it, photographing, drawing, drawing plans, etc. as he moved from the doorway to the final object. It was a work worthy of Reisner who was clearing the tomb of Hetepheres described earlier. One of the three gold coffins of King Tut remains in the tomb. The rest of the tomb furniture and objects continue to be the star attraction of the Museum in Cairo. A few items had a stellar tour of the U.S., 1976–79.[1]

## Mesopotamia

The French slipped back to Telloh in 1929. The Germans returned to the 110 acres of Uruk (biblical Erech; Genesis 10:10) in 1928 under Julius Jordan and later Arnold Noldeke. By careful stratigraphy they revealed a history stretching from 5000 B.C. to the Christian era. But Iraq had come under the aegis of John Bull. The British were out in force. In 1922 Gertrude Lowthian Bell established the Department of Antiquities. R. Campbell Thompson dug into Nineveh's 1850 acres (1927–32). Many lesser digs dotted the landscape. The most spectacular British work (1922–34) was at Ur, traditional city of Abraham, 220 miles south of Baghdad.

Sir Charles Leonard Woolley (1880–1960) was educated at St. John's and Oxford. He dug at Corbridge while an assistant curator of the Ashmolean Museum (1905–07) under Arthur Evans. He continued in Italy, Nubia (1907–11), Amarna (1921), the Syrian seaport of al-Mina (1936) and Tell Atchana (ancient Alalakh) in the Turkish Hatay region (1937–09, 1946–49). With Lawrence of Arabia and others, he dug at the Hittite site of Carchemish in upper Syria (1911–14, 1919).

Tell al-Muqayyar means "mound of pitch," perhaps from the pitch used as mortar in building the ziggurat. The mound had felt the spade before. A British consul at Basra, Major J.E. Taylor had dug in 1854. Among his finds was a baked clay cylinder of our friend, Nabonidus the archaeologist c. 550 B.C. The inscription identified Muqayyar as Ur of the Chaldees (Genesis 11:28). Later efforts were by R. Campbell Thompson and H.R. Hall. Woolley began in 1922 and when he quit 12 years later much more was known about the Sumerians. He summarized the status of knowledge in 1929 with his *The Sumerians*. He excavated in macrocosm as evidenced by the huge ziggurat. But he is most noted for what Wheeler called a *watchmaker's job*, one example of which is the reconstruction of a harp deteriorated to fragments and impressions in the dirt. In spite of this care, a colleague later described Woolley's methods as "slapdash."

The headline-catcher which came close on the heels of Carter's discovery of King Tut was the discovery of the Royal Graves, excavated 1926–29. Of 450 graves in the "death pit" cemetery, about sixteen were "royal." The burial of the monarch included his attendants! From six to eighty people were buried, presumably to serve the lord in the afterlife. This was noted earlier for Egypt, and for Reisner's excavation (1913) at Kerma. In Egypt humans were replaced by ushabti figurines. In Sumer the practice is unknown in later periods. It could represent human sacrifice, but this is not clear. Woolley also discovered a bed of silt — water-laid clay eight feet thick. At the time, the discovery was relayed to the world as evidence of the biblical Flood. Actually it is only one of many silt layers in various cities from various periods of time.

Gertrude Bell's will (1932) left money to start the British School of Archaeology in Iraq. The first chair of the committee was Sir Edgar Bonham-Carter. The School published the journal *Iraq*. Their first dig was at Arpachiyah (Tepe Reshwa), four miles east of Nineveh. Max Mallowan (later Sir Max of Nimrud fame) directed, fresh from his work with Woolley at Ur and R.C. Thompson at Nineveh. Among the fascinating discoveries were domed buildings up to thirty feet across, with access via rectangular hallways up to sixty feet long. These *tholoi* date c. 5000 B.C., preceding the Mycenean tholoi several thousand years. Figurines and other finds suggest the Arpachiyah tholoi were shrines.

The School's work switched to Chagar Bazar (1934–37) and then to Tell Brak, both in northeast Syria. At Brak, one of the outstanding discoveries was a series of four "eye temples" from c. 3000 B.C. The name is from thousands of black and while alabaster amulets, figurines with large eyes. Woolley in the meanwhile moved on to the two sites of al Mina (Posideium) and Atchana. The temples and tablets discovered there have added background to biblical studies.[2]

## For the Fathers

The ASOR established a branch in Baghdad in 1923. This Baghdad School, the Oriental Institute, Harvard, the University Museum and the Iraq Museum joined forces to dig Nuzi (1925–31), modern Yorghan Tepe near Kirkuk east of the Tigris River. Led by Edward Chiera, Robert H. Pfeiffer and Richard F.S. Starr, respectively, the expedition found 4000 tablets. These illuminate the background of Genesis 12–50 and the life of the Patriarchs. The Nuzians, c. 1500 B.C., were Hurrians, biblical Horites or Hivites. While forming a large element in the Kingdom of Mitanni in the Late Bronze Age (c. 1500–1200), they never formed a kingdom of their own. Except in the Bible, they were unknown until the appearance of their adopted cuneiform on an Amarna tablet and the discovery of their name in a Boghazkoy tablet in 1915. Since then, material has accumulated and in 1941 Ephraim Avigdor Speiser (1902–1965), Director of ASOR's Baghdad School (1934–47), Professor at the University of Pennsylvania and a brilliant linguist and historian, published a Hurrian grammar. Hurrians were probably at Ebla in Syria as early as 2500 B.C.[3]

## Syria

The French sphere of influence after World War I was in Lebanon and Syria. In 1921 Pierre Montet began work at Byblos, biblical Gebal (Ezekiel 27:9), twenty-five miles north of Beirut. After three more years, he was followed by Maurice

Dunand They found remains dating from 5000 B.C. through Crusader and Arab times. Byblos was a major seaport for exporting the cedars of Lebanon. We get our English world "bible" from Byblos, which means "books," perhaps itself derived from papyrus, Egyptian paper.

On the Mediterranean coast of today's Syria is a mound called Ras Shamra, "head of fennel," from the fennel plant. It is opposite Cyprus. The ruins came to light as noted earlier when a farmer's plow broke through the ceiling of a tomb near Minet el Beida. Beida was the seaport of the larger, more inland, Ras Shamra, ancient Ugarit. Claude Frederick Armand Schaeffer (1898–1982) excavated (1929–39, 1950ff) and found five major periods of occupation and a new culture, Ugaritic. Born in Alsace, Schaeffer studied archaeology at the Universities of Strasbourg and Paris. He also excavated Engomi (Alasia) in Cyprus.

Charles Virolleaud, Director of Antiquities for the French Mandate Government of Syria, investigated the tomb finds which included thirteenth century imports from Mycenae and Cyprus. The Academie des Inscriptions et Belles-Lettres (founded by Louis XIV in 1665) sent out an expedition under Schaeffer. Hundreds of clay tablets were found in Ras Shamra. These date from the fourteenth and thirteenth centuries B.C. They have added immeasurably to our knowledge of Canaanite culture. The inscriptions range from Egyptian to Cypriot to Akkadian. A number were in cuneiform, but in a new language called Ugaritic after the name of the ancient city known from the records of Amarna and Boghazkoy.

By 1930 Hans Bauer (1878–1937) had shown that Ugaritic was alphabetic and had identified seventeen signs. This completely unsuspected alphabet has thirty-two letters. The inventor(s) arbitrarily selected wedge forms to represent letters in an earlier alphabet. The origins of this earlier alphabet are unknown but go back as far as 1800 B.C. Three inscriptions (including a stone plaque from Shechem discovered in 1934) date to the seventeenth and eighteenth centuries. The script is called Early Canaanite. It developed into the North Semitic Alphabet (NSA) in contrast to the South Semitic in the Arabian Peninsula. This NSA is the ancestor of all alphabets in use today, moving from the Phoenicians to the Greeks, perhaps c. 1000 B.C., though this date is strongly debated.

The Ugaritic materials are of enormous value for their information on Canaanite religion, poetry, and historical background in the second millennium. Schaeffer found palaces and temples and a school where many of the tablets were found. One palace has sixty-seven rooms. An Amarna tablet refers to a destruction of Ugarit — half by fire and half "is not" — perhaps an earthquake. Schaeffer found evidence for a number of quakes in the history of the site, on which basis he constructed a rather "shaky" chronology for all of ancient Palestine.

Under André Parrot the French excavated Tell Hariri, the royal city of Mari (1933–38, 1951–56), after Bedouins looking for stones found a headless statue. The seven acre palace is impressive and so are the 25,000 tablets found there. The latter give background for Genesis 12–50, for the role of prophet, and for the history of the area. The Amorites set up a kingdom at Mari but were conquered by another Amorite kingdom, that of Hammurabi of Babylon, c. 1700 B.C. Earlier still, Mari was in conflict with the city of Ebla whose archives claim to have conquered Mari.[4]

## Palestine

In Palestine the British Mandate was set up after World War I. In 1920 the Department of Antiquities was established with John Garstang (1876–1956) in charge. Educated at Oxford, he dug with Petrie at Abydos in 1899 and excavated Meroe (1910–14) while Professor of Archaeology at the University of Liverpool. He helped organize the Palestine Archaeological Museum (endowed by John D. Rockefeller, Jr.) in Jerusalem. In 1948 he became Director of the British School of Archaeology in Ankara, Turkey and excavated Mersin. During his Palestine Mandate days, Garstang was also Director of the British School of Archaeology in Jerusalem, founded in 1919. He excavated (1930–36) Old Testament Jericho (Tell es Sultan), following up the German dig (1907–09). In turn Jericho was dug once more (1952–58) by Dr. Kathleen Kenyon. One of the most interesting things she found was a Neolithic tower first built around 8000 B.C., making Jericho the oldest fortified town known.[5]

One of the first excavation permits the new Department issued was to Clarence Stanley Fisher (1876–1942) and the University Museum (Philadelphia) for the excavation of Beth-shan. Fisher was an architect with the American expedition at Nippur (1898–1900) and with Reisner at Samaria. Later he worked with Reisner in Egypt and was Curator of Egyptian Antiquities in the University Museum (1915–25) and Professor of Archaeology for ASOR in Jerusalem (1925–42). He had dug at Memphis and elsewhere in Egypt and was a consultant in the Jerash (ancient Gerasa) excavation (1931) and to William Frederic Bade's (1887–1936) work at Tell en-Nasbeh, besides directing Beth-shan for several seasons and later Megiddo. Personality clashes made it difficult for him to stay long in any one place, but it is of interest that he spent his last years in Jerusalem working on a never-published corpus of Palestinian pottery and trying to help the children of the poor. Because he was an architect he concentrated on walls and buildings to the neglect of stratigraphy. His "section" drawings show walls and their elevations but not their debris layers (strata).

Ten campaigns at Beth-shan (1921–34) brought to light a city first settled c. 4000 B.C. with occupation continuing into the nineteenth century A.D. The most important finds were a series of temples with numerous cult objects. The excavations were the scientific model of the day. In spite of careful work by Fisher and successors Alan Rowe (1892–1968), trained by Reisner in Egypt, and Gerald Fitzgerald, the dating of the strata at Beth-shan was wrong. Their results were complicated by several inscriptions which seemed to date the temples in the Late

**Figure 4–7**    The Oasis of Jericho seen from the air. The difference between it and the surrounding desert is Ain Sultan, a strong spring that comes out near the foot of Tell Sultan, the Jericho of the Hebrew Scriptures.

Bronze Age (1500–1200 B.C.) However, the inscriptions had apparently been saved by the city's inhabitants, possibly as heirlooms. Subsequent study of the pottery lowered the dates so that the earliest temple is now dated in the time of Ikhnaton, c. 1350. Later temples range from 1290 on. The date of the last two temples is still in dispute, some saying c. 1000 while others claim they lasted through the Israelite period until Persian times, c. 400 B.C. Work has continued in phases (1972–83) led by Tsafir, Foerster and Yadin.

Fisher left Beth-shan to direct the University of Chicago's Oriental Institute dig at Megiddo (Tell el-Mutesellim). The Americans continued (1925–34) where the Germans had left off (1903–05). Megiddo was to be a model excavation and plans were made to dig the entire hill. When five layers of the twelve acre mound had been completely removed, this proved too expensive, even for a dig with Rockefeller funding. The excavators substituted a series of trenches. These told of settlement beginning around 4000 B.C. and continuing intermittently from then until the fourth century B.C. The results of the dig were impressive — temples, altars, cult objects and "stables." The last were related to the time of Solomon and his commercial horse trading (I Kings 9:15; 10:28). Yadin later dated them to King Ahab c. 750. They may not be stables but warehouses.

**Figure 4–3.**    Jericho Tower. Jericho's spring attracted people as early as 9000 B.C. This fortified tower makes it the oldest fortified site known.

**Figure 1-1.**    Jericho Tower interior. Early defenders went from ground level to the top via an inner staircase.

**Figure 4–5.**   The Gate of Megiddo.

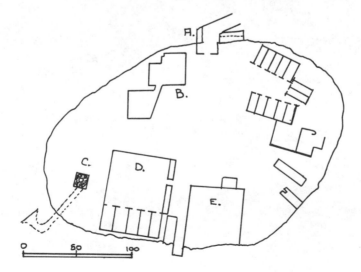

**Figure 4–6.**   Sketch plan of Megiddo: A. City Gate; B. Palace; C. Water Tunnel; D. "Stables;" E. Canaanite Altar. Drawn by J.E. Thompson.

**Figure 4–7.**    The City Gate at Beth-shan, an Egyptian outpost.

**Figure 4–8.**    Beth-shan. The drums of columns from the Byzantine Church, probably reused from the earlier Hellenistic-Roman temple.

**Figure 4–9.** A stele—slab of rock with writing on one side—of Pharaoh Ramses. The hieroglyphics outlined in white represent the name of Beth-shan, which helped to identify the site. While it was assumed the mound of Tell el-Husn ("Mound of the Fortress") was the ancient biblical city, it was still a guess until this and other inscriptions were found.

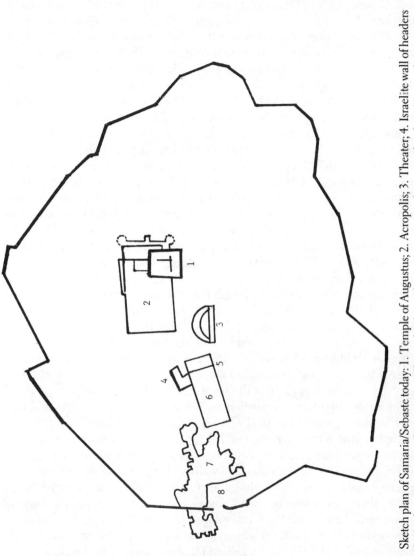

**Figure 4-10.**  Sketch plan of Samaria/Sebaste today: 1. Temple of Augustus; 2. Acropolis; 3. Theater; 4. Israelite wall of headers and stretchers; 5. Basilica; 6. Roman Forum; 7. Village of Sebastyeh; 8. Entrance to the mound today. (Drawn by Joyce E. Thompson)

In southern Palestine any survey of Near Eastern archaeology between the two world wars finds the excavation of Tell Beit Mersim as most significant. William Foxwell Albright (1891–1971), with a combination of luck and his own solid training, dug here (1926–32). The site is only seven and a half acres but has nearly complete stratigraphy dating from 2200–586 B.C. He identified it as biblical Debir (Joshua 10:38). Others equate Debir with Rabud, dug in 1968 by the Israeli archaeologist Moshe Kochavi. Albright's quick publication and the new clarity his well-stratified results brought to Palestinian pottery chronology account for the site's significance. His volumes (AASOR 12, 13, 17, 21–22) have been almost a "bible" for pottery typology though this is now being refined by work in progress today.

In spite of Reisner's careful work at Samaria, important remains there such as two round fort towers have had to be redated to a later period. This came after the work of J.W. Crowfoot, Kathleen Kenyon and others in a joint expedition by Americans, British and the Hebrew University (1931–33) and a British dig in 1935. Work continued under American and Jordanian auspices (1967) as part of a program to develop the site for tourism. The British School of Archaeology in Jerusalem under J. Basil Hennessy excavated the lower slope around the royal quarter. The publication of the 1930s campaigns, *Samaria Sebaste* I (1942), II (1938) and III (1957) by J.W. and Grace M. Crowfoot and Kenyon are landmarks in archaeological reporting.

Other important digs include the Jewish Palestine Exploration Society (now the IES) work at Hammath-Tiberius, Jerusalem, Ramat Rahel and Beth-Shearim. Lachish (Tell Duweir) was excavated (1932–38) but the work stopped when the director, J.L. Starkey, was murdered by bandits. Occupation at the site ranged from the Chalcolithic c. 3500 to the fourth century B.C. When a massive Middle Bronze Age fort wall went out of use, a Late Bronze temple was built and rebuilt in the *fosse* (moat) at the foot of the wall. The Lachish ostraca (writings on pieces of pottery) furnish important information on the development of scripts and language. Excavations were resumed (1973–83) by David Ussishkin.

Also noteworthy is the excavation of Teleilat Ghassul, a group of low mounds east of the Jordan River, near the Dead Sea. Chalcolithic finds include frescoes painted in geometric designs on plastered walls and a distinctive pottery which has since been found in other parts of the country. The pottery includes *cornets*, cups with a "V" shape, and butter or yogurt churns in a semi-bird shape. The excavations were carried out by the Pontifical Biblical Institute (R. Koeppel, A. Mallon, R. Neuville) from 1930–38. Work was resumed for a season (1960) by Robert North and again in 1967 and 1975–78, by J. Basil Hennessy and the British School.

In Transjordan or East Jordan, the Jerash excavations in the 1920s and 1930s represented a major American effort under Carl H. Kraeling of Yale. Renewed excavations (1982–   ) are extending those findings of the Hellenistic-Roman-Byzantine city.[6]

Figure 4–11.    The City Wall at Lachish.

## B.    AFTER THE BATTLES

World War II interrupted European and American excavation but gave new impetus to national archaeologists. The Egyptian Department of Antiquities emerged from European domination when the last French Director, Abbé Drioton, resigned in 1952. The Iraq Department and the Iraq Museum have sponsored many excavations. Turkish archaeology grew until by 1970, the Turks were digging as many (34) sites as foreign excavators in Turkey. The latter includes Bittel's continuing work at Boghazkoy. Since the war, an enormous amount of work has gone on all over the Near East. The excavations at Ugarit, Mari, Nippur, Jericho, Jerusalem, Gezer and Shechem have been noted. The Germans returned to Erech in 1954 under Heinrich Lenzen (1900–78), who also did some digging at Babylon in 1955–56. The Japanese entered Near Eastern archaeology in Iran, Iraq and Israel.

Max Edgar Lucien Mallowan (1904–78) was an Englishman of Austrian and French descent. An Oxford graduate (1925), he worked with Woolley at Ur and R.C. Thompson at Nineveh. He went on to dig nearby Arpachiyah and then directed work at Chagar Bazar and Tell Brak. Later he rose to fame with fourteen seasons (1949–63) at Nimrud, biblical Calah (Genesis 10:11–12), twenty miles south of Nineveh and Mosul. In addition to palaces and fortresses, he doubled the known number of ivory carvings. The results were published in two magnificent volumes with a third for maps and plans, *Nimrud and its Remains*; NY: Dodd, Mead, 1966. Mallowan was Director of the British School from 1947–61. He was almost unique among excavators in the publication of his results in a short time. Another of his claims to fame was his wife, Agatha Christie, the detective story writer whom he had met in Ur in 1930. She is reported to have quipped at one point that it is nice being married to an archaeologist — the older you get, the more interesting you become to him!

In 1964 the University of Rome began excavating Tell Mardikh in Syria. Its 140 acre tell has an acropolis that rises some fifty feet above the surrounding area. Paolo Matthiae directed the work. In 1968 a statue from c. 2000 B.C. was found with an inscription by King Ibbit-Lim of Ebla. This identified the site. The inscription was a dedication to Ishtar, so we also know something of his religion. In 1974–76, about 20,000 inscribed clay fragments and tablets were discovered. Their translation revealed a new empire with its own Northwest Semitic language from c. 2500 B.C., written in Sumerian script.

Early reports of translations caught public attention. It was said there were many connections with the Bible, such as the five cities of the plain in Genesis 14, including the infamous cities of Sodom and Gomorrah. One of the Eblite kings was named Ebrium, a name similar to Eber, an ancestor of Abraham. As excitement grew, so did conflict over the biblical connection. The controversy became quite bitter as carried out in the press and carried over into international politics. The biblical connection is now said to be "dead" (the early translations were all mistakes) but perhaps the controversy will speed publication of the tablets. This often bogs down in scholarly circles. The Nippur tablets are still not all translated.

Jerusalem, a long time favorite of archaeologists, was investigated again, by Kenyon (1961–67) fresh from the dig at Jericho (1952–58). The Israelis have dug several parts of the city. Since the old city came under Israeli jurisdiction in 1967, Israeli archaeologists have expanded their work to that portion of the city, as well as the City of David where Kenyon worked. Benjamin Mazar put in ten seasons on the Temple Mount south of the Haram esh-Sharif, the traditional site of Solomon's Temple. Nahman Avigad concentrated on the old Jewish Quarter in the southwest. Yigal Shiloh worked on Mount Ophel.

Gezer (I Kings 9:16) was re-dug (1964–73, 1984) by the Hebrew Union Biblical and Archaeological School, taking up where Macalister left off in 1909. In the 1930s, Madame Marquet-Krause excavated Ai (Joshua 8), but died before she could publish a final report. The site has been re-excavated (1964–68) by Joseph A. Callaway of Southern Baptist Theological Seminary, with the co-sponsorship of several other American schools. Lachish (Tell ed Duweir) was checked again. The solar shrine was re-excavated in 1966–68 by Yohanan Aharoni while the entire hill came back under investigation by David Ussishkin. Qumran, the "monastery" related to the Dead Sea Scrolls, was dug in the early 1950's by Roland de Vaux and others. Gibeon (Joshua 9:3) was dug (1956–62) by James B. Pritchard of the University Museum. Hazor (Joshua 11) was dug (1955–58) by Yadin and others, with new plans for digging again underway. The excavations of Hebron (Joshua 10:36) by Philip Hammond were interrupted by the war in 1967. Ashdod (I Samuel 5:1) began in 1970 under Moshe Dothan and a consortium of American schools. Caesarea was also begun in 1970 under the direction of Robert J. Bull of Drew University with a consortium of schools and museums.

In Egypt, dozens of rescues and reconstructions salvaged something from the rising waters of the new high dam at Aswan while rescue work has proceeded in Syria and Turkey to save something of sites to be lost behind the Euphrates dams. In the Jordan Valley and in East Jordan, digging has gone on at Deir' Alla, Tell es-Sa'adiyah and Tabqat Fahl (Pella), Araq el-Amir, Tell er-Rumeith, Umm el-Jimal, Umm Qais, Bab edh-Dhra', Sahab, Dhiban (Dibon), Tell Hesban, Buseirah, Machaerus, Tawilan, Petra, Amman and others.[7]

**Figure 4–12.**    Hazor. The remains of a warehouse.

In a sense the old method of simply digging a place out and clearing away the dirt has continued among the French. Their excavations at Ugarit and Byblos and at Engomi in Cyprus show great areas where the dirt has been cleared away. It is said that the French dig on a mass scale and interpret their findings from the mass of accumulated evidence. In contrast, the British have been said to excavate "in micro" and interpret the minutiae. A fine example is the impression of a reed mat at Jericho. Note that it was the impression the mat had left in the dirt when the mat decayed, not the mat itself. Besides this, which is no mean accomplishment in itself, the excavators traced the path of a termite which had eaten its way through or across the mat. One does not excavate mat impressions and worm holes with shovels! Another example is Hennessy's work at the Damascus Gate in Jerusalem. Some seventy layers or strata were noted, including forty resurfacings of the street since the times of the Crusaders.

Americans fit somewhere in between these two extremes, varying among themselves as to the degree to which an excavation will lean more heavily in one direction or another. The British method is called the Wheeler-Kenyon method. Sir Mortimer Wheeler and Miss Kenyon followed the methods of Pitt-Rivers. Americans would add Petrie, Reisner, Fisher and Albright. These methods include digging in "squares" (rather than tunnels, trenches, etc.), three-dimensional recording of the location of objects, and very careful stratigraphy (finding, studying, and making drawings of layers or strata of debris). American modifications include far greater attention to pottery typology, as with Albright. The difference between the "new" method of the British and the "old" method of the Americans is not always easy to see. Paul Lapp suggested that it was a matter of degree, with the Petrie-Albright technique emphasizing horizontal relationships including architecture. The Wheeler-Kenyon technique concentrates on vertical (stratigraphic) relationships. The differences are further obscured by Americans such as Lapp and Calloway who claimed they were using the Wheeler-Kenyon method, and by the fact that each excavator claims to be using the very latest scientific technique.

By way of footnote to these national traditions it should be said that the last excavations of Jericho and Jerusalem were cooperative efforts. Jericho teamed Miss Kenyon and ASOR while Jerusalem combined Miss Kenyon's wisdom with that of Pere Roland de Vaux (Ecole Biblique). The Royal Ontario Museum in Canada was another sponsor. De Vaux was the excavator of Qumran in 1952, also a joint venture with ASOR and others. The current work at Jerash was initiated by eight teams from Jordan, Great Britain, the United States, Australia, France, Poland, Spain and Italy. The Spanish and Italians continue while others are now concentrating on restoration.

A spirit of cooperation has developed over the past several decades. We can cite again the development of strong departments of antiquities in Near Eastern countries. Other parts of the world community are also taking an interest. Tokyo

**Figure 4–13.** Mat impressions are also excavated by Americans. This one was under a Cairn Burial at Bab edh-Dhra'. Photo courtesy G. Ernest Wright.

University and the Japanese Society for Near Eastern Studies have been digging in Iran, Iraq and Israel as noted earlier. Host countries have clamped down on the export of antiquities while Western nationalism has declined in intensity, leaving more room for the advancement of a purer science.[8]

## C.  CONTINUING TODAY

This historical survey has touched only lightly on some of the giants of the recent and current scene. William Foxwell Albright (1897–1971) was born in Chile of missionary parents and educated at Upper Iowa and Johns Hopkins Universities. He was the "great-grandfather" of American archaeologists in the Near East. His student, G. Ernest Wright had students in turn such as William G. Dever,

H. Darrel Lance and Joe D. Seger, directors of the Gezer Expedition. In turn Dever's students Seymour Gitin and Thomas Levy continue the tradition. Gitin is Director of ASOR's Jerusalem School and co-director (with Trude Dothan) of Tell Miqne (probably Philistine Ekron). Levy is assistant director of the School, with research in the Negev. Albright achieved expertise in ancient Near Eastern languages. By 1919 he was in Jerusalem, first as Fellow and then as Director of ASOR. He held the latter post until 1929 and again in 1934–36 when he was succeeded by Nelson Glueck (1900–71).

Albright was Professor of Semitic Languages at Johns Hopkins University (1929–58). He is sometimes credited with creating the discipline of Palestinian archaeology as it is known to Americans today. His bibliography had 1100 entries and he was still writing in the year of his death. In the reorganization of ASOR in 1970, the Jerusalem School was renamed The William Foxwell Albright Institute of Archaeological Research (AIAR) in Jerusalem.

Albright was a genius without modern parallel. His mind, work and publications covered the gamut of linguistic studies, field archaeology, pottery analysis, historical research, and historical and philosophical synthesis, to name only the highlights. His seminal work at Tell Beit Mersim was cited earlier. Unfortunately some of his other reports were not published with such dispatch, but these have been brought out by his students. He was instrumental in forming the Palestine Oriental Society in 1920 and was a frequent contributor to their journal. He edited the Bulletin of the ASOR (1931–68). His brilliant insights have often been confirmed by later work while his lesser thoughts are forgotten. His methods have been refined but his earlier work has often been established as correct. Tell el-Ful, for example, was re-excavated by Paul Lapp in 1964, confirming Albright's identification of the site as Gibeah, King Saul's (1020–1000 B.C.) fortress.

Paul Wilbert Lapp (1930–70) held a Ph.D. from the University of California and a Th.D. from Harvard. He was a student of both Albright and Wright. Lapp drowned in an undertow off the coast of Cyprus just prior to excavation at Idalion. Before his untimely death, he had spent two years as Professor of Old Testament and Archaeology at Pittsburgh University, and eight years successively as Annual Professor, Director and Professor of Archaeology of ASOR in Jerusalem. He directed several major digs — Ta'anach, Bab edh-Dhra', Tell er-Rumeith (Ramoth Gilead) and Araq el-Emir near Amman, besides participating at Shechem and other work. He published many of his results, in the tradition of Pitt-Rivers, Mallowan, and Albright, though final reports were not finished at the time of his death. These are being published by his wife Nancy and other colleagues. He estimated that ninety per cent of Palestine remains to be dug.

Nelson Glueck's work in surface survey, superseding that of Edward Robinson's, was mentioned under "Travellers" earlier. His work has been called one of the most important contributions to Palestinian archaeology of our time. Born in

**Figure 4–14.** Nelson Glueck and William Dever. Photo courtesy *Biblical Archaeologist*.

Cincinnati, he was educated at Hebrew Union College and the Universities of Cincinnati and Jena. He returned to HUC as an instructor in 1929 and rose through the academic ranks to the presidency in 1947. Just before his death, he was elected Chancellor. Besides directing HUC and its two branches in America, he started the HUC Biblical and Archaeological School in West Jerusalem. Intermittently (1932–33, 1936–40, 1942–47) he served as Director of ASOR in Jerusalem. He worked with Albright at Tell Beit Mersim and in 1931 began his famous surveys. From 1931–47 he explored the East Jordan region examining over 1500 sites. The southern desert of Palestine, the Negev, received his attention between 1952–64.

Using the techniques of pottery typology he built up a picture of the historical periods of occupation in these areas. Some of his most important clarifications concern the early Middle Bronze Age (nineteenth century B.C.) when semi-nomads settled in the Negev. These could be related to the movements described in the stories of the biblical patriarchs — Abraham, Isaac and Jacob. A second great time of settlement was from the thirteenth to the sixth centuries, including the Edomites, Moabites, Ammonites and Israelites. His explorations are summarized in five volumes of AASOR (1934–51). His studies included the excavation of Tell el-Kheleifeh (Ezion-geber? — I Kings 9:26) on the Gulf of Aqaba. Originally he thought the site contained evidence of a large smelter for copper ore in the time of Solomon. Subsequent study suggests the building may have been a fort or a granary.

From the second century B.C. to the second century A.D. the Nabateans ranged through the whole southern territory of today's Jordan and Israel. Glueck's work with this period was supplemented by his excavation of Khirbet et-Tannur, the isolated ruin of a Nabatean temple east of the Dead Sea. The results, with details of Nabatean religion and art, were published as *Deities and Dolphins*; NY: Farrar, Strauss, 1965. Among his other books are those cited earlier, *The Other Side of the Jordan* and *Rivers in the Desert*.

While Glueck's results have been modified, his technique of surface exploration has been continued, refined, and expanded throughout the Near East. In part this has been in response to the need to protect antiquities from modern construction. It is also part of the growing sense of the past as a national treasure. It has also served to facilitate the selection of excavation sites. Several digs have included regional exploration as a way of finding settlement patterns in relation to the site being excavated. The two American excavations of Shechem and Tell Hesban followed this plan, as have several Israeli and Jordanian efforts.

Dr. James A. Sauer has been a pre-eminent follower of Glueck's footsteps, with a far more refined pottery typology at his fingertips for a more accurate survey, and modern motor vehicles to facilitate movement. He has surveyed the Jordan Valley and parts of Syria in addition to supervising and acting as consultant for other area surveys such as the old territory of the biblical Moabites and the Yarmuk River area. Sauer was trained at Concordia College (Ann Arbor, MI) and Harvard. He worked at Ta'anach, Deir 'Alla, 'Araq el-Emir and Hesban. He has held positions in the AIAR and the American Center for Oriental Research in Amman. He was ACOR's Director and Professor of Archaeology (1975–81) as well as teaching at the University of Jordan and serving as a consultant to the Department of Antiquities of Jordan. He is currently Associate Curator of the Syro-Palestinian Section of the University Museum, succeeding James B. Pritchard, and President of the ASOR, following in the footsteps of his Harvard mentor, G. Ernest Wright. He also stands in the Albright tradition and his work continues through his students such as Jeffrey A. Blakely, who directs a dig in Yemen and earlier dug at Caesarea, with R.J. Bull, and Tell el-Hesi, with L.E. Toombs.

George Ernest Wright (1909–74) was educated at Wooster College, McCormick Theological Seminary and Johns Hopkins University. He began his field work under his seminary teacher, Ovid R. Sellers (1885–1974) in the excavation of Beth-zur in 1934. Later he worked with the pottery from Beth-Shemesh, published with Elihu Grant (Haverford). His main excavation was Shechem (1956–68), though his consultation direction of Gezer (1964–73) and Idalion in Cyprus (1971–74) also figures prominently. In his position as Parkman Professor of Divinity at Harvard and President of ASOR (1966–74), he continued to influence and promote American interests in Near Eastern archaeology through activities in Baghdad, Beirut, Cyprus, Jerusalem and Amman. His influence was greatly expanded through his book *Biblical Archaeology*, through excavation reports, and especially through his students. James Sauer was just cited. Darrell Lance teaches at Colgate

**Figure 4–15.** (Right to left) G. Ernest Wright, Lawrence T. Geraty and James Sauer confer about the excavation of Tell Hesban. Photo courtesy L.T. Geraty.

Rochester Divinity School. Joe Seger, now Director of the Cobb Archaeological
Institute of Mississippi State University, moved on from Gezer to excavate Tell
Halif. William Dever became Director of HUC-BAS and then of AIAR (1971–75).
Since then he has been at the University of Arizona in Tucson as Professor of Near
Eastern Archaeology. His work at Shechem is notable, as is his continuing excava-
tion in the Negev. Like Albright and Wright, Dever's numerous publications add
to the permanence of his contribution.

Another Harvard man was George M.A. Hanfmann, John E. Hudson Professor
of Archaeology emeritus (1911–86) who directed the Sardis excavation (1958–78)
sponsored by ASOR, Harvard's Fogg Art Museum, Cornell University, and the
Corning Museum of Glass. He published *Sardis: From Prehistoric to Roman Times*
(Harvard) and many preliminary reports, as well as studies on Etruscan sculpture
and Roman art. In 1978, he received the AIA Gold Medal for distinguished
archaeological achievement.

**Figure 4–16.** G. Ernest Wright (right) and Martin Noth at Shechem. The women stand in the doorway of the village school of Balata. Expedition rent money paid to put in electricity (the wire over the men's heads) and piped city water (the faucet and hose by Dr. Noth's right hand). Archaeology touches the economy of an area as well as its history!

**Figure 4-17.** Seymour Gitin and Alfred Gottschalk at Hebrew Union College Biblical and Archaeological School in Jerusalem.

**Figure 4–18.**    Dr. James B. Pritchard. Photo courtesy University Museum, University of Pennsylvania.

**Figure 4–19.**    Aerial view of Tabaqat Fahl, biblical Pella, looking west, general view of the central mound. Photo courtesy Dr. James A. Sauer.

**Figure 4–20.** Robert J. Bull, the Mukhtar (mayor) of Balata, E. F. "Ted" Campbell and Henry O. Thompson discuss the excavation of Tell Balata, ancient Shechem.

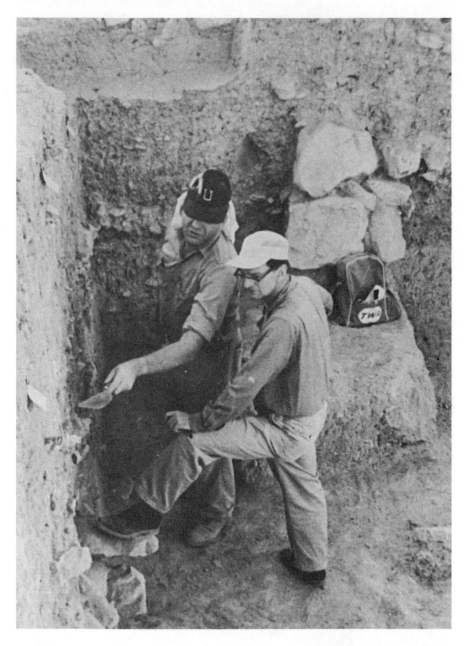

**Figure 4–21.**    Lawrence E. Toombs and Roger Boraas check the stratigraphy at Shechem.

**Figure 4–22.**   George E. Mendenhall (right) guides Moawiyah Ibrahim, Jalil Amr and Henry O. Thompson around the site of Umm Rujum in Jordan. Dr. Mendenhall found six inscriptions on a wall over the steps of a deep cistern. The six are in an archaic form of pre-Islamic Arabic, closely related to Thamudic and also Safaitic, known from much later times in Transjordan and the Hejaz. Photo courtesy Aethel Mendenhall.

James Bennett Pritchard was born in 1909 in Louisville, KY. He attended Asbury, Drew, and the University of Pennsylvania, where he eventually taught and served as Associate Director of the University Museum. He too began field work in 1934 at Beth-zur. Besides excavating at New Testament Jericho (Tulul Abu el-'Alayiq), he led the expeditions at Gibeon, Tell es-Sa'adiyeh in the Jordan Valley (biblical Zarethan? — Joshua 3:16), and Sarafand in Lebanon. Sarafand was the Phoenician city of Sarepta or Zarephath (I Kings 17:9). His wider influence however has been felt through the editing of two major volumes concerning the pictorial and literary record of the ancient Near East, *The Ancient Near East in Pictures* and *Ancient Near Eastern Texts Relating to the Old Testament.* His technical and popular reports of his excavations continue.

Lawrence Edmond Toombs (1919– ) was born in Canada and educated at Acadia, Toronto, and Drew Universities. He began field work with Kenyon at Jericho and served major roles at Shechem with G. Ernest Wright. He did preliminary work in 1967 with the Wooster College expedition to Pella, under Robert Houston Smith, and was archaeological advisor for the American work at Caesarea and Tell el-Hesi. He has also dug in Canada. He taught at Drew (1953–68) and continues teaching at Wilfred Laurier University in Waterloo, Ontario. In addition to numerous excavation reports, he has authored a number of biblical studies. Noted for his verve and humor, he is one of the most outstanding stratigraphers in the field today. His work also continues through his students such as Jeff Blakely (cited earlier with Sauer), Roger Boraas (Shechem, Tell Hesban, Khirbet Iskander) and the present writer.

Robert Jehu Bull (1920– ), Professor of Church History at Drew University, worked at Shechem and its extension to nearby Tell er-Ras on Mount Gerizim, at Ai, and at Pella, and served as Field Director at Khirbet Shema (1970–72). He began the Joint Expedition to Caesarea in 1971, supported by a consortium of over twenty schools and museums. He has served as Director of AIAR (1970–71) and founded the Drew University Institute for Archaeological Research. He has also dug in New Jersey. Part of the Albright-Wright tradition, he has students in turn such as J. Blakely (cited earlier) and the present writer.

There are many to add besides those already mentioned. Erich Schmidt (1897–1964) worked in Iraq. Rodney Stuart Young (1907–74) worked in Turkey. P. Sylvester Saller (1895–1976) dug on Mount Nebo and at Ain Karen and in Bethany. Herbert Gordon May (1904–77) dug at Megiddo. James Leon Kelso (1892–1978) was at Bethel. Harry Thomas Frank (1933–1980) and G. Glenn Rose (1928–81) dug at Hesi. There is a considerable list of current excavators in addition to those already mentioned and cited in footnotes. Among them: Dewey M. Beegle, Robert Boling, Edward F. Campbell, Rudolph Dornemann, Valerie Fargo, Lawrence T. Garety, Lawrence Herr, Delbert R. Hillers, John Holladay, Siegfried Horn, Philip J. King, Nancy Lapp, David McCreery, Machteld Mellink, George Mendenhall, Carol and Eric Meyers, Kevin G. O'Connell, S.J., Walter Rast, James Ross, Lawrence Stager, James F. Strange, Gus W. Van Beek, and Saul and Gladys Weinberg.[9]

Britain has provided a considerable contingent to the cause of Near Eastern archaeology. Several have already been noted. Earlier too, we cited Sir Robert Eric Mortimer ("Rik") Wheeler (1890–1976). Besides directing the National Museum of Wales and the London Museum, he rescued Pitt-Rivers' excavations methods from oblivion and put them to extensive use in England and India. He was Director General of Archaeology for Pitt-Rivers (1944–8). His book *Archaeology from the Earth* remains a major guide for field or dirt archaeologists. He started the University of London Institute of Archaeology in 1935–37, utilizing $30,000 raised by Petrie seven years earlier.

Pre-eminent among Wheeler's students is Dr. Kathleen Kenyon (1906–78), Principal (1962–73) of St. Hugh's College, Oxford. Born in London, she attended Somerville College, Oxford. Her archaeological career began in a sense before she was born, in the person of her father, Sir Frederick Kenyon. He was Director of the British Museum (1909–30) and a prominent biblical scholar and archaeologist.

She gained early field experience (1929) with Gertrude Caton Thompson at Zimbabwe, the African ruins. She worked with Wheeler (1930–35) at the Roman-British site of Verulamium (St. Albans) as well as assisting J.W. Crowfoot at Samaria (1931–35). She was secretary (1935–48) of Wheeler's Institute and then Lecturer in Palestinian Archaeology until 1962. Between 1936 and 1951 she dug at Roman and Iron Age sites in England and at Sabratha in North Africa.

The British School in Jerusalem was founded in 1919 but suspended operations from 1939–51. Miss Kenyon reopened it and served as Director until 1963. In 1952 she introduced the Wheeler-Kenyon method with her digs at Jericho (1952–58) and Jerusalem (1961–67). She became Britain's, and perhaps the world's, outstanding Palestinian archaeologist. In addition to reports, popular and technical, on Samaria, Jericho and Jerusalem, she wrote on many of the problems of Palestinian archaeology. Among her more famous dictums is the awareness that a tell should not be totally excavated because improved techniques twenty-five to fifty years hence may provide insight into a mound's history. The thought is supported by David Ussishkin, the Israeli archaeologist, among others, while it was opposed by Yohanon Aharoni.

Gerald Lankester Harding (1901–79) was born in Tientsin, China, and grew up in Singapore. He worked with Petrie at Tells Jemma, Farah, and el-Ajjul (1926–32) and at ed-Duweir (Lachish?) from 1932–36. In the latter year he became Director of the Department of Antiquities in Transjordan, now the Hashemite Kingdom of Jordan, a post he held until 1956. He salvaged a number of important tomb groups and dug on the Amman Citadel, founding the Amman Museum there. In addition to excavating Qumran and helping ensure the translation of the Dead Sea Scrolls, he led surveys and published inscriptions from the desert regions of Jordan, Saudi Arabia and the Aden Protectorates. He founded the *Annual of the Department of Antiquities* but is perhaps best known for his *The Antiquities of Jordan*, 2nd ed.; London: Lutterworth, 1967.

Crystal-Margaret Bennett was born in England and educated at Bristol and London Universities. She was Director of the British School in Jerusalem. Her work has included the Edomite sites of Umm el Biyara, Tawilan, and Buseirah. Diana Kirkbride (Mrs. Hans Helbaek; he was a famous Danish paleoethnobotanist, d. 1981) excavated in many places in Turkey, Lebanon, Palestine and Jordan. She was born in England, educated at the University of London, and began her field work with Kenyon at Jericho. She directed the excavation of the Neolithic village at Beidha in southern Jordan.

John Basil Hennessy (Australia) was cited earlier for his work in Samaria, Jerusalem and Ghassul. More recently he has been co-excavator of Pella. James Mellaart is most noted for his prehistoric studies in Palestine and especially Turkey. His excavations of Hacilar and Catal Huyuk extended our knowledge of city planning, architecture, art and religion back into the seventh millennium B.C. Peter J.Parr has done extensive work in Petra and in Arabia.[10]

**Figure 4-23.** The excavations of Jean Perrot near Beersheba revealed a series of underground rooms from c. 3500 B.C. Photo courtesy Consulate General of Israel (NY).

**Figure 4-24.** Avraham Biran, former Director of the Department of Antiquities in Israel and Director of the excavations at Tell Dan. Photo courtesy *Biblical Archaeologist*.

**Figure 4-25.** Yigael Shiloh. Based on findings from his excavations, Dr. Yigael Shiloh tells participants of the Biblical Archaeology Congress his theories of how the city of King David looked c. 3000 years ago. David's city, conquered from the Jebusites, was on Mt. Ophel, south of today's Old City. Ophel is a ridge between the Kidron Valley on the East and the Tyropolean Valley on the West. Photo courtesy Consulate General of Israel (NY).

**Figure 4–26.** The excavations of Yigael Shiloh. The monumental structure from King Solomon's Jerusalem which is believed to have supported buildings in an acropolis area. Photo: Isaac Harari, courtesy Consulate General of Israel (NY).

Among French archaeologists, the work of Schaeffer (1898–1982) at Ugarit and Engomi was cited earlier. The excavations of Jean Perrot (Palestine), Maurice Dunand (Lebanon) and Andre Parrot (Larsa, Lagash, Mari) are significant. The most notable in Palestine was Pere Roland de Vaux (1903–71), Professor of History and Archaeology at the French School of Archaeology in Jerusalem. He directed the School (1945–65) and excavated (1946–60) Tell el-Farah north (biblical Tirzah, I Kings 16:23). His work at Qumran and with the Dead Sea Scrolls is preeminent. His Tirzah excavation displays the wide open spaces of the French technique. But he commented on his digging with Kenyon in Jerusalem that it showed he could dig in a five meter square if he had to! He was followed at the Ecole Biblique by Pierre Benoit (1906– ) who arrived there in 1932 and rose to the position of director. Retired, he continues to write.[11]

In modern Israel, it has been said that every other person is an archaeologist. Besides some already mentioned, among the many are Itzhaq Beit-Arieh, Meir

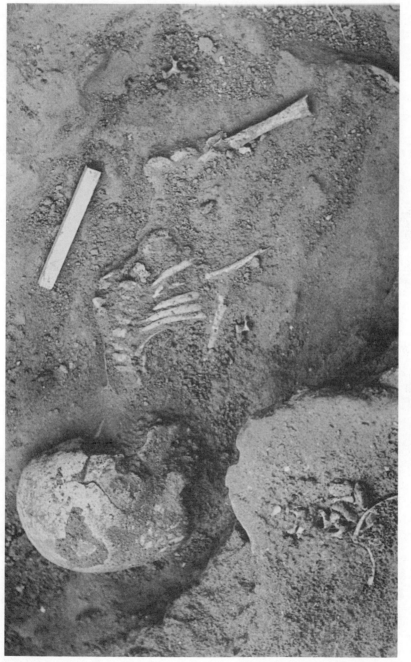

**Figure 4-27.** The excavations of Yohanan Aharoni at Beersheba found ancient skeletal remains. Photo courtesy Consulate General of Israel (NY).

**Figure 4–28.** Benjamin Mazar worked at Beth Shearim, famous for its Jewish cemetery. Photo courtesy Consulate General of Israel (NY).

**Figure 4-29.** Mazar's excavations in Jerusalem found Islamic, Byzantine and Roman remains east of the Dung Gate in the Old City wall, and south of the Mosque al-Aqsa, the round dome on the left. In the distance is the Mt. of Olives beyond the Kidron Valley (the tower on the top belongs to a Russian Orthodox convent).

Ben-Dov (field director for Mazar's Jerusalem dig), Moshe Dothan (Ashdod), Avraham Eitan (Director, Department of Antiquities), Israel Finkelstien, Jacob Kaplan, Moshe Kochavi, Avraham Malamat, Osmat Misch-Brandl, Ehud Netzer, and Shemuel Yeivin (1896–1982). Yeivin has been called the dean of Israeli archaeology. He studied under Petrie in London, served on excavation staffs in Egypt (1923–28) and Iraq (1929–37), excavated Tell el-'Areini (1956–61), was the first Director of the Israel Department of Antiquities and Museums in 1948, and founded the Department of Archaeology and Ancient Near Eastern Studies at the University of Tel Aviv. He published *The Antiquities of Israel* with Michael Avi-Yonah (1955) and *The Israelite Conquest of Canaan* (1971).

Yohanan Aharoni (1919–76) was born in Germany and went to Palestine in 1933. His earliest work was a survey out of which came his dissertation *The Settlement of the Israelite Tribes in Upper Galilee*; Jerusalem: 1957. He dug Ramat Rahel, Arad (with Ruth Amiran) and with Yadin at Masada and Hazor. The last seven years of his life involved Beersheba and the related sites of Tell Malhata and Tell Masos. During this period he was Professor of Archaeology at Tel Aviv University after earlier teaching at Hebrew University. He was sometimes seen as a maverick in archaeological method but his response was that methods must be adapted to a site and its problems rather than blindly followed. Like Wheeler, he emphasized horizontal excavation as well as vertical. Like Pitt-Rivers, he thought in terms of total excavation. In response to Kenyon's idea of leaving something for future excavators, he said that there are plenty of other mounds left for future excavators. In addition to his excavation reports and technical studies he is perhaps most well known for his *The Land of the Bible*, 2nd ed.; Philadelphia: Westminster, 1980.

Ruth Amiran is a "sabra" — born in Israel. She worked with E.L. Sukenik at Jerishe and Afuleh, and on the Ai dig with Marquet-Krause in the 1930s. Since then she has excavated at Hazor, Arad and Tell Nagila in addition to serving with the Archaeological Museum in Jerusalem and with the Israeli Department of Antiquities. She is perhaps most well known for her *Ancient Pottery of the Holy Land*; Jerusalem: Masada, 1963.

Benjamin Mazar (1906– ), Professor of Biblical History and Archaeology, and President (1953–61) of Hebrew University, was born in Germany and educated at the Universities of Berlin and Giessen. He worked with Albright at Tell Beit Mersim. Since then he has dug at Beth Shearim, Tell Qasile, and Engedi, and spent ten seasons at Jerusalem as mentioned earlier. Albright saw him as one of the founders of Israeli archaeology. Like Albright, his wide ranging scholarship includes archaeology in the context of geography, history, language, etc.

Eliezer Lipa Sukenik (1889–1953) was of Russian origin and was educated at the University of Berlin and Dropsie College in Philadelphia. He also worked with Albright, besides excavating Jewish tombs around Jerusalem. He studied the problem of the third wall north of Jerusalem, since identified by Kenyon as a hastily constructed defense wall in the second Jewish revolt crushed by the Romans in 135 A.D. Sukenik did major work on the Dead Sea Scrolls when they were first discovered in 1947, risking his life to bring them from Bethlehem to Jerusalem in the midst of gunfire.

Sukenik's son, Yigael Yadin (1917–1984), Professor of Archaeology at Hebrew University, was born in Jerusalem and educated at HU. He directed the dig (1955–58, 1969) at Tell el-Qedeh, biblical Hazor (Joshua 11) and was preparing to return at the time of his death to clear up unsolved problems. He dug at Megiddo (1960–71) to correct a number of errors there. He established that the stables, if such they be, are from the time of Ahab rather than Solomon. The excavation of caves at Nahal Hever (1960–61) near the Dead Sea added new information for the periods around 3500 B.C. and 135 A.D. His two year campaign at Masada (1963–65) — the large almond shaped, flat topped rock on the western shore of the Dead Sea — attracted 2000 volunteers from around the world. Yadin published preliminary results of his excavations as well as popular studies. His last and perhaps most famous now are *The Temple Scroll*, Vols 1–3; Jerusalem: IES, 1983, and *The Temple Scroll*; NY: Random House, 1985.[12]

Egyptian nationals came late to being field archaeologists in their own right. Ahmed Kamal (1849–1923) was the first in addition to being a long time curator of

**Figure 4–30.**    Dr. Yigael Yadin, Photo courtesy BAR.

the Cairo Museum. When the Director of Antiquities said that few Egyptians expressed any interest in archaeology, Kamal pointed out that the foreigners had not given his countrymen much opportunity to be interested. Salim Hassan (1887–1961) dug at Gizeh and Sakkarah and taught Egyptology at Cairo University. Abbé Drioton was succeeded by Mustapha Amer as Director of Antiquities. The Department has now been staffed by trained Egyptians including Zaki Sa'ad who dug at Helwan and Sakkarah, and the Coptic Labib Habachi (educated at Cairo University) who worked at Bubastis, Luxor, Nag Hammadi, and in the Delta. In addition to traditional enemies like weather, urban sprawl and development threaten many Delta sites. Fattah M. Sabbahy, Chief Inspector for the Department, excavated at Luxor.

Mohammed Zakaria Goneim (d. 1959) is probably most well-known in the western world for his work at Sakkarah. He was born in Egypt and received his diploma (1934) in Egyptology from Cairo University where he studied under Percy Newberry and Herman Junker. He began his career at Sakkarah as Assistant Archaeologist in the Department of Antiquities. He was Inspector of Antiquities successively at Aswan, Sohag, and Edfu (1939–43), when he became Conservator or Keeper of the Theban Necropolis. He was promoted to Chief Inspector of Antiquities for Upper Egypt (1946–51) and then to Keeper and Chief Inspector of Sakkarah. Here he made his famous discovery of a hidden — buried — unfinished pyramid of the Third Dynasty. Much publicity stirred interest in a sealed alabaster sarcophagus found inside a sealed tomb. The sarcophagus turned out to be empty — and so clean, it was obvious it had not been robbed but had never contained a burial. Goneim theorized that it was a *dummy burial*, possibly for the *ka* (roughly translated as "spirit") of the pharaoh. Goneim's work and career were unfortunately cut short by political and economic problems in 1956.

Dr. Ahmed Fakhry was born in 1905 and educated at the University of Cairo (1928) and in Belgium, England, and Germany. After completing his studies (1932) he served in the Egyptian Department of Antiquities and excavated at several sites. The most important of these were in the oases and among the pyramids, especially in the district of Dashour. Out of the latter work came his most well known book, *The Pyramids*; Chicago: University of Chicago, 1961. It has been translated into several languages. He also authored over twenty-seven books in various languages and over seventy articles. In 1952, he assumed the Chair of Ancient Pharaonic History of the Ancient Near East, in the College of Arts, University of Cairo, a post he held until he retired. He was a visiting professor in a number of countries and schools including the University of Jordan (1967–69).[13]

Among the pioneers in developing Iraqi archaeology are Fuad Suleiman Safar (1913–78) and Taha Baqir, both active in the Department of Antiquities and the University of Baghdad. Safar directed work at Hassuna, al 'Uqair, Eridu, and the Himrin Dam area. He also directed the excavations at the Parthian-Sassanian site of Hatra in northern Iraq for five years. Baqir worked principally at Aqar Quf, Tell Harmal, and Sippar. Mohammad Ali Mustapha dug at numerous places such as Nineveh, Hatra, Harmal, Tepe Gawra, Samarra, Aqar Quf, Sippar, Nippur, and Eridu. Behnam Nasir Abu al-Soof excavated at Khorsabad, Hatra, Nimrud, Ctesiphon, Seleucia, and Nippur. Subhi Anwar has worked at Hatra, Jarmo, and Warka. Tariq a-Wahhab Madhloom has dug at Nimrud, Ctesiphon, Nineveh, and Balawat. Wathiq al-Salihi directed work at Hatra. Ismail Hijar re-excavated Arpachiya. Saad Ayauh directed work at Babylon. The Department, under Dr. Isa Salman for many years and more recently Dr. Muayad Sa'id Demirji, has been very active in conservation and reconstruction and with excavation relating to these activities. The Department has been almost exclusively under Iraqi direction since 1934. Both Safar and Baqir have served as Director-General of the Department. Dr. Fawzi Rashid directed the new Iraq Museum in Baghdad. Iraqi archaeologists have dug over 100 sites while foreign expeditions also continue under the Danes, Soviets, Belgians, Dutch, Italians, and Japanese, as well as the Germans, British, and Americans.[14]

The Department of Antiquities in Transjordan was established in 1923. R.W. Hamilton was followed as Director by G.L. Harding. Dr. Awni Dajani (1917–68) was the first Jordanian Director (1956–68). He was educated at the American University of Beirut, Hebrew University, and the London Institute of Archaeology. He received his archaeological training from Kathleen Kenyon at Jericho and in London (Ph.D.). After teaching at the University of Jordan, an American-trained (University of Missouri) archaeologist, Dr. Adnan Hadidi, has headed the Department since 1977. He has excavated an Amman and the surrounding area, specializing in coins, pottery, and the history of archaeology. Under his direction, the Department has become self-sufficient and very active in the field and in publishing.

**Figure 4–31.**    Adnan Hadidi, Director of the Department of Antiquities of Jordan.

**Figure 4–32.** Moawiyah Ibrahim, Director, The Institute of Archaeology and Anthropology, Yarmouk University, Irbid, Jordan. Photo courtesy The Institute.

Foreign excavations have been warmly welcomed and encouraged. Dozens of excavations, surveys, and studies have taken place in recent years. A number of these have been chronicled in a series of International Conferences on the History and Archaeology of Jordan in 1980 (Oxford), 1983 (Amman), and 1986 (Tubingen). The several hundred participants have included over thirty-five Jordanian archaeologists. One could cite at random Sabri Abbadi, Abd'l Jalil Amr, Assem Bargouti, Ghazzi Bisheh, Zeidan Kaffafi, Nabil Khairi, Hanan Kurdi, Mujahid Muhasin, Nabil Qadi, Zahida Saffar, Safwan Tell, and Khair Yassine. A number of department staff and faculty of the University of Jordan have been trained in British and American schools.

Dr. Moawiyah Ibrahim was educated in Syria and Germany. After significant work with the Department at Ta'anach and Sa'adiyeh and directing the work at Sahab, he started a Department of Archaeology and an Institute of Archaeology at the new Yarmouk University. The Institute jointly sponsors the continuing Dutch

Figure 4-33.   Fawzi Zayadine, Assistant Director of the Department of Antiquities of Jordan.

excavations at Tell Deir Alla. A French-trained excavator, Dr. Fawzi Zayadin, has dug at Samaria, Petra, Kerak, and Hesban, co-directed Hajjar, and directed the Department's excavations of the Amman Citadel. He is currently Assistant Director-General of the Department. British, German and American-trained Mohammed Murshed Khadijah has worked at Amman, Petra, Hajjar, Biyara, Tawilan, Hesban, and Sahab. Rafiq Dajani worked at numerous sites, and published reports on Sahab and the Dolmens (standing stones, perhaps with religious or cultic importance, dated variously from the Iron Age back to the Paleolithic) before his death in 1974.

This listing serves as example and is not exhaustive. One could add many names in each area and other countries as well, such as the work of Roger Saidah (1930–79), Maurice Chehab, and Arnulf Kushke in Lebanon; or Martin Noth (d. 1968) and Siegfried Mittman in Jordan; or Namio Egami of Tokyo University in Iraq, in addition to names which have appeared elsewhere in the text and footnotes.[15]

**Figure 4–34.**    Muhammad Murshed Khadijah as foreman of the Tell Hesban excavations.
Photo courtesy L. T. Geraty.

## NOTES

1. Fred G. Bratton, *A History of Egyptian Archaeology* (New York: Crowell, 1968). R.G. Harrison
   and A.B. Abdalla, "The Remains of Tutankhamun," *Antiquity* 46, no. 181 (Mar. 72), pp. 8–14.
   N. Rambova, ed., *The Shrines of Tut-Ankh-Amon* (New York: Harper & Row, 1962). Katharine S.
   Gilbert, Joan K. Holt, and Sara Hudson, eds., *Treasures of Tutankhamun* (New York: Ballantine),
   1976. BGA, p. 419. CHP, pp. 185–199. CPHA, pp. 158–169. CCEA, p. 127. Caroline Stenger-
   Philippe, M.D. (Strasbourg University School of Medicine) claims six of the deaths of those who
   entered King Tut's tomb were due to an allergic reaction to anerobic mold which grew in the air-
   tight tomb. Milan Ruzicka, "Tomb explorers' mystery deaths linked to mold," DFP (30 July 85), p.
   14A. Actually, only one death can be "attributed" to the curse. Hugh Evelyn-White hung himself
   in 1924 because he believed, he wrote, "I have succumbed to a curse." Everyone who entered the
   tomb was, of course, doomed to die. But then, so are all human beings!
2. PDBW, pp. 49–50, 58. Woolley, *Ur of the Chaldees* (rev.; NY: Crowell, 1950), and *A Forgotten
   Kingdom* (Baltimore: Penguin, 1953). *Ur of the Chaldees* has been edited by P.R.S. Moorey and
   republished (Ithaca: Cornell, 1982). Richard L. Zettler, "Woolley's Ur Revisited," BAR 10, no. 5
   (Sep./Oct. 84), pp. 58–61. CCEA, pp. 494–495. Thorkild Jacobsen, "Ur (City)," IDB 4, pp. 735–
   738. David O'Conner, "Ancient Egypt and Black Africa — Early Contacts," *Expedition* 14, no. 1
   (Fall 71), pp. 2–9. Albert R. al-Haik, *Key Lists of Archaeological Excavations in Iraq, 1841–1965*
   (Coconut Grove, FL: Field Research Projects, 1968), p. xii. SBAF, pp. 181–186. WAFE, p. 125.
   BGA, p. 422. CHP, pp. 258–262. CPHA, pp. 256–272. Sir Max E.L. Mallowan, *Twenty-Five*

**Figure 4–35.**    Dolmens. There are some variations in design but two upright slabs of rock and another slab on top to form a kind of roof is a typical example.

*Years of Mesopotamian Discovery (1932–1956)* (London: British School of Archaeology in Iraq, 1956), and, "Recollections of C. Leonard Woolley," *Expedition* 20, no. 1 (Fall 77), pp. 3–4. Robert H. Dyson, Jr., "Archival Glimpses of the Ur Expedition in the Years 1920 to 1926," *Expedition* 20, no. 1 (Fall 77), pp. 5–23. Denise Schmandt-Besserat, ed., The Legacy of Sumer (Malibu: Undena, 1976).

3. James B. Pritchard, A. Henry Detweiler, and William F. Albright, "Ephraim Avigdor Speiser," BASOR 179 (Oct. 65), pp. 1–6. PDBW, p. 57. SBAF, pp. 192–195.

4. Peter C. Craigie, "The Tablets from Ugarit and Their Importance for Biblical Studies," BAR 9, no. 5 (Sep./Oct. 83), pp. 62–73. James M. Robinson, "An Appreciation of Claude Frederic-Armand Schaeffer-Forrer (1898–1982)," BAR 9, no. 5 (Sep./Oct. 83), pp. 56–61 (Schaeffer was Robinson's father-in-law). Charles F. Pfeiffer, *Ras Shamra, and the Bible* (Grand Rapids: Baker, 1962). Nina Jidejian, *Byblos Through the Ages* (Beirut: Machreq, 1968). SBAF, pp. 16–17, 232–250. PDBW, pp. 50–51. BGA, p. 421. Massima Pallotino, *The Meaning of Archaeology* (London: Thames and Hudson, 1968), p. 42. CHP, pp. 301–306. Hildegard Lewy, "Mari," IDB 3, pp. 264–266.

5. John R. Bartlett, *Jericho* (Grand Rapids: Eerdmans, 1983).

6. SBAF, p. 391 et passim. EAEHL, p. 441 et passim. BGA, p. 420. Alan Rowe, *The Topography and History of Beth-shan* (Philadelphia: University Museum, 1940). Henry O. Thompson, *Mekal: The God of Beth-shan* (Leiden: Brill, 1970). R.W. Hamilton, "Beth-shan," IDB 1, pp. 397–401. C.S. Fisher, *The Excavation of Armageddon* (Chicago: University of Chicago, 1929). Yigal Yadin, "Megiddo," IEJ 17 (1967), pp. 119–121. KAHL, pp. 308–313. W.F. Albright, "The Excavation of Tell Beit Mirsim I" (AASOR 12) (1932), "IA" (AASOR 13) (1933), "II" (AASOR 17) (1938), "III"

(AASOR 21–22) (1943). Moshe Kochavi, "Khirbet Rabud = Debir," TA 1 (1974), pp. 1–32. David Ussishkin, *The Conquest of Lachish* (Tel Aviv: TA University, 1982). James A. Sauer, "New Chalcolithic Wall Paintings at Ghassul," BA 42, no. 1 (Wint. 79), p. 9. J. Basil Hennessy, "Preliminary Report on a First Season of Excavations at Teleilat Ghassul," *Levant* 1 (1969), pp. 1–24, and, "Teleilat Ghassul," pp. 55–58 (in Studies in the History and Archaeology of Jordan ed. Adnan Hadidi; Amman: Department of Antiquities, 1982). William G. Dever, "Archaeology," IDBSV, pp. 44–52. Gus W. Van Beek, "Archaeology," IDB 1, pp. 205–206. Carl H. Kraeling, ed., *Gerasa: City of the Decapolis* (New Haven: ASOR, 1938). Iain Browning, *Jerash and the Decapolis* (Salem, NH: Merrimack, 1983). Rami G. Khouri, *Jerash* (London & NY: Longman, 1986). Fawzi Zayadin, ed., *Jerash Archaeological Projects, Vol. I* (Amman: Department of Antiquities, 1986).

7.  Andrè Parrot, "H. J. Lenzen (1900–1978)," *Syria* 55 (1978), pp. 400–401. Namio Egami, *Telul eth-Thalathat*, Vol. I (Tokyo: Yamakawa, 1959). Kiyoshi Ohata, *Tel Zeror*, Vols. I–III (Tokyo: Society for Near Eastern Studies in Japan, 1964–66). George G. Cameron, "Sir Max Mallowan, 1904–78," BA 42, no. 3 (Sum. 79), pp. 180–183. M.E.L. Mallowan, *Mallowan's Memoirs*; (New York: Dodd, Mead, 1977), and, *Early Mesopotamia and Iran* (New York: McGraw-Hill, 1965), and, *Twenty-Five Years*. BGA, p. 420. SBAF, pp. 200–204. Margaret E. Stout, "Calah," IDBSV, p. 122.

    Paolo Matthiae, *Ebla: An Empire Rediscovered* (Garden City: Doubleday, 1981). PAE. Chaim Bermant and Michael Witzman give an account of the problems through 1978 in their A *Revelation in Archaeology* (New York: Times, 1979). Much of the discussion has gone on in journals such as BA, BAR, CBQ, and others. Cf. Mitchell Dahood, "Eblaite and Biblical Hebrew," CBQ 44, no. 1 (Jan. 82), pp. 1–24, and, "The God 'Ya' at Ebla," JBL 100, no. 4 (Dec. 81), pp. 607–608.

    Ruth Amiran and Yael Israel, "Jerusalem," IDBSV, pp. 476–477. EAEHL, pp. 643–647. Kenyon, *Digging Up Jerusalem* (New York: Praeger, 1974). Mazar, *The Mountain of the Lord* (Garden City: Doubleday, 1975). Yigal Shiloh, *Excavations at the City of David 1978–1982*. (Jerusalem: IES, 1984). Meir Ben Dov, *In the Shadow of the Temple* (San Francisco: Harper & Row, 1986). Hershel Shanks, "Excavating in the Shadow of the Temple Mount," BAR 12, no. 6 (Nov./Dec. 86), pp. 20–38.

    There are several good descriptions of sites in Israel and Jordan now available. KAHL, pp. 313–43 gives a brief review. General sources include IDB, IDBSV, EAEHL, and Siegfried H. Horn, *Biblical Archaeology After Thirty Years (1948–1978)* (Berrien Springs, MI: Andrews University, 1978). SBAF lists sites throughout the Near East. Machteld J. Mellink, "Archaeology in Asia Minor," AJA 85, no. 4 (Oct. 81), pp. 463–479, is one of a series of reports for Turkey.

8.  Writing in 1965, Kenyon noted that the evidence of the Middle Bronze period at Byblos is "not easy to interpret. Byblos was excavated in a series of rigidly horizontal 'spits' (levees) of twenty centimetres. The true stratification was neither published nor observed, and the objects are published purely by spit and location, with no regard for the admittedly irregular contours of the site." "Archaeological Evidence from Palestine," CAH 1, Pt. 2 (1971), pp. 567–594 (published as a separate fascicle in 1965). The quote is p. 587. H. J. Franken claims that Petrie excavated in this manner. Franken and C.A. Franken-Battershill, *A Primer of Old Testament Archaeology* (Leiden: Brill, 1963), p. 7. William F. Bade wrote fifty years ago that it is a "delusion to think debris is in neat horizontal layers to be peeled like an onion. Sites are rarely level. There are hillocks and hollows into which deposits have accommodated themselves." A *Manual of Excavation in the Near East* (Berkeley: University of California, 1934), p. 60. Kenyon, *Digging Up Jericho* (London: Benn, 1957), p. 115. Neil A. Silberman, *Digging for God and Country* (New York: Knopf, 1982). Rami G. Khouri, "A Jewel in Jordan: The Greco-Roman City of Jerash," *Archaeology* 36, no. 1 (Jan./Feb. 85), pp. 18–25.

9.  Leona G. Running and David Noel Freedman, *William Foxwell Albright* (New York: Two Continents, 1975). Kenyon, "W.F. Albright (1891–1971), *Levant* 5 (1973), p. vi. G. Ernest Wright, ed.,

*The Bible and the Ancient Near East* (Garden City: Doubleday, 1961). Hans Goedicke, *Near Eastern Studies in Honor of William Foxwell Albright* (Baltimore: Johns Hopkins, 1971). Albright, *History, Archaeology and Christian Humanism* (New York: McGraw-Hill, 1964). Henry O. Thompson, "Biblical Archaeology: What's in a Name?," pp. 27–41 (in *Put Your Future in Ruins*, ed. Thompson; Bristol, IN: Wyndham Hall, 1985). Edward F. Campbell, Jr., "Paul W. Lapp: In Memoriam," BA 33, no. 2 (May 70), pp. 60–61. Delbert R. Hillers, "Paul W. Lapp in Memoriam," BASOR 199 (Oct. 70), pp. 2–4.

Albright, "Nelson Glueck in Memoriam," BASOR 202 (Ap. 71), pp. 2–6. Kay Prag, "Nelson Glueck (1900–1971): an Appreciation," *Levant* V (1973), pp. vii–ix. Gary Pratico, "Nelson Glueck's 1938–1940 Excavation at Tell el-Kheleifeh: A Reappraisal," BASOR 259 (Aug. 85), pp. 1–32. James A. Sauer, "Transjordan in the Bronze and Iron Ages: A Critique of Glueck's Synthesis," BASOR 263 (Aug. 86), pp. 1–26. CHP, pp. 307–311. Mo'awiyah M. Ibrahim, et al., "East Jordan Valley Survey, 1975," BASOR 22 (Ap. 76), pp. 41–66. W. Harold Mare, "1980 Survey of Abila of the Decapolis," BA 44, no. 3 (Sum. 81), pp. 179–180. Burton MacDonald, "The Wadi El Hasa Survey 1979," ADAJ XXIV (1980), pp. 169–183, and, "The Wadi el Hasa Survey, 1981," ASORN no. 3 (Nov. 81), pp. 8–15. Eric M. Meyers, et al., "The Meiron Excavation Project: Archaeological Survey in Galilee," BASOR 230 (Ap. 78), pp. 1–24. Aharoni, "Survey in the Galilee: Israelite Settlements and their Pottery," EI 4 (1956), pp. 56–64. Moshe Kochavi, ed., *Judaea, Samaria, and the Golan: Archaeological Survey 1967–1968* (Jerusalem: Carta, 1972). Ammon Ben-Tor, "The Regional Study — A New Approach to Archaeological Investigation," BAR VI, no. 2 (Mar./Ap. 80), pp. 30–44. S. Douglas Waterhouse and Robert Ibach, Jr., "The Topographical Survey," AUSS XIII, no. 2 (Aut. 75), pp. 217–233. "University Announcements," *Expedition* 23, no. 3 (Spr. 81), p. 2.

David Noel Freedman, "In Memoriam G.E. Wright," BASOR 220 (Dec. 75), p. 3. Peter J. Parr, "Obituary of Professor G. Ernest Wright," *Levant* 8 (1976), p. iii. Paul F. Jacobs, "Tell Halif/Lahav 1983 Season," ASORN 36, nos. 4–5 (Mar./Ap. 85), pp. 4–5. "ASOR-Affiliated Scholar Dies (Hanfmann)," ASORN 37, no. 3 (Ap. 86), p. 13. Henry O. Thompson, ed., *The Answers Lie Below: Essays in Honor of Lawrence Edmund Toombs* (Washington: University Press of America, 1984). Thompson, ed., *Put Your Future in Ruins: Essays in Honor of Robert Jehu Bull* (Bristol, IN: Wyndham Hall, 1985). Harry Thomas Frank, "Herbert Gordon May," *Oberlin Alumni Magazine* 74, no. 2 (Mar./Ap. 78), pp. 16–22. David W. McCreery, "A Tribute to James Leon Kelso," BA 42, no. 1 (Wint. 79), pp. 57–60. R.A. Coughenour, ed., *For Me to Live – Essays in Honor of James Leon Kelso* (Cleveland: Dillon/Liederbach, 1972). "Dr. Rodney Young, Archaeologist, 67," *New York Times* (27 Oct 74), p. L65. Crystal-Margaret Bennett, "The Rev. P. Sylvester Saller," *Levant* 9 (1977), p. iii. Hershel Shanks, "Harry Thomas Frank, 1933–1980," BAR 7, no. 1 (Jan./Feb. 81), p. 19. Michael D. Coogan, "Harry Thomas Frank, In Memoriam, 1933–1980," BA 44, no. 3 (Sum. 80), p. 178.

10. Wheeler, *Still Digging* (London: Joseph, 1955), and, *Alms for Oblivion* (London: Weidenfeld & Nicolson, 1977). Brian M. Fagin, "Sir Mortimer Wheeler," *Antiquity* 56, no. 217 (July 82), pp. 121–123. Jacquetta Hawkes, *Adventurer in Archaeology: The Biography of Sir Mortimer Wheeler* (New York: St. Martins, 1982). Kenyon, "Sir Mortimer Wheeler," *Levant* 9 (1977), pp. i–ii. A.J. Wilson, "Fifty years of archaeological teaching and research," IAMSN 7 (Dec. 84), pp. 4–6. Adnan Hadidi, "Kathleen Kenyon and her Place in Palestinian Archaeology," ADAJ 21 (1976), pp. 7–17. P.R.S. Moorey and Peter J. Parr, eds., *Archaeology in the Levant* (Warminster, England: Aris & Phillip, 1978). Moorey, "Prominent British Scholar Assesses Kathleen Kenyon," BAR 7, no. 1 (Jan./Feb. 81), pp. 46–48. William G. Dever, "Kathleen Kenyon (1906–1978): A Tribute," BASOR 232 (Fall 78), pp. 3–4. BGA, p. 420. "Kathleen Kenyon 1906–1978," BAR 4, no. 4 (Nov./Dec. 78), pp. 51–52. Joseph A. Callaway, "Dame Kathleen M. Kenyon (1906–1978)," BA 42, no. 2 (Spr. 79), pp. 122–125. A.C. Western, "Obituary: Dame Kathleen Kenyon, B.B.E.,"

*Levant* 11 (1979), pp. iii–iv. David Ussishkin, "Where Is Israeli Archaeology Going?," BA 45, no. 2 (Spr. 82), pp. 93–95. "In Memoriam Gerald Lankester Harding," ADAJ 23 (1979), pp. 198–200. Fred V. Winnet, "Gerald Lankester Harding 1901–1979," BA 43, no. 2 (Spr. 80), p. 127. *Iraq* 43, Pt. 1 (Spr. 81), p. i.

11. Paul W. Lapp, *Biblical Archaeology and History* (New York: World, 1969), p. 74. Thomas A. Collins, "Pere de Vaux and the Old Testament," BAR III, no. 2 (June 77), pp. 37–39. Nahum Sarna, "The Last Legacy of Roland de Vaux," BAR 6, no. 4 (July/Aug. 80), pp. 14–21.

12. Ussishkin, "Professor Shemuel Yeivin 1896–1982: 'In Memoriam'," TA 9, no. 1 (1982), pp. 1–2. Anson F. Rainey, "Yohanan Aharoni — The Man and His Work," BAR II, no. 4 (Dec. 76), pp. 39–40. "In Memoriam: Yohanan Aharoni," BA 39, no. 2 (May 76), p. 53. Crystal-Margaret Bennett, "Professor Yohanan Aharoni," *Levant* 9 (1977), pp. ii–iii. Albright, "The Phenomenon of Israeli Archaeology," NEATC, pp. 57–63. Benjamin Mazar, "Professor Eleazar L. Sukenik: In Memoriam," EI 8 (1967), p. 9. Nahman Avigad, "E.L. Sukenik — The Man and His Work," EI 8 (1967), pp. 9–11. Mayo Mohs, "Yigael Yadin: The Past is His Future," *Discover* 2, no. 8 (Aug. 81), pp. 74–79. William G. Dever, "Yigael Yadin: In Memoriam," BASOR 256 (Fall 84), pp. 3–5. Eric M. Meyer, "From the Editor's Desk," BA 47, no. 3 (Sep. 84), p. 131. Hershel Shanks, "Antiquities Director Confronts Problems and Controversies," BAR 12, no. 4 (July/Aug. 86), pp. 30–38, and, "Yigael Yadin 1917–1984," BAR 10, no. 5 (Sep./Oct. 84), pp. 24–29.

13. Labib Habachi, *Tell Basta* (Cairo: Supplement to Annales du Service des antiquites de l'Egypte, 1957), and, "Sixth-Dynasty Discoveries in the Jabal al-Tarif," BA 42, no. 4 (Fall 79), pp. 237–238. Christopher W. Wren, "Neglected Treasures of the Lower Nile," *New York Times* (4 Jan 81), p. 16E. M. Zakaria Goneim, *The Lost Pyramids* (New York: Holt, Rinehart and Winston, 1956). CHP, pp. 200–211. CPHA, pp. 128–129. My thanks to Dr. Mahmoud Samra and Dr. Adnan Hadidi for sharing the background of their colleague, Dr. Ahmed Fakhry.

14. Mu'ayad Sa'id Demirji, "Obituary: Prof. Fuad Safar," *Sumer* 34, no. 1 (1977), B-D, and, "Introduction," *Sumer* 34, Nos. 1–2 (1978), pp. 5–11. Max Mallowan, "Professor Fuad Safar," *Iraq* 40 (1978), p. i. Al-Haik, *Key Lists*, pp. xii–xvi, 34–55. PDBW, pp. 60–61. Edward Bacon, *Archaeology: Discoveries in the 1960s* (London: Cassell, 1971), pp. 185–192. Ismail Hijara, "Arpachiyah 1976," *Iraq* 42, Pt. 2 (Aut. 80), pp. 131–154.

15. Khair Yassine's excavations suggest the dolmens were burial sites in Early Bronze I. "The Dolmens: Construction and Dating Reconsidered," BASOR 259 (Aug. 85), pp. 63–69. Hadidi, *Studies*. Omar Jawad, "The Open Air Museum," Jordan 8, no. 1 (Spr./Sum. 83), pp. 2–9. "Roger Saidah, 1930–1979," Berytus 27 (1979), p. 5.

# ADDITIONAL READING

AIA, compilers, *Archaeological Discoveries in the Holy Land*. New York: Crowell, 1967.

Baramki, Dimitri C. *The Art and Architecture of Ancient Palestine from the Earliest Times to the Ottoman Conquest*. Beirut: PLO Research Center, 1969.

Ceram, C.W. *The March of Archaeology*. New York: Knopf, 1958.

Charles-Picard, Gilbert. *The Larousse Encyclopedia of Archaeology*. New York: Putnam's, 1972.

Daniel, Glyn E. *The Origins and Growth of Archaeology*. New York: Crowell, 1968.

Day, Alan E. *Archaeology: A Reference Handbook*. London, and Hamden, CT: Bingley and Linnet, 1978.

Edwards, I.E.S. et al. *The Cambridge Ancient History*, 3rd ed., Vols. I–II. Cambridge: Cambridge University, 1970–1975.

Frank, Harry Thomas. *Bible, Archaeology and Faith*. New York: Abingdon, 1971.

Frank, Harry Thomas. *The Biblical World*. New York: Harper & Row, 1975.

Garnett, Henry. *Treasures of Yesterday*. Garden City: Natural History, 1964.

Hendricks, Rhoda A. *Archaeology Made Simple*. Garden City: Doubleday, 1964.

Lloyd, Seton. *Foundations in the Dust*. New York: Thames and Hudson, 1981 (original 1947).

McCown, Chester C. *The Ladder of Progress in Palestine*. New York: Harper, 1943.

Mertz, Barbara. *Temples, Tombs and Hieroglyphs*. New York: Delta, 1964.

Miller, Madeleine S. and J. Lane. *Harper's Encyclopedia of Bible Life*. New York: Harper & Row, 1978.

Montet, Pierre. *Eternal Egypt*. London: Weidenfeld & Nicolson, 1964.

Painter, Floyd, ed. *Current Biographies of Leading Archaeologists*. Norfolk, VA: Chesopiean Archaeological Association, 1975.

Paintin, Elaine, ed. *The Illustrated Encyclopedia of Archaeology*. New York: Crowell, 1977.

Paor, Lima de. *Archaeology*. Baltimore: Penguin, 1967.

Poole, Lynn and Gray. *Men Who Dig up History*. New York: Dodd, Mead, 1968.

Rapport, Samuel B. and Wright, Helen, eds. *Archaeology*. New York: NYU, 1963.

Roux, Georges. *Ancient Iraq*. Baltimore: Penguin, 1964.

Sellman, R.R. *Ancient Egypt*. London: Methuen, 1960.

Shanks, Hershel and Mazar, Benjamin, eds. *Recent Archaeology in the Land of Israel*. Jerusalem and Washington: IES and Biblical Archaeology Society, 1984.

Silverberg, Robert. *Frontiers in Archaeology*. New York: Chilton, 1966.

Ward, William A., ed. *The Role of the Phoenicians in the Interaction of the Mediterranean Civilizations*. Beirut: AUB, 1968.

Williams, Walter G. *Archaeology in Biblical Research*. New York: Abingdon, 1965.

Wilson, John A. *Signs and Wonders Upon Pharaoh*. Chicago: University of Chicago, 1964.

Woolley, Leonard. *History Unearthed*. New York: Praeger, 1962.

Wortham, John D. *The Genesis of British Egyptology 1549–1906*. Norman: University of Oklahoma, 1971.

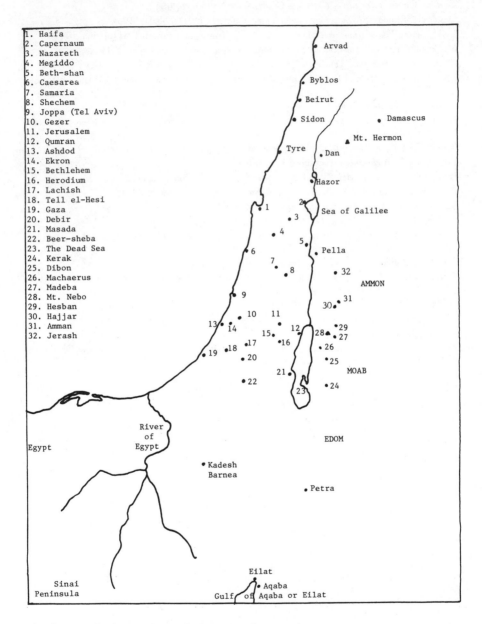

1. Haifa
2. Capernaum
3. Nazareth
4. Megiddo
5. Beth-shan
6. Caesarea
7. Samaria
8. Shechem
9. Joppa (Tel Aviv)
10. Gezer
11. Jerusalem
12. Qumran
13. Ashdod
14. Ekron
15. Bethlehem
16. Herodium
17. Lachish
18. Tell el-Hesi
19. Gaza
20. Debir
21. Masada
22. Beer-sheba
23. The Dead Sea
24. Kerak
25. Dibon
26. Machaerus
27. Madeba
28. Mt. Nebo
29. Hesban
30. Hajjar
31. Amman
32. Jerash

Arvad

Byblos

Beirut

Sidon          Damascus

Mt. Hermon

Tyre      Dan

Hazor

1        2    Sea of Galilee

3

4

5

6      Pella

7          32

8              AMMON

9

10    11            31
                30
13    14
      15    12    28   29
   17      16         27
18             26
   20                25
              MOAB
   21              24
22        23

EDOM

Kadesh
Barnea

Petra

River
of
Egypt

Egypt

Sinai
Peninsula

Eilat
   Aqaba
Gulf of Aqaba or Eilat

Sketch Map of Palestine (Drawn by Joyce E. Thompson)

SECTION III

# ARCHAEOLOGY
# AND SCIENCE[1]

In the past several decades the archaeological world has seen an explosion of knowledge that is simply mind-boggling. It has come through fascinating developments of the physical and biological sciences and modern developments of many kinds. Now, of course archaeology has long been a science (though some would say it is science with a soul of art while others insist it is art with a soul of science). A.C. Hogarth calls it a bridge across the great gulf between the sciences and the humanities. Some insist it is a study, a discipline, a pursuit of knowledge in its own right. But now, old and new theories and techniques from other sciences are being used or applied to archaeology to an amazing degree. This "new thing" (with apologies to Ecclesiastes) rose to such a crescendo that by 1970 people were talking about the "new archaeology," and by 1982, Robert C. Dunnell could speak of a "new" new archaeology.[2]

The vastness and complexity of this area of archaeology is reflected in a dizzying record of articles, books, reports, procedures, and experiments. In the literature today, we can find the possibility of recording music and voices from the surface of pottery or paintings. We can read about archaeomagnetism, the analysis of basalts and obsidian, dating by Potassium-Argon, the fluorine-uranium-nitrogen content of bone, pollen analysis, thermoluminescence, fission-tracks on glass, carbon 14, dendrochronology, and varves. Scientists have considered diffusion in ancient alloys, X-ray analysis, magnetic surveying, spectrographic analysis of jar handles and bronzes, stereoscopic photography, the infrared spectra of amber, the composition and source of Minoan and Mycenean pottery, the firing temperature of ancient pottery, the binding medium of oil paintings, the nature and source of pigments in paintings, the presence of trace elements and trace-trace elements (parts per million or *ppm*, and many other things that at first glance at least may not seem to have much to do with archaeology, at least as it has been traditionally understood.

Many of these studies are probably more significant for prehistoric archaeology and anthropology than for biblical studies. That is perhaps obvious for items like varve chronology (dating by the number of layers on ocean or lake beds left by the alternate melting and freezing of glaciers), pleistocene animals from millions of years ago, prehistoric bone, the origins of the dog, and deep-sea cores. However, Palestinian or biblical or Near Eastern archaeology might very well include many of the others. Some are quite obvious, like tree-ring dating (dendrochronology), the use of computers, the study of flint artifacts, obsidian analysis for date and origin, and the new ways of studying ancient pottery. These new scientific techniques are helping us to raise better questions in an already fascinating study called archaeology.

# CHAPTER 5

# Scientific Locators

## A. ELECTRONS

### Magnets

Magnetic surveying was successfully applied to archaeology in 1958. The magnetisim of the earth has been known for centuries. The common ordinary compass is based on this principle. It is common knowledge, too, that a compass is disturbed or thrown off by metals or nearby metallic ores. These deviations from the normal are called anomalies. They are measured in gamma. The standard magnetism of the earth ranges from 70,000 down to less than 30,000 gamma, depending on where you are on the globe. Quite small anomalies are caused by archaeological features such as accumulated humus in filled up ditches, anything that was subjected to heat such as a fireplace or a burned building as well as kilns, bricks, roof tiles and pottery. These have greater magnetism than ordinary dirt. Walls and rock structures have practically no magnetism at all. Archaeological anomalies range from 2–35 gamma for a ditch to as high as 100 gamma for a kiln. These variations can be measured by several different instruments.

The proton magnetometer was developed in the late 1950s. It is sensitive to anomalies of less than one gamma. Hydrogen protons in alcohol are disturbed by an artificial magnetic field, from a battery coil for example. The gyrations of the protons are proportional to the intensity of the earth's magnetic field. The magnetometer measures this intensity. Variations from the normal suggest buried features. The size of the variations or anomalies tell how deep the buried feature is. It

**Figure 5–1.** Dr. Elizabeth Ralph using a magnetometer at Sybaris. Photo courtesy the University Museum, University of Pennsylvania.

takes about four hours to cover an acre. The operator records the readings while a second person moves a detector around the area.

Working with the proton magnetometer in the search for Sybaris in southern Italy, the University Museum Applied Science Center for Archaeology found that this instrument only detected features three to ten feet deep, not enough for the deeply buried Greek remains. In 1964, they developed the rubidium magnetometer. It is 100 times as sensitive to magnetic changes. This instrument detects structures twelve to fifteen feet deep. Survey work can be done in one-fourth the time. The cesium magnetometer is even more sensitive. It can detect structures up to twenty feet deep. One can cover ten to twenty acres a day. All three instruments have been used in the Holy Land and elsewhere in the Near East.

The detector has been described as an aluminum pole one inch in diameter with a can as big as an economy-size fruit juice can on each end. Wires run from this sensor and the person carrying it to a second person who handles the batteries and recording meter, as much as fifty feet behind. From the batteries, another wire runs to another sensor set in the ground in the area being surveyed. A portable version of the cesium magnetometer can measure variations as low as 0.1 gamma. The measurements can be recorded on punch tape for computers. A computer can be programmed to produce a map with the anomalies on the printout. Sybaris was found. Later the Greek city of Ellis was surveyed. The entire city plan was found by magnetometer. More was learned in eight weeks than in the previous sixty years of occasional excavation.

A proton gradiometer or bleeper works on the same principle as the magnetometer. It is simpler to build, hence cheaper though not quite as sensitive as the proton magnetometer. The fluxgate magnetometer was developed in World War II to detect submarines. It uses small strips of *mu-metal* as detectors. Mu-metal is a nickel-iron-copper alloy which holds its magnetism longer than iron. The fluxgate is a bit heavy for field work but it is faster. It gives continuous readings in contrast to the intermittent proton magnetometer.

The pulsed magnetic induction locator was designed as a metal detector. It can find a penny up to sixteen inches away. It has been used to detect metal in tombs before going to the expense of opening them. It is also sensitive to other archaeological phenomena such as ditches, pits, and graves.

## Others

The above detectors involve magnetism. Resistivity surveying is another development. Geologists and civil engineers developed this about seventy-five years ago. It was applied to archaeology in 1946. Matter conducts electricity but resists it to various degrees. Put positively, some materials conduct electricity better than others. Copper is well known — it is used in electric wires. It has a low resistivity. Soil varies with the amount of water in it and especially the amount of minerals dissolved in the soil. Buried archaeological remains change the resistivity pattern because a filled up pit or ditch holds more moisture and is thus a better conductor, with lower resistivity. Buried walls have a higher resistivity. They are poor conductors. The variation is measured in several ways. The standard form is with four probes stuck in the ground. The probes are hooked up to meters. An electric charge is sent through the steel probes placed in the soil at spaced intervals. The resistivity is measured directly on a dial which registers any anomaly in terms of ohms. Newer instruments may have as many as thirty probes, which makes the process faster. A pocket-sized instrument was developed especially for archaeological work. It uses transistor circuits. While quite useful, there are problems. Boulders and some other natural features give anomalies similar to archaeological ones. The best work has been done on gravel subsoils and cave deposits. The method is effective for depths of up to six feet.

A radar unit has been developed for archaeological work. Signals penetrate the ground and react differently to sub-soil materials — soils, boulders, archaeological remains. The latter include walls, hollow spaces such as tombs, and metal objects over several centimeters in size. An American dime is 1.3 centimeters across. A laser based gold detector has been reported in the press. While currently used for treasure hunting, it may also be used for archaeology some day.

These types of exploration have not been used extensively in the Holy Land. The cesium magnetometer and resistivity surveying were main elements in Patrick E. McGovern's Beq'ah Valley Project in Jordan. The Beq'ah is unusual in the Near East for its rich, fertile soil in an almost self-contained valley, in contrast to the many gorges or wadis of parts of Jordan and Israel. McGovern knew of tombs already exposed or vandalized but used the techniques to find more, as well as in surveying the interior and exterior areas of building remains. The latter included megalithic structures associated with the Iron Age and the biblical Ammonites. Results of the survey were used to guide excavation which was limited by the usual shortage of time and money. The electronic guide was helpful though not infallible.

The Hebron excavations of Philip C. Hammond used the proton magnetometer and resistivity surveying. In a more extensive effort in Petra, Hammond used both methods to survey eighteen acres of the central city. He took nearly 16,000 readings, found 38 anomalies and excavated 2. One of these turned up previously unknown Nabataean houses. The other uncovered a Nabataean temple "of the winged lions." Phase X was a destruction level in both areas. It could be dated to Monday, 19 May, 363 A.D. An earthquake on this day is described in a recently published Syrian manuscript. The Petra effort covered about eighty per cent of the central city. In a less extensive survey at Tell Hesban, he looked for tombs, with limited results. A magnetometer was used at Caesarea on the

Mediterranean coast. Yigael Yadin used a mine detector in search of metal in the "Bar Koseba" cave of Nahal Tse'elim north of Masada. A magnetometer was used with limited success searching for mudbrick walls at Tell Maskhuta on the Suez Canal.

In 1960, a famous biblical archaeologist publicly declared that electronic detectors were the modern equivalent of that quaint superstition known as dousing rods. While the rocky hills of the Near East are not as good or as ideal for these new detectors as alluvial (water-laid) soil, these too appear in biblical areas. Perhaps the lack of or the limited use of electronic detectors is a matter of expense. Or perhaps it is a matter of cultural lag. Archaeologists like other scientists are not always open to new ideas, especially when someone else has suggested them.

An anomaly simulator was set up in Oxford to train operators of magnetometers. The Milan Polytechnical School and the Lerici Foundation have had courses in archaeological prospecting. These instruct in methods, scientific equipment, and technical facilities. A short course will not make a person an expert but can impart a firm working knowledge of the subject.[3]

## B.   ON THE MECHANICAL SIDE

The Lerici Foundation based its training program on several decades of experience. Much of that was with Etruscan cemeteries in Italy. Aerial photography helped authorities watch for grave-robbing. It also gave archaeologists a better idea of where the cemeteries were and how extensive they were. Ground surveys checked this information, especially using resistivity surveying. Carolo Mauillio Lerici pioneered new geophysical methods for prospecting for oil, gas, minerals, and water. He established the Foundation for this purpose in 1947.

An industrial engineer, Lerici turned his expertise to archaeology when he was looking for a design for his family tomb. His original contribution to archaeology was the Lerici periscope, which goes down through a drilled hole into a new discovered tomb. The periscope is upside down. It can rotate 360 degrees. Built-in lighting shows whether the tomb is worth excavating. Operators can even put in a camera and take pictures of the inside of the tomb without excavating it. A TV camera can be installed, and one tomb was drilled and then photographed "live" on Italian television.

Lerici has also used seismic recording. A small explosive charge sends shock waves through the ground. Underground features can sometimes be located by recording the pattern of the waves. A seismic shock can be also be created by putting a steel ball in the ground and hitting it with a sledge hammer.[4]

## C.    HEAVENLY ARCHAEOLOGY

### Beginnings

A country doctor and amateur archaeologist, J. P. Williams-Freeman thought that "one ought to be a bird in order to be a field archaeologist." Leo Deuel in telling the story of aerial archaeology, quotes Ecclesiastes 10:20, "a bird of the air will carry your voice, or some winged creature tell the matter." While it is doubtful that the poet had archaeology in mind, it is a reminder of what the bird's eye view might reveal. Deuel goes on to point out that the development of aerial archaeology goes with photography and flight. It is heavily tied to military interests. Gaspard Felix Tournachon ("Nadar") took a picture (daguerrotype) of Paris from a balloon tied to the ground, in October 1858, probably the first truly aerial photograph.

In the 1880s George Eastman developed his flexible film and Major Elsdale of the British Royal Engineers Balloon Establishment experimented with free, unmanned balloons and self-releasing cameras which could take more than one picture in a row. This method was used for the ruins near Agra in India by Charles F. Close (later Col. Sir Charles) in 1891, but the effort failed because of red tape. It was not until 1906 that the first real archaeological photo was taken. Lt. P.H. Sharpe, in a war balloon, accidentally took both a vertical and an oblique picture of Stonehenge in England.

Sir Henry Marston Wellcome experimented with box kites and remote controlled cameras in his excavations at Jebel Moya, in the Sudan in 1913. Both balloons and kites have been used by the Oriental Institute of Chicago, the former at Megiddo and the latter in Mesopotamia for the study of irrigation systems. Other excavations continue to utilize balloons or kites on occasion, but the typical excavation rarely mounts higher than a tall ladder for its aerial views.

### Heavier than Air

Charles Lindberg took a picture from his plane over Italy in 1909. After the war he carried out archaeological searches from the air over the American southwest and Yucatan. The airplane came of age in World War I, and with it came a new development in aerial archaeology. A number of accidental discoveries came in the Near East theater of operations. On the British side, Lt. Col. G.A. Beazeley, a sapper for the Royal Engineers, made repeated flights over the Tigris-Euphrates plain. He noted the outlines of old irrigation systems, and discovered "Old Samarra," built by the Caliph al-Mustasim sixty-five miles northwest of Baghdad. The city was nearly twenty miles long and may have had a population of 4 million. Air photographs clearly show the estates of the rich on the bank of the Tigris and both underground channels and canals of the city water system in the center of town. Squadron Leader Insull (who discovered Woodhenge in England), also flying in Iraq, found the site of Seleucia, the Hellenistic capital of Mesopotamia.

By and large archaeological discovery was a sideline, but the German Army launched a mission explicitly to photograph archaeological sites. Theodor Wiegand (who excavated Miletus on the Turkish coast and later was a president of German Archaeological Society) pursuaded the High Command to set up a unit for the protection of historical monuments (Denkmalschutzkommando) in the Near East. A pilot photographed ruins in the Negev and Sinai desert regions between Aqaba and the Mediterranean. While nothing new was found, the mission gave a tremendous overview of the area.

## How it Works

In the postwar years the development of aerial archaeology centered in England on Osbert Guy Stanhope Crawford (1886–1957). He had been with the Wellcome Expedition in the Sudan (1913) and realized the potential of the air in the conversation with Williams-Freeman noted earlier. He had flown survey flights for the RAF during the shooting, and afterwards had dug in Wales. In 1920 he became the Archaeological Officer (an office created for him) of the British Ordance Survey. He tried to get RAF photographs but failed until Williams-Freeman got him some in 1922, the year which Crawford calls the birth of aerial archaeology. Eventually Crawford started flying and taking his own pictures.

His discoveries do not concern us in the sense of actual sites, but the principles do. Crawford talks in terms of three kinds of sites: shadow sites, soil sites and crop sites. The first is based on the fact that small (eroded, sunken, etc.) mounds or ridges from old fortifications, burials, or buried remains in general, cast a shadow in slanting light (early morning, late afternoon). The shadows appear in vertical (taken from directly overhead) or in oblique (taken from an angle) pictures. These same ridges will reflect a direct light (the roundness foreshortens and condenses the light) and so appear as a brightness in relation to a darker surrounding.

Soil sites are those marked by ancient digging. Normally a subsoil is lighter (sand, gravel, less humus or organic matter) in color than topsoil. When a ditch or tomb is dug, the subsoil is brought to the top and the lightness appears clearly from above. The appearance might also be a darkness because the deeper soil of the silted-up ditch, or the refilled tomb, holds more moisture so the soil will be darker (as a wet towel is darker than a dry one). Cropsites (not limited to cultivated farm crops) are seen because the richer soil (depth, moisture) of ditches and tombs gives a more luxuriant (and hence darker green) growth. On the other hand, buried walls or streets have a shallower covering of soil and so give lighter growth which dies out more quickly in dry weather. Closely related to this is the preference of some plants such as poppies for deeper soil, so that they do not grow over a wall but grow profusely over a silted-up ditch.

This type of observation can sometimes be made from the ground, as noted in chapter one. The phenomenon was noted early on by William Camden (1551–1623), who saw that the grain was thinner over the streets of a buried Roman city in England. Sir Leonard Woolley's discovery of tombs in Egypt was cited earlier. He and a companion sat on a hillside late in the afternoon. The sun cast a shadow at just the right angle to make visible the slightly heaped-up gravel.

## System

Major George W.G. Allen (1891–1940) is credited by Crawford with a major advance in aerial archaeology. Until he read a report of Crawford's in 1930 and began using his private plane for systematic investigation, discovery had been at most an accidental affair. Allen took due note of the changes around Oxford with the seasons of the year. A field which showed nothing in November might reveal a Roman villa in June. He moved the new discipline into the era of a full-fledged practical technique with controls for climate, season, lighting, and vegetation.

**Figure 5–2.**    Masada from the shore of the Dead Sea.

**Figure 5–3.** Masada from the air.

## In the Near East

Antoine Poidebard (1878–1955) pioneered the new method in 1926 to explore hundreds of miles of Roman frontier in Syria. His "La trace de Rome dans le desert de Syrie" in 1934 completed a mission for the Geographical Society of France. Moving out from his professorship at the University of St. Joseph and a later French Air Force Chaplaincy in Beirut (he was a missionary in Armenia earlier), he developed his own techniques. Crawford's work did not reach him until 1928, by which time he had already discovered Tell Brak, a Sumerian and later an Akkadian city on the Habur River, north of Mari. He experimented with infrared film and learned to overcome the problems of atmospheric conditions beyond his control — intense light, dust, and heat. With the plane's wing as a shadow he pointed the camera into the sun but down at an oblique angle. Later he used his "counter-light" method in Algeria as well.

**Figure 5–4.**   A Roman siege camp from the top of Masada. An aerial view without benefit of airplane.

With his investigations of the Roman and Phoenician harbors of Tyre, Poidebard launched a new type of archaeological investigation. Crawford and Allen had already shown the necessity of coordinating aerial observation hand in glove with ground observation and excavations. Poidebard went underwater and coordinated investigations with divers and aerial observation. He was the first to demonstrate that underwater remains could be seen by aerial archaeology. He began with an excellent photo of a drowned villege on the bottom of Lake Homs in Syria and moved from there to a three year campaign (1935–37) which resulted in a complete map of both ancient harbors at Tyre ("Un grand port disparu, Tyre" 1939). Similar tri-phibian (Deuel's term) methods were used for the harbor of Sidon, elsewhere in Syria, and in North Africa. We will return to underwater archaeology shortly.

Erich F. Schmidt published *Flights Over Ancient Cities of Iran* in 1940. Three years before he had explored Persia from the air on behalf of the Oriental Institute. In one flight he saw 400 sites near Persepolis. One vertical view of Istakhr nearby showed the layout of the city — knowledge which the institute had earlier needed eighteen months to obtain. Similarly five minutes were spent on an aerial mosaic of Hatra. It had taken Walter Andrae weeks to get this for the German Oriental Society. This illustrates one major advantage of aerial archaeology. Historically the emphasis has been on discovery, but photogrammetry (map making from photographs) also plays a major role. The "look from above" has the advantage of showing relationships of the parts of a city or a ruin. By locating streets, buildings, fountains, and fortifications, that "look" can guide the excavator to just where he should dig.

We are concerned here not only with discovery, but also with plans and maps of a site. To this should be added a map of the area and of the whole country. Aerial mapmaking also contributes to archaeology by showing contours of the land, roads, water courses, irrigation, and other features related to ancient civilization. Of course, accurate maps are also quite helpful in finding one's way across the country and to the desired excavation site!

## Recent Developments

World War II brought further advances in film type and camera improvement. Camouflage detection contributed its part to aerial detective work. The debris covering archaeological sites has been called "natural" camouflage. Most of the archaeological activity came in Europe — the Etruscan discoveries of John Bradford from 1945 on (initiated with the use of British RAF photographs in Italy), Irwin Schollar of Bonn in the 1960s, and Dr. J. Kenneth S. St. Joseph.

St. Joseph was curator (1948) and later director (1962) of the Aerial Photography unit at the University of Cambridge. Aerial archaeology achieved academic status. He was initiated into the discipline when he and Crawford were looking for Roman remains in Scotland in 1939 in a joint foot and flight search. After service in the

Coastal Command of the RAF he returned to aerial archaeology. In 1945 he discovered more Roman sites in a few hours flying time than had been found in the previous 200 years.

In the early postwar years, A. Reifenberg, a British Army interpreter of aerial photographs, made aerial studies of such sites as Dothan and Mount Gerizim (Nablus) and the previously unknown Philistine harbor of Ashdod on the Mediterranean. In 1959 Nelson Glueck used aerial reconnaissance and aerial photos to supplement his ground survey of the Negev. An International Colloquium on Aerial Archaeology met in Paris in 1963 at the Sorbonne. In 1966 George E. Mendenhall made numerous flights over Jordan — both the East and West Banks — photographing with infrared and color film. In 1979, Diane Kennedy established an Aerial Photographic Archive for Archaeology in the Middle East in England at Sheffield University.

Infrared film has interesting potential for archaeology. It can detect heat on the leaves of plants. The leaf is cooled when moisture evaporates. Healthy plants give off moisture at a different rate than cut, wilting, drying, or diseased plants. That means they have different temperatures. This is one way of "seeing" through military camouflage. Plant life over buried remains reveals a difference also. When the plants grow over buried walls, the soil is shallower and the plants are thinner and dry out faster in dry weather, as noted earlier. Plants over the deeper soil beside the wall or the deeper soil of filled up ditches are more luxuriant, so they too have a different temperature.

The U.S. Air Force developed a multiband camera. It has nine lenses and records different spectra of light. One records the full spectrum as in ordinary cameras. The other eight record various sections of the light spectrum from ultraviolet to infrared. The camera was used by USAF working with the University Museum and the Cambridge Research Laboratory in the search for Sybaris.

Magnetometers are being used from the air to discover mineral deposits. There is a side-scanning radar which can penetrate to bedrock through dense foliage or into three feet of dry soil. These sensors developed during wartime now make it possible to discover building remains under heavy growth such as long uncultivated land or even jungle.

High altitude flying has been helpful in detecting archaeological remains. There are some types of fortifications that can only be seen from an altitude of 25,000 feet. Satellite photography is now in use as well. The U.S. Department of the Interior has a satellite program called LANDSAT. Earlier it was called Earth Resources Observation Satellite (EROS). Later the name was changed to ERTS (Earth Resources Technology Satellite).

LANDSAT 1 (ERTS-A) was launched in March, 1972. The second LANDSAT was launched in 1975. The program is concerned with natural resources. Studies range from water pollution to the growth of coral, the location of water in desert regions, the detection of minerals, geological studies, photogrammetry, plant disease, shore lines, old river and canal beds, schools of fish, etc. Satellite photogrammetry is especially useful. A single satellite picture covers the same area as 500 standard airplane pictures. And it does so more accurately, for the shadow effect remains constant in that moment while in planes it takes time to make that many pictures and the shadows change.

More directly significant are vegetation studies — the same decay, disease, and drought reactions already cited, as was change with the seasons. Satellites can locate features in November that did not appear in July and vice-versa. A satellite going around the earth year after year can study the same area on a seasonal or even a weekly basis. The LANDSAT satellites are in a sun-synchronous pattern. They orbit the poles and pass over the same spot at the same time every eighteen days. The European SPOT system sees any point on earth every 3.5 days.

Resolution (detection of things on earth) is now down to thirty-nine feet from 517 miles out in space. Military systems are said to have resolutions in inches. Some of the statements are hard to believe. One is that an object smaller than a Volkswagen can be pinpointed from 300 miles out. Another statement is that an object the size of a basketball can be spotted from 20,000 miles. From eighty miles out, one is supposed to be able to see a pack of cigarettes in a man's hand. But even if these reports are exaggerated, there can be little doubt that ancient buildings as well as cities can or will be detected. One can note parenthetically that this is not just a matter of detection in the sense of first-time discovery but of guidance for the actual excavation of a site. When faced with a five or 15 or 150 acre site, it is not always easy to decide where to put in the spade or pick. Aerial photography, including satellite photography or sensing, is already on the way to being a major resource in archaeology.

The concern with size and ground resolution may be misleading. Canals for example are narrow but long. Aerial photographs have revealed a canal on the eastern edge of the Nile Delta, east of the Suez Canal. One suggestion is that it goes back to the Middle Kingdom and the first pharaoh of the Twelfth Dynasty, Amenemhat I (c. 1991–1962 B.C.). A 2,000 year old network of canals was found by satellite radar in Guatemala. The Nazca lines of Peru have been studied from satellite photographs, though so far, these long geometrical formations have not yielded their origin or purpose.

Since people need water, ancient settlements had to have a source of water. Moisture can be detected by aerial sensors. In desert regions, the water sources may no longer be visible to the eye but might be found from the sky. One could call the satellite a "dousing rod in the sky." Several excavations have found sizable settlements, but no source of water. These might simply be dried-up but if they are still in existence, pictures or satellite sensors might give us a clue about water resources.

It is possible to study ancient river beds and shore lines. This could help us understand the formations of deltas and the silting process. In turn one would expect to find archaeological sites along the edge of water or under silt.

A new ground-penetrating radar aboard the space shuttle Columbia recorded valleys, old stream beds, and ancient or potential water sources under the Sahara Desert. In the Eastern Sahara in southwestern Egypt and northwestern Sudan, ground searchers guided by radar information found human artifacts from the Acheulian (200,000 years ago), Middle Palaeolithic (50,000 years ago) and Neolithic (10,000 years ago) periods.

The shoreline shows up in sharp relief on infrared film because of the strong contrast between land and water. Harbors and ancient living areas are easier to see on this sharper outline. Shipwrecks, harbors, and sunken cities are under water. Underwater archaeology by satellite may be able to look through the water to study them. The growth of coral reef is a part of the LANDSAT program. Reefs are frequently the scene of ancient shipwrecks. Their discovery could be added to a satellite survey.

The combination of air and sea reminds one of the work of Poidebard when he studied the harbors of Sidon and Tyre. This type of investigation is still going on in Greece and at Caesarea on the coast of Israel. Balloon and airfoil pictures contribute to photogrammetry, the discovery of underwater remains buried by mud, silt, or sand, and, actually aid day by day operations while these places are being dug or explored.[5]

## D. DOWN TO THE SEA

Poidebard's helmeted divers measured remains and took pictures, sometimes guided by local divers holding their breath in time-honored fashion. These were the first archaeological underwater photographs. They were supplemented by his aerial shots and stereophotographs which he took through a glass-bottomed bucket held on the surface. The latter allowed three-dimensional viewing of the underwater walls. From time immemorial, sponge divers and others without benefit of equipment have explored depths shallow and sometimes not so shallow. These divers, and more often fishermen with nets dragging the bottom, brought to the surface antiquities ranging from pottery jars to statues. The first diving suit recorded goes back to 1535 when Francesco Demarchi explored the Roman barges (probably of Caligula's time) at the bottom of Lake Nemi, Italy. Swimmers had made various attempts to salvage the ships using floats. Annesio Fusconi, a hydraulic engineer, used an eight-seat Halys diving bell in 1827, when he explored and took his turn at salvage. Mussolini finally had seventy feet of water pumped out of the lake to recover the ships, which were then burned by the Nazis in 1944.

Before Poidebaid's time, an Italian engineer, Giuseppe de Fazio (nineteenth century) had explored the sunken harbor of Puteoli near Naples, with the help of sponge divers. He was followed there by Robert Theodore Gunther, an Oxford archaeologist, who studied the ruins through a glass-bottomed box in 1901 and 1903. In 1910, Gaston Jondet discovered the underwater remains of the large harbor at Pharos near Alexandria. Harbors and sunken cities have been explored on the coasts of Yugoslavia, North Africa, the Black Sea, and the Caribbean (Port Royal), as well as in Lebanon and Palestine. An international team has been exploring the harbor of Caesarea Maritima, built by Herod the Great. Inland, underwater archaeology has ranged from the Canadian rapids (early trade goods), a *cenote* (sacred well of the Aztecs) in Mexico, land reclamation in Holland, the appearance of pile dwellings in Swiss lakes during times of drought, and the Sea of Galilee. The major focus of underwater work, however, has been on ship remains.

Here as with land surface archaeology, treasure and salvage were of prime importance in the beginning and still are. Treasure included $500,000 in gold and silver from a Spanish ship off Hispaniola in 1687. Salvage included the recovery of guns from sunken warships in the eighteenth and nineteenth centuries. In 1823 Charles Anthony Deane patented a helmet designed to give air to firemen in smoke-filled buildings. He and his younger brother John developed this for underwater exploration and recovery. For several years from 1828 on, John Deane recovered lost anchors and explored sunken ships for cannon and other objects around the coasts of England. Part of the importance of his work is in the sketches he had made before the items deteriorated in the air, and his sketches and descriptions of related marine biology including their accumulation ("concretion") on the objects. While Deane's work was salvage, he was also concerned with the historical significance of what he recovered. He published a diving manual in 1836 to describe the use of his helmet and suit.

Deane remained under shallow water for as long as five hours. Divers learned the hard way that in deeper water, extensive stays made them subject to the *bends*, now known to be caused by excessive nitrogen in the blood. By 1900, divers in suits similar to Deane's were limited to five minutes twice a day when working at considerable depths. The turn of the century marked the discovery of a Roman vessel from c. 80–65 B.C. in 180 feet of water off Antikythera, south of Greece. Its cargo of statuary was found by sponge divers who sought the help of government and antiquities authorities. This combination is seen by some as the beginning of underwater archaeology.

In method the divers were still limited to grabbing whatever could be tied to a rope and hauled to the surface. Large boulders were pulled off the wreck and tumbled into deeper water. Later, one of the "boulders" was brought to the surface and seen to be a large statue — on the murky sea bottom, encrusted with growth and mud, the "boulders" were not recognized as sculpture.

Spongers discovered a wreck containing classical antiquities three miles off the eastern coast of Tunisia at Mahdia. From 1908–13, they made dives in 130 feet of water to salvage columns and artifacts. Further salvage was conducted in 1948 by the French Undersea Group (GEES) under Commanders Tailliez and Cousteau, and in 1954–55 by the Tunisian Club of Underseas Studies. The latter group made a partial excavation of the ship, also Roman, dated to c. 80 B.C.

## Scuba

Jacques-Yves Cousteau (1910– ) was born in Gironde, educated at naval college, and served as a French naval officer. In 1942, he and Emile Gagnan invented the aqualung or *SCUBA* (Self Contained Underwater Breathing Apparatus) and modern underwater archaeology was under way. Like aerial archaeology's progress in relation to flying, underwater work has progressed along with diving. Much of it has been experimental and it was not until 1960 that a methodical excavation was carried to completion (a Bronze Age wreck off Cape Gelidonya, Turkey) by George Bass (1932– ), sponsored by the University Museum. Bass has a Ph.D. in classical archaeology from the University of Pennsylvania, an M.A. in Near Eastern archaeology from Johns Hopkins, and has worked with the American School of Classical Studies in Athens. He is Distinguished Professor of Anthropology at Texas A&M and serves as Archaeological Director of the affiliated Institute of Nautical Archaeology.

In some ways, underwater excavation is just like standard ground excavation. The concern for stratigraphy in a single shipwreck is rarely a matter of dating different historical strata but of determining the exact location of artifacts.— three dimensional recording. From this comes knowledge of cargo loading and ship construction, of the distinction between cargo and personal effects of the crew, as well as origin, ports of call, and the destination of the cargo. The difficulties of drawing top plans under water, with the problems of sea current (worse than wind on land) and still-limited stays at the site by divers, are being solved through photography.

## A New Medium

Apart from the problems of diving (Bass trains divers in a little over a week), underwater archaeology has developed several new techniques of its own. The mud and sand silted around a wreck and its cargo can be removed by air suction hose. Air pumped into the lower mouth of the hose or pipe (three to twelve inches in diameter) expands as it bubbles up to lighter pressure from the lower depths. This creates a suction within the tube, which pulls up water, sand, mud and small artifacts. Either the tube empties onto a surface barge where the water can run off, or it empties below the surface with a net to catch the objects while the current carries away the debris. Properly used, the air hose can excavate stratigraphically. Larger objects

**Figure 5–5.** Students inspect pottery shards from near the pinewood hull of the ancient Roman shipwreck off the coast of Caesarea, Israel, where archaeologists are excavating the ancient harbor completed by Herod in 10 B.C.E. Photo: Larry Roberts, courtesy Consulate General of Israel (NY).

can be hauled to the surface with ropes or floated to the surface with a balloon which is inflated after being tied to the object.

The opposite principle has also aided underwater archaeology by the invention of what Michael Katzev called a "magic air-wand." It is a pipe with a sharp tip and holes along the length of the pipe. Shoved into the sand, forced air through the holes loosens seaweed and the sand itself for easier digging. A water jet probe with a special nozzle to avoid backlash is also being used to clear sand away from underwater remains. The air lift vacuum has the advantage of taking debris to the surface where it can be screened for artifacts.

A plexiglass phone booth is being used in underwater archaeology. Its dome shape holds a capsule of air which is renewed from the surface. Set up near the dig, it provides a place to rest, and contact with the surface crew by phone. It is also an additional supply of air. One type has room for four people at once.

Coral and other growths or deposits frequently encrust objects on the sea floor. Sometimes these have to be chiselled and hammered off. Sometimes the lime encrusts a metal object which then decomposes, leaving an impression inside the crust which forms a natural mold. Cut open, the "mold" can be used with plaster of paris or rubber compounds to form a copy of the original.

Special precautions must be made for preservation since many things deteriorate when explosed to light and air, as in dry land archaeology. The major problem here is wood which is quickly ruined if allowed to dry from its water soaked condition. Treatment with polyethylene glycol is proving helpful. The glycol replaces the missing fibers of the wood with a waxy substance.

## The Near East

At first glance underwater archaeology might seem to be quite far removed from the deserts of the Near East. And yet we know that Egyptian ships were sailing along the Palestinian coast as early as 3000 B.C. Here as elsewhere artifacts appear in fishermen's nets and on the virtually harborless coast. For example, one shipwreck off Dor between Haifa and Tel Aviv, had ingots of tin (from Spain) and copper (from Cyprus). There are probably untold numbers of shipwrecks waiting in what Cousteau has called the Blue Museum.

The harbors are few, but of interest. Poidebard's work at Tyre and Sidon was cited earlier. When the Israelites from the east and the Philistines from the south invaded Palestine or Canaan, some of the Canaanites, according to one theory, were pushed into the narrow coastal lands of today's Lebanon. There they became a great sea-faring people, the Phoenicians. Anything that sheds light on these folk and their intimate contact with other ancient peoples, is potentially helpful. Bass' excavation at Gelidonya, for example, shows that Homer gave a reasonably accurate picture of sea-faring Phoenicians — the cargo of this ship was Cypriot copper but the personal belongings of the crew were Syrian-Phoenician.

## More and More

Bass notes that wrecks have been found by accident just as with many dry ground sites. The age of sea bottom exploration is just beginning in a systematic way. This has advanced with improvements in sight and sound equipment. The sound waves called sonar can be sent straight down. These can go through dozens of feet of sand. Side-scanning sonar has been used off the coast of Turkey. The sea bottom was searched for shipwrecks. Several were found. The device was developed as a way of mapping the ocean floor. It can work to depths of several miles but can also be used in as little as 150 feet of water. The system sends out sound waves sideways as much as 600 feet on each side to cover a path 1200 feet wide. The echoes from the sound waves give a profile of the sea bed. Irregularities can then be checked individually by divers or submarine for possible archaeological importance.

Proton magnetometers and induction detectors have been used underwater. The magnetometer bottle is put in a fiberglass shield and towed just above the sea bed. The surface vessel moves in ten foot wide paths over the area in survey. The method has been used along the Mediterranean coast. When a site has been

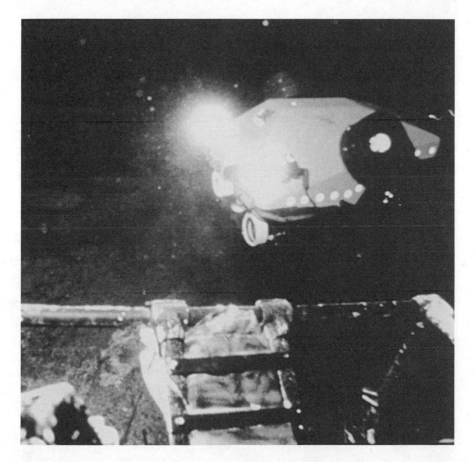

**Figure 5–6.**    The robot, Jason, Jr., used in exploring the sunken Titanic. It is part of the Argo/Jason system for underwater exploration. Plans are underway for its use in underwater archaeology in the Mediterranean. Photo courtesy Woods Hole Oceanographic Institution.

**Figure 5–7.** Alvin, the submersible used to explore the sunken ship, Titanic. Photo courtesy Woods Hole Oceanographic Institution.

located, and during its excavation as well, a metal detector can locate metals and guide the digging. A magnetometer was used to explore the bottom of Lake Superior which has a depth of 1300 feet, suggesting possibilities of the Sea of Galilee and the Dead Sea.

Closed circuit television has been used underwater. With a rudder for stability, the encased camera can be pulled by a cable behind the mother ship with a monitor on board. The camera has also been tied to an iron axle on wheels and moved over the bottom. The television camera can "see" better than the human eye at depths of up to 300 feet with only natural light. Mercury vapor lighting has been used as well. One underwater camera can be lowered to 30,000 feet. Up to 500 pictures can be taken in a single run with the use of strobe lighting.

Robert Ballard of the Woods Hole Oceanographic Institution led a French-American team that discovered the sunken liner Titanic 450 miles southeast of Newfoundland. The remains are 13,000 feet down. In the search, they used unmanned underwater television and camera vehicles, the Argo and the Angus (Accoustically Navigated Geological Underwater Survey) towed by the mother ship, Atlantis II. To explore the wreck, Ballard went down in a three-person sub, the Alvin, and took live television color videotapes with a lawn mower-sized robot called Jason, Jr. It was tethered to the Alvin with a 250 foot control cable used to direct its travels and its television cameras, which can rotate 170 degrees, over and inside the wreck. The expedition included 12 dives and netted 57,000 pictures and 50 hours of videotape. The United States Navy paid $220,000 to test Jason, Jr. No organic matter was found. The iron hulk is rusted. Copper and ceramic were well-preserved.

A one person "tow-vane" has been used to explore the sea bed. It is a steel capsule with a wrap-around plexiglass window. A surface vessel tows it. Vanes on either side can be used to glide the slightly buoyant capsule underwater and down to depths of as much as 300 feet. The operator looks at the bottom, takes pictures, and keeps in touch with the surface by phone.

A "space" suit nicknamed "Jim" after a pioneer diver, Jim Jarrett, has liquid filled spaces between metal plates. The suit can withstand pressures up to those found at a depth of 2,000 feet. Special equipment keeps air pressure equal to sea surface pressure. Oxygen is added and carbon dioxide is "scrubbed" from the air so that the one-person diving suit can theoretically stay below for up to forty-eight hours. It can operate without connection to the surface as a "free" agent, but was tested tied to a small submarine. It was used off the Hawaiian coast in depths of 1250 feet, the same depth as the Dead Sea.

One submarine that can be used is the two-man sub, the sixteen foot long Asherah, built in 1964. It was the first submarine designed especially for archaeology. It weighs four tons and can operate at depths of 600 feet. It can run for two to ten hours at speeds of up to four knots. The two people inside can communicate directly with divers working on a wreck. They can help excavate as well, by using a mechanical arm or a suction hose. From the sub, the operators can take pictures as the sub hovers or moves over the area. The operators can use natural light or floor lights on the sub. The Asherah has had extensive use in the eastern Mediterranean both in locating and in excavating shipwrecks.

An eighteen foot mini-sub designed by Cousteau weighs nine tons and can hold the pilot and two passengers. He named it "Deepstar 4000." It can work down to 4000 feet for as long as eight hours. It found a wrecked plane 2500 feet under the Pacific. The U.S. Navy's Deep Quest research sub recovered a plane from 3400 feet. Project FAMOUS (French-American Mid-Ocean Undersea Study) used a three-man French bathyscape, the Archimede, in 1973–74. They explored the Atlantic trench. The 60 foot, 200 ton, "yellow submarine" plunged to depths of 9000 feet. So did the three-man French submersible, Cyana, and the three-man American sub, Alvin. Each are one-third the size of the Archimede.

Cousteau set up an experimental village thirty-five feet beneath the surface of the Red Sea. Two men lived in a lower house at ninety feet for a week. They could work at 180 feet. His sub had an underwater garage so it could work at depths up to 1000 feet without resurfacing. In the Mediterranean, he had men living 600 feet down and working at 900 feet.

The Sea of Galilee, the Dead Sea, and the Gulf of Aqaba or Eilat, are part of a huge earth fault called the Rift Valley. The Dead Sea is 1250 feet deep in spots, while the Gulf reaches 6000 feet. Their exploration is now possible by sub, by "Jim," and by camera.

The same year that Bass swam into the Gelidonya wreck off Turkey, Edwin A. Link, the inventor, sailed into Caesarea twenty-five miles south of Haifa. The harbor of Herod the Great has probably sunk sixteen feet, maybe from earthquakes such as the one in 130 A.D. Link's ninety-one foot Sea Diver II is a 168 ton vessel especially designed for underwater archaeology with stabilizing bow jets, compressors, underwater viewing portholes, boom, work space, etc. The Reef Diver is a smaller version, carried on the Sea Diver's stern. The Reef Diver was trucked overland to the Sea of Galilee. It explored several areas including the shore of Magdala where the historian Josephus says the Romans and Jews fought a sea battle. The exploration was encouraging. The Israeli Department of Antiquities has people working full time on underwater archaeology. Their sea base is on the Carmel coast. They cooperate with the Undersea Exploration Society of Israel and with the sea workshop of the University of Haifa's Center for Maritime Studies.

*Saturation diving* is one of the more recent developments in underwater exploration. It uses special chambers attached to a mother ship. The chambers contain pressures equal to those at the diving depth. A mixture of helium and oxygen helps prevent *nitrogen narcosis* (the bends). The equipment is too expensive for ordinary undersea archaeology. However, several cooperative ventures have taken place between archaeologists and commercial and military divers. A navy diver helped explore the wreck of the Titanic, the work cited earlier as co-sponsored by the U.S. Navy.

Photography has made a great contribution to underwater work with photogrammetry. Stereophotography with three-dimensional pictures has cut the drawing of top plans to a fraction of the time it takes with the standard "measure and draw" process. Plans and map making from pictures were developed with fixed stationary cameras. Aerial survey cameras with housings for underwater were attached to the Asherah. Correcting lenses compensate for distortion and the index of refraction of water, and a depth difference gauge gives accuracies to one centimeter. A half hour dive with the Asherah gave the data for a three-dimensional plan of a whole wreck. Earlier methods would have taken dozens of dives and a month to do this. The excavation process as a whole can be photographed. The top plans can then be drawn later at headquarters with the use of stereoscopic viewers.

Before going on with the whole area of photoarchaeology, it can be noted that the development of underwater archaeology was aided by various national groups such as the U.S. Council for Underwater Archaeology and the Hellenic Federation of Underwater Activities, and those cited earlier — the French Undersea Group, the Tunisian Club of Undersea Studies, and the UES of Israel. Several world congresses have met in the past decades. The Fourth International Congress of Underwater Archaeology was held in Nice, France, in October 1971. The Committee for Nautical Archaeology at the Institute of Archaeology in London gives courses and seminars and technical advice. The American Institute of Nautical Archaeology was founded in 1973. Its first summer training program was at the site of Bass' work at Yassi Ada on the southwest coast of Turkey. Since then, their work has expanded to include other Mediterranean sites as well as African and American sites. In 1976, AINA established its permanent quarters in Texas with a joint program with Texas A & M University. It is a consortium of over twenty institutions and is allied with the AIA. The Conference on Underwater Archaeology meets annually with the Society for Historical Archaeology.

We might also note here the problem of looters or treasure hunters who look for gold, antiques, or simply for interesting objects. Some believe in "finders - keepers" but the problem is more extensive than ownership. As with dry land archaeology, objects torn from context lose historic and archaeological value. Looters destroy the ship or context so the shape, construction and other information is lost. Some countries have legislation to protect underwater remains in their coastal waters.[6]

# NOTES

1. This section is revised from an earlier edition printed in *The Biblical Archaeologist Reader* 3, ed. Edward F. Campbell, Jr. and David Noel Freedman (Garden City: Doubleday, 1970), pp. 335–344, which was a revision of "Science and Archaeology," BA 29, no. 4 (Dec. 66), pp. 110–135. Portions reprinted are by permission.

2. Hogarth, "Common Sense in Archaeology," *Antiquity* 46 (1972), pp. 301–304. The "gulf" of mutual incomprehension is what Charles P. Snow claimed lies between scientists and literary intellectuals. The latter might be seen as humanists in general. Snow, *The Two Cultures: And a Second Look — An Expanded Version of the Two Cultures and the Scientific Revolution* (New York: Cambridge University, 1964) (original 1959). David Wilson, *The New Archaeology* (New York: American Library, 1974). G. Ernest Wright, "The 'New' Archaeology," BA 38, nos. 3–4 (Sep./Dec. 75), pp. 104–115. Richard I. Ford, "Paleoethnobotany in American Archaeology," SAAMT 2 (1979), pp. 285–336. The SAAMT volumes are excellent examples of the new archaeology. Among the journals, one of the most prominent has been *Archaeometry*, published by the Research Laboratory for Archaeology and the History of Art, Oxford Unversity, since 1958. The University Museum of the University of Pennsylvania in Philadelphia has been on the forefront of new developments with the Applied Science Center for Archaeology. The MASCAN was published 1965–78. It has been replaced by the MASCAJ, 1, no. 1 (Dec. 78). There are many others, such as the Institute for Archaeo-Metallurgical Studies of the Institute of Archaeology, University of London, with an annual newsletter (IAMSN).

   Hogarth, "Common Sense," p. 301, claims "The fact is, of course, that there is no such thing as the New Archaeology. It is merely Newspeak Archaeology, tricked out in a whole wardrobe of new vocabulary apparently designed more to impress than to enlighten." In his view, the discoveries of science have been applied to archaeology for decades. Robert C. Dunnell, "American Archaeologist Literature: 1981," AJA 86, no. 4 (Oct. 82), pp. 509–529. The phrase, "new 'new archaeology' " is on p. 528. William Dever has called for a new biblical archaeology to grow out of dialogue between biblical archaeologists and Syro-Palestinian archaeologists.

3. Jack Anderson and Dale Van Atto. "Underwater Fortune Beckons Aquino," *The Washington Post* (10 Nov 86), p. C19, reports on the laser based gold detector being used in the Philippines. Bruce Bevan and Jeffrey Kenyon, "Ground Penetrating Radar for Historical Archaeology," MASCAN 11, no. 2 (Dec. 75), pp. 2–7. Sheldon Breiner, *Applications Manual for Portable Magnetometers* (Palo Alto, CA: Geometrics, 1973), and, "The Rubidium Magnetometer in Archaeological Exploration," *Science* 190, no. 3693 (8 Oct 65), pp. 185–193. Orville H. Bullitt, *Search for Sybaris* (New York: Lippincott, 1969). Oliver S. Colburn, "A Return to Sybaris," *Expedition* 18, no. 2 (Wint. 76), pp. 7–13. Hammond, "Cult and Cupboard at Nabataean Petra," *Archaeology* 34, no. 2 (Mar./ Ap. 81), pp. 34–37; and "Magnetometer/Resistivity Survey at Petra, Jordan — 1973," BASOR 214 (Ap. 74), pp. 39–41. A.C. Hayes and D. Osborner, "Fixing Site Location with Radio-Direction Finder at Mesa Verde," AA 27, no. 1 (1961), pp. 110–112. Burton MacDonald, "Tell El-Maskhuta," BA 43, no. 1 (Wint. 80), pp. 49–58. Patrick J. McGovern, "The Beq'ah Valley Project 1980," BA 44 (1981), pp. 126–128; and "The Baq'ah Valley, Jordan: A Cesium Magnetometer Survey," MASCAJ 1, no. 2 (June 79), pp. 39–41; and "The Baq'ah Valley, Jordan: Test Soundings of Cesium Magnetometer Anomalies," MASCAJ 1, no. 7 (June 81), pp. 214–217; and "The Beq'ah Valley Project 1980," ADAJ 25 (1981), pp. 356–357; and "Exploring the Burial Caves of the Baq'ah Valley in Jordan," *Archaeology* 35, no. 5 (Sep./Oct. 82), pp. 46–53. Irwin Scholler, ed., *Proceedings of the Eighteenth International Symposium on Archaeometry and Archaeological Prospection, Bonn, 14–17 March 1978* (Bonn: Rheinisches Landesmuseum, 1979). Glenn T. Seaborg, "Science and the Humanities: A New Level of Symbiosis," *Science* 144, no. 3623 (5 June 64), pp. 1199–1203. "Sybaris, a muddy prize," SN 94 (28 Dec 68), pp. 637–638. Roger S. Vickers

and Lambert T. Dolphin, "A Communication on an Archaeological Radar Experiment at Chaco Canyon, New Mexico," MASCAN 11, no. 1 (May 75), pp. 7–9. For general and continuing studies, see Archaeometry and MASCAJ.

4. Carlo M. Lerici, *A Great Adventure of Italian Archaeology: 1955–65, Ten Years of Archaeological Prospecting* (Milan: Lerici Foundation, 1965; and, "Periscope on the Etruscan Past," NG 116, No. 3 (Sep. 59), pp. 336–350. Fondazione Lerici Prospezioni Archeologiche, Via Vittorio Veneto 108, Roma 100187. CHP, pp. 407–412.

5. "Anthropology & Archaeology," SN 118 (1981), p. 404. Alison Betts, "The Search for a Desert Hill-fort," ILN 271, No. 7014 (Jan. 83), p. 58. Bruce W. Bevan, *Aerial Photography for the Archaeologist* (Philadelphia: University Museum, 1975). John Bradford, *Ancient Landscape: Studies in Field Archaeology* (London: Bell, 1957). CHP, pp. 387–393. CPHA, pp. 334–336. O.G.S. Crawford, *Archaeology in the Field* (New York: Praeger, 1953). Leo Deuel, *Flights Into Yesterday* (New York: St. Martins, 1969). Michael Evenari and Dov Koller, "Ancient Masters of the Desert," SA 194, no. 4 (Ap. 56), pp. 39–45. Raymond W. Fary, Jr., "Explorers from Space," *Journal of Geological Education* 15, no. 3 (June 67), pp. 99–104. William A. Fischer, "User Needs in Geology and Cartography," *The Proceedings of the Princeton University Conference on Aerospace Methods for Revealing and Evaluating Earth's Resources* (Princeton: Princeton University, 1970). Alexander F.H. Goetz and Lawrence C. Rowan, "Geologic Remote Sensing," *Science* 211, no. 4484 (20 Feb 81), pp. 781–791. Christopher L. Hamlin, "Machine Processing of LAND-SAT Data," MASCAN 13, nos. 1/2 (Dec 77), pp. 1–11. Elmer Harp, Jr., ed., *Photography in Archaeological Research* (Albuquerque: University of New Mexico, 1975). "Ideas and Trends: Secrets Under the Sahara," *New York Times* (28 Nov 82), p. 8E. D.L. Kennedy, "The Contribution of Aerial Photography to Archaeology in Jordan," (pp. 29–36 in Studies in the History and Archaeology of Jordan ed. Adnan Hadidi; Amman: Department of Antiquities, 1982). Thomas R. Lyons, ed., *Remote Sensing Experiments in Cultural Resource Studies:* (Albuquerque: National Park Service, 1976). Lyons and Thomas E. Avery, *Remote Sensing: A Handbook for Archaeologists and Cultural Resource Managers.* Sec. IV (Washington: Cultural Resources Management Division, National Park Service, U.S. Department of Interior, 1977). Lyons and G.L. Gumerman, "Archaeological Methodology and Remote Sensing," *Science* 172 (1971), pp. 126–132. J.F. McCauley, et al., "Subsurface Valleys and Geoarchaeology of the Eastern Sahara Revealed by Shuttle Radar," *Science* 218, no. 4576 (3 Dec 82), pp. 1004–1020. Loren McIntyre, "Mystery of the Ancient Nazca Lines," NG 147, no. 5 (May 75), pp. 716–728.

John A. Miles, "Field and Lab: Aerial Photography," BA 39, no. 1 (Mar 76), pp. 37–39. J. Wilson Myers and Eleanor Emlen Myers, "The Art of Balloon Archaeology," Archaeology 33, no. 6 (Nov./Dec. 80), pp. 33–40. L.W.B. Rees, "The Transjordan Desert," *Antiquity* 3 (Dec. 29), pp. 389–407. A. Reifenberg, "Archaeological Discoveries by Air Photography in Israel," *Archaeology* 3 (1950), pp. 40–46. Douglas G. Richards, "Water-penetrating aerial photography," IJNAUE 9, no. 4 (1980), pp. 331–337. Charles J. Robinove, "Future Applications of Earth Resource Surveys from Space," *AIAA Earth Resources Observations and Information Systems Meeting, 2–4 Mar 70* (New York: American Institute of Aeronautics and Astronautics Paper No. 70–302). Erich F. Schmidt, *Flights Over Ancient Cities of Iran* (Chicago: University of Chicago, 1940). Irwin Schollar, "The International Colloquium on Air Archaeology," *Antiquity* 37, no. 148 (Dec. 63), pp. 296–297. Mark Settle and James V. Taranik, "Use of the Space Shuttle for Remote Sensing Research," *Science* 218, no. 4576 (3 Dec 82), pp. 993–995. William H. Shea, "A Date for the Recently Discovered Eastern Canal of Egypt," BASOR 226 (Ap. 77), pp. 31–38. "SIR-A: A Radar Look from Space at the Rocky Earth," SN 120, no. 22 (28 Nov 81), p. 341. Amihai Sneh, Tuvia Weissbrod, and Itamar Perath, "Evidence for an Ancient Frontier Canal," *American Scientist* 63 (1975), pp. 542–548. Sneh and Weissbrod, "Nile Delta: The Defunct Pelusaic Branch Identified," *Science* 180 (1973), pp. 59–61. John K.S. St. Joseph, ed., *The Uses of Air Photography: Nature and*

*Man in New Perspective* (London: Baker, 1966). Warren Strobel, "News Gathering Goes into Orbit," Insight 2, no. 36 (8 Sep. 86), pp. 59–61. Erle Strohl, "Eye in the Sky," Barron's (23 Oct. 67), pp. 11, 20–21, 25. Henry O. Thompson, "Archaeology in Orbit," *Archaeology* 20, no. 3 (June 67), pp. 223–224, and "A New Development in Archaeological Air Photography," *Antiquity* 41, no. 163 (Sep. 67), pp. 225–227. "Underlines," *The Christian Century* 92, no. 22 (11–18 June 75), p. 591. U.S. Department of the Interior, *Geological Survey* (numerous releases). David Wilson, ed., *Aerial Reconnaissance for Archaeology* (London: Council for British Archaeology, 1975). The Nazca lines of Peru's southern pampas may be ritual lines for the agricultural calendar. Anthony F. Aveni, "The Nazca Lines: Patterns in the Desert," *Archaeology* 39, no. 4 (July/Aug. 86), pp. 33–39. They have been compared to the "kites" of the Arabian desert but these are for driving game.

6. AINAN 1, no. 1 (Spr. 74), continuing. J. Barto Arnold III, "Remote Sensing in Underwater Archaeology," IJNAUE 10, no. 1 (Feb. 81), pp. 51–62. Wendy Ashmore, "Historic Shipwreck Legislation," Newsletter AIA 4, no. 1 (Sep. 85), pp. 1, 4. Robert D. Ballard, "A Long Last Look at the Titanic," NG 170, no. 6 (Dec 86), pp. 698–727; and, "Project FAMOUS: II — Dive Into the Great Rift," NG 147, no. 5 (May 75), pp. 604–615. Ballard and J. Frederick Grassle, "Return to Oases in the Deep," NG 156, no. 5 (Nov. 79), pp. 689–705. George F. Bass, "Ancient Shipwreck Yields New Facts — and a Strange Cargo," NG 135, no. 2 (Feb. 69), pp. 282–300; and *Archaeology Beneath the Sea* New York: Walker, 1976; and, "The Asherah: A Submarine for Archaeology," *Archaeology* 18 (1965), pp. 7–14; and, "A Byzantine Trading Venture," SA 225, no. 2 (Aug. 71), pp. 22–31; and *Archaeology Under Water* (New York: Praeger, 1966); and, "A Bronze Age Ship-wreck at Ulu Burun (Kas): 1984 Campaign," AJA 90, no. 3 (July 86), pp. 269–296; and, *A History of Seafaring Based on Underwater Archaeology* (London: Thames and Hudson, 1972); and, "New Tools for Undersea Archaeology," NG 134, no. 3 (Sep. 68), pp. 402–423; and, "The Shipwreck at Serce Liman, Turkey," *Archaeology* 2, no. 1 (Jan./Feb. 79), pp. 36–43; and, "Underwater Archae-ology, Key to History's Warehouse," NG 124, no. 1 (July 63), pp. 138–156. Bass and Michael L. Katzev, "New Tools for Underwater Archaeology," *Archaeology* 21 (1968), pp. 164–173. Bass and Frederick H. van Doornick, Jr., "A Fourth-Century Shipwreck at Yassi Ada," AJA 75, no. 1 (Jn. 71), pp. 27–37. Lee Byrd, "Photos Sink Theories," DFP (31 July 86), pp. 1A, 18A, on the ship-wrecked Titanic. CHP, pp. 394–403. CPHA, pp. 332–333. John B. Corliss and Robert D. Bal-lard, "Oases of Life in the Cold Abyss," NG 152, no. 4 (Oct. 77), pp. 440–453. Jacques Cousteau, *The Silent World*; (New York: Harper & Row, 1953). Ron Church, "'Deepstar' Explores the Ocean Floor," NG 139, no. 1 (Jan. 71), pp. 110–129. "Deep Secrets," DFP (19 July 86), pp. 1C–2C. Frederic Dumas, *Deep-Water Archaeology* (London: Routledge and Kegan Paul, 1962). Dumas et al., *Underwater Archaeology* (Paris: UNESCO, 1972). Sylvia A. Earle, "A Walk in the Deep," NG 157, no. 5 (May 80), pp. 624–631. "Excavation, Sea Style," SN 89 (12 Feb. 66); p. 106. Donald Frey, "Saturation Diving — Nautical Archaeology's New Frontier," AINAN 4, no. 3 (Fall 77), pp. 1–5. Charles T. Fritsch and Immanuel Ben-Dor, "The Link Expedition to Israel, 1960," BA 24 (1961), pp. 5–9. Honor Frost, *Under the Mediterranean, Marine Antiquities* (Englewood Cliffs: Prentice-Hall, 1963). E.T. Hall, "The Use of the Proton Magnetometer in Underwater Archaeol-ogy," *Archaeometry* 9 (1966), pp. 32–44. Anthony F. Harding, "Pavlopetri, A Mycenean Town Underwater," *Archaeology* 23, no. 3 (June 70), pp. 242–250. Harp, *Photography*. J.R. Heirtzler, "Where the Earth Turns Inside Out," NG 147, no. 5 (May 75), pp. 586–603. Robert L. Hohlfelder, "Caesarea Beneath the Sea," BAR 8, no. 3 (May/June 82), pp. 42–47. "Ingots from Sea," IAMSN 2 (1981), p. 4. "Ingots from wrecked ship may help to solve ancient mystery," IAMSN 1 (1980), pp. 1–2. "Israel: Caesarea," IJNAUE 10, no. 2 (May 81), pp. 157–160. Gerhard Kapitan, *A Bibliography of Underwater Archaeology* (Chicago: Argonaut, 1966). Michael L. Katzev and Bates Littlehales, "Resurrecting the Oldest Known Greek Ship," NG 137, no. 6 (June 70), pp. 840–857. Donald H. Keith and Donald A. Frey, "Saturation Diving in Nautical Archae-ology," *Archaeology* 32, no. 4 (July/Aug. 79), pp. 24–33. Samuel W. Matthews, "New World of

the Ocean," NG 160, no. 6 (Dec. 81), pp. 792-833. Keith Muckelroy, ed., *Archaeology Underwater: An Atlas of the World's Submerged Sites* (New York: McGraw-Hill, 1980). John Lear, "Man's Return to his Ancient Home," SR (1 June 68), p. 45. Anna M. McCann and John D. Lewis, "The Ancient Port of Cosa," *Archaeology* 23, no. 3 (June 70), pp. 200–211. Alexander McKee, *History Under the Sea* (New York: Dutton, 1969). John P. Oleson, et al., "Caesarea Ancient Harbor Excavation Project (CAHEP): 1982 Season of Excavation," *Old World Archaeology Newsletter* 6, no. 3 (Nov. 82), pp. 12–14. A.J. Parker, "Fifth International Congress of Underwater Archaeology," IJNAUE 4 (1976), pp. 347–348. Mendel Peterson, *History Under the Sea: A Handbook for Underwater Exploration* (Washington: Smithsonian, 1969). Cemal Pulak and Donald A. Frey, "The Search for a Bronze Age Shipwreck," *Archaeology* 38, no. 1 (July/Aug. 85), pp. 18–24. Avner Raban and Robert L. Hohlfelder, "The Ancient Harbors of Caesarea Maritima," *Archaeology* 34, no. 2 (Mar./Ap. 81), pp. 56–60. Hans-Wolf Rackl, *Diving into the Past* (New York: Scribner's, 1968). Nan Robertson, "U.S. and French Divers Describe Exploration of Atlantic Abyss," *New York Times* (19 Oct 73), p. 3. C., and Alexis Sivirine, *Jacques Cousteau's Calypso;* (New York: Abrams, 1983). [The Calypso is one of his research ships.] "Robot readied for first foray inside Titanic," DFP (16 July 86), pp. 1A, 19A. "Robot sent to view remains on Titanic," DFP (18 July 86), p. 4A. Nancy Ross, "Crew still up for second lake dive," DFP (15 July 86), pp. 1B–2B, describes the research project in Lake Superior by Harbor Branch Oceanographic Institution of Fort Pierce, Florida. The four-person submersible, Johnson Sea Link II, and the parent ship, Seward Johnson, were used in the Atlantic Ocean search for the space shuttle Challenger. Joan du Plat Taylor, ed., *Marine Archaeology* (London: Hutchinson, 1965). SN 86 (10 Oct. 64), p. 233. Peter Throckmorton, *Lost Ships* (Boston: Little, Brown, 1964); and, "Ships Wrecked in the Aegean Sea," *Archaeology* 17, no. 4 (1964); and, *Shipwrecks and Archaeology* (Boston: Little, Brown, 1969). The *UNESCO Courier* 25 (May 72). Shelly Wachsmann and Kurt Raveh, "Underwater Investigations by the Department of Antiquities and Museums," IEJ 28, no. 4 (1978), pp. 281–283. Bart Ziegler, "Divers return to Titanic's grave," DFP (21 July 86), p. 4C, and, "Robot seeks staterooms of Titanic," DFP (17 July 86), p. 6A. For ongoing coverage, see AINAN and IJNAUE.

# Scientific Advances

## A.  PHOTOARCHAEOLOGY

Aerial and underwater archaeology show the interaction and the interdependence of procedures in archaeology. The earliest development of photography brought it into contact with archaeology. While he was working in Egypt, Sir Flinders Petrie developed a rubber hose with a lens in it so he could take pictures around a corner. Alexander Conze was the first to use pictures in archaeological reports. He dug at Samothrace near Greece from 1873–75. Then and now, our concern is record keeping and publishing as well as the discovery role so prominent in the searching techniques described earlier. Recording concerns the area before digging and during the excavation itself. Pictures are taken of remains *"in situ"* (in place, as they are found), of artifacts both before and after they are cleaned, of top plans, drawings, architectural remains, the balks — the sides of our digging square or trench which show the layers of occupation, often in living color. Reisner's intense use of photography was noted earlier. Today's improvements include color and light spectra beyond visible light, such as infrared and X-rays. These, plus television, aerial, and underwater phototgraphy, have been cited earlier. We can touch on a few more here.

Infrared has been used with manuscripts like the Dead Sea Scrolls. One example of this process derives from the cost of writing materials in ancient times. It was not unusual for a parchment (made from leather) or papyrus (paper made from reeds) to be erased and used over again. These re-used materials are called palimpsets. The earlier, erased writing can be read with the use of infrared. Infrared has been used to detect painted floors when the paint was invisible to the human eye. The famous shroud of Turin has been studied with both infrared and ultraviolet light. Infrared has aided the study of weaving and cloth dyes so we know more about ancient technology. Infrared light and the laser beam are both being used in surveying for archaeological sites.

X-rays are also being used in archaeology. An X-ray diffraction technique is used to check for deterioration of the Dead Sea Scrolls. The teeth of mummies have been X-rayed in the study of ancient disease and medicine (paleopathology). Mummies can be X-rayed without unwrapping them to show if there is any jewelry, special decoration, malformations in the skeleton, and to establish the cause of death (as when the skull is caved in or the neck broken), as well as to see if there actually is a mummy, that is, a body, inside the wrappings. Fake mummies have been detected in this way. A comparison of the famous King Tut's mummy with that of Pharaoh Smenkhkare shows strong similarities in bone structures. This has suggested that the two may have been brothers. Both were married to daughters of the so-called "heretic pharaoh" Ikhnaten. Pharaoh Ramses II, perhaps the pharaoh of the biblical Exodus, reigned for sixty-seven years according to inscriptions. Examination of his mummy suggests he was no more than fifty-nine when he died. The conflict in evidence is still under discussion. CAT scans have also been used on mummies to study the remains.

On a grand scale, X-rays have been used to study the second great pyramid at Giza in Egypt. Chephren's pyramid might have rooms in it like Cheop's pyramid, the biggest of the three at Giza. Using spark chambers set up inside the pyramid, investigators have checked for the presence of cosmic ray muons. When these unstable particles of the electron family go through matter, they lose energy and eventually stop. Empty spaces such as rooms within the pyramid would have altered their speed and direction. The results were negative. No evidence of rooms or empty spaces was found. The effort continues with the use of sound waves which go through rock and air at different speeds. The pyramids are also being studied from satellite photographs.

The photogrammetric techniques mentioned earlier have been applied to side views at places like Philae in Egypt and Petra in Jordan. New techniques and inexpensive equipment have been developed. The laborious, time-consuming drawing and measuring by hand of inscriptions and temple facades cannot be eliminated entirely. But photographs and drawings from them can aid and speed up the process. One aid is accuracy. In the process of excavation, color photographs preserve the memory of the colors found in digging as well as the contours of soil layers. This has been particularly valuable in beginning a new season of digging. Looking at last season's pictures reminds you of where you left off and what it all looked like. Whole pictures, including aerial views from ladders or balloons, give a sense of the whole when the excavation itself becomes fragmented during the course of the digging and help in relating one part of the excavation to another.[1]

## B.   COUNT OFF

Sooner or later computers were sure to get into the archaeological act. They are almost a standard part of every day living and scientific research. For over fifteen years, the possible uses of computers have been growing. Cited earlier were the use of computers for recording magnetometer surveys, and the electronic production of survey maps. A survey of ancient Moab used the Hewlett-Packard "Papa Bear" transit officially known as a "3820 distance meter." It uses a laser beam and a computer to pinpoint the horizontal and vertical location of sites. Television signals from spacecraft can be electronically corrected and printed out by a computer to give clear pictures.

A temple of Pharaoh Ikhnaten (c. 1370–1353 B.C.) is related to the temple complex at Karnak, now Luxor in Egypt. The stones of the temple were later removed and used throughout the complex in other projects. Over 100,000 sandstone blocks c. two feet high and ten inches wide have been found from this temple. Of these, 35,000 are decorated. Decorated blocks may number as many as 85,000 with a total of 250,000 blocks for the whole temple. It is a huge jigsaw puzzle of inscriptions, reliefs, and decorations. These features have been analyzed and the analysis fed into a computer. The temple may never be rebuilt on the ground but it has been partially reconstructed on paper. Architectural style, reliefs and inscriptions are gradually becoming known.

The use of computers in connection with artifacts is probably the greatest breakthrough. The computer was first used in archaeology for the recording of both newly discovered artifacts and material in storage or musuems. A computer terminal (actually a terminal hooked up by telephone to the computer 300 miles away) was first taken into the field and used during the excavation itself in 1971. Using several hundred categories and descriptive terms, projects have recorded, or are in the process of recording, the thousands of artifacts that are being dug up. Computer graphics can generate a picture of what pottery looked like by using these categories. Computerized reports can be used to study items already known and to study material dug up daily. The material of the immediate excavation can be compared with that of others. Writing and publishing archaeological reports has the greatest failure rate of any portion of the archaeological enterprise. But computerized data can revolutionize this process and make it possible to produce reports in record time. In turn, archaeologists may have to think up new excuses for not publishing reports.[2]

## C.   WHEN DID IT HAPPEN?

The date of archaeological material and sites is of the greatest importance. Biblical archaeologists want to relate their findings to the Bible, but any digger wants some idea of how old the place or the piece might be. All too often, objects are found or stolen or dug up by *pothunters* and tomb robbers. They rip things out of their historical context. Their history may be lost forever, though new techniques now available may reverse that statement. Apart from coins and dated inscriptions, it was not until stratigraphic methods of digging were developed that archeaology came into its own in terms of modern science. The chronological framework put the study of ancient remains on a firm scientific basis. Petrie's discovery of pottery typology was a tremendous advance. With or without inscriptions and coins, strata could be dated by changes in pottery styles. Today, new methods of dating have been discovered. Electronics play an important part in this new age of archaeology.

### Atomic Energy

Carbon 14 is made in the upper atmosphere of the earth. Cosmic rays bombard nitrogen 14 with neutrons. The nitrogen 14 loses a proton and an electron and gains two neutrons and becomes carbon 14. In the atmosphere today, there is one atom of carbon 14 for every million atoms of ordinary carbon 12. The radioactive carbon 14 combines with oxygen like ordinary carbon and thus mixes throughout the atmosphere. All living things take in this radioactive carbon from the air and do so at approximately the same standard rate. When the organism dies, no more radioactive carbon is taken in. The carbon 14 in the dead organism continues to break down as it did when the organism was alive but it is no longer being replenished. This disintegration or decay of the radioactive carbon proceeds at a half life rate of 5,730 (plus or minus 40) years.

An earlier half life of 5,568 (plus or minus 30) years is still recognized and used but the longer figure is generally recognized as more accurate. The half life figure means that if there is a total of one ounce of carbon 14 in the organism at death, 5,730 years later there would remain only a half ounce. The other half ounce would have broken down to nitrogen 14. After another 5,730 years, there would a quarter ounce of carbon 14. After another 5,730 years there would be one-eighth of an ounce, and so on until it was all gone.

One could put it another way. One gram of modern carbon has sixty billion atoms of radiocarbon. There are fourteen atomic disintegrations per minute. A sample 5,730 years old has seven disintegrations per minute while one twice as old as that, 11,460 years, would have three and a half. Instruments are available which detect a single disintegrating atom. Older or earlier methods of checking the carbon

14 content took larger samples. New methods can date a single thread. A carbon 14 test costs over $200. In 1980, commercial labs did about $3 million worth of work and the business is growing.

Carbon 14 was discovered in the 1930s. Willard F. Libby (1908–1980) began experimenting with carbon 14 for dating purposes in 1948. For his work in discovering this atomic clock, he received the Nobel prize. The method is good for materials up to about 50,000 years old. Current improvements could push this back to 100,000 years. A main source of error in working with materials being tested is contamination of the sample by roots and other modern or newer material. The exact amount of carbon 14 has also been a problem. The original and continuing studies were carried out on organic materials of known date. These include wood, peat, skin, cloth, shell, bone, horn, charcoal and other sources of carbon. The date might be known from historical records. Libby worked with acacia wood from the tomb of Djoser at Sakkara, the stepped pyramid of Egypt, which dates from 2700 B.C. Other materials might be dated by pottery typology, coins, tree ring dating, inscriptions, or analysis of handwriting. The accuracy of the method has been widely accepted. Robert W. Erich edited a book, *Relative Chronologies in Old World Archaeology*; Chicago: University of Chicago, 1954. Carbon 14 dating spread so rapidly that in 1965, the book was re-issued as *Chronologies of Old World Archaeology*. The "relative" was dropped because carbon 14 had given scholars so much assurance that they were right in their dating.

However, as work continued, both Libby's own and that of others, some carbon 14 dates did not agree with dates that were quite well known. It turns out that the earth's magnetic field has varied in intensity from 0.5 to 1.5 times its present value. Part of this discovery came through the study of the magnetization of artifacts that had been fired, such as pottery, kilns, clay pipes, rocks subjected to heat, and materials affected by the fires of destruction when an enemy burned the city. If material is heated to high enough temperatures, its electrons become aligned with the earth's magnetic field. Under the high temperature conditions, the electrons are "free" or loose enough to turn so they are attracted to the "magnetic" of the north pole and line up with magnetic north (in the northern hemisphere). The artifact is then slightly magnetic, just as one can magnetize a piece of metal with a magnet.

The intensity of this magnetization implies variations in the earth's magnetization. When the earth's magnetization increases, cosmic ray activity decreases and produces less carbon 14. The reverse is also true. The carbon 14 dates back to the time of Jesus of Nazareth are quite accurate. From there on back, carbon 14 tends to give too late a date. By 5000 B.C. this may be as much as 800 years too late. That is, carbon 14 might indicate the artifact is from 4200 B.C. when it is actually from 5000 B.C. This variation has now been calibrated so correction factors can be applied to both old and new carbon 14 dates. The variation in magnetism has also been plotted over the centuries. Now archaeomagnetism is itself a source of dating.

Corrections in the dates from carbon 14 are continuing. One source of correction is tree ring dating, or "dendrochronology," on which more later. Here it can be said that carbon 14 remains accurate enough to be both an independent means of dating and supportive evidence for other means. A wooden beam from Mount Ararat was identified as part of Noah's ark. Carbon 14 tests dated it however to the seventh–eighth centuries A.D.[3]

There are several other radioactive procedures for dating ancient remains. The F-U-N tests apply more to prehistoric materials. However, the series is of interest. Bones accumulate fluorine from the surrounding soil. The amount of fluorine gives an estimate of how long the bone has been in the ground. Bones lose protein, and the quantity remaining gives an estimate of age. Carbon remains in the ratio of 2.5:1 in comparison to nitrogen. The nitrogen test on bones indicates whether there is enough carbon for a carbon 14 test. The latter of course could then give an absolute age, that is, a date on the calendar such as 20,000 B.C., as well as (or in addition to) the nitrogen test's relative age. Bone absorbs uranium from the soil as an oxide such as $U308$ at a steady rate. A test for the quantity in very old bones gives a relative age. The amino acids in bones change form with age, a process called racemization. This change is being tested for dating significance.

Uranium is the main ingredient in atomic energy. The breakdown or disintegration or fission of this radioactive material has a dateable by-product. Fission track dating of glass is an example of this technique. As fission occurs, two particles are released. These smash into the material around the uranium atom. In glass, these particles leave tracks which can be brought out by etching with hydrofluoric acid and then counted visually. The method is good for a range of from twenty years to millions of years, but it needs high uranium-content glass. Glass here means not only man-made glass but volcanic glass such as obsidian.

Of related interest is the potassium-argon test for rocks. Radioactive potassium 40 decays to argon. This gas is caught in the rock, and measurements of the quantity of argon give an age for the time when the rock was formed. This was the method that dated the prehistoric human remains of "Zinjanthropus" to 1,750,000 B.P. (Before the Present). Louis S.B. Leakey and his family discovered these remains in Olduvai Gorge in East Africa. The fission track dating method was applied to pumice from the same area with similar results. Another radioactive substance that helps with dating is ionium. This is produced through the radioactive decay of $U234$. Ionium has a half life of 80,000 years.

The most relevant (to biblical archaeology), and most fascinating of all the new methods of dating, is thermoluminescence dating of ceramics. The concept was suggested in 1953 by Farrington Daniels of the University of Wisconsin. The phenomenon itself was first observed by Robert Boyle in 1663. All natural clays have small amounts of radioactive substances such as uranium, thorium, etc. Radioactive particles, especially alpha particles, push the electrons of other materials slightly out of kilter to slightly unstable levels. When a clay pot is baked to harden it, the electrons fall back to their stable level and the process starts over again. The amount of the accumulated unstable electrons can be measured. This in turn gives an estimate of when the material was originally fired.

A bit of pottery is ground to a powder and put on a thin steel or graphite plate. When it is flash-heated up to 100 degrees Centigrade per second, the electrons fall back into place. When they do, they give off a tiny bit of light (photons). The process gets its name from this combination of heat (thermo-) and light (-luminescence). All clays vary in the rate at which the natural alpha particles bombard other substances. They vary in susceptibility to alpha bombardments. The procedure requires an artificial bombardment to determine the susceptibility of each sample. This plus other correction factors gives the date of the pottery, or at least when it was made, with a reliability of plus or minus 300 years. This may be made as accurate as 100 years with further experimentation.

This means that thermoluminescence will probably never be a serious contender or competitor in biblical archaeology. Pottery typology can usually give a date to within 100 years and even less. But thermoluminescence, like carbon 14, is a very important external check on typology, and in those places where pottery typology is less defined, may provide new chronological pegs. Typologically dated potsherds or sherds dated by other means are being used to refine the method, but it is already accurate enough to detect museum forgeries while confirming the dates of other items where there was some doubt. Besides pottery, the method has been applied to glass, volcanic ash, slag from smelting metals, and burned flint.[4]

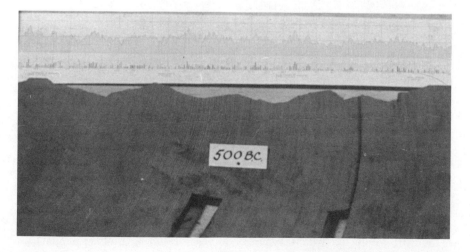

**Figure 6–1.**   Cross section showing tree rings that extend from 1100 B.C. to 1927 A.D. Photo courtesy Dr. Henry N. Michael.

**Figure 6–2.**    Portion of a bristle cone pine cross section of tree rings, magnified 20 times. There are 10 rings, hence 10 years, between the dots. Photo courtesy Dr. Henry N. Michael.

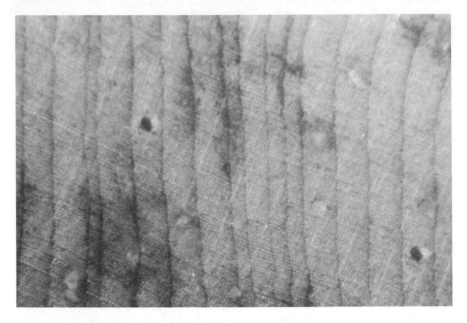

## Tree Rings and Volcanic Ash

Dendrochronology, the study of tree rings for dating purposes, was mentioned earlier. Tree rings were known in Aristotle's time. Leonardo da Vinci suggested they were growth rings. Using them as a method for dating was suggested in 1811 by DeWitt Clinton, builder of the Erie Canal. The method was developed (1904) by Andrew E. Douglas for the American southwest. Douglas was an astronomer who studied sunspots. He was looking for evidence of them in the growth record of trees. Each year of its life, a tree and some shrubs will add cells around the circumference of its trunk. This new layer of cells is called a growth ring. In dry years, the ring will be thin and in wet years it will be wide. By correlating the pattern of the rings of a series of trees, dendrochronologists obtain a floating chronology. This is like Petrie's floating chronology with pottery. He developed his sequence dating (S.D.) with changes in pottery styles. Eventually his S.D. changed from a *relative dating* (which one is older and which is younger) to *absolute dating* (on the calendar), by relating an S.D. with a dated event such as the destruction of a building dated by an inscription or the name of a known pharaoh.

**Figure 6–3.**   Drawing of tree rings by Kathleen Rogers illustrating how three different tree ring patterns are matched to give a continuous record longer than a single tree. Photo courtesy, Dr. Henry N. Michael.

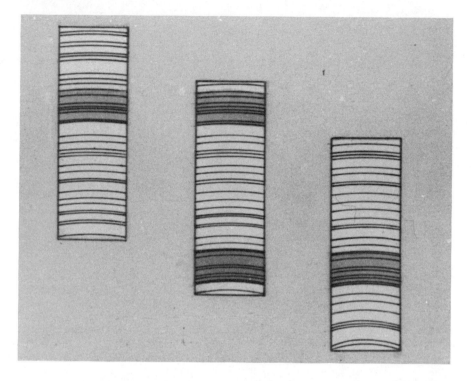

The floating chronology of the tree rings begins as a relative chronology. More recent rings could be dated to known events. Others have been dated by carbon 14, pottery typology, and other forms. Earlier we noted that dendrochronology is being used to correct carbon 14 dates. Some devotees claim an accuracy for tree rings to within a year. Others are more modest and suggest the method is accurate to within ten per cent. Charles Wesley Ferguson and his associates at the University of Arizona, with Henry N. Michael, have established a continuous chronology of over 8,200 years and floating chronology of 3,000 more which will eventually take us back to 9000 B.C. Some of the work has been done on the giant Sequoia or redwood trees of California. The longer work has been done on the bristlecone pine of the American southwest, especially found in eastern California's White Mountains.

Dendrochronology is now being used throughout the world, including the Near East. Bryant Bannister of the Laboratory of Tree Ring Research at the University of

**Figure 6–4.** Bristle cone pine growing on the upper mountain slopes. While they look dead, these trees are still very much alive and are as old as 4000 years. Photo courtesy Dr. Henry N. Michael.

Arizona has established a chronology for the Anatolian plateau. The Turkish area now has a floating chronology of over 800 years. Eventually it will be correlated with dated artifacts and historical events. Samples have also been collected in Egypt and Lebanon. The transport of logs in ancient commerce cautions researchers. The tree ring date is the time when the tree was cut down. The carbon 14 date marks the death of the tree also. In these drier areas of the world, a log might be preserved and be reused many times. Thus the date of the log might be older than the context in which it is found.

An interesting correlation of tree rings has been noted. Thin rings represent dry years. That probably meant a lower crop yield and even crop failure. There were thin rings in periods in which the Greeks pushed for independence, for example in the years 632–510 B.C. There were more Christian martyrs in the dry years of the second century A.D. than at other times. It may all be a coincidence, or it may mean that less food or lack of it stirred social unrest. Research continues.[5]

Pollen analysis *(palynology)* is another field developing in the Near East. Plants release thousands of pollen grains, the male part of the flower. These pollen grains fall as "rain" in the vicinity of the flower tree or plant, usually within a mile or two though sometimes the wind might carry the pollen for some distance. The cell wall of the pollen grain is quite resistant to decay. It lasts for centuries, especially in acidic soils since other soils encourage earthworms. Lake bottoms and bogs are also good preservation areas since the decay bacteria need oxygen.

Pollen grains are almost as distinctive as snowflakes in their variety of size, shape or structure. That means that the different species of plants can be identified. Pollen found in a dated context can tell us what kind of plants were growing in that time. In turn, as studies accumulate, paleobotanists develop pollen zones with details on the geographic spread and the duration of a given species. The chronology is first set by other means such as pottery or carbon 14. Then, the pollen analysis can itself be a form of dating. Though the time zone covers several thousand years, some of these can be subdivided in order to date a particular sample. The pollen grains or husks of the Turin shroud have been studied. They reflect Palestine and Turkey as well as medieval Europe.

*Obsidian dating* was developed several decades ago. Obsidian is a form of volcanic glass. One might ask what it has to do with the Bible apart from Sodom and Gomorrah. But artifacts are made from obsidian. Whenever a break exposes a fresh surface to the air, the obsidian starts absorbing moisture into the new surface. This process is called hydration. The rate of the hydration is more or less steady in a given area with the same climate. Humidity does not affect the rate. Chemical composition and temperature does. Cold slows and heat speeds the rate of hydration. By determining the rate and measuring the hydration layer, the approximate date when the artifact was chipped can be determined. Research continues here also. The hydration layer varies from 10 – 1000 millionths of an inch. The method has been used on objects dating from 1500 A.D. to an estimated 30,000 B.C.

Obsidian from Egyptian mummies and dated by Egyptian records has been used as a control in the hydration experiments. Since there is no natural obsidian in the Fertile Crescent, obsidian artifacts suggest trade or some kind of contact with Turkey or the Greek island of Melos where obsidian is found. This trade was in process as early as the eighth millennium B.C. Dates for these artifacts help us see patterns of commerce. Exact sources of obsidian are now being determined by X-ray analysis, which shows that different sources have different trace elements (rubidium, strontium, zirconium, etc.). By checking the artifacts and matching the trace elements, we can tell where the obsidian came from among the several known deposits.[6]

## D.   WHAT IS IT?

Obsidian hydration analysis means using a microscope. The microscope is not especially new to the archaeological world. It has been used to study small things such as coins and inscriptions. What is new is the extent and the variety of materials being used in microscopic studies and the way in which these are prepared. The microscopes themselves have become much more sophisticated. The electron microscope gives far greater and clearer resolution than anything dreamed of years ago. Microscopic analysis of stone can tell us something of its composition and perhaps where it came from, whether it was in the area or from a distance. Microscopic study of pottery may help us locate the clay beds used by the potter or it may tell something of how the pot was manufactured. The techniques of pottery manufacture are also being studied in a macroscopic way. We can go to a modern potter and watch and see how pottery is made today. Present methods can then be compared to what we know of ancient methods. The finished product of the modern potter can be studied under the microscope and the findings compared to ceramics of known ancient periods.

As with obsidian, microscopic study of glass is a means of dating by hydration. The method as applied to glass is disputed and needs further refinement, however, while obsidian is much more widely accepted. The study of metals under the microscope may give us clues to the source of ores and to methods of manufacture. The analysis of teeth has been used to compare ancient and modern sheep as well as human beings.

Perhaps the most important advance in microscopic study is the development of the thin section. A piece of the object is cut with a fine saw and then polished to sliver thinness. The finest particles in bone, rock, or pottery can then be examined.

One result in pottery analysis has been an increased interest in temper. Temper, such as straw (Exodus 5:15–18), sand, or ground up materials such as rock, shell or old pottery, is mixed into clay to bind it together. This prevents cracking in the dried and fired vessel. A pot from Gezer was found to have granules of basalt for temper. There is no natural basalt in that area. Perhaps the basalt was imported in the form of a bowl which was broken and then smashed for use in pottery. More likely, since basalt is a hard rock and it seems foolish to grind up basalt when there is so much sand around, the pottery itself was imported from a basalt area. The clay that the pot was made from had the trace element titanium. This makes it comparable to the soil of Galilee which is a basalt region.

Some of these materials can be used for *spectrographic analysis*. A substance is put between two electrodes, usually graphite. The material is ignited by a spark. The electrons of the electric discharge collide with the atoms of the element in the material being tested. This produces light. Since each element like iron, hydrogen, etc., has a place in the spectrum of light which is characteristic of that element in any combination or compound, the light given off tells us what elements are in the sample. This qualitative (what is there) test may also yield a quantitative (how much is there) analysis given by the intensity of the light in that portion of the spectrum. The method has been used on glass to determine composition, manufacturing process, and origins of materials. It has also been used on pottery and metal.

Spectrographic analysis is but one of several types of analyses that involve electronic studies. These range from lead and oxygen isotope studies, beta-ray backscatter detectors, neutron activation, and neutron absorption radiography, to the X-ray studies cited earlier. Some studies can be done on minute samples (microanalysis). Some can use a scraping, as off the bottom of a pottery vessel. If it is a valued museum piece, the less damage the better. Some forms of study are nondestructive and can be carried out on the item itself.

An electron micro-analyzer can study an area as small as 0.001 millimeter in diameter. Each layer of paint in a painting can be analyzed. The instrument can identify elements such as copper, iron, chloride, silicon, etc. In turn, these may give clues to the sources of the pigments and even the technique(s) of the artist. Sometimes elements or compounds can be found this way that have a known history of use. If the element was not used in painting before a certain date and the painting is claimed to be older, one can suspect it is a fake.

A portable field system for X-ray fluorescence spectrography can analyze metals, glass, glazed ceramics, and mineral specimens for elements in the periodic table above calcium. The fluorescence refers to the secondary X-rays excited out of the elements by a radioactive source. A new proton microprobe (non-portable) induces the emission of X-rays. It has a very sharp focus and can detect trace-trace elements.

Neutron activation involves neutron bombardment in an atomic reactor or from some other source of neutrons. The neutrons form radioactive isotopes with a half life unique to each element. In disintegrating to stable levels, the isotopes emit gamma rays at levels of energy special to each element. By reading this resultant radiation, the presence and quantity of the elements in the material can be known. This includes trace-trace elements. These and the trace elements cited earlier give a "fingerprint" profile which helps determine the origin of the material. The chemical profile or fingerprint analogy is the idea that trace elements are different in different places, just as the fingerprints of people differ. This has been used on metal, glass and pottery. One example is Palestinian bichrome (two colors) pottery. It is found in Palestine but it was made in Cyprus.

By way of contrast, Mycenean (Greek) style and Philistine pottery from Ashdod were both made locally rather than abroad. This fact together with the above methods and thermoluminescence can also be used to detect fakes. The appearance of copper arsenite in a painting, for example, means it was made after 1814 A.D. when this material came into use.

The techniques discussed here can be applied to metals. Measuring the specific gravity of an object can show which metals are present, since each retains its weight and displacement of water no matter what chemical combination it is in. A wide variety of chemical tests can be used on metals. High energy X-rays have revealed construction methods and modern repairs, the interlocking of part-iron, part-bronze weapons, and so forth. Electron microprobe studies have shown that an iron sword was made of meteoric iron. The same means can identify nonmetallic inclusions which identify the smelting process. Fingerprinting trace elements can lead to the source of the ore since ore bodies may be different from one region to another in these minute quantities of rare elements.

Metallurgy probably began with the use of naturally appearing or native copper. In some areas, copper appears as nodules in the vein of ore. This was hammered with stone tools into desired forms. One theory is that people in Iran discovered the process of smelting. It spread from there throughout the Near East. The people of Europe and Palestine were smelting copper as early as 4000 B.C. By 2500, the process was known throughout the Fertile Crescent and had spread to China, India and Southeast Asia.

As the use of copper spread, the area moved from the Stone Age to the *Chalco-lithic* (*chalco* = copper, *lithos* = stone) Age. In biblical areas, this is dated 4500–3300 B.C., though the limits are disputed. With the discovery of alloys, perhaps from natural mixes found in natural ores, the Bronze Age began. Culturally it is divided into EB, MB and LB: Early (3300–2000), Middle (2000–1500), and Late (1500–1200) Bronze.

Iron was used in natural and meteorite form. It was hammered into shapes at an early date. Smelting of iron may have originated in Turkey and been brought into Palestine by the Philistines (I Samuel 13:19ff). The Philistines were part of the "Sea Peoples." These may have helped bring down the Hittite Empire, c. 1200. They may have thus acquired the secrets of iron work. An alternate view comes from LB artifacts at Timnah at the Arabah between the Dead Sea and the Gulf of Eilat. The iron has a high copper content. A series of experiments show this iron came as a by-product of the copper smelting process which used an iron-oxide as one of the fluxes. Thus the discovery of iron smelting may have been an accident in the Egyptian copper mining and smelting operations here c. 1300–1150. An LB iron smelter is reported from Tel Yin'am southwest of the Sea of Galilee. This dates from before the Philistine arrival so it also raises a question about the origins of iron smelting. The earliest steel in the Near East has been found in Cyprus (Idalion), Palestine (Ta'anach), and Jordan (Baq'ah Valley). The last in the form of jewelry was found in a tomb dated c. 1200–1050. It was probably made in the area. Iron deposits were found less than ten miles away.[7]

The new processes described in this chapter continue to illuminate the development of ancient technology. A useful by-product for today is the modern exploitation of ancient ore beds and slag heaps. Primitive methods extracted only a portion of the metals. More metal can be obtained with modern techniques.

Chemists are involved in a number of the things described so far. This is a specific category of analysis in itself, however. Near Eastern and Palestinian archaeology has not made very full use of these newer methods. Too often we rely on visual observation alone, just looking at things to see what they are made of. That introduces a high degree of error. Sometimes it is hard to tell the difference between hard limestone, marble, alabaster, and similar stones. While archaeologists neglect the possibilities of chemistry and physics in the field, chemists and physicists continue to make their contribution in the lab.

Joseph V. Noble of the New York Metropolitan Museum of Art discovered the long lost formula for Egyptian blue faience after analyzing Egyptian natron by X-ray diffraction. It has at least a dozen substances in it. Experimenting with sand and copper, he produced blue faience with eighty-five percent sand, two percent copper, and thirteen percent natron. Frans Bruin and his coworkers at the American University of Beirut reproduced the famous royal purple of the Phoenicians. They followed the description of ancient writers such as Pliny and the 1907 effort of Paul Friedlander. They extracted .1 milligram from each animal — the sea snail called *murex trunculus*. The small amount accounts for the great mounds of shell heaps at Phoenician dye works on Mediterranean shores, and the cost of the "royal" purple. Bruin estimated one gram of dye as worth 10–20 grams of gold. They also found the murex dye is the chemical equal of a synthetic purple dye developed by German chemists in 1900!

Pottery typology continues its major importance for dating. Thermoluminescence has added new dimensions to this. The chemical and physical examinations described here have carried our concern with old pots far beyond the simple question of how old it is. We are dealing with questions of composition and the origins of clay, the origin of the pottery itself, who made it, and when and how was it made. Experiments with modern clay in firing techniques help show how ancient pottery was made. All of these concerns are set in the larger context of the aesthetics (decoration), the economic and technological development, and the sociological and psychological perspectives of entire cultures.

Organic materials and soils are another whole frontier of archaeological investigation. Pollen analysis was cited earlier for dating purposes. It can tell us what was growing when. The study of plant remains (*paleobotany*) is a larger picture of which pollen is a part. The origins of palaeobotany go back to the last century. The concern did not really catch on in archaeology until the 1950s. Some excavators however, have not yet discovered the importance of knowing what plants were around, were being farmed, or were used for food.

Similar studies are continuing for animal remains. *Paleozoologists* study the ancient fauna just as paleobotanists study the ancient flora. It is a question of the culture and economy in any period. For an earlier time, the date when animals and plants were domesticated is of interest. The current theory is that people settled down and built permanent dwellings before the domestication of livestock, rather than vice-versa. Perhaps the most fascinating new developments, however, are in the study of human skeletons. Simple observation, microscopic examination, X-ray studies, chemical tests, and other methods are applied in skeletal analyses. We learn about age, sex, cause of death, presence of disease, the practice of medicine, and diet. Related studies identify hair, skin, blood, leather, parchment, and fabrics. Source and method of manufacture and the date are but samples of the wealth of new information now available.

Aiding in these studies are flotation processes which recover major amounts of organic materials. A water separation technique separates soil from organic particles which tend to be lighter so they float. Chemicals like terpinol make the water froth and increase the separation of dirt and organic materials. Kerosene coats charcoal and helps it float. More seeds, nuts, bone fragments, charcoal, and other materials are being found and studied. The method was used at Gezer for a closely dated sequence of strata ranging from Late Chalcolithic to the Roman period. Up to a ton of dirt can be processed per day.

Soils are interesting in themselves. They are studied to determine crop areas, rates of erosion, how long a site was occupied or unoccupied, the effects of different soil types on corrosion and the preservation of artifacts such as fabrics, ceramics, glass, and metals. The preservation of pollen grains or husks in acid soil and under anerobic conditions was discussed earlier. The analysis of acidity, texture, organic and inorganic content, and color may tell us about the origin of soil, conditions and climate, and sometimes its date.

For several decades now, desert regions in the Near East have been studied to understand ancient soil engineering practices such as irrigation. In the southern desert of Palestine, the Negev, there are Nabataean remains which show the area was intensely cultivated. Rain averages less than four inches a year. By using terraces and small dams, water diversion and runoff channels, the Nabataeans sustained a considerable agriculture of grain and fruit for centuries. With the use of modern machinery, parts of the ancient system have been rebuilt and are in use today.[8]

## E.   MODERN MACHINERY

The use of earth moving machinery such as bulldozers is still a rare event in archaeology. In some cases, a bulldozer can be used to strip off disturbed topsoil. Modern transportation brings archaeologists and their supplies to a dig. Helicopters have been used at Masada and Petra. Masada is on a high plateau. Similarly at Petra, Umm el Biyara ("mother of cisterns") is a high plateau. Both are like the mesa in the western U.S. Umm el Biyara is identified by some as biblical Sela (I Kings 13:7; II Chronicles 25:11) but the date of excavated remains is a century later than the conquest described in the Bible.

Reconstruction, for study and for purposes of tourism, is more common today. It is also a way of consolidating the ruins to preserve them from time, the elements and vandalism. A unique bit of reconstruction was the well-publicized engineering feat at Abu Simbel in Egypt. The massive project cost over thirty-six million dollars and took five years. The statues of Ramses II (c. 1290–1224) and Queen Nefertari were moved from the base of the cliff to the top in order to escape the rising flood water of the Aswan High Dam. The move of over 200 feet was done by cutting the whole creation into over 1,000 blocks weighing 20–30 tons each. Some 300,000 tons of overlying rock were also moved. The temples were rebuilt under a rein-forced concrete dome which was then covered with sand and rock to resemble the natural surroundings of the area. The main statues were reassembled in front of the temples.

A less publicized but still monumental feat was the dismantling of the ancient buildings on the island of Philae in the Nile. The buildings were partially sub-merged by the 1902 dam but they stood out of the water at least part of the year. With the high dam, they would have been permanently submerged. Between 1972 and 1979 the Philae temples were taken apart. Over 37,000 blocks of stone were laid on the river bank. The island of Agilkia 1,000 feet downstream was rebuilt in the shape of Philae. Then the Philae structures were reconstructed on Agilkia. They are now in better condition than before the dams were built.[9]

## F.   TO BE CONTINUED. . .

The descriptions given thus far are only sketches of what is happening, but it is nec-essary to note that this is an expanding area of concern. The quantity and complex-ity of the data, the methods and types of application and potential application, are all part of this. But so is the rapidity of the advance. An article or book on the sub-jects is obsolete before it is published. Research now in the very early experimental stages may be established and methods now undreamed will show up on the archaeological horizon. This could be an argument for saving everything found in an excavation. Something may appear worthless today but be valuable tomorrow. Cremation remains and a good many things like bones and "extra" potsherds have been thrown away. Now there are ways of analyzing cremation remains and bones and sherds. In Near Eastern excavations such quantities of things are found it is impractical to save it all merely on the chance it might some day be useful. But the temptation is surely there, or should be.

And perhaps the point needs to be made again and again that a number of procedures described here are frequently so complex and time consuming and so expensive that they are not entered into lightly for every scrap of material that is dug up. But biblical archaeologists or Syro-Palestinian archaeologists or archaeologists anywhere in the world have at hand research tools that tantalize the mind with their possibilities. We are in a revolution like the Petrie-Fisher-Albright one which changed archaeology from a treasure hunt into a science.

A closing word might be tossed into the dog fight of dogma in the "new archaeology." On the one hand, one can close the mind to new developments and refuse to change. In his later years the innovative and imaginative Petrie became immune to change. The same has happened to others. Archaeologists who grew up in the field during Petrie's older years saw his ossification and inability to swing with the time. In the midst of the revolution of the 1960s and 1970s, these same figures had ossified in their own way.

A parallel phenomenon was cited earlier. We tend to think our way is best. Thus we look back on predecessors as contemptible examples of incompetence. The writings of Sir Mortimer Wheeler are touched with his superior attitude toward others. But time has its own way of dealing with our human pride. We might look with some humility upon the work of those who have gone before us. Careful reading of the literature will tell us that excavations that are now condemned were praised in their own day as the very best and latest thing in science. A little knowledge of history should perhaps suggest to us that what we consider the "best and the brightest" may some day be seen with loathing as total incompetence by our successors. Actually we all build on the work of those who have gone before, and their contributions could also be appreciated rather than condemned. Similarly, our own work might be presented with at least a tad of reserve.

On the one hand, we should keep an open mind to new developments in this great discipline called archaeology. On the other hand, we might do better than to declare our own work as the great Law of the Medes and Persians that changeth not regardless of conditions in the field or new discoveries in the laboratory. "New" archaeologists and "old" ones alike have much to learn. We may even have much to learn from each other![10]

# NOTES

1. John Badekas, ed., *Photogrammetric Surveys of Monuments and Sites* (New York: American Elsevier, 1975). Thomas W. Beale, "ASOR to Introduce New Photogrammetric Recording and Mapping System for Field Archaeologists and Epigraphists," ASORN no. 7 (May 82), pp. 1–3. Bruce Bevan, *Stereo Photography for the Archaeologist* (Philadelphia: University Museum, 1973).

Robert S. Bianchi, "Egyptian Mummies: Myth and Reality," *Archaeology* 35, no. 2 (Mar./Ap. 84), pp. 18–25. Virginia Bortin, "Science and the Shroud of Turin," BA 43, no. 2 (Spr. 80), pp. 109–117. CHP, pp. 413–415. V.M. Conlon, *Camera Techniques in Archaeology* (London: Baker, 1973). Maurice B. Cookson, *Photography for Archaeologists* (London: Parrish, 1954). A.R. David, "The Manchester Mummy Project," *Archaeology* 38, no. 6 (Nov./Dec. 85), pp. 40–47. Lee Edson, "Box Cameras were Never Like This," *Popular Mechanics* 126, no. 1 (July 66), pp. 66–69, 171–173. Elmer Harp, Jr., ed., *Photography in Archaeological Research* (Albuquerque: University of New Mexico, 1975). James E. Harris and Kent R. Weeks, *X-Raying the Pharaohs* (New York: Scribner's, 1973). R.G. Harrison and A.B. Abdalla, "The Remains of Tutankhamun," *Antiquity* 46, no. 181 (1972), pp. 8–14. Ethel S. Hirsch, "Infrared Photography and Archaeology," *Archaeology* 28, no. 4 (Oct. 75), pp. 260–266. *Infrared and Ultraviolet Photography* (Rochester, NY: Eastman Kodak Publication M–3, 1963). David H.O. John, *Photography on Expeditions* (New York: Focal, 1965). Sharon S. McKern, "Radiography: new tool for retrieving the wealth of the pharaohs," *Science Digest* 68 (July 70), pp. 8–13. Sidney K. Matthews, *Photography in Archaeology and Art* (London: Baker, 1969). "New Scientific Techniques to Measure Scroll Deterioration," BAR VII, no. 4 (July/Aug. 81), p. 48. "Newbriefs: Egyptian Mummy Undergoes Tests at Mayo Clinic," *Archaeology* 37, no. 1 (Jan./Feb. 84), p. 78 (CAT scan - Computerized Axial Tomography). Peter J. Parr, et al., "Photogrammetric Work at Petra, 1965–1968," ADAJ 20 (1975), pp 31–46. Samuel Pellicori with Mark S. Evans, "The Shroud of Turin Through the Microscope," *Archaeology* 34, no. 1 (Jan./Feb. 81), pp. 34–43. "Physics: Peering into the Pyramids," *Time* 89 (6 Jan. 67), p. 84. SBAF, p. 89. "Seeing Through the Pyramid," *New York Times* (17 Feb. 74), p. E14. A sealed chamber has been found in front of the pyramid. Farouk El-Baz, a space scientist, headed a research team to drill through the wall and photograph the interior and collect air to test its chemical compostion and compare it to today's atmosphere. Katie Tyndall, "Secrets of Old Air," *Insight* 2, no. 30 (28 July 86), p. 55. Dodo J. Shenhav, "Saving the Dead Sea Scrolls for the Next 2000 Years," BAR 7, no. 4 (July/Aug. 81), pp. 44–47, 49. Harold C. Simmons, *Archaeological Photography* (New York: NYU, 1969). Carl H. Strandberg, "Photoarchaeology," *Photogrammetric Engineering* 33, no. 10 (Oct. 67), pp. 1152–1157. Michael J. Walker, "Seeing the Unseen with Infrared," SN 90 (8 Oct 66), pp. 273–274. Stephen Weiner, et al., "Dead Sea Scroll Parchments: Unfolding of the Collagen Molecules and Racemization of Aspartic Acid," *Nature* 287 (30 Oct. 80), p. 820.

2. J. Barto Arnold III, "Archaeological Application of Computer Graphics," SAAMT 5 (1982), pp. 179–216, has an extensive bibliography, but primarily concerned with archaeology in the U.S. E.A. Bowles, ed., *Computers in Humanistic Research, Readings and Perspectives* (Englewood Cliffs: Prentice-Hall, 1967). Paul Buckland, "An Experiment in the Use of a Computer for On-Site Recording of Finds," *Scientific Archaeology* 9 (Jan. 73), pp. 22–24. D.F. Chantrey, et al., "The Sorting of Archaeological Materials by Computer and by Man: An Interdisciplinary Study in Pottery Classifications," *Scientific Archaeology* 14 (1975), pp. 5–31. *Computers in Anthropology and Archaeology* (White Plains, NY: IBM, 1971). "Computers Reconstruct the Appearance of an Egyptian Temple," *Archaeology* 22 (June 69), pp. 229–230. Martha Joukowsky, *A Complete Manual of Field Archaeology* (Englewood Cliffs: Prentice-Hall, 1980), pp. 297–303; and, "Computer Use in Pottery Studies at Aphrodisias," *Journal of Field Archaeology* 5, no. 4 (1978), pp. 431–432. James R. Kautz, "Tracking the Ancient Moabites," BA 44, no. 1 (Wint. 81), pp. 27–35. Susan Laflin, ed., *Computer Applications in Archaeology* (Birmingham: University of Birmingham, 1978). Paul S. Martin, "Trash and Computers = Archaeology," *Archaeology* 17 (Spr. 64), pp. 133–135. *Newsletter of Computer Archaeology, 1965–1979.* (Tempe: Department of Anthropology, Arizona State University). Donald B. Redford, "The Akhenaten Temple Project and Karnak Excavations," *Expedition* 21, no. 2 (Wint. 79), pp. 54–59. M. Rimon, "Appendix: Design of a Computer Program, Establishing the Family Relations of Individuals in the Jericho Tomb," BASOR 235 (Sum.

79), pp. 71–73. Irwin Schollar and F. Krickeberg, "Computer Treatment of Magnetic Measurements from Archaeological Sites," *Archaeometry* 9 (1966), pp. 61–71. Ray W. Smith, "Computer Helps Scholars Re-create an Egyptian Temple," NG 138, no. 5 (May 70), pp. 134–155. Smith and Redford, *The Akhenaton Temple Project, Vol 1, Initial Discoveries* (Warminster, England: Aris and Phillips, 1976). James F. Strange, "Recent Computer Applications in ANE Archaeology," (pp. 129–146 in *The Answers Lie Below* ed. Henry O. Thompson; Washington: UPA, 1984). John D. Wilcock, "A General Survey of Computer Applications in Archaeology," *Scientific Archaeology* 9 (Jan. 73), pp. 17–21.

3. J.R. Arnold and Willard F. Libby, "Age Determination by Radiocarbon Content: Checks with Samples of Known Age," *Science* 110 (1949), pp. 678–680. Lloyd R. Bailey, "Wood from 'Mount Ararat': Noah's Ark?," BA 40, no. 4 (Dec. 77), pp. 137–146. David L. Browman, "Isotopic Discrimination and Correction Factors in Radiocarbon Dating," SAAMT 4 (1981), pp. 241–295. Richard Burleigh, "W.F. Libby and the development of radiocarbon dating," *Antiquity* 55, no. 214 (July 81), pp. 96–98. Joseph A. Callaway and James M. Weinstein, "Radiocarbon Dating of Palestine in the Early Bronze Age," BASOR 225 (Feb. 77), pp. 1–16. John B. Carlson and Barbara Collins, "Advances in New World Archaeology in 1980," *Early Man* 3, no. 1 (Spr. 81), pp. 3–14. CHP, pp. 404–406. R.M. Clark and Colin Renfrew, "Tree-ring Calibration of Radiocarbon Dates and the Chronology of Ancient Egypt," *Nature* 243 (1973), pp. 266–270. "A Clay Pipe Cinch," *Discover* 2, no. 4 (Ap. 81), p. 11. G.H. Curtis, "A Clock for the Ages: Potassium-Argon," NG 120, no. 4 (Oct. 61), pp. 590–592. Willy Dyck, "Recent Development in Radiocarbon Dating" *Current Anthropology* 8, no. 4 (Oct. 67), pp. 349–351. "Ionium in Igneaous Rocks," SN 91 (3 June 67), p. 524. John S. Kopper and Kenneth M. Greer, "Paleomagnetic Dating and Stratigraphic Interpretation in Archaeology," MASCAN 12, no. 1 (June 76), pp. 1–3. Willard F. Libby, *Radiocarbon Dating* (Chicago: University of Chicago, 1952). Libby, et al., "Age Determination by Radiocarbon Content: World-Wide Assay of Natural Radiocarbon," *Science* 109 (4 Mar 49), pp. 227–228. Henry N. Michael, "Correcting Radiocarbon Dates with Tree Ring Dates at MASCA," University Museum Newsletter 23, no. 3 (Wint. 84–5), pp. 1–2. Evzen Heustupny, "A New Epoch in Radiocarbon Dating," *Antiquity* 44, no. 173 (Mar. 70), pp. 38–45. "Radiocarbon Dating Questioned," SN 92 (29 July 67), p. 119. Elizabeth K. Ralph, et al., "Radiocarbon Dates and Reality," MASCAN 9, no. 1 (Aug. 73), pp. 1–20. Robert Stuckenrath, "On the Care and Feeding of Radiocarbon Dates," *Archaeology* 18 (Spr. 65), p. 278. R.E. Taylor and Rainer Berger, "The Date of 'Noah's Ark'," *Antiquity* 54, no. 210 (Mar. 80), pp. 34–36. Gary A. Wright, "Bristlecone Pine Calibrations of Radiocarbon Dates: Some Examples from the Near East," AJA 77, no. 2 (1973), pp. 197–201. Frederick E. Zeuner, *Dating the Past — An Introduction to Geochronology* (London: Methuen, 1964).

4. Martin Aitken, "Thermoluminescence and the Archaeologist," Antiquity 51, no. 21 (Mar. 77), pp. 11–19; and, "Dating by Archaeomagnetic and Thermoluminescent Methods" (pp. 77–88 in The Impact of the Natural Sciences on Archaeology, ed. T.E. Allibone, et al.; London: Oxford, 1970). "A Bone to Pick: How to Date Bones," SN 120, no. 10 (5 Sep. 81), p. 151. Gary W. Carriveau, "Dating of 'Phoenician' Slag from Iberia using Thermoluminescence Techniques," MASCAN 10, no. 1 (July 74), pp. 1–2. G. Brent Dalrymple and Mason A. Lamphere, *Potassium Argon Dating: Principles, Techniques and Applications to Geochronology* (San Francisco: Freeman, 1970). Farrington Daniels, et al., "Thermoluminescence as a Research Tool," *Science* 117 (1953), pp. 343–349. Stuart Fleming reviews the early history of thermoluminescence in, *Thermoluminescence Techniques in Archaeology* (Oxford: Oxford University, 1979). Paul W. Levy, *Physical Principles of Thermoluminescence and Recent Developments in its Measurements* (Upton, NY: Brookhaven National Laboratory, 1974). Michael, "Correcting Dates." Elizabeth K. Ralph and Mark C. Han, "Dating of Pottery by Thermoluminescence," *Nature* 210 (1966), pp. 245–247. I. Skupinska-Lovst and Stuart J. Fleming, "A Scythian Figurine from Beth Shean," MASCAJ 1,

no. 3 (Dec. 79), pp. 76–77. The figurine is dressed in a Parthian or Partho-Roman style but the thermoluminescent dating of c. 110 years shows it to be a fake made in the last century. D.W. Zimmerman and J. Huxtable, "Thermoluminescent Dating of Upper Palaeolithic Fired Clay from Dolni Vestonice," *Archaeometry* 13 (1971), pp. 53–58. The oldest known clay objects are dated by thermoluminescence to an average of 35,600 B.P., and by related carbon 14 to c. 29,000 B.P.

5.  James F. Trefil, "Concentric clues from growth rings unlock the past," *Smithsonian* 16, no. 4 (July 85), pp. 46–57. A. Fahn, et al., "Dendrochronological Studies in the Negev," IEJ 13, no. 4 (1963), pp. 291–299. Nili Liphschitz and Yoav Waisel, "Dendroarchaeological Investigations in Israel (Taanach)," IEJ 30, nos. 1–2 (1980), pp. 132–136. Thomas H. Maugh II, "Tree Talk," *Science* 81, Vol. 2, no. 5 (June 81), pp. 68–70.

6.  Vaughn M. Bryant, Jr., and Richard G. Holloway, "The Role of Palynology in Archaeology," SAAMT 6 (1983), pp. 191–224. J.E. Dixon, et al., "Obsidian and the Origins of Trade," SA 218, no. 3 (Mar. 68), pp. 38–46. Stuart J. Fleming, *Dating in Archaeology* (New York: St. Martins, 1976). Irving I. Friedman and Robert L. Smith, "A New Dating Method Using Obsidian, Part I: The Development of the Method," AA 25 (1960), pp. 476–522. Freidman and W. Long, "Hydration Rate of Obsidian," *Science* 191 (1976), pp. 347–352. James Mellaart, *Earliest Civilizations of the Near East* (New York: McGraw-Hill, 1965). Henry N. Michael and Elizabeth K. Ralph, eds., *Dating Techniques for the Archaeologist* (Cambridge, MA: MIT, 1971). Joseph W. Michels, *Dating Methods in Archaeology* (New York: Seminar, 1973), and, "Archeology and Dating by Hydration of Obsidian," *Science* 158 (1967), pp. 211–214. Michels and Ignatius S.T. Tsong, "Obsidian Hydration Dating: A Coming of Age," SAAMT 3 (1980), pp. 405–444. Isadore Perlman and Joseph Yellin, "The Provenience of Obsidian from Neolithic Sites in Israel," IEJ 30, nos. 1–2 (1980), pp. 83–88. R.E. Taylor, ed., *Advances in Obsidian Glass Studies* (Park Ridge, NJ: Noyes, 1976). Gary A. Wright and Adon A. Gordus, "Distribution and Utilization of Obsidian from Lake Van Sources Between 7500 and 3500 B.C.," AJA 73, no. 1 (Jan. 69), pp. 75–77.

7.  "The Arabah Project," IAMSN 1 (1980), pp. 3–4. Michal Artzy, et al., "The Origin of the 'Palestinian' Bichrome Ware," JAOS 93 (1973), pp. 446–461; and, "The Tel Nagila Bichrome Krater as a Cypriote Product," IEJ 25, nos. 2–3 (1975), pp. 129–134, and, "Cypriote Pottery Imports at Ras Shamra," IEJ 31, nos. 1–2 (1981), pp. 37–47. Philip P. Betancourt, et al., "New Analysis Technique Developed," *Archaeology* 32, no. 4 (July/Aug. 79), p. 60. Leo Biek, *Archaeology and the Microscope*, (New York: Praeger, 1963). Ronald L. Bishop, et al., "Ceramic Compositional Analysis in Archaeological Perspective," SAAMT 5 (1982), pp. 275–330. Reuben G. Bullard, "Geological Studies in Field Archaeology," BA 38, no. 4 (1970), pp. 98–131. C.B. Donnan and C.W. Clewlow, *Ethnoarchaeology* (Los Angeles: University of California, 1974). Marie Farnsworth, et al., "Corinth and Corfu: A Neutron Activation Study of their Pottery," AJA 81, no. 4 (Fall 77), pp. 455–468. Judy Fischer, "The Glow of Forgery," *Science* 81, Vol. 2, no. 2 (Jan./Feb. 81), pp. 72–73. Albert E. Glock, "Ethnography in the Service of Archaeology," *Discovery* 1 (1975), pp. 4–5. "Ingots from wrecked ship may help to solve ancient mystery," IAMSN 1 (1 Nov 80), pp. 1–2. Maureen F. Kaplan, *The Origin and Distribution of Tell el Yahudiyeh Ware* (Goteborg: Aastroms, 1980); and, "Using Neutron Activation Analysis to Establish the Provenance of Pottery," BAR 2, no. 1 (Mar. 76), pp. 30–32. Arlette Leroi-Gourman, "The Archaeology of Lascaux Cave," SA 246, no. 6 (June 82), pp. 104–112. Harold Liebowitz, "Excavations at Tel Yin'am: The 1976 and 1977 Seasons," BASOR 243 (Sum. 81), pp. 79–94, and, "Excavations at Tell Yin'am, Israel," *Archaeology* 32, no. 4 (July/Aug. 79). pp. 58–59. Tom L. McClellan, "Chronology of the 'Philistine' Burials at Tell el-Far'ah (south)," *Journal of Field Archaeology* 6, no. 1 (1979), pp. 57–73. A. Millett and H. Catling, "Composition and Provenance: A Challenge," *Archaeometry* 9 (1966), pp. 92–97. "Mystery of Timna's iron solved by lead isotope fingerprinting'," IAMSN 6 (June 84), pp. 6–7. Vincent C. Pigott, et al., "The Earliest Steel in Transjordan,"

MASCAJ 2, no. 2 (1982), pp. 35–39. Anna Shepherd, *Ceramics for the Archaeologist* (2nd ed.; Washington: Carnegie Institute Publication 609, 1966). F.C. Thompson: "The Early Metallurgy of Copper and Bronze," *Man* 58 (1958), pp. 1–7. R.F. Tylecote, "The Composition of Metal Artifacts: A Guide to Provenance?," *Antiquity* 44, no. 173 (Mar. 70), pp. 19–25.

8. Curt W. Beck, ed., *Archaeological Chemistry* (Washington: American Chemical Society, 1974). Leo Biek, "Technology of Ancient Glass and Metal," *Nature* 178 (1956), pp. 1430–1434. Don R. Brothwell, *Digging up Bones* (rev.; London: British Book Center, 1977). Frans Bruin, "Royal Purple and the Dye Industries of the Mycenaeans and Phoenicians" (pp. 73–90 in *Societes et compagnies de commerce en orient et dans l'Ocean Indien*, ed. Michel Mollet; Paris: Ecole Pratique des Hautes Etudes, 1970). Frans Bruin, et al., "Electron spin resonance spectra of the basic indigoid dye radicals," *Journal of Organic Chemistry* 28 (1963), pp. 562–564. Earl R. Caley, *Analysis of Ancient Metals* (New York: Macmillan, 1964). David L. Clark, *Analytic Archaeology* (London: Methuen, 1968). I.W. Cornwall, *Bones for the Archaeologist* (rev.; London: Dent, 1974); and, *Soils for the Archaeologist* (rev.; London: Phoenix, 1966). Pam Crabtree, "Palaeoethnobotany at MASCA," *University Museum Newsletter* 22, no. 3 (Wint. 83–4), pp. 1–2. Robin W. Dennell, "Archaeology and Early Farming in Europe," *Archaeology* 31, no. 1 (Jan./Feb. 78), pp. 8–13. G.W. Dimbleby, *Plants and Archaeology* (London: Baker, 1967). J. Kenneth Eakins, "Human Osteology and Archaeology," *BA* 43, no. 2 (Spr. 80), pp. 89–96. John G. Evans, *An Introduction to Environmental Archaeology* (Ithaca, NY: Cornell University, 1978). K. Faegri and J. Iverson, *Textbook of Modern Pollen Analysis* (Copenhagen: Munksgaard, 1964). R.J. Forbes, *Studies in Ancient Technology*, Vols. IV and VIII (Leiden: Brill, 1964). Noel H. Gale and Zofia Stos-Gale, "Lead and Silver in the Ancient Aegean," *SA* 244, no. 6 (June 81), pp. 176–192. Zvi Goffer, *Archaeological Chemistry* (New York: Wiley, 1980). F.H. Goodyear, *Archaeological Site Science* (New York: American Elsevier, 1971). Joukowsky, *Manual of Field Archaeology*. Kenneth A.R. Kennedy, "Skeletal Biology: When Bones Tell Tales," *Archaeology* 34, no. 1 (Jan./Feb. 81), pp. 17–24. John Lear, "Peering Into Ancient Egypt Electronically," *SR* (3 Feb. 68), p. 60. Elizabeth McFadden, "Sleuth of 81st Street," *Newark Sunday News* (31 Dec. 67), p. 19 (Sec. 1). Patricia McBrown, "Chemistry Probing the Past," *SN* 94 (30 Nov. 68), pp. 552–553. D. J. Mack, "Short Tour of Archaeological Metallurgy," *Metal Progress* 76 (Dec. 59), pp. 94–98. Ora Negbi, "A Contribution of Mineralogy and Paleontology to an Archaeological Study of Terracottas," *IEJ* 14, no. 3 (1964), pp. 187–189. Frederic Neuburg, *Ancient Glass* (Toronto: University of Toronto, 1962). Paul T. Nicholson and Helen L. Patterson, "Ethnoarchaeology in Egypt: The Ballas Pottery Project," *Archaeology* 38, no. 3 (May/June 85), pp. 52–59. PRS, pp. 126–127. Glenn T. Seaborg, "Science and the Humanities," *Science* 144, no. 3623 (5 June 64), pp. 1199–1203, and, "Science Teams up with History and the Arts," *Chemistry* (Dec. 63), pp. 13–19. M.S. Tite, *Methods of Physical Examination in Archaeology* (New York: Seminar, 1972). Theodore A. Wertime, "A Metallurgical Expedition through the Persian Desert," *Science* 159, no. 3818 (1 Mar. 68), pp. 927–935. Robert K. Wilcox, "New Tests Support Holy Shroud Theory," *News World* (11 Dec. 77), p. 3B. David Williams, "Flotation at Siraf," *Antiquity* 47, no. 188 (1973), pp. 288–292. Richard R. Woodbridge III, "Acoustic Recording from Antiquity," *Proceedings of the Institute of Electrical and Electronics Engineers* 57 (Aug. 69), pp. 1465–1466.

9. *Abu Simbel News* 1, no. 4 (Mar. 69), Georg Gerster, "Abu Simbel's Ancient Temples Reborn," *NG* 135, no. 5 (May 69), pp. 724–744. William MacQuitty, *Abu Simbel* (New York: Putnam, 1965). Elda Maynard, "Philae Resurrected," *News & Notes of the Oriental Institute* 62 (May 80), pp. 1–3.

10. David H. Thomas, "The Awful Truth About Statistics in Archaeology," *AA* 43, no. 2 (1978), pp. 321–324. David P. Williams, "As a Discipline Comes of Age: Reflections on Archaeology and the Scientific Method," *Archaeology* 29, no. 4 (1976), pp. 229–231.

# ADDITIONAL READING

Aitken, Martin J. *Physics and Archaeology*. New York: Interscience, 1961.

Brill, Robert H. *Science and Archaeology*. Cambridge: MIT, 1971.

Brothwell, Don R. and Higgs, Eric S., eds. *Science in Archaeology*. New York: Praeger, 1970.

Charles-Picard, Gilbert, ed. *Larousse Encyclopedia of Archaeology*. New York: Putnam, 1972.

Dowman, Elizabeth A. *Conservation in Field Archaeology*. London: Methuen, 1970.

Fagan, Brian M., ed. *Avenues to Antiquity*. San Francisco: Freeman, 1976.

Hodges, Henry. *Technology in the Ancient World*. New York: Knopf, 1977.

Judson, Sheldon. 1961. "Archaeology and the Natural Sciences." *American Scientist* 49: 410–414.

Lamberg-Karlovsky, C.C., ed. *Old World Archaeology*. San Francisco: Freeman, 1972.

Linington, R.E. 1963. "Application of Geophysics to Archaeology," *American Scientist* 51: 48–70.

Openheim, A. Leo. 1973. "Towards a History of Glass in the Ancient Near East" *JAOS* 93: 259–266.

Ostermann, Robert. 1965. "Uncovering Keys: The Adventure of Archaeology." The National Observer (8 Feb 65), 20.

Pyddoke, Edward. ed. *The Scientist and the Archaeologist*. New York: Ray, 1963.

Rainey, Froehlich. 1966. "New Techniques in Archaeology." *Proceedings of the American Philosophcal Society* 110: 146–152.

Rainey, Froehlich and Ralph, Elizabeth K. 1966. "Archaeology and its New Technology." Science 153: 1481–1491.

Sherrat, Andrew. "The Revolution in Archaeology" pp. 25–28 (in The Cambridge Encyclopedia of Archaeology ed. Sherrat; NY: Cambridge University and Crown, 1980).

Stross, Fred H. 1971. "Application of the Physical Sciences to Archaeology." *Science* 171: 831–836.

SECTION

# DAILY LIFE IN BIBLICAL TIMES

Perhaps nothing more clearly illustrates the daily life of biblical times than the pottery which is so helpful in establishing the chronology of ancient life. In this section, ceramics — pottery and clay products in general — will be a theme or touchstone for the study of daily life. Pottery varied in shape, color, size, and quality. These changes reflect the differences among peoples, times, and usage as well as tastes. Of course, there are many other materials also and these are considered as well. Readers may remember the American emphasis on pottery in the history of the development of archaeology and see this focus as reflecting that history. And they would probably be right. But note that much of the new archaeology comes out of the American tradition as well. The new archaeology is concerned with the entire range of human experience.

# Life in General

## A.  THE ORIGINS OF POTTERY

We do not know for sure what the first pottery vessel was or where it was made or by whom. Clay sculptures were found at Lascaux in France. This cave art is dated c. 15,000 B.C. Figurines and geometric objects like clay balls were made as early as 8000 B.C. Pottery vessels appear c. 6000 B.C. One suggestion for the development of pottery comes from Jericho where excavators found plastered and modelled skulls and figures molded around a core of reeds. A large group of similar figurines have been found at Ain Ghazzal in Jordan. It seems a short step from molding with clay to molding a bowl. Perhaps it began with a clay depression in the floor which held rain water, and which may or may not have been "fired" or baked accidently by the family hearth. Eventually the hole was deepened and the sides built up and eventually it was cut free of the earth to form a free standing bowl. Another suggestion is that baskets were lined with clay. When set too near a fire the baskets caught on fire and burned, leaving a bowl or jar. It is speculation in any case. Excavations in Turkey suggest pottery may have been developed earlier there than elsewhere.

If the baking or firing of pottery was not discovered by the hearth accident, an alternate possibility is the lowly cook pot. After someone learned how to make a clay bowl, the lady of the house tried to cook with it and found that the fire made it permanently hard and that it held water much longer. (A friend commented to me that this theory does not hold water!) The cook pot tends to be the plainest and

**Figure 7–1.** A spouted jar c. 10 inches high, from Tomb A 43 at Bab edh-Dhra'. The decoration is in dark red paint. The handles are called ledge handles. Note the knobs on the shoulder in front of and to the sides of the spout. Photo courtesy G. Ernest Wright.

**Figure 7–2.** A perfume juglet c. 2 inches across, from Bab edh-Dhra' shaft tomb A 4. The lattice design decoration is in red paint. Photo courtesy G. Ernest Wright.

**Figure 7–3.** Left: A perfume juglet from the early 4th century A.D. It is c. 5 inches in diameter at the widest part of the body. It was set in the wall and protected by large slabs of the rock wall of Rujm al-Malfuf (Mound of Cabbages — a round tower) South in Amman. The tower was build c. 600 B.C. but re-used later. It was found by an American volunteer excavator, David Undeland.

Right: An "Assyrian" bottle, perhaps for perfumed oil, from c. 600 B.C. It probably post-dates the Assyrian presence but such fine ware may have been saved for some time. Similar bottles have been found in Jerusalem and other parts of the Holy Land. This one comes from Kirbet or Rujm al-Mekheizin, a square tower northeast of Amman on the campus of the Schneller School. Photo courtesy Department of Antiquities of Jordan.

**Figure 7–4.** Objects from Hesban. The glass bottles, with one exception, came from the tombs where they were preserved as long as the ceiling did not cave in. The same is true for the whole pottery vessels. Sometimes a broken vessel can be restored, in whole or in part.

ugliest of pots. It is usually coarse ware, seldom decorated, and frequently sooty from smoky fires. At times, cook pots had lids. At the time of the Patriarchs, cook pots had steam holes just under the rim. Sometimes there were no handles. They must have been picked up by the rim — a warm task — or simply left on the fire. At other times they had handles in style for the historical period.

Just when someone learned to use a kiln for baking or firing pots we don't know. A kiln of c. 3000 B.C. was excavated at biblical Tirzah but it was already an advanced design with a fire box underneath. The heat would have gone through flues around the pottery elevated above the box. This design suggests earlier ones but they have not been found or at least not recognized. A complete LB potter's workshop was discovered in a cave at Lachish. Pritchard found the remains of twenty-two kilns in one-fifth of an acre at Sarepta. This industrial area was in use from the LB to the Hellenistic Age. There were facilities for washing and mixing clay, and tanks for coating the pottery with "slip," a thin watery clay which helped seal the wall of the vessel to hold liquid better. When color was added to the slip it gave the finished product a different color.[1]

**Figure 7–5.**  A molded head with shell eyes.

## B.  WATER

The capacity of pottery to hold water conjures up visions of Near Eastern women gracefully carrying their water jars on their heads home from the village spring. Or you can picture them trudging through the water tunnels of Hazor, Ibleam, Gezer, or Megiddo; or up and down the staircase to the deep pool cut in solid rock at ancient Gibeon; or along the secret stairways at Megiddo and Tell es-Sa'idiyeh (biblical Zarethan or Zaphon). These stairways ran from the top of the tell to the spring at the bottom. They were dug into the hillside, roofed over like a tunnel, and presumably camouflaged to avoid detection by enemies. Water tunnels were sometimes constructed underground with vaulted roofs, as at Shechem and the East Jordan site of Muqibleh.[2]

Cisterns may have been in use by 3000 B.C. The more common interpretation is related to the invention of waterproof plaster in the LB Age. Albright suggested this made it possible for the Israelites to settle in the hill country c. 1250 B.C. in places that had not been occupied before, presumably for lack of springs. Without

**Figure 7–6.**    The Jordan River is shallow in some spots, "deep and wide" as in the American Spiritual, in other spots. It provided life-giving water for people, flocks, and irrigation. In the Jordan Valley there are many ancient tells and habitation sites.

**Figure 7–7.** The Pool at Gibeon.

water storage facilities it would not have been possible to live there in the dry season. By the ninth century B.C., many homes had their own cistern. These are common in Near Eastern villages today. When the cistern ran low (and got stale), or it was important to save the supply, the women and girls still carried water from the village spring or well.[3]

**Figure 7–8.** An ancient water reservoir at Umm el-Jimal ("Mother of Camels") in northeast Jordan is inspected by dig director Bert DeVries. In the background lies part of the ancient city built out of basalt blocks and slabs.

Water today is more often carried in five gallon tin cans. One can occasionally still see a skin water bag. These may have been in use before the water jar. The tomb painting of Beni-Hasan (c. 1890 B.C.) shows a group of Asiatics entering Egypt. One has a bag over his shoulder. An animal is butchered and skinned. The hide is turned inside out and the legs and body cuts of the hide are sewed together, with the hair side in. When filled with water the leather swells making the seams nearly water-tight. The bag "sweats" and keeps the water cool like the canvas bags still used by some on summer camping trips. Keeping liquids cool is also a property of pottery jars. The pottery "ebriq" or drinking jug breaks more easily than the tin or plastic ones more common today. But the ebriq keeps the water cooler!

The water pipeline is spreading rapidly in the Near East today, bringing water from springs, pumped wells, or storage facilities. Pipes of pottery are quite ancient both for drinking water and as drain pipes for rain and sewage. They go back at least to the MB Age and perhaps earlier. A sixth century B.C. copy of a third millennium Sumerian poem describes creation by the Babylonian god Marduk. He calls the spring which is in the sea a water pipe. The Minoans had drains c. 1900. MB drains were found at Hazor which also had an LB drainage channel partly made of old incense stands. Beth shan had street drains c. 1300. A pipeline of uncertain age was found in the Egyptian city of Ramses (Exodus 1:11). An extensive pipeline with two parallel lines of clay pipe brought water into the Greek city of Pella c. 600 B.C.

**Figure 7–9.**   An ancient reservoir at Umm el-Jimal has been restored to modern use by the Jordanian government for the bedouin of the area. In the winter rains the area gets little, but concentrated amounts of water gather in the normally dry wadis or gullies from which it can be channelled to places like these.

**Figure 7–10.** Drinking from a pottery ebriq (David Melring). The trick is not to spill water on your shirt! Photo courtesy L.T. Geraty.

A late Roman water pipe (still usable!) was discovered near Shechem. A first century A.D. Roman pipeline brought water from the hills to storage tanks cut in the rock at the seaport of Sarepta. The Romans also used lead piping. Some think their use of lead pipe and vessels induced lead poisoning and was a function in the downfall of the Roman Empire. The Romans are, of course, most famous for their aqueducts, two of which still stand at Caesarea on the Mediterranean coast. Sometimes the water channel of a Roman aqueduct was lined with tile.

Water was used extensively for irrigation in Mesopotamia and Egypt. Irrigation canals and methods are still being discovered and studied for their potential help in modern farming. The irrigation networks of the Nabataeans were cited earlier. Traditionally, the early Hebrews lived a nomadic or semi-nomadic existence (scholars are still debating this). Perhaps it was a mix of pastoralism and farming as in the story of Isaac. For most of their history, however, the Hebrews were farmers, with strong mixtures of commerce and fishing. Rain and sources of water were important for successful crops, for industrial activities, and for life itself.[4]

**Figure 7–11.**    Lamps. The changes in style from a simple bowl to a pinched lip nozzle to a closed top covers several thousand years.

## C.  LIGHT

Fire not only baked pottery and food. It provided light. We do not know when the first lamps were used. The cave paintings of Lascaux are deep inside the cave. The artists needed light of some kind. Early lamps were made of natural and carved stone. They probably burned animal fat and used juniper twigs for wicks. They were little more than small bowls or saucers. Such bowls have been found with a bit of blackened edge. They date as early as 3500 B.C. Someone finally made a slight dip in the lip for the wick. This became deeper as time rolled by and the pinch became pronounced. Finally the edges of the clay were folded over to form a spout. By the end of the Old Testament period, the entire top of the lamp was closed.[5]

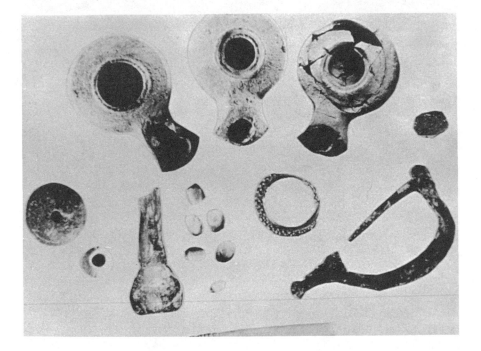

**Figure 7–12.** Objects from Hesban, Tomb G-10 (second rolling stone tomb, Early Roman in date). The lamps at the top are "Herodian." The name comes from Herod the Great in whose time this form first appeared. The style continued, however, until 70 A.D. The lower right hand corner is a fibula — a safety pin. Some countries keep all the finds while others share them with the expedition. The nation keeps the best finds for its national archives. Photo courtesy L.T. Geraty.

## D.   LUXURIES AND STAPLES

The lamps in biblical times probably burned olive oil, which brings us back to
other types of jars. Jars large and small were used to store the oil and other products
such as wine, fruit, grain and flour. Storage jars ranged from tiny perfume juglets
(pottery, alabaster, and later glass) a few inches high to huge objects three to six feet
high. The latter were probably not moved but sunken into the ground to make
them stand up and keep cool. At Gibeon, a series of cisterns carved down into
bedrock have an average temperature of sixty-five degrees. They may have been
reused for the storage of new wine, judging by the jars found in them.

**Figure 7–13.**   Olive mill. The large basin is filled with ripe olives and the round stone
rolled over them to break and bruise them. They were then put in a presser which squeezed
out the olive oil. The round stone has a hole for a long pole or tree branch which could be
fastened to an ox or donkey to roll it around. This mill is at Capernaum at the north end of
the Sea of Galilee.

**Figure 7–14.** Flour or grain mill. A family might use a saddle quern and rubbing stone. Larger units like this probably were for commercial use. Poles in the openings on the top piece could be attached to animals for power. This mill is also at Capernaum.

Archaeologists do not find the ancient oil or wine, of course, but sometimes some dregs or traces of material in the bottom of the jar have been analyzed. We also find grape and olive presses, and vats carved into a hilltop or inside a cave. At Shechem, what may have been a grape or olive press from the eighth and seventh centuries was found in the form of a large flat circular stone with grooves in it. The grooves led to a jar buried in the ground. An installation at Tell Dan, tenth to ninth centuries, has been interpreted as an olive press. The crushing vat was sunk in the ground for the first part of the process. Stone slabs on either side each had a groove leading to a sunken jar. The crushed olives could have been pressed here. Nothing was left of the pressing beams but the weight stones were found near by. These would have been hung on the end of the beam to increase the pressure and squeeze the oil out of the crushed olives. A large tomb in Yajuz in East Jordan near Amman was reused for olive oil production. The crusher was found in one corner and the press in another. Several old burial loculi had been plastered, presumably to store the fruit. Hestrin and Yeivin describe and illustrate a similar operation which was rebuilt and demonstrates the process. A large olive oil complex was discovered at Sarepta from the Hellenistic and Roman periods.

**Figure 7–15.**   Cosmetic palette. A number of these have been found in Near Eastern excavations. This one is from Tell Ureimeh near the Sea of Galilee. It is c. 4.5 inches in diameter. The center cavity may have been for grinding colors. A few have been found with different colors in the geometric designs. Perhaps the broad edge was for mixing colors. A few of these objects are quite plain but it is not clear if they are intended to be that way or if they are unfinished. They come in different kinds of stone. The cosmetics included rouge for cheeks and eye shadow. Photo courtesy the Israel Department of Antiquities and Museums.

**Figure 7–16.** Stone objects found at Shechem. The flat rocks are saddle querns — grain placed on them was ground for meal or flour with a rubbing stone. The large round rocks have a hole in the top and were used as door sockets. Doors swung on a pole or post like a wooden fence post of today.

It is not uncommon to find remains of fruit, raisins, nuts, various kinds of grain and even flour in the bottom of store jars. Some of these were smashed in the destruction of a house, a warehouse, or a temple where they would have been offerings to the gods. Sometimes they are found in tombs, as offerings for the dead. Bins, of stone and lined with clay, or underground pits, were also used for the storage of grain. The grain may have been "parched" for food but this is difficult to detect since the remains have often been burned and/or have decayed.

While the flour was stored in pottery, its preparation takes us to stone work. The common hand method was a large, flattish but slightly curved stone called a *saddle quern*. The grinding stone tended to be shaped more or less like a loaf of bread, perhaps more like a vienna loaf, flattened at both ends. Stone ground grain may have a bit of stone in it which may account for the generally poor teeth in older adults. A later development was the animal driven grinding mill which of course produced larger quantities and probably represents commercial milling of flour or the production of olive oil.

Moving in the other direction, we should note the mortar and pestle, perhaps still familiar in the modern pharmacy or drug store. These could be used for grinding small quantities of flour or spice. A tiny — one and a half inch high — cosmetic container, thirteenth century, had a pestle that fit snugly into the mortar which was in the form of a round or cylindrical box. Traces of rouge were still in it. A quite different style is a low flat bowl or a disc with a small depression in the middle. The wide flat edge was often decorated in designs, a few of which had colors in them when found though it is not clear if the color was decoration or from the cosmetics. One theory is that the cosmetic palette was for grinding the ochre and other sources of color though that name suggests the other theory, that it was used for mixing colors. It might have been used for both, of course.

Cosmetics and perfumes may also have been applied through burning. Incense burners are known from many periods. They are especially related to ancient worship. A small altar from the excavations at Lachish and similar ones from elsewhere have been interpreted as ritual incense burners. Albright reinterpreted the inscription on the Lachish altar to read, "Belonging to the daughter of Iyyos, son of Mahli the (royal) courier." Earlier it had been read as "Incense. . .to Yah" or Yahweh. The burning of cosmetics or perfumed oils would perfume the air, the clothing, and even the body. Modern perfumes and deodorants are "old hat" for the daily life of biblical times. Psalm 45 is a poem in honor of the king. Verses seven and eight say, "God has anointed you with the oil of gladness. . .; your robes are all fragrant

**Figure 7–17.** The remains of a "tabun" or oven. The later builders have cut through the mosaic floor of a church long since in ruins. The walls would have been built up of clay to form a dome with a hole in the top, to feed the fire and then to lay thin, pizza like layers of bread on the hot rocks in the bottom.

**Figure 7–18.** Tabun remains at Sarafand.

with myrrh and aloes and cassia." In Esther 2:12, candidates for Queen of Persia spent six months with oil of myrrh and six months with spices and ointments for women.

Grain was ground for bread which was baked in the form of flat loaves on a shallow pottery dish turned upside down over the fire. This method is still used by the bedouin though metal dishes are used today. Another method, more common in villages, is a dome-shaped oven with the lid on top. The walls are built up of clay or simply mud, sometimes with broken pieces of pottery mixed in, like rocks in cement or temper in pottery, to give it strength. Fire heated the rocks in the bottom. The ashes were scraped away and the flat loaves laid on the rocks until baked. An oven (*tabun* or *tannur*) was excavated at Shechem from c. eighth century B.C. After some discussion about how it was used, one of the citizens of Balata, Ibrahim Khalil, invited us to his home where his wife showed us how the tabun is used today! The large mills cited earlier and several passages in the Bible (Genesis 40:1; Hosea 7:4) suggest public bakers. The prophet Hosea may have been a baker by trade. Several large grinders were found at Capernaum from the early centuries A.D.

There is considerable information about food in the Bible in addition to archaeological remains. Among the latter are animal bones which probably indicate the meat people ate, though some were a source of milk and milk products and some were draft animals. Some bones indicate the wildlife of the area. In addition, paintings and carvings provide pictures of food. Inscriptions contain references to grain, fruit, and other foods.[6]

## E. INSCRIPTIONS

### Jar Handles

A large number of storage jar handles have been found which are inscribed with the Hebrew Letters for "lmlk." This means "to" or "belonging to" the king. The jars may have held taxes which were collected in the form of wine, grain, and other products before money was created in the form of coins. When the people wanted a king, Samuel warned them that a king would take a tenth of their grain for taxes, and their children for his bakers and servants (I Samuel 8:10–18). For some years, "lmlk" was thought to be a guaranteed measure like a modern bureau of standards but variable sizes of "lmlk" jars have now been found. Other interpretations of "lmlk" are that the jars held supplies for strategic military forts or wine from royal vineyards. The latter is suggested by the number of "lmlk" stamps which have the names of cities, such as Hebron, along with them.

The identification of ancient Gibeon was confirmed by the jar handles discovered there with the name of the city inscribed on them. A number of different marks, plus signs, circles, and so forth are found on jar handles. These have been interpreted as potters' marks, perhaps simply as a sign of who made the jar or perhaps of ownership. The latter may also be the case with seal impressions on a jar handle. The seal impression may have been equivalent to a signature.

### Seals

Seals were made of pottery or *faience* (a glazed sand paste) but more commonly were made of stone, especially gems or semiprecious stones. The seal may have been worn on a string around the neck. Jacob's son, Judah, apparently had one like this (Genesis 38:18). Alternately it may have been a ring, like the one the pharaoh gave to Joseph (Genesis 41:42). The seal in Egypt was a stamp seal, frequently made in the shape of a scarab beetle. The flat underside is engraved and when pressed into the moist clay of a jar, or the soft wax sealing a papyrus document, it leaves an impression of a name, an inscription, animals, deities, or a design. Stamp seals go back to the sixth millenium B.C. In Mesopotamia the seal was a cylinder, sometimes left with a ring on one end or more often with a hole bored lengthwise inside

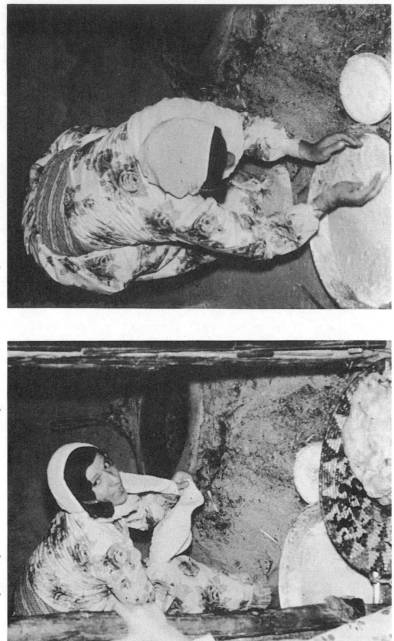

**Figure 7–19A and B.** Balata oven. Mrs. Ibrahim Khalil of the village of Balata shows how this style of tabun is used. Previously a fire inside the dome heated rocks in the bottom. The fire died down and the ashes were scraped away from the hot rocks. The thin bread dough was spread on it to bake and the lid put back on. Several finished pieces are on the tray on the right.

the cylinder for the string or wire. The cylinder was rolled over the clay forming an endlessly repeating scene. The impressions, called *bullae*, frequently survive on a chunk of wax or clay or pottery. Impressions on handles are especially common since the handles are thicker and stronger and more apt to last.

Large numbers of seals and impressions have been found in Palestine. Seals tells us about Egyptian and Mesopotamian influence, the nature of religion, and various elements of culture such as dress and the development of writing. Among the most interesting seals are those such as Jotham's. It was found at Tell el-Kheleifeh. The seal may have belonged to the Regent and later to King Jotham (750–735 B.C.), son of Uzziah, at the time of the prophet Amos. Other seals are those of Shema the servant of Jeroboam, king of Israel at that time; and one of Ushna the servant of Ahaz, later king of Judah in the time of Isaiah. The seal of Jaazaniah,

**Figure 7–20.**   Stamp seals. No. 5 is shaped like a scarab beetle (sacred in Egypt) with the design on the flat underside. It is c. 1 inch long. No. 22 has hole for a string. It may have been worn around the neck. No. 29 is a ring. The numbers are the registry numbers from the dig. i.e., No. 5 is the fifth object found and registered. These seals are from Khirbet al-Hajjar west of Amman. Photo courtesy the Department of Antiquities of Jordan.

servant of the king, c. 600, was found at Mizpah. It shows a fighting rooster on it. This may be evidence for the domestication of chickens in Palestine. Hebrew seals from c. 600 were found at Lachish. They were inscribed with such names as Nahum. An impression *(bulla)* has "Berechiah the scribe" (Jeremiah 36:4). Another has "Jerahmeel the king's son" (Jeremiah 36:26. The seal of "Milkom'ur, servant of Ba'al-yasha' " was cited earlier, from Tell el-'Umeiri (Hesban? Numbers 21:21; Abel-Keranim? Judges 11:33). Ba'al-yasha' may be the Ammonite King Baalis (Jeremiah 40:14). An important type of inscribed seal from the fifth and fourth centuries has "Yehud" (Judah) on it.[7]

## Coins

"Yehud" also appears on a class of coins from the fourth century B.C. At the time, Judah was a province of the Persian empire which allowed some subject people to coin their own money. Greek coins were more common in Palestine, as were Persian ones. Later the Maccabees also coined their own money, while in Roman times coins became very common and today can usually be bought from village children who find them on the surface. One of the oldest coins, c. 600 B.C., found in Palestine was discovered at Shechem. The oldest coin found in Jordan dates from c. 400 B.C.[8]

**Figure 7–21.** The oldest coin known from Jordan. A coin of Tyre dated c. 400 B.C. About the size of a U.S. quarter, the obverse shows a figure (god? king?) on a hippocampus or winged sea monster of Greek mythology, half horse (head and front legs) and half dolphin (tail). They are riding over the waves. The figure's right hand seems to hold the reins while the left has a bow and perhaps an arrow. A dolphin swims beneath the waves. The reverse shows the Athenian owl. On the other side of the bird are the shepherd's crook and the grain winnowing flail. In Egypt these symbolized royalty. It was found at Khirbet al-Hajjar on the western edge of Amman. Photo courtesy Department of Antiquities of Jordan.

## Literature

Inscribed handles, seals and coins help us study the development of writing. The study of writing — the way the letters are formed, the presence of different languages such as Hebrew, Aramaic, Akkadian, Greek, etc. — is called epigraphy. Discoveries on datable items or in datable layers or strata now make it possible to use writing itself to date artifacts.

The Dead Sea Scrolls were dated in this way. The Qumran monastery nearby was dated by coins and pottery typology. The linen used to wrap the scrolls has been dated by carbon 14. Epigraphy is so refined that it can even help date fragments of scrolls and sometimes single letters. The scrolls are mostly parchment, writing material prepared from skin. One scroll is made of copper. Very little papyrus has been found at Qumran but the Samaritan papyri were found in the Jordan Valley to the north and a number of papyrus scrolls and fragments were found in the Wadi Muraba'at to the south of Qumran. The latter are from the Simon Bar Koseba revolt (135 A.D.). They give insights into the revolt and Simon's control of territory, land ownership (by women as well as men), divorce customs, etc. Since virtually no remains of non-canonical biblical materials were found there, it is speculated that the canon, as established by the rabbinical academy at Jamnia (Jabneh) c. 90 A.D., had begun to take effect. This is in contrast to the Dead Sea Scrolls, which include large numbers of non-canonical materials.

Apart from the above, very few manuscripts have been found in Palestine. While it has a dry climate, there is sufficient moisture from winter rains and summer dew to decay the more perishable materials. This contrasts with Egypt, where ancient papyri are found, such as the Elephantine papyri. Stone does not decay but relatively few stone inscriptions have been found in Palestine. At Gezer, a small piece of soft limestone had a type of memory verse for the agricultural year scratched on it. It is dated to the tenth century. Hezekiah's water tunnel (dug 705 B.C.) had an inscription carved in the rock near the Siloam pool end. This tells how the digging parties listened for the sound of the picks of the other party digging toward them to get their bearings for further digging. Perhaps the most famous stone inscription is that of King Mesha in Moab, discussed in Section IV. Also described in detail there is an inscribed bronze bottle found at Tell Siran, which includes the names of three Ammonite kings.

Several Egyptian pharaohs left stone inscriptions in Palestine. Seti I and Ramses II left stelae at Beth-shan. Several have been found at Megiddo. Ramses II, and Shalmaneser III of Assyria, and other kings and conquerors have left relief carvings in the cliffs where the Dog River flows into the Mediterranean north of Beirut.

Among the many stone carvings, reliefs, and inscriptions in Egypt and Mesopotamia, a number shed light on the Bible. Hammurabi's stele (c. 1700) discovered in Susa where it was taken as raider's loot, has his law code carved on it. Some of the laws are very similar to biblical laws such as "an eye for an eye" (Par. 196; Exodus 21:24). At the top of the stele is a relief of Hammurabi before the sun god Shamash, like Moses before God. Pharaoh Merneptah's stele which mentions Israel, was found at Thebes. Shalmaneser's Black Obelisk was found in Nimrud. At the top of the stone is an inscription describing the scenes below, the way a modern book has captions under pictures. Sennacherib's reliefs from his palace in Nineveh illustrate Assyrian siege warfare and the treatment of captives. The inscription says he had the booty of Lachish paraded before him. His inscribed clay prism, now in the Oriental Institute, tells how he shut Hezekiah up in Jerusalem like a bird in a cage.

For inscriptions on clay, we should note again that archaeology has brought to light many thousands of clay tablets, written on while they were soft and then dried and frequently baked. When discovered in the moist earth of Mesopotamia, they may have to be baked again to preserve them. The Ebla tablets were baked by the fire that destroyed the city. The Cappodocian tablets tell us about Assyrian trade in Asia Minor c. 2000. The Execration Tablets curse Egypt's enemies c. 1800. The tablets of Mari (c. 1700) on the Euphrates refer to customs of the time of the Patriarchs, as do the Nuzi tablets c. 1500. The Amarna letters reflect political affairs in Palestine in the fourteenth century when the area was controlled by Egypt. The Ras Shamra (Ugarit) tablets provide information on Canaanite religion.

The tablets add immeasurably to reliefs such as "Baal of the Heavens" from Ras Shamra, or the little figurines of deities described later. Baal is a fertility figure whose worship was to guarantee the increase in crops, in livestock, and in human families. When the Israelites moved into the farming land of Canaan from the desert and the wilderness, it was a great temptation to worship Baal. The God of Israel was a desert, mountain, and war god who could hardly be expected to help with farming. It took the prophets a long time to convince people that all of nature is under God's control (Deuteronomy 8; Hosea 2:4).[9]

## Ostraca

The indestructible potsherd must be included here again. The scratch paper of the ancient world, sherds with writing on them, are called ostraca, from their use in ancient Greece in votes on ostracism. The Samaria ostraca, c. 750 or 800 B.C., and those of Lachish from 587, were cited earlier. Chemical analysis of the ink of the latter showed the ink was made from gallnut juice and soot. Other ostraca have been found in Beth-shemesh, Jerusalem, Tell Hesban and elsewhere. Over 200 (half Hebrew, half Aramaic) ostraca were found at Arad from c. 400 B.C. An ostraca at Izbet Sartah, perhaps biblical Ebenezer (I Samuel 4) has five lines of inscription. The last line is the Hebrew alphabet minus the "m" and "r." The writing is left to right rather than the more usual right to left. It may be from as early as 1200.[10]

In this Izbet Sartah alphabet, the letters "pe" and "ayin" are reversed from their usual order. The same is true in four acrostics (paragraphs arranged in alphabetical order) in Lamentations 1–3 and Proverbs 31. Ze'ev Meshel notes this along with the four *abecedaries* (alphabets) on the second *pithos* (large storage jar) found at Kuntillet Ajrud, forty miles south of Kadesh Barnea. Another inscription on this jar is a blessing. "Amaryau said to my lord. . .may you be blessed by Yahweh and his Asherah. Yahweh bless you and keep you and be with you. . ." It would be blasphemy to the Hebrew prophets to invoke the blessing of a goddess. The ending of "..yau" in Amaryau is a northern (Israel) type of ending in Hebrew names rather than the "..yahu" for Yahweh in southern (Judah) names. Similarly a stone bowl weighing 400 pounds is inscribed "(Belonging) to 'Obadyau son of 'Adnah, may he be blessed of Yahwe(h)." A second stone bowl had the inscription "Shema'yau son of 'Ezer." The first pithos had a blessing that is hard to read but it may have been "May you be blessed by Yahweh" followed by a word meaning protect or perhaps Samaria, the capital of the northern kingdom. The following word may be "his Asherah."

**Figure 7–22.**    Lion head in stone, held by Dr. Holt H. Graham. The head was probably a decoration on the Harianic temple on Tell er-Ras.

Two Phoenician inscriptions were found on plaster from doorjambs. One may include the phrases "..and in the (just) ways of El..," "..blessed be Ba'al in the day of..," and "..the name of El in the day of .." Hebrew letters were found on storage jars. Some had been carved in the clay before the pots were fired while on other jars, letters and names were added after the pottery was made. Meshel suggests these may represent offerings as in "q" for "qorban," "offering" (Mark 7:11). He thinks this may be evidence for priests at the site. His thought may be reinforced by remains of cloth preserved in the dry desert air. The cloth is linen and wool which was finely woven and sewn. The cloth is not from everyday work clothes such as one might find worn by shepherds in the area. The mix of linen and wool in a single garment is forbidden in Leviticus 19:19 and Deuteronomy 22:11. The combination of northern names and the mix of deities may reflect the time of Queen Athaliah (842–837 B.C.), the daughter of the Phoenician Queen Jezebel of Israel. The site may have been a stopover on a caravan or a pilgrimage route to Mount Sinai, where people asked for protection on the journey.[11]

All of this writing is a reminder that ancient Hebrews were familiar with the art. Some scholars have insisted that writing among the Hebrews developed late, and that the biblical materials were all written down at a later date, centuries after the events. That may be true for the Bible in the form we know it but at least some of it may have been written at the time, e.g., the court history of David in II Samuel 9:20 and I Kings 1–2. While excavation and exploration have not found many Hebrew inscriptions, there is hope for more. Enough have appeared to make it clear that daily life in biblical times included writing — law, letters, literature, customs, records (commercial and government), and religious texts.


# F.   ART, COMMERCE AND THE GODS

Writing, whether incised or inked, and seal impressions, were not the only things placed on pottery. The use of typology for dating purposes makes extensive use of decoration and decorative motifs. These varied in time and from people to people. They are an important indication of the arrival of new people, by conquest or peaceful migration. When an older style of pottery is replaced, especially by a layer of ashes on the older strata, we can assume a conquest. When the older pottery remains while new material appears, this may reflect new arrivals, or it may be evidence of trade.

Trade is widely evidenced in the Bible and the inscriptions. The Ebla tablets provide a picture of trade that stretched from Lebanon to Iran to the Sinai and to Asia Minor (Turkey). The Cappodocian tablets as cited earlier refer to Assyrian trade in Turkey. The Egyptian tale of Sinuhe says Sinuhe heard Egyptian spoken east of Byblos c. 1900. The excavations of Byblos suggest trade with Egypt as early

**Figure 7–23.** Philistine jug. The elliptical bodied birds and fish are typical of this style of pottery, which lasted c. 150 years.

as 3000. The Beni-Hasan painting of 1890 B.C. has an inscription that Asiatics have brought black pigment for eye paint with them from Transjordan. Besides cosmetics, perfume, jewelry, ivory, gold, and luxury items, there was trade in staples of grain, olive oil, and wine. Ebla traded in textiles, whose manufacture was controlled by the queen.

Albright's interpretation of "habiru" (Abram the Hebrew) as caravanaeers may suggest a hidden reference to trade in Genesis. While the translation is not widely accepted, there can be little doubt that there was trade as the extra-biblical evidence makes clear. Traders used donkeys in the Middle Bronze Age, going by the usual interpretation. It has been suggested that camels were not domesticated in large numbers until c. 1100 (Judges 6:5). Michael Ripinsky, however, claims that camels were domesticated before 3000, and by 1300 were common in Upper Egypt.

Solomon's trading activities were cited earlier. Israel, the northern kingdom, controlled more trade routes than Judah, the southern kingdom. This has led some to see Israel as the more commercial and cosmopolitan of the two. Hence it would

**Figure 7–24.** Lion and Dog Panel from Beth-shan. There are various interpretations of this unique scene. One is that the dog represents Gula, the goddess of protection, while the lion is Nergal, god of pestilence and disease, who is being driven away from the city.

**Figure 7–25.** Plaque figurines from Shechem. The rounded backs indicate a Late Bronze date.

be more open to foreign influences including religious idolatry and syncretism. In a later time, trade brought Greek pottery, coins, and artifacts several centuries before Alexander conquered the area.

A very distinctive trade pottery came from Cyprus in the Late Bronze Age (after 1500). The Cypriote milk-bowl gets its name from the milky white surface of the pottery. It is further distinguished by a ladder or lattice design in brown paint. One band of the decoration runs horizontally around the rim while a series of lattices or ladders run vertically down the sides of the bowl. Another distinguishing mark is its unique style of handle, called a wishbone because it resembles one. It is attached horizontally like a modern two handled kettle rather than vertically like a teapot or pitcher handle (the loop handle of storage jars). Eventually the Cypriote pottery was imitated locally in Palestine. The imitation has a less "milky" surface.

Distinctive pottery and other containers such as alabaster and other types of stoneware, and occasionally metalware, appear in Palestine from Egypt and Assyria. A "foreign" pottery with a special status is an unique Philistine pottery with antecedents in the Mycenean area. The Philistines may have come from Crete, though the biblical Caphtor is also equated with Asia Minor. The decoration has spirals and oval-shaped birds and fish. These are often separated in "panels" formed by lines of paint on the side of the jar. Large bowls with a strainer spout have been identified as beer mugs. Since there are so many, one might think the Philistines were great "guzzlers"!

Pottery decoration or art includes the use of clay for sculpture. We began with sculpture. Perhaps the most famous items in this group are clay figurines of deities. These are usually some form of the mother goddess. They help with chronology in a broad sense. In the Late Bronze Age, they were made in a mold that formed the front while the back was smoothed out — round or flat — in a plaque style. Later they were in the round. In addition to many female figurines, a number of figurines of gods have been found. They are often bronze, sometimes overlaid with silver or gold. The gods rarely appear in Israelite strata but the female figurine is common. Hebrew does not have a word for goddess and it may be the figurines were good luck charms to ensure pregnancy or an easy birth. There is no assurance that this is all, for the Canaanites and others put a strong emphasis on fertility as part of their religion.

One significant aspect of the fertility cult was the divine marriage during the New Year's festival. The king, representing the god, was married to a priestess representing the goddess. The symbolic marriage of the gods supposedly ensured the fertility of the land.

A tenth century cult vessel from Ashdod reveals another side of ancient worship. Molded figurines around the side of the cylinder of the stand under the bowl have been interpreted as musicians. Two are playing double-piped flutes while one plays a cymbal. An eighth century figurine from Ashdod is playing a small harp or lyre. Musical instruments are known in the Bible from paintings and carvings in the Ancient Near East and from actual instruments or parts of instruments found in digs. The latter include a shell trumpet, bone and silver flutes, cymbals, rattles ("sistrum"), harps (one at Ur was cited earlier) and the mouth-piece of a clarinet (found by Glueck at Kheleifeh). Bells and drums were also part of the "band." Music has been written for centuries. A Hurrian hymn deciphered from a cuneiform tablet of Ugarit, fourteenth century B.C., has been called the "world's oldest musical notation."[12]

Among pottery modellings are toys such as a toy chariot found in a child's tomb. The two-wheeled cart was in use among the Sumerians of Mesopotamia as early as 2800 B.C., but the war chariot was apparently introduced by the Hyksos who conquered Egypt c. 1700. The Egyptians learned from their conquerors. Later the Bible says the Israelites could not drive the Canaanites from the plain because the Canaanites had chariots of iron. These were probably wooden chariots protected by iron armor. David conquered enemies who used the chariot, but as a traditional foot soldier, he did not adopt this weapon. He hamstrung the horses so his enemies could not use them again (II Samuel 8:4). His son, Solomon, made up for this military shortsightedness. He not only had a chariot army; he even set up a trading venture in horses and chariots (I Kings 10:28f). It is of interest however, that there is no record of his chariots ever fighting a battle. [13]

Toys and games are not limited to pottery. There are several ivory gameboards from Megiddo, Debir, and Thebes (Egypt). A gameboard from Ur (twenty-fifth century) is made of stone and shell inlaid in bitumen. The last was common in ancient times. It floated in chunks in the Dead Sea. This may be the biblical "pitch" used on Noah's ark and Moses' basket in the bulrushes. It was also used to hold flint sickle blades in the wooden or bone haft until after David's time when iron sickles became common. [14]

Ivory carving was not limited to toys. Some of it reached the level of a very fine art. While not too common, one use was as furniture decoration. Amos (6:4) predicted woe for those who lie on beds of ivory in Samaria. The excavations there have produced a number of these decorative carvings. I Kings 10:18 says Solomon had an ivory throne. Amos and Solomon are a reminder that ivory inlay was probably restricted to the wealthy. The poor probably had no furniture at all. If they were lucky they had mats that served as chairs in daytime and beds at night.

Wood is very seldom preserved. Some carved wood at Ebla gives a tantalizing taste of craftsmanship. Partially preserved furniture was found in tombs dug into the rock near Jericho. One suggestion is that volcanic gases in this earthquake region may have been instrumental in preserving the wood. The wood in the great *tumulus* - burial mound - at Gordion in Turkey, may have been preserved by the constant humidity in the sealed tomb. Portions of it — perhaps the furniture of the fabulously wealthy King Midas — have been restored with modern technology. Occasionally remains of metal furniture are found in graves. Pottery models of furniture are also found in tombs.

Under the category of art and carving, we can refer once more to the engraved seals mentioned earlier. This engraving, or *glyptic* art, is an entire study in itself. It developed in different countries, so experts can use it as a means of dating the strata of a tell or as an indication of Mesopotamian or Egyptian influence. Cylinder seals have been found in Egyptian strata and tombs from c. 3000, suggesting Mesopotamian influence, probably through trade, at that early date.

Painting appears in pre-biblical times also. The cave paintings of France were cited earlier. Very little of this painting appears in the Near East. Frescoes of geometric design from c. 3500 were found on plastered walls at Ghassul on the northeast corner of the Dead Sea. With the Bronze Ages, paintings become common in Egyptian tombs but remain scarce elsewhere. In Palestine, the Kuntillet 'Ajrud excavation produced fragments of wall plaster with painted designs, animals, and human figures. The paintings of tombs at Mareshah were cited earlier. Several Roman tombs in north Jordan have frescoed walls and ceilings.

In contrast, the Egyptians frequently painted their tombs and temples. Their subject matter was the everyday life of hunting and fishing, farming, baking, dancing, etc. but they also show the royal family and the gods. These same subjects appear in the whole repertoire of Egyptian art — reliefs, pottery, wooden and pottery models, seals, and metal work.

For the Near East as a whole, painting is most common on pottery as described earlier. Occasionally people are depicted, especially in later Greek pottery though an early fragment from Beth-shan depicts a Canaanite woman and man. The two 'Ajrud pithoi cited earlier for their inscriptions contained a large variety of animal figures and several human figures as well. Two of the latter have been called Yahweh and the goddess Asherah. This would be blasphemy for the later Hebrew faith but would be no problem for a "syncretistic" — mixed — people as in the days of Queen Athaliah. More commonly there are animals, as in Philistine and Mycenean pottery, and designs, as with Cypriote pottery. Designs appear on pottery, from the earliest times through to today.[15]

# NOTES

1. Max E. L. Mallowan, "Ugarit," Antiquity 40 (Mar. 66), p. 30. Denise Schmandt-Besserat, "The Earliest Uses of Clay in Syria," Expedition 19, no. 3 (Spr. 77), pp. 28–42. Gary O. Rollefson, et. al., "The Neolithic of 'Ain Ghazal, Jordan" (in Preliminary Reports of ASOR-Sponsored Excavations 1980–1984 ed. Walter E. Rast; Philadelphia: ASOR, 1986). Paul T. Nicholson and Helen L. Patterson, "Ethnoarchaeology in Egypt: The Ballas Pottery Project," Archaeology 38, no. 3 (May/June 85), pp. 52–59. PRS, pp. 111–130.
2. James B. Pritchard, "The First Excavations at Tell es-Sa'idiyeh," BA 28, no. 1 (Feb. 65), pp. 10–17. HUCBAS Newsletter (25 Aug. 66), p. 4. Dan Cole, "How Water Tunnels Worked," BAR 6, no. 2 (Mar./Ap. 80), pp. 8–29. Henry O. Thompson and Bert de Vries, "A Water Tunnel at Muqibleh," ADAJ 17 (1972), pp. 89–90. Robert Bull, "Water Sources in the Vicinity," (pp. 214–228 in Shechem by G. Ernest Wright; New York: McGraw-Hill, 1965).
3. Moshe Dothan, "Excavations at Meser, 1956," IEJ 7 (1957), pp. 217–228, and, "Excavations at Meser, 1957," IEJ 9 (1959), pp. 13–29.
4. William H. Shea, "Artistic Balance Among the Beni Hasan Asiatics," BA 44, no. 4 (Fall 81), pp. 219–228. ANEP no. 3. Alexander Heidel, The Babylonian Genesis (Chicago: University of Chicago, 1951), p. 62, line 11. Yigael Yadin, Hazor (New York: Random, 1975), p. 268; and, Yadin et al., Hazor, vol. III–IV (Jerusalem: Magnes, 1961), pl. CXIV. Alan Rowe, The Topography and History of Beth-shan (Philadelphia: University of Pennsylvania, 1930), pl. 22:2. Pierre Montet, Everyday Life in Ancient Egypt (New York: St. Martins, 1958), p. 17. Photios Petsas, "Ten Years at Pella," Archaeology 17 (1964), p. 84, fig. 17. Yohanan Aharoni, "Excavations at Ramat Rahel," BA 24 (Dec. 61), p. 97, fig. 1. Robert J. Bull, "Caesarea Maritima — The Search for Herod's City," BAR 8, no. 3 (May/June 82), pp. 24–40. Victor H. Matthews, "Pastoralists and Patriarchs," BA 44, no. 4 (Fall 81), pp. 215–218; and, Pastoral Nomadism in the Mari Kingdom,

*ca. 1830–1760 B.C.* (Cambridge, MA: ASOR, 1978). Norman K. Gottwald, "Were the Early Israelites Pastoral Nomads?," BAR 4, no. 2 (June 78), pp. 2–7. Gershon Edelstein and Mardechai Kislev, "Mevasseret Yerushalayim: Ancient Terrace Farming," BA 44, no. 1 (Wint. 81), pp. 53–56. Amihai Sneh, et al., "Evidence for an Ancient Egyptian Frontier Canal," *American Scientist* 63 (1975), pp. 542–548. Michael Evenari and Dov Koller, "Ancient Masters of the Desert," SA 194, no. 4 (Ap. 56), pp. 39–45. Lawrence E. Stager, "Farming the Judean Desert during the Iron Age," BASOR 221 (Feb. 76), pp. 145–158. PRS, pp. 58–59, Fig. 27.

5.  Arlette Leroi-Gourham, "The Archaeology of Lascaux Cave," SA 246, no. 6 (June 82), pp. 104–112. Jean Perrot, "Bir es-Safadi," IEJ 5 (1955), p. 125. Varda Sussman, "Lighting the Way Through History," BAR II, no. 2 (Mar./Ap. 85), pp. 42–56.

6.  Wright, *Shechem*, p. 166, Figs. 89–90; p. 98. Gus W. Ahlstrom, "Wine Presses and Cup Marks of the Jenin-Megiddo Survey," BASOR 231 (Oct. 78), pp. 19–49. Lawrence E. Stager and Samuel R. Wolff, "Production and Commerce in Temple Courtyards: An Olive Press in the Sacred Precincts at Tel Dan," BASOR 243 (Sum. 81), pp. 95–102. Henry O. Thompson, "A Tomb at Yajuz," ADAJ 17 (1972), pp. 37–46; and, "Iron Age Cosmetic Palettes," ADAJ 16 (1971), pp. 61–70; and, "Cosmetic Palettes," *Levant* 4 (1972), pp. 148–150; and, "Cosmetics in Ancient Times," *Voice of the Holy Land* (in Arabic) 58 (Oct. 72), pp. 29–35. Ruth Hestrin and Ze'ev Yeivin, "Oil from the Presses of Tirat-Yehuda," BA 40, No. 1 (Mar. 77), pp. 29–31. PRS, pp. 129–130. Nancy Miller, "A Puzzle for Albright," BAR 8, no. 3 (May/June 82), pp. 65–68, re-interprets as an olive oil press what Albright guessed were dye vats at Debir. Albright, "The Lachish Cosmetic Burner and Esther 2:12" (pp. 25–32 in *A Light Unto My Path* ed. Howard N. Bream, et al.; Philadelphia: Temple, 1974). Albright: "The Beautician Reveals Secrets of Queen Esther's Cosmetic Aids," BAR 2, no. 1 (Mar. 76), pp. 1, 5–6. Nigel Groom, *Frankincense and Myrrh: A Study of the Arabian Incense Trade* (London: Longman, 1981). Jean Bottero, "The Cuisine of Ancient Mesopotamia," BA 48, no. 1 (Mar. 85), pp. 36–47. Richard H. Meadow, "The Study of Faunal Remains from Archaeological Sites," BA 46, no. 2 (Wint. 83), pp. 49–53.

7.  Pauline Albenda, "Of Gods, Men and Monsters on Assyrian Seals," BA 41, no. 1 (Mar. 78), pp. 11–22. William W. Hallo, "Glyptic Roles in the Biblical World," *Bible Review* 1, no. 1 (Feb. 85), pp. 20–27. David Ussishkin, "Royal Judean Storage Jars and Private Seal Impressions," BASOR 223 (Oct. 76), pp. 1–13; and, "The Destruction of Lachish by Sennacherib and the Dating of the Royal Judean Storage Jars," TA 4, nos. 1–2 (9177), pp. 28–60; and, "Answers at Lachish," BAR 5, no. 6 (Nov./Dec. 79), pp. 16–39. The seal impressions at Lachish are eighth century. Nadav Na'aman, "Hezekiah's Fortified Cities and the LMLK Stamp," BASOR 261 (Feb. 86), pp. 5–21. Nahman Avigad, "Jerahmeel & Baruch," BA 42, no. 1 (Spr. 79), pp. 114–118.

8.  Henry O. Thompson, "The Hajjar Coin: One of the Earliest Coins Yet Found in Jordan," forthcoming. John Wilson Betlyon, "Numismatics and Archaeology," BA 48, no. 3 (Sep. 85), pp. 162–165.

9.  Some inscriptions are magic spells. Charles D. Isbell, "The Story of the Aramaic Magical Incantation Bowls," BA 41, no. 1 (Mar. 78), pp. 5–16. Henry O. Thompson and Fawzi Zayadin, "The Tell Siran Inscription," BASOR 212 (Dec. 73), pp. 5–11.

10. Martin Noth, *The Old Testament World* (Philadelphia: Fortress, 1966), p. 220. Yohanan Aharoni, "Arad: Its Inscriptions and Temple," BA 31, no. 1 (Feb. 68), pp. 2–32; and, *Arad Inscriptions: Judean Desert Studies* (Jerusalem: IES, 1981). Aaron Demsky and Moshe Kochavi, "An Alphabet from the Days of the Judges," BAR 4, no. 3 (Sep./Oct. 78), pp. 22–30. Aron Dotan, "New Light on the 'Izbet Sartah Ostracon," TA 8, no. 2 (1981), pp. 160–172.

11. Ze'ev Meshel, "Did Yahweh Have a Consort?," BAR 5, no. 2 (Mar./Apr. 79), pp. 24–35. Pirhiya Beck, "The Drawings from Horvat Teiman (Kuntillet 'Ajrud)," TA 9, no. 1 (1982), pp. 3–68; and, "Kuntillet 'Ajrud: An Israelite Religious Center in Northern Sinai," *Expedition* 20, no. 4 (1978), pp. 50–54.

12. Albright, "Abram the Hebrew: A New Archaeological Interpretation," BASOR 163 (Oct. 61), pp. 36ff. Michael Ripinsky, "Camel Ancestry and Domestication in Egypt and the Sahara," *Archaeology* 36, no. 3 (May/June 83), pp. 21–27. "World's Oldest Musical Notation Deciphered on Cuneiform Tablet," BAR 6, no. 5 (Sep./Oct. 80), pp. 14–25. Anne D. Kilmer, "Music," IDBSV, pp. 610–612. Eric Werner, "Musical Instruments," IDB 3, pp. 469–476. Moshe Dothan, "The Musicians of Ashdod," BA 40, no. 1 (Mar. 77), pp. 38–39.

13. Vere Gordon Childe, *What Happened in History* (rev.; Baltimore: Penguin, 1965), p. 90. An example from Tell Agrab is illustrated opposite p. 225 in Ephraim A. Speiser, *At the Dawn of Civilization: A Background of Biblical History* (Rutgers: Rutgers University, 1964). Samuel Noah Kramer, *The Sumerians* (Chicago: University of Chicago, 1963), following p. 160.

14. ANEP, p. 212. The three ivory boards are nos. 213–215.

15. Hershel Shanks, "Ancient Ivory — The Story of Wealth, Decadence and Beauty," BAR 11, no. 5 (Sep./Oct. 85), pp. 40–53. R.D. Barnett, *Ancient Ivories in the Middle East and Adjacent Countries* (Jerusalem: IES, 1982). Kathleen M. Kenyon, *Amorites and Canaanites* (London: Oxford University, 1966), p. 75, fig. 40. Rachel Hachlili, "Ancient Burial Customs Preserved in Jericho Hills," BAR 5, no. 5 (July/Aug. 79), pp. 28–35; and, "A Second Temple Period Jewish Necropolis in Jericho," BA 43, no. 4 (Fall 80), pp. 235–240, reports on coffins preserved from the first centuries B.C. and A.D. Elizabeth Simpson and Robert Payton. "Royal Wooden Furniture from Gordion," *Archaeology* 39, no. 6 (Nov./Dec. 86), pp. 40–47. Bone was also used extensively in artistic carving. Elizabeth E. Platt, "Bone Pendants," BA 41, no. 1 (Mar. 78), pp. 23–28. W. Harold Mare, "Tomb Finds at Abila of the Decapolis," BA 45, no. 1 (Wint. 82), pp. 57–58. Meshel, "Yahweh Consort." Beck, "Horvat Teiman."

# Special Aspects
# of Daily Life

## A.  TUBALCAIN (GENESIS 4:22)

We have touched on metal a number of times. Pottery is involved with metallurgy in biblical times in a number of ways. The crucibles for melting down the ore and the metal ingots were ceramic. These crucibles are found in exploration and excavation with slag or bits of metal on their inner surfaces. Bellows appear in the Egyptian painting in the Beni-Hasan tomb and on the seal of Jotham from Kheleifeh. One form of bellows had a pottery nozzle which helped direct the air flow into the fire. Several of these were found at Shechem, which along with the pottery molds found there suggests that Shechem had a small bronze casting industry in the second millennium.

The molds found at Shechem were open-faced. Some double molds have been found — molds in two parts tied together with a hole at one end into which the molten metal was poured. Later the parts were separated leaving a metal product molded in the round. Molds were used for tools and weapons, jewelry, and other items. Some molds were made from stone. In earlier centuries glass objects, including jewelry, were formed in a mold though some were molded by hand, as was much metal jewelry. Blown glass was developed by the Romans. Some metal objects, especially softer materials like gold, were hammered or beaten into shape. Some hordes of miscellaneous metal objects may have been in storage to be melted down for jewlery or other purposes. Hordes have also been found containing jewelry, coins, etc. Schliemann's discovery of gold objects at Hissarlik was cited earlier, as were hordes of coins at Shechem and at Tell Hesban.

**Figure 8–1.**    A copper dagger with 4 rivets preserved, from Bab edh-Dhra' Charnel House A 41. Courtesy G. Ernest Wright.

The Arabah, part of the Rift Valley, south of the Dead Sea, had extensive copper deposits. Solomon's mines may have been near Timna near the Gulf. A copper smelting furnace was found there in 1965 and dated to c. 4000. This may be the oldest known furnace. Later furnaces have been discovered elsewhere, at Tell Abu Hawam and at Tell Zeror (LB in date). The possible development of economical methods of iron smelting by the Hittites was cited earlier. The secret was brought to Palestine by the Philistines. With the victories of Saul and David, the secrets of ironworking reached the hills — iron artifacts become more common in Israelite strata after 1000 B.C.[1]

## B.    CLOTHING

Paintings on pottery showing people indicate how people dressed. The paintings and carvings on temple and tomb walls, and on stelae and statues, provide more information. The Bible refers to skirts (I Kings 1:8), girdles or waistbands (II Samuel 18:11), sandals, and robes. Inscriptions and tablets describe clothing, sometimes as part of the tribute or the spoils of war in court records.

**Figure 8–2.** Crescent shaped battle axe made of copper from Charnel House A 44 at Bab edh-Dhra'. It was found less than 20 inches below the surface in a bone pile of mostly long bones and skulls some of which were removed before the picture was taken. Note the knob just below the bent haft. Courtesy G. Ernest Wright.

**Figure 8–3.** Metal Objects from Khirbet al-Hajjar. Nos. 21, 32, 24 are fibulas, the fore-runner of today's safety pin. No. 24 still works! No. 12 is a spatula for applying cosmetics. No. 37 is a needle. No. 20 is an arrowhead. No. 13 is a silver finger ring. No. 36 is the oldest coin found in Jordan and No. 29 is a ring seal. Photo courtesy Department of Antiquities of Jordan.

**Figure 8–4.**   Painting from the tomb of Beni Hasan. The tomb dates c. 1890 B.C. and shows Asians entering Egypt. Their clothing varies in style.

**Figure 8–5.**   Toggle pin. A thread through the hole tied it to the garment. When the pin was stuck through the edges of the robe, the extra thread was wound around it to keep it in place.

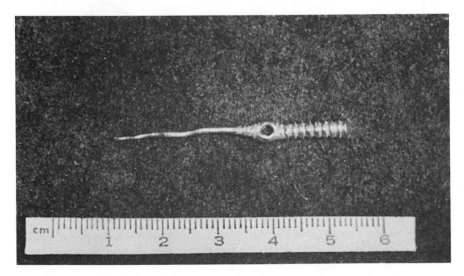

The clothing of Asiatics in the Beni-Hasan tomb painting (1890) is multi-colored, though two of the men wear white tunics or robes. A couple of men wear short skirts like Scottish and Egyptian kilts. The tunics of women and men both cover one shoulder though here too there is an exception, for one woman has a dress that covers both shoulders. A couple of the men are barefoot like the Egyptians, while others wear sandals. The women wear shoes or perhaps low boots as does one of the children.

The Assyrians, Egyptians, Philistines, and Hittites all wore kilts and robes of varying length. The Egyptians on the Mekal stela (Late Bronze Age) wear long skirts, while Mekal has a long robe. On the Black Obelisk of 842 B.C., some Hebrews wear what look like stocking caps, and shoes with turned up toes, Hittite style. Their tunics are like King Jehu's which is a short sleeved robe or tunic that comes down to his ankles. The women of Lachish (587 B.C.) and perhaps the men, wear similar tunics on the reliefs from Sennacherib's palace. Some of the men may be wearing a skirt and something like today's "T" shirt.

Clothing in Old Testament times did not have buttons. Excavations have produced a number of toggle pins, usually bronze. Perhaps there were iron ones which have rusted away. These are oversized straight pins with a hole in the middle for a string which held them on the garment. The pin was stuck through a fold or overlap of the robe and the loose string wound around both ends to hold it in place. The ancestor of the safety pin was invented about the tenth century. The triangular shaped "fibula" worked in the same way.

The coloring of cloth or thread was from some type of dyeing. The names "Canaan" (Akkadian) and "Phoenicia" (Greek) are often translated "purple" from the dye made from the murex shellfish (II Chronicles 2:7). The dye has been reproduced by modern chemists as noted earlier. Cloth was usually woven on looms in homes. An examination of textiles found in the Koseba caves (135 A.D.) showed several types of weave and dyes used in Roman Judea. The looms were probably of wood so there is little left, but large numbers of loom weights are found in excavations. The string of the loom may have gone over an upper beam or a tent pole and hung down on the other side. To keep it tight during the weaving process, a weight was attached to the loose end. These weights are made of pottery or of stone and shaped like a doughnut. Unusually large numbers of them were found at Beth-shan, suggesting a considerable weaving industry. In Ebla, as cited earlier, the queen controlled the weaving industry. She had factories staffed with women who were paid with grain.

An Akkadian tablet from Ugarit offers insight on the symbolism of clothing. The king divorced the queen and sent her back home to Amurru. Their son could choose to stay and become king some day or go with her and forfeit his claim to the throne. If he chose the latter, he was to leave his garments on the throne. Rummel compares this to the story of I Samuel 18:3–4. Jonathan, the son of Saul, gave his clothes and his armor to David. Jonathan gave up his claim to the throne.

The Joseph story in Genesis follows a similar pattern. When Joseph lost his cloak or clothing, he lost status and went into a pit or jail. When he received clothing, it was a symbol of status. His father gave him a special robe. Potiphar clothed him. The jailer clothed him to go before the pharaoh. Other examples are: Numbers 20:24–28 (Aaron is stripped of his garments which are put on Eleazer his son); I Kings 11:3–31 (the prophet Ahijah tore his new garment into twelve pieces and gave ten of them to Jeroboam); I Kings 19:19–21 (Elijah put his garment on Elisha); Isaiah 22:21 (Sheba's clothing will be given to Eliakim); Isaiah 47:1–2 (Babylon will be "unclothed"); Ezekiel 16:37 (Jerusalem will be stripped); Ezekiel 26:16 (princes of the sea will remove their robes); Hosea 2:3, 10 (Israel will be stripped); and Zechariah 3:3–7 (Joshua's filthy garments will be replaced with clean ones). We might add the story of Esther, who was clothed as queen, and the story of the prodigal son in the New Testament, who was clothed when he was restored to his role as a son. [2]

There are several places with a concentration of one kind of artifact. Beth-shan was cited earlier as was Ebla. There are other types of industry. I Chronicles 4:13–14 refers to the Valley of Craftsmen while verse 23 refers to the royal potteries of Netaim and Gederah; Jeremiah 37:21 refers to the bakers' street in Jerusalem, and Isaiah 7:3 to the fullers' field at Jerusalem. Avigad's excavations show that Jerusalem was a flourishing craft center for stone, pottery, and glass.

## C.  BRICKS AND BRICKLAYING

Clay or mud was a very common building material in biblical times and still is. When the Hebrews were slaves in Egypt, they made bricks (Exodus 1:14). A tomb painting of c. 1450 shows Syrians and Nubians making bricks for a temple. The clay or mud was commonly mixed with straw as a binding agent to keep the bricks from cracking when they dried, as with temper in pottery. When Moses asked the Pharaoh to let the people go, the Pharaoh responded with a stretchout, an old device in labor agitation. The Hebrews had to find their own straw, which took time. But their quota of bricks remained the same.

The Hebrew slaves are a reminder that the ancient world ran on a slave economy. There were also free peasants and skilled laborers. They were drawn into similar work for the government through tax in kind in the form of labor. The tax might be as high as one month out of three — a man might work two months for himself and one month in the government labor battalions called the "corvee" (I Kings 5:14). This was a common practice in the ancient Near East, so David (II Samuel 20:24) and Solomon were simply continuing an old practice.

The corvee was not limited to making mud bricks. Solomon used it for all his projects including quarrying stone for the foundations of his buildings. The latter

**Figure 8–6.** Roof roller. The indentation in the cylindrical end, matched by one on the other end, may have held a handle in place. The roller might have worked like lawn rollers today.

was a common form of construction — a stone foundation, varying from a single course of field stone to many. The bigger and more special buildings might have finely cut (dressed) ashlar blocks, especially around doors and windows. Walls of mud brick were built on the stone foundation or "socket," giving added height for a defense wall, or enclosing the rooms of a house or temple. The roof was normally of wooden beams laid from one wall to another, perhaps with a column or series of columns in the middle for larger rooms. The beams were overlaid with small branches, then brush or reeds, and the top was plastered mud. After a winter rain, the mud would *percolate* — get little holes in it. The mud was then packed down with a stone roller. These cylindrical stones are found in excavations. Sometimes a new layer of mud or clay would be plastered over the old. Roofing from an eighth century house at Shechem showed five such layers.

The temple at Schechem had a foundation seventeen feet thick in 1650 B.C. G. Ernest Wright suggested this meant a building two to three stories high. A city wall at Gezer is fifty feet wide. The mud brick wall above this socket must have been reminiscent of the ziggurats of Mesopotamia. The latter were made entirely of mud brick. The outside layers were baked or burned brick, making them more resistant to erosion. Raw mud brick, exposed to the weather and not kept under regular repair, would soon deteriorate or simply dissolve back into plain dirt. Archaeologists have occasionally dug right through this raw brick without knowing it. With care it can be distinguished. Baked brick is more substantial but it too tends to disintegrate. Both contribute to the buildup of a tell as described in chapter one.

Later inhabitants might simply build right on top of the debris. At times they would dig down into earlier strata and take out the stone from earlier foundations. This was easier than cutting new stone or hauling it from the mountains. The pit or trench this left would fill with debris and form what archaeologists call a robber trench or pit. Stone was sometimes used for whole walls as well as foundations and was commonly used for door sockets, the frames of city gates, and columns in larger buildings.

**Figure 8–7.** A close-up of the construction at Umm el-Jimal, the black basalt city in northeast Jordan. The round window is cut from several blocks of stone. The stair to the upper floor and the landing there are made of long thin slabs of basalt.

Figure 8–8.   Umm el-Jimal.  Extensive use was made of the Roman arch during the Roman and Byzantine periods. Barely visible above the arches are slabs of basalt cantilever slabs that formed part of the roof or ceiling.

Figure 8–9.   An underground room hollowed out of rock. At the far end a door led out to the side of the hill. Tell Siran. Photo courtesy Department of Antiquities of Jordan.

The earliest dwellings were caves. Since tents were made of skins or other perishable materials, the date of the first tent is unknown. Sometimes the outside edge of the tent was held down against the wind with rocks and debris. These circles have been found from early times. Some early dwellings were pits dug into the ground, probably roofed over with skins or perhaps brush. Such dwelling pits of c. 4000 were found at Beth-shan, c. 5000 at Jericho. Bir es-Safadi and several other sites in the southern Negev had underground rooms hollowed out of the *loess* (wind drift) soil. Tell Siran in Jordan had underground rooms of uncertain date hollowed out of rock.

Remains of both round and square or rectangular construction have been found. The poor lived in small round huts of brush but there were large round *tholoi* — beehive shape — in Greece and Syria. They may have been temples or tombs. A beehive-shaped mud house style is still used in northern Syria — the heat rises and keeps the dwelling cool in the summer. An interesting variant in the round and square construction is the *apsidal* house. It has one round and one rectangular end. The form appears c. 3600 at Meser and c. 3000 at Beth-shan. The style is used for temples in later Greece and Turkey (Sardis, c. 600) and appears in cave temples in India, perhaps through Hellenistic influence.

## D.  RELIGION

The temples draw our attention to religion, which formed an intricate part of daily life in biblical times. Figurines were cited earlier. No idols have been found in Palestine that could be related to the Hebrew God. Either the Second Commandment against images was obeyed, or the idols were destroyed or have not yet been found or been recognized. The idolatry condemned in the Bible is that of other gods, especially of Baal, the Canaanite fertility god.

Israelite religion before the temple of Solomon apparently made free use of Canaanite "high places" such as Gibeon (I Kings 3:4) or earlier places such as the Shechem temple (Judges 8:33; 9:46). Later, this was condemned by the Deuteronomic editor of the history that runs from Deuteronomy to the end of II Kings, in favor of Solomon's temple. A major exception is Elijah's rebuilding of an old altar on Mount Carmel (I Kings 18:30).

Several altars, or what may have been high places, have been found in and around Palestine. One of the most famous is the huge oval altar of c. 1900 B.C. at Megiddo. Joshua's altar on Mount Ebal may have been found and a high place may have been uncovered at Tell Dan, but both are still debated. Several high places have been found at Petra in southern Jordan. Albright thought they were funerary shrines, like the monument to Absalom mentioned in the Old Testament (II Samuel 19:17). The latter is not the Absalom's monument visible today in the

**Figure 8–10.**    The oval altar at Megiddo. It was in use c. 1900 B.C. and probably represents a Canaanite high place.

Kidron Valley by Jerusalem. The Kidron Valley monument dates from the Hellenistic period, c. 200 B.C. There was an Israelite temple at Arad which continued from Solomon's time to Josiah's. Its destruction may have been part of Josiah's reform to concentrate worship in his capital. Earlier, Arad had a high place. Aharoni thought the sacred site may have been the Kenites'. They were Moses' in-laws. The temple at Lachish was also built on the site of an earlier high place.

Later interpretation of the commandment against idols was that it was against representation of anything on earth or in heaven. That was certainly not the case with Solomon's temple. The Bible describes many decorations. Nor was it the interpretation of the synagogues of the early Christian period. These had beautiful mosaics with many motifs from nature. Paintings and frescoes also indicate the decorative art of the synagogue which continued until at least 250 A.D. (Dura Europas on the Euphrates River) and continued in Christian churches. A synagogue was discovered at Nabratein in Galilee. A portion of an ark of the covenant was found there, recognizable from artistic scenes already known. The stone "ark" presumably contained a copy of the Torah, the most sacred portion of Hebrew scripture. The broken ark was itself not sacred — it was reused in rebuilding during the next period.[3]

**Figure 8–11.**   The Beer-sheba horned altar, reconstructed. Photo courtesy *The Biblical Archaeologist*.

**Figure 8–12.**   The Temple of Hercules on Jabel Qalat, the acropolis of ancient Rabath Ammon (Amman).

**Figure 8–13.**   The High Place of Petra. The square high place on one of the highest mountains above the city, contrasts to a round high place within the city itself.

**Figure 8–14.**    Petra altar. At one end of the square high place is a circular altar with a channel for the blood of the sacrificed animal to run off to a lower area.

**Figure 8–15.**    Temple of Samaria. The large steps indicate the size of the temple, built by Herod the Great to honor his patron Emperor Augustus Caesar. The city was renamed Sebastiya, for the emperor Augustus' personal name.

**Figure 8–16.**    Temple of Apollo at Corinth.

**Figure 8–17.**    The Parthenon. This famous building on the Acropolis of Athens was a temple to Athena and later a Christian Church and later a Muslim mosque. Now it is a museum. Holy sites tended to retain their holiness for centuries. A major example of this is the 4000 year old tradition of the Dome of the Rock in Jerusalem.

**Figure 8–18.** The Haram esh-Sharif — The Sacred Enclosure — the platform built by Herod the Great for his remodelling of the Second Temple (516 B.C. — 70 A.D.). The remodelling was finished in 64 A.D. The Dome of the Rock — Muslim shrine built by Abd al-Malik in 685 A.D. It stands over the traditional site of the Temple of Solomon ("Master of all the genies") and the Rock (hence its name) where Abraham the Prophet and ancestor of the Arabs almost sacrificed Isaac.

**Figure 8–19.**    The Haram esh-Sharif with the fountain for washing before prayer, and the Mosque al-Aqsa.

A group of small altars, usually of limestone, have been found in Palestine. One from Megiddo, tenth century, is about eighteen inches high. The top is concave and the four corners stick up suggesting horns. When David's general Joab tried to escape Solomon's vengeance, he went to the tent shrine and caught hold of the horns of the altar. This was an ancient symbolic way of seeking sanctuary from one's enemies, but he was killed anyway (I Kings 2:28ff). Since these altars seem too small for animal sacrifice, they may have been incense altars, perhaps even for private homes. A whole class of pottery vessels and objects have been called incense stands. They range from one to over two feet in height.

The exact use of other cult objects is not as clear. Some are in the form of little houses, one or two stories high. An object called a kernos ring is a hollow pottery ring which might have been worn on the head during religious rituals. On the ring were ceramic animal heads, fruit, vases, and lamps. The ring may have contained a libation which poured from an animal mouth when the wearer bowed. Another clay object, sometimes found in Palestine but more common in Mesopotamia, is a model liver. Priests would serve as diviners. The sacrificial animal was butchered and the lines on the liver studied as omen signs for the future — whether the king should go to battle, etc. Clay models of the livers may have been to train student priests or to preserve readings. Livers and other objects could be made of metal. Solomon had many bronze objects in the temple (I Kings 7:13ff), along with decorations of gold and ivory and wood carvings (6:14ff).

Inscriptions have added considerable information on religion. The model livers were frequently inscribed. Stelae were often inscribed though the art they contain may contribute as much to our knowledge as the writing. The Ras Shamra tablets are particularly helpful for religious studies. Included in religion are many ancient laws and customs, described as gifts of the gods. Orthodox Judaism has developed an extensive system of dietary laws based on the biblical injunction against boiling a kid in its mother's milk (Exodus 23:19, 34:26; Deuteronomy 14:21), a custom still practiced by Arab bedouin in the 1930s. A Ras Shamra tablet says that the most proper way to honor the gods is with a young kid boiled in milk. The honored guest of the desert nomads once received the same delicacy. Perhaps the biblical prohibition was to keep the Hebrews away from pagan practices, lest they be enticed to worship the deities involved.[4]

# E.   ILLNESS, TOO

Ancient peoples, like people today, became sick and suffered from various diseases. We include this here because of the relationship between health and religion. Today it is often called psychosomatic medicine. Ancient peoples appealed to the gods for life and health, and though epidemics and death were punishment by the gods. The temple was the first hospital. The priests were the first doctors. Pottery figurines of the ancient world show such problems as elephantiasis and tetanus. These figurines have been found in the western hemisphere also. Some were left in temples as votive offerings in hope of healing, or in gratitude for healing.

Ancient literature offers some knowledge of health problems. The Bible contains many "medical" references, such as that to leprosy in Numbers 12:10. Ancient medical texts are more magical in character, prescribing rituals to end an epidemic or drive out "demons" (mental illness?). Egyptian medical papyri contain lists of illnesses and treatments, including dental work. One of the most remarkable ancient inscriptions is a Hurrian text on the worm and the toothache. It is a religious incantation coupled with practical instructions to the dentist to use a pin to grab the foot of the "worm" (the nerve?) and pull it out.[5]

Skeletal remains are an important source of medical and dental knowledge. Tombs are of interest for their pottery and other artifacts, but the skeletal remains indicate life expectancy and nutrition as well as dental cavities, tetanus, bone lesions, tumors, etc. The skeleton of a woman found at Tell Hesban had a calcified tumor inside the rib cage suggesting the cause of death. X-rays of Egyptian mummies reveal the dental problems of the pharaohs. Ramses II had over 22 cavities. The wounds have killed them also appear. Primitive doctors or medicine men knew something about setting broken bones. A fascinating practice is called trepanning. Surgeons cut holes in the skulls of patients in prehistoric Jericho, later Lachish, and various parts of the Old World and the New. Some of these operations were at least partially successful because bones had grown back together. The purpose of the operation is obscure. One can guess that in the days B.A. (Before Aspirin), it was a drastic treatment for migraine. Instead of the hammers shown inside the head in modern commercials, ancient man had a picture of a demon pounding the inside of the head, trying to get out, so they cut a hole to let him out![6]

## F.   HEREAFTER

As early as Neanderthal Man, 50,000 years ago, people began to bury artifacts with their dead. This practice implies some religious belief in an afterlife. Pottery was included once it was invented. The pottery was carefully laid in the grave. Since many burials were in natural (Genesis 23) or artificial caves in the rock, burials are the main source of whole pottery vessels. Even if the roof of the cave fell in, and crushed the contents, the pieces would all be there. Pottery can now be dated with little more than a piece of rim. But it is always helpful to see what the whole vessel looked like and dating may depend on a combination of features such as bases and handles.

Toggle pins in graves suggest clothing. Samuel's ghostly look (I Samuel 28:14) suggests he was buried in his robe. Artifacts also included tools and weapons and even food. A series of burials at Jericho, possibly of Amorites, are called dagger tombs. The only artifact in each tomb was a bronze dagger. A very rich tomb, c. 1200 B.C. at Tell es-Sa'idiyeh, had a bronze wine service set — a tray, a bowl (as a cup), a strainer, and a jug. Another tomb whose skeleton was imbedded in a slab of bitumen, had a bronze sword, spearheads, arrowheads, etc. The model furniture at Lachish and the wooden furniture at Jericho was cited earlier. The latter may be more common than current evidence indicates since wood decays so rapidly.[7]

There were many types of burials. The Hyksos buried beneath the floor of the house, perhaps so the dead would always be with them. This may be the model for Samuel's burial (I Samuel 25:1). The practice persisted in the case of children. We occasionally find infant remains under building foundations, especially large public buildings like temples and palaces. These have been interpreted as child sacrifices to give the building a long life. But the infant mortality rate was so high that many of these could be foundation burials rather than sacrifices.

Multiple burials appear before 3000. One tomb might have few or as many as 300 individual burials. A tomb might be used once or over centuries. It wa swork to cut a tomb out of solid rock, and expensive to hire workers to have it done, so the multiple burials may have been simply practical. However, some were family tombs as with Abraham's cave at Machpelah or the tombs of kings (I Kings 11:43, 14:31).

The many natural caves in the hills of Palestine are still used for burials, especially by the poor who cannot afford a present day Christian or Muslim burial. When a tomb was reused, earlier remains might be covered with dirt that had sifted in or by a partly fallen ceiling. Thus tombs may have strata just as tells do. If the bones of earlier inhabitants were still exposed, they might be carefully preserved or simply pushed aside. Some tombs have evidence of secondary burial — that is, a nomadic people would bury their dead immediately while following the seasonal pasture, and when they returned to their permanent or winter headquarters, they would disinter the remains for burial in the family tomb. Examples might be a tomb with all long bones and no fine bones (fingers, feet, etc.), or a tomb with more skulls than other skeletal remains. [8]

Cremation was practiced as early as 3000 B.C. (I Samuel 31:12) as shown by the charred remains of bones in and around a fire-pit in a tomb. One of the most fascinating instances of cremation is a series of "charnel houses" discovered in a large cemetery on the eastern side of the Dead Sea, at Bab edh-Dhra. Hundreds of bodies were cremated in addition to standard burials performed during the third millennium. Hundreds of pottery vessels have been found in charnel houses and in the conventional burials. Paul Lapp, the first excavator, judged by the number of houses and tombs left unexcavated that this huge cemetery contained three million pottery vessels. [9]

We cannot leave the subject of pottery and burials without reference to pottery coffins. Pottery urns, called *ossuaries*, in which to place bones after the flesh decayed were being made in the Chalcolithic Age c. 3500. Multiple burials of up to a hundred ossuaries have been found. One type is about one foot wide by two feet long by two feet high. They are painted with designs and shaped like a house. Perhaps this is what the houses of the era and area looked like. Others are shaped like animals or simply round. Large numbers of stone ossuaries have been found in Jewish tombs of the first centuries B.C. and A.D. One type is a chest with a lid on top.

**Figure 8–20.** A stone lined tomb covered with a slab roof. It was mostly robbed before the archaeologists arrived, but they did find an articulated torso near the back of the chamber. Bab edh-Dhra'. Courtesy G. Ernest Wright.

**Figure 8–21.** Charnel House A41 at Bab edh-Dhra'. This was a mudbrick rectangular building with a large slab of rock for a threshhold (under the meter stick) and a cobbled floor. The entryway was probably sealed by a mudbrick wall. In the center of the building is a large pile of bones and pots that were heavily burned while the pile in the left foreground was only partly burned. The entryway area had been robbed before archaeological excavation. Two daggers made of copper were found near the half meter stick on the right side of the picture. Courtesy G. Ernest Wright.

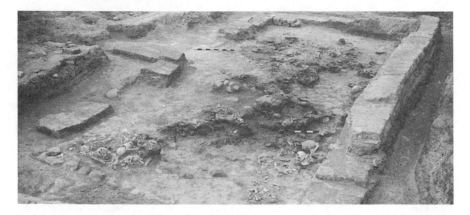

**Figure 8–22.** Bones and pots piled together in one corner of Charnel House A42. The large pot in the upper left hand corner is from the next pile. This group just below the surface is a representative group for the Charnel Houses. Bab edh-Dhra'. Courtesy G. Ernest Wright.

**Figure 8–23.** A shaft tomb at Bab edh-Dhra'. Each of the five boulders blocks a dome shaped chamber with a pile of disarticulated bones in the middle, a line of skulls and pots heaped around the wall. This is tomb A68. Courtesy G. Ernest Wright.

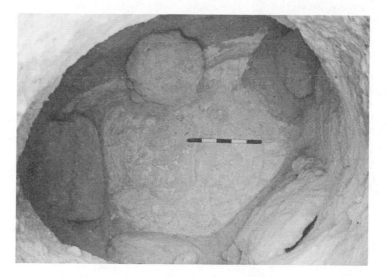

**Figure 8–24.** Shaft tomb A43 chamber with pots along the wall. Note the spouted bowl on the left, decorated in vertical lines of paint. Bab edh-Dhra'. Courtesy G. Ernest Wright.

**Figure 8–25.** Shaft tomb A69 chamber with long bones on top of small bones. Vessels were apparently new and unused when placed in the tomb. The central bowl is shiny from burnishing — smoothing the vessel before baking with a smooth stone or bone. The burnishing both decorates and helps the baked pottery hold liquid better. Bab edh-Dhra'. Courtesy G. Ernest Wright.

**Figure 8–26.** Shaft tomb A72 with perfectly preserved bowls and pots. Note long bones laid on top of disarticulated small bones, i.e., this is a secondary burial. These bones were gathered from an earlier burial after the decay of the flesh, and re-buried here. Bab edh-Dhra'. Courtesy G. Ernest Wright.

**Figure 8–27.** A rolling stone tomb at Tell Hesban, perhaps like the tomb of Joseph of Arimathea in which the body of Jesus was lain after the crucifixion. The round disc rock rolls in a trench for most of these tombs. Here it rolls between two walls.

**Figure 8–28.** The interior of the rolling stone tomb at Hesban showing the loculi (singular "loculus") after excavation. There were four loculi on each of three sides of a central room. The door is in the fourth side coming in from the slope of the hill.

**Figure 8–29.** Roman tomb with door, at Hesban. One speculation is that the facade is modelled after the home of the deceased. The door still swings in its sockets!

**Figure 8–30.** Anthropoid coffin. These have been associated with the Philistines or at least the Sea Peoples. They may have been introduced by even earlier Myceneans.

**Figure 8–31.** The Tomb of "Absalom" in the Kidron Valley actually dates from c. 250 B.C.

It varies from one and a half to three feet long. Many are inscribed in Hebrew, Aramaic, or Greek with the names of the deceased and sometimes those of his ancestors. These have the familiar ring of Jewish names in the New Testament — Jesus, Mary, Joseph, Ananias, etc. One of Jesus the son of Joseph created a small stir when it was found!

The Egyptian poor were simply buried in the sand, but the wealthy had elaborate burials. The pyramids are an extreme example. The body was embalmed for several months and put in a coffin. Jacob and Joseph were embalmed (Genesis 50:2 and 26) but neither practice was carried on by the Hebrews in general. Egyptian coffins were usually of wood (King Tut's three coffins are of gold) and had a lid in the shape of a person wrapped like a mummy. In Palestine, a number of pottery coffins, called "anthropoid sarcophagi," have been found in several places and dating from several periods. One type found at Beth-shan, from the fourteenth century and perhaps later, has been related to the "Sea Peoples" or to the Myceneans, hired by the Egyptians as mercenary soldiers. Wright has related these and several in southern Palestine with the Philistines. This type had one unit shaped like a slipper so they are called *slipper sarcophagi* at times. A second unit served as a lid. Stylized or realistic features were molded on the lid.

Coffins were made of stone also. Some were elaborately carved, especially in Egypt and Phoenicia where they date from before 2000 down to Roman times. One of the more famous is that of Ahiram of Byblos, tenth century. He is shown seated on a throne receiving gifts and greetings from his attendants. His throne may be like Solomon's (I Kings 10:18ff).

In Palestine, the practice of building monuments above ground did not begin until the Hellenistic Age. The monuments in the Kidron Valley, including Absalom's cited earlier, date from this period. The monument which the original Absalom set up for himself (II Samuel 18:18) may have been a stele or simply a large upright stone. The so-called Tombs of the Kings in northern Jerusalem originally had a monument above ground. These tombs were of the royal family of Adiabene which had converted to Judaism. The tombs date to about 50 A.D. [10]

Queen Helena of Adiabene forms an example of the prominent role of women in the ancient Near East. Queens are known among Arab tribes. Queen Zenobia of Palmyra was a strong opponent of the Romans. The Queen of Ebla was cited earlier. In Egypt, Nefertiti had a considerable influence in the court of Pharaoh Ikhnaten. Earlier we note not Queen Hatshepsut but Pharaoh Hatshepsut. Her father, the incarnation of the god Horus, pronounced her a man and she reigned as the incarnation of Horus after her father's death.

This discussion of illness and death based on artifacts, tombs, and inscriptions is a reminder that life in ancient times was not easy. The transitoriness of life was the message signalled by war, famine, pestilence, and disease. It is tempting to romanticize the earlier picture of women gracefully carrying water pots on their heads. But these were heavy and for the carriers it was more like work than romance. Farming was work and so were the tasks of the corvee, cutting rocks and timber and building roads with primitive tools.

Carol Meyers of Duke University has perceptibly combined social insight, biblical studies, and archaeology to suggest that in an earlier day, women and men shared this rough life. There were priestesses as well as priests, queens as well as kings. Women and men were "co-laborers in the vineyard." The creation stories suggest a certain equality. In Genesis 1 this is quite clear where women and men are created together as the last creatures created — the epitamy of divine creation. In Genesis 2 the man is created lower than (before) animals, and is passive and submissive. She cites the widespread appearance of female figurines from the Old Stone Age to the Late Bronze Age and the prominence of the goddesses as well as gods in the pantheons of the ancient Near East.

The Late Bronze Age was a time of plagues that decimated the population. The Hebrew conquest and settlement destroyed cities. The Hebrews populated new lands in the hill country of Judah where they could now give thanks to waterproof plaster for cisterns. They needed to increase the population to replace the dead and to cultivate the land. The result was not the restriction of women's roles (which came later) but a concentration on child production as their contribution to the socio-economic situation. By the time of David with the corvee and the slave wife harems, the role of women changed from economic contribution to subordination, away from a covenant of freedom and equality which the Hebrew slaves made with Yahweh at Mount Sinai. So the daily life of women moved from equity to oppression.[11]

While not everyone will agree with Meyers' interpretation, it is a reminder of another of her statements that the ultimate goal of archaeology is not the potsherd or even the shrine. Archaeology is truly valuable when it brings us closer to the people who produced the artifacts, and when we get some glimpse of the function and meaning of those artifacts in the lives of the people who owned them. We are again reminded of Wheeler's aphorism that we are not digging up things, but people.[12]

# NOTES

1. R.F. Tylecote, "From Pot Bellows to Tuyeres," *Levant* 13 (1981), pp. 107–118. R.J. Forbes, *Studies in Ancient Technology*, Vol. VIII (Leiden: Brill, 1964), pp. 113–115. Moshe Kochavi, "Tel Zeror," IEJ 15, no. 4 (9175), pp. 253–255. Elizabeth E. Platt, "Triangular Jewelry Plaques," BASOR 221 (Feb. 76), pp. 103–111. Joe D. Seger, "Reflections on the Gold Hoard from Gezer," BASOR 221, pp. 133–140. Ora Negbi, *The Hoards of Goldwork from Tell el-Ajju* (Goteborg: Aastroms, 1970). K.R. Maxwell-Hyslop, *Western Asiatic Jewelery, c. 3000–612 B.C.* (London: Methuen, 1971). Alix Wilkinson, *Ancienty Egyptian Jewellery* (London: Methuen, 1971). Theodore A. Wertime and James D. Muhly, eds., *The Coming of the Age of Iron* (New Haven: Yale, 1980).
2. Shea, "Beni Hasan Asiatics." "Israel's Soil Yields New Knowledge," *Land of the Bible Newsletter*, no. 30 (Jan. 63), p. 1. Stan Rummel, "Clothes Maketh the Man — An Insight from Ancient Ugarit," BAR 2, no. 2 (June 76), pp. 6–8. PRS, p. 126. Glenn T. Seaborg, "Science and the Humanities: A New Level of Symbiosis," *Science* 144 (1964), pp. 1201–1202.
3. Nahman Avigad, "Jerusalem Flourishing: A Craft Center for Stone, Pottery, and Glass," BAR 9, no. 6 (Nov./Dec. 83), pp. 48–65; and, *Discovering Jerusalem: Recent Archaeological Excavations in the Upper City* (Nashville: Nelson, 1983). Adam Zertal, "Has Joshua's Altar Been Found?," BAR 11, no. 1 (Jan./Feb. 85), pp. 26–43 (Zertal says "Yes.") "How can Kempinksi Be So Wrong?," BAR 12, no. 1 (Jan./Feb. 86), pp. 43, 49–53. Aharon Kempinski, "Joshua's Altar — An Iron Age I Watchtower," BAR 12, no. 1 (Jan./Feb. 86), pp. 42, 44–49. Albright, "The High Places in Ancient Palestine," *Vetus Testamentum Supplement* 4 (1957), p. 242. Valerie M. Fargo, "Temples and High Places," BA 40 (May 77), pp. 54–55. Eric M. Meyers, et al., "The Ark of the Nabratein Synagogue — a First Glance," BA 44, no. 4 (Fall 81), pp. 237–243. Meyers and Meyers, "American Archaeologists Find Remains of Ancient Synagogue Ark in Galilee," BAR 7, no. 6 (Nov./Dec. 81), pp. 24–39. Christopher J. Davey, "Temples of the Levant and the Buildings of Solomon," *Tyndale Bulletin* 31 (1980), pp. 107–146. Henry O. Thompson, "Apsidal Construction in the Ancient Near East," PEQ 101 (July/Dec. 69), pp. 69–86.
4. Mervyn D. Fowler, "Excavated Incense Burners," BA 47, no. 3 (Sep. 84), pp. 183–186. Nelson Glueck, *The Other Side of the Jordan* (rev.; New Haven: ASOR, 1970), p. 4.

5.  J. Gourevick, "Recorded in Clay," Abbottempo, pp. 16–21. Paul Chalioungui, "The Medical Objects in the Cairo Museum," *Egypt Travel Magazine* 103 (Mar. 63), pp. 6–17. Stuart Fleming, "Life in Ancient Egypt: Harsh Realities," *Archaeology* 35, no. 4 (July/Aug. 82), pp. 72–73. Faye Marley, "Relics Show their Merits," SN 90 (12 Nov. 66), pp. 396–397. Carol Meyers, "The Roots of Restriction: Women in Early Israel," BA 41: no. 3 (Sep. 78), pp. 91–103. C.J. Brim, *Medicine in the Bible* (New York: Froben, 1936). ANET, pp. 100–101, 347–348. Joseph Zias and Karen Numeroff, "Ancient Denistry in the Eastern Mediterranean," IEJ 36, nos. 1–2 (1986), 65–67.

6.  M.S. Goldstein, "The Paleopathology of Human Skeletal Remains" (pp. 391–400 in *Science in Archaeology*, rev., ed. Don R. Brothwell and Eric C. Higgs; New York: Praeger, 1970). J. Kenneth Eakins, "Human Osteology and Archaeology," BA 43, no. 2 (Spr. 80), pp. 89–96. SN 91 (25 Mar. 67), p. 280. *Life* 62 (7 Ap. 67), pp. 57–58. Fleming, "Life in Ancient Egypt." Rebecca Huss-Ashmore, et al., "Nutritional Inference from Paleopathology," SAAMT 5 (1982), pp. 395–474.

7.  James B. Pritchard, "The First Excavations at Tell e-Saidiyeh," BA 28, no. 1 (Feb. 65), pp. 14–17.

8.  Joseph A. Callaway, "Burials in Ancient Palestine: From the Stone Age to Abraham," BA 26 (Sep. 63), pp. 74–91. Nahman Avigad, "The Tombs in Jerusalem," EAEHL, pp. 627–641. Eric M. Meyers, "Secondary Burials in Palestine," BA 33, no. 1 (Feb. 70), pp. 2–29. L.Y. Rahman, "Ancient Jerusalem's Funerary Customs and Tombs — Part One," BA 44, no. 3 (Sum. 81), pp. 171–177; and, "..Part Two," BA 44, no. 4 (Fall 81), pp. 229–235; and, "..Part Three," BA 45, no. 1 (Wint. 82), pp. 43–53.

9.  "Have Sodom & Gomorrah Been Found?," BAR 6, no. 5 (Sep./Oct. 80), pp. 26–36. William C. van Hattem, "Once Again: Sodom and Gomorrah," BA 44, no. 2 (Spr. 81), pp. 86–92. Walter A. Rast, "Bab-edh-Dhra" and Numeira," BA 40, no. 4 (Dec. 77), p. 135. David N. Freedman, ed., *Preliminary Excavation Reports* (Cambridge: AASOR 43, 1978). Water E. Rast and R. Thomas Schaub, *The Southeastern Dead Sea Plain Expedition: An Interim Report of the 1977 Season*; (Cambridge: AASOR 46, 1980).

10. WBA, pp. 245–246.

11. Meyers, "Roots of Restriction." Edward F. Campbell, Jr., "Moses and the Foundations of Israel," *Interpretation* 29 (1975), pp. 141–154. B.F. Batto, *Studies on Women at Mari* (Baltimore: Johns Hopkins, 1974). A van Selms, *Marriage and Family Life In Ugaritic Literature* (London: Luzac, 1954). Rivkah Harris, "Woman in the Ancient Near East," IDBSV, pp. 960–963. Phyllis Trible, "Woman in the Old Testament," IDBSV, pp. 963–966. Robin Scroggs, "Woman in the NT," IDBSV, pp. 966–968, notes that in contrast to the subordination of women in Mediterranean cultures, Christianity initially accepted women with equality. However, it soon reverted to the old ways. The worship of goddesses continued throughout the centuries. Robert A. Oden, "The Persistence of Canaanite Religion," BA 39, no. 1 (Mar. 76), pp. 31–36. Drawings and inscriptions from the eighth century B.C. have raised the question, "Did Yahweh Have a Consort?," BAR 5, no. 2 (Mar./Ap. 79), pp. 24–35 by Ze'ev Meshel.

12. Quoted by BAR 3, no. 4 (Dec. 77), p. 58, from Carol L. Meyers, *The Tabernacle Menorah: A Synthetic Study of a Symbol from the Biblical Cult* (Missoula, MT: Scholar's, 1976), p. 2. Fleming, "Life in Ancient Egypt." Wheeler, *Archaeology from the Earth* (Baltimore: Penguin, 1954), p. 15.

# ADDITIONAL READING

Anati, Emmanuel. *Palestine Before the Hebrews*. New York: Knopf, 1963.

Bailey, Albert E. *Daily Life in Bible Times*. New York: Scribners, 1943.

Ben-Tor, Ammon. 1979. "Tell Qiri: A Look at Village Life." BA 42 (no. 1): 105–113.

Contenau, George. *Everyday Life in Babylon and Assyria*. New York: Norton, 1966.

Edelstein, Gershon and Gibson Shimon. 1982. "Ancient Jerusalem's Rural Food Basket." *BAR* 7 (no. 4): 46–54.

Frank, Harry Thomas. *Discovering the Biblical World*. Maplewood, NJ, and New York: Hammond, and Harper & Row, 1975.

Heaton, E.W. *Everday Life in Old Testament Times*. London: Batsford, 1956.

Kenyon, Kathleen M. *Archaeology of the Holy Land*. 4th ed.; NY: Norton, 1979.

Oppenheim, A. Leo. *Letters from Mesopotamia*. Chicago: University of Chicago, 1967.

Posener, Georges. *Dictionary of Egyptian Civilization*. New York: Tudor, 1959.

Saggs, H.W.F. *Everyday Life in Babylonia and Assyria*. New York: Putnam, 1965.

Sameh, Waley-el-dine. *Daily Life in Ancient Egypt*. New York: McGraw-Hil, 1964.

Severy, Merle, ed. *Everyday Life in Bible Times*. Washington: NG Society, 1967.

de Vaux, Roland. *Ancient Israel*. New York: McGraw-Hill, 1961.

White, J.M. *Everyday Life in Ancient Egypt*. New York: Putnam, 1963.

# ARCHAEOLOGY
# ILLUMINATES THE BIBLE

The Hebrew Scripture, the Christian Old Testament, covers several thousand years or more of history. Archaeology illuminates virtually all of it or at least every age of the Bible. The first portion of this section concentrates on Genesis 1–11. Many scholars do not think these chapters are historical. This means that "bibilical history" includes archaeological background for the Bible without necessarily proving or disproving the literal history. Archaeological data does not "prove" the Bible, does not prove it right nor prove it wrong. My concern is to show the role archaeology plays in studies of the Bible.

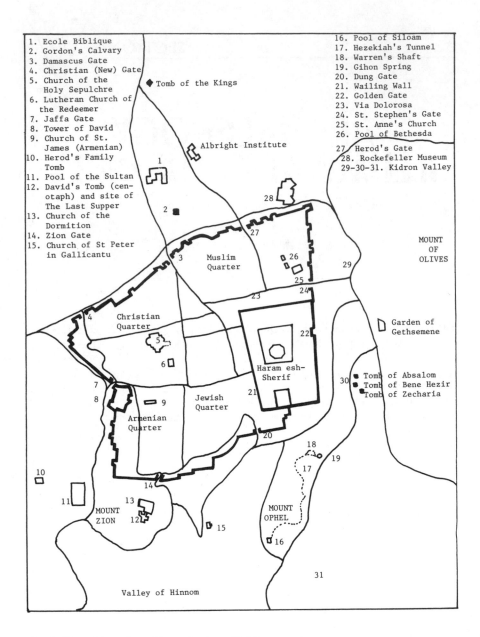

1. Ecole Biblique
2. Gordon's Calvary
3. Damascus Gate
4. Christian (New) Gate
5. Church of the
   Holy Sepulchre
6. Lutheran Church of
   the Redeemer
7. Jaffa Gate
8. Tower of David
9. Church of St.
   James (Armenian)
10. Herod's Family
    Tomb
11. Pool of the Sultan
12. David's Tomb (cen-
    otaph) and site of
    The Last Supper
13. Church of the
    Dormition
14. Zion Gate
15. Church of St Peter
    in Gallicantu

16. Pool of Siloam
17. Hezekiah's Tunnel
18. Warren's Shaft
19. Gihon Spring
20. Dung Gate
21. Wailing Wall
22. Golden Gate
23. Via Dolorosa
24. St. Stephen's Gate
25. St. Anne's Church
26. Pool of Bethesda
27. Herod's Gate
28. Rockefeller Museum
29-30-31. Kidron Valley

Tomb of the Kings

Albright Institute

MOUNT
OF
OLIVES

Muslim
Quarter

Christian
Quarter

Haram esh-
Sherif

Garden of
Gethsemene

Tomb of Absalom
Tomb of Bene Hezir
Tomb of Zecharia

Jewish
Quarter

Armenian
Quarter

MOUNT
ZION

MOUNT
OPHEL

Valley of Hinnom

Sketch Plan of Jerusalem (Drawn by Joyce E. Thompson)

# The Pentateuch

## A. GENESIS 1–11

The opening chapters of Genesis are stories of creation, the first woman and man, the paradise of Eden, Abel and Cain, the flood, and the tower of Babel. There are many theories about these stories. The theories can be seen in terms of two extremes and a broad middle way. Biblical literalists insist that every single word in the Bible is true, including words added by translators to clarify the Hebrew, Aramaic and Greek, and including scholarly guesses where we do not know the original. On the other hand there are those who consider these eleven chapters fiction which should be ignored. In between are a variety of middle positions. "The stories are true as a whole though we need not insist every word is literally true." "The stories are an honest attempt to write history. The material is in an historical format. In the end, sincere or not, we must see the stories as simply untrue." Other theories claim these are stories of faith. They are poetry that is a way of expressing truth though, like poetry anywhere, anytime, it is not literally true, by the very nature of poetry. These are myths, myths not in the sense of fairy tales but as a symbolic way of telling the Truth. This last ideas is *mythopoeic*, from the Greek words "to make myth."

### Creation

The archaeological background for these stories is not strictly archaeological. Geologists claim the earth is several billion years old instead of a few thousand indicated in Genesis 5, 10–11. The Irish Archbishop Ussher decided the world was not created in 4004 B.C. The figure was put in a marginal note in some Bibles, and for some people it is now as sacred as the text. Pottery was invented c. 6000 B.C., so we are already pre-Ussher. The potassium-argon test dates the first humans at about 2.4 million years ago. An "atomic clock" using uranium for measurement puts the formation of the world at 4.5 billion years.

In addition to these scientific theories, the creation stories in the Bible contain various accounts. There are four different concepts of creation in the Hebrew Scriptures (Genesis 1 and 2; Proverbs 8, and that of the ancient Near East), plus one in the New Testament (John 1). The first story is that of Genesis 1:1–2, 4a (first part of verse 4). The world begins as watery chaos. People are the final product — women and men are created in the divine image. The rest of chapter 2 contains a quite different story. The world is created dry, so God waters it. A man is created lower than the beasts while a woman is the eiptome, the crown of God's creation. God saved the best for last.

The first story is similar to evolutionary theory. The second has a different sequence. The modern theory of evolution stemming mostly from Charles Darwin is widely accepted though never proven. It relies heavily on the fossil record. Here again archaeology overlaps geology as well as anthropology, paleontology, paleobotany, paleozoology, etc. There is nothing about the semi-human apes called *australopithecines* (southern ape) in the Bible. There is no mention of the small female nicknamed "Lucy." Our biblical narrative does not include the humanoids Zinjanthropus (c. 2 million years ago) or Neanderthal (c. 100,000 years ago). The bibilical doctrine stresses God as creator. Evolution talks about natural development. The two are not necessarily contradictory although some think they are. [1]

More immediately related to archaeology is data which provides the ancient Near Eastern background for the Bible. Excavations have found tablets and inscriptions of several creation stories. The most well known is the Mesopotamian "Enuma Elish" (Akkadian for "when above"). The tablets were found in the British digs at Nineveh and Kish and the German work at Ashur. The original deities, Apsu and Tiamat, fresh and salt water, come together and produce the gods. Later the older deities are irritated by the noise of the younger and plan to kill them. [2]

The "children" decide to fight. They are led by their champion, "Marduk," the god of Babylon. He wins. He kills Tiamat in the form of a snake or dragon, the monster of chaos. He cuts her in half. One half is used to create the earth and the other half is used to create the heavens. This resembles the firmament and the separation of waters in Genesis 1. What is not so obvious in English is the meaning of the original Hebrew test. Genesis 1:2 says "darkness was upon the face of the deep." The English "deep" is the Hebrew "tehom," from the same root as Tiamat. The dragon of the Akkadian story has been demythologized to be simply the deep or the ocean. The sea is under God's control as part of his created order.

Figure 9–1.    Ebla — The Archives showing some of the clay tablets as they fell on the floor. Photo courtesy *The Biblical Archaeologist*.

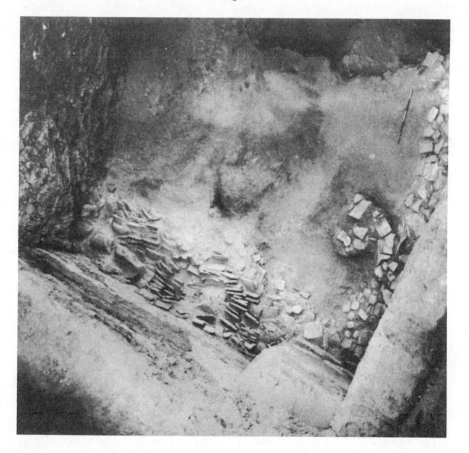

The Enuma Elish is probably behind other references such as Amos 7:4, Isaiah 27:1, Psalms 89:10, and Job 26:12. The Hebrew writers used the themes, myths, motifs, stories, and literary devices of the people around them. They reworked these ancient elements into a monotheistic faith which usually gave quite different meanings from the original. The ancient stories were de-mythed, if you will, historicized. They became descriptions of what God has done in history. The Hebrews used the language of their day to write of the mighty acts of God. If we were to write today, we would probably use language appropriate to the space age with moon walks and interplanetary probes, satellites and space shuttles, neutrons and mesons, black holes and stellar dust.[3]

## Eve, Adam and the Kids

One interesting biblical story is the creation of man from dust or clay in Genesis 2:7. The story of Eve's creation from Adam's rib is also part of this creation narrative (Genesis 2:21–23). Excavations at Jericho and 'Ain Ghazzal uncovered several types of figure modelling. Several human skulls have features filled out in flesh-tinted clay with shells for eyes. Several figures are made of clay on a core of reeds. Ruth Amiran suggested the reeds represent bones. Perhaps such figures are related to the creation story. Sumerian literature also contains the story of man created from clay and then filled with the breath of life. In that tradition, people were created to do the work and relieve the gods of effort.[4]

The tablets found at Ebla are being published. There is a lively debate about their relevance for biblical studies. Preliminary reports present claims and counterclaims. Several are of interest for biblical studies. One claim is for a creation story. Giovanni Pettinato translated three texts with the words:

> Lord of heaven earth:
> the earth was not, you created it,
> the light of day was not, you created it,
> the morning light you had not (yet) made exist.

Mitchell Dahood cited a name, "Temple of the Creator" and another, "Temple of the Word." He translated a term, "the Voice has created." These concepts resemble God's creation by word or voice as in Genesis 1:3, Psalms 33:6 and John 1:1. Creation by word or divine command is also found in Egyptian creation traditions.[5] Another claim is that the name Adam has now appeared in Ebla tradition as one of their fourteen provincial governors. It has been found only once before, in Old Akkadian. Eve was unknown outside the Bible until recently. The name appears in an economic tablet at Ebla.[6] Final publication should be interesting but the argument will continue even then. That is the nature of academics.

The Garden of Eden story (Genesis 3) also has an ancient Near Eastern background. "Enki and Ninhursag" is a Sumerian story of paradise in the land of Dilmun. Dilmun has been identified with the island of Failaka near Kuwait or the island of Bahrain in the Arabian Gulf. Danish excavation there uncovered Early Bronze settlements from c. 2500. A scene on a University Museum "bulla" has been interpreted as Eve and Adam cringing under the overhanging body of a snake. The impression, c. 3000 B.C., was found in Level VIII at Tepe Gawra.[7]

"Dumuzi and Enkimdu" is a story about a contest between a farmer god and shepherd god for the hand of a goddess, who chose the farmer. There is no goddess in the Cain and Abel story (Genesis 4). There is no word for goddess in Hebrew. Farmer Cain and Shepherd Abel each bring an offering to God who favors the shepherd. Some interpret this as the nomadic Hebrews being contrasted with the farmer Canaanites. The Patriarchs of Genesis 12–50, Moses, and the Hebrews wandering in the wilderness were all living as nomads.

One way in which ancient material illuminates the Bible is by suggesting alternate readings of the text, the words of the Bible. Mayer I. Gruber has suggested that Cain was angry with Abel because Cain was depressed. He follows modern psychoanalytic theory but finds support in ancient texts. Genesis 4:5 says Cain's "countenance fell." In verse 6, God asks "Why has your countenance fallen?" In the Akkadian myth, "The Descent of Ishtar," the goddess goes to the underworld Papsukal, the vizier of the great gods, mourns her going. His "countenance was fallen, his face was clouded." In the Gilgamesh epic, Siduri, a tavern keeper, sees Gilgamesh. She asks "Why are thy cheeks wasted, is sunken thy face, is so sad thy heart, are worn thy features?" In both contexts, we have depression rather than anger. Here as in the tehom/Tiamet case, is an example adding meaning to the text.[8]

## High Water

The story of the flood in Genesis 6–8 may be as old as 10,000 B.C. The last glaciers melted then. Tremendous amounts of water may have flooded the earth. Albright has pointed out that American Indians were at the southern tip of South America c. 6500. The Indians had a flood tradition. They may have derived this from the melting of the American glaciers. Many people believe the Indians came to the new world by the Alaska-Siberian land bridge. They may have brought the flood tradition with them. If there is a common origin to all the flood stories, this is the oldest dateable folk tradition we have, according to Albright.

The flood has been called a parable or euphemism for invasion. A type of fortress in central Asia is called an "ark," as in Bukhara in today's Uzbekistan. Invaders flooded the land and inhabitants and their animals took refuge in the ark, perhaps on a mountain top. Remains of floods in the form of silt layers have been found in Iraq. In his reports from Ur, Woolley refers to the flood layer. Such layers have been found in several cities, dated centuries apart. They are evidence that the Tigris and Euphrates Rivers flooded. The Egyptian Nile flooded every year before construction of the Aswan high dam. There is no flood evidence in Palestine.

Related to the search for physical evidence of the biblical flood are the repeated attempts to find Noah's ark on Mount Ararat in northeastern Turkey. The Bible uses a general phrase, "the ark came to rest on the mountains of Ararat" (Genesis 8:4). Nearby, Antiochus I (280–261 B.C.) founded the Phrygian city of Apameia Kibotos. His mother's name was Apameia. Kibotos is Greek for ark. Several coins of the city show the biblical tradition. One has the Roman Emperor Trebonianus Gallus (251–253 A.D.) on one side. On the other is an ark. It is shown as a box. Both the Greek and the Hebrew word "tebah," mean box as well as ark. On the coin, the lid of the box is open. A woman and man peer out. On the side is the Greek "Noe" (Noah). Overhead is a dove with an olive branch. To the right is another scene. A woman and man stand with arms raised, presumably Noah and his wife giving thanks.

The Bible says mountains. Tradition specifies Mount Ararat. There are seven other mountains associated with the ark but recent interest has focused on the 16,950 foot extinct volcano, Jabel al-Harith, known in the West as Mount Ararat. The search has claimed discovery of timbers from a large shadow under the glacial ice 14,000 feet above sea level. The timber was tested for carbon 14 and gave a date of c. 700 A.D., a bit late for Noah's ark. A monastery was built for pilgrims coming to Mount Ararat. It was destroyed by a landslide in 1840 A.D. Perhaps the timbers are from the monastery. Turkish authorities sometimes ban search to avoid friction with the USSR just across the border. The Soviets think Americans searching for the ark are spies.[9]

Like the creation story, the flood tradition has parallels in ancient Mesopotamia. Atrahasis is a Babylonian Noah. A Sumerian tradition was found in the American excavations at Nippur in the 1890s. The Sumerian Noah is Ziusudra of Shuruppak, modern Tell Fara dug by Robert Koldewy in 1902–03 and Eric Schmidt in 1930. The Akkadian parallel is the Gilgamesh story. These tablets were in the library of Ashurbanipal at Nineveh and are part of the Layard-Smith story cited earlier. Two copies of the Gilgamesh story are reported from Ebla. Hittite and Hurrian versions were found at the capital of the ancient Hittites, Hattusas (modern Boghazkoy), in Turkey.[10]

When his friend Enkidu died, Gilgamesh began to worry about dying himself. He heard about an immortal named Utnapishtim. Gilgamesh went to look for and finally found Utnapishtim. The latter explained his immortality as a gift of the gods after he survived the flood. The god Ea had warned him and told him to build an ark. He was to take a pair of each type of animal with him into the boat. He did all this. The flood came and he and the ark survived.

The similarities to the biblical tradition are clear. Differences are also interesting. The Mesopotamian gods decided to destroy humans because they made too much noise as with the creation story and the younger gods. In the Bible God decided on the flood because of human sin (Genesis 6:5–7). Noah did not receive immortality. Tikva Frymer-Kensky notes that in the Atrahasis Epic, the noise came from overpopulation. The flood was to relieve the problem. After the flood, measures were introduced to keep production down. These included the creation of barren women and the death of newborns. In part this is an etiololgy, an explanation of origins as in the case of evil (Adam and Eve ate the forbidden fruit). However, this evil was really meant for good — the survival of humanity. In Genesis 9, God repeats the creation story "Be fruitful and multiply and fill the earth." Later, in Exodus 23:26, he promises the Hebrews that the women will not miscarry or be barren. After the flood, God gave Noah and his sons new laws. Frymer-Kensky sees a structural parallel between the two stories. In Atrahasis, the overpopulation is solved by flood and restricted life. In Genesis the problem is sin. The solution is flood and new laws. She may be right though one can note that in Genesis 6:3 God limits life to 120 years. She is surely correct when she says the differences need to be studied as well as the similarities. [11]

The moral element of the flood is in the Adam and Eve episode of the forbidden fruit and Cain's murder of Abel. In Genesis 6 there is a story about the sons of God having intercourse with the daughters of men. There is no direct archaeological analogy to this story. There are many traditions of divine-human sexual relations. Greek myths have many such stories. According to tradition, the pharaoh of Egypt was the offspring of such a union. Collectively, however, these stories may not be concerned with sex but sin. They are etiologies — stories about origins. Genesis 3:14 explains why the snake crawls on its belly. Verses 17–19 tells why people work for a living. The Hebrew writer knew these old stories but rewrote them to show the origin of sin and God's concern with right and wrong. The Amarna letters and Pharaoh Ikhnaten were described earlier. His worship of the sun disc has been called monotheism. He worshipped other gods so he was not a monotheist. The worship of one god as the main deity is called "henotheism." The real contrast however, is the lack of moral concern as in Genesis 1–11. This is largely missing in Mesopotamia as well. [12]

Sin did not disappear with the flood. Noah got drunk and cursed his grandson Canaan. Canaan had done nothing wrong. This may be more of the nomad versus shepherd theme. Wine represents farming (cultivation, the vine). The semitic Canaanites of Palestine were farmers. [13]

## Man's Reach Must Exceed his Grasp

In Genesis 11, people build the tower of Babel to reach heaven, to escape future floods. The ancient Mesopotamians made artificial mountains where they worshipped their gods. The mud brick towers are called ziggurats. Their ruins still exist at Nippur, Nimrud, Ashur, and other sites. The ziggurat may have been the inspiration for the tower of Babel story. The ziggurat at Babylon may have been *the* inspiration. The Hebrew for Babylon is "babel." The tower, named Etemenanki, was built with the temple of Marduk on top. Herodotus, the Greek historian, described it as eight stories high. Others say it was in ruins by his time and the time of Alexander the Great. In 323, Alexander cleared the rubble to rebuild the ziggurat but died before he could. By contrast, Speiser finds the inspiration in the Enuma Elish which includes a description of the building of the city of Babylon. [14]

After all this "data" we are left with relatively few conclusions or probabilities. We can paraphrase the familiar: Yes, Virgina, there is a universe. Just how this

**Figure 9–2.**    Ziggurat at Ashur. Ashur was one of the capitals of ancient Assyria. A temple probably stood at the top of the ziggurat.

came to be is open to some question. The details have not been proven scientifically. The biblical versions differ in detail but agree it was God and not Marduk who created the world. The creation was intentional and not an accident which may be the real differences between the Bible and some modern theories. For Genesis 1–11, archaeology provides some rich background to illuminate the text and suggest how and why the biblical writers produced the biblical stories. The significance of this will be considered in Section VI.[15]


## B. GENESIS 12–50

Here again there is a variety of opinions. As with Genesis 1–11, some insist every word is literally true. Others see these chapters as mere fiction.[15] Some interpret Genesis 1–11 as myth and claim that Genesis 12–50 contain legends about Hebrew ancestors. An example of this is the suggestion that Abraham, Isaac, and Jacob were not historical figures but gods. The stories are stories of deities, stories which have been redone or demythologized to make them about people. Abraham, according to this theory, is the moon god Sin (pronounced "seen" as with Nabonidus). Ur and Haran are prominent cities in the Abraham story (Genesis 11:31). They were centers of worship for the god Sin. [16]

Related to this is the concept that the Patriarchs are eponymous ancestors. [17] Jacob is the ancestor of the Israelites, Esau of the Edomites, Uncle Laban of the Aramaeans, and so on. Of course they could fulfill this role and still be historical persons. Others see the Patriarchs as the personification of the tribes, as Uncle Sam is the personification of the United States, or as a corporation is a legal person before the law. Abraham pursued the four kings in Genesis 14:14 with 318 warriors. This would imply a tribe of over a thousand non-fighting men, women and children. [18] Genesis 34:25ff describes the capture of Shechem by Jacob's sons, Simeon and Levi. We do not ordinarily think of two men singlehandedly capturing a city. So it has been conjectured this was two *tribes* capturing Shechem. In turn, this may be part of the conquest story under Joshua, when the Hebrews controlled the city but did not conquer it. Perhaps their relatives were living there. Here again, one can note the Patriarchs could be leaders of tribes and still be historical individuals. The point is, there was more going on than the bare outline of the biblical stories reveal.

## Topography

The archaeological background for Genesis 12–50 is in several categories. One category is topographical or social conditions. This includes density of population, the free movement of peoples in and through the area, and the mixed ethnic nature of the population. This category also includes farm products and food, commercial products, lifestyle, and other aspects of an area and an era.

The Patriarchal period in biblical history is much like the Middle Bronze Age c. 2000–1550. The cities are few and far between. People are a mix of Amorites, Egyptians, Hurrians, Hittites, and others. [19] The Hittites in this list were, until recently, suspect — unknown outside the Bible. Like the more recently discovered Empire of Ebla, the Hittites were only a name. The excavation of Hattusas and the discovery of the tablets there changed this view. [20] The Tale of Sinuhe, c. 1950, is about an Egyptian who fled the possible wrath of the pharaoh. He went to live with the Amorites east of Byblos on the coast of today's Lebanon. He lived there as a semi-nomad. The Amorites were close enough to the desert to hunt wild game like Esau in the Bible. They also grew an occasional crop like Isaac in Genesis 26:12. The Execration Texts of Egypt c. 1991–1778 and the eighteenth century texts of Mari in today's Syria, give a similar picture. People were free to move from one area to another. Abraham moved from Ur to Haran to Canaan to Egypt and back to Canaan. Jacob moved from Canaan to Haran and back and eventually to Egypt.[21]

This freedom of movement may have been facilitated by the Hyksos. This mixed people controlled the delta of Egypt and the whole of Canaan from c. 1710–1570. The Egyptians called them the "Rulers of Foreign Lands." While they were in control of Egypt, someone like Joseph might very well have risen to prime minister (Genesis 41:40–44). The tomb of Beni-Hasan 160 miles south of Cairo, c. 1890, has a painting on the wall, still in vivid color. It shows Asians entering Egypt, not unlike Jacob and his family coming during the time of famine (Genesis 46:6). Their leader, Ibsha or Abi-shar, is called a heqahasut, the origin of the word "Hyksos." Pharaoh Haremhab, c. 1350, is pictured on the wall of his tomb. He was asked about some starving Asians who begged of pharaoh a home "after the manner of your fathers' fathers since the beginning." Haremhab's answer is missing in the inscription but the Asians' response is there, praising the pharaoh, so he must have granted their request. A later inscription, c. 1200, is about a frontier official. He sent word to the pharaoh of hungry nomads who sought refuge in Egypt. Here again the implication is of an old practice going back centuries.[22]

## Literary

The story of Joseph raises the category of literature as in Genesis 1–11. There is an Egyptian "Tale of Two Brothers" found in a payrus from about 1225. The wife of the older brother tried to seduce the younger but he refused. She went to her husband and accused the younger brother of attempted rape. The younger fled his brother's wrath. Later, the older found out the truth and killed his unfaithful wife. He went to look for his brother and found him and they were reconciled. In the Joseph story with Potiphar's wife, Joseph was imprisoned (Genesis 39:7–20).

A statue of King Idrimi of Alalakh is dated c. 1450. Woolley found it in today's Turkey, on the Orontes River. The statue has an inscription. Idrimi describes the jealousy of his older brothers. They are reconciled later (Genesis 37:3–33; 50:15–21). There is also a tradition concerning seven years (Genesis 41:17–30). An Egyptian inscription has a tradition of seven lean years when the Nile did not overflow, and fertilize the land with a new layer of mud. The tradition may go back to 2800 though the inscript is from the end of the second century. There are various means of divining the future in Idrimi's story, as in Joseph's. Dreams appear in Egypt, as part of an Egyptian guide for interpreting dreams. The known manuscript is c. 1300 but it goes back to the Middle Bronze Age judging by its use of language and grammar. The interpretive principle is one of similarity of sounds or puns like Joseph's interpretation of pharaoh's dream.[23]

## It's the Law

Another category of data concerns a series of texts, especially the Hurrian texts from Nuzi 150 miles north of Baghdad, about 90 miles south of Mosul, ancient Nineveh. In the Nuzi texts, and older ones as well, are customs, laws, mores, and regulations with parallels in Genesis 12–50. Among these are adoption proceedings. Some of these are like Abraham and his servant Eliezer (Genesis 15:2). Unless Abraham had a biological son, his servant would inherit the property. Jacob may have been an adopted son of Laban. Hurrian custom forbade the adopted son taking a wife who was not a daughter of his adopted father (Genesis 29:14, 31:50–55). The household gods which Rachel stole from her father (31:19) may represent the title deeds of Laban's property which she considered her own and Jacob's according to the customs of adoption and marriage.[24]

Genesis 15 is a primitive ritual with the "cutting of a covenant." To make or form a covenant is to "cut a covenant." This is a technical phrase found in a fifteenth century text from Qatna in Syria. Cutting an ass in half is a ritual known from Mari.

**Figure 9–3.** The mosque at Hebron marks the traditional site of Machpelah, the burial cave Abraham purchased from Ephron the Hittite.

**Figure 9–4.** The interior of the mosque at Hebron. The cenotaph on the left is one of the empty tombs — memorials to the patriarchs.

In ancient Shechem, people worshipped the lord of the covenant (Baal berith). The Shechemites were the "sons of Hamor," the sons of the ass (Genesis 34). Their covenant may have involved cutting a covenant by cutting an ass in half rather than a sheep or heifer. The ass had some kind of orthodoxy in the covenant ceremony for at Mari an official insisted on an ass and opposed the young animal and lettuce (?) brought by one of the people. Abraham "cut a covenant," but with a heifer, goats, and pigeons.

The Cappadocian tablets found in Turkey are from the nineteenth century. Here the covenant is between the head of a clan and his personal god, as in Genesis 15 with Abraham, Genesis 26 with Isaac, and Genesis 38 with Jacob. The Hittites had laws and customs also. In Genesis 23 Abraham's purchase of the land followed Hittite law. If he accepted the field as a gift, he would owe feudal service to the former owner. By paying what appears as an excessive price of 400 shekels (whole villages were sold for 100) he avoided those duties. The silver was paid at the current merchant rate — a technical term known from Old Babylonian and used as early as the laws of Eshnunna c. 2000.

Victor Matthews has done a close study of Genesis 21:22–32 and 26:12–22, the interactions of Abimelech, the king of Gerar, and the patriarchs Abraham and Isaac. These show parallels with the rest of the ancient Near East in terms of water rights and land use between the settled peoples and the nomads or semi-nomads who roamed the area. This included the recognition of boundaries of influence and means of peaceably settling disputes.[25]

The customs of Genesis 12–50 have so many parallels with ancient Mesopotamia that John Bright thought the Patriarchs were closer to Middle Bronze Mesopotamia than later Israel. The Patriarchs may have brought the laws of Mesopotamia, such as those of Hammurabi, into Hebrew tradition. The law code of Hammurabi dates c. 1700 but is based on older codes such as those of Eshnunna and Lipit-Ishtar. These have close parallels in the Bible such as Exodus 21:23–25.[26]

## What's in a Name?

The names of the Patriarchs constitute a unique type of data. These names do not fit well into any later period of history. Of the thirty-eight names in Patriarch tradition, twenty-seven do not occur in the later history of the Bible. However, they are normal for the Middle Bronze Age. This includes the Amorites and Hyksos, the Mari tablets and Execration texts, but the names come from all over the Fertile Crescent. Several are claimed to appear in the texts from Ebla from c. 2500.[27]

## Hbrw

A people called Habiru or Khapiru are found in the records of the Fertile Crescent throughout the second millennium. They were not a class but an element in society, not unlike migratory workers today. They were of several races, different language groups, different origins. Siegfried H. Horn has compared the Habiru to "Displaced Persons," a term familiar from the post-World War II years. Habiru appear in the inscriptions as slaves, bandits, mercenary soldiers, government officials, and sometimes as wealthy individuals. They may have led a gypsy type of life.

The two words, Hebrew and Habiru, are very much alike. However, the Habiru were so widespread in geography and time there is no way they could be biblical Hebrews. Alternately, the Hebrews may have been Habiru, one family of a variegated collection of people or an element in society. One could pick out a family named Smith among migrant workers and follow them for several generations as they move about the country. The Smiths would then be migrants, but migrants would not all be Smiths.

It is the Patriarchal lifestyle that relates the biblical Hebrews to the Habiru, rather than ethnic origins. They were footloose, sometimes wealthy (Abraham and Jacob), sometimes aggressive in attacking cities (Simeon and Levi), sometimes rising to high positions (Joseph) and later on, enslaved in Egypt. The Egyptians at times fought and at times enslaved Habiru or 'Apiru as the term is spelled in hiero-glyphs. This was especially the case during the New Kingdom, the Eighteenth and Nineteenth Dynasties, c. 1550–1200.[28]

In summarizing the discussion, there is also an argument from silence. No data contradicts significant elements of the Patriarchal tradition. Of course, one would hardly look for scientific evidence of the angel and Jacob in a wrestling match. We will probably not find the remains of the roast leg of lamb which Abraham shared with God and two of his lieutenants. Sarah's great beauty at the age of eighty has so far escaped the archaeological spade, and the modern cosmetic industry! One could humorously hope to find a petrified tree trunk with a heart carved on it with Cupid's arrow and the inscription in good biblical Hebrew or the Akkadian lingua franca, "Abe loves Sari, July 4, 1776 B.C." Seriously speaking, the Patriarchs were of little or no significance in the empires through which they moved and among which they lived. We will probably never have court records about them, though the impossible has happened before and may happen again. What we do have is a clear picture of the life and times of the Middle Bronze Age which is much like that of Genesis 12–50. To be sure, this does not prove they were historical indi-viduals, nor does it prove any father-son-grandson relationship.[29] But the biblical record is at least as believable as the many other reconstructions which have been suggested.[30]

## C. EXODUS AND COVENANT

The extremes in viewpoint continue for this section of the Bible. Some say it is all literally true, while others think it never happened. In between is a spectrum of belief — one often shading into another. Some are concerned with essential truth, believing something happened though they do not know what and they deny the story as a whole.

### Miracles

Some think the plagues of Exodus 7:8–11:10 happened indeed, but interpret them and the crossing of the Red Sea (Exodus 14) as natural phenomena. The plagues, except for the tenth, the death of the first-born, have been seen in modern history. This has usually occurred after the annual flood of the Nile. The water turned to blood (7:14–25) is presented as a seasonal event when the Blue and White Nile come together with the red silt eroded off the uplands. Strong winds have blown the water back (Exodus 14:12) from the shore of Lake Timsah, sometimes identified as the Sea of Reeds.[31]

Several ingenious efforts have related the disappearance of the lost continent of Atlantis to the story of the Exodus. A variant has been the disappearance of an

**Figure 9–5.**   The Nile Delta from space. The light areas are well watered. The lower left hand corner light spot is the Faiyum depression, 15 meters below sea level, irrigated by Nile River water via a canal. The Rosetta branch of the Nile is on the left side of the Delta with the city of Alexandria on the upper left of the triangle. The Damietta branch of the Nile is off to the right. Cairo (El Qahina) is in the center of the picture. The narrow light line from the Delta to the left (now the Suez Canal) is an ancient branch of the Nile, perhaps an ancient canal, connecting the Delta with the Bitter Lakes on the right edge, center of the picture. The Delta is 7500 square miles (20,000 square kilometers) and has a population of c. 45 million people. The photo was taken by Astronauts Thomas K. Mattingly II and Henry W. Hartsfield, Jr. during a 7 day trip in space. Photo courtesy NASA # 82–HC–496.

island in the Aegean Sea or the Red Sea. The theory is that the island sank, perhaps from volcanic action. Water rushed into the hole, drawing water away from shore in Egypt several hundred miles away, so the Hebrews could get across. The backwash was a tidal wave which caught the Egyptians and swamped them in their chariots.

The island of Thera or Santorini thirty miles north of Crete is a candidate. An eruption c. 1500 is said to have destroyed the Minoan civilization on Crete. A tidal wave destroyed the pursuing Egyptians. The theory elaborates the smoke and the fire of the volcano as the Hebrews' pillar of cloud by day and of fire by night. Leon Pomerance dates this event c. 1200 or possibly 1190–1180. He bases this on the widespread destruction of Mediterranean settlements and civilizations and the arrival of the "Sea Peoples." The latter were refugees rather than destroyers. They were easily defeated by Ramses III c. 1190–80. Others claim the curvature of the earth would make it impossible to see Thera's smoke and fire from Egypt.

This theory has been around for several years. More recently Hans Goedicke related it to an inscription of Pharaoh (Queen) Hatshepsut, (c. 1487–1468) whose statues show her with the Egyptian ceremonial beard. This wife and sister of Tuth-mosis II suppressed her stepson, Tuthmosis III (c. 1490–1436). According to Goedicke, the inscription is about Asiatics in Avaris. She allowed them to leave, but the earth swallowed their footsteps at the direction of the Primeval Father (Nun, the primeval water) who came unexpectedly. An older translation suggests the Asiatics were the Hyksos from the previous century. The father was the sun god, Re, "who comes at his (appointed) time."[32]

Still antoher theory is that a comet came close to the earth and its gravitational pull parted the waters to let the Hebrews through.[33] A simpler suggestion is that they were on foot. They found their way through the swampy water. However, the heavy chariots of the Egyptians bogged down in the swamp or sea of reeds. That made them easy targets for Hebrew bows and arrows.[34]

## Other Ideas

A different type of theory is that the traditions of the Exodus were derived from dif-ferent tribes. The Sinai tradition came from northwest Arabia which has the nearest volcanoes. The Wilderness Wandering tradition is from another tribe as is the Exodus and the Conquest. Later, these tribes coalesced into one people in Canaan, and the traditions also became one as though the events had happened to all the tribes as one people.[35]

There were a number of Egyptian names among the Hebrews according to the book of Exodus. These names were common to the thirteenth century according to the archaeological data. The Hyksos of Joseph's day had their capital in the delta. Earlier and later the capital was in Upper Egypt in Thebes. The Nineteenth Dynasty c. 1300–1200 were descendents of the Hyksos. They re-established the capital in the delta. The Joseph story suggest the capital was in the delta. His family settled in the land of Goshen on the eastern edge of the delta, not far from his court. When Seti I c. 1300 and Ramses II c. 1290–1224 rebuilt the old Hyksos capital, they enslaved some Habiru. These were cheap labor to build the city of Ramses or

Figure 9–6.     Ramses II (c. 1290–1228 B.C.), sometimes suggested as the pharaoh of the Exodus. Photo courtesy the Egyptian State Tourist Administration.

Rameses and its support cities such as Pithom (Exodus 1:11). The city of Rameses was also called Tanis, Zoan, and Avaris in various periods of history. The architectural remains there from the time of Ramses II may identify him as the pharaoh of the Exodus.[36]

## The Route

When the Hebrews were ready to leave, they went toward the Sea of Reeds, Hebrew "Yam Suph." The Egyptian text, Anastasi II c. 1230, refers to the "Papyrus Marsh" near Rameses. The Hebrews went past Baal-zephon (14:2), present day Tell Defneh; Elim (15:27), present day Wadi Gharandel; Dophkah (Numbers 33:12), and Egyptian mining center called Serabit el-Khadem; and Rephidim (Exodus 17:1), the Wadi Refayid. These all point to the location of Mount Sinai in the Bible as the present day Jabal Musa in the southern end of the Sinai peninsula. There are no volcanoes here. However, fire and smoke are traditional ways of representing the presence of a god or goddess. At Sinai the same phenomenon of fire and smoke can be found in desert storms (lightning and dark clouds or dust), if one must have a naturalistic explanation. However, no one assumes the tabernacle in the wilderness or the later temple of Solomon were volcanoes even though Moses and later Isaiah saw fire and smoke in their meetings with God.[37]

## Covenant

The Covenant at Sinai can be compared to political treaties found in the ancient Near East. The Hittite suzerainty treaties have close parallels. The treaties between equals are paralleled in the Bible in other covenants like that between Jacob and Laban in Genesis 31. The suzerainty treaty is between a superior and inferior, between a king and a vassal ruler, between a leader and his loyal follower.[38] The basic elements of the treaty are an historical prologue which relates what the king has done for the vasal or his father. After this come the demands of the treaty. The gods are witnesses of the treaty which is to be properly cared for in the sanctuary. It is a religious document. Blessings and curses come with the keeping of the violation of the treaty.

This is all paralleled in the Bible. The whole of Exodus 1–15 might be seen as the historical prologue. It is all summarized in Exodus 20:2, "I am the Lord thy God who brought you up out of the land of Egypt." The demands follow in the Ten Commandments. The various codes of law such as the Holiness Code follow. Some scholars today see the bulk of the laws as being incorporated into the literature at a later date, perhaps as late as the Exile in the fifth or even the fourth century. The Hebrews do not have the gods as witnesses, for that would violate their monotheism. However, in a later covenant ceremony in Joshua 24, he sets up a stone for a witness (verse 27). The blessings and curses may have been carried out in a ritual at Shechem (Deuteronomy 27; Joshua 8).[39]

Once again, this is not a matter of proof. The probabilities of the archaeological data do not prove anything. Even if one could prove these events all happen naturally, that would not prove that the Exodus happened. People in the ancient world did not distinguish between natural and supernatural events as people do today, if they bother to think about the supernatural at all. The real significance of the miracles is not the miraculous, but our understanding of God. Does he or does he not act in the world? The biblical writers thought God does. The data does not prove the Bible correct in this nor does it prove the Bible is incorrect. But in identifying the places of the Exodus route and by providing background to understand the covenant and other aspects of the life of that time, archaeology at least helps us see the biblical material in an historical and geographical context.[40]

# NOTES

1. Donald Johansen and Maitland Edey, *Lucy: The Beginnings of Humankind* (New York: Simon and Schuster, 1981).
2. ANET, pp. 60–72. TDOTT, pp. 3–16. Alexander Heidel, *The Babylonian Genesis* (2nd ed.; Chicago: University of Chicago, 1951). NERT, pp. 80–84. The tablets date from the first millennium B.C. Scholars date the contents to the Old Babylonian period on the basis of language and context. This is the time of King Hammurabi, c. 1750, and of the biblical Patriarchs. "Akkadian" refers to the language and the empire, c. 2360–2180, of Akkad (Agade), founded by Sargon I. Akkadian became a "lingua franca" (common language) throughout much of the Near East for a millennium. Jared J. Jackson, "Tiamat," IDB, 4 p. 639. ANEP, nos. 523, 670, 691. Tiamat may appear in the Ebla tablets as Tiamatum. PAE, pp. 47, 238, 248, 259. Thorkild Jacobsen called a Sumerian version of the tradition, "The Eridu Genesis," JBL 100, no. 4 (Dec. 81), pp. 513–529. Eridu was the first city to have a king. Ziusudra was king and priest at the time of the great flood. The text says that An, Enlil, Enki, and Ninhusaga (Nintur) created people. Parallels in other myths suggest to Jacobsen that only the last two deities were involved. Cf. also W.G. Lambert and A.R. Millard, *Atra-hasis: The Babylonian Story of the Flood* (Oxford: Clarendon, 1969).
3. William F. Albright, *New Horizons in Biblical Research* (London: Oxford, 1966), pp. 33–34. Another example of this type of analysis is Delbert Hillers, "Amos 7, 4 and Ancient Parallels," CBQ 26 (1964), pp. 221–225. The phrase "demythologize" is associated with the New Testament scholar Rudolph Bultmann. Bernhard W. Anderson, "Creation," IDB 1, pp. 725–732.
4. Kathleen M. Kenyon, *Digging Up Jericho* (London: Benn, 1957), pp. 60–64. Amiran, "Myths of the Creation of Man and the Jericho Statues," BASOR 167 (Oct. 62), pp. 23–25. Similar skulls are known from Oceania. L.Y. Rahmani, "Ancient Jerusalem's Funerary Customs and Tombs, Part One," BA 44, no. 3 (Sum. 81), pp. 171–177. "Sumerian" refers to the language and literature of the people of unknown origin who established city-states in Mesopotamia c. 3000 to c. 2400 when they were conquered by Sargon I of Akkad. Sumerian culture had a renewal in the Third Dynasty of Ur c. 2160–1900. Samuel N. Kramer, *The Sumerians* (Chicago: University of Chicago, 1963); and, *Sumerian Mythology* (New York: Harper, 1961); and, "Sumerian Literature," BANE, pp. 249–266. Thorkild Jacobsen, "Formative Tendencies in Sumerian Religion," BANE, pp. 167–278.

The origin of man from clay is a motif found earlier, "Creation of Man by the Mother Goddess," ANET, pp. 99–100. NERT, pp. 76–77. It is now known to be part of a longer work, "Atrahasis," another flood story. Lambert and Millard, *Atra-hasis. ANET Supplement*, pp. 512–514. NERT, pp. 90–93. Tikva Frymer-Kensky, "What the Babylonian Flood Stories Can and Cannot Teach Us About the Genesis Flood," BAR 4, no. 4 (Nov./Dec. 78), pp. 32–41. Robert A. Oden, Jr., "Transformations in Near Eastern Myth: Genesis 1–11 and the Old Babylonian Epic of Atrahasis," *Religion* 11 (Jan. 81), pp. 21–37.

5. PAE, p. 244. Dahood, "Afterword: Ebla, Ugarit and the Bible," PAE, pp. 272–311. NERT, pp. 4–5. In this Memphis theology, the god also rests after his creating (Genesis 2:2–3) but he names things as in Psalm 147:4, while in Genesis 2:19–20 it is Adam who names things, or at least names the animals. ANET, pp. 3–7.

6. Mitchell Dahood, "Are the Ebla Tablets Relevant to Biblical Research?," BAR 6, no. 5 (Sep./Oct. 80), pp. 54–60. The literature on Ebla is quickly reaching astronomical proportions. The debate can be followed in BAR and BA and other journals. Mildred Freed Alberg produced an award winning film, "The Royal Archives of Ebla." Paolo Matthiae, excavation director, published *Ebla* (Garden City: Doubleday, 1981; Italian 1977). The first epigrapher, Giovanni Pettinato, wrote PAE (cf n. 2). A highly readable story is Chaim Bermant and Michael Weitzman, *Ebla: A Revelation in Archeology* (New York: Times, 1979). SBAF, pp. 242–246. Pettinato continues to publish in the journal *Oriens Antiquus*, while Matthiae and his official team publish a new journal, *Studi Eblaiti*. The debate continues. Cf. J.D. Muhly's review of Matthiae and Pettinato in BAR 7, no. 6 (Nov./Dec. 81), pp. 9–12. *The Museum of Belshazzar's Sister* (Philadelphia: University Museum, 1937) pp. 6–7.

7. ANET, pp. 37–41 (Dilmun). P.V. Glob and T.G. Bibby, "A Forgotten Civilization of the Persian Gulf," (pp. 165–173 in *Old World Archaeology* ed. C.C. Lamberg-Karlovsky; San Francisco: Freeman, 1970). Bibby, *Looking for Dilmun* (New York: 1969). ANET, pp. 41–42 (shepherd and farmer).

8. Gruber, "Was Cain Angry or Depressed? Background of a Biblical Murder," BAR 6, no. 6 (Nov./Dec. 80), pp. 35–36, and, a more detailed study "The Tragedy of Cain and Abel: A Case of Depression," *The Jewish Quarterly Review*, N.S. 69, no. 2 (1979), pp. 89–97. ANET, pp. 107–109 (Ishtar), 72–98 (Gilgamesh). Albright claims Siduri was the goddess of life in *History, Archaeology and Christian Humanism*; (New York: McGraw-Hill, 1964), p. 147. "Life" is the issue in all three examples.

9. T. Burton Brown, "The Flood," *Archaeology* 16 (1963), p. 134. G. Ernest Wright, ASORN 3 (Oct. 70), pp. 1–2. Sam Cohen, "Turkey Has Decided to Halt Expeditions That Are Searching for Noah's Ark," *Des Moines Register* (16 Aug. 70), p. G10 (In subsequent years the Turks permitted these expeditions, then halted them, then permitted them again). Woolley, *Excavations at Ur*; (New York: Crowell, 1965). John Bright, "Has Archaeology Found Evidence of the Flood?," BA 5 (Dec. 42), pp. 55–62. Yaakov Meshorer, "An Ancient Coin Depicts Noah's Ark," BAR 3, no. 5 (Sep./Oct. 81), pp. 38–39. Lloyd R. Baily, "Wood from 'Mount Ararat': Noah's Ark?," BA 40, no. 4 (Dec. 77), pp. 137–146 (extensive bibliography); and, *Where is Noah's Ark?* (Nashville: Abingdon, 1978). Fernand Navarra, *Noah's Ark: I Touched It!* (Plainfield, NJ: Logos, 1974). William H. Stiebing, Jr., "A Futile Quest: The Search for Noah's Ark," BAR 2, nos. 2 (June 76), pp. 1, 13–20. Howard M. Teeple, *The Noah's Ark Nonsense* (Evanston: Religion and Ethics Institute, 1978). Dahood, "Are the Ebla Tablets Relevant?" p. 55, notes that "tabah" has not been found outside of biblical Hebrew until now. It appears in Eblaite in the form of "ti-ba." The name, Noah, has also been unique to Hebrew but may appear in Eblaite as the name of a place, the "Island of Repose," the Island of Noah.

10. ANET, pp. 42–44 (Ziusudra), 72–98 (Utnapishtim), 104–106 (Atrahasis; cf. n. 5 above). TDOTT, pp. 17–26. John H. Marks, "Flood (Genesis)," IDB 2, pp. 278–284. PAE, pp. 37, 74, 75, 95, 238.

Edmond Sollberger, *The Babylonian Legend of the Flood* (London: British Museum, 1971). Jacobsen, Eridu Genesis.

11. Frymer-Kensky, "Babylonian Flood Stores" and, "The Atrahasis Epic and its Significance for our Understanding of Genesis 1–9," BA 40, no. 4 (Dec. 77), pp. 147–155. Lambert and Millard, *Atra-hasis*. Jacobsen, "The Eridu Genesis," also emphasized both differences and similarities. The moral element of the Bible is one way it differs from the ancient Near Eastern traditions.

12. Albright, *History*, p. 153.

13. Harry Thomas Frank, *Bible, Archaeology and Faith* (New York: Abingdon, 1971), p. 111.

14. Andre Parrot, *The Tower of Babel* (London: SCM; 1955); and, *Babylon and the Old Testament* (New York: Philosophical Library, 1958). Speiser, *Genesis* (Garden City: Doubleday, 1964), p. 75. Thorkild Jacobsen, "Babel," IDB 1, p. 334, and, "Babylon (OT)," IDB 1, pp. 334–338. James Wellard, *Babylon* (New York: Schocken, 1972). Henry W.F. Saggs, *The Greatness that was Babylon* (New York: Hawthorn, 1962). Joan Oates, *Babylon* (London: Thames and Hudson, 1979). SBAF, pp. 188–192. Robert Koldewey, *The Excavations at Babylon* (New York: Macmillan, 1914). The Iraqi government is now rebuilding Babylons ziggurat. For some scientific pondering about creation, "Shaken Atheism: A Look at the Fine-Tuned Universe," see Rolston, Holmes III. *The Christian Century*, 103, no. 37 (3 Dec. 86), pp. 1093–1095.

15. Thomas L. Thompson, *The Historicity of the Patriarchal Narratives* (New York: De Gruyter, 1974). S.H. Hayes and J.M. Miller, eds., *Israelite and Judean History* (London: SCM, 1977).

16. R. Lansing Hicks, "Abraham," IDB 1, pp. 14–21 (the meaning of the name, Abraham, is uncertain), and, "Isaac," IDB 3, pp. 728–731, and, "Jacob (Israel)," IDB 3, pp. 782–787. Speiser, *Genesis*, pp. 80–81, discusses the problem of "Ur of the Chaldeans." The Chaldeans came to Mesopotamia a thousand years later than the usual date for Abraham. The Ur excavated by Woolley is Sumerian Ur in southern Iraq. It is not called Chaldean in ancient Near Eastern literature. Though it is a magnificent site, whether it was Abraham's city is debated. Anon., "Ur of the Sumerians," Baghdad no. 7 (Aug. 73), pp. 12–22. C.J. Gadd, "Ur," AOTS, pp. 87–101. Thorkild Jacobsen, "Ur (city), IDB 4, pp. 735–738. SBAF, pp. 181–186. Cyrus H. Gordon has suggested Ur is near Haran which Speiser called Abraham's birthplace. Speiser thought Ur and Haran might have been linked because of moon worship. Gordon also noted an Ur in the Ebla tablets which he thinks adds support to his argument. "Where is Abraham's Ur?," BAR 3, no. 2 (June 77), pp. 20–21, 52. Gordon, "Haran (Place)," IDB 2 (1962), p. 524. Kay Prag, "Haran (Place)," IDBSV, p. 387.

17. The term "eponymous" is Greek for "given as a name," from "epi," "upon" and "onyma," "name." An eponymous person, real or mythical, is the source of the name of a people, country, etc. Amerigo Vespucci (Latin, Americus Vespucius), 1451–1512, an Italian navigator, was the eponym of "America."

18. The Kings had defeated the rebellious cities of Sodom, Gomorrah, Admah, Zeboiim, and Bela or Zoar (Genesis 14:2). The first two and Zoar are also in Genesis 18:16–19:30. Sodom and Gomorrah are described in the Bible as cities destroyed by God as punishment for their sin. Once again we see the moral element in biblical narrative. Scholars have argued for years over the location or even the existence of these five cities. A recent guess is that they are the archaeological sites Bab edh-Dhra', Numeira, Safi, Feifa, and Khanazir on the southeast corner of the Dead Sea. They came to an end, several by fire, c. 2300. Ebla was destroyed about the same time. Among early reports on the Ebla tablets was a statement that the five city names appear in the tablets. The claim is disputed and denied. A later report left out Admah. The expedition's new epigrapher, Alfonso Archi, in "Are the 'Cities of the Plain' Mentioned in the Ebla Tablets?," BAR 7, no 6. (Nov./Dec. 81), pp. 54–55, answered "No." It is, of course, of interest that the name Sodom appears at all as "Si-da-mu(ki)" (the "ki" means it is a place) even if it is not the town by the Dead Sea.

The disputed Ebla evidence and the end of Bab edh-Dhra' brought a suggestion for a new date for Abraham. That has since been dropped. Future translation and excavation should be interesting. "Have Sodom and Gomorrah Been Found?," BAR 6, no. 5 (Sep./Oct. 80), pp. 27–36. Van Hatten, "Once Again: Sodom and Gomorrah," BA 44, no. 2 (Spr. 81), p. 87092. David Noel Freedman, "The Real Story of the Ebla Tablets and the Cities of the Plain," BA 41, no. 4 (Dec. 78), pp. 143–164; and, Freedman, ed., *Preliminary Excavation Reports* (Cambridge: AASOR 43, 1978). Walter E. Rast and R. Thomas Schaub, "Preliminary Report of the 1979 Expedition to the Dead Sea Plain, Jordan," BASOR 240 (Fall 80), pp. 21–61. Archi, "Cities of the Plain" PAE, p. 287. Suzanne Richard, "Toward a Consensus of Opinion on the End of the Early Bronze Age in Palestine-Transjordan," BASOR 237 (Wint. 80), pp. 5–34. J. Penrose Harland, "Sodom," IDB 4, pp. 395–397, and, "Gomorrah," IDB 2, p. 440. SBAF, p. 483.

19. William H. Stiebing, Jr., claims the Patriarchs cannot be dated to MB I (c. 2000–1900) when the land was entirely nomadic. He thinks they could be in MB II (c. 1900–1550), when cities such as Shechem were inhabited once more. He thinks the name Canaanite (merchant? of purple) belongs to the LB Age. However, the word is reported in the Ebla tablets. "When was the Age of the Patriarchs? . . . of Amorites, Canaanites, and Archaeology," BAR 1, no. 2 (June 75), pp. 17–24. Kathleen Kenyon, Amorites and Canaanites (London: British Academy 1966); and, *Archaeology of the Holy Land*, (4th ed.; New York: Norton, 1979), and, *The Bible and Recent Aracheology* (Atlanta: Knox, 1978). R. Lansing Hick, "Patriarchs," IDB 3, pp. 677–678. Beer-sheba is one of the places named by the Patriarchs. Genesis 21:31 says it is of Abraham's time, and Genesis 26:33 links it with Isaac. The excavations revealed nothing earlier than c. 1250. Either the Fathers are to be dated much later than MB, or Beer-sheba was not a city then, or the Patriarchal Beer-sheba has not been found. Ze'ev Herzog dates the Patriarchs later. "Beer-sheba of the Patriarchs," BAR 6, no. 6 (Nov./Dec. 80), pp. 12–36. Yohanan Aharoni, "Nothing Early and Nothing Late: Re-Writing Israel's Conquest," BA 39, no. 2 (May 76), pp. 55–76, and, "Tel Beer-sheba," EAEHL, pp. 160–168. SBAF, pp. 315–321.

20. Kurt Bittel, *Hattusha* (New York: Oxford, 1970). Albrecht Goetz, "Hittite and Anatolian Studies," BANE, pp. 316–327. O.R. Gurney, "Boghazkoy," AOTS, pp. 105–116; and, *The Hittites* (rev.; Baltimore: Penguin, 1966). Aharon Kempinski, "Hittites in the Bible — What Does the Bible Say?," BAR 5, no. 4 (Sep./Oct. 79), pp. 20–45. Ignace J. Gelb, "Hittites," IDB 2, pp. 612–615. Michael C. Astour, "Hittites," IDBSV, pp. 411–413. SBAF, pp. 219–229. James G. McQueen, *The Hittites and their Contemporaries in Asia Minor* (Boulder: Westview, 1975).

21. ANET, pp. 18–22 (Sinuhe). Victor H. Matthews, "Pastoralists and Patriarchs," BA 44, no. 4 (Fall 81), pp. 215–218. In contrast, Norman K. Gottwald argues that the Patriarchs were settled farmers. Bovines were raised only in settled areas so they were stock breeders. So were the Hebrews in Goshen (Exodus 12:32, 38). "Were the Early Israelites Pastoral Nomads?," BAR 4, no. 2 (June 78), pp. 2–7, and, *The Tribes of Yahweh* (Maryknoll, NY: Orbis, 1979), pp. 435–463. He claims the basic social conflict of the ancient Near East was not nomad versus farmer, but country versus city. He calls for archaeological investigation of rural areas. That is happening as more archaeologists take a regional approach, studying the surrounding area, as at Shechem and Hesban. It was implicit in the surveys of Glueck, Benjamin Mazar, Moshe Stekel, Aharoni, and Kochavi. Cf. Aharon Kempinski, "Israelite Conquest or Settlement? New Light from Tell Masos," BAR 2, no. 3 (Sep. 76), pp. 25–30. Glueck, *The Other Side of the Jordan* (rev.; Cambridge: ASOR, 1970). Ammon ben-Tor, "The Regional Study — A New Approach to Archaeological Investigation," BAR 6, no. 2 (Mar./Ap. 80), pp. 30–44. Sean Freyne's study is regional — *Galilee from Alexander the Great to Hadrian, 323 B.C.E. to 135 C.E.: A Study of Second Temple Judaism* (Wilmington: Glazier, 1980). Edward B. Banning, "The Research Design of the Wadi Ziqlab Survey, 1981," ASORN no. 8 (June 82), pp. 4–8. Burton MacDonald, "The Wadi el Hasa Survey, 1981," ASORN no. 3 (Nov. 81), pp. 8–15. An example of a small town (c. forty houses) excavation is Givat

Sharett near Beth Shemesh. Dan Bahat, "Did the Patriarchs Live at Givat Sharett?," BAR 4, no. 3 (Sep./Oct. 78), pp. 8–11. Khirbet al-Hajjar represents a small fortified village east of Amman. Henry O. Thompson, "The Ammonite Remains at Khirbet al-Hajjar," BASOR 227 (Oct. 77), pp. 27–34. One might add that a regional framework is involved in aerial photography and archaeology. This is necessarily so with satellite sensing.

One aspect of this whole concern is the identification of peoples and movements. The Patriarchal movements have been identified with the Amorites who have been variously dated to EB and MB. They are at times credited with the widespread destructions c. 2300. Some think Amorites spread over centuries not unlike Europeans moving to the Americas after 1492 (almost five centuries now). Kathryn A. Kamp and Norman Yoffee caution against simplistic solutions, including those of farmer versus nomad and rural versus urban. "Ethnicity in Ancient Western Asia During the Early Second Millennium B.C. Archaeological Assessments and Ethnoarchaeological Prospectives," BASOR 237 (Wint. 80), pp. 85–104. Kenyon, *Amorites*. William Dever, "The EB IV - MB I Horizon in Transjordan and Southern Palestine," BASOR 210 (Ap. 75), pp. 37–63. WBA, pp. 41–42. Alfred Haldar, "Amorites," IDB 1, pp. 115–116; and, *Who Were the Amorites?* (Leiden: Brill, 1971). Herbert B. Huffman, "Amorites," IDBSV, pp. 20–21.

22. Nahum M. Sarna, "Exploring Exodus: The Oppression," BA 49, no. 2 (June 86), pp. 68–80. ANET, pp. 328–329 (Execration Texts), 259 (nomads). ANEP no. 3 (Beni-Hasan painting). William H. Shea, "Artistic Balance Among the Beni Hasan Asiatics," BA 44, no. 4 (Fall 81), pp. 219–228. Thomas A. Lambdin, "Hyksos," IDB 2, p. 667. John van Seters, "Hyksos," IDBSV, pp. 424–425; and, *The Hyksos* (New Haven: Yale, 1966). Jack Finegan, *Let My People Go* (New York: Harper & Row, 1963), p. 3. Siegfried H. Horn, "What We Don't Know About Moses and the Exodus," BAR 3, no. 2 (June 77), pp. 22–31.

23. ANET, pp. 23–25 (two brothers). This story also appears in Hinduism. ANEP no. 452 (Idrimi). ALbright, "Some Improtant Recent Discoveries: Alphabetic Origins and the Idrimi Statue," BASOR 118 (1950), pp. 11–20. ANET, p. 295 (dreams), pp. 31–32 (seven years). Orval S. Wintermute, "Joseph Son of Jacob," IDB 2, pp. 981–986. W. Lee Humpheys, "The Joseph Story," IDBSV, pp. 491–493.

24. ANET, pp. 219–220. M.A. Morrison and D.I. Owen, eds., *Studies on the Civilization and Culture of Nuzi and the Hurrians in Honor of E.R. Lachman* (Winona Lake, IN: Eisenbrauns, 1981). E.A. Speiser, "Hurrians," IDB 1, pp. 664–666; and, "Nuzi," IDB 3, pp. 573–574. Frederick W. Bush, "Hurrians," IDBSV, pp. 423–424. Barry L. Eichler, "Nuzi," IDBSV, pp. 635–636. C.J. Mullo Weir, "Nuzi," AOTS pp. 73–86. WBA, pp. 43–44. The materials actually date from early LB, c. 1500. They reflect earlier use, however, Cf. Tikva Frymer-Kensky, "Patriarchal Family Relationships and Near Eastern Law," BA 44, no. 4 (Fall 81), pp. 209–214. The Nuzi date and related data led W.G. Lambert to claim that the book of Genesis dates after 1500. "The Babylonian Background of Genesis," *The Journal of Theological Studies* 16 (1965), p. 300. Similarly, van Seters thinks the Patriarchal stories were created over a thousand years after MB Age. They date to the Exile (586–538) and later. *Abraham in History and Tradition* (New Haven: Yale, 1975); and, "Patriarchs," ISBSV, pp. 645–648. Nahum M. Sarna reviewed van Seters' book and notes its shortcomings. Among these are elements of the tradition that later were against the law such as marriage to a half sister. "Abraham in History," BAR 3, no. 4 (Dec. 77), pp. 5–9. Van Seters replied these examples were ambiguous even in the Exilic period. "Dating the Patriarchal Stories," BAR 4, no. 4 (Nov./Dec. 78), pp. 6–8. Cf. also T.L. Thompson, *Patriarchal Narratives*.

25. One of the customs cited by Speiser, *Genesis*, pp. 92–94, 151–152, is the idea of a wife being a sister (Genesis 12:10–20; 20:1–18; 26:6–11). Speiser thought three Nuzi tablets showed that the status of sister was conferred on a wife as a kind of adoption procedure which then gave her a higher status than simply being a wife. Several scholars now say Speiser misinterpreted the tablets. The three Genesis episodes now have no explanation beyond the fear of Abraham and Isaac who needed

a good excuse. Much of modern scholarship sees the three stories as simply different versions of one story. Cf. Sarna and van Seters, *Abraham in History*; David Noel Freedman, "A New Approach to the Nuzi Sisterhood Contract," JNES 2, no. 2 (Sum. 70), pp. 77–85; and, anon., "The Patriarchs' Wives as Sisters — Is the Anchor Bible Wrong?," BAR 1, no. 3 (Sep. 75), pp. 22–24, 26.

One of the more unusual customs is in Genesis 24:2–9. Abraham has his servant take an oath. Eliezer is told to put his hand under Abraham's thigh. R. David Freedman notes that Old Babylonian legal documents from c. 1700 include oath-taking ceremonies. The person taking the oath is to do so in the presence of the deity, i.e., in the temple. If unable to go to the temple, the oath taker can hold a symbol of the deity while taking the oath. Freedman suggest that circumcision was a sign of the covenant and hence of God's presence. So Eliezer took his oath accordingly. "'Put Your Hand Under My Thigh' — The Patriarch Oath," BAR 2, no. 2 (June 76), pp. 3–4, 42. SBAF, p. 192. John Gray, "Baalberith," IDB 1, p. 331. W.L. Reed, "Shechem (city)," IDB 4, pp. 313–315; and, "Shechem, Tower of," 4, p. 315. George E. Mendenhall, "Covenant," IDB 1, pp. 714–723. Martin Noth, *The Laws in the Penteuch and Other Essays* (London: Oliver & Boyd, 1966). Abraham bought a burial cave from Ephron the Hittite (Genesis 23) at today's mosque of Hebron. On Genesis 23, cf. Speiser, pp. 169–173. Manfred R. Lehmann, "Abraham's Purchase of Machpelah and Hittite Law," BASOR 129 (Feb. 53), pp. 15–18. ANET, pp. 188–197. Nancy Miller, "Patriarchal Burial Site Explored for the First Time in 700 Years," BAR 11, no. 3 (May/June 85), pp. 26–43.

26. BHI, p. 70, 79. ANET, pp. 150–161 (Lipit-Ishtar), 161–163 (Eshnunnal), 163–180 (Hammurabi). The last is also in TDOTT, pp. 27–37. A. Leo Oppenheim, "Hammurabi," IDB 2, pp. 517–519. Victor H. Matthews, "The Wells of Gerar," BA 49, no. 2 (June 86), pp. 118–126.

27. BHI, pp. 77–78. Dahood, "Are the Ebla Tablets Relevant," pp. 55–56.

28. Moshe Greenberg, *The Hab/piru* (New Haven: American Oriental Society, 1955). Albright's suggestion for Habiru as donkey caravaneer was cited earlier. See his "Abram the Hebrew," BASOR 163 (Oct. 61), pp. 36–54; and, *Yahweh and the Gods of Canaan* (New York: Doubleday, 1968), pp. 51–79. Cf. also Mendenhall, "The Hebrew Conquest of Palestine," BA 25 (Sep. 62), pp. 66–87. BHI, p. 92094. "Siegfried Horn Replies," BAR 3, no. 4 (Dec. 77), pp. 47–48. WBA, pp. 42–43. Alfred Haldar, "Habiru, Hapiru," IDB 2, p. 502. Michael C. Astour denies the identification of the Habiru and the biblical Hebrews. "Habiru or, more correctly, Hapiru," IDBSV, pp. 382–384. In a provocative study of Deuteronomy 29:12, Rav A. Soloff suggests Hebrew/Habiru refers to those who enter a covenant. See his "The Initiated" (pp. 319–330 in *The Answers Lie Below* ed. Henry O. Thompson; Washington: UPA, 1984).

29. One can note, however, that such divergent historians as John Bright (BHI, p. 91) and Martin Noth *The History of Israel* (New York: Harper, 1958, p. 121) agree that Abraham, Isaac, and Jacob were historical figures. Bright follows Albright in believing the archaeological data confirms much of the biblical material while Noth, especially for the early history of Israel (pre-monarchy), thinks the archaeological data is to be interpreted differently. Noth is more concerned with the literature of the Bible.

30. The late Père Roland de Vaux, along with many others, thought the Patriarchal stories were originally separate traditions. The stories have been divided differently and even splintered. One way is to see three cycles of stories — Abraham and Isaac, Jacob, and Joseph. A later editor, perhaps the so-called "J" or Yahwist writer c. 950 B.C., put the traditions together creating a family tree. While widely accepted as a theory, it is beyond proof or disproof. Cf. de Vaux, "The Separate Traditions of Abraham and Jacob," BAR 6, no. 4 (July/Aug. 80), pp. 22–29, excerpted from *The Early History of Israel* (Philadelphia: Westminster, 1978). Cf. Julius Wellhausen, *Prolegomena to the History of Ancient Israel* (New York: Meridian, 1957) (original 1878). Kendrick Grobel, "Biblical Criticism," IDB 1, pp. 407–413. Simon J. De Vries, "Biblical Criticism, History of," IDB 1, pp. 413–418. Henry Cazelles, "Biblical Criticism, OT," IDBSV, pp. 98–102. Henry O.

Thompson *Approaches to the Bible* (Syracuse: Center for Instructional Communication, 1967). Martin Noth, *A History of Pentateuchal Traditions*; (Englewood Cliffs: Prentice-Hall, 1972) (original 1948). Noth separated the traditions into what he considered originally unconnected stories. Robert Polzin shows how Noth used the same guideline to call one tradition "early" and another "late" without explaining what he was really doing. Polzin sees Noth and other literary critics as mythmakers as defined by Mircea Eliade in *Myth and Reality* (New York: Harper & Row, 1963), pp. 76–79; and, Claude Levi-Strauss, *The Savage Mind* (Chicago: University of Chicago, 1966), p. 22. Cf. Polzin, "Martin Noth's A History of Pentateuchal Traditions," BASOR 221 (Feb. 76), pp. 113–120.

31. Charles F. Aling, *Egypt and Bible History* (Grand Rapids: Baker, 1981). Greta Hart has made a detailed study of the natural events. "The Plagues of Egypt," *Zeitschrift fur die Alttestamentliche Wissenschaft* 69 (1975), pp. 84–103; and 70 (1958), pp. 48–59. Cf. also Brevard S. Childs, *The Book of Exodus* (Philadelphia: Westminster, 1974), pp. 153–162, 215–239. Finegan, *Let My People Go*, pp. 47–57, 77–89. Horn, "What We Don't Know," pp. 29–31. Mordechai Gilula thinks the death of the first born (Exodus 11:4–6, 12:29–30) was originally an Egyptian concept. It appears in the Pyramid Texts (twenty-fifth to twenty-first centuries) and the Coffin Texts (twenty-first to eighteenth centuries). "The Smiting of the First-Born — An Egyptian Myth?," TA 4, nos. 1–2 (1977), pp. 94–95. A similar effort to find a "natural" explanation has been made for other biblical miracles. Cf. John F.A. Sawyer, "Joshua 10:12–14 and the Solar Eclipse of 30 September 1131 B.C.," PEQ 104 (July-Dec. 72), pp. 139–146.

The biblical name, Jethro, Moses' father-in-law (Exodus 3:1) has not been noted outside the Bible before. Dahood thought he had found it in Eblaite and in Ugaritic. PAE, pp. 281–282.

32. Leon Pomerance, *The Final Collapse of Santorini (Thera): 1400 B.C. or 1200 B.C.?* (Goteborg: Aastroms, 1970). C. Doumas, ed., *Thera and the Aegean World*, Vols. I-II: *Papers and Proceedings of the Second International Scientific Congress, Santorini, Greece, August 1978* (London: 1978, 1980). B. Michael Blaine, "Santorini," *Footnotes* 1 (1981), 1–5. James Mann, "New Finds Cast Fresh Light on the Bible," *U.S. News* 91, no. 8 (21 Aug. 81), pp. 38–40.

Hershel Shanks, "The Exodus and the Crossing of the Red Sea, According to Hans Goedicke," BAR 7, no. 5 (Sep./Oct. 81), pp. 42–50. ANET, pp. 230–231. John A. Wilson, *The Culture of Ancient Egypt* (Chicago: University of Chicago, 1951), pp. 160, 174–175. Ronald Schiller, "The Explosion that Changed the World," *Reader's Digest* (Nov. 67), pp. 122–127. "Archaeology: How a Civilization Disappeared," *Time* (6 May 66), notes that Greek archaeologist Spridon Marinatos suggested as early as 1939 that Thera's volcanic eruption destroyed the Minoans.

In response to Goedicke's theory, Charles R. Krahmalkov suggested the destruction of the Egyptians was on the Red Sea. The Hebrews crossed it by boat from the port of Qoseir, east of Thebes. Goshen was in the Theban area and the Hebrews left by the old trade route through the Wadi Hammamat. "A Critique of Professor Goedicke's Theories," BAR 7, no. 5 (Sep./Oct. 81), pp. 51–54. He based his theory on an analysis of Exodus 15 which he considers an eyewitness account. Eliezer D. Oren suggested the crossing was at Lake Bardawil on the northwest coast of Sinai. In 1977, a team of archaeologists under his direction experienced a sudden flooding of the area during a violent winter storm. "How Not to Create a History of the Exodus — A Critique of Professors Goedicke's Theories," BAR 7, no. 6 (Nov./Dec. 81), pp. 46–53. C. Leroy Ellenberger, letter to editor, BAR 8, no. 1 (Jan./Feb. 82), p. 14.

33. This is associated most prominently with the work of Immanuel Velikovsky. He did not propose archaeological data for his theories but rather suggested a combination of traditions from various parts of the world. Carl Sagan has made a thorough analysis of Velikovsky's ideas in "A Scientist Looks at Velikovsky's 'Worlds in Collision'," BAR 6, no. 1 (Jan./Feb. 80), pp. 40–51 and p. 11.

34. L.S. Hay, "What Really Happened at the Sea of Reeds?," JBL 83 (Dec. 64), pp. 397–403.

35. Cf. Noth, *Pentateuchal Traditions*. This theory would fit with Krahmalkov's.

36. BHI, p. 119. SBAF, pp. 262–264. Finegan, *Let My People Go*, pp. 3–46. Horn, "What We Don't Know." Pithom (Exodus 1:11) was once identified with Tell el-Maskhuta, now near the Suez Canal. Later it was identified as Succoth (13:20). Excavations there have found several tombs of the MB Age but no occupation earlier than c. 600 B.C. Burton MacDonald, "Tell el-Maskhuta," BA 43, no. 1 (Wint. 80), pp. 49–58. In contrast, Nahum M. Sarna cites inscriptions found there from the time of Ramses II. The site was also known as Tjeku in Egyptian. Sarna, Exploring Exodus, suggests modern el-Khatana or Qantir as the most likely location for the city of Rameses. He views the Nineteenth Dynasty as descendents of an ancient family in the region who had long supplied the priesthood for the worship of the god Seth. Menehem Haran, "The Exodus," IDBSV, pp. 304–310. John J. Bimson, *Redating the Exodus and Conquest* (Winona Lake, IN: Eisenbraun, 1981). Bimson dates the Exodus in the fourteenth century.

37. BHI, pp. 122–123. SBAF, pp. 261–262. Finegan, *Let My People Go*, pp. 77–100. G. Ernest Wright, "Exodus, Route of," IDB 2, pp. 197–199. WBA, pp. 60–65. Horn, "What We Don't Know," pp. 29–31. The location of Sinai is still being debated. Emmanuel Anati, "Has Mount Sinai Been Found?," BAR 6, no. 4 (July/Aug. 85), pp. 42–57, thinks it is in northeast Sinai.

38. There is an extensive literature on covenant and treaties. WBA, pp. 99–101. BHI, p. 144. Mendenhall, *Law and Covenant in Israel and the Ancient Near East* (Pittsburgh: Biblical Colloquium, 1955); and "Covenant," IDB 1, pp. 714–725. Murray Newman, *The People of the Covenant* (New York: Abingdon, 1962). Klaus Baltzer, *The Covenant Formulary* (Philadelphia: Fortress, 1971). Shalom M. Paul, *Studies in the Book of the Covenant in the Light of Cuneiform and Biblical Law* (Leiden: Brill, 1970). Dennis McCarthy, *Old Testament Covenant* (Atlanta: Knox, 1972). Paul A. Rieman, "Covenant, Mosaic," IDBSV, pp. 192–197. Henry O. Thompson, *Eternal Love: Biblical Covenants and Modern Man* (forthcoming). C.F. Whiteley puts the whole covenant tradition, including the Ten Commandments, in the time of King Josiah's reform, c. 621 B.C. "Covenant and Commandments in Israel," JNES 22 (1963), pp. 37–48.

39. Henri Cazelles, "Ten Commandments," IDBSV, pp. 875–877. Samuel Greengus, "Law in the OT," IDBSV, pp. 533–537. Walter J. Harrelson, "Law in the OT," IDB 3, pp. 77–89; "Ten Commandments," IDB 4, pp. 569–573; and, "Blessings and Cursings,"IDB 1, pp. 446–448. *Polzin, Moses, and the Deuteronomist* (New York: Seabury, 1980). Mendenhall, *Law and Covenant*.

40. Childs, *Exodus*, pp. 282–283. The data sometimes raises as many questions as it offers answers. The problem of Beer-sheba was cited earlier. A similar one exists for Kadesh-barnea. The Hebrews spent many years there (Numbers 13–20), usually dated thirteenth century. But recent excavations found nothing earlier than the tenth century. Rudolph Cohen, "Did I excavate Kadesh-Barnea?," BAR 7, no. 3 (May/June 81), pp. 2–33; and, "The Excavations at Kadesh-Barnea," BA 44, no. 2 (S pr. 81), pp. 93–107. Moshe Dothan, "Kadesh: Barnea," EAEHL, pp. 697–698. Perhaps the ancient site has not been found. Cohen notes alternatives.

    For a thorough study of literary and archaeological data, see Dewey M. Beegle, *Moses, The Servant of Yahweh* (Grand Rapids: Eerdmans, 1972). An interesting parallel exists between the birth stories of Moses and Sargon the Great. His mother put him in a basket of rushes and sealed the lid with bitumen. She put him in the river which floated him to "Akki the drawer of water," who raised him (ANET, p. 119; NERT, pp. 98–99). Similarities to the Moses story are clear. There are also differences. Sargon's mother was a "changeling," perhaps a prostitute. His father was unknown. His mother gave birth in secret. He grew up a gardener and became a king. Moses grew up in a palace and became a shepherd.

# CHAPTER 10

# Joshua-Kings

## A. TRANSITION: CONQUEST, SETTLEMENT

### Conquest

The extremes appear once more. For some the conquest is literally true. For others it is completely false. The "via media" includes theories like a slave uprising of Habiru instead of a conquest or in response to Joshua's small band proclaiming freedom. One theory claims a gradual infiltration of families or tribes. These became a new people in the time of Samuel. Some argue for a series of little conquests instead of one big one. Related to this is the idea that the Habiru of the Amarna letters were near Shechem, and they were an early movement of Hebrews. Another theory is that the Calebites came from Sinai and took over the south.

The biblical narrative says Joshua did not capture all of Canaan (Joshua 15:63; 16:10; 17:12–16). Canaanite city states continued a long time. Jerusalem was Jebusite. Beth-shan remained an Egyptian fort and then a Philistine one. The latter controlled the coast where Egyptians had continued long after Joshua. The Bible says some areas were taken by other leaders. Similarly, the Supreme Allied Commander in a modern war may get the credit of battles fought by subordinates. Some see Joshua 1–11 as a different story than Judges 1. The latter lists cities which continued independent or under Egyptian-Philistine control. Some claim this is evidence of no conquest or a very minimal one. Further data is Hebrew inability to invade from Sinai (Numbers 14:40–45) or Edom (Numbers 20:14–21).[1]

The archaeological data is mixed. Glueck said the two kingdoms of Edom and Moab did not develop until the thirteenth century. They were there when the Hebrews came through. That suggests they came after 1300. New evidence says there was some occupation there in the period 1800–1300. Bennett found no urban settlement before the ninth century. Perhaps there was a strong tribe or tribes still nomadic or semi-nomadic. Glueck's chronology is of interest, to go back to the Exodus. Ramses was pharaoh about 1290. If the Hebrews went past Edom after 1300, it would have been around 1250.[2]

However, there are several problems. Moses led the conquest of Heshbon. Excavation of Tell Hesban found nothing earlier than 1200. Perhaps the name moved as with Jericho. Jericho itself had very little Late Bronze material — Kenyon said erosion may have washed it away, but no valid conclusions can be drawn about the walls tumbling down (Joshua 6). Excavation at Ai showed no occupation in the Late Bronze Age for Joshua to conquer (Joshua 9). The nearby Bethel (Modern Beitin) however, had a major destruction in the thirteenth century. There was also a change in culture. The mounds of Tell ed-Duweir (Lachish; Joshua 10:31–32),

**Figure 10–1.** Aerial view of Tell Deir' Alla, looking southwest. Photo courtesy Dr. James A. Sauer.

Tell Beit Mersim (Debir?; Joshua 10:38–39), Tell el-Qedah (Hazor; Joshua 11:1–15) and Ras al-'Aln (Aphek; Joshua 12:18) were also destroyed in this period. By contrast, the places not conquered according to Judges 1 and Joshua 13, do not show evidence of conquest in this period. Shechem was not conquered, but the Israelites were in control (Joshua 8, 24) and we can only guess how or why.[3]

One theory holds that these cities destroyed each other. Others deny this claim, saying the evidence is ambiguous. The biblical story seems as reasonable to some as scholarly speculations of today. More information comes from the Merneptah stele, c. 1220, the earliest known reference to Israel outside the Bible. Pharaoh Merneptah claims he completely destroyed Israel. It is one of the ironies of history that Merneptah is remembered for the people he claimed to have eliminated. The stele has hieroglyphs indicating Israel was a recognizable people but not a settled geographical group. This is what one would expect so soon after the conquest. Both the Bible and aracheology suggest the rest of the land was conquered piecemeal, a little at a time. Control was not final until David, and even he did not take Philistine land.

In summary, it is at least possible that a conquest took place. The initial blitzkrieg was partially successful at best. The data is too unclear to be dogmatic. Archaeology provides little data on the distribution of territory among the tribes and their settlement. Some border cities representing tribal boundaries have been identified.[4]

## Balaam

There is a fascinating interlude in the biblical conquest of Transjordan that now is supported by archaeological data. To ward off the invading Hebrews, the Moabite King Balak sent for a diviner, Balaam the son of Beor, to curse the invaders (Numbers 22–24). At first God does not let him go. Balak sent more messengers, so God said OK and then changed his mind and sent an angel to stop Balaam. Balaam the diviner could not see the angel but the donkey could! That says something about Balaam's spiritual power. Eventually they arrived but instead of a curse, Balaam gave a blessing. He could only do what God told him to do.

Hendricus Jacobus Franken excavated Deir 'Alla in the Jordan Valley. In 1967, a sharp-eyed worker saw writing on a bit of plaster. Further investigation found two large though fragmentary inscriptions. The plaster may have been on a wall. Franken thinks it was a stele. Stratigraphy and epigraphy suggest a date c. 700 B.C. This is debated as are the contents of the two inscriptions.

At least one inscription is about Balaam the son of Beor who had a dream about doom for the city. The destruction was planned by the gods for the natural order had gone awry. Mild animals became wild and vice versa. Poor women were using myrrh as though they were rich. The next morning Balaam was sad. When asked about it, he told about his dream. It would seem the plan was averted and the city saved. People put up the inscription as a memorial but Balaam was doomed to die for thwarting the plans of the gods.

While even the most liberal dating does not put the inscription back to the time of the biblical Balaam, one could postulate the Deir 'Alla inscription commemorates an ancient event. The repetition of the name and the father-son combination is certainly striking. It is also of interest that the Deir 'Alla Balaam is more like the biblical prophets (Isaiah 13:9–11 and Joel 2:1–3) who prophesied doom for sinful people, than like the biblical Balaam who was for hire to bless or to curse. It will be interesting to follow the debate as scholars argue over the translations and interpretations.[5]

## B. THE JUDGES

The period of the Judges is usually estimated as c. 1200–1020. The war in Judges 4–5 has Deborah as Judge and Barak as general. Her name, as a place, the city of Taanach, and perhaps the name of Sisera are said to be in the Ebla tablets. "Sisera" has not previously been found outside the Bible. Deborah and Barak may have been like prophets and kings. The prophet gave the king the word of the Lord as Deborah gave the word to Barak. Judges 5:19 refers to Taanach and Megiddo. Judges 1:27 says these cities were not conquered by Joshua. They were destroyed c. 1125 judging by archaeological data. Deborah and Barak were active while the cities still existed, before 1125. They could be located in the time of Joshua if he had not yet conquered Hazor. A number of scholars see the reference in Judges 4:2 to Jabin, King of Hazor, as a later addition to the text. Alternately, Jabin could have continued or there could have been a later king who still claimed to be king of Hazor. Others think Megiddo and Taanach were destroyed in the fight referred to in Judges 4–5 so Deborah and Barak would date c. 1125. Judges 9 is about Abimelech who destroyed Shechem. That destruction was c. 1150, so his father, Judge Gideon, would have been Judge in about 1175, earlier than the more traditional 1100.[6]

### Philistines

Early in the period of the Judges, the so-called *Sea Peoples* arrived in Canaan. They had tried to capture Egypt c. 1190. Ramses III (c. 1198–1166) defeated them, and then hired them as mercenaries to guard his frontier posts. Their artifacts have been found on the southern border of Egypt and in Palestine. He may have made a virtue out of necessity — they were too strong to destroy outright. Beth-shan was one of Ramses' outposts. A seated statue of him was found there. One of the tribes was

**Figure 10–2.**    Ramses III defeated the Sea Peoples. He had the event commemorated on the wall of his temple at Thebes. The feathered headdresses have been compared to those of American Indians. A precedent for them is known from Crete and other areas.

named Palashtu, Peleset, Prst or Philistines. They came from Caphtor, perhaps Crete. Palestine was named after them by the Romans though some credit Herodotus who called them Palastinoi. They settled on the southern coast in an area that became known as Philistia. Their five main cities (pentopolis) were Gaza, Ashkelon, Ashdod, Gath and Ekron. Tell es-Safi is a current guess for Gath. Ekron is equated with Tell Miqneh where a joint Israeli (Trude Dothan) - American (Seymour Gittin) dig began in 1981.

Philistine pottery had a distinctive type of decoration as noted earlier. It marks their territory and territorial expansion for 150 years. It has been found at Aphek (I Samuel 4:1) where it disappeared with the next level of occupation, presumably Israelite. Before that later victory, however, the Philistines carried the day. The Israelites had camped at Ebenezer, "stone of help." Kochavi has identified Ebenezer with today's 'Isbet Sartah. Excavation shows occupation ended as Israelite occupation of Aphek began, after the destruction of the Philistine Aphek.[7]

Earlier, c. 1200, the Sea Peoples were credited with destroying the Hittite Empire and the city state of Ugarit. A letter from Ugarit was found in the pre-Philistine level at Aphek. The Hittites had found an economical way to refine iron ore. Perhaps the Sea Peoples learned of this process and brought it with them. The Philistines were able to work iron and the Israelites were not. I Samuel 13 says they had to go to Philistia to get their iron tools sharpened. Excavations have found very few iron artifacts in the Hebrew hill country at this time.

Gradually the Philistines began to expand. At the height of their power, they may have controlled the entire coastal plain and the Esdraelon to Beth-shan (Haifa to the Jordan River). They may even have begun to move down the Jordan Valley in a pincer movement around the Hebrews. The excavation of Shiloh, Tell Seilun 20 miles northeast of Jerusalem showed a destruction c. 1050. Perhaps this took place after the defeat at Aphek (I Samuel 4). The Israelites continued to fight under the leadership of Samuel and then Saul, their first real king.[8]

## Others

The Hebrews had a number of enemies in this period of the Judges. The Midianites made quick raids across the desert on their camels. They were finally stopped by Gideon. After the battle, Gideon was offered the kingship but declined. "God is your king." His son Abimelek ("my father is king") had no such scruples. He set himself up as king of the city state of Shechem. When the people tired of his rule, they rebelled so he destroyed the city c. 1150, including the temple of Baal Berith. Excavations show it was not rebuilt until Jeroboam I made it his capital c. 922 (I Kings 12:25).[9]

The Canaanites were defeated in a general sense but were still very much around "in the days when the Judges ruled." The Hebrew and Philistine conquest of the main part of Canaan or Palestine pushed some Canaanites into the northern region, especially the coastal plain of today's Lebanon. Here at Sidon and Tyre, they took to the sea. They became what the Greeks called Phoenicians. As mentioned earlier, the name is from the Greek "phoinike" from "phoinix," "red purple (wool)." "Canaan" is from the Akkadian "kinahna," or "kinahhu" or perhaps from the Hurrian "knaggi." "Ka-na-na" is said to be in the Ebla tablets. It is the royal purple from the murex shellfish, royal because only the wealthy could afford it (I Maccabees 4:25).

The Phoenicians c. 1100 furnished the Greeks with the alphabet we still use. These seafaring Semites sailed all over the Mediterranean and may have sailed around the continent of Africa. They established colonies and commerical trading posts on the island of Sardinia west of Italy, had colonies in Spain, founded the famous city of Carthage in North Africa, and may have had colonies on the Atlantic. Some say they went as far as England and now and then someone suggests they reached the Americas. King Hiram of Tyre was a friend and commerical partner of David and Solomon.[10]

In Judges 18 and Joshua 19:47–48, the biblical record says the tribe of Dan could not conquer its tribal allotment near the coast. They moved north and took Laish or Leshem, an ally of Sidon. They renamed it Dan, today's Tell el-Qadi (Mound of the Judge) at the source of the Leddan River, one of the sources of the Jordan River, at the base of Mount Hermon. Later Israel is described as extending "from Dan" in the north "to Beer-sheba" in the south (I Samuel 3:20, II Samuel 24:15; I Kings 4:25; I Chronicles 21:2). The Israelis renamed the ancient ruins Tell Dan. It lies twenty-five miles east of Sidon and Tyre on the road to Damascus. The Sidon alliance suggests the Phoenicians controlled an extensive inland area but the control was not very solid. The site is being excavated by Avraham Biran. He has identified Stratum VI, c. 1150, as the tribe of Dan's occupation level.[11]

In this period of the Judges, the Canaanites did not just sit back and let the Hebrews take over. The Canaanites continued to fight back. So did the peoples in the Transjordan region. The Moabites took back some territory. Several megalithic towers around Amman, ancient Rabbath Ammon, may date from this period as the Ammonites continued to develop and expand in their area. The fighting back and forth, as with Judge Jephthah and others, may account for some other destructions found in excavations.[12]

## Neighbors

It has been suggested that the Israelite tribes were associated in an *amphictyony* (Greek for "neighbors"), a confederation around a temple or in support of a common worship. One well known amphictyony was the Etruscans of Italy. They may have migrated from today's Turkey. There were amphictyonies among the Greeks and among the Sea Peoples. The Philistines may have had one. If the Hebrew tribes were organized in this way, they were unique with their central worship around a portable shrine rather than a fixed temple. The tabernacle apparently moved from place to place such as Gilgal, Shiloh, Shechem, and perhaps elsewhere. The Hebrews often borrowed elements from the surrounding culture and adapted them to their own use. The amphictyony had both political and military functions as the Bible amply demonstrates. [13]

## C. THE UNITED MONARCHY

Pressure from the conquering Philistines and the example of other kingdoms like Ammon, Moab, and Edom, may have combined to bring changes to the Israelite tribes. According to the book of Samuel, the people wanted a king and kingdom rather than the old amphictyony.

### Samuel

Samuel was the midwife for the birth of the monarchy. Today he would be called a kingmaker. In some ways he was a typical Judge. He led the people in military battle or at least inspired them as Deborah had. He judged or decided among them in disputes. Yet in other ways he was more like a priest. Like his mentor Eli, Samuel performed sacrifices and prayed on behalf of his people. Yet again, he was a prophet. He was a spokesman for God. He called his people to account for their sin and to repent even as the classical prophets did for centuries. Samuel is probably the most important biblical figure after Moses. While both Abraham and Moses were called prophets, Samuel is *the* prophet, the "father" of Hebrew prophecy. As Moses can be called the Lawgiver, Aaron is the founder of the priesthood. David, the sweet singer of Israel, founded psalmody as Solomon fathered the wisdom movement. Samuel is the father of prophecy.

The ancient Near East had known prophecy for several centuries. There is a type of prophecy in the Mari tablets c. 1750. The prophetic stories include one of a man who brought a message to the king from one of the gods. This type of activity may appear in the Ebla tablets c. 2350 though we must wait for further publication to be sure. Such political and military prophecy may form the background of the Deborah and Barak story in Judges 4–5. Oracles and prophecies of well-being or woe, or a king coming to power, were common in Egypt and Mesopotamia.

In an earlier day, the *baru*, or diviner, was a standard role in society. The story of Balaam was cited earlier. Some diviners were priests who examined the livers and entrails of sacrificial animals. From these "readings" they decided the future. Is this the place the gods want us to form a colony? Is this the time to go to war? Shall I buy this land? Ancient peoples needed to know when or where to carry out the gods' will. One called the diviner or priest rather than the stockbroker. The Egyptian Tale of Wenamon c. 1100 tells of a young man who fell into an ecstatic trance. In this state, he prophesied as Saul and the sons of the prophets did later. Apart from special individuals like Abraham and Moses, the earliest Hebrew prophets were spirit-filled ecstatics. In a religious frenzy, filled with the spirit of God, they prophesied (Numbers 11). Later there were regular bands of these ecstatics called "sons of the prophet." Samuel apparently organized them in some way for I Samuel 19:20 says he stood as head over them, in charge of them.[14]

The battle with the Philistines at Ebenezer was during Samuel's childhood. The probable destruction of ancient Shiloh at this time was cited earlier. Eli's death and the end of the shrine left the way open for Samuel to move from altar boy to high priest. I Samuel 7 describes his active life as Judge and priest (7:6). He gathered the people at Mizpah, perhaps Nebi Samwil about five miles northwest of Jerusalem, though Mizpah is more commonly identified with Tell en-Nasbeh seven and a half miles north of Jerusalem. Nasbeh was excavated by William F. Bade in 1926–35. It had been occupied c. 3000 and then abandoned until the eleventh century. A section of city wall and several private homes were found from the town of Samuel's day. In I Samuel 7:16, we read that Samuel was like an early Methodist circuit rider. He travelled on a circuit from one place of worship to another. His circuit was Mizpah to Bethel to Gilgal and back home to Ramah.

Bethel is modern Beitin, the site of Jacob's dream of angels climbing up and down a ladder to heaven (Genesis 28:19; 35:1–6). It was cited earlier as part of the conquest, a possible alternative to the story of Ai. The site was excavated by Albright in 1927 and 1934, and by Kelso in 1954, 1957, and 1960. The excavation found several phases of the Iron I (1200–900) period. Phase 3 at Bethel ended c. 1025. This may have been the time of Samuel with Phase 4a that of Saul and David. Architecture was of poor quality in both phases but the pottery improved remarkably from Phase 3 to Phase 4a, perhaps reflecting improved living conditions under the monarchy.

Gilgal ("circle of stone") appears in Joshua 4:19. Its exact location is unknown. In the book of Joshua it seems to be close to Jericho. Khirbet al-Mafjar, one and a half miles north of Jericho, has been suggested as the site of Gilgal. Here, in Samuel, one would expect the stone circle to be closer to the other sites. Perhaps there was more than one "circle." Ramah was Samuel's home (I Samuel 1:19, 2:11). In 1:1, it is called Ramathaim in Ephraim, which may be Rentis, sixteen miles east of Tel Aviv. Some have suggested Beit Rima twelve miles northwest of Bethel. There is also a Ramah in Benjamin, modern er-Ram, about five miles north of Jerusalem. This fits the context of 7:16–17. In a later time, it was traditional that priests came from the tribe of Levi. If Samuel was an Ephraimite, either this was an exception, or the Levitical tradition came later, or the Levites were a professional group rather than a biological tribe.[15]

**Figure 10–3.** The Tower of "David" with a more recent mosque minaret rising from the ruins. The tower is actually part of the fortifications of Herod the Great on Mt. Zion, near the Jaffa Gate on the left and the platform of his palace off to the right of the picture, now part of the Armenian Quarter.

## Saul

Samuel anointed first Saul and then David as king of Israel. Saul's rustic fort head-quarters at Gibeah (I Samuel 15:34) have been excavated. Albright dug there in 1922–23 and in 1934. Paul Lapp did some more digging in 1964. The town was founded, perhaps by the tribe of Benjamin, in the twelfth century B.C. This may have been the town destroyed by other Israelites (Judges 19–20). An eleventh century fort may have been Philistine (I Samuel 13:3). Fortress II, late eleventh century, is probably Saul's. An iron plowshare found there is one of the earliest known Israelite iron objects. The fort was destroyed, perhaps after Saul's death, by the Philistines near Beth-shan.[16]

Excavations at Beth-shan by the University Museum, 1921–33, found a small stele. The upper register is a bas relief of the god, Mekal. The Egyptian hiero-glyphic inscription, a mortuary prayer on the lower register, suggests he was a *chthonic*, or underground, god of life and death. *Necromancy*, the cult of the dead, might also be represented by figurines and a snake in decoration. Necromancy was banned by Saul. However, before the battle at Beth-shan, he was desperate. Samuel was dead and Saul felt isolated with no word from the Lord. So he went to a necromancer, the witch at Endor. The Bible describes how she brought Samuel up from the dead. Unfortunately for Saul, Samuel's prophecy was the same bad news Samuel gave Saul earlier. Saul was going to die. The Philistines won the bat-tle and hung his body on the walls of Beth-shan — the city of Mekal, the city of the House (beth) of the Dead (Sheol) or the place of asking (sha'ul) of the dead.[17]

## David

The Hebrew monarchy developed when the surrounding nations were weak. The two ends of the Fertile Crescent; Egypt and Mesopotamia, were not building empires that included Palestine. Thus the Philistines and Hebrews had a free hand to fight each other. The Philistines won some battles, like Aphek and Beth-shan. They lost the war. Thanks in large part to the leadership of David, the Hebrews survived. They not only survived but David went on to conquer most of the area except his own household (II Samuel 13–18).

One of the puzzles of his conquests is that he clearly beat the Philistines. Yet he did not annex their territory. Why not? One guess is that this omission is due to the old ties he had with them when he was their ally and he was fleeing the insane wrath of King Saul. David served Achish, king of Gath, who gave David the town of Zik-lag (I Samuel 27:1–8). Ziklag has been identified with Tell esh-Shari'a, northwest of Beersheba. It was dug, 1972–78 by Eliezer Oren of Ben Gurion University. Level VIII contained Philistine pottery.

G. Ernest Wright thought David was respecting Egyptian territory claims. Egypt had been in and out of the area for a thousand years. The Philistines may have been allowed by Egypt to settle there as noted earlier. Thus Philistia was at least a sphere of influence even if it was no longer Egyptian territory as such. Some credence for this view is provided by several ideas of government which David seems to have borrowed from Egypt. The lists of his officers in II Samuel 8:16–18 and 20:23–25 have parallels in Egypt. This continues with Solomon in I Kings 4:17 (cp. also 18:3 and II Kings 18:18). The tradition of David and music was cited earlier (I Samuel 16:23). Tradition says he authored the book of Psalms. Scholars debate this but there are psalms which have parallels in the hymns of Egypt. Perhaps the ties with Egypt were closer than the Bible indicates. David may even have arranged the mar-riage of Solomon to an Egyptian princess.[18]

Jerusalem is one of the most intensely excavated places on earth. It was here that the Palestine Exploration Fund began its search for "illumination of the Bible." In 1927, Macalister cleared a wall on the eastern slope of Mount Ophel, David's city. He thought it was the wall defending the Jebusite city which David conquered though its people said that could not be done. The wall was repaired in ancient times so Macalister thought David had repaired it. More recently, Kenyon dated this wall to the time of Nehemiah (fifth century). It was reinforced by the Hasmoneans (first century). Yigael Shiloh has unearthed a massive "glacis" (fortified slope) outside the wall which the Hasmoneans added to the defense. The Jebusite and Davidic wall is further down the slope. The structure is nine feet thick and was built c. 1800. It was used until the Babylonian destruction in 587. There were no houses outside — down the slope. David's city was confined to the Ophel. On the western side of Jerusalem, Mount Zion, is the Tower of David. It was built c. 25 B.C. by Herod the Great as part of his palace.[19]

In II Samuel 2:12–17 there is an earlier story of David's forces fighting the troops of Ishboseth or Ishbaal, son of Saul. The armed units met "at the pool of Gibeon." While excavating el-Jib in 1956, James Pritchard found a huge well or shaft in the bedrock. It is thirty-seven feet across. A spiral staircase cut in the rock leads down inside. At thirty-five feet there is a floor, but a tunnel continues the spiral stair down through the bedrock another forty-five feet. At the bottom is a kidney-shaped pool, perhaps for collecting water from the water table. Pritchard considers this the pool of Gibeon in David's time.

A second water system is a long stepped tunnel which runs under the city walls and out to a spring at the edge of the hill. The walls are dated twelfth–eleventh, and tenth centuries. This makes the tunnel later, perhaps in the time of Solomon. The upper beginning of the tunnel may have been dug to avoid the "pool," indicating the pool was already there, so the pool is earlier. Dan Cole now reasons the pool was a thirty-seven foot cistern for water storage. The additional forty-five foot stretch was dug later, probably in the ninth century B.C.[20]

II Samuel 5:6–10 is the story of David's capture of Jerusalem. The Jebusites mocked him saying he could not capture the city. But David challenged his men to "get up the water shaft." I Chronicles 11:4–9 says it was Joab who did it and became chief of staff. The Gihon Spring gets its name from "gicha," "to gush forth." It pulsates irregularly, bubbling up larger amounts of water than usual. About fifty feet inside Hezekiah's tunnel (more later) is a horizontal branch tunnel through the bedrock. It leads to a vertical shaft up through the rock. This is Warren's shaft, named for Captain Charles Warren who explored it in 1867 for the PEF. The shaft rises fifty-two feet to a horizontal tunnel over sixty feet long which runs under the ancient city wall to a stepped tunnel rising closer to the surface. This brings one to both a horizontal tunnel leading out to the edge of the hill and to a vertical shaft opening inside the ancient walls.

Recent clearing and study by Yigal Shiloh shows this system was still being used in Roman times. When was it first dug? We do not know. It may have been the water shaft scaled by Joab. Outside the Gihon is a channel that has been traced along the edge of the hill, leading down along and to lower parts of the Kidron Vally. The water in this system may have been used for irrigation. The channel may date from the time of Solomon.

At Megiddo, excavations found a sunken walkway or gallery from Solomon's time. It was dug under the city wall. A stair went down the side of the hill to an underground room with a spring. The staircase, dug into the side of the hill, would have been roofed and camouflaged to hide it from an enemy, like the staircase at Tell es-Saidiyeh. A second system, a tunnel dug through the bedrock to the same spring, probably is from the time of King Ahab c. 869–850 B.C.[21]

## Solomon

The Kingdom of Israel was a well established fact when Solomon schemed to get the throne. He maintained much of it and may have expanded a bit. Towards the end of his reign, the Bible says he lost Edom and Damascus but he may have expanded into Philistine areas and into the Negev desert. However, his main effort was internal development. The biblical record describes a major building program. The emphasis is on the temple. No recognized archaeological evidence has been found for the temple itself. The Israelite temple at Arad may be similar in some ways. The Arad temple was built in the tenth century Stratum IX. It was used through Stratum VII, and destroyed near the end of the seventh century, perhaps in the reform of Josiah. The Samaritan altar on Mount Gerisim is supposedly modelled after the Jerusalem temple. But that would be the second temple, completed c. 516, after the Babylonian destruction of Solomon's temple in 587. Several ideas about what it looked like have been developed, partly on biblical description and partly on what is known of tenth century temples. Solomon's temple was built by Phoenicians so it was presumably of Phoenician design.[22]

Some of his other construction is noted in I Kings 9:15ff. In the past, a number of things have been mistakenly attributed to Solomon. The smelting center at Tell el-Kheleifeh has been reexamined. It may be a granary or fort. The copper mines and slag heaps in the Arabah represent activity before 1150 and in Roman times according to the more recent work of Beno Rothenburg.[23]

Part of Solomon's wealth was in gold from the fabled Ophir (I Kings 9:26–28, 10:11; II Chronicles 8:17–18) as well as taxes and gifts from such people as the Queen of Sheba. The location of Ophir is uncertain. The gold of Ophir is mentioned on an ostracon, c. 700, from Tell Qasile on the Mediterranean. The ships of Tarshish (I Kings 10:22) brought Solomon gold and silver but also ivory, apes, and peacocks. This sounds like Africa. It seems logical to connect the verses and locate

Ophir in Africa. A geological survey has reexamined the gold mines of Saudi Arabia. The mines at Mahd adh Dhahab, "cradle of gold," could have produced the enormous amount recorded for Solomon and earlier for David (I Chronicles 29:4). Solomon's income (I Chronicles 29:4) was 666 talents of gold, about 815,184 ounces.[24]

The archaeological showplace for Solomon's career has also shifted. Ever since the Oriental Institute, Breasted's brainchild, dug Megiddo in the 1930s and uncovered Solomon's stables, these unusual buildings have been part of biblical archaeology. Yadin's more recent work suggests they belonged to Ahab of the northern kingdom, 100 years after Solomon. There are even those who question that the buildings were stables, rather than simply warehouses. However, Yadin also showed there is a Solomonic gate at Megiddo and similar gates at Hazor and Gezer.[25]

Solomon's "glory" is further shown by his palaces. The Bible says he spent thirteen years building his palace in Jerusalem and only seven building the temple. Obviously the palace was a more elaborate work. If there are any remains of either, they are probably under Herod's temple platform, today's Haram esh-Sharif. The Phoenicians were involved here as well as with the temple, so one would expect the design to be Phoenician. David Ussishkin suggested parallels with the "bit-hilani," the palace pattern of northern Syria. That is the case with the two palaces discovered at Megiddo. There is no biblical description of these so we can only go by the archaeological remains. One entered a rectangular reception hall through an elaborate portico on the long side of the rectangular building. A small side room is off one end of the reception or entrance hall. The main room is behind both of these. Other small rooms are beyond or beside the main room.[26]

The new excavations at Gezer found additional evidence of tenth century destruction. The city was then rebuilt. The destruction may have been by the pharaoh who captured the city and gave it to Solomon as part of the dowry of the Egyptian princess who married Solomon (I Kings 9:16). Abraham Malamat suggested that the pharaoh is Siamun, c. 976–958. He thinks Siamun made a major expedition into Philistia. He may have conquered Ashdod also. If Malamat is right, the marriage may have sealed a peace treaty between Egypt and Israel. The northern and eastern borders were secure. Solomon's huge armed forces could have responded to the Egyptian threat. This could account for Solomon's fortification of Gezer and other sites. The threat of an Egyptian invasion was real.

The Bible does not mention his forts in the south. They were destroyed when Pharaoh Shishak went from threat to reality and invaded shortly after Solomon's death. The original dates of the forts are disputed like most things in the Bible and in archaeology. Cohen, who dug several, thinks they were Solomon's and guarded his southern trade.[27]

Solomon's commercial activities conflicted with the trade of the Sabeans. By this time they had established a kingdom in the lower Arabian peninsula, the area of today's Yemen. The Queen of Sheba came to Jerusalem to discuss the situation. She was apparently successful in these trade negotiations (I Kings 10:13). Solomon went on to become the middleman in the horse and chariot trade between Egypt and today's Turkey, then the old Hittite territory, which by Solomon's time was neo-Hittite. These areas had been known for these products for several centuries (I Kings 10:26–29).

In spite of his supposed wealth, Solomon went heavily into debt (balance of trade) to the Phoenicians for his construction program. He ceded twenty cities to Hiram and still had problems. He set high taxes and used the corvee — taxes in kind in the form of labor. These were a burden on the people and contributed to the break up of the empire after his death. Still, excavations show an increase in prosperity during the monarchy. The Israelite house was better constructed than the peasant homes of the fourteenth and thirteenth century Canaanites. The culture in general became quite uniform over the next few hundred years.

David's Egyptian connection was cited earlier. E.W. Heaton called Solomon the pharaoh of Israel. He thinks the scribes of Solomon's court found models in their Egyptian counterparts. They wrote the Annals of Solomon (I Kings 3–11) and described him in the same terms — wealth, wisdom, commerce — as Egyptian scribes used for the pharaohs. Among others, Hatshepsut and Ramses III sent expeditions to Punt. So Solomon sent shipping expeditions for luxury and trade. The story of Wenamun represented commercial relations with the Phoenicians, so Solomon had his trade with Hiram of Tyre. David laid the foundations for Egyptian style government; Solomon developed the massive bureaucracy of empire. The civil service, the division of the country into administrative districts, taxation, and corvee all followed Egyptian models. Egyptian influence may have been even more extensive. The Bible says Solomon wrote 3000 proverbs and 1005 songs (I Kings 4:29–34). There are many parallels between the wisdom literature of Israel and Egypt. Without ascribing all of Israel's wisdom literature of Solomon, he can still be seen as its inspiration and patron saint. The wisdom of the entire Near East could have influenced Israel but the Egyptian may have been particularly influential through Solomon's court.[28]

## D. THE DIVIDED MONARCHY

Solomon was followed by his son Rehoboam. People asked for relief from taxes and the corvee but Rehoboam took a hard line and promised more of the same and worse. As if to add insult to injury, Rehoboam sent his message with Adoram, the man in charge of the corvee. People stoned him to death (I Kings 12:18). David had

**Figure 10–4.**   Ahab's Wall. Samaria construction. The stretcher-header technique has a block placed lengthwise (a rectangle to the viewer) followed by two blocks with square ends showing. It was prominent in the time of King Omri and his son, King Ahab.

an Adoram in charge of forced labor (II Samuel 20:24). Solomon had Adoniram, son of Abda, in charge of forced labor (I Kings 4:6). Rehoboam's Adoram may have been the same person though by this time he would have been along in years. Nahman Avigad published a seal inscribed, "Belonging to Pela'yahu who is over (in charge of) the corvee." It dates to the seventh century. The name Pelaiah appears in Nehemiah 8:7 and other later sources. The seal, however, indicates the importance of this government official and it suggests the institution of the corvee lasted for centuries.[29]

## Israel

Jeroboam was a labor battalion captain under Solomon. He had tried to revolt but failed. After Solomon's death, he came back from refuge in Egypt. When Adoram relayed King Rehoboam's demands, Jeroboam raised the traditional cry of revolt. "To your tents, O Israel." The northern tribes seceded from the union (I Kings 12).

Traditionally the area was made up of 10 out of 12 tribes. By this time the tribes were no longer distinct, but from c. 922–721, this northern tribe was known as Israel, or the Northern Kingdom of Israel. The two southern tribes of Benjamin and Judah were called Judah or the Southern Kingdom, 922–587.

Jeroboam set up his capital at Shechem (I Kings 12:25). Some remnants of casemate wall discovered at Shechem may be a part of his rebuilding of the old cult center. I Kings 13:17 may indicate he set up a second headquarters in Tirzah, seven miles northeast. Tirzah is identified with Tell el-Farah North (to distinguish it from another Farah in the south). Roland de Vaux excavated here 1946–60. The site is larger than Megiddo and twice the size of Jericho so it was more important than biblical references suggest.

Jeroboam could have set up a worship center at Shechem on the ruins of the temple to the covenant god, Baal-berith. Instead he set up two religious shrines to compete with Solomon's temple — at Bethel ("house of God") and Dan (I Kings 12:29). In each place he set up a golden calf. He told the people, "Behold your Gods." He also made houses on high places. THe Hebrew here is "beth bamah," pl. "bamoth" (I Kings 12:27–31). They were the infamous high places condemned by the prophets and the Deuteronomic School which wrote the history from Deuteronomy to Kings (cf. I Kings 3:3; Jeremiah 19:3–5). Biran's excavations at Dan have uncovered what he calls a cultic center, possibly that of Jeroboam. It is big — about half an acre in size. The open air platform measured about twenty-two by sixty feet, built of cut limestone blocks on a rough stone base. The first one, "Bamah A," is tenth century. Very little survived from a destruction of the stratum. It was rebuilt to measure sixty by sixty-two feet. This Bamah B is c. 850 in date, the time of Ahab. Bamah C is c. 800–750. The area was still used for worship in the Roman period.

Early in Jeroboam's reign, his old friend and protector, Pharaoh Shishak (c. 940–915) invaded (I Kings 11:26, 40). He raided both Judah and Israel. He plundered Jerusalem, including the temple with all the wealth Solomon supposedly accumulated there. Shishak listed the cities he conquered on the walls of the temple at Karnak as earlier pharaohs had done. Some historians suspect he may have enlarged his own list over reality by copying names from the earlier lists. However, a stele of Shishak's was found in Megiddo and destruction layers of several of these cities such as Gezer are attributed to him. He may have gone to the old Egyptian smelting center in the Arabah, perhaps to reclaim the copper working industry there.[30]

In 876, an army general named Omri became king of Israel. He left Tirzah (I Kings 16:17, 23) with a half-built palace and fortifications and started a new capital at Samaria (I Kings 16:22–24). Excavations suggest a possible Chalcolithic settlement 2000 years earlier. Debate continues on whether there was a settlement when Omri bought it or whether it was a farm. He bought it from its owner though

he presumably could have simply taken it. Extensive remains have been found in
the excavation. Much of what one can see there now belongs to a later time — that
of Alexander, Herod, and the Crusaders. However, at least some of the ruins
uncovered go back to Omri and his son Ahab. The construction technique is a distinctive "headers and stretcher" type. Two blocks are laid so their ends show. A
third block is laid lengthwise. Looking at the finished wall, the viewer sees a line of
two squares followed by a rectangle.

   In 853, Ahab joined a group of allies — Syrian, Transjordan and Palestinian
states — to fight the advancing Assyrians. The Battle of Qarqar stopped the Assyrians. The Assyrian King Shalmaneser III (c. 859–824) recorded his "victory" on a
stele. His scribe listed Ahab as having the largest number of chariots — 2000 out of
the allies' 3940. Ahab had 10,000 out of the 60,000 troops. Assyrian records show
that Shalmaneser had only 2000 chariots. He tried again in 849, 848, 845, and
841. He finally succeeded. By this time the alliance had split. Hazael (c. 842–806)
had seized power in Damascus and Jehu (c. 842–815) had assassinated the entire
ruling family of Omri and most of the Davidides of Judah.[31]

**Figure 10–5.**    Figurine of Baal.

Yadin's suggestion that the stable remains of Megiddo belonged to Ahab was cited earlier. The archaeological remains seen today are for the most part from Ahab's time. That includes the great shaft dug through bedrock and the tunnel at the bottom that leads to the spring.

The prophet Elijah was Ahab's nemesis (I Kings 17–21). Ahab was married to Jezebel, a Sidonian princess (I Kings 16:30–33). Perhaps through her influence, Ahab worshipped Baal and made an Asherah. This idolatry was sin enough but he added to it gross social injustice (I Kings 21). The story opens with Elijah pronouncing drought. Then the Lord told Elijah to go hide by the brook Cherith. When the brook dried up, he was told to go to Zarephath, which belongs to Sidon (I Kings 17:9). Zarephath is identified with Sarafend, excavated by Pritchard as noted earlier. I Kings 17:17–24 tells how Elijah brought back to life the son of a widow with whom he stayed. The deed was commemorated in a painting in Dura-Europas synagogue on the Euphrates River. In the Christian tradition later there was a church and tower at Sarepta in memory of Elijah. No remains of these have been found. But a temple of Ashtart, Phoenician Tanit, was found.

THE SILOAM INSCRIPTION

**Figure 10–6.** The inscription was cut out of the wall of the Siloam Tunnel (Hezekiah's Tunnel) and taken to the Istanbul Museum. Photo by Siegfried H. Horn, courtesy of Horn Archaeological Museum.

Omri had probably reconquered the Moabites. In his grandson's time, the Moabites regained their freedom according to the Bible. This is reflected in the famous Mesha stone. The inscribed stele was found in 1868 at Dhiban (Dibon) east of the Dead Sea, forty miles south of Amman (Isaiah 15:2, Jeremiah 48:18). King Mesha describes his victory over the house of Omri and his building of Dibon. U. S. and Canadian excavators in 1950–55 uncovered a royal quarter in the southeast corner of the city which may have been the work of Mesha. [32]

The Omri family was destroyed in 842 in a bloodbath by his army general Jehu. Later, Jehu bowed and paid tribute to Shalmaneser III, who had the event recorded in pictures as well as writing. The Black Obelisk of Shalmaneser has a series of panels in bas-relief. One shows Jehu with his face on the ground. The Assyrians continued to refer to the Northern Kingdom as the House (Land) of Omri. This may simply be because that was their first contact with the kingdom. It may also be that they thought Jehu was an Omride. Jehu's long reign was not good for Israel's material welfare. It was not until his grandson, Jeroboam II, that the country recovered financially.

Jeroboam (c. 786–746) led the country to the greatest prosperity it had ever known. The prophet Amos (c. 750) did not see this as a blessing. He called down the wrath of God, or rather he heard God's message to Israel and spoke forth for God, "Thus sayeth the Lord . . ." He prophesied the destruction of the houses of ivory and of those who lay on beds of ivory (3:15; 6:4). Samaria had continued as the capital of the northern kingdom. Excavations there found ivory carvings which may have decorated the walls and furniture then. The Samaria ostraca may have come from Amos' time also. These potsherds, the scratch paper of the ancient world, contain receipts for wine and oil. This may represent taxes in kind before coinage was widespread. [33]

Amos' predictions were not long in coming. Tiglath-pileser III (c. 745–727) ushered in a period of Assyrian domination over Palestine that lasted more than 100 years. Assyrian records include both Judah and Israel. Several rebellions in Israel, with quick changes of kings and intrigue with Egypt, led to Assyrian reprisals. The Assyrians under Shalmaneser V (c. 726–722) and then Sargon II (c. 721–705), attacked the city of Samaria which fell in 721. Sargon's records claim he took thousands of captives and exiled them to various parts of the empire to prevent future troublemaking.

These captives have disappeared from history but have given rise to the tradition of the ten lost tribes of Israel. We have no archaeological evidence they migrated to the shores of South or North America and became the American Indians as some have claimed. Nor do we have any archaeological data they migrated to the British Isles to start the British Empire as the new Promised Land giving Britannia the right to rule the world. There are those looking for such evidence and hoping to find it. Many may have escaped the Assyrian dragnet

by simply going south to Jerusalem. Its population increased from c. 5000 to
c. 25,000. In addition, new settlements were started in the hills of Judah. Sargon
brought people from other parts of his empire to repopulate Samaria and the old
Northern Kingdom. Some think this new population is the origin of the Samaritans while others claim the Samaritans emerged in the time of Nehemiah or even
later, after Alexander the Great.[34]

The Assyrian campaigns of 735 and 721 devastated a number of sites. Shechem,
ten miles from Samaria, was destroyed. Excavations have found destruction layers
from this period at Dothan, Bethel, Megiddo, Hazor, Beth-shan, Dan, and elsewhere. According to II Kings 15:29, Hazor was conquered in the days of Pekah,
king of Israel (c. 737–733). Excavations here found a storage jar with a Hebrew
phrase scratched in the shoulder, "Belonging to Pekah." It was a common name of
the time but it is at least possibly a reference to the king.[35]

## Judah

While the northern kingdom of Israel lasted 200 years, the southern kingdom of
Judah lasted almost 350. The difficulty of dating some of the southern border forts
was cited earlier. King Rehoboam, c. 922–915, may have built some to protect the
southland. They did not help much, as Shishak's invasion made clear. But Judah
survived and at times even prospered. Jehoshaphat, c. 873–849, tried to revive
Solomon's maritime trade (I Kings 22:48). He failed and the rebuilt port city of
Ezion-geber or Elath declined. It may have been destroyed by the Edomites who
succeeded in rebelling against his son Jehoram, c. 849–842 (II Kings 8:20). Jehoram's son, Ahaziah was killed in 842 by Jehu in the bloodbath cited earlier.
Ahaziah's mother, Athaliah, the daughter of Queen Jezebel, took over the throne
of Judah, 842–837. Ze'ev Meshel, the excavator of Kuntillet Ajrud, has suggested
this site was occupied in Athaliah's day. Inscriptions there indicate the worship of
Baal and Asherah as well as Yahweh.

Period III at Elath has been related to the work of King Uzziah, c. 783–742 (II
Kings 14:22). A seal from this stratum is inscribed, "Belonging to Jotham,"
Uzziah's son and successor, c. 742–715. He may have been there as governor.
Nachman Avigad interpreted the symbol on this seal as a stylized bellows. He
relates this to the metallurgy of the area. The ram on the seal may be a pictorial
version of the city name since the Hebrew for ram, " 'il," is similar to Elath, " 'ilt."

Uzziah had a strong interest in farming. He developed the Negev or at least it
underwent extensive development in this period. The result was the densest population for the area since the nineteenth century. The Iron Age II (c. 900–600 B.C.)
forts and new agricultural villages come from the time of Uzziah (II Chronicles
26:10). Tell Beit Mersim contained a large installation of the related olive oil industry at this time.[36]

From an archaeological perspective, Hezekiah, c. 715–687, is probably the most famous of the Judean kings. Egypt was led by a vigorous Ethiopian conqueror, Piankhi. After a long absence, Egypt was once again meddling in Palestinian affairs. Hezekiah was drawn into the plots and counterplots for revolt against the Assyrians. He began with a religious reform (II Chronicles 29). This included removing elements of Assyrian worship which had been introduced into the country, especially into Solomon's temple. This was rebellion against the Assyrian warlords. In preparing for the counterattack from the Assyrians, he had a tunnel dug from the Gihon spring. The tunnel went through the ridge called Mount Ophel and ended in the pool of Siloam (II Kings 20:20). The spring was presumably covered and hidden from the enemy.

The tunnelers moved in the wrong direction several times so the tunnel curves back and forth underground. The straight distance from spring to pool is 1200 feet. The tunnel is 1752 feet long. It was discovered in 1838 by the American explorer Edward Robinson. It was cleared in 1910 by the Parker Mission which was searching for the mythical lost treasure of Solomon. In 1976, the Israeli government cleaned it again to make the tunnel safe for tourists. The venturesome can wade through it though those with claustrophobia are advised against it.

**Figure 10–7.** Hezekiah's water tunnel.

**Figure 10–8.** This bas-relief decorated Sennacherib's palace. It shows the Assyrians attacking (on the left) the biblical city of Lachish. On the lower right, the city has surrendered and people are led away captive. Photo courtesy British Museum.

Near the Siloam end of the tunnel, an inscription was carved in the wall describing the final meeting of the diggers. They dug from both ends at once. As they got closer to each other, there were several misdirections which can still be seen in the tunnel. But the inscriptions say they listened to the digging of the other party and then dug in that direction until they finally met. The inscription is in the Museum of the Ancient Orient in Istanbul. Kenyon suggested that originally the Siloam pool was an underground cistern with an overflow tunnel out to the valley in the south. Eventually the roof caved in and left the open pool seen today.[37]

The tunnel did not stop the Assyrian King Sennacherib, 704–681, from conquering the territory of Judah. In one of his inscriptions, he claims he shut Hezekiah up in Jerusalem like a bird in a cage. He captured forty-six towns of Judah. Among the most important, at least to him, was Lachish, probably Tell ed-Duweir, twenty-five miles southwest of Jerusalem. Stratum III is probably the Lachish he conquered, but there has been considerable debate over this. Sennacherib had a large bas-relief of the battle and his capture of the city installed as wall panels in his palace in Nineveh. Excavators of Lachish found the crest of an Assyrian helmet, like those pictured on the relief in Nineveh.

**Figure 10–9.** A reconstruction of the Assyrian attack and capture of Lachish. Photo courtesy British Museum.

Sennacherib did not capture Jerusalem. II Kings 19:33 says the angel of the Lord killed the Assyrian troops and saved the city. The Greek historian Herodotus describes a plague of mice that ate the bow strings and other leathers of the army. Some have thought this meant a bubonic plague. The evidence has been inconclusively debated. Some have suggested that the miraculous deliverance came in another attack on Jerusalem in 688. In the first attack in 701, this theory says that Hezekiah bought his way out of his gilded cage. A seal impression from this period is inscribed "Belonging to Yehozarah the son of Hilqiyahu servant of Hezekiah." This was probably King Hezekiah. In Isaiah 36:3 and II Kings 18:18 there is a royal steward of Hezekiah named Eliaqim son of Hilqiyahu. Perhaps the seal belonged to a brother. The well-known stamped jar handles reading "lmlk," "to the king" or "belonging to the king," come from this period. This may represent taxes in kind, or they may have been jars of produce from the king's estates. As cited earlier, Na'aman thinks they are supplies for the fortified cities of Judah. [38]

Hezekiah's son Manasseh, c. 687–642, inherited the throne. He reversed Hezekiah's reformist policy and reinstated Assyrian worship in the temple of Jerusalem. With one possible exception (II Chronicles 33:11) he remained a loyal vassal to Assyria. It was probably a necessity. Assyria was at the height of its power. The Assyrian kings Esarhaddon and Ashurbanipal included Manasseh in their lists of tribute payers.[39]

**Figure 10–10.**    The Zion Gate in the Old City wall is on Mt. Zion, to which the city spread in Hezekiah's time or earlier, perhaps from an influx of refugees from the destruction of Samaria in 721 B.C. The foundations date from the Roman period. The gate leads in to the Armenian Quarter today.

**Figure 10–11.**    Qumran. Siegfried Horn (right foreground) inspects. The original fortification of the site was in the Iron Age. It may have been done by King Hezekiah.

Manasseh's grandson Josiah, 640–609, reversed things once more. He returned to Hezekiah's reformist position. As before this meant removing Assyrian elements from the temple in Jerusalem. He went much further. II Kings 22:8 tells of a book discovered during his repairs to the temple. The book is commonly identified with Deuteronomy ("second law"). In II Kings 23:8 we read that Josiah defiled the high places from Geba to Beersheba, perhaps following Deuteronomy 12. This may be reflected in the destructions at Beersheba, Arad, Bethel, Shechem, and Beth-shan. Among the removals from the Jerusalem temple were "the horses that the kings of Judah had set up in honor of the sun at the entrance to the house of the Lord" (II Kings 23:11). In her excavation outside the city wall, Kenyon found a cult center. There were two repositories of sacred or dedicated objects — pottery, figurines and miniature furniture. Among the animal figurines are some with a disk between the ears. This may represent the sun and the figurines are examples of or miniature model horses of the sun.[40]

Josiah succeeded in his revolt because the great bloody empire of Assyria was about to meet its bloody end. The Babylonian Chronicles are official records which give us a year by year description of how Nabopolasser, 625–605, rose to power in Babylon. With the help of his more famous son Nebuchadnezzar, 605–562, as leader of the army and several allies, Assyria was destroyed. The prophet Nahum sang the death song over the Fall of Nineveh in 612. A horde of seals, c. 600, found in the re-excavation of Lachish, includes the name Nahum which also appears on an ostracon from Arad. The Assyrians retreated to Haran and Carchemish but the end came in 605. While the issue was still in doubt in 609, Pharaoh Necho, 610–594, led his Egyptian armies through Palestine to help Assyria. We do not know if this was out of loyalty to his Assyrian masters or if this was a shrewd move to keep a weakened Assyria as a buffer state between Egypt and the conquering Babylonians or Chaldeans as they are sometimes called. King Josiah of Judah tried to stop Necho and was killed in battle at Megiddo. The destruction of Megiddo Stratum II may relate to this conflict.[41]

Necho's efforts were successful for four years, but futile once Nebuchadnezzar had finished off the Assyrians in 605. He moved on to take over Palestine. For seven years, his control was questioned but not challenged. In 598, King Jehoiakim, 609–598, encouraged by Egypt, rebelled against the Chaldeans. Jehoiakim conveniently died as the Chaldeans besieged the city and left his son, Jehoiachin, 598–597, to be captured and exiled to Babylon. In his excavation of Babylon, 1899–1917 A.D., Koldewey found some ration records inside the famous hanging gardens of Nebuchadnezzar. These records indicate that Jehoiachin was still considered a king in 592 and was receiving royal treatment as described in II Kings 25:20.

The Babylonians chose Jehoiachin's uncle, Zedekiah, 597–587, to be king. He rebelled ten years later only to have Jerusalem captured once more. This time the city and the temple of Solomon were destroyed. The Babylonians appointed Gedeliah as governor who moved the capital to Mizpah although he was murdered by Ishmael in 582. Archaeological evidence for the Babylonian campaigns has been found in several cities of Judah. A seal impression from the last Judahite occupation of Lachish has an inscription "Belonging to Gedaliah who is over the house." It is not impossible that this is the governor. The designation, "over the house," is ascribed to Jotham, the son of Uzziah in II Kings 15:5. A seal found at Tell en-Nasbeh (Mizpah) says "Belonging to Jaazaniah, servant of the king." This may be one of the captains of Judah's army in Gedaliah's time (II Kings 25:23; Jeremiah 40:8).

The Lachish ostraca were cited earlier. Several of these pieces of pottery have whole letters written on them that are concerned with the defense of the city. The letters include names like Yirmiyahu (Jeremiah) and Mattanyahu (Mattaniah = Zedekiah, II Kings 24:17). The ostraca are in Hebrew but a number of Aramaic inscriptions have been found from this period. The use of this language was rising and soon spread to the whole region as a new "lingua franca" or common language as Akkadian had been earlier and Greek would be later. Aramaic lasted through the time of Jesus of Nazareth. The Aramaic papyri of Elephantine are of special interest in the fifth century exilic period.[42]

Several ostraca from Arad are also of interest. One is a letter ordering troops to Ramath-negeb. The last line is "Lest Edom should come there." Evidently they were expecting an attack by Edomites. Ramath-negeb appears in the Bible from an earlier period (Joshua 19:8; I Samuel 30:27). Its exact location is unknown. Nachman Avigad reports on two "bullae" — lumps of clay used to seal documents like the wax used on papyri and also in more recent history. The stamp of the owner or sender was put in the clay with a stamp seal or cylinder seal that rolled across the clay. One of Avigad's reads "Belonging to Berechiah, son of Neriah the scribe." The other says "Belonging to Jerahmeel the king's son." Berechiah is probably a long form of Baruch, Jeremiah's scribe. We may have here a seal impression from "Baruch the son of Neriah" who wrote the scroll for Jeremiah (Jeremiah 36:4). In Jeremiah 36:26, King Jehoiakim ordered Jerahmeel the king's son and others to seize (arrest?) Baruch and Jeremiah. Avigad also published a seal "Belonging to Seraiah, son of Neriah." This may be Baruch's brother (Jeremiah 32:12; 51:59), chief chamberlain of King Zedekiah. Jeremiah sent an oracle against Babylon with Seraiah who went there with Zedekiah.

Some have suggested "son of the king" was a functional title rather than a biological one. Avigad prefers the royal lineage. A seal he published earlier says "Belonging to Manasseh son of the king." Manasseh was king c. 687–642. He was only 12 when he began his reign. The seal dates from c. 700 B.C., so it probably does not refer to the king but to another prince or a royal official.[43]

## East of the River

Seals and inscriptions provide some information for the Transjordan area for this time. Several Ammonite seals have names of kings and officials. Two seals belonged to women: "Alyah maid-servant of Hanan'el" and "'NMWT maid-servant of DBLBS." "Maid-servant" is probably a court official paralleled in other seals like "Adonipelet servant of Amminadab" and "Adoninur servant of Amminadab." Women officials in Ammon may reflect a higher status for women in this desert kingdom. "Amminadab" means "My god 'Amm is generous" or "My people (kinsman) are generous (noble)." It is a common biblical name (Numbers 1:7, etc.) as well as the name of a king of the Ammonites on Cylinder C of the Assyrian King Ashurbanipal c. 667.

In 1972, a bronze bottle about six inches long was found at Tell Siran on the campus of the University of Jordan. Inscribed on the bottle are eight lines of script.

> The works of Amminadab, King of the Ammonites
> The son of Hissal'el, King of the Ammonites
> The son of Amminadab, King of the Ammonites
> a vineyard and the gardens and the 'thr
> and cisterns.
> May he rejoice and be glad
> for many days and long years.

**Figure 10–12.**    The Tell Siran Bottle, 7th century B.C. The corroded bronze bottle as it was found "in situ."

This is the first complete Ammonite inscription discovered and the longest one, by one letter. Ecclesiastes 2:4–6 reads:

> I made great works; I built houses and planted vineyards for myself;
> I made myself gardens and parks, and planted in them all kinds of fruit trees.
> I made myself pools from which to water the forest of growing trees.

The last line of the Siran inscription is echoed in a verse (12:27) in Ezekiel, "Son of man, Behold, they of the house of Israel say, 'The vision that he sees is for many days hence, and he prophesies of times far off.'" Scholars do not think Solomon wrote Ecclesiastes but he may have been the inspiration for it. The point here is simply that gardens and vineyards were an acceptable activity of kings. This appears in the story of Ahab, who wanted Naboth's vineyard to expand the king's garden (I Kings 21:1–2). It was common among Muslim kings in a later day — Baghdad, Persia, India, Turkey.

**Figure 10–13.** After cleaning by Mohammad Murshed Khadijah.

The contents of the bottle were a mix of wheat and barley. A carbon 14 test gave a date of 460 B.C., at least 150 years later than the inscription. This may be due to modern contamination after the bottle was opened and the ancient grain exposed to the air. It is not impossible though unlikely that the grain was put in this much later.

There is some debate over which Amminadab on the bottle is the one on Ashurbanipal's Cylinder C and how the two seals relate to these two on the bottle. Frank Cross thinks the Amminadab of the seals and cylinder are all the same person, who is the grandfather of the grandfather (line three) on the bottle.

**Figure 10–14.** A drawing of the entire inscription. The unknown word, " 'thr" curves around the bottom of the bottle.

**Figure 10–15.** The form of the letters suggest a date of c. 700 B.C. For example, the second letter, "b" is mostly open at the top so it looks like a "y" but one is closed like "9" or "g." The 16th letter, the Semitic "ayin," is mostly open and shaped like a "u" but one is closed like an "o." The older closed forms are 8th century while the open forms are 7th century. The transition took place c. 700. However, Frank Moore Cross, Jr., dates the inscription c. 600.

CHARACTERS on TELL SIRAN BRONZE BOTTLE
DRAWN by BERT DE VRIES
SCALE 0   1   2   3 CM.

In I Samuel 11 (c. 1020 B.C.) and II Samuel 10:2, there is a reference to Nahash, king of the Ammonites. The name also appears in the Deir 'Alla text of c. 700. In II Samuel 10:2 there is a reference to his son Hanun, c. 990. Shobi was another son of Nahash (II Samuel 17:27). Solomon married an Ammonitess, Naamiah, who became the mother of Rehoboam, Solomon's successor. Perhaps she was a sister or daughter. Ba'asha' the son of Ruhubi was the Ammonite king c. 853 according to the monolith inscription of Shalmaneser III. Ba'asha' fought along with Ahab at Qarqar. The next known king would be Shanip or Shanipu c. 733.

**Figure 10–16.** A seal impression in baked clay, possibly a stopper for a bottle. Found at Tell el 'Umeiri in Jordan. The inscription reads, "Belonging to Milkom'ur servant of Ba'alysa'." Published by permission L. T. Geraty.

**Figure 10–17.** A drawing of the 'Umeiri seal impression. Photos courtesy The Horn Archaeological Museum, Andrews University. Published by permission L.T. Geraty.

There is an inscription on the base of an Ammonite statue of a king found in Amman. The inscription has recently been retranslated to read "Ycrah'azar son of Zakir son of Shanib." Shanib is probably the Shanip of Assyrian records, the Annals of Tiglath-pileser III, c. 733. Thus Shanib was followed by Zakir and Yerah'azar. The Annals of Sennacherib refer to Buduili or Bod'el as king of the Ammonites c. 701. He appears again in the records of Esarhaddon, c. 680–669 as Puduil and yet again in Ashurbanipal's records c. 668. Cross has published a seal inscribed "Belonging to byd'l servant of pd'l." This pd'l may be the king. Cross dates the seal to the time of Sennacherib. There is another pd'l seal from c. 600. Avigad published a seal saying "Belonging to Bod'el son of Nadab'el."

In 667, Ashurbanipal's Cylinder C names Amminadab as king. His son, says Cross, is unknown. Then comes Amminadab (line three on the bottle), Hissal'el, and Amminadab. Ba'lys appears as an Ammonite king in Jeremiah 40:14. He plotted with Ishamel c. 581 to murder Gedaliah, the governor in Mizpah. A seal impression in baked clay, possibly a jar stopper for a bottle, was found at Tell el'Umeiri southwest of Amman. The inscription says "Belonging to Milkom'ur servant of Ba'alysa'." It is possible that Hanan'el and DBLBS from the seals noted earlier are also Ammonite kings. They could fit in c. 620 B.C. or earlier.[44]

The Moabite inscription of Mesha was cited earlier. Several Assyrian inscriptions refer to Moab and Moabite kings. Shalamanu was king in the time of Tiglath-pileser III, c. 745–727. Kammusunadbi and Musuri were kings in Sennacherib's day, c. 704–681. Musuri was still king in Ashurbanipal's time (Cylinder C). Several seals have the name Kemosh (Chemosh) the god of Moab, as well as personal names and officers of the kings. Chemosh appears in the texts of Ebla ("[d]ka-mi-ish," "[d]ka-me-ish") and of Ugarit ("kmt") and in the Syrian city name of Carchemish, "the market of Chemish."

From further south from Umm el-Biyara at Petra, there is a seal with the name Qos-gebar, king of Edom. Qos or Qaus was an Edomite god. Gebar = Hebrew "gibbar" a hero or bold one as in the name *Gabriel* (mighty one of God) in Daniel 8:16. Both Esarhaddon and Ashurbanipal include Qaus-gabri as king of Edom in their records. Earlier, Tiglath-pileser III said that Qaus-malaku of Edom paid tribute. Sennacherib also lists an Aiarammu as king of Edom. At Tell el-Kheleifeh, seal impressions on jars included the name Qaus'nl.[45]

# NOTES

1. This "weakness" is eliminated if we follow those scholars who think there was an invasion from the south. They see this in the Caleb stories of Numbers 14; Joshua 15:16–17, 21:12; Judges 1:12–13; and Samuel 30:14. Cf. Robert F. Johnson, "Caleb," IDB 1, pp. 482–483. Excavations in Edomite territory suggest little or no urban settlement before the ninth century. If there was no Edom at the time of Moses there would not have been any weakness or fear of Edom, unless the Edomites were simply a strong tribe. Crystal-Margaret Bennett, "Edom," IDBSV, pp. 251–252; "A Brief Note on Excavations at Tawilan, Jordan, 1968–1970," *Levant* 3 (1971), pp. v–vii; and, "Excavations at Buseirah, Southern Jordan, 1977," *Levant* 9 (1977), pp. 1–10. John R. Bartlett, "The Rise and Fall of the Kingdom of Edom," PEQ 104 (Jan.–June 71), pp. 26–27. Manfred Weippert, "The Israelite 'Conquest' and the Evidence from Transjordan" (pp. 15–34 in *Symposia* ed. Frank Moore Cross; Cambridge: ASOR, 1979).

2. Glueck's evidence was based on pottery found on the surface in the Transjordan region, now the Kingdom of Jordan. More recent work there provides evidence of occupation throughout the Bronze Ages. Thomas L. Thompson, "Observations on the Bronze Age in Jordan," ADAJ 19 (1976), pp. 109–111. James R. Kaute, "Tracking the Ancient Moabites," BA 44, no. 1 (Wint. 81), pp. 27–35. J. Maxwell Miller, "Archaeological Survey South of Wadi Mojib," ADAJ 23 (1979), pp. 79–92; and, "Survey of Central Moab," BASOR 234 (1979), pp. 43–52. Burton MacDonald, "The Wadi El-Hasa survey 1979," ADAJ 24 (1980), pp. 169–183; and, "The Wadi el-Hasa Survey 1981 (Southern Jordan)," BA 45, no. 1 (Wint. 82), pp. 58–59. Albert Leonard, "Kataret es-Samra: A Late Bronze Age Cemetery in Transjordan?," BASOR 234 (Spr. 79), pp. 53–65. Mo'awiyah M. Ibrahim, et al., "East Jordan Valley Survey, 1975," BASOR 222 (Ap. 76), pp. 41–66. Robert H. Smith, "Pella of the Decapolis," *Archaeology* 34, no. 5 (Sep./Oct. 81), pp. 46–53. Patrick E. McGovern, "Explorations in the Umm ad-Dananir region of the Baq'ah Valley 1977–1978," ADAJ 24 (1980), pp. 55–67; and, "Exploring the Burial Caves of the Baq'ah Valley in Jordan," *Archaeology* 35, no. 5 (Sep./Oct. 82), pp. 46–53. J. Basil Hennessy, "Excavation of a Bronze Age

Temple at Amman," PEQ 98 (July–Dec. 66), pp. 155–162. Vronwy Hankey, "A Late Bronze Age Temple at Amman," *Levant* 6 (1974), pp. 139–178. Moawiyah M. Ibrahim and Gerrit van der Kooij, "Excavations at Tell Deir 'Alla," ADAJ 23 (1979), pp. 41–50. Adnan Hadidi, "The Cemetery at Tell es-Sa'idiyeh," ADAJ 24 (1980), p. 213. Ibrahim, "Second Season of Excavation at Sahab, 1973," ADAJ 19 (1974), pp. 55–61.

However, the Tell Hesban dig and Bennett's excavations show or suggest a lack of urban occupation until the Iron Age. See "Edom," Buseirah, and "Moab," IDBSV, p. 602. Gary Pratico, "A Reappraisal of Nelson Glueck's Excavations at Tell el-Kheleifeh," ASORN no. 6 (Mar. 82), pp. 6–11. Duane W. Roller says the 'Ain La'ban oasis in northern Edom was occupied continuously from early Neolithic times until the second century A.D. See "The 'Ain La'ban Oasis: A Nabataean Population Center," AJA 86, no. 2 (Ap. 82), pp. 282–283. A recent study by Robert G. Boling assembles the archaeological data for demographic patterns in the second millenium. Without the Bible, we would have to invent a similar story to account for the evidence, *The Early Biblical Community in Transjordan*; Sheffield, England: Almond, 1987.

3. Roger S. Boraas and Lawrence T. Geraty, "The Long Life of Tell Hesban, Jordan," *Archaeology* 32, no. 1 (Jan./Feb. 79), pp. 10–20. Geraty, "The 1976 Season of Excavations at Tell Hesban," ADAJ 21 (1976), pp. 41–53. Siegfried H. Horn, "Heshbon," IDBSV, pp. 410–411. Kathleen M. Kenyon, "Jericho," EAEHL, pp. 550–564; KAHL; and, *Digging Up Jericho* (London: Benn, 1957). George M. Landes, "Jericho," IDBSV, pp. 472–473. Joseph A. Callaway, "Ai," EAEHL, pp. 36–52; "AI," IDBSV, pp. 14–16; "Excavating Ai (et-Tell)," BA 39, no. 1 (Mar. 76), pp. 18–30; and, "Was My Excavation of Ai Worthwhile?," BAR 11, no. 2 (Mar./Ap. 85), pp. 68–69 (Callaway answered "Yes"). James L. Kelso, et al., *The Excavation of Bethel (1934–1960)* (Cambridge: ASOR, 1968). Nahum M. Sarna cites the abrupt end of Canaanite culture and its replacement by a culture which appears to be that of seminomads in the process of settling down. The conquest under Joshua is the only theory that accounts for all the data. "Exploring Exodus," BA 49, no. 2 (June 86), pp. 68–80. David Ussishkin, et al., "Excavations at Tel Lachish," TA 5, nos. 1–2 (1978), pp. 1–97. Ussishkin, "Lachish," EAE HL, pp. 735–753. Ussishkin and Christa Clamer, "A Canaanite Temple at Tell Lachish," BA 40, nos. 2 (May 77), pp. 70–76. Albright, "Tell Beit Mersim," EAEHL, pp. 171–178. Michael C. Astour, "Debir," IDBSV, p. 222. Yadin, "Hazor and the Battle of Joshua — Is Joshua 11 Wrong?," BAR 2, no. 1 (Mar. 76), pp. 3–4, 44; "Hazor," EAEHL, pp. 474–495; "Hazor," IDBSV, pp. 387–390; and, *Hazor*; (New York: Random, 1975). Victor R. Gold, "Hazor," IDB 2, pp. 539–540. Moshe Kochavi, "The History and Archaeology of Aphek—Antipatris," BA 44, no. 2 (Spr. 81), pp. 75–86. G. Ernest Wright, "Shechem," EAEHL, pp. 1083–1094, and, *Shechem* (New York: McGraw-Hill, 1965). Edward F. Campbell, Jr., "Shechem (city)," IDBSV, pp. 821–822. Lawrence E. Toombs, "The Stratigraphy of Tell Balata," ADAJ 17 (1972), pp. 99–110. Adam Zertal, "Has Joshua's Altar Been Found?," BAR 11, no. 1 (Jan./Feb. 85), pp. 26–43. Zertal says "Yes." Zertal, "How Can Kempinski Be So Wrong?," BAR 12, no. 1 (Jan./Feb. 86), pp. 43, 49–53. Others say "No." Aharon Kempinski, "Joshua's Altar — An Iron Age I Watchtower," BAR 12, no. 1 (Jan./Feb. 86), pp. 42, 44–49. Manfred Weippert, "Canaan, Conquest and Settlement of," IDBSV, pp. 125–130, and, *The Settlement of the Israelite Tribes in Palestine* (London: SCM, 1971). J. Maxwell Miller, "Archaeology and the Israelite Conquest," PEQ 109 (July–Dec. 77), pp. 87–93. Volkmar Fritz goes back to the Habiru theory for the Negev based on his excavations. The new inhabitants had already been in steady contact with the Canaanites for some time and had adopted or adapted their culture. They had already become semi-sedentary — thirty per cent of their livestock was cattle. They established peaceful villages — no walls, no destruction levels — that lasted for several hundred years. "The Israelite 'Conquest' in the Light of Recent Excavations at Khribet el-Meshash," BASOR 241 (Wint. 81), pp. 61–73. Benjamin Mazar suggests gradual settlement by Hittite elements as well as Israelites. "The Early Israelite Settlement in the Hill Country," BASOR 241 (Wint. 81), pp. 75–85.

4. Martin Noth, *The History of Israel* (New York: Harper, 1958). Kempinski, reads the data as settlement rather than conquest. Unoccupied hill country was settled by Israelites judging by the pottery, while major sites remained in Canaanite hands. "Israelite Conquest or Settlement: New Light from Tell Masos," BAR 2, no. 3 (Sep. 76), pp. 25–35. Kathleen Kenyon makes a similar observation in *The Bible in Recent Archaeology* p. 43. Both refer to Yohanan Aharoni. Cf. his *Archaeology and the Land of Israel* (Philadelphia: Westminster, 1982); and, "New Aspects of the Israelite Occupation in the North," NEATC, pp. 254–267. Yadin reads Aharoni's evidence in the opposite direction. He answers positively, "Is the Biblical Account of the Israelite Conquest of Canaan Historically Reliable?," BAR 7, no. 2 (Mar./Ap. 82), pp. 16–23. Abraham Malamat tells how it was done in his "How Inferior Israelite Forces Conquered Fortified Canaanite Cities," BAR 7, no. 2, pp. 24–35; and, "Israelite Conduct of War in the Conquest of Canaan," pp. 35–55, in *Symposia*.

5. Jacob Hoftijzer and G. Van der Kooij, *Aramaic Texts from Deir 'Alla* (Leiden: Brill, 1976). Jacob Hoftijzer, "The Prophet Balaam in a Sixth Century Aramaic Inscription," BA 39, no. 1 (Mar. 76), pp. 11–17. The date in the title was an insertion of the editor — cf. "erratum," BA 39, no. 3 (Sep. 76), p. 87. H.J. Franken announced the find in *Vetus Testamentum* 17 (1967), pp. 480–481. Henry O. Thompson, "Balaam in the Bible and at Deir 'Alla," BA 49, no. 4 (Dec. 86); "The Story of the Deir 'Alla Texts," ibid. Several reviews have been published with critiques pro and con. Joseph A. Fitzmeyer, CBQ 40, no. 1 (1978), pp. 93–94. Jonas C. Greenfield, *The Journal of Semitic Studies* 25, no. 2 (1980), pp. 248–252. Stephen A. Kaufman, "Review Article: The Aramaic Texts from Deir 'Alla," BASOR 239 (Sum. 80), pp. 71–74. Baruch A. Levine, "Review Article: The Deir 'Alla Plaster Inscriptions," JAOS 101, no. 2 (Ap.–June 81); pp. 195–205. Alexander Rofe, *The Book of Balaam (Numbers 22:2–24:25): A Study in Methods of Criticism and the History of Biblical Literature and Religion* (in Hebrew) (Tel Aviv: Simor, 1979). He includes a discussion of the Deir 'Alla inscriptions and claims the language is Midianite. Within the biblical story, he thinks the donkey is the biblical writer's attempt to burlesque Balaam's prophecy. The book is reviewed in BA 45, no. 1 (Wint. 81), p. 61. P. Kyle McCarter, Jr., "The Balaam Texts from Deir 'Alla: the First Combination," BASOR 239 (Sum. 80), pp. 49–60, studies the first major portion of the plaster inscription. He thinks it was on a wall and compares Kuntillet 'Ajrud where black and red ink on plaster texts were also found. Here some were still attached to a wall. Cf. Ze'ev Meshel and Carol Meyers, "The Name of God in the Wilderness of Zin," BA 39, no. 1 (Mar. 76), pp. 6–10. The perversion of the natural order is the complaint of the Egyptian prophet in "The Admonitions of Ipu-Wer," ANET, pp. 441–444. Cf. also Andre Lemaire, "Fragments from the Book of Balaam Found at Deir 'Alla," BAR 11, no. 5 (Sep./Oct. 85), pp. 26–39. Jo Ann Hackett, *The Balaam Text from Deir 'Alla* (Chico, CA: Scholars, 1984).

6. PAE, pp. 279, 284. "Yigael Yadin on 'Hazor, The Head of All Those Kingdoms'," BAR 1, no. 2 (June 75), pp. 3–4, 15; and, "Megiddo," IDBSV, pp. 583–585. Yohanan Aharoni, "Hazor and the Battle of Deborah — Is Judges 4 Wrong?," BAR 1, no. 4 (Dec. 75), pp. 3–4, 26. Aharoni and Yadin, "Megiddo," EAEHL, pp. 830–856. Robert G. Boling, *Judges* (Garden City: Doubleday, 1975). Albert E. Glock, "Taanach," EAEHL, pp. 1138–1147; and, "Taanach," IDBSV, pp. 855–856, *Stratigraphy*.

7. Kochavi, *History and Archaeology*, Aphek, p. 92. Kochavi and Aaron Demsky, "An Israelite Village from the Days of the Judges," BAR 4, no. 3 (Sep./Oct. 78), 19–21. Amihai Mazar, "Additional Philistine Temples at Tell Qasile," BA 40, no. 2 (May 77), pp. 82–87. "The Kibbutz Sasa Kernos," BAR 2, no. 2 (June 76), pp. 5, 29, is one of the most complete kernos rings known in Palestine. Others are known from Beth-shan, Gezer, Ashdod, and Megiddo. The last one is the most complete.

8. Trude Dothan, *The Philistines and Their Material Culture* (New Haven and Jerusalem: Yale and IES, 1982); and, "What We Know About the Philistines," BAR 8, no. 4 (July/Aug. 82), pp. 20–44.

G. Ernest Wright, "Fresh Evidence for the Philistine Story," BA 29, no. 4 (Sep. 66), pp. 70–86. P. Kyle McCarter, Jr., *I Samuel* (Garden City: Doubleday, 1980). A late thirteenth century iron smelter found at Tell Yin'am had Mycenean ware but no Philistine pottery with it. An earlier wave of Sea People may have brought their knowledge of smelting to the Esdraelon/Jezreel area long before the Philistines held Beth-shan and killed Saul here. Harold Liebowitz, "Excavations at Tell Yin'am, Israel," *Archaeology* 32, no. 4 (July/Aug. 79), pp. 58–59; and, "Excavations at Tel Yin'am: The 1976 and 1977 Seasons," BASOR 243 (Sum. 81), pp. 71–94. T. Stech Wheeler, et al., "Iron at Taanach and Early Iron Metallurgy in the Easter Mediterranean," AJA 85, no. 3 (July 81), pp. 245–268. Theodore A. Wertime and James D. Muhly, eds., *The Coming of the Age of Iron* (New Haven: Yale, 1980). Muhly, "How Iron Technology Changed the Ancient World and Gave the Philistines a Military Edge," BAR 8, no. 6 (Nov./Dec. 82), pp. 40–54. T.C. Mitchell, "Philistia," AOTS, pp. 405–427. Jonas C. Greenfield, "Philistines," IDBSV, pp. 666–667; and, "Philistines," IDB 3, pp. 791–795. KAHL, pp. 221–239. Edward E. Hindson, *The Philistines and the Old Testament* (Grand Rapids: Baker, 1971). Nancy K. Sanders, *The Sea Peoples* (London: Thames and Hudson, 1978). S. Wachsman, "The Ships of the Sea Peoples," IJNAUE 10, no. 3 (1981), pp. 187–220. Marie-Louise Buhl and S. Holm-Nielsen, *Shiloh* (Copenhagen: National Museum, 1969). Holm-Nielsen, "Shiloh (city)," IDBSV, pp. 822–823. "Did the Philistine Destroy the Israelite Sanctuary at Shiloh? . . . The Archaeological Evidence," BAR 1, no. 2 (June 75), pp. 3–5. William L. Reed, "Shiloh," IDB 4, pp. 328–330. Israel Finkelstein, "Shiloh Yields Some, But Not All, of Its Secrets," BAR 12, no. 1 (Jan./Feb. 86), pp. 22–41, on Israeli excavations 1981–1984.

9. George M. Landes, "Midian," IDB 3, pp. 375–376. Charles F. Kraft, "Gideon," IDB 2, pp. 393–395. Toombs, *Stratigraphy*, op. cit. Wright, *Shechem.*

10. Samuel W. Matthews, et al., "The Phoenicians," NG 146, no. 2 (Aug. 74), pp. 149–189. Donald Harden, *The Phoenicians* (New York: Praeger, 1962). John Gray, *The Canaanites* (New York: Praeger, 1965). Frank M. Cross, *Canaanite Mythology and Hebrew Epic*; (Cambridge: Harvard, 1973). Arvid S. Kapelrud, "Phoenicia," IDB 3, pp. 800–805; and, "Tyre," IDB 4, pp. 721–723. Alfred Haldar, "Canaanites," IDB 1, pp. 494–498. Lloyd B. Jensen, "Royal Purple of Tyre," JNES 22, no. 2 (Ap. 63), pp. 104–118. Sabatino Moscati, *The World of the Phoenicians* (New York: Praeger, 1968). James D. Muhly, "Homer and the Phoenicians," Berytus 19 (1970), pp. 19–64. William Ward, ed., *The Role of the Phoenicians in the Interaction of Mediterranean Civilizations* (Beirut: AUB, 1968), p. 168. James B. Pritchard, "The Phoenician City of Sarepta," *Archaeology* 24, no. 1 (Jan. 71), pp. 61–63; "The Phoenicians in their Homeland," *Expedition* 14, no. 1 (Fall 71), pp. 14–23; PRS; and, *Sarepta* (Philadelphia: University Museum, 1975). Nina Jidejian, *Tyre Through the Ages* (Beirut: Mashroq, 1969). William Culican, *The First Merchant Ventures: The Ancient Levant in History and Commerce* (London: Thames and Hudson, 1966). Joseph Naveh, "The Greek Alphabet," BA 43, no. 1 (Wint. 80), pp. 22–25.

Carthage has been excavated by an international team sponsored by UNESCO. See C.M. Wells, "Recent Excavations at Carthage," AJA 86, no. 2 (Ap. 82), pp. 293–296. Canadian and U.S. archaeologists participate through ASOR, the Oriental Institute, the Harvard Semitic Museum, and the Kelsey Museum of the University of Michigan. Cf. *Excavations at Carthage Conducted by The University of Michigan*, Vols. I–VII. Ann Arbor; University of Michigan, (1975–1978). Lawrence E. Stager, "Carthage 1977: Punic and Roman Harbors," *Archaeology* 30, no. 3 (May 77), pp. 198–203. Freedman, *Preliminary Excavation Reports*, Cambridge: 1978. AASOR 43, "Carthage," IECW, pp. 110–112. John G. Pedley, ed., *New Light on Ancient Carthage* (Ann Arbor: University of Michigan, 1980).

11. Biran, "Tell Dan — Five Years Later," BA 43, no. 3 (Sum. 80), pp. 168–182; "Tell Dan," EAEHL, pp. 313–320; and, "Dan," IDBSV, p. 205. Gus W. Van Beek, "Dan. 2," IDB 1, pp. 759–760. John C.H. Laughlin, "The Remarkable Discoveries at Tell Dan," BAR 7, no. 5

(Sep./Oct. 81), pp. 20–37. SBAF, pp. 347–353. P.H. Vaughn, *The Meaning of 'bama' in the Old Testament* (London: Cambridge University, 1974).

12. Siegfried H. Horn, "Ammon, Ammonites," IDBSV, p. 20. George M. Landes, "Ammon, Ammonites," IDB 1, pp. 108–114. SBAF, pp. 489–491.

13. Michael C. Astour, "Amphictyony," IDBSV, pp. 23–25. He concludes that the Israelites did not have an amphictyony but a loose confederation of tribes similar to the confederations in the Mari tablets. It has also been suggested they were neither a political nor a military group. A.D.H. Mayes, *Israel in the Period of the Judges* (London: SCM, 1974). C.H.J. De Geuss, *The Tribes of Israel: An Investigation into Some of the Presuppositions of Martin Noth's Amphictyony Hypothesis* (Amsterdam: Van Gorcum, 1976). B.D. Rahtjen, "Philistines and Hebrew Amphictyonies," JNES 24 (1965), pp. 100–104. George E. Mendenhall, *The Tenth Generation* (Baltimore: Johns Hopkins, 1973); and, "'Change and Decay in All Around I See': Conquest, Covenant, and The Tenth Generation," BA 39, no. 4 (Dec. 76), pp. 152–157. Roland de Vaux, "Was There An Israelite Amphictyony?," BAR 3, no. 2 (June 77), pp. 40–47. He says "No," because Israel did not have a central sanctuary with a council of delegates to run the amphictyony. Edward F. Campbell and G. Ernest Wright, "Tribal League Shrines in Ammon and Shechem," BA 32, no. 4 (1969), pp. 104–116. Michael Grant, *The Etruscans* (London: Weidenfeld and Nicolson, 1980).

14. James S. Ackerman, "Prophecy and Warfare in Early Israel: A Study of the Deborah-Barak Story," BASOR 220 (Dec. 75), pp. 5–13. Hans Goedicke, *The Report of Wenamun* (Baltimore: Johns Hopkins, 1975). ANET, pp. 441–452 (oracles and prophecies), 482–483 (Mari), 25–29 (Wenamon). ANETS, pp. 604–607 (oracles and prophecies), 623–632 (Mari). NERT, pp. 118–128. P. Kyle McCarter, *I Samuel* (Garden City: Doubleday, 1980), pp. 164–188, 327–331. WBA, pp. 97–98.

15. David Diringer, "Mizpah," AOTS, pp. 329–342. Chester C. McCown, et al., *Tell en-Nasbeh*, Vols. I–II (Berkeley-New Haven: ASOR, 1947). McCown, *The Ladder of Progress in Palestine* (New York: Harper, 1943). Mogen Broshi, "Tel en-Nasbeh," EAEHL, pp. 912–918. James Muilenburg, "Mizpah," IDB 3, pp. 407–409; and, "Gilgal," IDB 2, pp. 398–399. Boyce M. Bennett, Jr., "The Search for Israelite Gilgal," PEQ 104 (Jan.–June 72), pp. 111–122. The root "gll," means "rolled away." Kelso, *The Excavation of Bethel*; "Bethel," EAEHL, pp. 190–193, and, "Bethel," IDB 1, pp. 390–391. McCarter, *I Samuel*, pp. 204, 49–66. William H. Morton, "Ramah, 3.4," IDB 4, p. 8. Peter R. Ackroyd, *The First Book of Samuel* (Cambridge: Cambridge University, 1971), pp. 18–32, 64–68. Samuel's mother was Hannah (I Samuel 1:2). An eighth century seal with this name is known from Tell ed-Duweir. John R. Bartlett, "The Seal of HNH from the Neighborhood of Tell ed-Duweir," PEQ 108 (Jan.–Jun. 76), pp. 59–61.

16. Lawrence A. Sinclair, *An Archaeological Study of Gibeah: Tell el-Ful* (New Haven: AASOR 34–35 (1954–1956)), 1960, pp. 1–52, and, "Gibeah," EAEHL, pp. 444–446. Paul Lapp, "Tell el-Ful," BA 28, no. 1 (1965), pp. 2–10. Nancy L. Lapp, et al., *The Third Campaign at Tell el-Ful* (Cambridge: AASOR 45, 1979). WBA, pp. 121–124. Morton, "Gibeah," IDB 2, pp. 390–391. Carl Graesser, "Gibeah (of Benjamin)," IDBSV, pp. 363–364. Graesser does not think the fortress was Philistine.

17. Henry O. Thompson, *Mekal: The God of Beth-shan* (Leiden: Brill, 1970). Frances James, *The Iron Age of Beth-shan* (Philadelphia: University Museum, 1966). Alan Rowe, *The Topography and History of Beth-shan* (Philadelphia: University Museum, 1930). WBA, p. 96. H. BarDeroma, in his paper " 'Ye Mountains of Gilboa'," PEQ 102 (July–Dec. 70), pp. 116–136, thinks Saul died at Aphek.

18. Oren, "Ziklag — A biblical city on the edge of the Negev," BA 45, no. 2 (Sum. 82), pp. 155–166. WBA, pp. 96, 124–126. Eugene H. Maly, *The World of David and Solomon* (Englewood Cliffs: Prentice-Hall, 1965). ANET, pp. 369–371. NERT, p. 40 is a hymn of Amun as a shepherd, similar to Psalm 23 and to David's own life. Johannes Hempel, "Psalms, Book of," IDB-3,

pp. 942–958. Claus Westermann, "Psalms, Book of," IDBSV, pp. 705–710. Siegfried Horn, "The Crown of the King of the Ammonites," AUSS 11, no. 2 (July 73), pp. 170–180. Horn compares the crown David captured in Ammon (II Samuel 12:30; I Chronicles 20:2) with those on statues found in and around modern Amman, but dating from the Iron Age, perhaps between 1000 and 600 B.C.

19. Kenyon, *Jerusalem* (New York: McGraw-Hill, 1967), pp. 19–53; *Royal Cities of the Old Testament* (New York: Schocken, 1971), pp. 13–35; *Digging Up Jerusalem* (New York: Praeger, 1974); "Jerusalem: History of the Excavations," EAEHL, pp. 591–597; and, *The Bible and Recent Archaeology*, pp. 44–66. Benjamin Mazar, "Jerusalem," EAEHL, pp. 579–591, and, *The Mountain of the Lord* (Garden City: Doubleday, 1975). Yadin, ed., *Jerusalem Revealed* (Jerusalem. IES, 1975). Meir Ben-Dov, *In the Shadow of the Temple*; San Francisco: Harper & Row, 1986. Millar Burrows, "Jerusalem," IDB 2, pp. 843–866. Ian W.J. Hopkins, *Jerusalem* (Grand Rapids: Baker, 1970). Yohanan Aharoni, "The Building Activities of David and Solomon," IEJ 24, no. 1 (1974), pp. 13–16. Aharoni thought David fortified Dan and Beersheba and that Megiddo palaces 1723 and 6000 are David's rather than Solomon's. Yigal Shiloh, *Excavations at the City of David I* (Jerusalem: Qedem vol. 19, 1984). Hershel Shanks, "The City of David After Five Years of Digging," BAR 11, no. 6 (Nov./Dec. 85), pp. 22–38.

20. Dan Cole, "How Water Tunnels Worked," BAR 6, no. 2 (Mar./Ap. 80), pp. 8–29. Pritchard, *Gibeon* (Princeton: Princeton University, 1962); *The Water System at Gibeon* (Philadelphia: University Museum, 1961); and, "Gibeon," EAEHL, pp. 446–450. William L. Reed, "Gibeon," AOTS, pp. 231–243.

21. Yigal Shiloh, "Jerusalem's Water Supply During Seige," BAR 7, no. 4 (July/Aug. 81), pp. 24–39; "Excavating Jerusalem," *Archaeology* 33, no. 6 (Nov./Dec. 80), pp. 8–17; and, "The City of David Archaelogical Project: BA 44, no. 3 (Sum. 81), pp. 161–170. Shiloh and Mendel Kaplan, "Digging in the City of David," BAR 5, no. 4 (July/Aug. 79), pp. 36–49. Dora J. Hamblin, "Bearing Witness to City of David's Life and Death," *Smithsonian* 13, no. 4 (July 82), pp. 72–82. Neil A. Silberman, "In Search of Solomon's Lost Treasures," BAR 6, no. 4 (July/Aug. 80), pp. 30–41. Arie Issar, "The Evolution of the Ancient Water Supply System in the Region of Jerusalem," IEJ 26, nos. 2–3 (1976), pp. 130–136. Robert S. Lamon, *The Megiddo Water System* (Chicago: University of Chicago, 1935). Cole, "Water Tunnels." Yadin, *Hazor* pp. 226–247, and, "A Rejoinder," BASOR 239 (Sum. 80), pp. 19–23.

22. WBA, pp. 137–146. Fig. 91, p. 139 has a suggested reconstruction of the temple. Cf. also Paul L. Garber, "Reconstructing Solomon's Temple," BA 14, no. 1 (Feb. 51), pp. 2–24. Kenyon, *Jerusalem*, pp. 54–62. Jean Quellette, "Temple of Solomon," IDBSV, pp. 872–874. William F. Stinespring, "Temple, Jerusalem," IDB 4, pp. 534–560. Aharoni, "The Israelite Sanctuary at Arad," FGNDBA, pp. 25–39. Christopher J. Davey, "Temples of the Levant and the Buildings of Solomon," *Tyndale Bulletin* 31 (1980), pp. 107–146. Carol L. Meyers, "The Elusive Temple," BA 45, no. 1 (Wint. 82), pp. 33–41. She asks "Was There a Seven-Branched Lampstand in Solomon's Temple?," BAR 5, no. 4 (Sep./Oct. 79), pp. 46–57. She does not think so. She traces the symbol to the tabernacle in the wilderness (Exodus 25:31–40, 37:17–24) and finds it reappearing in the Second Temple, c. 516 B.C.–70 A.D. However there is no mention of it in Solomon's temple. The tabernacle itself may have been put inside the Holy of Holies of Solomon's temple. Richard E. Friedman, "The Tabernacle in the Temple," BA 43, no. 4 (Fall 80), pp. 241–248. If Friedman is right, one would expect the tabernacle equipment to be in the temple also, so the menorah would be there as well.

23. "Nelson Glueck and King Solomon — A Romance That Ended," BAR 1, no. 1 (Mar. 75), pp. 1, 10–1, 16. Glueck, "Ezion-geber," BA 28 (1965), pp. 70–87; and, "Tell el-Kheleifeh," EAEHL, pp. 713–717. Beno Rothenberg, *Timna* (London: Thames and Hudson, 1972). Simon Cohen, "Ezion-geber," IDB 2, pp. 213–214. Eleanor K. Vogel, "Tell el-Kheleifeh," IDBSV, pp. 869–870.

24. Lois Berkowitz, "Has the U.S. Geological Survey Found King Solomon's Gold Mines?," BAR 3, no. 3 (Sep. 77), pp. 1, 28–33. "U.S. Geological Survey Locates Biblical Ophir," BA 39, no. 3 (Sep. 76), p. 85.
25. "Megiddo Stables or Storehouses?," BAR 2, no. 3 (Sep. 76), pp. 1, 12–18. Yadin, "In Defense of the Stables at Megiddo," ibid., pp. 18–22. James B. Pritchard, "The Megiddo Stables — A Reassessment," NEATC, pp. 268–276. He suggested they are storerooms. WBA, pp. 130–137. Kenyon, *Royal Cities*, pp. 36–70. William G. Dever, "Gezer," IDBSV, pp. 361–362. Gus W. Van Beek, "Megiddo," IDB 3, 335–342. R.W. Hamilton, "Gezer," IDB 2, 388–389. Israel Finkelstein thinks the great outer wall over fifty feet thick was built in the post-Solomonic period, perhaps by King Asa who built Mizpah (I Kings 15:22) and other cities (II Chronicles 14:5–6). "The Date of Gezer's Outer Wall," TA 8, no. 2 (1981), pp. 136–145.
26. Ussishkin, "King Solomon's Palaces," BA 36, no. 3 (Sep. 73), pp. 78–105, and, "Was the 'Solomonic' City Gate at Megiddo Built by King Solomon?," BASOR 239 (Sum. 80), pp. 1–18. Yadin, "Megiddo," IDBSV, pp. 583–585, and, "A Rejoinder." Yigal Shiloh, "Solomon's Gate at Megiddo as Recorded by its Excavator, R. Lamon, Chicago," *Levant* 12 (1980), pp. 69–76. As noted earlier, Aharoni thinks David built the palaces rather than Solomon (IEJ 24, pp. 13–16).
27. Malamat, "The First Peace Treaty Between Israel and Egypt," BAR 5, no. 4 (Sep./Oct. 79), pp. 58–61. Rudolph Cohen, "The Iron Age Fortresses in the Central Negev," BASOR 236 (Fall 79), pp. 61–79. Ze'ev Meshel suggested they were built by King Saul after he defeated the Amalekites (I Samuel 14:48, 15:1–9). "Horvat Ritma — An Iron Age Fortress in the Negev Highlands," TA 4, nos. 3–4 (1977), pp. 110–135.
28. Jacob M. Myers, "Solomon," IDB 4, pp. 399–408. Dorothea W. Harvey, "Sheba, Queen of," IDB 4, pp. 311–312. Pritchard, ed., *Solomon & Sheba* (London: Phaidon, 1974). Nigel Groom suggests the Queen of Sheba came from a Sabean merchant colony in north Arabia. Cf. his *Frankincense and Myrrh: A Study of the Arabian Incense Trade* (London: Longmsn, 1981). John A. Thompson, "Horse," IDB 2, pp. 646–647. John W. Wevers, "Chariot," IDB 1, pp. 552–554. E.W. Heaton, *Solomon's New Men* (New York: Pica, 1974). NERT, pp. 44–63. ANET, pp. 412–425. On Mesopotamian wisdom literature, cf. NERT, pp. 133–145, and ANET, pp. 425–430, 434–440, 589–604. Sheldon H. Blank, "Proverbs, Book of," IDBXV, pp. 702–704. James L. Crenshaw, "Wisdom in the Old Testament," IDBSV, pp. 952–956. Robert B.Y. Scott, *Proverbs – Ecclesiastes* (Garden City: Doubleday, 1965).
29. Avidgad, "The Chief of the Corvee," IEJ 30, nos. 3–4 (1980), pp. 170–173.
30. Moses Aberbach and Leivy Smolar, "Jeroboam," IDBSV, pp. 473–475. Hugh B. McLean, "Jeroboam," IDB 2, pp. 840–842. G. Ernest Wright, *Shechem* (New York: McGraw-Hill, 1965). Roland de Vaux, "Tell el-Fara'a, North," EAEHL, pp. 395–404. William L. Reed, "Tirzah," IDB 4, pp. 652–653. John A. Wilson, "Shishak," IDB 4, pp. 337–338. ANET, pp. 242–243, 263–264. BHI, pp. 226–236. KAHL, pp. 260–281.
31. Hugh B. MacLean, "Omri," IDB 3, pp. 600–601; and, "Ahab," IDB 1, pp. 61–63. A. Leo Oppenheimer, "Shalmaneser," IDB, 4, p. 305. ANET, pp. 276–281 (Shalmaneser). M. Elat, "The Campaigns of Shalmaneser III Against Aram and Israel," IEJ 25, no. 1 (1975), pp. 25–35. Nadav Na'aman says the 2000 is a scribal error. It may have been 200. Ahab is listed third which suggests a smaller number than the first two. To Na'aman 2000 is impossibly expensive for a small kingdom like Israel. "Two Notes on the Monolith Inscription of Shalmaneser III from Kurkh," TA 3, no. 3 (1976), pp. 89–106. Kenyon, *Royal Cities*, pp. 71–110. Nachman Avigad, "Samaria," EAEHL, pp. 1032–1050. Hennessy, "Samaria," IDBSV, pp. 771–773. Peter R. Ackroyd, "Samaria," AOTS, pp. 343–354. Gus W. Van Beek, "Samaria," IDB 4, pp. 182–188.
32. Pritchard, *Sarepta*. PRS, pp. 26, 37–40, 131–148. The Dura Europa painting is reproduced on p. 38, Fig. 14. Richard W. Corney, "Mesha, King of Moab," IDB 3, p. 357. A. Douglas Tushingham, "Dibon," EAEHL, pp. 330–333; and, *The Excavations at Dibon (Dhiban) in Moab*

(Cambridge: AASOR 40, 1972). ANET, pp. 320–321. NERT, pp. 236–240. BHI, pp. 236–249. Max Miller, "The Moabite Stone as a Memorial Stele," PEQ 196 (Jan.–June 74), pp. 9–18.

33. MacLean, "Jehu," IDB 3, pp. 817–818; and, "Jeroboam," IDB 3, p. 842. Alberto R. Green, "Sua and Jehu: The Boundaries of Shalmaneser's Conquest," PEQ 111 (1979), pp. 35–39. Van Beek, "Samaria," p. 184. Avigad, "Samaria," pp. 1032–1050. ANET, pp. 280–281 (Jehu), 321 (Samaria ostraca), 284–287 (Sargon). BHI, pp. 249–263. James W. Ward, "Amos," IDBSV, pp. 21–23. James D. Smart, "Amos," IDB 1, pp. 116–121. David Ussishikin, "The 'Camp of the Assyrians' in Jerusalem," IEJ, nos. 3–4 (1979), pp. 137–142. Robert M. Talbert, "Assyria and Babylonia," IDBSV, pp. 73–76. Oppenheim, "Assyria and Babylonia," IDB 1, pp. 262–304; and, "Sargon," IDB 4, pp. 222–224.

34. Mogan Broshi, "Estimating the Population of Ancient Jerusalem," BAR 6, no. 2 (June 78), pp. 10–15; "Evidence of Earliest Christian Pilgrimage to the Holy Land Come to Light in Holy Sepulchre Church," BAR 3, no. 4 (Dec. 77), pp. 42–44; "Digging Up Jerusalem — A Critique," BAR 1, no. 3 (Sep. 75); and, "The Expansion of Jerusalem in the Reigns of Hezekiah and Manasseh," IEJ 24, no. 1 (1974), pp. 21–26. Yigal Shiloh, "The Population of Iron Age Palestine in the Light of a Sample Analysis of Urban Plans, Areas, and Population Density," BASOR 239 (Sum. 80), pp. 25–35. Hillel Geva, "The Western Boundary of Jerusalem at the End of the Monarchy," IEJ 29, no. 2 (1979), pp. 84–91. ANET, pp. 284–287 (Sargon).

35. Shulamit Geva, "A Reassessment of the Chronology of Beth Shean Strata V and IV," IEJ 29, no. 1 (1979), pp. 6–10. Ephraim Stern, "Israel at the Close of the Period of the Monarchy," BA 38, no. 2 (May 75), pp. 26–54. ANET, pp. 282–284 (Tiglath-pileser). BHI, pp. 265–274. WBA, pp. 147–166. Yadin, Hazor, pp 175–183.

36. MacLean, "Uzziah," IDB 4, pp. 742–744; and, "Jotham," IDB 2, pp. 999–1000. Lawrence E. Stager, "Agriculture," IDBSV, pp. 11–13; and, "Farming in the Judean Desert during the Iron Age," BASOR 221 (Feb. 76), pp. 145–158. Frank M. Cross, Jr., "El-Buqei'a," EAEHL, pp. 267–270. WBA, pp. 183–191. Vogel, "Tell el-Kheleifeh," p. 870. Nachman Avigad, "The Jotham Seal from Elath," BASOR 163 (Oct. 61), pp. 18–22. Glueck, "Kheleifeh, Tel," EAEHL, pp. 713–717. Nancy Miller, "A Puzzle for Albright," BAR 8, no. 3 (May/June 82), pp. 65–68.

37. Cf. the water systems discussed earlier, and, "Hezekiah's Tunnel Re-Opens," BAR 2, no. 2 (June 76), pp. 9–12. Naseeb Shaheen, "The Siloam End of Hezekiah's Tunnel," PEQ 109 (July–Dec. 77), pp. 107–112; and, "The Sinuous Shape of Hezekiah's Tunnel," PEQ 111 (July–Dec. 79), pp. 103–108. ANET, p. 321 (Siloam inscription). Kenyon, Jerusalem, pp. 70–77; Royal Cities, pp. 139–140; and, The Bible and Recent Archaeology, pp. 67–82. MacLean, "Hezekiah," IDB 2, pp. 598–600.

38. For a complete analysis of the two campaign theory, see BHI, pp 296–308. Siegfried H. Horn, "Did Sennacherib Campaign One or Twice Against Hezekiah?," AUSS 4 (1966), pp. 1–28. David Ussishkin, "Answers at Lachish," BAR 5, no. 6 (Nov./Dec. 79), pp. 16–39; "The Destruction of Lachish by Sennacherib and the Dating of the Royal Judean Storage Jars," TA 4, nos. 1–2 (1977), pp. 28–60; and, "Excavations at Tel Lachish," TA 5, nos. 1–2 (1978), pp. 1–97. Nadav Na'aman, "Hezekiah's Fortified Cities and the LMLK Stamp," BASOR 261 (Feb. 86), pp. 5–21. Anson F. Rainey, "Taharqa and Syntax," TA 3, no. 1 (1976), pp. 38–41. Ruth Hestrin and Michal Dayagi, "A Seal Impression of a Servant of King Hezekiah," IEJ 24, no. 1 (1974), pp. 27–29. Olga Tufnell, "Lachish, AOTS, pp. 304–305. Oppenheim, "Sennacherib," IDB 4, pp. 270–272. ANET, pp. 287–288 (Sennacherib), 321–322 (ostraca). Stern, "Israel at the Close," p. 30. G.W. Ahlstrom, 2"Is Tell Ed-Duweir Ancient Lachish?," PEQ 112 (Jan.–June 80), pp. 7–9. Ahlstrom says "No" and suggests Tell 'Etun southeast of Duweir. He follows Alt and Beyer in this and thinks 'Etun fills a gap in the line of forts that Hezekiah had constructed along his southern and southwestern border.

39. ANET, pp. 291–294 (Esarhaddon). BHI, pp. 309–315. Oppenheim, "Ashurbanipal," IDB 1, pp. 256–257. MacLean, "Manasseh, 2," IDB 3, pp. 254–255.

40. MacLean, "Josiah," IDB 2, pp. 996–999. Norbert Lohfink, "Deuteronomy," IDBSV, pp. 229–232. Gerhard Von Rad, "Deuteronomy," IDB 1, pp. 831–838. ANET, pp. 294–300 (Ashurbanipal). Wright, Shechem, p. 166 (Level VI destroyed by Josiah?). Aharoni, "Arad," EAEHL, pp. 85–86; and, "Arad: Its Inscriptions and Temple," BA 31, no. 1 (1968), pp. 2–32. Hershel Shanks, "Yigael Yadin Finds a Bama at Beer-sheba," BAR 3, no. 1 (Mar. 77), pp. 3–12. Yadin, "Beer-sheba: The High Place Destroyed by King Josiah," BASOR 222 (Ap. 76), pp. 5–17. Rainey, "Beer-Sheva Excavator Blasts Yadin — No Bama at Beer-Sheva," BAR 3, no. 3 (Sep. 77), pp. 18–21. "Yadin Answers Beer-Sheva Excavator," BAR 3, no. 4 (Dec. 77), pp. 3–4. "A Jerusalem Celebration — of Temples and Bamot," BAR 3, no. 3 (Sep. 77), pp. 22–24. "The Mystery of the Horses of the Sun at the Temple Entrance," BAR 4, no. 2 (June 78), pp. 8–9.
41. WBA, p. 177. Oppenheim, "Nebuchadnezzar," IDB 3, pp. 529–531. John A. Wilson, "Necho," IDB 3, pp. 530–531. ANET, pp. 303–311 (Nabopolasser and Nebuchadnezzar), 569 (Nahum). Land of the Bible Newsletter 46 (Jan.–Mar. 67), p. 2. D.J. Wiseman, Chronicles of the Chaldean Kings (626–556 B.C.) in the British Museum (London: British Museum, 1956).
42. Kenyon, Jerusalem, pp. 78–104. BHI, pp. 305–331. WBA, pp. 167–182. Herbert G. May, "Jehoiachin," IDB 2, pp. 811–813. MacLean, "Zedekiah," IDB 4, pp. 948–949. ANET, p. 308 (Jehoiachin), pp. 321–322 (Lachish ostraca). Tufnell, "Lachish," pp. 305–306. Ussishkin, "Answers . . .," pp. 20–23. TDOTT, pp. 80–81, 84–86, 224. Charles F. Pfeiffer, Exile and Return (Grand Rapids: Baker, 1962).
43. Aharoni, "Three Hebrew Ostraca from Arad," BASOR 197 (Feb. 70), pp. 16–42; and, "Arad," EAEHL, pp. 86–88. ANET pp. 568–569. Avigad, "Jeremiah and Baruch," BA 42, no. 2 (Spr. 79), pp. 114–118; "'Baruch the Scribe and Jerahmeel the King's Son," IEJ 28, nos. 1–2 (1978), pp. 52–56; "The Seal of Seraiah," EI 14 (1978), pp. 86–87; and, "A Seal of 'Manasseh Son of the King'," IEJ 13, no. 2 (1963), pp. 133–136.
44. Avigad, "Ammonite and Moabite Seals," NEATC, pp. 284–295. The letters DBLBD are not clear. Fawzi Zayadine and Henry O. Thompson, "The Ammonite Inscription from Tell Siran," Berytus 22 (1973), pp. 115–140; and, "The Tell Siran Inscription," BASOR 212 (Dec. 73), pp. 5–11. Frank M. Cross, Jr., "Notes from an Epigraphist's Notebook," CBQ 36 (1974), pp. 486–494. Thompson, "A Note on the Tell Siran Inscription," forthcoming. William H. Shea, "The Siran Inscription: Amminadab's Drinking Song," PEQ 110 (1978), pp. 107–112. Robert B. Coote, "The Tell Siran Bottle Inscription," BASOR 240 (Fall 80), p. 93. Zayadine, "Rabbat Ammon and Its Citadel," Jordan 7 (1975), pp. 23ff. Hans Helbaek, "Grain from the Tell Siran Bronze Bottle," ADAJ 19 (1974), pp. 167–168. Corey, "Nahash," IDB 3, p. 397; and, "Hanun," IDB 2, p. 523. Edward R. Dalglish, "Shobi," IDB 4, pp. 339–340. Lansing Hicks, "Naamah," IDB 3, p. 490. Landes, "Ammon, Ammonites," IDB 1, pp. 108–114. Horn, "Ammon, Ammonites," IDBSV, p. 20. Avigad, "Two Ammonite Seals Depicting the 'Dea Nutrix'," BASOR 225 (Feb. 77), pp. 63–66. Charles Krahmalkov, "An Ammonite Lyric Poem," BASOR 223 (Oct. 76), pp. 55–57. ANET, p. 294 (Shalmaneser; Amminadbi), 279 (Ba'asa), 282 (Sanipu), 287 (Buduili), 291 (Puduil). Larry G. Herr, "The Servant of Baalis," BA 48, no. 3 (Sep. 85), pp. 169–172. Milkom was the god of the Ammonites. The servant's name means "the light of Milkom."
45. Horn, "Why the Moabite Stone Was Blown to Pieces," BAR 12, no. 3 (May/June 86), pp. 50–61; and, "The Discovery of the Moabite Stone," (pp. 497–505 in The Word of the Lord Shall Go Forth, ed. Carol L. Meyers and Murphy O'Connor; Winona Lake, IN: Eisenbrauns, 1983). ANET, pp. 282, 287, 291, 294. Avigad in NEATC, pp. 289–292. PAE, pp. 291–292. Stern, "Israel at the Close." Vogel, "Tell el-Kheleifeh," p. 870. Bennett, "Buseirah," Levant 6 (1974), pp. 4, 19. NERT, p. 246.

# CHAPTER 11

# Exile-Maccabees

## A. THE EXILIC PERIOD

In the three retaliations by the Chaldeans in 597, 587, and 581 B.C., many people were killed. In addition, the Chaldeans, or Neo-Babylonians, followed the Assyrian pattern of deporting large numbers of people. That is especially true of 587 B.C., often called *the* Exile because this was when the temple and the city of Jerusalem were destroyed. The archaeological data suggests that many cities were destroyed and not reoccupied. In some cases, they were never reoccupied. Perhaps a distinction should be made between the devastated cities of Judah and the less hard hit areas of the old northern kingdom. At least some occupation continued though some towns also died out. Samaria seems to have been continuously occupied.

Events in Palestine are somewhat hidden over the next 50 years. Fragmentary inscriptions tell of several military efforts by Nebuchadnezzar, including an invasion of Egypt. The biblical book of Obadiah suggests that the Edomites moved into the southern Negev desert and into southern Judah. They may have simply taken the opportunity to occupy nearly vacant land or they may have been under pressure from the Arabs moving in from the Arabian peninsula.

In Babylon, Nebuchadnezzar was followed by Amel-Marduk (562–560 B.C.). In his excavations of Susa, the old Elamite and later Persian capital in Iran, De Morgan found a vase with the inscription, "Palace of Emel-Marduk, King of Babylon, son of Nebuchadnezzar, King of Babylon." The vase may have been taken from Babylon as loot from a raid, or as tribute. In the Bible, he is called Evil-mero-dach. According to II Kings 25:27–30, he released Jehoiachin from prison. He was followed by his brother-in-law, Nergal-shar-usur, or Neriglissar (560–556 B.C.). He could be the captain or Rabmag of Jeremiah 39:3, 11–14, who put Jeremiah under the care of Gedeliah. Neriglissar died and left his throne to his son Labashi-Marduk who was still a minor. He was removed by the last king of the Chaldeans, an Aramean noble named Nabonidus (c. 556–539).

Nabonidus' mother was from Haran and he himself was a devotee of the Moon god Sin, noted earlier as a suggested background for Terah and Abraham as they moved from Ur to Haran (Genesis 11). Nabonidus excavated and restored old temples, making him one of the first if not the first archaeologist in history. He may have been rebuilding old temples as a way of curbing the Marduk priesthood, as Ikhnaten and his father had curbed the priests of Amon in fourteenth century Egypt. Then again, it may have been simple devotion. We do not know why he moved to the desert oasis of Tema in 552 B.C. Here again, it may have been for religious reasons or to curb the military and commerical power of the Arabs.

The story of Nabonidus is part of the background for the book of Daniel. Many modern scholars see Daniel as being written much later, in the years 168–165 B.C., the time of the Maccabees, about whom more later. Here we note that Belshazzar is named as king of Babylon (Daniel 5). The Babylonian records tell us that before Nabonidus left for Tema, he designated his son Belshazzar to rule Baby-lon. In a prayer to Nannar and in another to the god Shamash, Nabonidus asks the god's favor for his son, Belshazzar. Among the Qumran material centuries later there is a manuscript which is described as a prayer of Nabonidus.[1]

We have relatively little archaeological evidence for the exiles in Babylon. They were settled near the Chebar Canal between Babylon and Nippur (Ezekiel 1:1–3). They were near Tell Abib (Mound of the Flood), Tell Harsa, Tell Melah, and Kaiphia (Ezekiel 1:1–3, 3:15; Ezra 2:59, 8:17). The records of a banking and tax collection agency, Marashu and Sons, were found in Nippur by the American expedition there at the turn of the century. These materials date between 445 and 403 B.C. Among their customers were Jews who may have been descendents of the exiles who did not return to Palestine when they had the chance. Inscribed Hebrew bowls also suggest that Jews lived in the area for several hundred years.

In later times, great rabbinical schools of learning developed in Mesopotamia. The Jewish Talmud consists of two main parts, the Mishna (written down c. 200 A.D.) and the Gemara. There is both a Palestinian (c. 400 A.D.) and a Babylonian (c. 500 A.D.) Gemara (there is only one Mishna). Usually when people refer to the Talmud, they mean the Babylonian version. The Jewish scholars who developed this Babylonian Gemara may have been descendents of these early exiles, though they may have been augmented by later exiles after the Jewish revolts against Rome in 70 and 135 A.D.

## B. THE PERSIAN PERIOD

### The Return

Cyrus the Great (c. 550–530 B.C.) conquered Babylon in 539. He allowed exiled peoples, including Jews, to return to their homelands. Some did, but obviously many chose to remain in their new country. They had grown up there so it was as much their country as anyone's. Cyrus' conquest is recorded on the Cyrus Cylinder. In this record, he gives Marduk the credit for his victories and announces his permission for exiled people to return to their homelands if they wish to do so. In Ezra 1 and 6, we have a similar decree for the people of Judah, the Jews.[2]

At least some Jews did return to Jerusalem. The returnees laid the foundation for the new temple and then found themselves struggling merely to survive. It was not until 515 B.C., with the encouragement of the prophets Hagagi and Zecharia, that the temple was actually rebuilt. This was about seventy years after its destruction. Some have suggested this as the fulfillment of Jeremiah's prophecy that the Exile would last seventy years. But the first returnees went back within fifty years, and others straggled back over the next several centuries. The rebuilt temple is called the second temple. It sometimes gives its name, the period of the second temple, to the entire period from 515 B.C. to the destruction of Jerusalem in 70 A.D.

**Figure 11–1.**    The Island of Elephantine. Papyrii found here tell of a Jewish temple here in Egypt. Photo courtesy Barry J. Beitzel, *The Moody Atlas of Bible Lands* (Chicago: Moody Press, 1985).

For all its importance, we do not know much about it. Asher S. Kaufman investigated a wall uncovered in the Haram esh-Sharif, the Muslim area of Herod the Great's temple platform. The small portion of wall was uncovered just east of the present Dome of the Rock. By comparing these remains with the literary sources, he believes he has a tentative plan of the second temple. A shrine of the Persian period at Lachish has been called Israelite. The shrine has also been associated with Geshem the Arab. It follows the general plan of court, inner court, and holy of holies, and may be a clue to the construction of the second temple in Jerusalem.

Another shrine in Lachish dates to the time of the Maccabees or Hasmoneans. This Hellenistic period shrine has also been called Israelite. There was a temple at Elephantine c. 400 B.C. but no remains of it have been found. A building at Araq el-Amir in Transjordan has been called a temple. It dates to c. 200 B.C. It is doubtful that it gives a picture of the second temple. The excavation at Tell er-Ras was noted earlier. The cube or rather half cube built of uncut stones, measuring sixty by sixty by thirty feet, may be an altar. It seems doubtful it is the whole temple. For the time being, we can only assume that if there are remains of the second temple (or other remains, if Kaufman has already found some remains), these are buried under the Haram esh-Sharif, Herod's massive rebuilding of this second temple.[3]

During the exiles of 597–581, at least part of the depopulation of Judah came because people fled the advancing Chaldeans. Many went to Egypt (Jeremiah 43:5–7). A group of these probably originated the colony of Jews known from Elephantine. We know of them through the papyri discovered on the Island of Elephantine, located at the First Cataract of the Nile River. These Jews guarded Egypt's southern border as mercenary soldiers for Egypt. They were there when Cambyses (c. 530–522 B.C.), Cyrus' son and successor, conquered Egypt in 525 B.C. The Elephantine Jews remained as a garrison for the Persians. One papyrus tells of their temple and its destruction c. 410, by an Egyptian mob. The letter asks permission to rebuild the temple. They received that permission. They had first asked Yohanan, the Jewish high priest in Jerusalem, and Bagoas, the governor of Judah. Then they wrote to Delaiah and Shelemiah, sons of Sanballat, governor of Samaria, and Arsames, Persian Satrap of Egypt (455–407 B.C.). The Elephantine Jews had a religion which some say was polytheistic because of offerings to such names as Ashim-bethel (cf II Kings 17:30), Anathbethel, or AnathYahu. Anath is the name of the Canaanite fertility goddess. Anathbethel may also mean the "sign of bethel [the house of God]." So it is not clear whether these Jews were monotheistic or polytheistic. The last of the papyri is dated c. 399 B.C. One guess is that the colony was destroyed in one of the Egyptian rebellions against Persian rule.[4]

## Esther

The story of Esther is set in the Persian period of Jewish history. The Persian king is called Ahasuerus. If this is Xerxes, son of Darius I (522–486), the story of Esther falls in the period 486–465. If Ahasuerus is Artaxerxes as suggested by the Septuagint (Greek) form of the Old Testament and the Jewish historian Josephus, the time is 465–424. Xerxes is Greek for the Persian Khshay-arsha which may be equivalent to the Hebrew Aashwerosh, for Ahasuerus. A Persian finance officer named Marduka (Mordecai) was in the capital of Susa c. 486 B.C. Many scholars today see the story as a romance, rather than literal history. Its purpose is to explain the origin of the festival of Purim. It has been noted also that Mordecai's name equals the name of the Babylonian god Marduk while Esther is a form of the Goddess Ishtar. The Hebrew writer may have historicized a Babylonian myth. The book refers to prayer but does not refer to God, at least in its Jewish and Protestant limits. The later Greek additions do have God specifically mentioned. It is the only biblical book which has not yet been found among the manuscripts of the Dead Sea Scrolls.[5]

## Nehemiah and Ezra

By 445 B.C., Jews had spread (we use the terms *dispersion, Diaspora*) as far as Sardis in Western Turkey. We do not know just how or when they arrived. It is not impossible they were descended from the "Lost Tribes" in 721 B.C., or were part of the scattering in 597–581. They had spread throughout the Persian Empire and may have gone there for trade and commerce. This date, however, brings us to the time of Nehemiah, governor of Jerusalem (445–433). He was, of course, a governor on behalf of the Persian Empire. He had been appointed by Artaxerxes (465–424). The temple had been rebuilt by 515, but the city walls remained in ruins. Nehemiah's first task was to rebuild these city walls and make the city a safe place in which to live. The Bible says he did this in fifty-two days (Nehemiah 6). Kenyon identified the wall or at least part of it, on the eastern edge of David's city, Mount Ophel. As noted earlier, when this wall was found by Macalister in the 1920s, he thought it was Jebusite and Davidic. Kenyon's work shows it to be Nehemiah's but it was strengthened later by the Maccabees. One thing this means is that Nehemiah's wall was much smaller in circumference than the earlier Jebusite-Davidic city. To judge by his difficulties in getting enough people to live there, the area circled by the wall was more than adequate.[6]

Rebuilding the city wall did not make everyone happy. Even during the repairs, Nehemiah faced opposition from Sanballat in Samaria, Geshem the Arab, and Tobiah the Jewish governor of Ammon (Nehemiah 2:19). Sanballat is a good Babylonian name, Sin-uballit, suggesting that the governor was himself a Babylonian, and a worshipper of the god Sin. However, his sons were Delaiah and Shelemiah, combinations with the name of God, Yahweh. This suggests that Sanballat worshipped Yahweh. He and his family may have been part of the origins of the Samaritans cited earlier.

The Persian province of Arabia at this time included southern Palestine as far north as Hebron and Lachish. A Persian villa in Lachish may have been Geshem's headquarters. Remains of the Persian period have been found at Tell el-Hesi, Tell Jemmeh, and Tell el-Fara south, as well as further south. The province may have extended to the Nile Delta or the old land of Goshen, the Wadi Tumeilat. A temple of the Arabian goddess Han-Allat was found at Tell el-Maskhuta cited earlier at the eastern end of Tumeilat and once thought to be biblical Succoth. Some silver objects in the Brooklyn Museum came from Maskhuta. A bowl has an inscription, "Qayne (Cain) son of Gasm king of Qedar." Gasm may be the Geshem or Gashum of the above trio of Sanballat, Tobiah, and Geshem. The bowl is dated to c. 400 B.C., which would date Geshem between 450 and 425 B.C. Several other names appear in inscriptions from this time frame. A "bulla" (seal impression) dating c. 500 B.C. has the name HNNH, possibly Hanani(h), one of Nehemiah's brothers (Nehemiah 1:2, 7:2) or Hananiah (7:2), the commander. The name appears at Elephantine also.[7]

As noted, the Elephantine papyri say Yohanan was high priest in Jerusalem c. 410. In Ezekiel 10:6, the high priest was Yohanan. According to Nehemiah 12, Yohanan was a sucessor to Eliashib (Nehemiah 3:1), high priest during the time of Nehemiah. This relates to other evidence that Ezra followed Nehemiah instead of coming first as the biblical record now indicates. A few years earlier, the Passover papyrus, c. 419 B.C., suggests a Persian attempt by Darius II (423–404) to regulate the rituals of Elephantine. The orders came through Jerusalem and Hananiah (Nehemiah's brother?). This would argue that Ezra's reading of the Law which regulated rituals took place in Jerusalem before 419. Perhaps the suggested guess of 428 B.C. is as close as we can come for the date of Ezra.[8]

It was under the Persians that the restored people came to be known as Jews, people of Yehud. Yehud (Aramaic for Judah) was the official name of the province. The letters YHD and occasionally YHDH appear on seals, seal impressions, and coins which came into use in this time. The Yehud coins continue into the third century B.C. where some have the portrait of Ptolemy I Soter (304–282 B.C.). The Yehud stamps on jars have been found in Persian contexts from the sixth to the fourth centuries B.C., including places like Jerusalem. Some jars are stamped "Jerusalem." Persia allowed a number of her subject peoples to make their own coins. In Palestine, these were in the Attic style with the Athenian owl on one side. Tyrian coins have a "hippocampus", a kind of sea horse, on the other side.[9]

# C. THE HELLENISTIC PERIOD

Greek influence began in the Near East long before the conquests of Alexander the Great (336–323). Greek pottery appeared as early as the seventh century, following a long tradition of imports from the Aegean area, Crete and Cyprus. Greek coins or coins in the Greek style, such as the Attic just mentioned, made their way into Near Eastern trade long before the great conqueror. The remains of an early eighth century Greek colony have been excavated at Sukas on the Syrian coast. Finds include a Greek style temple which was later replaced by a Phoenician type. A Greek inscription with Ionian names dates from c. 600 B.C. Cyrus H. Gordon has suggested reverse influence in seeing the western Mediterranean as a Phoenician lake during the second millennium, 2000–1000 B.C. If he is correct, contact between the two areas was earlier and much more extensive than commonly supposed. His views have not been widely accepted.[10]

The flow of commerce is represented in the following centuries by, among other ,things, a distinctive Hellenistic jar handle called Rhodian after the Island of Rhodes in the Aegean. The large angular handle is often decorated and frequently inscribed with names, sometimes the name of the potter, and sometimes with dates. Generally, this type of handle dates from the fourth to second centuries B.C.[11]

At the site of Dan in the north by Mount Hermon, the sacral area continued to function as a cult center. An inscription on a ten by six inch limestone piece has three lines in Greek and one in Aramaic. The latter is badly damaged. The Greek says Zoilos made a vow to the "god who is in Dan." In the south at Khirbet el-Kom, between Hebron and Lachish, an ostracon reflects a similar bilingual situation c. 250 B.C. The Greek text is written from the perspective of Nikeratos, the receiver of thirty-two drachmas. The Aramaic is written from the viewpoint of the payer, Qos-yada, an Edomite.[12]

## Alexander

Alexander's conquest of Palestine (I Maccabees 1:1–8) did not initiate Greek culture and artifacts in Palestine. But that event in 332 B.C. certainly accelerated the process. We have little or no record of how he came into control of the central hill country of Palestine. Perhaps it simply fell to him as a by-product of his conquest of Syria, the Palestinian coast and Egypt. Josephus tells us that the people of Samaria accepted his rule. Later they burned down the house of Alexander's governor, Andromachus, and burned the governor alive. Alexander retaliated and destroyed Samaria. He rebuilt it as a Greek city. His round Hellenistic towers have been uncovered and can be seen there today. They are forty feet across and still stand over twenty-five feet high. A Macedonian garrison was settled in the new city. This was but one of many examples of Greek colonies which Alexander and his successors established all through his domains.

The ancient site of Shechem was reoccupied at this time. It had been abandoned for 150 years. This new construction may reflect Alexander's treatment of Samaria. The people who survived and were no longer able to live in Samaria went to ancient Shechem. Josephus and probably Ben Sirach 50:26 refer to the Samaritans at Shechemites. Their Levels IV (331–250 B.C.) and III (250–190) show a well planned and prosperous city. This is probably also the time they established their temple on Mount Gerizim. Josephus says there was a governor of Samaria named Sanballat. His daughter Nicaso was married to Manasseh, a brother of the Jerusalem high priest Jaddua III. Manasseh was expelled from the priesthood by the elders of Jerusalem. Sanballat received permission from Darius III (336–330 B.C.) and then from Alexander, to build his son-in-law a temple on Gerizim. The story is suspect because of its similarity to Nehemiah 13:28 when a daughter of Sanballat I was married to a son of the high priest Joiada I, 100 years earlier. But Josephus refers again to a temple on Mount Gerizim when it was called the temple of Zeus Hellanios. In Maccabees 6:2, it is called the temple of Zeus Xenius, Zeus the Friend of Strangers.

In 1964, 1966, and 1968, Robert J. Bull of Drew University excavated Tell er-Ras, the northern and most prominent of Gerizim's three peaks. He found remains of a building, probably a temple of Zeus built by the Roman Emperor Hadrian c. 135 A.D. To form a foundation for this temple, the Roman engineers had put down a massive fill of cement and rubble. The fill was in and around a half cube cited earlier as made of uncut field stone. The structure had been surrounded by a wall of uncut stone, about five feet thick and over fifteen feet high. It formed a rectangular courtyard 135 feet wide. The wall was built on bedrock except for a corner sunk in soil. Third century B.C. Hellenistic potsherds were found in the foundation trench at this point. This could date the half cube to the third century, as much as a century after Alexander. The outside wall, of course, could be a later addition. Bull has suggested the half cube was the Samaritan altar of sacrifice. According to Josephus, the temple of Gerizim was modelled after the temple in Jerusalem.[13]

Alexander's destruction of Samaria may also be reflected in the Samaritan manuscripts found in 1962 in caves near the Jordan River, nine miles north of Jericho. They were found in the Wadi ed-Daliyeh by the Ta'amireh bedouin who had found the Dead Sea Scrolls in 1947. In fact, the later excavation of Daliyeh was assisted by Muhammed edh-Dhib Hassan who found the Dead Sea Scrolls when he threw a rock into a cave while looking for a lost goat. Daliyeh papyri eventually reached the market and came to the attention of Mr. Yusef Saad, Curator of the Palestine or Rockefeller Archaeological Museum, and Père Roland de Vaux of the French School of Archaeology in Jerusalem. They contacted Paul Lapp of the American Schools of Oriental Research. Together they found the caves, which were then excavated in January 1963 and February 1964.

The papyri are very fragile and in many fragments. The largest has only twelve lines. Papyrus 1, the best preserved, is incomplete. Its preservation may be accidental but it was sealed with seven seals when found. Several papyri are precisely dated. In our calendar they have such dates as 4 March, 354 B.C., and 19 March, 335 B.C. The papyri are legal and administrative records. These include the sale of a slave. This is of interest because all three parties — the slave, seller and buyer — have Yahwistic names: Yehohanan, Hananiah and Yehonour. The legal and administrative nature of the papyri plus the jewelry found, suggests that the skeletons in the cave where the papyri were found were upper class people from the city, trying to escape Alexander's vengeance. Perhaps they hid in the cave but were found by his troops and killed. Over 300 skeletons were found in the excavation.

The new materials add to our knowledge of the development of Aramaic writing. They also give us additional names of governors of Samaria, Papyrus 4 has a line, "(before yes)ua' son of Sanballat and Hanan the prefect." Papyrus 5 refers to "(Yash)yahu, son of (San)ballat." Papyrus 8 includes the phrase "before (Ha)naiah governor of Samaria." Frank Cross has suggested the Sanballat of Nehemiah 2:10, 19, 3:33, etc., is Sanballat I. The Sanballat of these papyri is his grandson, Sanballat II, perhaps the son of Delaiah mentioned in the Elephantine papyri. Josephus' Sanballat would then be Sanballat III, grandson of Sanballat II.[14]

Alexander founded the city of Alexandria in Egypt in 331 B.C. He settled a large number of Jews in the city and gave them considerable privileges. Alexander's general, Ptolemy I Soter (304–282) took over the Egyptian and Palestinian portions of Alexander's empire. He was followed by Ptolemy II Philadelphus (285–246). According to the Letter of Aristeas, Aristeas was a courtier in Philadelphus' court. In his letter, Aristeas tells his friend Philocrates what happened. Philadelphus' librarian had collected over 200,000 books but had no Greek translation of the Jewish laws. So Philadelphus sent a letter to the high priest in Jerusalem and asked for seventy-two translators to make the translation. Aristeas and Andreas delivered the letter to Eleazer the high priest, who sent the seventy-two elders back to Alexandria with Aristeas and Andreas. The translation was completed in seventy-two days. The Letter of Aristeas is generally seen as an historical romance. Scholars tend to see the Septuagint (abbreviated LXX) as growing out of the needs of the Jews in the Diaspora. Greek had become the lingua franca, replacing the Aramaic common to the Persian Empire.[15]

## Hellenization

An interesting example of the Hellenization of Palestine is Tell Sandahannah, probably the town of Marisa or Maresha (Joshua 15:44; II Chronicles 11:8, 14:9–14, 20–37; Micah 1:15). By 250 B.C., it had replaced ancient Lachish as the main town in the southwest foothills of Judah. The Phoenician names on its tombs suggest the presence of a colony of Sidonians. While the older generation had Semitic names, the younger generation had Greek names. A number of Greek magical curses on limestone tablets also came from the second century.

A temple which has been called a Jewish temple was built, c. 200 B.C., forty-four yards from the Persian temple and over the buried remains of an earlier Canaanite high place. In Jerusalem, Jason's tomb has been dated to c. 200–175 B.C. The so-called tomb of Absalom in the Kidron Valley on the east side of Jerusalem may date to this period.[16]

## Decapolis

Another important development in this period was the Decapolis (Mark 5:20); at least its roots are seen here. The Decapolis was a loose federation of ten cities. They were semi-autonomous, part of the empire but also self-governing. No one is quite sure when or how they started. The term does not appear before the first century A.D., but the concept goes back at least to Pompey and perhaps to Alexander. One guess is that he or his successors were involved. Jerash (Gerasa), for example, may have been founded by Alexander's general Perdiccas twenty miles east of the Jordan and twenty-six miles north of Amman. The site was excavated in 1925–1935 by the British and American team cited earlier, including Yale and the ASOR. Pella and Dion are Macedonian names and may have started with Alexander's troops, such as those he settled in Samaria. Robert H. Smith, however, notes that Pella is also a Hellenized form of the ancient name, Pihilum, which reappears in the Arabic name, Tabaqat Fihl or Fahl. Amman is ancient Rabbath Ammon (Deuteronomy 23:3; I Kings 11:5; Nehemiah 4:7). It was rebuilt by Ptolemy II Philadelphus c. 265 B.C. and renamed Philadelphia. His governor was a man named Tobiah according to the Zenon Papyrus.

No one is quite sure what the "ten" cities were either. Pliny, c. 75 A.D., listed Scythopolis (Beth-shan), Hippos, Gadara (Um Qeis), Pella, Philadelphia, Gerasa, Dion, Canatha, Damascus, and Raphana. Josephus seems to exclude Damascus though he gives no list. Some add Abila, between Dion and Gadara. Scythopolis (city of the Scyths) was the only one west of the Jordan River. The ten form a triangle extending into the desert. That location may give a clue as to their function. They formed a bastion of Greek and later Roman loyalty against the "Sons of the East" (probably the Arabs) who had moved into the area after Nebuchadnezzar destroyed Rabbath Ammon. Later on they were strongholds against the Maccabees. The cities were on or near ancient trade routes so they were commercial centers as well as military establishments.

The Beth-shan excavations by the University Museum in the 1920s and 30s have been cited several times. Pella, seven miles southeast of Beth-shan, has been under

**Figure 11–2.**    A series of large caves were excavated in a cliff overlooking the castle of Araq el-Amir. Outside of one is the name "Tobiah" carved in the face of the cliff.

excavation for some years. Gadara, 15 miles north of Pella, is also under excavation. It sits high on a hill overlooking the Sea of Galilee five miles northwest. This may be the Gadara of the Gadarene demoniac in Matthew 8:28–34; Mark 5:1–19; Luke 8:26–39. Abila is currently being excavated. Preliminary finds include tombs with fresco paintings. The pottery dates the tombs to the second and third centuries A.D.

## Transjordan

Since most of the Decapolis cities are in Transjordan, the references above are already to the eastern side of the Jordan River. Here we can add the site of Araq t0 el-Amir (Castle of the Prince) which has fascinated people for years. Large caves,

**Figure 11–3.** Araq el-Amir — "The Castle of the Prince" — in Jordan. It may have been a temple or a palace and may have been associated with the Tobiad family in the Ezra-Nehemiah stories.

perhaps family burial vaults, appear in a ridge high over the west bank of the Wadi es-Sir. Outside two of these is the name Tobiah, carved in the rock. It is the name of Nehemiah's enemy (Nehemiah 2:10). Tobiah is a Yahwistic name (tob yah, perhaps, Yahweh is good). Whether this cave belonged to this Tobiah or his family has been disputed. The mound below was occupied in the eleventh century B.C. and then abandoned until 200 B.C. One excavator, Paul Lapp, identified the site as the fortress Tyros built by the Tobiad Hyrcanus early in the second century B.C.

About 1600 feet southwest of the mound on a kind of plateau reaching out into the edge of the Wadi, there are building remains. The most prominent is called the Qasr al-Abd, the castle of the servant. This Arab name may reflect Nehemiah 2:10 where Tobiah the Ammonite is called the servant. While the Arab name implies a castle, others have thought it was a temple, sometimes identified as the temple of Hyrcanus. It dates to c. 200–175 B.C.

**Figure 11–4.** Araq el-Amir. Detail of construction shows remains of a frieze of lions which decorated the top of the wall of the castle.

**Figure 11–5.** Araq el-Amir. The feline fountain is made of dolomite and is red and white in color. The cat's mouth originally had a stream of water coming through. It is carved from a single block of stone and was found along the base of the "temple" or "palace" or "castle."

**Figure 11–6.** Araq el-Amir. Detail of construction of the castle showing the close fitting blocks — evidence of high quality workmanship. Above the meter stick is a "crow-step" design common in Nabataean architecture. Below the meter stick, a full block down, a slab leans against the building. The slab obscures part of a drainage system built into the construction.

Southwest of Amman, Esbus (Tell Hesban), was rebuilt c. 250 B.C. after being abandoned for 250 years. The early Hellenistic period (Stratum XXI) lasted until 198 B.C., the year of the conquest of Antiochus III (223–187 B.C.), whose ancestor Seleucus I Nicator (311–281) had teamed up with Ptolemy I to take over Alexander's empire. Seleucus then established himself in Babylon and finally Syria, where he started the Seleucid kingdom. Hesban Stratum XX, Late Hellenistic, lasted until the Roman Conquest in 63 B.C. Stratum XX had a city wall about five feet thick. This may be the level occupied by John Hyrcanus in 128 B.C.

We turn now to these Maccabees or Hasmoneans. [17]

## The Hasmoneans

The Hellenization discussed earlier was under the Ptolemies. It was low-key and relatively benign. It was simply present as a growing part of the lifestyle and culture. When Antiochus III conquered the territory, the way opened for more aggressive Hellenization on the part of another branch of Alexander's successors. The struggles between the Seleucids and Ptolemies did not end with Antiochus' victory in 198. They continued off and on and were still in process when Antiochus IV Epiphanes (175–163 B.C.) came to the throne. In 168, he tried to force the Jews to worship him as a god (I Maccabees 1:10–61). Some of the Jews revolted under the leadership of a priest named Mattathias at Modein (I Maccabees 2:1–69), seventeen miles northwest of Jerusalem. He was a descendant (great grandson?) of a man named Asmonaios or Hashmon, so the family of Mattathias is known as the Hasmoneans. Just as often they are called Maccabees.

Mattathias's son Judas took over the leadership (165–160) after his father's death. He was nicknamed maccabee or "hammer" perhaps because of his hammering of the enemy during the fight for freedom from the Seleucids (I Maccabees 3–9). This revolt is considered by some to be the background for the book of Daniel (168–165 B.C.) which has been called the "Manifesto of the Maccabees." It is also called the "manifesto of the Hasidim," the religious group or movement which developed to support the Hasmoneans as long as they were fighting for religious freedeom. When the Hasmoneans later turned to political freedom and territorial gain, the Hasidim withdrew their support.

Judas captured Jerusalem or most of it, at least. He restored the purity of the temple, an event which is still celebrated in the festival of Hanukkah. The fight was carried on until the Maccabees had established a kingdom. At its widest extent, it covered much of David's old empire, including the Transjordan region. It lasted until 63 B.C. when the Romans took over. The remains of Maccabean activity appear frequently in excavations. In Jerusalem, the strengthening of Nehemiah's wall was cited earlier. That included a massive glacis laid down the slope which had the happy (for us) coincidence of preserving older remains underneath as well as helping the defense of the Hasmonean city by exposing attackers to missiles from the top of the wall.

The American excavations at Gezer found a large domestic complex from the late second century B.C. It has three living units around a central courtyard. A Rhodian jar handle was stamped in Greek, "of Simon." Whether this was Simon the Maccabee (143–134 B.C.) we cannot tell, but it is possible. On the floor of the house were Hellenistic potsherds of the foldover type. A coin of 144 B.C. had the name of Demetrius II Nicator, Seleucid king from 145–140, and 129–125. Under the floor was a coin of Antiochus VII Sidetes (138–129). In the earlier excavations of Macalister, Reich has identified seven *mikvaot* (ritual baths) from the Hasmonean occupation. Gezer had been a Seleucid stronghold for the first decades of the Maccabean struggle. According to I Maccabees 9:52, the Seleucid general Bacchides had consolidated control there at the death of Judas the Maccabee in 160 B.C. It was not until 142 that the city capitulated to Simon or Simeon (I Maccabees 13:41), who put his son John in charge of the Jewish garrison in the fortress they built (Verse 47). John became John Hyrcanus who was king from 134–104.

Marisa, cited earlier, was also a Seleucid stronghold (I Maccabees 5:66; II Maccabees 12:35). It was not captured until Hyrcanus took it and all of Idumea, the old southern territory of Judah. He forced the Idumeans (Edomites) to be circumcised and become Jews, according to Josephus. Later, his son Judas Aristobulus I (104 B.C.) did the same to the Galileans. Aristobulus died within a year and was followed by a second son of Hyrcanus, Jonathan, better known by his Greek name, Alexander Janneus (103–76). A bulla from Jerusalem reads, "Jonathan High Priest of Jerusalem." Judging by the script and historical circumstances, Avigad thinks the seal belonged to Janneus although his great uncle, Jonathan Maccabee (160–142) was high priest in his time. It was Janneus who extended the kingdom to its largest territorial holdings though his father Hyrcanus gave him a good start. It may have been Hyrcanus who took over Hesban in the Transjordan region. It was Hyrcanus who destroyed the Samaritan temple on Gerizim. According to Josephus, this was in 128 B.C. The archaeological data for this is not yet available.

Hyracanus also destroyed Samaria and Shechem c. 108–107. Janneus went on to capture Pella and Jerash in 83–82. He built a fortress at Machaerus on the east side of the Dead Sea, fifteen miles southeast of the Jordan River. Perhaps he needed to hold the eastern territory against the Nabateans. It may have been Janneus who built the Hasmonean palace in the Wadi Kelt near Jericho. There were a series of aqueducts carrying water from the springs four and ten miles to the north as well as from Old Testament Jericho, Ain es-Sultan. They had this portion of the Jordan Valley blooming like a rose, as one big well-watered garden produced grain for the rest of the country.

**Figure 11–7.**   Qumran. One interpretation is that scribes sat cross-legged on the lower shelf and wrote the Dead Sea Scrolls on the "tables." Another theory is that they sat on the "benches" and used the lower level for foot rests while writing.

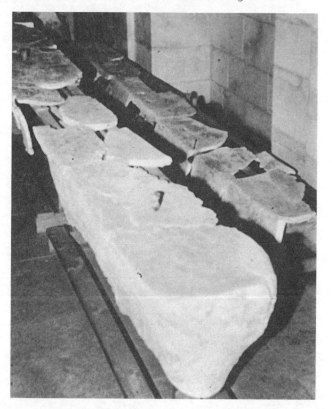

The palace at Tulul Abu al-Alayk has been explored in excavations by Ehud Netzer of Hebrew University who began digging there in 1973. Mudbrick walls have been uncovered which still stand twenty feet high. It may have been a two-story building over 160 feet square, built around a central court. At least some of the walls had molded stucco and frescoed plaster. Painted borders around floral designs give the appearance of marble panels. Northeast of the palace, Netzer found a swimming pool sixty by a hundred feet wide by twelve feet deep. Nearby were six ritual baths. This pool may be the one where Herod the Great had the Hasmonean high priest Aristobulus III drowned in 36 B.C. At that time, the palace would have been in the hands of Herod's mother-in-law, Alexandra, daughter of the Hasmonean Hyrcanus II (63–40 B.C.). Herod was married to Aristobulus' sister, Mariamne.[18]

**Figure 11–8.** Qumran. The partially rolled "Thanksgiving Scroll," one of the original Dead Sea Scrolls, contains 40 psalm-like hymns all starting with the words, "I thank thee, O Lord." Photo courtesy Consulate General of Israel (NY).

**Figure 11–9.** Opening a scroll. One of the Dead Sea Scrolls was reportedly opened with a penknife and guts. A tweezers proved helpful also in this example of a Hebrew magical text being opened here by Jalil Amr and Henry O. Thompson. A glass plate under the scroll helps protect the fragile papyrus. When the scroll is completely unrolled, another glass plate will go on top and protect it from further damage. The contents were identified by Dr. George E. Mendenhall. Photo by Mrs. Mendenhall.

## Qumran

Sometime during the Maccabean period, the ruling forces in the temple irritated and perhaps persecuted some fellow Jews who then left and found refuge in the wilderness on the northwest shore of the Dead Sea, eight and a half miles south of Jericho. They rebuilt a seventh century building, perhaps a fort of King Hezekiah. We call their construction the monastery of Qumran. The story of the discovery of the Dead Sea Scrolls in 1947–48 has appeared in several versions. According to one, a bedouin boy, Muhammad edh-Dhib was looking for a lost goat. He threw a rock into a cave and heard something break. It turned out to be a pottery jar. He and his friends of the Ta'amireh tribe found eight scrolls which eventually came to an antiquities dealer in Bethlehem and thence to Eleazer L. Sukenik, the father of Yigael Yadin, and to the Syrian Orthodox archbishop Mar Athanasius Samuel. Samuel's scrolls were identified as authentic at the ASOR through John Trevor's photographs sent to William F. Albright. In 1954, Samuel sold his five scrolls through an intermediary to Yadin for $250,000. All eight scrolls ended up in Israel where a special Shrine of the Book was built to display them and to keep them from deteriorating in today's light and moisture.

The caves and the ruin called Khirbet Qumran and the nearby building complex at the springs known as Ain Feshka were excavated by Pére de Vaux, the Palestine Archaeological Museum, and the Department of Antiquities of Jordan (then under Lankester Harding). The ASOR assisted in the search of the many caves in the area. Some thirty-seven caves produced pottery, and eleven caves produced manuscript materials. Cave 6 was the first cave found by the Bedouin. The monastery is a building complex measuring 260 by 330 feet. There were three strata. Level la was occupied in the period 150–100 B.C. There were eleven Seleucid coins, including three dated between 132 and 130 in the reign of Antiochus VII. This initial level may have been settled in the time of Simon the Maccabee (142–134) or Hyrcanus (134–104). One coin of the latter was found. The monastery was extensively rebuilt in the time of Alexander Janneus (103–76) though the excavators note this could have occurred in the latter part of Hyrcanus' reign. Some 143 coins of Janneus were found. This Phase 1b lasted until a huge earthquake in 31 B.C. The cracks in the ground and buildings can still be seen today. Josephus included the quake in his Jewish history. The site was more or less abandoned for a time but then rebuilt about 4 B.C. This Phase 2 was destroyed by the Romans in 68 A.D. at the beginning of the First Jewish Revolt (66–72 A.D.).

Qumran is the source of some 600 manuscripts or fragments known as the Dead Sea Scrolls. The sectarians who wrote or preserved these materials are very likely the sect called Essenes. They copied the scriptures including every book but Esther. (At least we have not yet found any portion of Esther.) There is still material waiting to be published, however. The Qumranites also wrote their own rules and regulations, and they had an extensive body of their own literature. The latter included such things as the "War between the Sons of Light and the Sons of Darkness." Needless to say, they were the Sons of Light and their enemies were the Sons of Darkness. Human nature has not changed lately. Cross has suggested the Qumranites arose out of several power struggles, first between the Seleucids and the Maccabees, and then between the Maccabees who proclaimed themselves high priests and other priestly families who also claimed the office. Jonathan, the second ruling Maccabee brother, 160–143, accepted the office of high priest from his enemies(!) in 152 (I Maccabees 9:19–12:53). He was made high priest by the Seleucid Alexander Balas (150–145 B.C.) during part of his struggle for the throne with Demetrius I Soter (162–150). The Dead Sea Scrolls refer to a Wicked Priest. Some claim Jonathan was the Wicked Priest. Cross thinks the wicked priest is Simon (143–134), the last of the Maccabee brothers. A Qumran commentary on the prophet Habakkuk says the wicked priest was called faithful but was faithless. I Maccabees 14:35 calls Simon faithful. Simon (I Maccabees 13–16) and his eldest and youngest sons were murdered by his son-in-law after Simon rebuilt Jericho. The Qumran commentary on Joshua 6:26 suggests the murder of the three Hasmoneans fulfilled Joshua's prophecy that whoever rebuilt Jericho would lose his eldest and youngest son.

Much of the light these materials shed on the Bible involves textual criticism, the concern with the correct or original text of the Bible, and the development of writing. Part of the light is the way in which we can see they applied scripture to their own day, not always taking in the clear meaning of the original text or realizing it had already been fulfilled. Their way of life also tells us something about the pluralism of Jewish Palestine during the rise of Christianity, itself a sect of Judaism (though it survived to outgrow its mother while the Qumranites perished). They, like the early Christians, saw themselves as the remnant, the New Israel, in whom the prophecies of the Hebrew scriptures would be fulfilled.

Where mainstream Jews and Christians talk about a Messiah, the desert sect had at least two and perhaps three. They looked for a messiah of Aaron and a messiah of Israel. The first was a priestly messiah of the tribe of Levi (Deuteronomy 33:8–11), the traditional tribe of priests. The second was a military prince who would come from the tribe of Judah (Numbers 24:17). This would be a Davidic messiah. A prophet-to-come is also a messiah figure (Deuteronomy 18:18).

The Teacher of Righteousness is a prominent figure in the Scrolls. Early reports on the Scrolls identified him with Jesus of Nazareth. The Teacher was probably an historical person, perhaps the founder of the sect or a major figure in its early years. He may have been an ex-high priest, which points to the years 159–152 for which we have no high priest of record in Jerusalem. The Teacher may have simply been one of the Zadokites, the priestly family or group which claimed the priesthood back to the time of David (II Samuel 8:17). Josephus said there was more than one settlement of the Essenes. One of these may have been found on the shore of the Dead Sea, ten miles south of Qumran, at 'En el-Ghuweir. [19]

# NOTES

1. KAHL, pp. 282–304. BHI, pp. 341–392. Jacob Neusner, "Archaeology and Babylonian Jewry," in NEATC, pp. 331–343. James D. Newsome, Jr., *By the Waters of Babylon: An Introduction to the History and Theology of the Exile* (Atlanta: Knox, 1979). James A. Sanders, "Exile," IDB 2, pp. 186–188. P. Kyle McCarter, "Obadiah 7 and the Fall of Edom," BASOR 221 (Feb. 76), pp. 87–91. A. Leo Oppenheimer, "Nebuchadnezzar," IDB 3, pp. 529–530; "Nabonidus," IDB 3, pp. 493–495; and "Evil-Merodach," IDB 2, p. 183. ANET, pp. 305–315, 560–563. TDOTT, pp. 81–91, 222–223. John Gray, *Archaeology and the Old Testament World* (New York: Harper & Row, 1965), pp. 189–198. D. J. Wiseman, *Chronicles of the Chaldean Kings* (London: British Museum, 1956). Charles F. Pfeiffer, *Exile and Return* (Grand Rapids: Baker, 1962), pp. 83–87. George A. Barton, *Archaeology and the Bible* (Philadelphia: American Sunday School Union, 1916), p. 479.

2. Ran Zadok, "West Semitic Personal Names in the Marasu Documents," BASOR 231 (Oct. 78), pp. 73–78. Michael D. Coogan, *West Semitic Names in the Marasu Documents* (Missoula: Scholars Press, 1976). Matthew W. Stolper, "A Note on Yahwistic Personal Names in the Marasu Texts," BASOR 222 (Ap. 76), pp. 25–28. Mark J. Dresen, "Cyrus," IDB 1, pp. 754–755. TDOTT, pp. 92–96. ANET, pp. 315–316. WBA, pp. 202–211. John A. Boyle, ed., *Persia: History and Heritage* (London: Henry Melland, 1978). Robert Collins, *The Medes and Persians* (New York: McGraw-Hill, n.d.). J. A. de Gobineau, *The World of the Persians* (Geneve: Minerva S.A., 1971). Sylvia A. Matheson, *Persia: An Archaeological Guide* (Park Ridge, NJ: Noyes, 1973).

3. Kaufman, "The Eastern Wall of the Second Temple at Jerusalem Revealed," BA 44, no. 2 (Spr. 81), pp. 108–115. Yohanan Aharoni, "Temples, Semitic," IDBSV, pp. 874–875. William F. Stinespring, "Temple, Jerusalem," IDB 4, pp. 534–560. Olga Tufnell, *Lachish III: The Iron Age* (New York: Oxford, 1953), pp. 141–145, pl. 24. Bruce T. Dahlberg, "Sheshbazzar," IDB 4, pp. 325–326; and, "Zerubbabel," IDB 4, pp. 955–956. Gray, *Archaeology*, pp. 185–186.

4. ANET, pp. 222–223, 491–492, 548–549. TDOTT, pp. 256–269. NERT, pp. 252–253. SBAF, pp. 268–270. Emil G. H. Kraeling, "Elephantine Papyri," IDB 2, pp. 83–85; and, *The Brooklyn Museum Aramaic Papyri* (New Haven: Yale University, 1953). Arthur E. Cowley, *Aramaic Papyri of the Fifth Century B.C.* (Oxford: Clarendon, 1923).

5. W. Lee Humphreys, "Esther, Book of," IDBSV, pp. 279–281. Dorothea W. Harvey, "Esther, Book of," IDB 2, pp. 149–151. Bruce T. Dahlberg, "Mordecai," IDB 3, pp. 437–438. Carey A. Moore, *Esther* (Garden City: Doubleday, 1971). William A. Hallo, "The First Purim," BA 46, no. 1 (Wint. 83), pp. 19–26.

6. Shemaryahu Talmon, "Ezra and Nehemiah (Books and Men)," IDBSV, pp. 317–328. Jacob M. Myers, *Ezra–Nehemiah* (Garden City: Doubleday, 1965). Ephraim Stern, "Archaeological Research in the Period of the Return to Zion" (pp. 69–74 in *Recent Archaeology in the Land of Israel* ed. Hershel Shanks and Benjamin Mazar; Jerusalem and Washington: IES and Biblical Archaeology Society, 1984).

7. I. Rabinowitz, "Aramaic Inscriptions of the Fifth Century B.C.E. from a North-Arab Shrine in Egypt," JNES 15 (1956), pp. 1–9. W. J. Dumbrell, "The Tell el-Maskhuta Bowls and the 'Kingdom' of Qadar in the Persian Period," BASOR 203 (1971), pp. 33–44. WBA, p. 207. Gray, *Archaeology*, pp. 185–186. ANET, p. 657. Nachman Avigad, "A New Class of 'Yehud' Stamps," IEJ 7, no. 3 (1957), pp. 146–153.

8. Cf. BHI, pp. 392–403 for a complete discussion of alternate theories. Robert H. Pfeiffer, "Ezra and Nehemiah," IDB 2, pp. 215–219. Ezra 7:7–8 says he came in the seventh year of Artaxerxes, but does not say which Artaxerxes it was. There were three: I (465–424), II (404–358), III (358–338). This could put Ezra in 458, 398, or 351. The second and third are too late, as noted. The first is too early. Josephus says it was Xerxes. There were two of them: I (486–465), II (423 — only one year). This would put Ezra in 479 which most consider too early. Albright suggested the numeral 30 had

dropped out of the text. Subtracting 30 + 7 from 465 gives us 428 as his guess for when Ezra came. Cf. *The Biblical Period*, p. 64, n. 133.

9. WBA, pp. 205–206. Shiloh, "Excavating Jerusalem," *Archaeology* 33, no. 3 (Nov./Dec. 80), p. 13. Arnold Spaer, "Some 'Yehud' Coins," IEJ 27, no. 4 (1977), pp. 200–203. Avigad, "A New Class."

10. "Greeks in Phoenicia," *Archaeology* 17 (1964), pp. 206ff. Gordon, *Before the Bible* (New York: Harper & Row, 1962); in paperback as *The Common Background of Greek and Hebrew Civilization* (New York: Norton, 1961). Ya'akov Meshorer, "The Holy Land in Coins," BAR 4, no. 1 (Mar. 78), pp. 32–38. Moshe Dothan, "An Attic Red-Figured Bell Krater from Tel 'Akko," IEJ 29, nos. 3–4 (1979), pp. 148–151. Lee I. Levine, "Archaeological Discoveries From the Greco-Roman Era," pp. 75–87 in Shanks and Mazar, *Recent Archaeology*.

11. Yohanan Landau and Vassilios Tzaferis, "Tel Istabah, Beth Shean: The Excavation and Hellenistic Jar Handles," IEJ 29, nos. 3–4 (1979), pp. 152–159. Yigal Shiloh, "City of David Excavations 1978," BA 42, no. 3 (Sum. 79), pp. 165–171.

12. John C.H. Laughlin, "The Remarkable Discoveries at Tell Dan," BAR 7, no. 5 (Sep./Oct. 81), p. 34. Avraham Biran, "Tell Dan, 1976," IEJ 26 (1976), pp. 204–205. Lawrence Geraty, "The Khirbet el-Kom Bilingual Ostracon," BASOR 220 (Dec. 75), pp. 55–61. Aaron Skaist, "A Note on the Bilingual Ostracon from Khirbet el-Kom," IEJ 28, nos. 1–2 (1978), pp. 106–108. William G. Dever, "Khirbet el-Qom," EAEHL, pp. 976–977.

13. Lawrence E. Toombs, "The Stratigraphy of Tell Balata," ADAJ 17 (1972), pp. 108–109 and pl. II. Wright, *Shechem* (New York: McGraw-Hill, 1964), pp. 170–184; "Shechem," EAEHL, pp. 1091–1094; and, "The Samaritans at Shechem," HTR 55 (1962), pp. 357–366. WBA, pp. 211–213. Bull, "Tell er-Ras," EAEHL, pp. 1015–1022; "The Excavation of Tell er-Ras on Mt. Gerizim," BA 31 (1968), pp. 58–72; and, "Mount Gerizim," IDBSV, p. 361. Nachman Avigad, "Samaria," EAEHL, pp. 1032–1046. J.D. Purvis, "Samaritans," IDBSV, pp. 776–77. John Bowman, "The History of the Samaritans," *Abr-Nahrain* 18 (1978–1979), pp. 101–115. Robert T. Anderson, *Studies in Samaritan Manuscripts and Artifacts* (Cambridge: ASOR, 1981). R.J. Coggins, *Samaritans and Jews: The Origins of Samaritanism Reconsidered* (Atlanta: Knox, 1975). Nigel Turner, "Alexander," IDB 1, pp. 77–78. Edward F. Campbell, Jr., "Jewish Shrines of the Hellenistic and Persian Periods," CS 159–167. BHI, pp. 414–416.

14. Paul W. Lapp, "Bedouin Find Papyri Three Centuries Older than Dead Sea Scrolls," BAR 4, no. 1 (Mar. 78), pp. 16–24. Paul W. and Nancy L. Lapp, *Discoveries in the Wadi ed-Daliyeh* (Cambridge: AASOR 41, 1974). Frank M. Cross, "The Historical Importance of the Samaria Papyri," BAR 4, no. 1 (Mar. 78), pp. 25–27; and, "Papyri of the Fourth Century B.C. from Daliyeh," FGNDBA, pp. 41–62.

15. IECW, pp. 30–31. Harold R. Willoughby, "Alexandria," IDB 1, pp. 79–81. Turner, "Alexander," p. 77. Robert A. Kraft, "Septuagint," IDBSV, pp. 807–815. John W. Wevers, "Septuagint," IDB 4, pp. 273–278. Overlapping dates for Ptolemy I and II probably means a coregency, three years when they shared the rule. Gunther Zuntz, "Aristeas," IDB 1, pp. 219–221. He says the Letter of Aristeas dates to c. 100 B.C.

16. Michael Avi-Yonah, "Maresha," EAEHL, pp. 782–790. Thomas O. Hall, Jr., "Maresha (City)," IDBSV, pp. 566–567. Victor R. Gold, "Mareshah," IDB 3, pp. 263–264. Gabriel Horowitz, "Town Planning of Hellinistic Marisa: A Reappraisal of Excavations After Eight Years," PEQ 112 (July–Dec. 80), pp. 93–111. Sidney B. Hoenig, "Jason," IDB 2, pp. 804–805. Edward R. Dalglish, "Absolom," IDB 1, pp. 22–23. Bernard Boyd, "Lachish," IDBSV, p. 526. Aharoni, "Trial Excavation in the 'Solar Shrine' at Lachish," IEJ 18 (1968), pp. 157–169; and, "Lachish: The Excavation of the Solar Shrine," EAEHL, pp. 747–749. Gideon Foerster, "Architectural Fragments from 'Jason's Tomb' Reconsidered," IEJ 28, no. 3 (1978), pp. 152–156. L.Y. Rahmani, "Jason's Tomb," IEJ 17, no. 2 (1967), pp. 61–100; and, "Ancient Jerusalem's Funerary Customs and

Tombs," BA 45, no. 1 (Wint. 82), pp. 43–53. Benjamin Mazar, *The Mountain of the Lord* (Garden City: Doubleday, 1975), p. 226, dates this tomb to the first century B.C.

17. D.C. Pellet, "Decapolis," IDB 1, pp. 810–812. Shimon Applebaum, "Gerasa," EAEHL, pp. 417–428. W. Harold Mare, "1980 Survey of Abila of the Decapolis," BA 44, no. 3 (Sum. 81), pp. 179–180; and, "Tomb Finds at Abila of the Decapolis," BA 45, no. 1 (Wint. 82), pp. 57–58. Kenneth W. Clark, "Gerasa," IDB 2, pp. 382–384. SBAF, pp. 491–494 (Jerash). Carl H. Kraeling, *Gerasa, City of the Decapolis* (New Haven: ASOR, 1938). Adnan Hadidi, "The Roman Town-Plan of Amman," (pp. 210–222 in *Archaeology of the Levant* ed. Peter Roger Stuart Moorey and Peter J. Parr; Warminster: Aris and Phillips, 1978). Michael Avi-Yonah and Ephraim Stern, "Rabbath-Ammon," EAEHL, pp. 987–993. Aharon Kempinski, "Besh-shean," EAEHL, pp. 207–210. Frances James, "Beth-shean," EAEHL, pp. 215–225. Robert H. Smith, "Pella of the Decapolis," IDBSV, pp. 651–652; *Pella of the Decapolis*, Vol. I (Wooster: College of Wooster, 1973); "Preliminary Report on the 1979 Season of the Sydney-Wooster Joint Expedition to Pella," ADAJ 24 (1980); pp. 13–14; "Pella of the Decapolis," *Archaeology* 34, no. 5 (Sept./Oct. 81); and, "Preliminary Report on a Second Season of Excavation at Pella, Jordan," ADAJ 25 (1981), pp. 311–326. Anthony McNicoll and J. Basil Hennessy, "The Winter Session," ADAJ 24 (1980), pp. 14–40. Hennessy, et al., "Preliminary Report on a Second Season of Excavation at Pella, Jordan," ADAJ 25 (1981), pp. 267–309. McNicoll and Smith, "Tabaqat Fahl — Pella (1981)," ADAJ 25 (1981), pp. 358–359; and, "The 1979 Season at Pella of the Decapolis," BASOR 240 (Fall 80), pp. 63–84. Smith, McNicoll and Hennessy, "The 1980 Season at Pella of the Decapolis," BASOR 243 (Sum. 81), pp. 1–30. Ute Wagner-Lux and Karel J.H. Vriezen, "A Preliminary Report on the Excavations at Gadara (Umm Qes) in Jordan from 1976 to 1979," ADAJ 24 (1980), pp. 157–161. Fawzi Zayadine, "Excavations at Petra (1976 and 1978)," ADAJ 23 (1979), pp. 185–197. Foerster, "Architectural Fragments." Robin M. Brown, "Excavations at 'Iraq el-Emir," ADAJ 23 (1979), pp. 17–30. Paul W. Lapp, " 'Iraq el-Emir," EAEHL, pp. 527–531; "Soundings of 'Araq el-Emir (Jordan)," BASOR 165 (1962), pp. 16–34; and, "The Second and Third Campaign at 'Araq el-Emir," BASOR 171 (1963), pp. 8–39. M.J.B. Brett, "The Qasr el-'Abd: A Proposed Reconstruction," ibid., pp. 39–45. Nancy L. Lapp, "The Hellenistic Pottery from the 1961 and 1962 Excavations at 'Iraq el-Amir," ADAJ 23 (1979), pp. 5–15. Campbell, "Jewish Shrines," pp. 162–164. Roger S. Boraas and Lawrence T. Geraty, "The Long Life of Tell Hesban, Jordan," *Archaeology* 32, no. 1 (Jan./Feb. 79), p. 13. Siegfried H. Horn, "Heshbon," EAEHL, p. 512. Seleucus I became king in 304 B.C.

18. Jonathan A. Goldstein, *I Maccabees* (Garden City: Doubleday, 1976). Moshe Perlman, *The Maccabees* (New York: Macmillan, 1973). BHI, pp. 416–429. IECW, pp. 415–416 (Seleucus), 244 (Hyrcanus), 32 (Alexander Jannaeus). Nachman Avigad, "A Bulla of Jonathan the High Priest," IEJ 25, no. 1 (1975), pp. 8–12. Harry M. Orlinsky, "Maccabees, Maccabean Revolt," IDB 3, pp. 197–201. Nigel Turner, "Hasmoneans," IDB 2, pp. 529–535. Louis F. Hartman and Alexander A. DiLella, *The Book of Daniel* (Garden City: Doubleday, 1977). Daniel is the name of a wise king in the Ugaritic tale of Aqhat (NERT, pp. 225–226; ANET, pp. 149–155). This ancient tradition may be the Daniel of Ezekiel 14:14, 20 and 28:3. Jack Finegan, *Archaeology of the New Testament* (Princeton: Princeton University, 1969), p. 15. Joe D. Seger, "The Search for Maccabean Gezer," BA 39, no. 4 (Dec. 76), pp. 142–144. William G. Dever, "Gezer," EAEHL, pp. 442–443. Ronny Reich, "Archaeological Evidence of the Jewish Population at Hasmonean Gezer," IEJ 31, nos. 1–2 (1981), pp. 48–52. Suzanne F. Singer, "The Winter Palaces of Jericho," BAR 3, no. 2 (June 77), pp. 1, 6–17. Ehud Netzer, "The Hasmonean and Herodian Winter Palaces at Jericho," IEJ 25, nos. 2–3 (1975), pp. 89–100; and, "The Winter Palaces of the Judean Kings at the end of the Second Temple Period," BASOR 228 (Dec. 77), pp. 1–13. Netzer, et al., "Jericho from the Persian to the Byzantine Periods," EAEHL, pp. 564–575. Uriel Rappaport, "The Birth of the Hasmonean State," pp. 173–177 in Shanks and Mazar, *Recent Archaeology*.

19. The literature on the Dead Sea Scrolls and on Qumran is voluminous. Frank M. Cross, *Ancient Library of Qumran* (rev.; Grand Rapids: Baker, 1980). Cf. also Cross and Shemaryahu Talmon, *Qumran and the History of the Biblical Text* (Cambridge: Harvard University, 1975). Cross, "The Dead Sea Scrolls and the People Who Wrote Them," BAR 3, no. 1 (Mar. 77), pp. 1, 23–32, 51. Joseph A. Fitzmeyer, "The Dead Sea Scrolls and the New Testament after Thirty Years," *Theology Digest* 29, no. 4 (Wint. 81), pp. 351–367. Reviewed in BAR 8, no. 5 (Sep./Oct. 82), p. 6. Charles F. Pfeiffer, *The Dead Sea Scrolls and the Bible* (Grand Rapids: Baker, 1969). FGNDBA. SBAF. WBA, pp. 216–220. Geza Vermes, "Dead Sea Scrolls," IDBSV, pp. 210–219. Turner, "Alexander," IDB 1:78. Otto Betz, "Dead Sea Scrolls," IDB 1, pp. 790–802. Dodo J. Shenhav, "Saving the Dead Sea Scrolls for the Next 2000 Years," BAR 7, no. 4 (July/Aug. 81), pp. 44–49. Harry Thomas Frank, "How the Dead Sea Scrolls were Found," BAR 1, no. 4 (Dec. 75), pp. 1, 7–11, 14–16, 28–30. Jerome Murphy-O'Conner, "The Essenes in Palestine," BA 40, no. 3 (Sep. 77), pp. 100–124. Merlin D. Rehm, "Zadok the Priest," IDBSV, pp. 976–977. Pessach Bar-Adon, "Another Settlement of the Judean Desert Sect at 'En el-Ghuweir on the Shores of the Dead Sea," BASOR 227 (Oct. 77), pp. 1–25. George W.E. Nickelburg, Jr., "Simon — A Priest with a Reputation for Faithfulness," BASOR 223 (Oct. 76), pp. 67–68. Roland de Vaux, "Qumran, Khirbet — 'Ein Feshka," EAEHL, pp. 978–986; and, *Archaeology and the Dead Sea Scrolls* (London: Oxford University, 1973). Michael Wise, "The Dead Sea Scrolls: Archaeology and Biblical Manuscripts," BA 49, no. 3 (Sep. 86), pp. 140–154. Qumran and DSS studies have continued in the biblical and archaeology journals and in the journal, *Revue de Qumran*, Vol. 1 (1971) + (Paris: Gabalda).

# CHAPTER 12

# The Roman Period

The sons of Alexander Janneus, Hyrcanus II (63–40) and Aristobulus II (67–63), quarrelled over the throne and the high priesthood. Both appealed to the Roman general, Pompey. In 64 B.C., Pompey had made Syria a Roman province. After asking Pompey to step in and decide the issue, Aristobulus changed his mind. He fortified himself in Jerusalem where he was able to hold out against Pompey for three months. Pompey captured the city and sent Aristobulus to Rome in chains. He set Hyrcanus up as high priest, but not king. This ended the Hasmonean kingdom and inaugurated the Roman rule of Palestine which was to last for centuries.

## A. THE HERODIANS

### Herod the Great

As noted earlier, the Maccabees had converted the Idumeans (Edomites) to Judaism. Hyrcanus II had an Idumean friend named Antipater whose father, Antipater, was governor of Idumea under Alexander Janneus. During the civil war between the two Hasmoneans, Antipater backed Hyrcanus. After the Romans took over, Antipater supported each successful Roman general in turn during the turmoils of the Roman Empire. He was murdered in 43 B.C. He had set up his sons Herod and Phasael as governors of Galilee and Judea. His very able but very unscrupulous son, Herod, was later called Herod the Great. Herod was king by

**Figure 12–1.** Qasr Azraq (Azraq Castle). Built by the Romans on the desert commercial route in the Oasis of Azraq. It was revived as a military post in World War I when used as a camp headquarters for Lawrence of Arabia. Today, the pools of Azraq, in the heart of the desert with its wild life, have become an interesting attraction for visitors. Jordan Information Bureau, Washington, D.C.

Roman appointment over all of Palestine from 40 B.C. to his death in 4 B.C. It was during his later years that Jesus of Nazareth was born (Matthew 2:1). At the beginning of his reign, a son of Aristobulus II, Matthias Antigonus (40–37 B.C.) captured and held Jerusalem for three years with the help of the Parthians from Persia. With Roman help, Herod drove the invaders out and captured Jerusalem. One of his wives was Mariamne, as cited earlier. She was a Hasmonean princess, daughter of Alexandra, and granddaughter of Hyrcanus II.

The archaeological remains of Herod are significant and magnificent even in their ruined state. He built eleven fascinating fortresses such as Machaerus ("The Sword"). The Arabs called it Mukawer. The Maccabees had fortified this peak which towers 150 feet above the Arnon Valley on the eastern side of the Dead Sea. Pompey's general Gabinius destroyed the fortress in 63 B.C. Herod rebuilt it and made it a retreat for himself as well as a bastion against the East. He probably reached it by boat across the Dead Sea. The fortress was in Perea, later governed by Herod's son, Herod Antipas who imprisoned and beheaded John the Baptist at Machaerus, according to Josephus. It was later occupied by the Zealots in the First Jewish Revolt, and destroyed once again in 72 A.D. by the Roman Commander Lucilius Bassus. A preliminary season of excavation by E. Jerry Vardamn in 1968 explored the foundations of Herod's work, the cistern carved out of the mountainside and what may have been an aqueduct from inland springs. Major work is now under way under Stanislas Loffreda, Vergilis Corbo, and others.

Herodium, Jebel el-Fureidis ("mountain of small paradise"), is a truncated cone, seven and a half miles south of Jerusalem. It was excavated by Corbo for the Studium Biblicum Franciscanum (1962–67), with additional work by Gideon Foerster and Ehud Netzer (1967–72). The fortress is a round construction 262 feet across. On the east side is a tower sixty feet across and still preserved to a height of fifty-seven feet. On the north, south, and west are semi-circular towers on the outside of the main wall. Inside is a garden 100 feet long, an elaborate bath in Roman style, and luxurious quarters. Herod apparently built the Herodium as a mausoleum, his burial place, as well as a fortress. An aqueduct brought water from Solomons' pools south of Jerusalem. On the lower land below the mountain were a number of buildings including a pool, possibly for swimming, and what may have been a hippodrome. The Zealots later took over this fortress too, and it was also destroyed by the Romans under Lucilius Bassus. In the Second Jewish Revolt (132–135 A.D.), it was a command post for the Zealot commander, Bar Kochba (or Koseba) and was destroyed by the Romans yet again. There is another Herodium near Mount Nebo in Perea.

Perhaps the most fascinating of Herod's fortress palaces is that of Masada, another former Hasmonean fort. It was excavated by Yadin, 1963–1965. Masada is an isolated rock which rises between 600 and 800 feet in height. It is a bit like a western mesa in the U.S. The top is shaped like an almond or a boat and measures 1800 x 900 feet. On one end is a hanging palace built on a series of ledges on the northern tip of the "boat." The top had large storerooms as well as a palace, an extensive bath, and related buildings. Masada's fame comes from a later incident at the end of the First Jewish Revolt. The Zealots had taken over the fort as a "last stand." The Romans under Flavius Silva surrounded Masada and breached the wall from a ramp they built up the side. When they entered the fort, Josephus tells us the Romans found the nearly 1,000 Zealot defenders had murdered each other

**Figure 12–2.**    Air view of Masada, ancient Jewish fortress. On the top of the plateau are remains of warehouses and Herodian buildings. On the left side of the hill are three terraces with remains of Herodian palaces. Beyond the hill on the left, the remains of a Roman siege camp can be seen on the valley floor, from the siege of 72 A.D. when the Romans surrounded the Zealots fortified on top of the plateau in Herod's old fortress. Photo courtesy Consulate General of Israel (NY).

and committed suicide rather than be taken prisoner. In his excavations, Yadin found several skeletons which he related to this story. Israeli army recruits are sworn into the army at dawn on the top of Masada with the vow that Masada will not fall again. Tourists can reach the plateau by cable car or by walking up the tortuous Snake Path.

Herod built whole cities such as Caesarea Maritima on the Mediterranean coast. It is named in honor of Caesar Augustus. Earlier, the Sidonians may have had an outpost known as Straton's Tower, probably named for the second of two kings named Abdashtart at the end of the Persian period. The Hasmoneans had controlled the area and Pompey made it a Roman colony. Herod completely rebuilt the city on a grand scale, with an artificial harbor, sewers that were flushed out by

**Figure 12–3.** Masada. Close up view of the Herodian fortress. Photo courtesy Consulate General of Israel (NY).

**Figure 12–4.**    Masada. Close up view of the middle terrace of Herod's Palace. Photo courtesy Consulate General of Israel (NY).

the sea, a long row of warehouses for goods going in and out of the port (one of which became a temple to the god Mithraeus in the third century B.C.), and aqueducts that brought fresh water from the north from over twelve miles away. Later (second century B.C.) the city had a 4,500 seat theater and 38,000 seat hippodrome. The theater was excavated, 1959–63, by A. Frovo of the Instituto Lombardo in Milan. It has been partially restored and is now in use for plays and concerts. J. Ory, A. Negev, and Michael Avi-Yonah participated in explorations, 1945–62. Caesarea has been under excavation since 1971 by an American consortium of schools and museums. Robert J. Bull has directed the work.

Herod was followed by his son Archaelaus in this area. The son was removed for incompetence in 6 A.D., and after that Judea was governed by Roman procurators. Caesarea was their residence. The most well known of these was Pontius Pilate who gave the order for the crucifixion of Jesus. An inscribed stone was later reused as a step for the theater. The inscription reads, "Pontius Pilate, Prefect of Judea."

**Figure 12–5.** Caesarea Maritima, an aerial view. The two "fingers" sticking out into the Mediterranean Sea at the top of the picture are the "moles" of Herod's harbor. The building remains below it are the Crusader fortress. In the left center, the long rectangle is the Roman hippodrome. Stretching from it and curving up to the right is the Byzantine city wall. Photo courtesy Caesarea Joint Expedition.

**Figure 12–6.** Caesarea. This Herodian warehouse vault was reused as a Mithraeum — a temple to the god Mithraeus, a favorite of the Roman legions. Photo courtesy Caesarea Joint Expedition.

Many of the visible ruins at Samaria date to the time of Herod. That includes a temple to Augustus on the high point of the mound. He renamed the city Sebaste in honor of his patron. Sebaste is Greek for Augustus. Among Herod's other temples is one at Esbus, Tell Hesban, noted earlier. The foundations for the temple may have been found by excavations there. A later Byzantine church was built on the summit of the mound and thoroughly reused stones of an earlier building dated to the time of Herod. He adorned Hebron and Mamre with his constructions in honor of the Patriarchs. Abraham is the traditional ancestor of both the Hebrews and the Edomites. Examples of the finest Herodian masonry can be seen there today. Some of the large blocks are twenty-five feet long and three feet high. They were put together without mortar but so closely fitted it is difficult to put a knife blade in the joints except where weathering has taken place. Herod's palaces in the Wadi Qelt near Jericho have been excavated recently. Built on the Hasmonean foundations cited earlier, the sunken gardens and pools fed by aqueducts added to the luxury of large buildings decorated in frescoes, mosaics, and marble.[1]

## Jerusalem

From the perspective of biblical history, the temple and the construction that is most important is of course in Jerusalem. Herod rebuilt the second temple (originally built in 515 B.C.) on a tremendous scale. It was finally completed in 64 A.D., just six years before it was destroyed by the Romans in the First Revolt, when Titus conquered Jerusalem. His victory is recorded on the Arch of Titus at the end of the Forum in Rome. A relief carved on the inside of the arch shows Jewish prisoners carrying a menorah, the seven-branched candelabra, being paraded through the streets of Rome. The temple was thoroughly demolished, perhaps illustrating Jesus' statement (Matthew 24:2) that the temple would be torn down without one

**Figure 12–7.**    Jerusalem from the Mt. of Olives. The old city wall as seen today dates from the Muslim ruler, Suleiman the Magnificant who conquered the city from the Crusaders. The Golden Gate shown here is closed. Tradition says the Messiah will enter the city through this gate, so the story goes that Suleiman had it closed to prevent anyone else ruling the city. In rebuilding the walls, Suleiman followed previous lines and in places the lower reaches of the wall are Herodian.

**Figure 12–8.** The Haram esh-Sharif. The platform built by Herod the Great has been rebuilt several times as shown by the smaller stones near the top. The silver dome of the Mosque al-Aqsa is at one end while the Golden Dome of the Rock is in the middle. Herodian masonry is clear on the left at the Wailing Wall.

stone left standing upon another. In 1871 and 1935, stones were found with a Greek inscription, "No alien may enter within the barrier and wall around the temple. Whoever is caught (violating this) is alone responsible for the death (-penalty) which follows."

While the temple was demolished, the platform Herod constructed has remained largely intact. It is a trapezoid, shorter on the north and west, 910 feet on the south, 1,575 feet on the east. The most significant portion of it is the western side popularly known as the Wailing Wall. Through the centuries, Jews came here

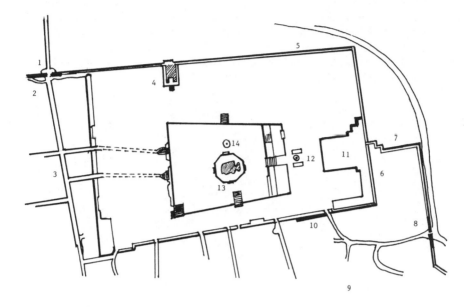

**Figure 12–9.**    Sketch Plan of the Haram and Vicinity: 1. St. Stephen's Gate [down: to the Kidron Valley and the Mt. of Olive; up: to . . . ] 2. St. Anne's Church; 3. Via Dolorosa; 4. Golden Gate; 5. Outside wall of Herod's Platform; 6. Area of Mazar's excavations; 7. City Wall of Suleiman; 8. Dung Gate; 9. Jewish Quarter [area of Avidgad's excavations]; 10. Western Wall of Herod's Platform — "Wailing Wall;" 11. Mosque al Aqsa; 12. Fountain; 13. Dome of the Rock [inside is an outline of the rock]; 14. Dome of the Chain where tradition says Muhammad the Prophet tied his horse. Drawn by J.E. Thompson.

to remember the sorrows of their people and to pray. Since 1967, that practice has been resumed after a twenty year long interruption. At that time, too, Benjamin Mazar of Hebrew University began excavating around the southwest corner and along the south wall of the platform. Among the fallen stones found in Mazar's excavations, one has a partially preserved inscription, "To the place of trumpeting . . ." An Herodian street has been uncovered along with a monumental stair on the western side at the south end. A portion of the broad staircase from the street up to the southern (Huldah) gates into the temple area has also been found.

Herodian remains appear in the wall around the Old City of Jerusalem. One of its gates, on the north side, east end, is called Herod's Gate, though the gate itself is of a later date. The Damascus Gate on the north side, middle section, is from later on in the Roman period. The Jaffa Gate on the western side has a tower popularly known as David's tower but dating from the time of Herod. It is usually called the

**Figure 12–10.**   The Western Wall. On the western side of the Haram esh-Sharif is a clear portion of the Herodian platform. For centuries, Jews have come here to mourn the fate of the temple, so it is called the Wailing Wall. The fence down the middle separates the women on the near side and the men on the far side. At the far end is a series of arches. They are called Wilson's arches and represent a bridge that once spanned the Tyropoean Valley which was once 70 feet deep before being filled with debris.

Herodian Tower of Phasael and is part of the Citadel which is now open to the public. Herod built a huge (985 by 330 feet) platform here on Mount Zion, the western hill of the big "U" of Jerusalem. Mount Ophel, the other leg of the "U," is the city of David and the Jebusites and of Nehemiah. The Zion platform might be seen as an architectural balance to the temple platform. Its foundation walls were thirty-three feet thick and from ten to thirteen feet high. Here Herod built a magnificent palace surrounded by courtyards and gardens. At the northern end, Josephus says Herod erected three towers which he named after his children Phasael

**Figure 12–11.** The Jaffa Gate (so called because the old road led from here to Jaffa now next to the new city of Tel Aviv) belongs to the Old City wall of Suleiman the Magnificent but its foundations are Herodian as is David's tower on the right.

**Figure 12–12.** The Damascus Gate (so called because the old road led from here to Damascus) is part of the wall of Suleiman the Magnificent. Its foundations are much older. People are walking across a bridge which replaced the ancient roadway excavated by J. Basil Hennessy.

**Figure 12–13.** The Roman foundations of the Damascus Gate, excavated by Hennessy. The arch dates from the time of Herod Agrippa, King of Israel, grandson of Herod the Great.

**Figure 12–14.** Herod's Gate is part of the Old City wall of Suleiman the Magnificant but like the other gates of Jerusalem, the foundations here date from the Roman period.

**Figure 12–15.**    The family tomb of the Herodian family. This is a rolling stone tomb, perhaps like the one Jesus was buried in.  Herod himself was supposedly buried in his fortress at Herodium but his tomb has not been found yet.

**Figure 12–16.** One of the newly developed archaeological gardens next to the walls of Jerusalems's Old City. In the rear are buildings of the reconstructed Jewish Quarter. Both inside and outside remains are preserved open to public view. Photo courtesy Consulate General of Israel (NY).

and Hippicus and his wife Mariamne. The visible one remaining is usually called Phasael's though some consider it Hippicus. It more nearly fits the dimensions of Hippicus as given by Josephus. Excavations in this area have been carried out by a number of scholars over the years. C.N. Johns worked at the Citadel, 1934–40. More recently, Ruth Amriran, A. Eitan, D. Bahat, and Mogen Broshi have excavated here.

Excavations in the Jewish Quarter of the Old City have uncovered large, well-built houses of the Herodian period. We could even call them mansions. Some had frescoed walls like Masada, beautiful mosaic floors, fine imported Italian pottery (some of it a fine thin red ware called "terra sigilatta"), and the usual cooking pots, lamps, and other household items. The bathrooms and ritual baths were standard as well. The Romans invented blown glass. Molded glass had been around for centuries but the thin blown glass was new and expensive. Many fragments of this commodity have been found in the excavations Avigad began in 1969. A menorah was incised in the plaster wall of one house.[2]

**Figure 12–17.**    The Via Dolorosa with the Ecce Homo ("Behold the Man") Arch, so called from Pontius Pilate's words to the crowd at Jesus' trial. On either side of the main arch is a smaller one, hidden in the building construction. More recent excavation shows this arch is from the time of Hadrian, c. 135 A.D., over 100 years after Jesus and Pilate.

## The Nazarene

The Palestine of Jesus was the Palestine of Herod the Great and his sons Archaelaus and Herod Antipas and the Roman procurators who followed Archaelaus. The archaeological remains are the remains of the first half of the first century A.D. The discovery of a synagogue at Capernaum was exciting. Jesus had been there. The building was of white limestone, sixty-five feet long and two stories high. The synagogue remains we see are from the fourth or fifth century. Underneath are the basalt walls and floor of an earlier building which is probably a synagogue also and very likely the one where Jesus preached (Mark 1:21–28; Luke 5:31–37).

The remains of an octagonal Byzantine church lie eighty-four feet south of the synagogue. The church remains date to the fourth and fifth centuries. Under these are the basalt rock walls of a first century A.D. house, which may have been built in the first century B.C. This house has been identified as the home of the Apostle Peter where Jesus stayed and may have lived for a time (Matthew 8:14–16; Mark 2:1–5).[3]

In Jerusalem, Jesus walked in the porches of the temple of Herod the Great. The colonnade or the Porch of Solomon ran along the outer wall along the east side and overlooked the Kidron Valley. On one corner of the temple precincts was a fortress called the Antonia. The Apostle Paul was imprisoned there (Acts 21:27). Jesus may have been tried before Pilate here (Mark 15). Some years ago, the Sisters of the Convent of Zion needed more space so they began to enlarge their basement. They found an ancient pavement and asked Father Louis H. Vincent to investigate. He concluded it was the pavement of the Antonia, six and a half feet below the present street level. John 19:13 says Pilate's judgment seat was in a place called the pavement, the "lithostratum." Above ground is the "ecce homo" arch, named from John 19:5 where Pilate said, "Behold the man." The arch is part of a triple-arched gateway from the Hadrianic city of Aelia Capitolina. The pavement discovered by the Sisters is now known to be part of the gateway entrance from 135 A.D.

The "Pools of Bethesda" (John 5:2) were identified for a time with two large reservoirs near the Church of St. Anne (which honors the Virgin Mary's mother). These are now known to be Hasmonean in date. The Bethesda Pool where Jesus healed the lame man may be a nearby cave which collected water from an ancient stream. One suggestion is that it was red because of the soil, which suggested the idea of blood and hence of healing powers. The lame man in verse 7 says, "When the waters are troubled," suggesting movement in the water, perhaps from intermittent gushing like the Gihon Spring.

In John 4:4–42, we read the story of Jacob's well. Near Shechem, at the foot of Mount Gerizim, the Greek Orthodox Church owns a well called Jacob's well. It is presently inside a partially constructed church, in an underground room. The Old Testament does not mention this well, but it is one of the few things archaeologists do not argue about.

**Figure 12–18.** The Via Dolorosa in the Christian Quarter, closer to the Church of the Holy Sepulchre. The actual roadway followed by Jesus is several feet underground.

**Figure 12–19.** The Christian Gate leads into the Christian Quarter of the Old City of Jerusalem. This gate was made 100 years ago for the visit of Kaiser Wilhelm to the City. It did not exist in the time of Jesus and has no archaeological significance though tourists often assume so. The foundations here as elsewhere are Roman since Suleiman the Magnificent followed the earlier line of the wall when he had it rebuilt.

Back in Jerusalem, the street called the Via Dolorosa marks the path Jesus took from the Antonia to his crucifixion. The site of Calvary and the tomb of Joseph of Arimathea is traditionally under the Church of the Holy Sepulchre. This is inside the wall of the Old City. In 1867, General Charles "Chinese" Gordon stood on the wall of Jerusalem near the Damascus Gate. He was nicknamed from the Boxer Rebellion in China and later lost his life at Khartoum fighting the Muslim Mahdi who wanted to drive out the British. Gordon looked across the road to a hill with a Muslim cemetery on top. On the side of the hill, in the striation of the rock, he saw the outline of a skull and thought of "Golgotha," the "place of the skull." This must be Calvary, he thought, outside the city walls. There is a rolling stone tomb at the bottom of the hill. Today there is a lovely garden here called the Garden Tomb or the Protestant Calvary. This tomb is part of a larger group of tombs from the Iron Age.

**Figure 12–20.** St. Stephen's (for the first Christian martyr) or The Lion Gate (note two lions on each side of the top of the gate) of Jerusalem. Straight ahead is The Via Dolorosa; to the right is St. Anne's Church; to the left is The Dome of the Rock; the Kidron Valley is behind the viewer.

**Figure 12–21.** The Church of the Nativity at Bethlehem. The foundations date to the time of Constantine, c. 330 A.D. It was built on what was believed to be the site of Jesus' birth.

**Figure 12–22.** The Church of the Nativity, interior. The columns date from Crusader times. The high altar is over the cave where tradition says Jesus was born. During repair of the building, archaeologists found the floor of the Constantinian Church c. 1.5 feet below the main floor shown here.

In more recent times, excavations by Ute Wagner Lux, Kathleen Kenyon, and Israeli archaeologists suggest that the site of the Church of the Holy Sepulchre was outside the walls in Jesus' day. Between the hill of Calvary and the city wall, was a deep rock quarry. This has been confirmed by evidence from under the Church. Restoration and repairs since 1960 have involved a number of excavations which show that the quarry dates back to the seventh century B.C. It was filled in during the first century B.C. and used as a garden or orchard and as a cemetery. Hadrian rebuilt the city after the Second Jewish Revolt in 135 A.D. He built a temple of Aphrodite on this site.[4]

**Figure 12–23.**    The Church of the Holy Sepulchre. The building seen here is basically that of the Crusaders with more recent repairs and additions. It is built over the church built by the Roman Emperor Constantine c. 330 after his mother, Helena, found remains of the true cross in a cave. Earlier, there was a Hadrianic temple here, c. 135, built by Hadrian as part of Aelia Capitolina. It is possible the site was chosen to cover over the Christian site of Calvary and the burial cave of Jesus.

**Figure 12–24.**    The ruins of Gamla in northern Israel are silent reminders of the Jewish zealots' stand against Roman forces. Photo: Israel Talby, photo courtesy Consulate General of Israel (NY).

## B. THE FIRST REVOLT

The First Jewish Revolt, 66–72 A.D., was a watershed for both Jewish and Christian history. The Zealots rebelled against the oppressive regimes of the Procurators, though their agitation over the years was part of the problem, with both sides escalating the issues. Gamla or Gamala was one of the first casualties. The "Masada of the North" was in the Golan Heights up above the northeast corner of the Sea of Galilee. The siege lasted only four weeks. Here too Josephus tells us the defenders committed suicide rather than surrender to the Romans. The Hasmoneans had been here first as well. Their ritual baths have been found and, as at Masada and Herodium, there may have been a synagogue. These three synagogues are the earliest for which we have physical evidence.

What may be the earliest archaeological data for a synagogue is an inscription from Shedia near Alexandria. It is from the time of Ptolemy III Euergetes (246–221 B.C.). The inscription refers to the house of prayer of the Jews. A later Alexandrian inscription is from 37 B.C. A Jewish tradition says the Romans destroyed 480 synagogues in Jerusalem. They have not yet been found. A Roman building under the fourth century A.D. synagogue at Caesarea has been called a house synagogue, possibly to be identified with the "Synagogue of the Revolt" destroyed in 66 A.D. according to the Talmud. A first century A.D. Greek inscription says Theodotus the son of Vettenus built a synagogue for those coming from abroad. Some have related this to Acts 6:9, "The synagogue of the Freedmen."

The destruction of Machaerus, Qumran, the Jerusalem temple, Herodium, and Masada, were cited earlier. It is of interest to note that among the Masada excavations was a Qumran type scroll, that is, one that is identical to a Qumran Cave IV scroll. Yadin interpreted this as suggesting Qumranites (Essenes) were at Masada rather than suggesting that the Qumranites were Zealots or that the Masada defenders were Essenes. Perhaps some of the Qumranites escaped the destruction of the monastery and took refuge at Masada. Perhaps Qumran materials were circulating in Palestine.[5]

## C. TO BE CONTINUED . . .

Just where one ends the history of the people of the Old Testament is a scholarly debate. John Bright ends with Judas the Maccabee's restoration of temple worship. This is reasonable. The book of Daniel is probably involved here. According to many, it is the last or youngest of the Hebrew Scriptures. Thus we come to the end of the Jewish bible, the Tenak, and the Protestant Old Testament. The Eastern Orthodox and Roman Catholic Old Testament, however, contains later material so there is also justification for continuing a bit further, as we do in this text.

**Figure 12–25.** Gamla. Mountaintop view in Israel's north, with a sign telling visitors about Gamla and its siege. Photo: Israel Talby, photo courtesy Consulate General of Israel (NY).

**Figure 12–26.** The Beit Alpha Synagogue had beautiful mosaic floors. It is of interest that showing human and animal figures was acceptable when this floor was created. Photo courtesy Consulate General of Israel (NY).

**Figure 12–27.** The Madaba Map dates from the late 500s, perhaps 600 A.D. It was found heavily damaged but still readable in part. The lower right corner shows the Nile River delta. In the middle is the Dead Sea. The view here is looking toward the east as many ancient maps did, instead of toward the north as today. The faces of the boat men were deliberately removed, perhaps by Muslim conquerors who objected to the representation of any living creature, but the church itself may have been destroyed by Persians in their conquest of 614 A.D. The map is an important part of the history of map making. Photo courtesy the Friends of Archaeology of Amman.

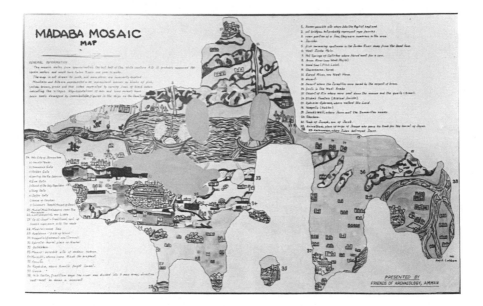

Martin Noth extends his work to 135 A.D. and the Roman crushing of the Second Jewish Revolt in the time of the Emperor Hadrian (117–138 A.D.). This too was a landmark in religious history. The Romans destroyed the city of Jerusalem and rebuilt it as a pagan city, Aelia Capitolina, with a pagan temple in place of the temple of Herod. The Byzantines (Eastern Romans — they had their capital at Byzantium, or Constantinople) continued the Roman Empire and the Roman history of Jerusalem. The excavations of the 1970s have revealed additional elements of this later Aelia Capitolina. These details include the main street or Cardo. It is known from the Byzantine period from a sixth century A.D. map of Jerusalem.

The map is part of a partially preserved map of Palestine, Transjordan, and Egypt now in the floor of a church in Madeba in the area of ancient Moab, in today's Kingdom of Jordan. A portion of the Cardo was excavated in 1976 by Avigad. In the modern rebuilding of the Jewish Quarter of the Old City, the Cardo has been kept open for public viewing.

In time, Aelia Capitolina also disappeared. In 638 A.D., the Muslims took Jerusalem. The Umayyad Caliph Abd el-Malik (685–705) built the Dome of the Rock on the site of Solomon's temple. The Muslim shrine was consecrated in 691. It was refurbished and given an anodized aluminum dome in 1967. The surrounding area is called the Haram esh-Sharif ("the noble sanctuary"). It is sacred to Islam because of their tradition that Muhammad the Prophet visited this site.

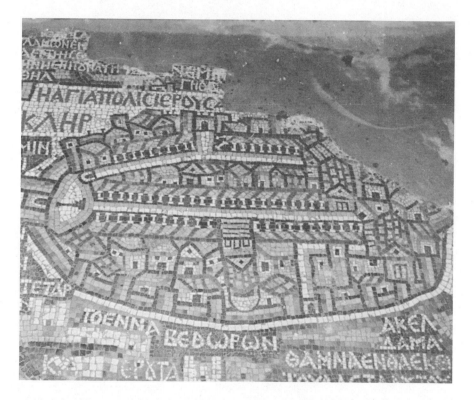

**Figure 12–27B.** The Madaba Map of Jerusalem. The main street north-south is a straight white line. The Church of the Holy Sepulchre appears upside down in the lower middle of the picture. If one stood on the church floor on the Jordan River–Dead Sea side and looked at the map, the Holy Sepulchre would, of course, be "right side up." Photo courtesy of the Jordan Information Bureau, Washington, D.C.

**Figure 12–27C.** The Church of the Apostles, Madaba. This is one of many beautiful mosaics that escaped the iconoclasts. It was probably covered with debris and hidden from view. This supports the theory that these churches were destroyed by Persians 20 years before the 635 A.D. conquest by Muslims who officially tolerated "People of the Book" such as Jews and Christians. Not all Muslims were opposed to representation of living creatures. The Umayyads of Damascus decorated several of their desert castle hunting lodges in elaborate fashion with people, animals and plants.

The crusaders made the Dome of the Rock into a church in 1100 A.D. In 1187, the Muslim leader Saladin recaptured Jerusalem and restored the Muslim and Jewish habitation and traditions. The Romans had barred Jews from the city in 135 A.D. but by the third century, this ban had been relaxed. The Crusaders reinstated it though they had already killed most of the Jews. While the Jews were barred for a time, they did not disappear from the country. Literary references suggest their presence and their synagogues even where we do not have data of archaeology for the second century. Christians were there from the time of Jesus but there is no clear evidence of churches until Constantine.

**Figure 12–28.**   Qasr Amra. A triple vaulted and domed little building with frescoed siesta rooms and ornate steam baths. Built early in the 8th century by the Omayyad Caliph Walid I as a hunting lodge and bath. Ceilings and walls were covered with frescoes. Photo courtesy Jordan Information Bureau, Washington, D.C.

We have moved into and beyond the Talmudic period. Judah the Prince codified the Mishna c. 200 A.D., but its sources go back at least to the first century B.C., to his ancestor, Rabbi Hillel, who lived from c. 60 B.C. to 20 A.D. Hillel the humanist and his conservative opponent, the strict Rabbi Shammai, were Pharisees who were contemporaries of Herod the Great. Christianity usually begins its history with Herod.[6]

**Figure 12–29.** The Cilician Gates. This pass through the Taurus Mountains would have been used by Paul in traveling from his home in Tarsus in the south into the central part of Asia Minor, today's Turkey.

**Figure 12–30.**    Laodicea. The Apostle Paul started a church here.

Thus Herod and the Romans might be a logical stopping place for the main concerns of this book, along with the advance references to Qumran, Masada, and the Zealots which we have already cited. It is tempting to go on with additional descriptions of the magnificent Roman ruins of Jerash, Amman, Bosra, and Caesarea, or the Hadrianic temple remains on Tell el-Ras. The Roman work at Petra and the history of the Nabataeans overlaps the era covered here. The Nabataeans took over the old Edomite territory and the trade routes across southern Palestine. In the time of Paul they had extended their control up the old King's Highway from the Gulf of Aqaba (Elath), Tell Hesban, Ammon, Jerash, and Umm el-Jimal (the black basalt city in the desert) to Damascus.[7]

**Figure 12–31.** Ephesus. Paul worked here for several years. The Letter to the Ephesians is traditionally for the church here.

**Figure 12–32.** Mars Hill in Athens. Paul preached to the philosophers here, on the side of the Acropolis, but had little response.

**Figure 12–33.** The Shops and Forum of Corinth are inspected by Dr. Roger Boraas of Upsala College. Paul worked here for several years. The First and Second Letters to the Corinthians are traditionally his letters to the church he established here.

Some word should be said about the scrolls found in caves in the Wadi Muraba'at and Nahal Hever. They are from the time of (and some are in the hand of) Bar Kochba or Koseba, whom Rabbi Akiba hailed as the messiah, the son of the star (Numbers 24:17) in the Second Revolt. And thus we could move on into the first millennium of the present era, with the later Romans, the Byzantines, and the Arabs and their Muslim successors, not to mention the Christians including the later Crusaders whose castles still dot the land. We could follow the Apostle Paul through Turkey and Greece and on to mighty Rome with all the archaeological remains along the way. We could explore plans and mosaics of the early synagogues and churches including those at Dura Europas (c. 250 A.D.) on the Euphrates River in Syria and in other parts of the Roman Empire. The fabulous fourth century A.D. manuscripts of Nag Hammadi or Chenoboskion in Egypt could be considered, because of their importance for understanding early Christianity and Gnosticism. But we need to stop somewhere. Or shall we say, in the words of an old friend, "To be continued . . ."[8]

**Figure 12–34.**    The Apostle Paul appealed to Caesar to make sure he got a fair trial, a right of every Roman citizen.

**Figure 12–35.** The Roman Forum and the Senate building (on the left).

**Figure 12–36.** The Triumphal Arch of Titus, conqueror of Jerusalem. Inside, a bas-relief shows Jewish captives carrying a menorrah, a seven branched candlestick, perhaps loot from the Temple before it was destroyed in 70 A.D.

**Figure 12–37.**    The Colosseum where later Christians were thrown to the lions.

**Figure 12–38.**    The interior of the Colosseum. The floor is gone. The pillars beyond the gate are the walls of underground rooms and dungeons where the wild animals and prisoners were kept.

# NOTES

1. Nigel Turner, "Hasmoneans," IDB 2, pp. 529–535. IECW, pp. 368–369 (Pompey), 45 (Antipater), 232–233 (Herod the Great), 233 (Antipas). Michael M. Grant, *Herod the Great* (London: Weidenfeld and Nicolson, 1971). Samuel Sandmel, "Herod (Family)," IDB 2, pp. 585–594. August Strobel, "Observations About the Roman Installations at Mukawer," ADAJ 19 (1974), pp. 101–127. Stanislas Loffreda, "Preliminary Report on the Second Season of Excavations at Qal'at el-Mishnaqa — Machaerus," ADAJ 25 (1981), pp. 85–94. Nigel Turner, "Machaerus," IDB 3, pp. 217–218. William R. Farmer, "John the Baptist," IDB 2, pp. 955–962. Harry Thomas Frank, "Herodian Fortresses," IDBSV, pp. 408–409. A. Segal, "Herodium," IEJ 23, no. 1 (1973), pp. 27–29. Ehud Netzer, "Searching for Herod's Tomb," BAR 9, no. 3 (May/June 83), pp. 30–51. Herod was supposedly buried at Herodium. E. Jerry Vardaman, "Herodium: A Brief Assessment of Recent Suggestions," IEJ 25, no. 1 (1975), pp. 45–46, and, "A History of Herodium," (pp. 58–81 in *The Teacher's Yoke* ed. Vardaman and J.L. Garrett; Waco: Word, 1964). Thomas O. Hall, Jr., "Herodium," IDBSV, pp. 409–410. Gideon Foerster, "Herodium," EAEHL, pp. 502–510. Robert W. Funk, "Herodium," IDB 2, pp. 595–596, and, "Masada," IDB 3: pp. 293–294. Yadin, *Masada: Herod's Fortress and the Zealot's Last Stand* (New York: Random House, 1966); "Masada," EAEHL, pp. 793–816; and, "Masada," IDBSV, pp. 577–580. SBAF, pp. 429–438. Robert J. Bull, ed., *The Joint Expedition to Caesarea Maritima*, Vol. I of Charles T. Fritsch, et al., *Studies in the History of Caesarea Maritima* (Missoula: Scholars Press, 1975). Bull, "Caesarea," IDBSV, p. 120; and, "Caesarea Maritima: The Search for Herod's City," BAR 8, no. 3 (May/June 82), pp. 24–40. Janet Crisler, "Caesarea World Monument," BAR 8, no. 3, p. 41. Robert L. Hohlfelder, "Caesarea Beneath the Sea," BAR 8, no. 3, pp. 42–47, 56. Hohlfelder, et al., "Sebastos: Herod's Harbor at Caesarea Maritima," BA 46, no. 3 (Sum. 83), pp. 133–143. Abraham Negev, "Caesarea," EAEHL, pp. 270–274, 279–285. David C. Pellett, "Caesarea," IDB 1, pp. 479–480. John H. Humphrey, "A Summary of the 1973 Excavations in the Caesarea Hippodrome," BASOR 218 (Ap. 75), pp. 1–24. Gus W. Van Beek, "Samaria," IDBSV, pp. 182–188. Avigad, "Samaria," EAEHL, pp. 1032–1050. Siegfried H. Horn, "Heshbon," EAEHL, pp. 510–514. Victor R. Gold, "Hebron," IDB 2, pp. 575–577; and, "Mamre," IDB 3, p. 235. Shimon Appelbaum, "Mamre," EAEHL, pp. 776–778. Netzer, "Herod's Tomb." James L. Kelso and Dimitri C. Baramki, *The Excavation of New Testament Jericho* (Cambridge: AASOR 29–30, 1955). James B. Pritchard, *The Excavation of Herodian Jericho 1951* (Cambridge: AASOR, 1958). Finegan, *Archaeology of the New Testament*. WBA, pp. 221–247. Lee I. Levine, "Archaeological Discoveries from the Greco-Roman Era," (pp. 75–87 in *Recent Archaeology in the Land of Israel* ed. Hershel Shanks and Benjamin Mazar; Jerusalem and Washington: IES and Biblical Archaeology Society, 1984).
2. Meir Ben-Dov, "Temple of Herod," IDBSV, pp. 870–872; and, *In the Shadow of the Temple*; San Francisco: Harper & Row, 1986. William F. Stinespring, "Temple, Jerusalem," IDB 4, pp. 534–560. Carol L. Meyers, "The Elusive Temple," BA 45, no. 1 (Wint. 82), pp. 33–41. Michael Avi-yonah, "Jerusalem," EAEHL, pp. 597–627. Mazar, *The Mountain of the Lord* (Garden City: Doubleday, 1975); "Excavations Near Temple Mount Reveal Splendors of Herodian Jerusalem," BAR 6, no. 4 (July/Aug. 80), pp. 44–59; and, "Herodian Jerusalem in the Light of the Excavations South and Southwest of the Temple Mount," IEJ 28, nos. 4 (1978), pp. 230–237. Yadin, ed., *Jerusalem Revealed* (Jerusalem: IES, 1975). Ruth Amiran and Yael Israeli, "Jerusalem," IDBSV, pp. 475–477. Aaron Demsky, "When the Priests Trumpeted the Onset of the Sabbath," BAR 12, no. 6 (Nov./Dec. 86), pp. 50–52. J. Basil Hennessy, "Preliminary Report of Excavations at the Damascus Gate Jerusalem, 1964–66," *Levant* 2 (1970), pp. 2–27. Cedric N. Johns, "The Citadel," QDAP 14 (1950), pp. 121–190. Hillel Geva, "The 'Tower of David' — Phasael or Hippicus?" IEJ 31, nos. 1–2 (1981), pp. 57–65. Avigad, *Archaeological Discoveries in the Jewish Quarter of*

*Jerusalem: Second Temple Period* (Jerusalem: IES and The Israeli Museum, 1976); "How the Wealthy Lived in Herodian Jerusalem," BAR 2, no. 4 (Dec. 76), pp. 1, 23–35; and, "Jerusalem — 'The City Full of People'," (pp. 129–140 in Shanks and Mazar, *Recent Archaeology*. "Herod's Family Tomb in Jerusalem," BAR 9, no. 3 (May/June 83), pp. 52–59, suggests the traditional tomb near the King David Hotel is not that of Herod's family. He thinks the site is north of the Damascus Gate at a site discovered over a hundred years ago by Conrad Schick.

3. James F. Strange and Hershel Shanks, "Synagogues Where Jesus Preached Found at Capernaum," BAR 9, no. 6 (Nov./Dec. 83), pp. 24–31; and, "Has the House Where Jesus Stayed in Capernaum Been Found?" BAR 7, no. 6 (Nov./Dec. 82), pp. 26–37. Strange, "Capernaum," IDBSV, pp. 140–141. Strange and Eric M. Meyers, *Archaeology, The Rabbis and Early Christianity* (Nashville: Abingdon, 1981). The Franciscan Friar Gaudentius Orfali excavated at Capernaum in the 1920s. Since 1968, the work has been carried on by two Franciscan fathers, Virgilio Corbo and Stanislas Loffreda. Corbo, *The House of St. Peter at Capharnaum* (Jerusalem: Franciscan Press, 1969). Loffreda, "The Late Chronology of the Synagogue of Capernaum," IEJ 23 (1973), pp. 37–42; and, *A Visit to Capharnaum* (6th ed.; Jerusalem: Franciscan Printing Press, 1978). G. Bushnell, *New Memoirs of Saint Peter by the Sea of Galilee* (Jerusalem: Franciscan, 1969). Igzazio Mancini, *Archaeological Discoveries Relative to the Judeaeo-Christians* (Jerusalem: Franciscan, 1970), pp. 100–105. Avigad, "Capernaum," EAEHL, pp. 286–290. Pellet, "Capernaum," IDB 1, pp. 532–534. Baruch Kanael, *Die Kunst der Antiken Synagoge* (Munchen: Ner-Tamid-Verlag, 1961), pp. 18–25. James L. Kelso, *An Archaeologist Looks at the Gospels* (Waco: Word, 1969). Finegan, *Archaeology of the New Testament*, pp. 50–56. Yoram Tsafir, "Ancient Churches," pp. 97–107 in Shanks and Mazar, *Recent Archaeology*.

4. John Wilkinson, *Jerusalem as Jesus Knew It: Archaeology as Evidence* (London: Thames and Hudson, 1978). Kenneth W. Clark, "Antonia, Tower of," IDB 1, pp. 153–154. D.J. Wieand, "John V.2 and the Pool of Bethesda," *New Testament Studies* 12 (1965–1966), pp. 392–404. Clark, "Beth-Zatha," IDB 1, p. 404. Pellet, "Jacob's Well," IDB 2, p. 787. S.G.F. Brandon, *The Fall of Jerusalem and the Christian Church* (London: SPCK, 1978). Robert H. Smith, "Holy Sepulchre, Church of," IDBSV, pp. 413–415. Clark, "Holy Sepulchre," IDB 2, pp. 625–626. Charles Couasnon, *The Church of the Holy Sepulchre* (London: Oxford University, 1974). Joachim Jeremias, *Jerusalem in the Time of Jesus* (Philadelphia: Fortress, 1969). Gabriel Barkay and Amos Kloner, "Jerusalem Tombs from the Days of the First Temple," BAR 12, no. 2 (Mar./Ap. 86), pp. 22–39. Barkay, "The Garden Tomb," ibid., pp. 40–53, 55–56. Rolling stone tombs are found at the Tombs of the Kings of Adiabene, first century A.D., north of the Damascus Gate and Herod's Gate, and at the traditional site of Herod's family tomb in West Jerusalem across the valley from the Jaffa Gate, near the King David Hotel. Cf. also the examples at Tell Hesban cited earlier. See also Joseph A. Kohlbeck and Eugenia L. Nitowski (Sister Damian), "New Evidence May Explain Image on Shroud of Turin," BAR 12, no. 4 (July/Aug. 86), pp. 18–29. Sister Damian "studied sixty-one rolling stone tombs in Palestine/Transjordan, dating from the Early Roman through Byzantine periods (63 B.C. to 640 A.D.)." Dan Bahat, "Does the Holy Sepulchre Church Mark the Burial of Jesus?" BAR 12, no. 3 (May/June 86), pp. 26–45.

5. Helmut Merkel, "Zealot," IDBSV, pp. 979–982. William R. Farmer, "Zealot," IDB 4, pp. 936–938. "Gamla: The Masada of the North," BAR 5, no. 1 (Jan./Feb. 79), pp. 12–19. Lee I. Levine, *Ancient Synagogues Revealed* (Jerusalem: IES, 1981). Isaiah Sonne, "Synagogue," IDB 4, pp. 476–491. Hershel Shanks, *Judaism in Stone: The Archaeology of Ancient Synagogues* (New York: Harper & Row, 1979). Pierson Parker, "Freedman, Synagogue of," IDB 2, p. 325. Eric M. Meyers, "Synagogue, Architecture," IDBSV, pp. 842–844; "Ancient Synagogues in Galilee: Their Religious and Cultural Setting," BA 43, no. 2 (Ap. 80), pp. 97–108; and, "Synagogues of Galilee," *Archaeology* 35, no. 3 (May/June 82), pp. 51–58. Meyers, et al., *Ancient Synagogue Excavations at Khirbet Shema', Upper Galilee, Israel, 1970–1973* (Durham: Duke University,

AASOR 42, 1976). Michael Avi-Yonah, "Caesarea: The Synagogue," EAEHL, pp. 277–279; and, "Synagogues," EAEHL, pp. 1129–1138. WBA, pp. 221–247. Yadin, *Masada*. Doren Chen, "The Design of the Ancient Synagogues in Judah: Masada and Herodium," BASOR 239 (Sum. 80), pp. 37–40. Moshe Dothan, "Research on Ancient Synagogues in the Land of Israel," pp. 89–96 in Shanks and Mazar, *Recent Archaeology*.

6. BHI. Noth, *The History of Israel* (New York: Harper & Brothers, 1958). Avi-Yonah, *Jerusalem The Holy* (New York: Shocken, 1976); and, "Medeba," EAEHL, pp. 819–823. Edward D. Grohman, "Medeba," IDB 3, pp. 318–319. "The Ancient Cardo is Discovered in Jerusalem," BAR 2, no. 4 (Dec. 76), pp. 19–21. Rivka Gonen, "Keeping Jerusalem's Past Alive," BAR 7, no. 4 (July/Aug. 81), pp. 16–23. Chen, "Dating the Cardo Maximus in Jerusalem," PEQ 114 (Jan./June 82), pp. 43–45. Robert L. Wilken, "From Time Immemorial? Dwellers in the Holy Land," *The Christian Century* 103, no. 23 (30 July – 6 Aug. 86), pp. 678–680. Judah Goldin, "Hillel (The Elder)," IDB 2, p. 605. Albright, AOP.

7. Carl H. Kraeling, ed., *Gerasa* (New Haven: ASOR, 1938). Rami G. Khouri, *Jerash* (New York: Longman, 1986); and, "A Jewel in Jordan: The Greco-Roman City of Jerash," *Archaeology* 38, no. 1 (Jan./Feb. 85), pp. 18–25. Crystal-Margaret Bennett, "Excavations at the Citadel (al Qal'a), Amman, 1977," ADAJ 23 (1979), pp. 151–159; and, "Excavations on the Citadel (al Qal'a), Amman, 1978," ibid., pp. 161–176. Adnan Hadidi, "The Excavation of the Roman Forum at Amman (Philadelphia), 1964–1967," ADAJ 19 (1974), pp. 71–91. Nelson Glueck, *Deities and Dolphins: The Story of the Nabataeans* (New York: Farrar, Strasuss, and Giroux, 1965). John I. Lawlor, *The Nabataeans in Historical Perspective* (Grand Rapids: Baker, 1974). Philip C. Hammond, *The Nabataeans — Their History, Culture and Archaeology* (Goteborg: Paul Astroms Forlag, 1973); "New Light on the Nabataeans," BAR 7, no. 2 (Mar./Ap. 81), pp. 22–41; "New Evidence for the Fourth Century A.D. Destruction of Petra," BASOR 238 (Sep. 80), pp. 65–67; and, "Petra, the Timeless," *Archaeology* 39, no. 1 (Jan./Feb. 86), pp. 18–25. Abraham Negev, "Petra," EAEHL, pp. 943–959. Ian Browning, *Petra* (Park Ridge, NJ: Noyes Press, 1973). Simon Cohen, "Nabataeans," IDB 3, pp. 491–493. John R. Bartlett, "From Edomites to Nabataeans: A Study in Continuity," PEQ 110 (Jul.–Dec. 78), pp. 53–66. Bert De Vries, "Research at Umm el-Jimal, Jordan, 1972–1977," BA 42, no. 1 (Wint. 79), pp. 49–55.

8. Yadin, *The Finds From the Bar-Kokhba Period in the Cave of Letters* (Jerusalem: IES, 1963); and, *Bar-Kokhba* (London: Weidenfeld and Nicolson, 1971). Joseph Aviram, et al., "Judean Desert Caves," EAEHL, pp. 665–694. Joshua Prawer, "Archaeological Research on the Crusader Period," (pp. 115–126 in Shanks and Mazar, *Recent Archaeology*. Kelso, *An Archaeologist Looks*; and, *An Archaeologist Follows the Apostle Paul* (Waco: Word, 1970). Edwin Yamauchi, *The Archaeology of New Testament Cities in Western Asia Minor* (Grand Rapids: Baker, 1980). Mancini, "Archaeological Discoveries." Finegan, *Archaeology of the New Testament*. "Churches," EAEHL, pp. 303–313. Rudolf Cohen, "Monasteries," EAEHL, pp. 876–885. Clark Hopkins, *The Discovery of Dura Europas* (New Haven: Yale University, 1979). Andrew K. Helmbold, *The Nag Hammadi Gnostic Texts and the Bible* (Grand Rapids: Baker, 1967). James M. Robinson, ed., *The Nag Hammadi Library* (New York: Harper & Row, 1977); and, "The Discovery of the Nag Hammadi Codices," BA 42, no. 4 (Fall 79), pp. 200–224. Bastiaan Van Elderin, "The Nag Hammadi Excavation," BA 42, no. 4 (Fall 79), pp. 225–231. Geroge W. MacRae, "Nag Hammadi," IDBSV, pp. 613–619. Enid Schmuch, "Research Team Explores Mediterranean Background of Early Christianity," *Harvard Divinity Bulletin* 12, no. 5 (June–July 82), pp. 10–13.

# ADDITIONAL READING

Adler, Rudolph J. *Biblical Beginnings: Archaeology and the Roots of Scripture.* Englewood Cliffs: Prentice-Hall, 1985.

Blaiklock, E.M. *The Archaeology of the New Testament.* Nashville: Nelson, 1984.

Boyd, Robert T. *A Pictorial Guide to Biblical Archaeology.* Eugene, OR: Harvest House, 1981.

Bronner, E. Raymond. *King Solomon's Temple.* Thousand Oaks, CA: Artisan Sales, 1979.

Bronner, Leah. *Biblical Personalities and Archaeology.* New York: Bloch, 1975.

Castel, Francois. *History of Israel and Judah From the Beginnings to the Second Century A.D.* Mahwah, NJ: Paulist, 1985.

Chiat, Marilyn. *Handbook of Synagogue Architecture.* Decatur, GA: Scholars Press, 1982.

Cornfeld, Gaalyah and Freedman, David Noel, eds. *Archaeology of the Bible — Book by Book.* San Francisco: Harper & Row, 1982.

Davis, John J. and Whitcomb, Jonn C. *A History of Israel.* Grand Rapids, MI: Baker, 1980.

Grant, Michael. *The History of Ancient Israel.* New York: Scribner, 1984.

Hadidi, Adnan, ed. *Studies in the History and Archaeology of Jordan II.* Amman: Department of Antiquities, 1985.

Harrison, R.K. *Major Cities of the Biblical World.* Nashville: Nelson, 1985.

Hoppe, Leslie J. *What Are They Saying About Biblical Archaeology?* Mahwah, NJ: Paulist, 1984.

Lewis, Jack. *Archaeology and the Bible.* Abilene, TX: Bible Research, 1975.

Lewis, Jack. *The Archaeological Background to Bible People.* Grand Rapids: Baker, 1981.

Millard, A.R. *The Bible: What Can Archaeology Prove?* Phillipsburg, NJ: Presbyterian and Reformed, 1982.

Murphy-O'Connor, Jerome. *The Holy Land: An Archaeological Guide from Earliest Times to 1700.* New York: Oxford, 1980.

Neilson, Francis. *From Ur to Nazareth.* Brooklyn: Revisionist Press, n.d.

Orlinsky, Harry M. *Understanding the Bible Through History and Archaeology.* Hoboken, NJ: Ktav, 1969.

Orlinsky, Harry M. *The Israel Exploration Journal Reader.* 2 vols.; Hoboken, NJ: Ktav, 1982.

Parmalee, Alice. *A History of the People of Israel.* Wilton, CT: Morehouse, 1980.

Perkins, Ann L. *The Comparative Archaeology of Early Mesopotamia.* Chicago: Oriental Institute, 1977.

Powell, Ivor. *Bible Treasures.* Grand Rapids: Kregel, 1985.

Ramsey, William M. *Letters to the Seven Churches.* Grand Rapids: Baker, 1985.

Sawyer, John F. and Clines, David J. *Midian, Moab, Edom: The History and Archaeology of Late Bronze and Iron Age Jordan and North-West Arabia.* Winona Lake, IN: Eisenbrauns, 1983.

Soggin, J. Albert. *A History of Ancient Israel.* Philadelphia: Westminster, 1985.

van der Woude, A.S., ed. *The World of the Bible.* Grand Rapids: Eerdmans, 1985.

Vos, Howard F. *Archaeology in Bible Lands.* Chicago: Moody, 1977.

Vos, Howard F. *An Introduction to Bible Archaeology.* Chicago: Moody, 1983.

Wiseman, Donald J., and Yamauchi, Edwin. *Archaeology and the Bible.* Grand Rapids: Zondervan, 1979.

Wiseman, P.J. and D.J. *Ancient Records and the Structure of Genesis: A Case for Literary Unity.* Nashville: Nelson, 1985.

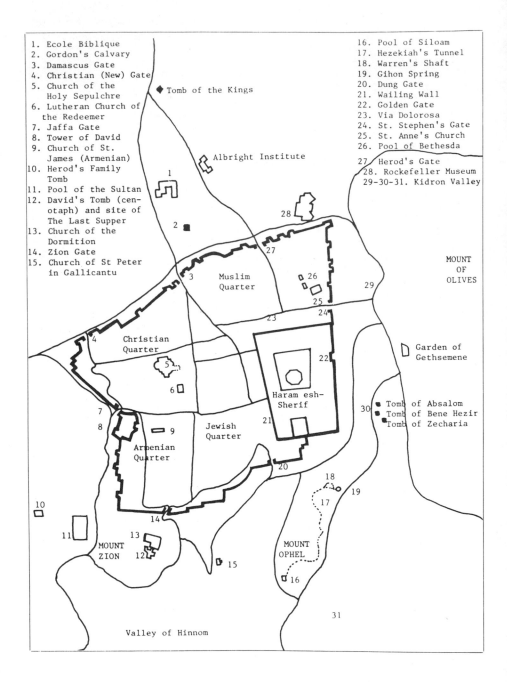

1. Ecole Biblique
2. Gordon's Calvary
3. Damascus Gate
4. Christian (New) Gate
5. Church of the
   Holy Sepulchre
6. Lutheran Church of
   the Redeemer
7. Jaffa Gate
8. Tower of David
9. Church of St.
   James (Armenian)
10. Herod's Family
    Tomb
11. Pool of the Sultan
12. David's Tomb (cen-
    otaph) and site of
    The Last Supper
13. Church of the
    Dormition
14. Zion Gate
15. Church of St Peter
    in Gallicantu

16. Pool of Siloam
17. Hezekiah's Tunnel
18. Warren's Shaft
19. Gihon Spring
20. Dung Gate
21. Wailing Wall
22. Golden Gate
23. Via Dolorosa
24. St. Stephen's Gate
25. St. Anne's Church
26. Pool of Bethesda

27. Herod's Gate
28. Rockefeller Museum
29-30-31. Kidron Valley

Tomb of the Kings

Albright Institute

MOUNT
OF
OLIVES

Muslim
Quarter

Christian
Quarter

Garden of
Gethsemene

Haram esh-
Sherif

Tomb of Absalom
Tomb of Bene Hezir
Tomb of Zecharia

Jewish
Quarter

Armenian
Quarter

MOUNT
ZION

MOUNT
OPHEL

Valley of Hinnom

Sketch Plan of Jerusalem (Drawn by Joyce E. Thompson)

# ARCHAEOLOGY AND RELIGION

Archaeologists have been digging up temples and altars and the material remains of religion ever since archaeology began. They have also excavated remains of related interest such as burial remains, which may indicate something about beliefs, concerning the afterlife, a religious concept. Religion is also a major aspect of many of the inscriptions found by travelers and diggers since time immemorial. If one thinks of religion only in terms of the supernatural or of pure spirit, it could be said that archaeology really has nothing to do with religion. We do not dig up God although we occasionally dig up gods and we do not dig up Spirit though we come upon the reflections of spirits from time to time. But of course religion is far more than this. Or to put it in more immediate terms, excavation reveals the human aspects of faith even though it does not uncover the Subject.

# CHAPTER 13

# Artifacts in Religious Perspective

## A. CAVEATS

"Let the buyer beware" is an old caveat, or warning. The warning here concerns the narrow view that theology consists only of systematic theology. This view would restrict theology and perhaps all of religion to non-material concepts or dogmas about faith. One is reminded of the old cliche that "some folks are so heavenly minded, they are no earthly good." What does "archaeo-logy" — the study of the old — have to do with "theo-logy" — the study of God? The "old" is something dug up, not an abstract idea about God. While Psalm 18 may say that God has a nose, it also says God is a Spirit. We do not dig up too many spirits in excavation, let alone the Spirit of the Living God. George E. Mendenhall has suggested there is a tremendous gulf between archaeology and theology.[1]

While theology is literally the study of God, in common usage it means the study of religion. It might be restricted to the study of ideas about religion, although theology is sometimes concerned with the ideas behind the use and design of material things such as altars and buildings. Theology is also involved in the application of ideas, as in ethics. There are more definitions, but here perhaps, it is enough to caution against too strict an interpretation of theology as being only a matter of ideas or only concerned with the non-material.

On the other hand, archaeology seems to be only a matter of material artifacts which have survived the centuries. However, by their material location, design, and other characteristics, these artifacts suggest the ideas of their makers and builders. This point is particularly clear in prehistoric archaeology. Here, the only source of human ideas, including theology, is in the material artifact alone. A specific example of this might be the shrines and religious art, dating back to 7000 B.C., found at Chatal Huyuk in Turkey. The usual eroticism is lacking, leading the excavator to suggest that "If the Chatal Huyuk religion is a creation of women, one has the rare opportunity of exploring Neolithic woman's mind by studying the symbolism she used in her effort to comprehend and influence the mysteries of life and death."

Geoffrey Bibby notes that the body found in a Danish bog had his throat cut and in addition had a specially twisted rope, a "torque," as a hangman's noose around his throat. Bibby admits that "archaeologists have often been accused of calling in hypothetical gods and cult practice whenever they find anything they cannot explain by obvious mundane means . . . But how else is one to explain . . ." this find except as a sacrifice to a fertility goddess?[2]

We may indeed be over-interpreting. Yet, for any time period, it is legitimate to ask questions about material artifacts. How were these things used? Why did they make them this way? Why did they make this item of gold instead of stone? Why did they use these at all? In one sense, it is true that we are digging up things. But actually, we are digging up people.

In this line of inquiry, however, there is a very real scale of increasing difficulty as we move from one question to another.

The interpretation of prehistoric (pre-written records) data, says C.F.C. Hawkes, includes four "inferences." We can find out how things were made simply by appropriate examination. Describing economic structures from the archaeological data is more difficult but still relatively easy. The social, political, or religious organization is something else again. Take, for example, the foundation of a large hut. It is obviously significant. Was it a chief's hut, or a medicine man's? Was it a temple, or some other public building? The fourth inference, and the most difficult, concerns religious institutions and spiritual life. On the basis of material remains, what did people believe? Hawkes claimed that the degree of difficulty is related to the move from the material to the non-material, from the generically animal to the more specifically human.[3]

L.S.B. Leakey suggested that about 100,000 years ago, people began to have abstract thoughts — to invent the world of spirits, supernatural beings, and gods; to take an interest in nature and the environment. While the context of his assertion does not specify the basis for his conclusion, the list of evidence would include burials with artifacts which presumably were for use of the dead in some type of afterlife. Albright suggested religion began 150,000 years ago. Neanderthal people were the first people that we know about who gave a definite burial to the dead. The body was in a flexed, fetal position on its side, with stones set around it to form an oval. The body had been sprinkled with red ochre which may have symbolized blood or life. To be sure, we do not know that this was a burial, in the sense that we can "prove" it, but it is a reasonable "inference" or interpretation. The suggested dates for this beginning are, of course, speculative. One could speculate that abstract thoughts and religion were present with the first human beings — "the more specifically human." Melvin Konner, a biological anthropologist at Harvard, uses the figure, 10 million years, for the dawn of awe, of sacred attentiveness, of wonder. He calls wonder the hallmark of our species. In any case, one need hardly limit the beginning of thought to the appearance of burials or artifacts in graves. That is only our first material evidence of such thought.[4]

## B. THE BIBLE

We are not limited, of course, to speechless walls and artifacts. Among the material things archaeologists find are writings — letters, inscriptions, myths, records, and notes. These writings reflect the ideas of people in that day, as well as their history, daily life, economy, hopes, fears, children, politics, and religion. The writings discovered by archeologists, and the Bible itself, are literary. Thus biblical archaeology is not limited to the interpretation of non-literary artifacts. The Bible is a book of religion. Theology, in the broad sense noted earlier, is the study of religion. As a book of religion, then, the Bible is a book of theology, or a theological book. To be sure, there are those who would call it a book of life rather than theology. And there are other labels one could give it. The Bible has been studied sociologically and historically. It can be studied for its psychological insights, its philosophical insights, and even its scientific data. But in the end, its significance in the world, and specifically the Western world, has been its religious significance as the foundation of Judaism, Christianity, and Islam. Specifically too, it has been not simply a source of inspiration but an authority and a symbol of authority. We hear references to the "bible" of the auto mechanic, or of the social worker, or of the government bureaucrat. *The* Bible, this foundation, this source of inspiration, this authority, is theological.[5]

When the Palestine Exploration Fund of Great Britain was started in 1865, its aims were to investigate the archaeology, topography, geology, geography, manners, and customs of Palestine, "for biblical illustration." The essence of it all is in the last two words, as Kathleen Kenyon has pointed out.[6] This "biblical illustration," or "illumination," was a major motive in the beginnings of biblical archaeology. Since the document is theological, one could argue that biblical illumination is a theological concern and biblical archaeology is a theological enterprise. This may be overstating the case. From the Jewish, Christian, and Islamic perspectives, everything is theological. Since the universe was created by God, and since human life is meaningless apart from its Creator, all existence, i.e., everything, has theological significance. But in common language, this overstates the case. Most people do not think that the color of a person's hair has theological significance, especially in this day of color rinses! The color red, as for blood, has theological significance. It was a *red* heifer that the Hebrews were to sacrifice and burn to ashes for their purification. Our folklore says a redhead is supposed to have a sharp temper. But one would hardly move from such examples as these to the idea that "red" has to have theological significance every time it appears, whether on a barn, in the name of a ball club, a car, or a sunset. So one could question the idea that everything in the Bible is theological and since biblical archaeology illuminates the Bible, that everything about biblical archaeology *must* be theological.

In fact, this motivation for archaeology has rendered biblical scholars suspect as scientists. Some have claimed that biblical scholars are out to "prove" the Bible. There are literalists who would like to see this as archaeology's primary purpose (see apologetics, later). But the attack is unwarranted. G. Ernest Wright noted the origins of modern Palestinian or biblical archaeology in the humanist concern for historical research. The interest in proving the veracity of the Bible was an afterthought. Indeed, the initial discoveries, such as that of the Babylonian flood tradition, if anything, created difficulties for the literalist position.

Biblical archaeology is a science in its own right, with the limits and responsibilities of other science. This means using scientific methods in gathering data. This means examining that data and interpreting it as objectively and as honestly as possible. Albright welcomed the entry of Japanese archaeologists into the Near East. Their Buddhist and Shinto backgrounds would not have a biblical bias. Albright thought that if we have been as scientific as we should have been, our results and those of the Japanese archaeologists will be the same. It should hardly be necessary to add that archaeology as a science includes the interpretation of its data. Certainly chemical, nuclear, sociological, botanical, and other scientific data can be utilized by others outside the specific discipline. It is not inconceivable that a chemist might make a discovery which he would then ignore. Normally, however, a chemist is interested in the interpretation, significance, and relevance of his discovery and of chemistry in general. An archaeologist is interested in artifacts, including inscriptions, his own discoveries, and those of others. That interest rarely stops with the discovery, but continues to the interpretation, and the use of the new knowledge.[7]

This concern with illuminating the Bible may seem to contradict all that was said earlier. Actually, this is not the case because the Bible remains a theological book. What then, is the relevance of the science of archaeology to biblical theology? Relevance is a matter of application. Physics becomes relevant to biology when a radioactive isotope is used to trace the circulation of the blood. The techniques and methods of astronomy become relevant to biblical studies when astronomy can be used to date a biblical event. A raid by an Assyrian king can be dated because his reign is dated in the modern calendar. The lists of Assyrian kings can be synchronized with an eclipse or astral movements. The techniques and methods of scientific archaeology become relevant to biblical studies when this scientific data is applied to the life and times of people and events in the Bible. This brings us back to where we started — the Bible is a theological work. Biblical archaeology does not prove biblical theory, but it illuminates a theological book. In this sense, biblical archaeology is a theological activity.

There is more than this, however. Theology is not a single, monolithic thing and never has been. It has developed in the Western world into several different branches.[8]

# NOTES

1. Mendenhall, "Between Theology and Archaeology," *Journal for the Study of the Old Testament* 7 (1978), pp. 28–34. He notes that the Bible will be understood in its own context by neither discipline in isolation. Gordon Kaufman has declared that "The proper business of theology (theos-logos) is the analysis, criticism and reconstruction of the image/concept of God. . ." The straitjacket is loosened, however, by his conclusion "that theology should now be conceived as essentially the attempt to construct imaginatively a theistic worldview." See his "Theology as Imaginative Construction," JAAR 50, no. 1 (Mar. 82), pp. 73–79. My suggestion is that archaeology provides the imagination with a few things to work with for its reconstruction. In fact, without those things, we would not even know what the worldview was except as an imaginary construct.

   My own struggle with a definition of theology turns on a Christian who said theology is Christian and only Christian. He said that I have no right to apply the term to other aspects of religion, or other religions. This latter view and Kaufman's original thesis would eliminate most of what has been practiced throughout Christian history as theology, the Queen of the Sciences. To speak to the latter speaker's narrow, jingoistic chauvanism, Giles Gunn takes Kaufman to mean "that theological reflection is an intellectual activity generic to virtually all religious traditions rather than specific to one." See his "On the Relation Between Theology and Art in the Work of Gordon D. Kaufman, JAAR 50, no. 1 (Mar. 82), pp. 87–91. Any similarity in all this to archaeology as a vendetta, is purely intentional. See further notes 7 and 8.

2. Jacquetta Hawkes, ed., *The History of Mankind: Prehistory*, Vol. I, Part 1; (New York: Mentor, 1963). V. Gordon Childe, *What Happened in History?* (rev.; Baltimore: Penguin, 1965), p. 22. James Mellaart, "A Neolithic City in Turkey," SA 210, no. 4 (1964), pp. 94–104. Geoffrey Bibby, "The Body in the Bog," Horizon 10, no. 1 (Wint. [Jan.] 68), pp. 45–51. Sir Mortimer Wheeler, *Alms for Oblivion* (London: Weidenfeld and Nicolson, 1966), pp. 47–72. L.R. Binford, "Archaeology as Anthropology," *American Antiquity* 28 (1962), pp. 217–225. S.R. and L.R. Binford, eds., *New Perspectives in Archaeology* (Chicago: Aldine, 1968). Gordon R. Willey, "A Consideration of Archaeology," *Daedalus* 106, no. 3 (Sum. 77), pp. 81–95.

3. C.F.C. Hawkes, "Archaeological Theories and Methods: Some Suggestions from the Old World," *The American Anthropologist* 56 (1954), pp. 161–162. A similar caution is voiced by Berta Stjern-quist who then proceeds with her interpretation in "New Light on Spring-cults in Scandinavian Prehistory," *Archaeology* 17 (1964), p. 180. D.P. Dymond pleads for total archaeology, in which

we include material and non-material (i.e., all) aspects of our subject. *Archaeology and History: A Plea for Reconciliation* (London: Thames and Hudson, 1974). Carolyn Elliott, "The Religious Beliefs of the Ghassulians c. 4000–3000 B.C.," *PEQ* 109 (Jan.–June 77), pp. 3–25.

4. Barbara Tuffy, "The Ascent of Man," SN 91 (25 Feb. 67), p. 188. Childe, *What Happened?*, p. 21. Shirley Gorenstein, *Introduction to Archaeology* (New York: Basic Books, 1965), pp. 143–145. Albright, "The Impact of Archaeology on Biblical Research—1966," FGNDBA, pp. 1–14. G.F.S. Brandon, "The Origins of Religion: Theory and Archaeology," *History Today* 17, no. 4 (Ap. 67), pp. 264–271. Konner, "The Tangled Wing," *Psychology Today* 16, no. 5 (May 82), pp. 91–2.

5. Henry O. Thompson, *Approaches to the Bible* (Syracuse: Center for Instructional Communication, 1967). For the sociological approach, see especially the works of Norman K. Gottwald, e.g., *The Tribes of Yahweh* (Maryknoll: Orbis, 1979). Cf. also his "John Bright's New Revision of A History of Israel," BAR 8, no. 4 (July/Aug. 82), pp. 56–61; and, "Sociological Criticism of the Old Testament," *The Christian Century* 99, no. 14 (21 Ap. 82), pp. 474–477.

6. KAHL, p. 1.

7. Wright, "Archaeology, History and Theology," *Harvard Divinity Bulletin* 28 (Ap. 64), pp. 85–96; "Is Glueck's Aim to Prove the Bible is True?" BA 22, no. 4 (Dec. 59), pp. 101–108; and, *The Old Testament and Theology* (New York: Harper & Row, 1969). The attacks and counter-attacks are reminiscent of Wheeler's remark that archaeology is not so much a science as a vendetta (*Alms for Oblivion*, p. 153n). Joe D. Seger, "Why We Dig — At Gezer," *The Hartford Quarterly* 7, no. 4 (Sum. 67), pp. 9–39. Herbert G. May, "Why Do They Dig?" *Religion in Life* (Aut. 66), p. 603 (offprint). Albright, "The Impact of Archaeology," p. 1; and, "Archaeological Discoveries and the Scriptures," *Christianity Today* 12, no. 19 (21 June 68), pp. 3–5. Paul Lapp, *Biblical Archaeology and History* (New York: World, 1969). David L. Clarke, *Analytical Archaeology* (London: Methuen, 1968). Siegfried H. Horn, "Recent Illumination of the Old Testament," *Christianity Today* 12, no. 19 (21 June 68), pp. 5–7; and, *Biblical Archaeology After 30 Years (1948–1978)* (Berrien Springs, MI: Andrews University, 1978). James Kautz, "Some Questions of the Role of Archaeology and Biblical Studies," *Perspectives in Religious Studies* 5, no. 2 (Fall 78), pp. 155–162. SBAF, pp. 153–169. William G. Dever, "Biblical Theology and Biblical Archaeology: An Appreciation of G. Ernest Wright," HTR 73, nos. 1–2 (Jan.–Ap. 80), pp. 1–15; and, "Retrospects and Prospects in Biblical and Syro-Palestinian Archaeology," BA 45, no. 2 (Spr. 82), pp. 103–107. Eric M. Meyers, "The Bible and Archaeology," BA 47, no. 1 (Mar. 84), pp. 36–40. Henry O. Thompson, "What's in a Name," (pp. 27–41 in *Put Your Future in Ruins*, ed. Thompson; Bristol, IN: Wyndham Hall, 1985).

The idea that the archaeologist is merely to report findings and never interpret them has sometimes been ascribed to the British. One notes that Wheeler, Kenyon, and others interpreted their finds. In my own case, an American historian told me I had no right to interpret what I found. In contrast, Alfred Von Rohr Sauer says that "archaeologists need to recognize that their task is to determine the nature of archaeological evidence and then to evaluate and to interpret to the best of their ability the evidence they have uncovered." Cf. his "The Meaning of Archaeology for the Exegetical Task," *Concordia Theological Monthly* 41, no. 9 (Oct. 70), pp. 519–541. Alan P. Sullivan also cites the view on non-interpretation of data. "Inference and Evidence in Archaeology: A Discussion of the Conceptual Problems," SAAMT 1 (1978), pp. 183–222.

8. Whether and how theology is to be divided into branches is debated, as are so many things. Frank L. Cross, ed., *The Oxford Dictionary of the Christian Church* (New York: Oxford University, 1957), p. 1344. The divisions used here are fairly common. Vergilius Ferm, *Concise Dictionary of Religion* (New York: Philosophical Library, 1951); and, *An Encyclopedia of Religion* (New York: Philosophical Library, 1954). Van A. Harvey, *Handbook of Theological Terms* (New York: Macmillan, 1964). *Webster's Third New International Dictionary (Unabridged)* (Springfield, MA: Merriam, 1965). James Hunt, "What is Theology?" public lecture, Syracuse University, 9 May 65.

# CHAPTER 14

# Theology

## A. TRADITIONAL DISCIPLINES

### Apologetics

One branch of theology is called "apologetics," the "apologia" or defense of the faith. This is sometimes seen as a defense of Christianity. In its larger sense, it is the defense of religion or of a cause. Archaeology has contributed to the defense of the faith. Archaeology does not "prove" the Bible. There are details in the Bible that are beyond what we normally think of as provable. How would one prove, for example, Sarah's great beauty at the age of eighty, or Jacob's wrestling match with an angel? But archaeology has provided enough data for the background and illumination of Genesis 12–50 that these chapters cannot be dismissed out of hand as mere fiction. This confirmation (not "proof") of the basic historicity of a major unit of the Bible serves as a "defense" of it. The cautious tone of both the paragraphs above and the theories about probable events contained in chapters 9–12 suggest that we must not claim too much for archaeology in the branch of theology called apologetics. On the other hand, we do not need to claim too little either. Archaeology *has* made a contribution. And to pretend that it has not, or to ignore the contribution, is very unscientific.

### Natural Theology

Another branch of theology is "natural theology." We look at nature, and reason from nature to God. The sun is the source of light, and of life, so people reason that

425

God or the creator of the sun is the source of life. Data from archaeology tells us that the various elements of nature in the ancient world were either deities (sun, moon, storm, river) or aspects of deity (thunder is the voice of the storm god). In the Bible we find the Hebrew writers saying these are not deities but things made by a Creator, or aspects of the Deity.

We will come back to the comparison with ancient Near Eastern religions later. Here it is enough to note what is perhaps the more common understanding of natural theology. It is not simply a theological understanding of nature. Natural theology refers to knowledge of the Divine without Divine revelation. We gain this knowledge by the competence of our own reason. Judging by literary remains (including the Bible), ancient people made no distinction between the sacred and the secular, the natural and the supernatural. William F. Albright, however, suggested that the Hebrew Scriptures mark an epoch in human thinking. The Hebrews reasoned from the incongruities of naturalistic polytheism (known to us through the data of archaeology) to an empirically recognized unity of nature. This type of reasoning is scientific, antedating by several thousand years the unity science sees in the molecular construction of matter or in the origin of humanity. This reasoning is also a form of natural theology. It is a theological understanding acquired through reason, although the Hebrew would not say that this was a human reason unaided by God. Archaeology has helped us understand what is involved by supplying the context for this "natural theology."[1]

## Practical Theology

This branch of theology includes liturgy, worship, and the administration of the religious organization. Burial practices might be included here. Archaeology has uncovered temples, altars, and cult objects in abundance. These suggest the concepts of worship of the users. J.G. Davies has suggested that Christian church architecture and decoration (mosaics, baptismal fonts) reflect the then current concept of "church" worship, the sacraments, etc. The same might be said of the synagogue or the structures of other religious groups. Ancient ritual is only partly illuminated by material artifacts. We are aided in our interpretation by paintings, carvings, and literature. The kernos ring was worn on the head of the priest or priestess. We sometimes find the rings, or more often, fragments of them. The hollow ring was worn on the head like a crown, with small pottery vessels or animal heads from which the sacred libation could pour.[2]

Absolute certainty is hard to obtain in any field of knowledge, and our present concern is no exception. No matter how well-preserved the floor plan of a temple may be, our interpretation is always approximate. And yet, if one finds a small inner sanctuary in relation to a large outer court, it is surely reasonable to assume that the people remained in the outer area and only the priests approached the deity in the "holy of holies." The discovery of altars with the skeletal remains of a bull nearby may not prove anything, but it surely suggests sacrifice. It also suggests that the bull was a sacrificial animal sacred to the deity.

Today, neither Judaism nor Christianity practice animal sacrifice. But we still worship with our "offerings," which are brought to the "altar." We still have priests and religious leaders.

## Moral Theology

Perhaps under the influence of the prophets, the Judeo-Christian tradition often suggests the practical application of theology in terms of everyday living. Here we move into the area of theology sometimes called "moral theology." The term "ethics" may be more widespread today. Ethics has philosophical roots as well as theological sources (in the West, these two disciplines have become separated, while in some non-Western systems, e.g., Buddhism, they remain together). Some see no distinction between the word ethics (Greek "ethos") and the word morals (Latin "moralis"). The words simply come from two different languages. Others suggest "morals" are the "shoulds" and "should nots" of life, like the Ten Commandments, whereas ethics asks the philosophical question, "Why?" Ethics is concerned with the reason for the moral code or standard. If one says the reason is "the Good" or "God," metaethics asks about this standard beyond (Greek "meta") the reason. Moral theology or theological ethics as well as philosophical ethics considers this whole area of concern.

The Bible is a book very concerned with morality. By contrast, Mesopotamian deities did not cause the flood out of any moral concern. An ancient deity (male or female) might slaughter people by the thousands for no reason at all. But this is not the whole picture. Rachel Levy observes that some of the hymns of Egypt and Sumer show a sense of sin, humility, and desire for services that is more than ceremonial. There is even an idea that right-doing is better than sacrifice, couched in words similar to the Hebrew prophets. "More acceptable is the character of one upright of heart than the ox of him that doeth iniquity." But she goes on to say that in Palestine alone we have the history of a nation devoted from the beginning to a single purpose: "to maintain by faith and conduct a direct relationship with its God." Eichrodt represents a similar school of thought, when he claims that primitive covenant rituals lack the moral basis and orientation which belong to the essence of Israelite ritual. Childe notes that immortality in the pyramid age of Egypt was assured by spells and ritual purity. Moral virtue was helpful, but in turn, immortality was not used as a motive for moral virtue, nor did Sumerians and Egyptians pray for help to be honest, just, or charitable.[3]

In the ancient world, all law comes from deity. Hammurabi's law code stele shows him before Shamash the sun god. Moses received the Law from God on

Mount Sinai. Eichrodt points out, however, that Hammurabi's law is explicitly his, with Shamash mentioned at the beginning and end, while Israelite law is the Law of Yahweh. Later, the phrase "Law of Moses" appears and becomes prominent, but religion, law, and morality remain interwoven. Eichrodt also notes the higher value placed on human life, as opposed to property, the abolition of gross brutality, and the rejection of class distinction in the administration of justice. In these regards, Israelite law is superior to ancient Near Eastern law in general as well as Hammurabi's.[4]

Many of the laws of the Bible have parallels in other law codes of the ancient world. Archaeology, which has recovered these other codes, helps us understand the background and development of moral theology. One interpretation is that God handed the Laws to Moses on Mount Sinai and they were diffused, spread out to other people, from there. A more common interpretation is that many of the laws of the Bible were borrowed from the surrounding cultures. There was no distinction between natural and supernatural, secular or sacred. What happened in nature was the will of God. What happened in law was the will of God.

It may be important to emphasize that ancient Near Eastern parallels or background do not in themselves pass judgment on the validity of a particular law or moral concept, any more than the history of chemistry, beginning with alchemy, determines the validity of chemistry today. While there have always been people who question the Ten Commandments, others would insist they are still valid. And the fact that people have not yet lived up to them, for example, the law against coveting other people's goods, does not invalidate the laws themselves. Other laws, such as "an eye for eye and a tooth for a tooth," are not taken literally today. In historical context, this constituted an advance in law. In Hammurabi's day, it meant a limitation on a formerly unlimited revenge. A further advance appears in the Bible, for it supports equal treatment before the law. Rich and poor, king and commoner, slave and free, were all to have the same treatment, the same punishment for the same offense. Here is a moral concept which the modern world is still unable to put into practice, as witnessed by the civil rights movement in America, apartheid in South Africa, the distinctions made in the supposedly classless society of Communist Russia, and the lack of justice for the poor the world over. America is often accused of having one system of justice for the poor and another system for the rich. We have not yet reached the equality of either Hammurabi or the Bible.[5]

## Systematic Theology

"Moral theology" is sometimes simply included in "systematic" or "dogmatic theology." The larger category, as the word "systematic" suggests, is basically a matter of putting theological concerns into systematic form. No branch of Judaism or Christianity has ever succeeded in completely limiting its dogmatic theology to the Bible. Yet, this book has usually received at least lip service as the recognized source of the ideas or dogmas delineated in systematic theology. The Old Testament or Hebrew Scriptures is basic to both Judaism and Christianity with respect to these ideas. But the Bible is not written in systematic form. This has led some to argue that any attempt to systematize biblical ideas cannot help but distort them. This is a danger, to be sure, which must not be taken lightly. On the other hand, if done carefully, there is no basic reason why one cannot see what the Bible has to say about God, Humanity, the World, and then proceed to arrange this in systematic form. Archaeology, as one might suggest, contributes to this "carefully."

John Gray has suggested that "archaeology sets the word of God in its proper context so that dogmatic theology may draw neither more nor less from a passage than that context warrants." He sees archaeology promising a factual and objective counter-balance to theology's flights of fancy and to denominational dogmatics.[6]

Biblical ideas are not all on one plane. As just pointed out in the section on moral theology, some concepts may remain valid to this day. There is probably no responsible person, who would insist on taking an "eye for an eye" literally. The concept of God as a God of war has had its up and downs. Jehu slaughtered hundreds of people in his rise to the throne, apparently with the approval of the prophets. A century later, Hosea, the prophet of love, implied that the blood of Jezreel (where Jehu murdered the royal families of Judah and Israel) needed atonement. Or again, we ourselves are selective in our use of biblical ideas. Jacob Petuchowski has commented on this. We do not say, "Be thou vengeful as God is vengeful." We say, "Be thou loving as God has loved you." This combination of constancy, change, and interpretation is a part of the historical development of the Judeo-Christian tradition.

Archaeology has contributed to our understanding of this history. No systematic or dogmatic theology that is going to take the Bible seriously can ignore the contribution of biblical archaeology to our understanding of this book. The systematic theologian must understand as clearly as possible what the Bible means. This writer would venture one step further with a personal value judgment and say that any systematic theology that fails to take the Bible seriously, and hence any that fails to take biblical archaeology seriously, can hardly claim to stand in the Judeo-Christian tradition.

## Historical Theology

The historical development of a religion comes under the branch of theology called "historical theology." This discipline is sometimes reserved for the study of Christian or church history. Like apologetics, however, it has a broader definition.

Most people are familiar with history, in the sense of dates and people, but history is not merely a matter of battles and knowing when which kings ruled. There is also the history of ideas. In the sense that everything has theological significance, we could say that all ideas have theological significance. In everyday language, however, most of us do not think of ideas about the combustion engine, or the invention of the water wheel, as theological ideas. The theology of technology or the theological response to technology is a major concern today. Still, theological ideas are ideas about God, human nature, and our human relationship with the natural world. When did these ideas, such as monotheism, life after death, love and justice, human sisterhood and brotherhood, and moral responsibility first appear? The very asking of the question assumes that these ideas did not all together drop with the first rain after creation. Indeed, the world is only now learning to live in a non-slave economy. Slavery has only recently been abolished in some countries and there are those who claim it still exists in some parts of the world. A non-slave economy is not a new concept. When did it first appear? How did it develop along the way? These are questions that the historian of ideas must ask and then search for the answers.[7]

In the Judeo-Christian tradition, religious ideas or theology, are closely related to the Bible. What are the religious ideas there? When did they first appear on the horizon of history? Where did they come from and with or by whom? What happened to these ideas later? Did they catch on right away or take a while? Were they accepted, then ignored and forgotten, and revived at a later date?

The Passover is an idea-loaded ritual that remains a part of Judaism to this day. According to the record of a reform by King Josiah, the Passover had been forgotten since the days of the Judges, but Josiah revived it (II Kings 23:22).

Archaeology provides artifacts and texts which help us approximate the historical origins and development of theological ideas. George Mendenhall and others have drawn attention to the parallels between ancient Near Eastern political covenants and the Covenant form as it appears in the Bible. A hundred years ago, major scholars claimed that the Hebrews had no concept of creation or at least they did not develop their concept of creation until a later date. Archaeology, however, has revealed many ancient Near Eastern influences upon the religion of ancient Israel. Most of the surrounding peoples had fully developed creation concepts by the year 2000 B.C., and perhaps as early as 3000. This should at least raise an eyebrow regarding the claim that Israel did not develop its understanding until 500 B.C. A re-examination of the biblical material, even on the basis of the hundred year old concepts of literary criticism, shows that the Hebrews had a clear understanding of God as Creator by the time of the monarchy — the so-called "J" or Yahwist writer c. 950 B.C. — and probably already with Moses.

## B. COMPARATIVE RELIGION

One could, I suppose, see the study called "History of Religions" or "Comparative Religion" as simply a branch of Historical Theology. Since its development, however, this study or discipline has expanded beyond being simply the history of ideas. It includes cultural, political, military, and other elements in the context of a religion. A study of Hinduism divorced from its context in India would be thoroughly inadequate. What has really happened though, is something in reverse. We live in a world come of age. It has finally dawned on us that one cannot understand India without understanding Hinduism! This has occurred in no less a place than the U.S. Supreme Court, which has banned state-sponsored worship (prayers, Bible reading as a morning ritual) but which has also given approval for the academic study of religion. This support, incidentally, has opened the door to the development of courses in religion in state-sponsored schools, from kindergartens to graduate schools.

At first glance, the whole idea might seem so obvious as to be absurd. It is utter nonsense to try to understand Western civilization without the Judeo-Christian tradition. Indeed, the history of Europe in the Middle Ages *is* church history! Whether this is good or bad, is, of course, a value judgment perhaps best left to the individual. To what degree the Judeo-Christian tradition influenced, failed to influence, or was influenced by Western civilization, is also debated and must be examined in detail. But to deny its *presence* is as foolish as the ignorant graduate student who could not understand why people in India were starving. All they had to do, he thought, was butcher the cows wandering all over India, and live on beef.

### The Ancient Near East

The impact of archaeology on comparative religious study is perhaps obvious. Indian archaeology is shedding considerable light on the history and development of that area, including its religion. Biblical archaeology has given us huge amounts of information on the religions of the ancient Near East. Of course, everything that comes to light on these religions is not of comparative value for the Bible. But much of it is. Some of this has already been cited in chapters 9–12. The Hebrews borrowed rather freely. As a general principle, we might keep in mind the claim that what they borrowed, they transformed in terms of their own faith. We might keep in mind here, too, that while there are many similarities between the Hebrew religion and the religions of the ancient world, there are also differences.

### Hebrew Religion

There is some debate over just when the Hebrew religion really developed. Some say it began with Abraham, while others say it began with Moses. Some relate it to the beginning of the monarchy or the time of the Hebrew prophets. One could say that Hebrew religion, and what grew out of it as Judaism, Christianity, and Islam, has always been in the process of development. Some Christians, for example, still do not see anything wrong with racism, perhaps the greatest evil of our time. But with this continuing development in mind, one could say that the basic elements of the faith were there by the time of Moses (ascribing the Ten Commandments to him or his time) with roots going back to the Patriarchal Period (the concept of covenant), while granting the impact of the temple upon the development of the official ritual.

## Canaanite Religion

During a significant portion of the time of this development, the Hebrew religion was in contact with Canaanite religion. It has been said that it is easier to understand what a person is saying if you know what he or she is fighting. Hebrew religion fought the Canaanite religion of Baalism, which was basically a fertility religion. They fought it on many fronts, but there were at least two major grounds for the battle. One was idolatry and the other was adultery. The commandment is clear enough: You will have no other gods before you. This should have been sufficient grounds to avoid Baal worship. The commandment against adultery is equally clear. This appeared because a main feature of Canaanite religion was its cultic prostitution. This was not Hollywood or Madison Avenue exploitation of sex, but a primitive magic. We are familiar with the voodoo doll. One pokes pins in it and the enemy jumps. The Baal worshipper had intercourse with the cult prostitute and assured the fertility of his crops and flocks.

Baal is the male principle. Mother Earth is the female principle. Baal rains upon the Earth, impregnates her, and she produces the grass and grain necessary for both animal and human life. The worshipper, in imitating Baal's action, by impregnating the temple prostitute or female attendant of the deity, helped bring the desired fertility to the land. Bernard W. Anderson has pointed out that the farmer in ancient times would no more neglect this "scientific" necessity for his farming than the modern farmer would neglect crop rotation, hybrid seeds, and the right kind of fertilizer.

The problem was compounded for the Israelite because of past associations. God had helped his people conquer the land. In Sinai, he had been a mountain and a desert God. What could he possibly know about farming? When in Canaan, do as the Canaanites do. Hebrew religionists fought back by outright opposition. The pig, sacred to Baal and a number of other ancient deities, was banned, a a ban which remains today as part of kosher food laws for orthodox Jews. Demonology, witchcraft, necromancy, and related activities were also banned. Gerhard von Rad has suggested that the first commandment was explicitly directed against demonology, rather than against the great pantheons of Mesopotamia and Egypt.[8]

Baalism was also "fought" by adoption of its leading premises. Bismarck borrowed the planks out of the socialist platform and established health insurance long before England or the U.S. even thought seriously about it. A prime example of this in Judaism's conflict with Baalism is that fertility was ascribed directly to God (Hosea 2:8; Jeremiah 2; Elijah in I Kings 18:1). Baal concepts were also "transformed." Some have thought that Hosea's use of the marriage metaphor for the relationship between God and Israel does not have his own marriage in the background but the sacred marriage of the fertility gods. In addition to the imagery of Baal and Mother Earth, Mesopotamians, and perhaps Canaanites, also included in their annual New Year's Festival a sacred marriage. The king, representing the deity, married a temple prostitute or priestess, representing the goddess. This may be the background for Ezekiel's metaphor in Ezekiel 16, in which God finds a baby girl (Israel) left in the wilderness to die (exposure was a common way of getting rid of unwanted children, especially girls). He rescues the child, and when she has grown into a beautiful woman, "marries" her. However, she is not grateful for all that her "husband" has done, but runs off with other lovers (gods).

## Egyptian Influence

The word, "archaeology," has not been mentioned for several paragraphs and yet it has been silently assumed all through these last sentences. We know about sacred marriages and fertility concepts from the discoveries of religious texts, especially those of Ras Shamra and Mesopotamia. One of the current question marks for the comparative religious study of the Bible and the ancient Near East is the influence of Egypt. We know that Egypt was a land of many idols — in human form, in animal form, in combinations. Perhaps one reason for the commandment against idols was this Egyptian background.

Long before Joseph or Moses appeared on the scene, the Egyptians had developed what is called "wisdom literature." Some of it is like the books of Proverbs, Job, or Ecclesiastes. Some say that the Joseph stories have their background in the Egyptian wisdom movement. Mesopotamia had its wisdom literature also and may have influenced Hebrew thought, but we have several passages, such as Proverbs 22:17–23:14, which are so similar to Egyptian materials, that these must have been known to the Hebrew writers. One of the most interesting passages in the Bible is Proverbs 8 where wisdom is personified as a woman who was with God during the creation of the world. R.B.Y. Scott has argued persuasively that this is not Wisdom as an entity separate from God, but a kind of principle binding the universe together.

In our discussion here, we might think that the woman represents the fertility myth again. This is not impossible, but here there is the twist that in this case, wisdom in her guise as a woman calls to men to *avoid* sexual entanglements. However, the focus in this passage is on the Hebrew word, "amun," which is sometimes translated "little child" and sometimes "master workman" (RSV). This is Scott's binding principle. Amun is also the name of one of the most important gods in Egypt. One might see here a parallel with the use of "tehom" or "deep" in Hebrew (Genesis 1:2) as a cognate of Tiamat, the watery dragon of chaos in the Mesopotamian creation myth. The Hebrew writer may have taken the name of the Egyptian god, Amun, and transposed it, as a being or concept subordinate to the Almighty, as the "deep" is subject to his power in Genesis and elsewhere. Amun and Tiamat are not gods, say the Hebrew writers. These so-called gods are only creatures or attributes of the God of Israel.[9]

Amun is sometimes seen as the "sole creator" of the world. This concept may have been influenced by the religion of Ikhnaton. Ikhnaton's religion has been suggested as the source of Moses' monotheism. This is not impossible, but on the whole, it is doubtful on several counts. One is that the pharaoh and his family worshipped the old sun god, Re, under his name, the Aton, represented by the sun disc. The people of Egypt, however, continued to worship the pharaoh (Ikhnaton) as the god Horus as they did before, and after, Ikhnaton. In addition, we can note that Ikhnaton was crowned pharaoh by the two gods, Set and Horus, like all Egyptian pharaohs were crowned, and we have found at least one prayer by Ikhnaton to another god.

Another reason is that Moses' religion has a strong ethical emphasis (cited in the section on moral theology) which seems to be lacking in Atonism. This is not to say there were no moral or ethical principles in Egyptian life. When a person died, he went to the Judgement, and made a "Negative Confession," copies of which have been found. Included are such things as disclaimers for murder and theft. The confession is called "negative" because all the statements are on the order of "I did not . . ." We also have in Egyptian records a piece called the "Eloquent Peasant." A peasant was robbed by a nobleman along the way. He protested to the prince. His plea for justice was so eloquent that the prince kept him around for a while repeating the plea just because it was interesting to hear. He finally granted the peasant his cause and got his grain back for him.

Atonism was not monotheism. Ikhnaton's religion was influenced by the rebellion of his father against the rich and powerful priests of Amun. Still, the hymn to the Aton describes him in monotheistic terms. This hymn may or may not have influenced Moses, but it surely influenced the writer of Psalm 104. Several verses there (e.g., verses 20–30) are very similar to the Aton hymn.

Yet another Egyptian deity was the god Set, who helped his nephew (or brother) Horus crown the pharaohs of Egypt. This was their only cooperation, however. According to one tradition, Set had killed his brother Osiris, who later became the god of the dead. Horus, Osiris's son, fought Set for vengeance and for control of Egypt. He got the latter. In ancient times, Set was the god of Upper Egypt, and

Horus was the god of Lower Egypt, which is why both crowned the pharaoh. Eventually, however, Set became the god of foreign lands, including Palestine or Canaan. Set's worship was promoted by the Hyksos who conquered Egypt in 1710 B.C. Their control of Egypt may form the background for the Joseph stories. Later the Hyksos were expelled (1570 B.C.) and the god Amun, of Thebes, gained the ascendency. But the Nineteenth Dynasty of Seti and Ramses II revived the worship of Set, c. 1310 B.C. Thus he was a prominent god in the household of pharaoh, where Moses was presumably raised.

Set was the god of pestilence. Note the plagues which God brought on the Egyptians. Set was the god of storm and the desert. Note the darkness (perhaps a sand storm) of the ninth plague, God's leadership of his people through the desert of Sinai and later Transjordan, and the smoke and fire on Mount Sinai which have been compared to a storm. Set was also the god of foreign lands, and God had power in foreign lands. Set was represented by many animals. Among these were the pig, the hippopotamus, the crocodile and the bull. The pig was rejected by the Hebrews. We hear little or nothing about the middle two, except as creatures of God (Job 40:15; 41:1). The bull, however, does fit into Hebrew religion. In what was later considered idolatry, Moses' brother Aaron set up a golden calf in the wilderness for the people to worship. Later, when Jeroboam I started the Northern Kingdom of Israel, he set up a golden calf in Bethel and another one in Dan. It has been pointed out that these may have been pedestals for the invisible God to stand on, rather than idols in their own right. [10]

The bellow of a bull is also of interest. God speaks out and it sounds like thunder, or the bellow of a bull. In the poetry of the Psalms, God comes riding on the wings of a storm, with thunder as his voice and lightning as his weapons. Set is significant for us in yet one more point. He was an opponent of Horus. The pharaoh was traditionally Horus incarnate. Like Set, God opposed Horus, that is, the pharaoh.

These religious influences of Egypt on the development of Hebrew religion are highly speculative. What we can say is that the Bible presents God in a certain fashion. We can describe several characteristics in Egyptian religion during the time the Hebrews were supposedly there. And we can note that in general, they "fought" other religions by borrowing and transforming their ideas to harmonize with their own religion. There are other ways in which Egypt may have influenced Israel. Earlier we touched on the possible parallels between David's government and Egyptian government officials. Religion and government were combined in ancient times for most peoples. In Egypt, this was particularly the case, since the pharaoh was supposed to be both a god and the son of a god. The Hebrew king was not considered divine, but we might see this Egyptian belief as background for describing the Hebrew king as the "Son of God."

## Mesopotamia

Very few Mesopotamian kings were considered divine. One of these was Naram-Sin, grandson of Sargon, who established the Akkadian empire and whose birth story is similar to Moses. Naram-Sin is shown on a stele, climbing the sacred mountain, and wearing horns, symbol of divinity. As a rule, however, the Meso-potamian king was considered the servant of the god. In this sense, Hebrew king-ship was more like the Mesopotamian form than the Egyptian. At the time the Hebrew monarchy was formed, however, the more immediate model was probably Edom, Moab and the Canaanite city-state kings, with whom the Hebrews had con-tact, rather than Mesopotamia, which their ancestors had left long ago. Meso-potamian influence has already been cited for the book of Genesis. The background for Genesis 1–11 is Mesopotamian mythology, but is is demytholo-gized. The background for Genesis 12–50 is largely a matter of laws and customs. The conquests of Assyrians and Babylonians left their mark, as well.

A very interesting suggestion for the theological importance of archaeological data has been made regarding Hezekiah's tunnel. While the tunnel did not stop Sennacherib from devastating the countryside, the tunnel did help Hezekiah hold Jerusalem. This may have aided in elevating Hezekiah to the status of a "savior-king." He is one of only two kings from the whole divided monarchy to get genuine praise instead of the censure which the Deuteronomic historians gave to all the other kings. Since Isaiah had predicted that the city would not fall, the tunnel may have helped give him status along with his declaration that God would deliver them, if only people would trust in Him. The developing concept of a Messiah in the line of David, and the importance of Jerusalem, may also have gained by the tunnel's "saving presence." The point of course, is that the city was not conquered at that point. The discovery of the tunnel gives us an insight into how that hap-pened, which in turn may have contributed to the above theological concepts.

In a later time, Persian influence was probably felt in several ways. There was political support for the rebuilding of the temple, and for the governors, Nehemiah and Ezra. That included the former's rebuilding of the walls of Jerusalem and the promotion of the latter's laws, for example the passover at Elephantine. More direct religious influence might be connected to what is known as "Persian dual-ism." Zoroaster had started the religion of Ahura Mazdah which he promoted as a member of the court of Darius the Great's father. Darius put Ahura Mazdah's name on the inscription on the Behistun mountain. In Zoroastrianism, Ahura Mazdah was the god of light. At first, this was monotheism and Ahura Mazdah and his followers were opposed by the principle of darkness or evil and those who follow or live by evil, i.e., Zoroaster's enemies. Later this principle itself became a god, Angra Mainyu. The principle of light against darkness, good against evil, became a part of Judaism. This was touched on in the discussion of Qumran, where one of the Dead Sea Scrolls has been called, "The War between the Sons of Light and the Sons of Darkness." Dualism may be more familiar to the average reader in the concepts of heaven and hell and the battle between God and the devil.[11]

## Other Parts of the Ancient Near East

In addition to a comparative religious study of Egypt and Mesopotamia, and all our knowledge of these areas today by way of archaeological discovery, one should add other areas and peoples such as the Hittites who were not even known as anything but a casual name in the Bible (Genesis 23) until their entire civilization came to light through archaeological exploration. They are of particular interest because their form of political covenant has been most clearly preserved. In between Palestine and the Hittites is another newly discovered culture. The city of Ebla was in Syria, between today's Hama and Aleppo. The kingdom controlled or influenced a large area. Just what, if any, influence it had on biblical history remains to be seen. There has been considerable controversy. Hopefully, more of the thousands of tablets discovered there will be translated soon and published, and so provide a clearer judgment. One could add to these the influence of Arabia, which is only beginning to come under systematic exploration.[12]

The Aegean is yet another source of influence. Pottery and other traded goods were being imported into Palestine during the second millenium B.C. This seems to have largely stopped with the disruptions of the Sea Peoples and the invasion of the Hebrews. By the seventh century, pottery and Greek coins appear in excavated strata. Presumably this was a matter of trade. Later, Alexander conquered the area. He personally did not live long enough to do much of anything except punish the Samaritans for murdering his governor, as cited earlier. But as noted there, Alexander came not merely to conquer, but to spread Greek culture. His successors continued this diffusion. The Ptolemies accomplished this transformation benevolently. Greek influence, attitudes toward the body (running naked in athletic games, for example) and to life in general, the development of philosophy, religion, and commerce all began to cross over into Jewish life and culture. A large number of Jews lived in relative peace in Egypt. At one time, the city of Alexandria was heavily Jewish in population.

In daily language, these Jews had long since changed from Hebrew to Aramaic. Now they turned to Greek. Around 250 B.C., the Torah (Pentateuch) was translated into Greek. As described earlier, it came to be called the Septuagint because of the tradition that seventy-two (usually abbreviated to simply LXX) scribes had translated it. Eventually the LXX came to include fifteen writings which were not accepted by the academy of Jewish rabbis who gathered at Jabneh or Jamnia under Johanan ben Zakkai after the First Jewish Revolt. About 90 A.D., they decided what was Scripture or "canon" (standard, rule). They followed three main principles — a work had to be in Hebrew; it had to be prophetic (N.B.: prophecy stopped with Ezra and Nehemiah c. 400 B.C.); and it had to agree with the Torah. For one reason or another, the fifteen writings were not accepted. They are called the Apocrypha, and are part of the Roman Catholic Old Testament which is based on the LXX. Some of them are included in the Eastern Orthodox Bible as well. Protestants, following the lead of Martin Luther, go back to the Jamnian canon. The Dead Sea Scrolls date to before 68 A.D., when Qumran was destroyed. This was before Jamnia. Numerous non-canonical works were found among the Dead Sea Scrolls. By contrast, the Bar Koseba writings found in the Wadi Muraba'at, date from c. 135 A.D., after Jamnia. The writings include canonical materials but no Apocrypha.

Archaeological data attest to the widespread nature of Judaism, in the diaspora, and helps us to understand the move to Greek, which became the common language of the Mediterranean world. For a long time, scholars thought that the New Testament was written in a special kind of Greek. The discovery of large numbers of Greek papyri — business documents, letters, and the like, show that New Testament Greek or "koine" Greek was the common everyday Greek of the time. The New Testament, however, was written in a "koine" influenced by Hebrew and Aramaic. Albright pointed out a similar phenomenon in the Dead Sea Scrolls.[13]

A very special development in religious doctrine came under the impact of the Seleucid (Antiochus IV Epiphanes) persecution of the Jews in Palestine, and the attempt to force Greek culture on the Jews. This was the internal development of the concept of the afterlife. Since this was only partly influenced by external ideas, we should end our survey of archaeology, "Comparative Religion" and the Bible, and turn to a concern which has been referred to several times. This is the concept of history itself.

# NOTES

1. Albright, *History, Archaeology and Christian Humanism* (New York: McGraw-Hill, 1964), pp. 99–100; *New Horizons in Biblical Research* (London: Oxford, 1966), p. 32; *Archaeology, Historical Analogy & Early Biblical Traditions* (Baton Rouge: Louisana State University, 1966), and, "Archaeological Discoveries . . . and the Scriptures," *Christianity Today* 12, no. 19 (21 June 68), pp. 3–5. A similar thought is expressed by Walther Eichrodt in his *Theology of the Old Testament*, Vol. 1 (London: SCM, 1960), p. 41. Jack W. Provonsha, "Revelation and History," AUSS II (1964), pp. 109–119.
2. Davies, "Architecture and Theology," *Expository Times* 73 (May 63), pp. 231–233.

3. G.R. Levy, *Religious Conceptions of the Stone Age and Their Influence on European Thought* (New York: Harper & Row, 1963), p. 196. The quotation is from the Papyrus Petersburg, called "The Instruction of King Meri-Ka-Re," ANET, p. 417. Alan Gardiner, "New Literary Works from Ancient Egypt," *Journal of Egyptian Archaeology* 1, no. 1 (Jan. 14), p. 34. Eichrodt, *Theology*, p. 43. V. Gordon Childe, *What Happened in History?* (rev.; Baltimore: Penguin, 1965), pp. 145–146. George E. Mendenhall, "Between Theology and Archaeology," *Journal for the Study of the Old Testament* 7 (1978), p. 29.

4. Eichrodt, *Theology*, pp. 75–80, with numerous citations.

5. Keith W. Whitelam, *The Just King: Monarchial Judicial Authority in Ancient Israel* (Sheffield: JSOT Supplement 12, 1979). Henry Frankfort, *Kingship and the Gods* (Chicago: University of Chicago, 1948).

6. Gray, *Archaeology and the Old Testament World* (New York: Harper & Row, 1962), p. v; "Towards a Theology of the Old Testament: The Contribution of Archaeology," *Expository Times* 74 (Aug. 63), pp. 347–351; and, "Recent Archaeological Discoveries and Their Bearing on the Old Testament," (pp. 65–95 in *Tradition and Interpretation*, ed. George W. Anderson; Oxford: Clarendon Press, 1979).

7. Dorothy M. Slusser and Gerald H. Slusser, *Technology — The God that Failed* (Philadelphia: Westminster, 1971). Gabriel Vahanian, *God and Utopia: The Church in a Technological Civilization* (New York: Seabury, 1977).

8. Bernard W. Anderson, *Understanding the Old Testament* (3rd ed; Englewood Cliffs: Prentice-Hall, 1975). Gerhard von Rad, *Moses* (London: Lutterworth, 1960). J.A. Black, "The New Year Ceremonies in Ancient Babylon: 'Taking Bel by the Hand' and a Cultic Picnic," *Religion* 11 (Jan. 81), pp. 39–59. Paul E. Dion, "Did Cultic Prostitution Fall into Oblivion during the Postexilic Era? Some Evidence from Chronicles and the Septuagint," CBQ 43, no. 1 (Jan. 81), pp. 41–48. Alfred von Rohr Sauer, "The Meaning of Archaeology for the Exegetical Task," *Concordia Theological Monthly* 41, no. 9 (Oct. 70), p. 524.

9. Personal communication, Bruce D. Rahtjen.

10. Albright, *From the Stone Age to Christianity* (2nd ed; Garden City: Doubleday, 1957), p. 299. Sauer, "The Meaning of Archaeology," p. 525. In Hindu traditions, the god Shiva rides a bull named Nandi.

11. A.T. Olmstead, *The History of Persia* (2nd ed; Chicago: University of Chicago, 1969). S.G.F. Brandon, ed., "Dualism," (p. 250 in *A Dictionary of Comparative Religion* (New York: Scribner, 1970). Yigael Yadin, *The Scroll of the War of the Sons of Light Against the Sons of Darkness* (1962).

12. Paola Mattiae, *Ebla* (Garden City: Doubleday, 1981). PAE. Mendenhall, *Law and Covenant in Israel and the Ancient Near East* (Pittsburgh: Biblical Colloquium, 1955); and, "Covenant," IDB 1, pp. 714–725. Dennis J. McCarthy, *Old Testament Covenant: A Survey of Current Opinions* (Atlanta: Knox, 1972).

13. Albright, *New Horizons*, p. 37.

# CHAPTER 15

# The Theology of History

## A. THE PAST

To begin with, we must note the emphasis upon history and the uniqueness of history in the Judeo-Christian tradition. Both Judaism and Christianity are historical faiths. By this we do not simply mean that one can point out their beginnings on a calendar of the centuries. It is rather that the major people and events which have shaped them, and to which they turn again and again for guidance, inspiration, and indeed, their very reason for existence — these events and people are historical. This contrasts with other traditions such as Hinduism or modern existentialism. Even Marxism with its dialectical history is essentially nonhistorical. Many people today find history a dull subject which they would just as soon ignore. And yet we *are* our past. We can never completely get away from it. We can only attempt to understand it and profit by the understanding. This becomes painfully apparent when anyone asks, "What is Christianity?" or "What is Judaism?" These questions cannot be answered in a vacuum. We must turn to the past in order to understand the present, if we are going to be able to face the future with intelligent understanding.

Amos Elon has suggested a connection between nationalism and archaeology. It is a connection underlined with historical details by Neil Asher Silberman. Elon sees the birth of archaeology in Europe as coinciding with the rise of nationalism. Jewish settlers in Palestine in the late nineteenth and early twentieth centuries paid little attention to the antiquities of the land. Theodore Herzl, the founder of Zionism, had very little interest. Today, it is said that every Israeli or at least every other one, is an archaeologist at heart. When Yadin called for volunteers to excavate Masada, thousands responded — from all over Israel and from all over the world. Yet there are very few American Jewish archaeologists. A similar phenomenon might be noted in the case of the response to Alex Haley's book, *Roots*, which traces the origins of his black ancestors to West Africa.[1]

## Identity

There are events which might be called "the touchstones of history." The Fourth of July is such an event. This formative event gives identity to America and Americans, whether we arrived yesterday or 200 years ago. The Bible also has its touchstones or formative events. The formative event for the Hebrews was the Exodus. The establishment of the monarchy, and the later development of the idea of a Messiah, and the building of Solomon's temple might be considered as formative events. It is surely no accident that we have more detail in the Bible about these formative events than about the hundreds of years before and after. Jews continue to look back to Moses and the Exodus. Christians look to the Christ event in the New Testament, while continuing to hold the Old Testament sacred as scripture. Again, we can note that the life of Jesus is quite sketchy, until we come to the "Passion" narrative — the crucifixion and resurrection and the events immediately around these traditions.

It is interesting to realize that the Fourth of July is a kind of cultic re-enactment of the historical event of the "first" Fourth of July. Judaism has its cultic re-enactments in Passover, Rosh Hoshannah, Yom Kippur, circumcision, bar mitzvah, etc. For some, these are mere "sops" or sentiment over the religion of our ancestors. But Jews who are grounded in their faith know the Covenant at Sinai was not made only with their ancestors but with them. Christians know that the Mass or Lord's Supper establishes a relationship between themselves and their Lord. But this existential involvement cannot be divorced from the past. Indeed, it makes very little sense without the "original" Exodus and Supper. These formative events of history point us to a theological concept.

## B. GOD AND HISTORY

God is one who acts in history. The mighty acts of God are recorded in the Bible. God is involved in history. According to the biblical record, God started history, and in general terms at least, He controls history, which is moving toward his goals. Basically, the view of history in the Bible is linear. History had a beginning and it is moving toward a goal. The mighty acts of God are events along the time line called history. This contrasts with the Greek view of history as cyclical (history repeats itself every 5000 years or more) or earlier ancient Near Eastern cyclical views related to the changing seasons and the fertility cycle.

The major exception in the Bible is the book of Judges. Here the Hebrews fell away from God and began going around in circles — circles of sin, God's punishment (oppression by their enemies), their repentance, and God's deliverance. The last came in the form of a judge, a military leader who led them in battle to defeat their enemies. While the judge lived, the people remained loyal to God. The judge died, they sinned, etc. The history as we now have it is surely stylized around this concept, for many of the judges appear to be quite local in their activity and probably overlapped chronologically. The message remains. "In tune with the infinite," people go forward. In rebellion, they run around in circles.

The point remains too that God is not aloof from His creation, somewhere off on Cloud Nine enjoying the sunshine. He acts in history. He is involved in history. The Bible takes history very seriously and it is no accident that the Hebrews were the world's first historians. Their history and history writing had a theological base. Archaeology is concerned with that history.

Albrektson has pointed out that other peoples saw their gods active in history. Their gods helped them in battle, gave and took away thrones, health, wealth. We cannot pretend this concept is unique with the Hebrews, though John Gray insists that "the large perspective of the consistent purpose of God in history characteristic of the great prophets of Israel" is still without parallel in the ancient Near East. Admittedly not all of the truth in the Bible is historical. Much of it is ahistorical or nonhistorical. The wisdom literature (Proverbs, Ecclesiastes, Job, some of the Psalms) has little or no historical referent. But the sense of history and the importance of history is clear for much of the Bible.[2]

## C. NO IVORY TOWER

Theological ideas do not exist in a vacuum. They have a context. We cannot understand these ideas without their context. For Christians to talk about Christ, that is, Joshua the Messiah, without any knowledge of what the Messiah is or was or was supposed to be, is like trying to hang an idea in an empty space. Why should God be labeled as the giver of fertility? Obviously a knowledge of Baalism and the long struggle between it and Hebrew religion is a necessary background. But why shouldn't it be sufficient to simply study the Bible itself? Why or how does archaeology come into the picture?

Perhaps two actual cases will help make the point. For a long time, an older scholarship, which is still influential, drew a sharp dichotomy between prophet and priest. The prophet is the great moralist in ancient Israel, calling upon the people to follow the will of God in a new, radical way. The priest represents the status quo, whose only concern is peace and order at any price, so that the mechanics of the official cult, from which he receives his living, can be maintained. Something of the background of Hebrew prophecy in ancient Near Eastern religion was cited earlier. As one studies the textual and artifactual remains of the ancient world, however, it appears that the priests and diviners with their sacrificial animals and clay model livers for divining the future are not really very different in principle from the ecstatic prophets who worked themselves into a religious frenzy in order to prophesy. These cultic prophets help us to see that for the most part, ancient prophets functioned as a part of the official cult. This new data has led to a re-examination of the biblical material itself. We find that such figures as Samuel, Jeremiah, Ezekiel, and perhaps Isaiah were prophets *and* priests, while others such as Elijah carried out priestly activities. In an examination of the cultic summaries of the Bible, such as Joshua 24, Lawrence E. Toombs has shown that these are not mere mechanical elements of the cult. They are recitals of the mighty acts of God. The cultic summaries are as fully involved in history as the rest of the Old Testament. Priest, like prophet in Israel, had the responsibility of keeping these "acts" before the people. When priests or prophets or anyone else failed in their responsibilities before God, a man like Amos or Jeremiah denounced them all and pronounced God's judgment. [3]

John Gray also notes that the acceptance of an earlier date for the Psalms has given us a greater appreciation of religion in this period. At the very time the priesthood was supposed to be bogged down in sterile legalism (according to the school of thought stemming from Julius Wellhausen in 1868), the Psalter (in an earlier form than what we have today) was the "hymn book" of the temple. To this Gray feels we should also add the "humanist voice of the wisdom literature," to give a fuller picture. Subsequent literary criticism suggests this period was one of dynamic vitality with the editing or writing of Ruth, Jonah, Zechariah, Isaiah 56–66, the wisdom literature, the Apocrypha, and Apocalyptic materials. [4]

A second case is the Hebrew belief in an afterlife. The traditional view is that the Hebrews had no belief in an afterlife. Rather, they believed that the blessing of God was a long and good life here and now, ending with an honorable burial in the family tomb. It has also been suggested that the Hebrews saw their immortality in either their children or their people or both. Some have been willing to recognize the concept of an afterlife in the idea of Sheol, the place of the dead. A few references in the Bible, plus descriptions in Mesopotamian and Greek literature, picture Sheol (Hades) as a dry dusty place where all the dead, good and bad alike, continue a partial existence. The traditional view is that God did not have control over Sheol, at least not until a later time and development in Hebrew thought. However, archaeology has illuminated two aspects of this theological idea and its historical development.

## Comparison

One is the comparative material just mentioned. Major exceptions to the idea of a dry dusty place where all the dead go are the Elysian Fields for heroes in Greek thought, and the paradise of becoming one with Osiris, the god of the dead in Egyptian thought. If one failed to pass the last judgment (in which the heart was weighed in a balance against the feather of Ma'at, the concept of truth and justice), a monster stood by waiting to devour the failure. This is not quite the moral concept it seems, since the standard grave goods included careful instructions, including magical incantations, to ensure one's passing the judgment test.

## The Grave

Grave goods are another aspect which have particular significance. When we find weapons, pottery and various other artifacts in a grave, including Israelite graves, some would say these are only symbolic. American folk humor has a story of Pat and Mike who were business partners. They agreed that if one should die before the other, the living partner would deposit the dead man's half of the business in the coffin and bury it with him. Pat died. On the day of the funeral, Mike walked up to the casket and said, "Well Pat, here's your half of the business," and put in a check. If we go back to Hawke's caution at the beginning of this section, we can recognize that it is very difficult to determine the motives for putting *anything*, even a symbol like a check, in a grave. But the artifacts do suggest that there was some type of belief that the dead would need these grave goods in the afterlife. In early Mesopotamia (the royal graves of Ur excavated by Woolley) and Egypt, servants, guards, horses, and other items belonging to the dead person were buried with him. Later, especially in Egypt, this concept was transposed from the slaughter of live servants to paintings on the wall, and to models of bakeries, farms, and bodyguards. Why were these things put in the grave? One reason might be some type of belief that the dead would need them in the afterlife.[5]

## Personality

Turning back to the Old Testament, we find that Jacob expected to die of a broken heart. But he looked forward to Sheol where he would see Joseph, supposedly killed by wild beasts (Genesis 37:35). Some would claim this is mere metaphor. Where did the metaphor come from? Obviously someone believed that there was enough personality in Sheol so Jacob would recognize his son. Saul knew Samuel in the story of the witch of Endor (I Samuel 28). We, of course, do not believe in ghosts so we will dismiss this story as "metaphor." But someone believed this. It appears again in Isaiah, where the inhabitants of Sheol recognize the king of Babylon when he arrives (Isaiah 14). This idea of recognizable personality in Sheol also appears in the Mesopotamian story of Gilgamesh, who visited his friend Enkidu in Sheol.

## Rest

We also find in the Bible the idea of "rest in peace." Burial is necessary lest the spirit be forced to wander around the earth and, in anger for lack of rest, try to harm the family who should have buried the dead one. This concept is common to the entire ancient Near East, including Greece. It reflects the demonology which von Rad suggested is the background for the first commandment against other gods. It reflects the whole realm of the occult, including necromancy, which Saul banned and then practiced, or perhaps practiced before converting to Yahwism, and returned to it in his desperate need. This concern with the dead, including offerings at the grave to placate the spirits of the dead, we now know was common in the ancient world. It reached its most elaborate form in Egypt, with the mummification of the dead, the pyramids and funerary temples, all of which reflected concepts of immortality. The preservation of the physical remains of the dead was still important in Judaism in the first centuries B.C. and A.D., as we know from the ossuaries, which were used to store the defleshed bones of the dead. We could include here the preservation of King Uzziah's bones, and the inscription discovered some years ago, requesting or demanding that the bones be left in peace.[6]

It is inconceivable that all of this would not affect ancient Israel and the Hebrew concept of the afterlife. Indeed, the archaeological and biblical data combine to show that ancient Israel was affected from the beginning. Later on, the Seleucid persecution (168 B.C.) prematurely killed loyal followers of God. The development of the idea of heaven for these loyal followers and hell for their enemies is but the product of a long history of ideas. These ideas come from many sources such as Persian dualism, but the development occurs within Judaism itself.

## Angels and Demons

One more example might help. The excavation of Beth-shan produced a fourteenth century B.C. stele of the god Mekal. He was a god of fertility and death who had power to confer either health or death. His name is identical in Egyptian hieroglyphics with that of the later archangel in charge of heaven, Michael ("Who is like God?"). We have here the transformation of a pagan deity into a supernatural being in Hebrew or Jewish thought. A similar process is revealed by the identification of the Philistine god of Ekron, Baalzebul, with the devil, the angel or demon in charge of hell. This reflects on pagan concepts of gods of the dead. The God of Israel was never called the god of the dead, but a re-examination of the evidence points up his power to destroy, or send to the grave, and to bring people back from the dead. In other words, he controlled Sheol (Psalms 30:3).

We have much to learn about the Hebrew concept of the afterlife, e.g., just how were the dead to use their grave goods? This learning will be facilitated by archaeological discovery and subsequent re-examination of the biblical material itself.

## D. ARCHAEOLOGY AND REVELATION

Everything said thus far about biblical archaeology and theology has involved biblical "illumination." Without this, one could go so far as to say biblical theology does not exist. This is an overstatement, of course, for even without archaeology, the biblical theologian still has the Bible itself with which to work. But our discussion thus far should make it abundantly clear that archaeology contributes heavily to biblical theology, and to theology in general.

We remain with many questions, but two are of further interest here. One is about the concept of revelation. One concept of revelation is that God does not reveal ideas about himself, which the faithful are then left to subscribe to as a creed or article or dogma of faith; instead, God reveals himself. This direct experience of the divine has always been the goal of the mystic. However, not even the mystic operates in a vacuum. He has a context. Without it, he would not recognize the divine when he "saw" it. Archaeology is concerned with the context of the mystic or simply of the believer, because this context is historical. Archaeology's relation to history should be clear by now. But as a matter of fact, it is difficult to see how God could reveal himself to the mystic, or simply to the believer, without also revealing something "about" himself. Archaeology is also interested in these "abouts" or ideas of God or other propositional concepts of religion. This brings us to our final question about archaeology and theology.

### Scientific Proof

It has been suggested that archaeology can neither prove nor disprove theological concepts. Archaeology cannot confirm theology, nor can it open the realm of faith. One's immediate response to this is, "but of course, that is obvious." But perhaps now, presupposing the rest of this book, we can suggest that the correct response is a "yes" *and* a "no." Archaeology cannot prove that today there is or is not an afterlife, any more than a history of the development of sociology proves that today there is, or is not, a valid discipline or study called sociology. At the rate the sciences change, one could say that today's superstition is yesterday's scientific knowledge, while today's knowledge is tomorrow's superstition. But a knowledge of the history of sociology does "prove," that is, it shows, how it developed. Without this, we might not know what it is we are trying to prove or why we are bothering with it at all. As van Beek has put it, the barrier of time stands between us in our modern world and the Bible in its ancient world. Archaeology has broken the barrier. Another way of looking at this concern with proof is Philip Watson's suggestion that biblical theology as a scientific discipline tries to understand the theological content of the Bible and to give an accurate description of it. The biblical theologian is not trying to say whether biblical theology is true. He is trying to say what it is.[7]

The question of whether Moses was or was not a monotheist is a theological concept which archaeology supposedly can neither prove nor disprove. And yet, we can note that some claim Moses could not have been a monotheist, arguing that the very concept of monotheism is too abstract for that day and age. Archaeology has provided enough data to show that such a notion is false. Abstractions abound in the comparable literature of the ancient Near East. In the end, it is true that archaeology does not prove Moses was, or was not, a monotheist. But archaeology certainly shows that it was possible in Moses' world to have such abstract ideas. Archaeology is concerned with contexts, the historic concepts, and the ancient possibilities for belief in God. In the end, it is true it neither proves nor disproves His existence. One could close with the observation that belief that God exists, or belief that God does not exist, is a matter of faith and not subject to proof of any kind, archaeological or otherwise. Albright put it this way: "The profoundest intuitions of faith are not subject to logical proof—but neither are the axioms on which all science and technology are erected."[8]

# NOTES

1. Elon, *The Israelis: Founders and Sons* (New York: Holt, Rienhart and Winston, 1971), pp. 282–283. Silberman, *Digging for God and Country: Exploration, Archaeology and the Secret Struggle for the Holy Land, 1799–1917* (New York: Knopf, 1982). Haley, *Roots* (Garden City: Doubleday, 1976). Albright, "The Phenomenon of Israeli Archaeology," NEATC, pp. 57–63. "In America, Biblical Archaeology Was — and Still Is — Largely a Protestant Affair," BAR 8, no. 3 (May/June 82), pp. 54–56.
2. Bertil Albrektson, *History and the Gods* (Lund, Sweden: Coniectanea Biblica, 1967). John Gray, "Recent Archaeological Discoveries and their Bearing on the Old Testament," (pp. 65–66 in *Tradition and Interpretation*, ed. George W. Anderson; Oxford: Clarendon, 1979). G. Ernest Wright and R.H. Fuller, *The Book of the Acts of God* (Garden City: Doubleday, 1957).
3. Toombs, "History and Writing in the Old Testament," *The Drew Gateway* 31, no. 3 (Spr. 61), p. 144. Toombs sees such biblical re-examination as one of the results of a stimulation of biblical studies by archaeology. This stimulation is a major contribution of archaeology to theology. Cf. also his "Archaeology and Theological Studies," *The Drew Gateway* 32, no. 1 (Aut. 61), pp. 26–34.
4. Gray, "Towards a Theology of the Old Testament: The Contribution of Archaeology," *Expository Times* 74 (Aug. 63), p. 350. Walter Harrelson, "Christian Misreadings of Basic Themes in the Hebrew Scriptures," *Quarterly Review* 2, no. 2 (Sum. 82), pp. 58–66.
5. V. Gordon Childe, *What Happened in History?* (rev.; Baltimore: Penguin, 1965), pp. 41–42, 142–156.

6. WBA, p. 247. Lloyd R. Bailey, Sr., *Biblical Perspectives on Death* (Philadelphia: Fortress, 1979).
7. Gus W. Van Beek, "Archaeology," IDB 1, p. 205. Philip S. Watson, "The Nature and Function of Biblical Theology," *The Expository Times* 73 (1962), p. 200.
8. Albright, *History*, p. 322. The potential for abstract thought has also been supported by other studies. Cf. Nathan A. Scott, Jr., *The Wild Prayer of Longing* (New Haven: Yale, 1971), pp. 27–42. Howard Gardner, *The Quest for Mind* (New York: Knopf, 1973). Claude Levi-Strauss, *The Savage Mind* (Chicago: University of Chicago, 1966).

# ADDITIONAL READING

Albright, William F. 1958. "Return to Biblical Theology." *The Christian Century* 1328–1331 (offprint).

Archer, G.L. 1970. "History and Recent Theology." *Bibliotheca Sacra* 127: 3–25, 99–115, 195–210.

Cross, Frank M. *Canaanite Myth and Hebrew Epic: Essays in the History of the Religion of Israel.* Cambridge: Harvard University, 1973.

Mead, Sidney E. *History and Identity.* Missoula: Scholars Press, 1979.

Pannenberg, Wolfhart. *Revelation as History.* New York: Macmillan, 1968.

Robinson, James, and Cobb, John, eds. *Theology as History.* New York: Harper & Row, 1967.

Smith, N.H. 1967. "Archaeology and the Minister." *The Drew University Magazine* 1: 7–9.

Sullivan, Alan P. "Inference and Evidence in Archaeology: A Discussion of the Conceptual Problems" (in SAAMT 1:183–222).

# Glossary

**Abecedary.** An alphabet used as a model for students or a student copy of the alphabet, sometimes the native tongue plus a foreign one.

**Absolute dating.** Calendar dating — it can be given a specific year or span of years on the calendar, e.g., 1500 B.C. See **relative dating**.

**Acrostic.** A poem or paragraph arranged in alphabetic order, so each line or stanza begins a new letter.

**Aerial archaeology.** The study of a site from a height, a balloon, a plane or a satellite.

**Amphictyony.** A group of tribes or peoples united around a temple or in support of a common worship.

**Amulet.** An object worn to ward off sickness or evil or to ensure good fortune. It may be a simple bone or an elaborately carved figurine. Seals may have been worn on a string around the neck as amulets.

**Anthropoid sarcophagi.** Coffins with human features modelled on the lid.

**Apsidal construction.** Round on one end and square on the other.

**Archaeology.** Study of the archaic or old. It has become an elaborate discipline involving excavation and study of ancient ruins and artifacts. As an academic discipline, it may stand alone or be part of anthropology, biblical studies or religious history, classical (Greece and Rome) studies or general history. There are a number of other related disciplines such as papyrology and epigraphy.

**Area.** A portion of the excavation, sometimes part of a field (equals "plot"), sometimes the term is used instead of "field." An area may consist of one or more squares.

**Artifact.** Man-made objects as distinct from structures or natural remains such as bones or plants but the term is sometimes extended to mean any ancient material.

**Ashlar.** Building stone cut or squared.

**Balk** or **baulk.** A segment or wall of earth — often c. 3 feet thick — left between squares as a check on the stratigraphy, and for convenience in moving around the area, or simply the vertical side of the excavation trench or square.

**Barrow.** Burial mound over one or more burials which may be in chambers. The mound may be round, long, or saucer-shaped. See **tumulus.**

**Bulla.** An impression left by a seal in clay or wax used to close a document or storage jar.

**Burial loculi.** Roman and other tombs may have a central room with rectangular holes carved out from the sides of the room where bodies were placed.

**Carbon 14 dating.** Carbon 14 is a radioactive isotope of carbon 12, produced from nitrogen 14 under cosmic radiation. The isotope breaks down at a steady rate; its half life is 5730 plus or minus 40 years. By measuring the amount left in an organic substance, the date the plant or animal died can be determined.

**Casemate wall.** A wall system with an inner and outer wall with crosswalls connecting them which divided the space into rooms. These might be used for living space, storage, or guard rooms.

**Cenote.** Aztec sacred wells — not man-made but natural sink holes fed by ground water. Artifacts, probably religious offerings, have been recovered from them by divers.

**Chalco.** Copper — in common archaeological talk, a short form for chalcolithic.

**Chalcolithic.** The archaeological age when stone was still used but the use of copper was beginning, hence a copper/stone age.

**Charnel house.** A structure for the burial of the dead or the secondary deposition of bones, as at Bab edh-Dhra.

**Chthonic.** Underworld, as with deities who ruled the underworld and/or had power over life and death, illness and health.

**Coptic.** Egyptian writing using the Greek alphabet plus five signs adapted from earlier language. It replaced demotic and in turn was replaced by Arabic, but continues as the ritual language of the Coptic Church in Egypt.

**Cornet.** A pottery cup with a "V" or horn shape, found at Ghassul and related sites.

**Corvee.** A labor battalion made of people whose labor was a tax paid to the government in the form of work.

**Cuneiform.** Wedge-shaped writing used in Mesopotamia, Persia and Hittite areas. It was originally picture writing and became stylized with the use of the reed pen or stylus — triangular or wedge-shaped in cross section or when sharpened to a point which was pushed into soft clay of tablets. The Babylonians and Assyrians had about 600 symbols.

**Demotic.** Greek, "people" — a more cursive but simplified form of Egyptian writing. See **hieroglyphics.**

**Dendrochronology.** Measuring dates by the study of growth rings in trees and shrubs.

**Determinative.** A symbol used in hieroglyphics to show the true sound or meaning of a word.

**Diaspora.** A scattering through, e.g., the world, as with the Jewish people scattered by persecution and migration outside the Holy Land (Hebrew, "galut" — forced exile).

**Dilettante.** Lover of the fine arts — pejoratively, a dabbler, or one who claims a skill he does not really have.

**Dispersion.** See Diaspora.

**Ebriq.** A pottery drinking jug.

**Epigraphic survey.** A systematic search of an area such as Egypt to record the inscriptions.

**Epigraphy.** The study of writing — translating, classifying.

**Faience.** In Egypt, sand paste, baked to fusion into glass — used for seals, amulets, etc. In classical studies, a fine grade of porcelain originating in Faenza in northern Italy and hence the name, "faience."

**Fertile crescent.** James Breasted's term for a crescent shaped area from Canaan to Mesopotamia, sometimes extended to include the Nile River valley. Its fertility is in contrast to the Arabian and other deserts and to the mountains of Armenia and Iran.

**Field.** A designated excavation portion of the tell with one or more squares, sometimes equivalent to "area" and sometimes composed of one or more areas.

**Field or "dirt" archaeology.** Excavation as contrasted to laboratory or library study of artifacts, reports, etc.

**Flotation.** Excavated earth is put in water; lighter items like carbon will float to the surface.

**Fosse.** Moat or ditch around a site as a defensive measure.

**Foundation trench.** Sometimes a wall is built directly on the surface of the ground but more often, a trench is dug and the first courses or foundation of the wall are below ground, for stability. Excavation done perpendicular to the ancient wall can find this trench. The artifacts in it are an indicator of the date when the wall was built.

**F-U-N test.** Fluorine, uranium, nitrogen tests for age, usually of bone. The fluorine and uranium are absorbed from the soil. The nitrogen is part of the organic matter of the bone.

**Glacis.** A plaster slope outside a defensive wall — an enemy trying to get up the slope would be exposed to troops defending it. See **terra pisee.**

**Glyptic art.** Carving on small stones or gems as in seals or amulets.

**Henotheism.** The worship of one god without denying the existence of others.

**Hieratic.** "Priestly" — the cursive (hand writing as contrasted to printing) form of Egyptian hieroglyphics. Later usage was largely limited to the priests.

**Hieroglyphics.** Literally "sacred carvings." Egyptian hieroglyphics are pictures or symbols (over 600) representing sounds, syllables or words. It is the most ancient form of Egyptian writing. See **Hieratic, demotic, Coptic.**

**"In situ."** "In place" — found in place or as it was found. An artifact is not always found in the place where it was used.

**Kernos ring.** A hollow ring, perhaps worn on the head like a crown, with small pottery vessels, fruit or animal heads rising from the ring. It may have been filled with a sacred libation which would pour out as the priest or priestess bowed before the altar or idol.

**Layer.** Stratum or level of earth or occupation debris, often designated a **locus.**

**Level.** Layer or stratum — also used in surveying to indicate height above sea level. Level is sometimes used as equivalent to locus.

**Lingua franca.** Technically a mixed language such as pidgin English; used in this text as the common language of an area in a given time. Akkadian was wide spread in the second millennium, Aramaic in the latter part of the first, Greek in the time of Jesus, English today. Originally it meant the language of the Franks (French), equated with "European" in Arabic, and Lingua Franca was a mixed Mediterranean language of commerce.

**Lithos.** Stone, as in Chalcolithic Age and lithostratos — stone layer or pavement.

**Loculi.** See **burial loculi.**

**Locus** (s.), **loci** (pl.). A general term used to indicate some aspect of the excavation such as a wall, a room, a pit or a stratum. Numbers are given to loci and the numbers are put on artifacts to record their find spot and used to indicate the item in discussion. The term "level" is sometimes used as equivalent to locus.

**Magnetometer.** A meter/magnet combination utilizing hydrogen or other substances used in measuring the magnetic force of the ground, which may indicate the presence of architecture, tombs or artifacts.

**Malacology.** The study of shells — snails, clams, molluscs.

**Mastaba.** Fore-runner of the pyramid — a four-sided structure with a flat top, serving as a tomb or covering a burial chamber.

**Mikvaoth.** Hebrew ritual baths for women to purify themselves after their menstrual periods.

**Monotheism.** The worship of one god, usually with the denial that others exist.

**Mudir.** Chieftain.

**Mukhtar.** Mayor.

**Murex.** The purple dye, sometimes called royal purple because it was expensive, made from the "murex trunculus" shellfish found along the coast of Phoenicia, today's Lebanon.

**Mythopoeic.** Literally "to make myth" — this may not be "myth" in the sense of fiction or fairy tale but a story to illustrate a truth.

**Necromancy.** The worship of the dead, or deities of the underworld, which sometimes included the use of witches or seances.

**Nitrogen narcosis.** The bends — diving at great depths allows nitrogen to build up in the blood stream where it bubbles and can cause death.

**North Semitic Alphabet.** The NSA comes from the northern Semitic area — Sinai to Syria — in contrast to the SSA from southern Arabia. NSA is the ancestor of alphabets used today. Ugartic used the NSA.

**Numismatist.** Specialist in coins.

**Obelisk.** A four-sided pillar tapering to a pyramid at the top. It often has inscriptions or pictures carved on the four sides. Egyptian obelisks were often made from a single piece of stone.

**Obsidian.** Volcanic glass. The name is from Obsius who discovered it in Ethiopia according to Pliny.

**Obsidian dating.** When broken, as in making artifacts, the new surface absorbs moisture at a given rate. Measuring this hydration gives a time for the break, when the artifact was made.

**Ossuary.** A box of pottery or stone used for the burial of bones after the decay of the flesh.

**Ostracon** (s.), **ostraca** (pl.). Writing on a potsherd. The name comes from the Greek use in voting whether to ostracize an offender.

**Palaeobotany.** Study of ancient plant remains.

**Palaeontology.** Study of fossil animal remains; human palaeontology studies the origins of man.

**Palaeozoology.** Study of ancient animal remains.

**Palynology.** Pollen analysis.

**Paper squeeze.** Wet paper, layer by layer, is put on an inscription and carefully brushed into the carving. Left to dry and then removed, it gives an impression of the letters.

**Papyrology.** The study of papyrus materials.

**Papyrus.** Egyptian writing material, made from the reed *cyperus papyrus*. The term is the source of the English word "paper."

**Parchment.** Writing material made from animal skin, usually sheep or goat. The term comes from ancient Pergamum in western Turkey where the process developed in the second century B.C.

**Period.** Time of occupation as Period VI in the history of a site. There may be sub-periods or phases such as a rebuilding of VIa in VIb; some use stratum in this sense. The word is also used for archaeological periods such as Early Bronze Age, Iron Age, etc.

**Phase.** Subdivision of a period or stratum, sometimes used as a temporary designation in digging before stratigraphy is clear.

**Photoarchaeology.** The use of photography in archaeology.

**Photogrammetry.** Using pictures to make maps.

**Pithos.** A large pottery storage jar.

**Pitt-Rivers (A.H. Lane-Fox) method.** See **three dimensional recording.**

**Plan.** Drawing usually to scale of the horizontal layout of a building or excavated area.

**Plot.** Part of an excavation field or area.

**Pollen analysis.** Plants have their own distinctive pollen, the outer husk of which resists decay. Study shows the kinds of plants in a given period.

**Pot hunters.** People who dig up pottery and other artifacts for private collection or sale, normally without regard to stratigraphy or accurate recording.

**Potsherd.** A sherd or piece of pottery broken from a pottery pot or vessel. Rims, bases, handles, decoration and other aspects are useful in dating. See **typology.** Pottery typology was developed by Petrie.

**PPM** — parts per million — a measurement concept for trace-trace elements — the amounts in a substance are too small for percentages.

**Prediluvian.** Before the Flood (Genesis 7).

**Probe trench.** A small area, often a portion of a square, c. 3 feet on a side, which is dug as a test of the buried strata. Used as a guide to the digging of the rest of the square. Also called **trial trench.**

**Reis.** Egyptian director, as for an area in antiquities or in an excavation.

**Relative dating.** Something, such as an artifact, is younger or older in relation to something else, but the calendar date may be unknown — cf. **absolute dating.**

**Resistivity survey.** Measuring the electrical conductivity of the earth to detect buried remains.

**Robber trench** or **ghost wall.** A filled in ditch left from the removal for re-use of the stones of a wall.

**Saddle quern.** A large, flat, slightly concave rock used for grinding grain by hand. The grinder was often a flat based, rounded stone, usually basalt or similar stone.

**Scarab.** Ancient Egyptians made seals in the form of the sacred scarab beetle (Scarabaeus sacer). The seals were flat on the bottom, round on top with the head and folded wings indicated. The flat base was usually inscribed with hieroglyphics or symbols, perhaps the name of the owner.

**SCUBA.** Self-Contained Underwater Breathing Apparatus — the aqualung — an oxygen tank is strapped on the swimmer's back and she breathes through tubes while under the water; invented by Cousteau and Gagnan.

**Sea Peoples.** A general name for a variety of tribes that invaded or migrated into the eastern Mediterranean — Syria to Egypt. Their origins are debated; Libya, Turkey, Cyprus, and Crete are suggested.

**Seal.** Ancient peoples sealed documents or indicated ownership with a mark or seal often made by a carved object. Seals in Mesopotamia were usually cylindrical and rolled over the wax of the seal or the clay of the pottery jar or clay tablet. In Egypt, the seal was often a scarab seal. The scarab is a form of stamp seal which also came in other shapes. The seals were inscribed with symbols or inscriptions, sometimes with the name of the owner. The form, the symbols, or where known, the name, might indicate the date of the seal, and hence the locus where it was found.

**Section.** Scale drawing, usually 1:25, of the vertical sides of the excavation square or trench.

**Sequence Dating.** The types as found in earlier and later strata. Petrie developed pottery typology on this basis. In time, he was able to put a calendar date on the items in sequence.

**Shawabti.** See **ushabti**.

**Sherd** or **shard.** Anglo-Saxon "fragment" — short form of potsherd.

**Slipper sarcophagi.** Coffins, usually made of baked clay, shaped like a shoe or slipper, usually with a lid that closed the opening. The lid often had a human face and sometimes arms molded on it. See **anthropoid sarcophagi.**

**Socket.** The hollowed out stone used for the lower end of a door post in which the door turned as it swung open and shut; sometimes the stone foundation for a mudbrick wall.

**Spectrographic analysis.** Elements such as copper and iron have their own place in the spectrum of light. Measuring the electronic discharge of a substance tells what elements are present; the intensity of the light tells how much is present.

**Sphinx.** An Egyptian statue with the body of a lion and the head of a person, ram or hawk, perhaps a symbol of the pharaoh as the sun god. *The* Sphinx is near the pyramids at al Jizah (Giza) near Cairo.

**Square.** The basic unit in excavation — in Kenyon's work, the standard size was 5 meters on a side. In practice, the unit may be smaller or larger and may take other shapes, rectangular, trapezoidal, etc., depending on the space available to dig.

**Stela** or **stele** (s.), **stelae** (pl.). Greek for "post" — in architecture and archaeology, an upright slab of stone with an inscription, symbols and/or picture(s) carved on one side, like older style markers in graveyards. In ancient times, they were monuments marking battles, devotion (prayers), and other events. They were used as boundary markers in some cultures.

**Steno's Law.** The principle of superposition or stratification. Nicholas Steno (1638–1686), geologist, physician and Roman Catholic priest, suggested sedimentary rocks were similar in structure to the seabed. The lower layers were deposited first and hence are older in time. The geological term was borrowed by archaeologists to describe the deposition of debris layers from sequential human occupation of a city or place.

**Stereophotography.** Three dimensional photography.

**Strata** (plural), **stratum** (s.). Layer, as of earth, in geology and archaeology. Some use the term as equivalent to "period."

**Stratigraphy.** Literally the writing ("graphe") of strata — the accumulated strata of a tell and by extension the finding, the study, the recording, and the interpretation of the strata.

**Surface exploration.** Early travellers recorded the names of places and identified ruins. Nelson Glueck studied the pottery found on the surface of ancient sites and used pottery typology to date the sites.

**Tabun** or **tannur.** Beehive shaped oven with thick clay walls.

**Tel** (Hebrew) or **tell** (Arabic). An artificial hill or mound formed from the ruins of an ancient settlement.

**Terra pisee.** Beaten earth used in building instead of mud brick; in defensive ramparts, usually plastered to prevent erosion and plant growth. See **glacis**. The ramparts are sometimes identified with the Hyksos who ruled Egypt c. 1600 B.C.

**Theology.** Literally the study of God — in practice the study of ideas about God and of religion in general.

**Thermoluminescence.** A heat and light test for radioactive particles — the amount indicates the age of the material.

**Tholus** (s.), **tholoi** (p.). Round or domed structures with the dome coming to a point like a beehive, often used as tombs, sometimes with rectangular hallways or entry ways.

**Three-dimensional recording.** Shows where an artifact was in the mound, vertically and East-West horizontally. Developed by Pitt-Rivers.

**Toggle pin.** An oversized straight pin of bronze or copper with a hole in the middle for a long string which held it on the garment. The pin was used to hold folds of the robe together and the string wound around it to keep it in place.

**Trial trench.** See **probe trench**.

**Tubalcain.** The originator of metallurgy in the biblical tradition in Genesis 4:22.

**Tumulus.** Burial mound. See **barrow**.

**Typology.** The study or science of types. Pottery typology is the ordering of pottery — jars, bottles, cooking vessels, bowls, lamps — by types — shapes and decoration varied over time so the types are an indication of date. Some vessels appear in some periods but not others so they may be indicators of date. Typology is also applied to weapons, clothing, tombs, architecture, and other artifacts.

**Ugartic.** The language of Ugarit, the civilization centered on the city of Ugarit at the site of Ras Shamra near the coast of Syria opposite the island of Cyprus. The city was destroyed about 1200 B.C.

**Ushabti figures.** Small carved or molded figures of people, livestock etc. found in tombs in the Nile Valley. They may have been substitutes for live humans earlier interred with their master to serve him in life after death, and hence the name, which means "answerer."

**Wadi.** Arabic for gully or canyon.

**Wheeler-Kenyon method.** Following Pitt-Rivers, Sir Mortimer Wheeler, followed by his student, Kathleen Kenyon, excavated stratum by stratum in small areas of the tell, giving a vertical view of the history of occupation.

**Ziggurat.** Four-sided mound of mud brick built in Mesopotamia with a temple on top. They may have been substitute mountains for the mountain people who conquered the area. Ziggurats have been suggested as the background of the Tower of Babel story in Genesis 11.

# Sources

Blakely, Jeffrey A., and Toombs, Lawrence E. *The Tell el-Hesi Field Manual*. Cambridge: ASOR, 1980.

Bray, Warwick, and Trump, David. *The Penguin Dictionary of Archaeology*. Baltimore: Penguin, 1972.

Lance, H. Darrell. *Excavation Manual for Area Supervisors*. New York: HUCBAS, 1967.

Dever, William G., and Lance, H. Darrell, eds. *A Manual of Field Excavation: Handbook for Field Archaeologists*. New York: Hebrew Union College—Jewish Institute of Religion, 1978.

McKechnie, Jean L. *Webster's New Twentieth Century Dictionary of the English Language*. 2nd ed. New York: Collins-World, 1976.

Shechem and Hesban staffs. Personal communications.

Toombs, Lawrence E. *Excavation Manual*. Wooster, OH: College of Wooster, 1966.

Wheeler, Mortimer. *Archaeology from the Earth*. Baltimore: Penguin, 1956.

# Index

The index is to proper names and themes which are developed in the text, excluding notes and bibliographies. The illustrations (see xix–xxiv), abbreviations (see xv–xvii), and most glossary terms (see 451–458) are not repeated here.